The Nonprofit Handbook

**Everything You Need to Know to Start
and Run Your Nonprofit Organization**

Fifth Edition

Gary M. Grobman

White Hat Communications

Harrisburg, Pennsylvania

White Hat Communications
PO Box 5390
Harrisburg, PA 17110-0390
(717) 238-3787 (tel)   (717) 238-2090 (fax)
Web Site: http://www.whitehatcommunications.com

The material in Chapter 4 and Chapter 17 of this publication is authored by Michael Sand and is reprinted with permission. The author gratefully acknowledges the contributions Mr. Sand has made to the material that comprises Chapter 16. The material in Chapter 7 is authored by Gerald Kaufman and is reprinted with permission. The material in Chapter 8 is authored by Gerald Kaufman and Gary Grobman. Much of the material in Chapter 10 was rewritten by Melanie Herman of the Nonprofit Management Risk Center (NMRC). Some of the material in Chapter 21, 22, and 23 is based on the book *Fundraising Online: Using the Internet to Raise Serious Money for Your Nonprofit Organization* by Gary M. Grobman and Gary B. Grant and is reprinted with permission. Some of the material in Chapter 23 is based on the book *The Nonprofit Organization's Guide to E-Commerce* by Gary Grobman (White Hat Communications, 2001). The material in Chapter 28 is authored by Dr. Pam Leland, and is reprinted with permission from the author. Some of the material in Chapter 31 is co-authored by Gary Grobman, Gerald Gorelick, and Frederick Richmond, and it is used with permission from the authors.

Corrections to this publication, if any, will be posted at:
http://www.whitehatcommunications.com/nphome.htm

IMPORTANT DISCLAIMER: This publication is intended to provide general information and should not be construed as legal advice or opinions concerning any specific facts or circumstances. Consult an experienced attorney if advice is required concerning any specific situation or legal matter. Neither the author nor the publisher make any warranties, expressed, or implied, with respect to the information in this publication. The author and publisher shall not be liable for any incidental or consequential damages in connection with, or arising out of, the use of this book.

Contact the author in care of White Hat Communications, or by e-mail at:
gary.grobman@paonline.com

Printed in the United States of America.

Library of Congress Cataloging-in-Publication Data

Grobman, Gary M.
 The nonprofit handbook : everything you need to know to start and run your nonprofit organization / Gary M. Grobman. -- 5th ed.
    p. cm.
 Includes bibliographical references and index.
 ISBN-13: 978-1-929109-20-3 (5th edition)
 ISBN-10: 1-929109-09-1 (3rd edition)
 ISBN-10: 0-9653653-2-8 (2nd edition)
 ISBN-10: 0-9653653-7-9 (1997-1998 national edition)
 1. Nonprofit organizations--United States--Management--Handbooks, manuals, etc. I. Title.
HD62.6.G762 2008
658'.048--dc22
                              2008003721

Table of Contents

Board Responsibilities
How Boards Function Effectively
Holding High-Quality Board Meetings
Relationship Between Board Members and Staff Members

The Mission Statement
The Vision Statement
Examples of Mission and Vision Statements

Introduction
Purpose of Strategic Planning
Making the Decision to Develop a Strategic Plan
Benefits of Strategic Planning
Costs of Strategic Planning
A Sample Strategic Planning Model

Overview
Current Board Functioning
A New System of Board Governance
Conclusion

Introduction
Ethics in the Nonprofit Environment
Accountability
Conflict of Interest
Disclosures
Accumulation of Surplus
Outside Remuneration
Salaries, Benefits, and Perquisites
Personal Relationships
Standards of Excellence
Taxpayer Bill of Rights II—Intermediate Sanctions
Codes of Ethics
Conclusion

Government Grants
Finding Corporate Support
Hiring a Consultant

Introduction
Researching the Grantor
Sections of a Grant Application

Legal Requirements for Lobbying
Expense Reporting Requirements
Effective Strategies for Lobbying and Advocacy
501(h) Election
IRS Regulations on Lobbying
Contacts With Legislators

Introduction
Individual Political Activities
Penalties
Quasi-Political Activities

Introduction
Menu of Nonprofit Communications Tools

Practical Applications of the Internet
The World Wide Web
How to Find Resources on the Web
Directories
Domain Names
How to Register a Domain Name
Developing Your Own Web Page
Encouraging First-Time Visitors
Encouraging Repeat Web Site Visits
Let Visitors Know About Your Site

Add Features That Attract Visitors
Blogs
Electronic Newsletters
HTML-Formatted E-Mail and Newsletters
Podcasts
Online Communities
Challenges of Online Communities
Internet Etiquette (a.k.a. Netiquette)
Problems With the Internet
Useful Internet Resources for Nonprofits

Chapter 22. Fundraising on the Internet

Introduction
Advantages of Internet Fundraising
Disadvantages of Internet Fundraising
Direct Mail
Prospect Research
Major Gifts
Special Events
Capital Campaigns
Online Fundraising Strategies
"Donate Here" Buttons
Cause-Related Marketing
Tribute Gifts
Personal Fundraising Pages

Chapter 23. Nonprofit E-Commerce

Introduction
Build, Buy, or Rent?
Setting Up an Online Store
Online Auctions
Online Charity Malls
Search Engine Marketing
Advertising
Miscellaneous Issues

Chapter 24. Forming and Running a Coalition

Introduction
The Coalition
Structures of Coalitions

Advantages of Forming a Coalition
Disadvantages of Coalitions
To Form a Coalition or Not
How to Form a Coalition

Office Equipment
Staffing Patterns
Stationery/Logo
Filing Systems
Computer
Hardware/Software
Basic Hardware Decision—Apple or IBM-Compatible
Typical Software for Nonprofits
Credit Card Sales
Computer Communications/Internet
Postal Service Issues

Introduction
Federal Unrelated Business Income Tax (UBIT)
Differences Between Nonprofits and For-Profits

Sales and Use Tax-Exemptions
Why User Charges May Not Be the Answer
Justification for the Charitable Tax Exemption

Education
Planning
Documentation
Communication
Collaboration
Discussion

Factors That Trigger Merger Consideration
How to Begin

Steps to a Merger
Budgeting
Obstacles to Merger
Legal Requirements

Chapter 30. Quality Issues

Introduction
Why Quality is Important to Nonprofit Organizations
The Cost of Poor Quality
Quality in the Nonprofit Organizational Context

Chapter 31. Change Management

Total Quality Management
Business Process Reengineering
Benchmarking
Outcome-Based Management
Large Group Intervention

Chapter 32. Organization and Program Evaluation

Introduction
What is Program Evaluation?
Why Program Evaluation is Performed
Who Performs a Program Evaluation
Planning for Program Evaluation
Conclusion

PART II: A Student Guide to Nonprofit Organizations

Chapter 33. Defining and Describing the Nonprofit Sector

Definition of Nonprofit Organization
Models of Nonprofit Organizations
Classification of Nonprofit Organizations
Differences Between Private Foundations and Public Charities
How Organizations are Funded
Legal Definition of Charitable Organization and Tax Exemption
Size and Growth of the Voluntary Nonprofit Sector
Nonprofit Taxonomies
Assets of the Sector

Boundaries of the Sector
Differences Among the Sectors

Introduction
Modern Roots of American Charitable Law and Organizations
Faith-Based Initiatives

Public Goods Theory
Market Failure Theory
Market Failure and High Transaction Costs
Pluralistic Theory
Externality Theory
Contract Failure Theory
Subsidy Theories
Consumer Control Theory
Non-Economic Theories
Pluralistic Theory
Mediating Structures
Theory of the Commons
Are Nonprofits Altruistic or Self-Maximizing?

Introduction
Trend 1: Terrorism and the Fear of Terrorism
Trend 2: The Demographics of the United States
Population is Changing
Trend 3: Most Nonprofits are Taking Advantage of the
    Technological Revolution, but a Digital Divide
    Threatens to Divide the Sector into "Haves" and
    "Have Nots"
Trend 4: The Nonprofit Sector Should Expect
    Increased Government Scrutiny, as Well as More
    Regulation and Accountability Requirements
Trend 5: Government Funding is Drying Up at a Time
    When Demand for Services Will be Increasing
Trend 6: Donor Attitude Changes Will Profoundly
    Affect How Charities Raise Funds
Trend 7: The Nonprofit, For-Profit and Government

Sectors Will Continue to Converge
Trend 8: The Nonprofit Sector Workforce is
    Professionalizing
Conclusion
References

Foreword

Joe Geiger, Executive Director
Pennsylvania Association of Nonprofit Organizations (PANO)

Congratulations! You have decided to be a part of the fastest-growing segment of business development in the United States. You are considering joining, or have already joined, over a million other nonprofits in the United States. They come in all sizes, shapes, and colors. The nonprofit sector's heritage includes helping in an emergency, encouraging the human spirit, educating and shaping values and goals, and being the first to offer a hand.

You have chosen to be a vital link in developing the fabric of the community. From the time our ancestors landed on Plymouth Rock (or staffed the Welcome Wagon that greeted those who did), people have worked together in formal organizations to better the human condition. The nonprofit sector has always been in the forefront of improving our society and the human condition.

Today, the nonprofit sector is in a very challenging period. Nonprofits are experiencing ever-growing scrutiny and demands for accountability. Service demand is increasing. There is more competition for charitable dollars. The public and government both are demanding that nonprofits improve their efficiency. This book will help you respond to these challenges.

As the Executive Director of PANO, I am pleased to be a part of the 5th edition of *The Nonprofit Handbook*. Every week, callers to PANO ask questions: Should we start up? How do we get our tax exemptions? Where can we find grant funds? Should we merge? Should we contract with a for-profit to help us fundraise online? I am pleased to have a practical tool that can help answer these questions. This book will help to keep you on track. It is also an extraordinary resource for those who already manage or serve on the boards of nonprofit organizations. With practical advice on fundraising, communications, lobbying, personnel management, grantsmanship, and scores of other issues, it is a must for every nonprofit executive to have.

In summary, *The Nonprofit Handbook* is at the top of the list of essential tools to have on your bookshelf. This book is must reading. While it will have value as a reference tool to be consulted when needed, I highly recommend that you read the book cover-to-cover to familiarize yourself with the panoply of issues facing the modern nonprofit in every state of our United States.

J.M.G.
January 2008

Introduction

Americans of all ages, all stations in life, and all types of disposition are forever forming associations. There are not only commercial and industrial associations in which all take part, but others of a thousand different types—religious, moral, serious, futile, very general and very limited, immensely large and very minute. Americans combine to give fetes, found seminaries, build churches, distribute books, and send missionaries to the antipodes. Hospitals, prisons and schools take shape in that way. Finally, if they want to proclaim a truth or propagate some feeling by the encouragement of a great example, they form an association. In every case, at the head of any new undertaking, where in France you would find the government or in England some territorial magnate, in the United States you are sure to find an association.

—Alexis de Tocqueville
Democracy In America
1835

Little has changed about the American propensity to form benevolent associations in the 173 years since de Tocqueville wrote the above words. The modern charitable institution, however, may bear little resemblance to the typical charity of the 19th century. Burgeoning demands for services, increased government regulation, keen competition for funds, the advance of technology, demographic changes, and the public's changing perception of our institutions have all worked to increase the challenge to those in leadership positions with nonprofit organizations.

In our highly competitive, individualistic society, the nonprofit sector provides a way to express our humanitarian values, to preserve our cultural heritage, to promote various causes, to educate, and to enlighten. It is often through coming together in nonprofit organizations that our citizens exercise their constitutional rights to petition their government, engage in free speech, and exercise their freedoms of assembly and religion.

Nonprofits play a unique role as an intermediary between the citizens and their government. They maintain and transmit values to a degree that government has been unable to do.

Perhaps most important of all, nonprofits formulate much of the moral agenda for society. One only has to think of the response to the September 11, 2001 terrorist attacks, the environmental movement, rape crisis and domestic violence centers, public subsidies of arts and humanities, public awareness of AIDS and support of AIDS programs, and countless other issues that people coming together in voluntary organizations were able to put on the nation's agenda.

Virtually every single American is touched in some way by the services of this country's nonprofit organizations. Organizations such as institutions of religious worship, civic groups, hospitals, day care centers, libraries, colleges, symphonies, art museums, the Red Cross, Salvation Army, and the American Cancer Society work in partnership with government and the public to improve our lives and those of our neighbors. According to the Internal Revenue Service, there were 1,585,479 organizations that were exempt under Section 501(c) in FY2006, 1,064,191 of which were 501(c)(3)s (see Chapter 33).

Historically, the primary distinguishing characteristic of the nonprofit sector is that it is mission- and value-driven. Nonprofit organizations exist to accomplish some social good, however that may be defined. A set of values and assumptions underlies this view of the voluntary sector, including altruism, benevolence, cooperation, community, and diversity. The privileges granted to the sector and public expectations are grounded in this belief.

Nonprofits in the United States sometimes take the form of soup kitchens, such as Our Daily Bread in Harrisburg, Pennsylvania, which operate on a shoestring budget and charge their clients virtually nothing for their services. They also take the form of enterprises such as hospitals, with budgets in the hundreds of millions of dollars, which often act in ways very much like their for-profit counterparts, seeking to maximize revenue and capture market share.

In January 2000, a Dauphin County (PA) Common Pleas Court county judge ruled against the tax exemption eligibility for Hershey Medical Center (HMC), affiliated with Penn State University. One of his objections was that the facility paid salaries to some individuals on staff in excess of a half-million dollars annually. Like almost all hospitals, HMC enters into sophisticated business arrangements. A couple of years ago, the hospital merged with Geisinger, a for-profit health system. The merger collapsed, chiefly as a result of conflicting organizational missions and cultures between the two parent organizations, in addition to financial and operational difficulties.

In contrast to the soup kitchen, the financial aspects of decision-making are of paramount importance to HMC's decision-making strategy. Yet, as one wag pointed out on the tangible benefits of a nonprofit being selected as a "Point of Light" by the White House, even a "point of light" has to pay the electric bill.

Neither Hershey Medical Center nor Our Daily Bread, about ten miles away from each other, is atypical of the nonprofit sector. While they may appear to be as different as night and day, they also share many things in common. Both depend on government grants, as well as donations from foundations, businesses, and individuals, to keep them operating in the black and to supplement fees for service. Both provide free services to those who are unable to pay for them. Both depend on volunteers. Both are governed by a board of directors, whose members do not share in any surplus revenues that may be generated, and that consists of unpaid volunteers from the community.

These are some of the aspects that differentiate nonprofit organizations from their government and private sector counterparts that also provide inpatient health care and food services. Nonprofit organizations, especially those qualified under section 501(c)(3) of the Internal Revenue Code, occupy a special and unique place in American society. Their uniqueness has many attributes.

All such organizations are supported by the nation's taxpayers. They are exempt from federal and state income tax. Contributors, for the most part, can deduct their contributions from their federal income tax (and from their state income taxes in most states). They are eligible to have their postage subsidized by the federal government. Many are exempt from state and local sales and property taxes.

Some people, including those who formulate tax and regulatory policies that apply to charities, have a vision of charitable organizations that resembles those of the 19th century. In that vision, staff consists of volunteers. Recipients of services are too poor to provide for themselves. Funding comes from wherever it can be found. An example of what this looked like is described on the Web site of Yale University's School of Medicine:

> *A 19th century hospital was predominantly a charity institution, although from the beginning, some patients paid for their stays. It was intended for the worthy poor, for*

sailors, and for other strangers in town. People of means, such as the donors who were members of the General Hospital Society of Connecticut, would receive medical care in their homes, and not in a hospital. The hospital as yet offered no advantages over home care. Physicians served in the hospital without salary on a rotating basis as attending physicians. They did so as a form of charity and civic duty, but hospital service also provided valuable experience, professional recognition, and the possibility of training students in the wards.

from *Connecticut and New Haven's First General Hospital: Hospitals in the Nineeenth-Century;* Harvey Cushing/John May Whitney Medical Library; Yale University School of Medicine; *http://www.med.yale.edu/library/exhibits/hospitals/*

Benjamin Franklin convinced the Pennsylvania Legislature to participate in chartering the nation's first hospital, Pennsylvania Hospital. He received a commitment to match £2000 donated by private individuals with a like amount appropriated by the state government. Founded in 1751, the institution was created "to care for the sick poor of the Province and for the reception and care of lunaticks" (source: *In the Beginning: The Story of the Creation of the Nation's First Hospital; http://www.uphs.upenn.edu/paharc/features/creation.html;* University of Pennsylvania Health System, 2003).

The modern charitable institution, however, may bear little resemblance to the typical charity of the 19th century. Burgeoning demands for services, increased government regulation, keen competition for funds, the advance of technology, demographic changes, and the public's changing perception of our institutions have all worked to increase the complexity of decision-making to those in leadership positions with nonprofit organizations. Pennsylvania Hospital, started with perhaps a handful of employees, has evolved into the University of Pennsylvania Health System, with a workforce measured in the tens of thousands, making it one of the largest private employers in the entire state. Other nonprofits, such as educational institutions and other integrated health care systems, are on the roster of the state's largest employers. In fact, one such institution, The University of Pennsylvania, is the largest nongovernmental employer in Pennsylvania other than Wal-Mart (source: *http://www.aadet.com/article/Pennsylvania*).

The nonprofit sector's participation in the American economy is impressive. According to a November 2006 study of the Urban Institute's National Center for Charitable Statistics, nonprofit organizations account for 5.2% of the nation's economic output and pay 8.3% of all salaries and wages (source: *Nonprofit Almanac,* 2007), with 2004 revenues of more than $1.4 trillion and assets of $3 trillion. Of the 27.7 million organizations of all types in the United States in 1998, 1.626 million, or 5.8%, were federally tax-exempt, and these nonprofit organizations accounted for 6.7% of the $7.3 trillion in national income when the value of volunteer time was included. The IRS says that 1,585,479 organizations were tax exempt under Section 501(c) in FY 2006, and about 100,000 of these are new 501(c)(3) organizations created since 2003.

Most Americans recognize the value of nonprofit organizations in society. Of more than 130 million individual tax returns filed nationally for tax year 2004 by individuals and couples, 38.566 million claimed a tax deduction for charitable giving, totaling more than $122.875 billion in deductions, according to the IRS. Many more billions of dollars were donated by persons who do not itemize, or who do not bother to declare the value of their charity on their tax returns. The business community also donates billions of dollars each year to charitable institutions.

According to the June 2007 annual report of *Giving USA,* published by the American Association of Fund-Raising Counsel Trust for Philanthropy, total charitable giving by individuals, corporations, and foundations increased by 4.2% in 2006 over the previous year to an estimated $295 billion. Additionally, billions of hours annually are volunteered to nonprofits. According to the Bureau of Labor Statistics of the Department of Labor, 61.2 million persons 16 and over volunteered for an organization at least once between September 2005 and September 2006, 26.7% of the population. Statistics from the Independent Sector Web site are even more encouraging, estimating that 44% of adults volunteer, and that the value of their service is valued at $239 billion annually. Annually, Independent Sector calculates the value of an hour of volunteer time, which for 2006 is $18.77. With more than 15 billion hours in volunteer time annually, this is certainly substantial. As those who volunteer can attest, the value to society, such as the relief of human suffering, far exceeds the dollar value.

It is difficult to foresee and anticipate all of the barriers that stand in the way of a nonprofit organization's creation and survival. One thing is certain—there will be barriers. Forming and running a nonprofit corporation, or any corporation, is a major challenge. Yet it is known that the accomplishments such organizations can achieve far exceed what any single person, operating without an organizational structure, can achieve alone.

Starting and running a nonprofit corporation in the 21st century requires political acumen, immense technical skill, vision, physical and mental stamina, and, perhaps most of all, luck and a sense of humor.

In the fall of 1984, the Internal Revenue Service, because of a computer glitch, lost $300 million in federal tax withholding payments of 10,000 companies. Even after the snafu was discovered, thousands of the companies received curt letters threatening that the government would seize their property and bank accounts if the tax payments were not made within 10 days. As a nonprofit executive who was on the receiving end of one of these letters, I can certify that "maintaining a sense of humor" was not easy at that time. Yet in the years after that IRS debacle, several more calamities beyond my control afflicted the nonprofit I ran.

There were times when running a nonprofit was no picnic. And then there were times when it was the most fun I ever had. I would like to think that if a publication such as *The Nonprofit Handbook* had been around when I first started, my job would have been easier.

Purpose of the Handbook

As one might expect, a plethora of laws, regulations, court decisions, and other government policies apply to nonprofit corporations.

The purpose of this handbook is to provide answers to questions such as:

1. What does one have to do to form a nonprofit corporation?
2. What are the advantages and disadvantages of incorporating?
3. How does a nonprofit organization qualify and apply for 501(c)(3) status?
4. What kind of paperwork is involved in typical nonprofit operations?
5. What should be in a nonprofit corporation's bylaws?
6. How does a nonprofit organization qualify for discount bulk mailing privileges?
7. How does a nonprofit organization qualify for a state sales tax exemption?
8. Can a nonprofit organization engage in unrelated activities that generate income?
9. Will the tax exemption of a nonprofit organization be at risk if it engages in lobbying?
10. How do nonprofit organizations use the Internet to increase revenues?

This handbook cannot purport to answer every conceivable question, but it does attempt to provide sources for answers to many of the questions posed by nonprofit board members and staff. It also provides references to primary source material, much of it available on the Web, on important state and federal laws and regulations, sources for some of the most useful government forms, and sound advice about many nonprofit management issues.

For each state and the District of Columbia, this handbook provides basic information about incorporation, lobbying registration and reporting, income and sales tax exemptions, and registration to conduct charitable solicitations. The names and addresses of the appropriate government contact offices are provided. It also provides the addresses of useful Web sites where additional resources may be found.

What's New in the Fifth Edition

Among the new features that appear in this edition are—

- A new chapter on organization and program evaluation
- Charts and graphs illustrating the growth of the sector
- An expanded section on financial management
- An expanded chapter on the use of the Internet for fundraising

Who Can Use This Book

This handbook will be a useful reference for—

- Those who are considering forming a nonprofit corporation.

- Those who need to keep current on laws, regulations, and court decisions that affect nonprofit organizations, including executive staff and board members of existing nonprofit organizations.

- Those who will benefit from the advice included in this handbook on running a nonprofit organization, such as fundraisers, lobbyists, public affairs consultants, staff and leadership of funding organizations, and government officials, in addition to those who serve as the staff and board members of nonprofit organizations and their associations.

- Those who are students of nonprofit management at both the graduate and undergraduate levels. Beginning with the third edition, this book includes chapters on the definition of the nonprofit sector, history of the nonprofit sector, and academic theory that has been developed to explain why the sector exists. A new chapter has been added beginning with the fourth edition on *The Future of the Nonprofit Sector,* giving students (and practitioners alike) a perspective on important developments and trends that suggest what the future holds for the sector.

This is the fifth edition of this publication. Every effort has been made to make this *Handbook* as useful and free from errors as possible. It is the intent of the author to seek corrections as well as suggestions for improving this publication, and to incorporate these contributions in future editions. A survey/order form has been included in the Appendix to provide feedback to the author and publisher.

Acknowledgments

The author gratefully acknowledges the contributions of scores of individuals and organizations to this book. Among them are Kathleen Steigler and Linda Grobman, who edited the first edition of the *Pennsylvania Non-Profit Handbook,* on which this book is based; Michael Sand, who wrote the chapter on boards, as well as the chapter on applying for grants; and Bob Mills, Esq., who was the initial author of the chapter on volunteer and staff liability, which has since been completely revised, updated, and expanded, thanks to the efforts of Melanie Herman of the Nonprofit Management Risk Center. Thanks are due also to those who reviewed and edited specific chapters of the previous editions, including Terry Roth, Esq.; W. Barney Carter; George Bell, Esq.; Bill Knoll, Classification Reform Instructor for the U.S. Postal Service; Otto Hofmann, Esq.; Phil McKain; Jim Fritz, Esq.; Frederick Richmond; the late Steve Zneimer; Jim Redmond; Elizabeth Hrenda-Roberts; Ron Lench; Christine Finnegan; Joan Benso; Dick Shelly; John Briscoe; and Ken Wickham. Patricia Mogan, Standards for Excellence Officer of the Pennsylvania Association of Nonprofit Organizations (PANO), updated the section in Chapter 8 related to the Standards for Excellence program. I wish to thank John Hope, Linda Grobman, Barbara Blank, and Judy Grobman who reviewed and edited this edition and/or previous editions of this book.

I am also appreciative of the contributions to this publication made by Gerald Kaufman, executive director of the Awbury Arboretum Association, whose essay on governance of nonprofit charities and contribution to the chapter on nonprofit ethics deserve to be shared with every board member and staff person who is affiliated with a charity. Dr. Pam Leland deserves kudos for her thoughtful chapter on how to respond to property tax exemption challenges. Joel Cavadel, an attorney from York, PA, made many contributions to the section on mergers and consolidations, for which I am most grateful. Dr. Roger Lohmann of West Virginia University reviewed parts of the Student Guide to Nonprofit Organizations. Esther Hyatt of Virginia Commonwealth University reviewed the chapter on evaluation. Nearly a score of members of the teaching section of the Association for Research on Nonprofit Organizations and Voluntary Action (ARNOVA) reviewed chapters of *An Introduction to the Nonprofit Sector,* a textbook based on the third edition of *The Nonprofit Handbook.* Some of their suggestions have been incorporated into this 5th edition. Some of the material in the chapter on change management was adapted from material on outcome-based management jointly written by Frederick Richmond and myself, and from material on large group intervention that Gerald Gorelick and I wrote together. Gary Grant and I wrote the material that comprises Chapter 22, *Fundraising on the Internet,* which I feel makes a significant contribution to the value of this edition.

Finally, a word of thanks to the Pennsylvania Association of Nonprofit Organizations, particularly to its executive director, Joe Geiger, for participating in this fifth edition. PANO is the authority Pennsylvania nonprofits turn to for information, products, services, and training to make them the best they can be.

G.M.G.
January 2008

Part I

For Practitioners

White Hat Communications

Quick Start Guide
to Forming a Nonprofit Organization

The following provides an overview of the major steps involved in starting up a nonprofit corporation. The order in which these appear below is not necessarily the most efficient in every case (and many steps can be accomplished simultaneously), but it should be sufficient for most startups. Obviously, the procedures will vary by state, and changes in laws and regulations will occur that may modify the contents of this list. Because this book does not provide legal advice relating to any specific fact situation, I recommend that you consider consulting a qualified attorney before starting up any corporation.

1. Choose the general purpose and mission of the organization, and write a description of it in a single sentence.
2. Conduct research to see—
   - whether there is a sufficient need for a new organization with that purpose
   - whether other organizations are already providing the service you propose to provide
   - who and how many will likely seek to be served by your organization
   - what federal, state, and local laws and regulations will apply to your organization
   - whether you will have enough startup income to finance initial expenses, and whether you can generate enough income (through sales of goods and services, grants, or donations) necessary to sustain your organization
   - whether there is sufficient interest in your community to build a board of directors for this organization.
3. Prepare a business and marketing plan if your startup is likely to require a substantial investment in startup funding.
4. Choose a unique business name, and check on its availability.
5. Choose an Internet domain name based on that name.
6. Choose a legal address for your organization.
7. Obtain an EIN number (your taxpayer identification number) from the Internal Revenue Service by filling out a Form SS-4. (This can be obtained online at: http://www.irs.gov/pub/irs-pdf/fss4.pdf by using the forms and publications finder using the term "SS-4" or by calling 1-800-829-FORM.)
8. Choose incorporators.
9. Prepare and file your incorporation papers with the appropriate state office.
10. Place any legally required advertisements about the incorporation of your organization.
11. Obtain any required local business licenses.
12. Obtain business insurance, and consider obtaining directors' and officers' insurance.
13. Register with your state's charitable regulation agency, if you will be required to do so.
14. Find out about legal requirements relating to employees if you plan on having them, such as federal income tax and Social Security tax withholding, state and local payroll tax procedures, unemployment insurance, and workers' compensation insurance; prepare job descriptions for staff, and develop personnel policies for employees.
15. Prepare draft organization bylaws.
16. Hold an organizational meeting of the board of directors and approve bylaws, approve organization bank accounts, elect organization officers, and schedule subsequent meetings.
17. Open a bank account for the organization.
18. Set up the organization's accounting/bookkeeping, financial reporting system, and other record-keeping systems.

19. Obtain office space if required, business cards, stationery, office equipment, and supplies.
20. Obtain an Internet host, publicize your e-mail address, and build your Web site.
21. Obtain any required state sales tax licenses if you will be required to collect sales tax on items you sell.
22. Apply for mailing permits.
23. If eligible, apply for a federal tax exemption using Form 1023 for 501(c)(3) status and Form 1024 for exemption under other sections of the Internal Revenue Code.

Chapter 1
The Decision to Incorporate

> **Synopsis:** Among the advantages of incorporating an organization are limits on liability, lower taxes, and increased organizational credibility. Among the disadvantages are loss of centralized control and increased paperwork, time, and expense of running a corporation.

Introduction to Incorporation

A corporation is a legal entity formed for business activities. Under state and federal laws, a corporation is treated as a separate "person" for purposes of making contracts, paying taxes, and being liable for the consequences of business activity. A nonprofit corporation, also called a "not-for-profit" corporation in some states, generally is not permitted to issue shares of stock, and does not provide shareholders with dividends from the profits that are received from operating the business. While nonprofit corporations can and do make profits, these profits may not inure to the benefit of the "owners" of the corporation— the board of directors or trustees. Rather, these profits must be used to operate and maintain the organization. Some states place limitations on the types of activities that are the primary purpose of the nonprofit corporation.

Generally, there are three classes of nonprofit corporations:

1. Funding agency (e.g. United Way, Jewish Federation, private foundations)

> The primary purpose of these organizations is to allocate funds, either those solicited as private donations or those already accumulated in an endowment or private fortune, for other agencies that provide actual services. Many of these organizations restrict their grants of funds to groups that provide a narrow range of services of interest to the funding organization. A Jewish federation is likely to make contributions solely to Jewish-affiliated organizations or others that principally serve the Jewish community. The United Way generally provides funding to social service agencies. Some foundations restrict their contributions to organizations promoting services for women, health-care related studies, or arts and humanities agencies.

2. Membership organizations (e.g. Common Cause, the Sierra Club, League of Women Voters)

> These organizations exist primarily to provide services (such as advocacy, information sharing, and networking) for their members, usually with a specialty of expertise.

3. Service agencies (e.g. hospitals, schools, day-care centers, family services)

> These organizations exist to provide specific services to the public. They often charge fees on a sliding scale for their services to fund the bulk of their budgets.

Each type of organization operates differently in many significant ways.

The decision to incorporate is a mere formality for most leaders who envision a large organization with employees, contracts, offices, property, and equipment. Corporate status in general, and nonprofit corporate status in particular, provides many advantages. Maintaining an unincorporated organization with annual revenue and expenditures comfortably in five figures is cumbersome at best, if not impossible. It is at the low end of the scale where the decision to incorporate is most important.

It would be ludicrous to consider incorporation for the Saturday morning running group get-together, which collects two dollars from each of its eight members to pay for the refreshments after the run. Yet, when the group expands to three hundred members, dues are collected to finance a race, the municipality demands that the club purchase insurance to indemnify against accidents, and the club wants a grant from an area foundation to purchase a bus to transport its members to area races, then incorporation is clearly the option of choice.

Advantages and Disadvantages of Incorporation

The **advantages** of incorporation are the following:

1. Limited Liability. Of all the reasons to seek corporate status, this is perhaps the most compelling. Under all state laws, the officers, directors, employees, and members of a corporation, except under very limited and unusual circumstances, are not personally liable for lawsuit judgments and debts related to the organization. Thus, the personal assets of the organization's executive director or board members are not at risk in the event of a successful suit brought against the corporation, or in the event the organization goes out of business while owing money to its creditors. The assets of an organization may be minimal, while the individuals running it may have substantial assets. Corporate status protects those personal assets. Many people won't even consider participating in the leadership of an organization unless their personal assets are shielded by incorporation.

The Congress and many state legislatures have enacted laws that are designed to expand the liability protection afforded to nonprofit boards of directors and volunteers (see Chapter 10).

2. Tax Advantages. In the absence of incorporation, income accruing to an individual running an organization is subject to federal, state, and local taxes at the individual rate, which is likely to be substantially more than the corporate rate. In the case of nonprofit incorporation, an organization can be exempt from many taxes, depending upon its type.

For organizations that are charitable, educational, religious, literary, or scientific, 501(c)(3) tax-exempt status is particularly attractive (see Chapter 9). Most states exempt corporations that have federal tax-exempt status from state corporate income tax. Certain types of charities may be exempt from state sales and use tax and local property taxes, as well. Many types of charitable institutions, such as colleges and hospitals, which have substantial property holdings, would be taxed beyond their abilities to operate if they were denied tax exemptions. Many funding sources, such as government, foundations, and the public, will not make contributions to an organization that is not exempt under Section 501(c)(3), since this status provides a tax exemption to the contributor and assures that there is at least some minimal level of accountability on the part of the organization.

3. Structure, Accountability, Perpetuity, and Legally Recognized Authority. When people and organizations interact with a bona fide corporation, they have confidence that there is some order and authority behind the decision-making of that entity. A reasonable expectation exists that the corporation will continue to honor agreements even if the principal actor for the organization dies, resigns, or is otherwise disassociated from the organization. They know that there is a legal document governing decision-making (as detailed in the bylaws), succession of officers, clear purposes (as detailed in the Articles of Incorporation), a system for paying bills, accounting for income and expenses, and a forum for the sharing of ideas on policy and direction from the corporation's board members. So long as the necessary papers are filed, the organization will continue in perpetuity regardless of changes in leadership. This gives such organizations an aura of immortality, which is seen as an advantage in planning beyond the likely tenure of an individual board chairperson or executive director.

4. Ancillary Benefits. Nonprofit incorporation can provide lower postage rates (see chapter 25); access to media (through free public service announcements); volunteers, who would be more hesitant volunteering for a comparable for-profit entity; and the so-called "halo effect," in which the public is more willing to do business with a nonprofit because of a real or perceived view that such an organization is founded and operated in the public interest.

5. Strength of Collegial Decision-Making. Decision-making in an autocracy is clearly easier and more efficient than in an organization run as a democracy. Yet, there is a value in making decisions by building a consensus among a majority of members of a diverse, volunteer, community-based board. Members of a board often bring different experiences and talents and provide information that would otherwise not be available in making decisions. Issues are often raised that, if overlooked, could possibly result in disastrous consequences for the organization.

The **disadvantages** of nonprofit incorporation are the following:

1. Loss of Centralized Control. Many organizations are formed and run by a charismatic leader with a vision of how to accomplish a particular task or mission. Decision-making is enhanced without the distractions of the scores of issues that relate not to the actual mission of the organization but to the internal management of the organization. The very act of forming a nonprofit corporation can be draining—preparing and filing Articles of Incorporation, negotiating bylaws, finding quality colleagues to serve on a board of directors, hiring qualified staff if necessary, and dealing with the myriad of personnel issues that emanate from hiring staff, preparing budgets, raising money, and preparing minutes of board meetings. Even finding a convenient time and place where the board can meet to ensure that a quorum is present can pose a troublesome and potentially overwhelming problem at times.

Incorporation is a legal framework that trades off the advantages addressed earlier in this section with some serious disadvantages. Decisions can no longer be made in a vacuum by one person without oversight or accountability, but are legally under the purview of a board of directors. Decisions have to withstand scrutiny of *all* persons on the board, some of whom may be hostile or have personal axes to grind. By definition, boards of directors are committees, and committees often make decisions that are compromises to mollify members with divergent viewpoints and competing interests.

For those used to making quick decisions "on the fly" and who revel in not having their decisions subject to second-guessing, modification, or otherwise being meddled with, incorporation can be a personally shackling experience and can dilute one's control over the organization.

2. Paperwork, Paperwork, Paperwork. Even in the smallest nonprofit corporation, the paperwork load related to corporate status can at times be overwhelming. There are deadlines for virtually every filing. Keeping ahead of the paperwork wave requires discipline, commitment, and a sense of humor. Forms get misfiled, or otherwise lost in the bureaucracy or mail.

In some cases, failure to handle this paperwork can result in criminal penalties. There are penalties for missed filings (e.g., failure to file a timely 990 federal tax return results in a $20/day penalty, up to a maximum of $10,000, or 5% of the agency's gross revenues, whichever is smaller—and $100/day up to $50,000 for organizations with annual gross receipts exceeding $1 million). As soon as the first employee is hired, the paperwork wave accompanying that is substantial.

In the first year, the filings can be intimidating, time-consuming, and frustrating. A new corporation must develop a bookkeeping system that is understandable by the accountant who will perform the audit and prepare the financial reports, pass resolutions, file forms to open up corporate savings and checking accounts, order checks, file tax returns, and pay taxes. There are many federal, state, and local taxes, each of which requires its own filing at different times of the year. A new corporation must also reconcile savings and checking accounts, prepare board meeting announcements and minutes, devise a system to pay bills, and establish a process for the reimbursement of expenses. Other tasks it must accomplish are filing forms to protect its corporate name, preparing an annual report, adopting a personnel policy, purchasing office equipment, renting an office, preparing budgets, writing fundraising letters, and finding and retaining board members.

Few of these tasks have a direct impact on the actual work of the agency, but typically they will consume more time during the initial year after incorporation than does the work related to the actual mission of the organization.The only consolation is that after a few years, one becomes familiar with the required filings. Then they become routine and just a minor nuisance.

3. Expenses in Money and Time. Significant resources are required to establish a corporation and run it efficiently. No law prohibits running a corporation from one's home with a staff of volunteers. Legally, the only monetary requirement is to pay a fee to file Articles of Incorporation. Yet, doing so often sets off a chain of events that dramatically increases the organization's complexity. Opening up corporate bank accounts, doing expense reports, filing taxes, and doing the paperwork described above are difficult to accomplish solely with volunteer labor. Raising the funds necessary to hire a person to do all of this work—in addition to coordinating the actual work related to carrying out the actual mission of the organization—adds to this burden, and requires even more filing and paperwork.

Many of these tasks would be required even in the absence of a decision to incorporate. One can avoid much of the "wasted" time and energy by keeping "small," but this places a substantial limit to what one can accomplish. Experiencing the disadvantages of incorporation is the cost one incurs to receive the substantial benefits.

Nonprofits and Private Benefit

Nonprofit corporation status provides many advantages over comparable for-profits. Yet this status is not conferred without a cost. Generally, nonprofits must operate differently and with different motivations than their for-profit counterparts. There is a general legal doctrine that prohibits nonprofits from acting in a manner that results in "private inurement" to individuals, i.e., the transfer of earnings or profits from the corporation to its "owners." The basic principle at work here is that a for-profit is intended to benefit its owners, whereas a nonprofit is intended to further a purpose.

In the 2001 book *Starting & Managing a Nonprofit Organization,* author-attorney Bruce R. Hopkins provides a useful chapter on the issue of private inurement in nonprofits.

There is nothing illegal or unethical about nonprofits selling goods and services and generating income. Nonprofits are becoming more sophisticated in finding new revenue sources to supplant the loss of government funds (see Chapters 22 and 23). Yet, nonprofits are distinguished from their for-profit counterparts by the destination of any profit. Chapter 26 includes a list of many of the important differences between nonprofits and for-profits.

Tips:

- Review your state's nonprofit laws and decide whether your organization is willing to be subjected to the limitations and accountability required by these laws.

- Avoid incorporating if it is essential to maintain complete control of the organization, and if it is possible to keep the scale of operations small.

- Contact someone who runs a nonprofit corporation of similar size and type envisioned for your organization. Ask questions about paperwork requirements, office equipment, rental space, and the benefits and pitfalls of running such a corporation.

- If leaning toward incorporation, identify potential incorporators/board members who are—

    a. Accessible, and not spread too thin among many other competing organizations
    b. Potential contributors to the organization
    c. Experienced fundraisers
    d. Knowledgeable about the issues of concern to the organization
    e. Respected and well-known in the community
    f. Experienced in legal, accounting, and nonprofit management issues.

- If you find the requirements of incorporating your own organization too intimidating, consider seeking a fiscal sponsor (see Chapter 11).

White Hat Communications

Chapter 2
Steps to Incorporation

Synopsis: Organizational leadership must file the appropriate forms with the state to incorporate an organization. Among important decisions to be made are choosing the corporate name, opting whether to have members, and choosing corporate purposes.

Introduction to Incorporation

While incorporation is a legal procedure, it does not require the services of a lawyer. However, lawyers with training and experience in state nonprofit law can be useful in reviewing, if not preparing, Articles of Incorporation and bylaws that are consistent with both statutory requirements and the purposes of the organization.

State libraries, law school libraries, and many public and private libraries have a set of books that have all of the state laws codified by topics that typically include "corporations." Make sure in researching current law to refer to the most up-to-date supplement for use in the current year. This supplement will include all changes made to state laws since the law books were first printed.

Role of Incorporators

Incorporators are those persons legally responsible for forming the corporation. It is common for one person to serve in this capacity, although several people may sign the Articles of Incorporation form as formal incorporators. Some states require more than one incorporator (see the state directory of this book).

Incorporators frequently play a more active role than solely being a name on the Articles of Incorporation filing. If they act to promote the interests of the new corporation (e.g., raise funds, recruit personnel, negotiate leases, or purchase property for the organization), their legal status is augmented by the responsibility of serving in a fiduciary capacity. This legal status confers on them the duty to take actions in the best interest of the corporation rather than their own personal interest, and to disclose any conflicts of interest that may occur in their business dealings on behalf of the corporation.

By law, the incorporators make agreements on behalf of the corporation while it is in the process of legal formation. These agreements have no legal effect until they are approved by the corporation's board of directors, once the corporation legally exists. As a result, incorporators who make these agreements must make it clear to the other party that the agreement is not binding until the corporation exists as a legal entity and its board ratifies the agreement.

Once the Articles of Incorporation are filed and the state government agency with jurisdiction over incorporation (usually the Department of State) approves them, incorporators have no formal status, with one exception. They are invited to be present at the organizational meeting required by law, at which the board of directors is selected.

It is a common practice that the incorporators include members who will be serving on the first board of directors. Thus, care should be taken as to the qualifications of incorporators, since they may continue their association with the corporation as directors.

Choosing a Corporate Name

One of the most important and basic decisions in forming a corporation is choosing a corporate name. This name will be the organization's corporate identity, and the image created by it provides the first impression held by those outside of the corporation. "Short" and "descriptive" are two desirable characteristics in a corporate name. Many nonprofit organizations choose a name that gives the connotation of helping, or otherwise doing charitable activities in the public interest, rather than implying a for-profit motive.

If the organization plans to apply for 501(c)(3) status, it should avoid names that would be suitable for organizations whose activities are clearly not eligible for this status. The organization may wish to consider suitable acronyms comprising the first letter of each word of its name, but cute or frivolous acronyms often give an unprofessional impression. It is useful to check if any other organization is using the prospective name by using Internet search engines and the U.S. Patent and Trademark Office's database (see below).

The process of having to change a corporate name after incorporating and operating as a nonprofit often results in time-consuming and costly activities, such as changing the logo (see Chapter 25); reprinting stationery, business cards, checks, and brochures; and changing all of the legal forms relating to Articles of Incorporation, bank accounts, and contracts.

For obvious legal reasons, the name must be unique in the state of incorporation, although it is usually legal to adopt a name similar to another existing corporation after receiving permission from that corporation and filing the necessary forms to do so. Typical state laws permit the name to be in any language, but require that it be expressed in English letters or characters. For more information about the limitations on corporate names, consult the state directory of this book, and call the contact office with specific questions.

You should perform a name search with the state agency of jurisdiction to ensure that no other corporation, active or inactive, is using an identical or similar name. Almost every state permits the name to be reserved for a modest fee prior to incorporation, typically for a 120-day period.

Many corporations also choose to do a national name search and take steps to register their names with the United States Patent and Trademark Office as trademarks. This can be done only for those organizations that will be marketing goods and services interstate. The fee is $375 for paper filing and $325 for electronic filing using the Trademark Electronic Applications System (TFAS), which provides registration for ten years, assuming the owner certifies that the trademark has active status. Obviously, if an organization has trademarked its name, it is not available for your use, even if that organization is headquartered in another state.

For more information or to obtain the correct forms, contact the Patent and Trademark Office:

U.S. Patent and Trademark Office (USPTO)
Commissioner for Trademarks
U.S. Department of Commerce
PO Box 1451
Alexandria, VA 22313
(571) 272-1000
(800) 786-9199
Web site: http://www.uspto.gov/teas/

Basic information about trademarks can be accessed at:
http://www.uspto.gov/

Choosing Corporate Purposes

It is generally advisable to state broad corporate purposes in a manner that permits the corporation to grow and change direction without requiring its Articles of Incorporation to be amended. However, the purposes should be specific enough to permit the corporation to be eligible for 501(c)(3) status, if this is expected.

The Internal Revenue Service has provided guidance on drafting a purpose statement that will facilitate a successful 501(c)(3) eligibility determination. Two examples illustrate clauses that will satisfy the IRS:

"1. charitable and educational purposes within the meaning of IRC 501(c)(3).
"2. To grant scholarships for deserving junior college students residing in Gotham City."

"To operate a hospital" is an example of a purpose that is unacceptable to the IRS. The explanation provided by the IRS is that the purpose is ambiguous, since a hospital may be exempt or not exempt, depending upon how it is operated.

The IRS provides language that nonprofit organizations may use if they choose a broad corporate purpose consistent with the first example:

This corporation is organized exclusively for one or more purposes as specified in Section 501(c)(3) of the Internal Revenue Code or the corresponding section of any future federal tax code, including, for such purposes, the making of distributions to organizations that qualify as exempt organizations under Section 501(c)(3) of the Internal Revenue Code, or the corresponding section of any future tax code. The corporation shall not carry on any other activities not permitted to be carried on by a corporation exempt from Federal income tax under 501(c)(3) of the Internal Revenue Code of 1954, as amended (or the corresponding provision of any future United States Internal Revenue law).

A second consideration when devising the purpose statement to facilitate exemption is to provide that the organization benefits an indefinite class of individuals, not specific persons. For example, if the purpose of the organization is intended to be establishing a scholarship fund for specific members of a family who were orphaned by the September 11th World Trade Center disaster, the purpose should be "to grant scholarships to deserving American students orphaned by terrorist attacks" rather than "to grant scholarships to the children of John A. Smith."

Research similar organizations and review their Articles of Incorporation to obtain ideas on framing your own organization's Articles of Incorporation. Some states have limitations on how broad these purposes can be in the Articles (see state directory beginning on page 375).

Choosing to Have Members or No Members

"Membership" in the legal sense has a different meaning than those in an organization who pay dues. In the context of incorporation, having members refers to providing broad governance authority beyond an organization's board of directors. In general, it is desirable for most nonprofit corporations to have no members. This will ensure that all power and authority will be maintained by the board of directors, and it will prevent the difficult legal problems of expelling an individual member should that occasion arise. It is also expensive and time-consuming to conduct elections, change bylaws, and make major organizational decisions when all members have the legal right to participate. Outsiders, including those who would pay dues in exchange for participating in organizational programs and activities, can still participate in the activities of the nonprofit corporation without being legal members who are entitled to vote on the affairs of the corporation.

As with almost every issue, there are exceptions to this. Many organizations will find it desirable for each participant in the organization's programs and activities to have an equal voice in the internal governance of the organization. Many individuals bristle at the fact that a nonprofit organization's governance is often controlled by a self-selected group of individuals that some times are perceived by members to be elitist, paternalistic, or secretive about the organization's affairs. Some feel that having legal members is more egalitarian and democratic.

Additional Provisions

Many corporations that wish to qualify for 501(c)(3) status add a provision that will facilitate tax-exemption approval. One such provision is a statement forbidding the corporation from engaging in partisan political activity on behalf of, or in opposition to, a candidate or substantially engaging in lobbying. The language for this provision can be adopted from 501(c)(3) itself:

> No substantial part of the activities of the corporation shall be the carrying on of propaganda, or otherwise attempting to influence legislation, and the corporation shall not participate in, or intervene in (including the publishing or distribution of statements) any political campaign on behalf of any candidate for public office except as authorized under the Internal Revenue Code of 1954, as amended.

A second provision required for Section 501(c)(3) eligibility relates to corporate dissolution:

> Upon the dissolution of the corporation, assets shall be distributed for one or more exempt purposes within the meaning of Section 501(c)(3) of the Internal Revenue Code, as amended or supplemented, or shall be distributed to the federal government or to a state or local government for a public purpose. Any such assets not so disposed of shall be disposed of by the District Court of the county in which the principal office of the corporation is then located, exclusively for such purposes or to such organization or organizations, as said Court shall determine, which are organized and operated exclusively for such purposes.

A third provision required by the IRS for Section 501(c)(3) eligibility relates to private inurement. All states require similar language as a condition for incorporating as a nonprofit:

> No part of the net earnings of the corporation shall inure to the benefit of, or be distributable to, its members, trustees, officers, or other persons, except that the corporation shall be authorized and empowered to pay reasonable compensation for services rendered to the corporation and to make payments and distributions in furtherance of the purposes set forth herein.

Once the Articles of Incorporation are filed and approved, be sure that all actions taken on behalf of the Corporation will clearly indicate that they are actions for the corporation and not on behalf of individuals. Otherwise, such individuals may be personally liable for fulfilling the terms of contracts and other agreements, such as paying rent, staff salaries, telephone installation costs, and so on. One way to indicate that persons are acting on behalf of the corporation is to explicitly sign legal contracts and other documents as follows:

(corporate name)
By (individual's signature)
(individual's corporate title)

Tips:

- Review the legal requirements of state laws for nonprofits to make sure the organization can and is willing to comply with them.
- Have a lawyer review, if not draft, the Articles of Incorporation.
- Include in the Articles of Incorporation additional provisions to enhance the prospects for achieving the appropriate federal tax status if such status is desirable. See Chapter 9 for additional details.
- Choose a short and descriptive corporate name.
- Check out your prospective name using popular Internet search engines, such as Google *(http://www.google.com)* and Yahoo! *(http://www.yahoo.com)*. Having a corporate name that is not unique in the world may not be illegal, but it could be confusing.
- Review publications published by the Small Business Administration (SBA) that will help you start up and run your organization.

White Hat Communications

Chapter 3
Bylaws

Synopsis: Bylaws provide general policy guidelines for nonprofit corporations. There are statutory provisions that go into effect automatically in the absence of comparable bylaw provisions.

Introduction to Preparing Bylaws

Every corporation must have a set of bylaws that provides for its internal management and regulation. A sample set of bylaws is included in the Appendix that may provide guidance to those seeking language for bylaws that would be appropriate for a nonprofit organization.

Perhaps the best advice on formulating organizational bylaws can be found in the publication *Robert's Rules of Order Newly Revised,* 10th Edition, published in November 2000 by Perseus Books ($37.50). The 802 pages in the book contain an invaluable wealth of knowledge not only on parliamentary procedure but also on organizational leadership. This book provides guidance on drafting certain bylaw provisions, and includes a sample set of bylaws. An abridged, inexpensive paperback parliamentary guide, *Robert's Rules in Brief,* published in 2004, is available (Da Capo Press, 176 pages, $6.95).

Each state has individual requirements for the content of bylaws for nonprofit corporations, although these requirements tend to be similar. Beyond legal requirements, corporate bylaws are a necessary and important document, and great thought and care should be exercised as to what will be included in them.

Typical bylaws include provisions governing the following internal procedures and policies of the nonprofit corporation:

1. The purposes of the corporation, consistent with any federal tax law limitation or state laws governing lobbying or other activity
2. Limitations of liability of directors, consistent with state law
3. Types of officers
4. Terms, powers, and succession of officers
5. Location of principal office
6. Whether the corporation will have members, or whether all powers will be vested in a board of directors
7. How directors will be selected and how vacancies will be filled
8. How many directors there will be
9. Length of terms of board of directors, limits on consecutive terms, and if and how such terms will overlap with other board members
10. Terms under which a member of the board of directors can be disqualified
11. Conditions under which the annual meeting and other regularly scheduled board meetings are held
12. How unscheduled meetings of the board may be called
13. Terms under which notice of board meetings must occur
14. What constitutes a quorum for the transaction of business
15. How many directors are required to approve an action
16. Whether actions of the board may be ratified through the mail or by conference call, or require directors to be present at a meeting

17. Power of the chairperson (or president) to appoint committees, and to provide for rules, powers, and procedures of such committees
18. Whether alternates may be empowered to represent directors, and who selects them
19. Who is responsible for preparing board meeting minutes and for storing and using the corporate seal on official documents
20. Who is responsible for keeping and reviewing the corporate books, and dispersing corporate funds
21. How amendments may be made to the bylaws
22. Terms and conditions regarding compensation, if any, paid to directors
23. What committees are authorized, and what powers and duties they have
24. The terms under which the corporation will be dissolved.

Legal Requirements of Bylaws

Each state has laws providing for some minimum standards with respect to nonprofit corporation bylaws.

Most of these laws provide rules on many of the above bylaw options in the absence of explicit directions in the nonprofit corporation's bylaws. Thus, it is important to place provisions in the bylaws that will be intended to supersede these statutory legal guidelines, if the directors feel that the guidance provided in law is not acceptable to the corporation.

Among the bylaws provisions that deserve the highest consideration and thought are the following, with some comments about the issues they raise:

Quorum Requirements

A quorum is the minimum number of members or directors required to be present for a meeting to be held for the legal transaction of business. The purpose of a quorum requirement is to assure that actions are taken by a representative number of duly authorized participants rather than by an elite few. Standard advice, in the absence of relying on any statutory requirement, is to set the quorum at the minimum number of people who will be expected to attend a meeting, taking into account emergencies, adverse weather conditions, or conflicts with competing meetings. If the bylaws permit it, board members may participate in meetings and be counted as part of a quorum if they are in communication by speaker phone or by conference call.

Since actions cannot be taken legally at board meetings without a quorum present, it is best to begin with a conservatively low quorum requirement. Then change the bylaws to increase that number as appropriate. Otherwise, it is possible that the corporation will never have a quorum for its meetings, even if the sole purpose of the meeting is to change the bylaws to decrease the number of directors constituting a quorum.

Voting Rights

Boards need to vote to formally demonstrate that they have taken actions. Many organizations can be effectively run by consensus rather than by formal voting, but even the most congenial and tolerant boards will eventually face issues that will divide them. In the absence of a provision in the bylaws, action may be taken at a board meeting with the approval of a majority of directors who are present at the meeting. Nothing prohibits a two-thirds vote from being required to ensure that actions are closer to representing a consensus. A two-thirds vote may be suggested for changing bylaws, or for changing membership dues requirements. Generally, a majority vote is sufficient for most routine board decisions, and avoids the inability to take positions and actions that can occur as a result of a two-thirds voting requirement.

Selection of Officers

Many organizations are attracted to the democratic notion of offices being opened to all. With such a policy, any director can run for an office, ballots are prepared, and the winner is selected by the majority (or plurality) of voters from the board of directors or the membership at large. Other organizations feel that democracy puts at risk an orderly succession and threatens the existing power structure. Orderly succession can be accomplished by providing for a nominating committee, appointed by the chairperson, which selects a slate of officers. This slate is then perfunctorily approved by the full board. Both systems have their advantages and disadvantages.

Some organizations utilize a third alternative that combines the two. The nominations committee recommends a slate of candidates, but the procedures permit other candidates to run as well.

Executive Committees

Board meetings may occur at regular intervals, but issues arise in the interim that demand immediate attention. In such cases, it is valuable to have a mandated procedure for taking legally legitimate actions in the absence of board meetings. The mechanism to accomplish this is the executive committee, provided for in the corporate bylaws. While the executive committee typically is comprised of the corporation's officers, many state laws authorize executive committees comprised of one or more directors appointed by the board. Typically, by law, the executive committee has all of the power and authority of the full board with the following exceptions:

- The executive committee cannot fill vacancies on the board.
- The executive committee cannot adopt, amend, or repeal bylaws.
- The executive committee cannot have powers inconsistent with the resolution passed by the board establishing it.

Tips:

- **Review state law with respect to corporate bylaws. Identify which provisions are required, which provisions apply only in the absence of a different provision in the bylaws, and which act to pre-empt the statutory guideline.**

- **Give careful consideration to the more important bylaw provisions, such as—**

  - **Quorum requirements**
  - **Succession of officers**
  - **Powers of the executive committee**
  - **Voting by the board of directors**

- **Have an attorney review the bylaws to ensure that they are in compliance with state law, and ensure that the organization's desires with respect to internal decision-making will be consistent with efficient operating procedures.**

- **Schedule an organizational meeting to approve the bylaws, and distribute a draft of proposed bylaws before this meeting.**

- **After a final version of the bylaws is approved, provide a final copy of the bylaws to all members of the board of directors.**

Chapter 4
Nonprofit Boards of Directors

by Michael A. Sand

Synopsis: It is a critically important function for nonprofit organizations to find and retain qualified, experienced board members and officers. Board meetings generally have a routine order of business and provide the forum for making organizational policy.

One important requirement of a nonprofit organization is the formation of a board of directors. The board has the responsibility to set policy for the organization in accordance with all applicable laws and to see to it that the policies are implemented.

Board Formation

The size of the board should depend on the needs of the organization. If the board's role is strictly policy-making and the policies are implemented by a qualified staff, a small board might be more appropriate. However, if extensive board time is required for fundraising or implementing programs, then a much larger board is in order.

The number of board members is set in the bylaws. One effective technique is to set a minimum and maximum number of board members and to allow the board to determine its own size within these parameters. Then the board can start small and add members as the need arises.

The term of board members must be included in the bylaws. Board members should have fixed terms of office. One common practice is for all board members to have three-year terms, with one-third of the members being elected each year. In this way, board continuity is assured. Some boards allow their members to serve an unlimited number of terms; other boards wish to limit the number to ensure new members with fresh ideas.

The election process should also be spelled out in the bylaws.

Most organizations have a nominating or governance committee that is responsible for recommending new board members to the full board. Additional candidates for board membership can be nominated either in advance or from the floor at the election.

The titles, duties, length of term, and process for the election of officers should be spelled out in the bylaws.

Organizational Officers

The elected officers of most organizations are similar:

Chairperson, Chair, or President
Leads the meetings of the organization. Appoints committee chairs. Either signs checks or delegates this duty to another individual.

Vice-Chair
Assumes the duties of the president or chair in his or her absence, or upon his or her death or resignation. In many organizations, is given specific responsibilities,

either in the bylaws or by vote. In some organizations, automatically becomes the next president.

Secretary
Either takes minutes at the board meeting or approves the minutes if taken by another individual. Responsible for all official correspondence.

Treasurer
Responsible for finances of the organization. Usually makes financial reports to the board and signs checks.

Getting Good Board Members

Many organizations are finding it more difficult than ever to attract excellent board members. This is due to many factors, such as the large increase in the number of nonprofit boards, the increasing number of women in the work force, and the fact that upwardly mobile professionals often relocate.

To ensure excellence, many nominating committees meet several times during the year rather than just once to search for potential board members. One effective technique is to strive for a diverse board, and to list the types of characteristics desired. Some might be:

- *Expertise*: Some board members should have personnel management, fiscal, fundraising, or legal expertise.

- *Ages*: It is helpful to have older people represented, as well as youth and individuals in between.

- *Races and Religions:* All major races and religions in the community should be represented on a diverse board.

- *Backgrounds:* It would be helpful if some board members had corporate backgrounds, some were government leaders, and others had served on the boards of other nonprofit groups.

- *Users of the service:* Many boards include representatives of the client population being served.

The nominating committee or board development committee can search throughout the year for individuals with these characteristics, who are then asked if they want to be considered for board membership.

Each board should have a list of board member responsibilities. These might include attending board meetings on a regular basis, serving on at least one standing committee, and participating in fundraising. The list of duties should be provided to each prospective board member, and no board member should be elected who will not agree to meet these responsibilities.

Keeping Good Board Members

One technique for keeping good board members is to require all new board members to participate in an orientation program before they attend their first board meeting.

The first step in the process is to receive and review materials that all board members should have received previously. These include—

- Articles of Incorporation
- Bylaws
- Funding applications
- Personnel, fiscal, and other board policies
- Annual reports
- Names, addresses, phone numbers, and biographical sketches of other board members and key staff members
- List of committees and committee duties
- Minutes of the last several board meetings
- Audits, budgets, and recent financial statements.

The second step is to hold a meeting with the board chair and the executive director. This provides an opportunity to ask questions about the materials received, visit the staff offices and programs, get an update of current issues, and review board member responsibilities.

Other steps to encourage productivity of board members include—

- Give board members specific projects. A board member who serves as the chair of a committee or who has specific fundraising responsibilities is more likely to stay active.
- Keep board meetings interesting.
- Thank board members for their work.
- Have social events periodically, in addition to formal board meetings.

One other technique is to remove unproductive board members quickly and replace them with new and productive ones.

Other ways to increase board productivity include—

- Have a policy in the bylaws that missing a specified number of board meetings without a reason will result in automatic dismissal.
- Re-elect only board members who have been meeting their responsibilities.
- Call board members who have not been active to ask them if there are any problems. In some cases, the chairperson should ask for their resignation if they do not agree to meet board responsibilities.

Board Responsibilities

Members of boards of directors have the following duties:

Personnel

The board hires the executive director. This is the board's most important responsibility. It then makes assignments to the executive director and monitors the executive director's performance. It is appropriate for the board or its Personnel Committee to do a formal performance appraisal of the executive director at least annually. The board approves salary scales and job descriptions for the other staff members, who are hired by the executive director. The board approves the personnel policies for the organization.

Finance

The board approves budgets for the organization. No funds are expended unless the funds are included in a budget approved by the board. The board approves spending reports, which are submitted on a regular basis.

Fundraising

All applications for funds are submitted to the board before being submitted to funding sources. The board also approves plans for special events fundraising, and board members are expected to participate in fundraising events.

Planning

Board members approve short- and long-range plans for the organization. They then monitor the effectiveness of the agency's programs to see if it has met the goals outlined in the plans.

Board Development

The board selects new board members and adopts procedures to see that excellent board members are selected and continue to serve.

Public Relations

Board members are aware of all of the organization's activities and encourage participation in appropriate activities by the community.

Advising

Board members advise the executive director on policy implementation as requested.

How Boards Function Effectively

Boards set policies only through a majority vote of their members at board meetings, unless the bylaws provide otherwise. For boards with staffs, one effective method of policy-making is to ask the staff to draft proposed policies. These policies are then sent to a board committee for review.

The chair of each committee should be a board member appointed by the board president. Members of committees are usually selected by the committee chair and may include non-board members.

All committees are advisory, except that the bylaws may permit the executive committee to act on behalf of the board between board meetings. Once a committee has approved a proposed policy, it is submitted to the board for approval. The board may delegate authority to committees to implement some decisions.

Board members who want a policy to be adopted begin the discussion by making a motion that it be approved. If another board member seconds the motion, discussion can begin; if not, the motion fails.

Once a motion is seconded, the chairperson opens the floor for discussion. Members are recognized by the chairperson before they may speak, and they can discuss only the motion on the floor. When the discussion has ended, the chairperson announces that a vote will be taken.

The easiest way to vote is by a show of hands. The secretary can then record the vote. If a majority approves a policy, it becomes the board's policy (unless the bylaws provide otherwise). It is the responsibility of the executive director to implement that policy.

The executive director receives instructions from the board at a board meeting. It is improper for individual board members to give assignments to any staff member without prior board authorization.

Holding High-Quality Board Meetings

One key factor in getting and keeping excellent board members is the quality of the board meetings. If board meetings are unproductive, board members tend to be unproductive.

An important technique for improving board meetings is to do as much planning *before the board meeting* as possible.

This might include:

- Sending a notice of the date, time, and location of the meeting to the members several weeks before the meeting. Even if the board meets the same day of each month at the same place and time, a reminder notice is important.

- Giving the board members the telephone number of the individual (usually the chairperson) to call if they cannot attend the meeting. This way, the chairperson can get input on important items from individuals who cannot attend the meeting. Also, if a quorum will not be present, the meeting can be canceled in advance.

- Notifying members of important items to be discussed at the meeting. For major items, information or issue papers might be included in the meeting notice packet.

- Including as many written items as possible with the meeting notice rather than distributing them at the meeting. This may include the minutes of the previous meeting and the treasurer's report, for example. Members then have an opportunity to read items before the meeting, and members who do not attend the meeting are kept up-to-date more effectively.

- Developing a preliminary agenda before the meeting. Committee chairs who will be asked to report at the meeting should be notified. Background reports should be developed for important issues.

The board meetings should start on time. Once the members know that every board meeting starts on time, it is much more likely that they will be prompt. Each board meeting should start with the distribution of a written agenda. The agenda should be as detailed as possible, listing each separate item to be voted on.

Once the secretary announces that a quorum is present, the chairperson asks all those present if there are any additional items for the agenda. Thus, there will be no surprises, and the chairperson can run the meeting more effectively. The chairperson has the option of referring new items to committees or postponing items until future meetings.

A typical order of business at a board meeting is as follows:

- *Approval of the Minutes of the Previous Meeting.* A formal vote is needed to approve the minutes. Minutes should be distributed to all members and should not be read aloud at the meeting.

- *Chairperson's Report.* The chairperson should state before each item whether it is informational only or requires board action. The chairperson should remind the members that only policy-making recommendations require board action.

- *Executive Director's Report.* This report should be in writing. If it is lengthy, it should be distributed before the meeting. The executive director should then highlight important aspects of the written report and take questions.

- *Committee Reports.* Committee reports should be in writing unless they are very brief. After giving the report, the committee chair should make specific motions when board action is required. Only policy items require board action; no board action is required when the committee chair is simply providing information.

- *Unfinished Business.* The only items belonging in this section are ones raised at previous board meetings. The chairperson should remind the members when the item was raised originally and why it was postponed.

- *New Business.* Major items of business are discussed as part of the chairperson's report, executive director's report, or committee reports. At the beginning of the meeting, members are asked if they have additional agenda items, and the chairperson has the option of placing some of these items under New Business.

- *Good and Welfare.* Many organizations provide an opportunity for members and guests to make short announcements, raise issues to be discussed at future meetings, or comment on items of interest.

- *Adjournment.* No formal action is needed. The chairperson announces the date, time, and place of the next meeting, reminds the members of steps to be taken before the meeting, such as committee meetings, and adjourns the board meeting.

After the board meeting, the minutes are sent to board members for their review. The minutes must include a list of attendees and the motions made and votes taken. Additional information may be included at the pleasure of the board. Many organizations include only the minimum required, and the minutes do not include individual comments made at the meeting. While the minutes need not be taken by the board secretary, they should be distributed under the signature of the board secretary.

Relationship Between Board and Staff Members

The board of directors sets policy for the organization. Several examples of the types of policies set by the board are provided above. The only way policy can be set is by a majority vote of the board at a board meeting (unless the bylaws provide otherwise).

The executive director (or chief executive officer) attends all board meetings, and is responsible for implementing the policies set by the board. The executive director hires other staff members (whose salary levels and job descriptions have been approved by the board) to assist in implementing these policies.

When an item arises at a board meeting, the chairperson rules whether the item is a policy matter. If so, a vote of the board is required for action to be taken. If the item is not a policy matter, no board vote is taken. The purpose of the discussion is to provide guidance to the executive director on non-policy matters.

The executive director researches sources of funds and develops grant applications. Before a grant application can be submitted to a funding source, it should be approved by the board.

Certain types of communications between board members and staff members are not appropriate. For example, individual board members may not give assignments to staff members. Assignments are given to the executive director by vote of the board at a board meeting. The executive director is responsible for assigning tasks to other staff members.

Staff members should not complain to individual board members about programs, assignments, or policies. Complaints should be made according to specific procedures established by the board.

When a board member volunteers to help out in the office, that person must be treated as a staff person and no longer wears the "board hat." The executive director remains the person to make assignments to that person.

Tips:

- Develop a list of typical decision areas that are likely to arise in the course of routine corporate operations and reach a board consensus on whether the decisions should be made by—

    a. The executive director alone
    b. The executive director, in consultation with the board
    c. The executive director, in consultation with the board chairperson
    d. The board alone
    e. The chairperson alone
    f. A committee of the board.

    Review, revise, and update this list annually.

- Consider adopting a policy on the responsibilities and privileges of board members, and include a conflict-of-interest policy. A sample conflict of interest policy is provided in Form 1023 of the Internal Revenue Service, and more information may be found on the Web at:

http://www.nonprofits.org/npofaq/16/59.html

Chapter 5
Mission and Vision Statements

Synopsis: Mission and vision statements provide a foundation for your organization's future and help keep it focused on the purposes for which it was created. The mission statement includes the core organizational purpose. The vision statement describes the ideal future of the organization. Both are useful in maintaining the stability of organizations.

Every nonprofit organization should have a mission statement and a vision statement. Many nonprofit executives are confused about the difference between the two, and this is not surprising since organizational consultants disagree among themselves about what these should contain.

The Mission Statement

The mission statement should be a succinct description of the basic purpose of the organization, including the nature of the work to be carried out, the reason it exists, and the clients and constituencies it is designed to serve. It may also include some principles and values that are to guide the organization, although these can be enumerated in a separate values/principles statement.

The mission statement serves several purposes.

First, it is a core document guiding basic decision-making for the organization. The mission statement can effectively place constraints on decision-making that is inconsistent with the organization's core purpose, and thus provide a mechanism for organizational stability. Any decision made by an organization that would result in activities that contradict the mission statement should either not be implemented, or should require a major soul-searching by the organization's board of directors.

A second purpose is to provide the organization's board and staff with a useful short description of the organization. This permits all who work with the organization to be on the same page with respect to core purpose. The mission statement serves an important public relations function by explaining to important stakeholders, such as funders, government regulators, and clients, what the organization is about.

A third purpose is to serve as a way to focus all of your organization's staff and board on the primary reason for the organization's existence, so that internal activities and politics that might conflict with the true purposes of the organization can be reined in and resources are not diverted to purposes inconsistent with the core mission.

Many mission statements contain two parts, although the first part is sufficient. The first part is often referred to as the "umbrella," a short overview of the purpose of the organization. For example, the Pennsylvania Jewish Coalition's mission is "to monitor legislative and regulatory developments in Harrisburg that affect Pennsylvania's organized Jewish community." During the 13 years I served as the executive director of that organization, I must have recited that mantra a thousand times, and I can still do so in my sleep. This statement served an important purpose. It kept me focused on state matters at a time when there was a vortex of legislative and regulatory activity in Washington that threatened to divert me from doing the narrow task for which I was hired. Another purpose is that the funder, legislator, or member of the press who heard me recite it generally understood the role and essence of the organization.

A second part of the mission statement, which many, including myself, consider to be optional, provides further detail. One way to do this is to add the following after the umbrella: "In support of this mission, we..." followed by general, bullet-pointed objectives relating to, for example, increasing public awareness about the organization's goals and objectives; meeting the needs of clients; providing quality services; and maintaining relationships with officials from the government, the media, the advocacy community, and the public.

The Vision Statement

The vision statement is related to, but clearly different from, the mission statement. Its purpose is to convey the ideal future of the organization—what it hopes to become in the eyes of its board, staff, and stakeholders. One purpose of the vision statement is to inspire those in the organization to achieve goals. Another is to help frame decisions made by the organization in the context of achieving these goals.

Among the issues that might be appropriate in a vision statement include the organization's place in society, its intended growth, its use of new technology, quality improvement, its reputation in the community, and how the public perceives the organization's effectiveness and efficiency. Other topics could be how it will serve as a good organizational citizen in the community and a measurement of the degree to which it hopes to contribute to solving (or mitigating) particular social problems.

One of the best guides I have found on the preparation of mission statements and vision statements is a 1996 book, *A Guide to Strategic Thinking: Building Your Planning Foundation* by George Morrisey (Jossey-Bass).

Examples of Mission and Vision Statements

The following are examples of mission and vision statements.

Mission Statement of the Delaware Association of Nonprofit Agencies (reprinted with permission):

Our mission is to increase the effectiveness of Delaware's nonprofit organizations. To achieve this, DANA will do the following:

> *-Promote understanding and support as an advocate for the efforts of nonprofits through public education activities.*

> *-Provide a network for ongoing information and activities which assist nonprofits in areas such as training, purchasing, managing, fundraising and public relations.*

Vision Statement of California State University, Monterey Bay (CSUMB)
http://csumb.edu/site/x11547.xml

Vision Statement of Africare
http://www.africare.org/about/about.html

Vision Statement of the Young Adult Library Services Association (YALSA)
http://www.ala.org/ala/yalsa/aboutyalsab/yalsavisionstatement.cfm

Vision Statement of the Forestville (CA) Planning Association:
http://www.forestvillefpa.org/about/vision.html

Vision Statement of the Pennsylvania Society of Association Executives (PASAE):
http://www.pasae.org/about/mission_vision.asp

Online Resources to Explore

The Grantsmanship Center: How to Write a Mission Statement
http://www.tgci.com/magazine/98fall/mission.asp

Dilbert.com's Mission Statement Generator
http://www.dilbert.com/comics/dilbert/games/career/bin/ms.cgi

Leader to Leader Institute: Drucker Self-Assessment Tool—How to Develop a Mission Statement
http://www.pfdf.org/leaderbooks/sat/mission.html

Alliance for Nonprofit Management: What's In a Mission Statement?
http://www.allianceonline.org/FAQ/strategic_planning/what_s_in_mission_statement.faq

Raise Your Voice: How to Write a Mission Statement
http://www.compact.org/scec/getstarted/howto-mission.html

Tips:

- **Keep your mission statement focused on a narrow, specific purpose, to an extent that your organization won't be seen as potentially duplicative of other organizations in your area. In other words, carve out your own organizational niché, highlighting a unique service or serving a unique population of clients.**

- **Don't try to put too much into your mission statement; a single sentence is usually sufficient.**

- **Consider the mission and vision statements of similar organizations. You can find many examples on the World Wide Web.**

- **Periodically revisit your mission and vision statements to determine if they might be constraining your organization from adapting to new environmental conditions.**

Chapter 6
Strategic Planning

Synopsis: Formal strategic planning is not for every organization. All stakeholders must be committed to successfully develop and implement a strategic plan. Although such plans require a major investment in money and time and have other institutional costs and risks, the benefits include enhancing the agency's ability to respond to internal and external threats.

Introduction

Strategic planning is a formalized process by which an organization makes a study of its vision for the future, typically for three years or more from the present. A strategic plan is an important management tool that can help agency leaders consider the effects of advances in technology, changing markets for its services, the effects of government funding cutbacks, or the emergence of other organizations (both for-profits and nonprofits) that provide similar, competing services.

Agency CEOs often are so involved with putting out fires and responding to the exigencies of day-to-day operations that it is a luxury to set aside time to think about the position of the organization even a year into the future. An agency's board is often ill equipped to consider changes in agency structure and operations in the context of a regular board meeting.

Purpose of Strategic Planning

In his 1994 book *The Rise and Fall of Strategic Planning,* Henry Mintzberg lists four reasons for organizations to do strategic planning: to coordinate their activities, to ensure that the future is taken into account, to be rational, and to control. Strategic planning is designed to suggest remedies for agency problems before they blow up. Deep cuts in government grants, changes in markets, advances in technology, competition from for-profit businesses, and changes in demographics in an agency's service area all crystallize the need to change the basic way an agency does business.

Virtually all successful large for-profit businesses engage in a formal strategic planning process. The conventional wisdom is that businesses that do so, regardless of whether they are for-profit or nonprofit, are more successful over time than those that do not. However, Mintzberg cites scores of academic studies that show mixed results as to the benefits of strategic planning in business and industry, and concludes that the value of strategic planning is nebulous at best.

Putting that aside, a periodic strategic planning process provides the framework for a long-term assessment of emerging threats, and the opportunity to develop creative strategies to respond to them. The intent here is not to encourage or discourage nonprofits to engage in a formal strategic planning process; rather, it is to raise issues to consider in the event that this endeavor, for whatever reason, is under consideration.

Strategic planning requires the investment of both money and time. For most nonprofits, both are scarce. Thus, it is important that agency leaders systematically evaluate whether the benefits of preparing, updating, and implementing a periodic strategic plan outweigh the costs. Strategic plan preparation often involves the hiring of an outside consultant, plenty of meetings, and the involvement of board members, agency staff, and other agency stakeholders for an extended period of time.

The strategic planning process is fraught with danger. The contents of a final strategic plan often are totally at odds with the vision of the agency leader who first suggested preparing one. The planning committee dynamics are often uncontrollable by the people who provide the agency with leadership. Agency leaders may be uncomfortable sharing the agency's dreams and aspirations, its "dirty little secrets," and proprietary financial projections with a professional outside consultant, and may be even more reticent with community members of the planning committee. Yet, many agencies that successfully complete a strategic planning process improve their performance. Participating board members feel a renewed connection and bond to both the agency and their colleagues. Agencies that don't plan for the future, whether in a formalized process or informal board retreats, often suffer the consequences.

Strategic planning in the for-profit sector has been popular for several decades. In the for-profit world, strategic planning has the advantage of having each member of the committee, virtually by definition, already in agreement on the basic mission of the organization; that is, in short, to make as much profit as possible. There will be differences, of course, as to the methods used to accomplish this. In a nonprofit, there is not always agreement on the mission from the outset. In a hospital situation, for example, some planning committee members may view the mission as providing quality health care to the community. Some may feel it is to teach medical students, advance life-saving technology, increase "market share" by gobbling up other health care institutions, or serve populations not served by other institutions.

In a for-profit setting, the outcomes are easily measurable—net profit and market share are statistics easily compiled. In the nonprofit sector, consumer satisfaction, community benefit, and image in the community often are considered more important than bottom-line net revenue, and they are difficult to measure satisfactorily. In the nonprofit sector, board members may actually be concerned if the institution is making too much net revenue and not providing services to sectors of the market that would clearly result in revenue shortfalls. It is the nature of nonprofits that the institution is not motivated by private profit motive and, in theory, this can create conflicts. As a result of government cutbacks, tensions are mounting within nonprofit boards as they wrestle with difficult decisions concerning how to ease the financial crunch while maintaining traditional markets.

Making the Decision to Develop a Strategic Plan

The motivation for initiating a strategic plan comes from many sources:

> **Board Members.** Board members who have participated in successful strategic planning as a result of their service on other nonprofit boards are often the source for initiating a strategic plan. Board members who run their own businesses or work for for-profit companies that routinely develop strategic plans also may raise this issue. Many who serve on nonprofit boards see strategic planning as a management and governance tool equal in importance to budgeting, and they cannot imagine an organization that doesn't initiate a formal process to look inward at least once every half-decade.

> **Funders.** Some funders require the development of a strategic plan before they make grants to nonprofit charities. These funders want evidence that their contributions will be used prudently and cost-effectively and will influence the direction of the organization. A strategic plan developed as a result of such a requirement by a funder would obviously highlight changes in the organization's programs that are the direct result of the contribution.

Retirement of a Long-Term CEO. Many nonprofits were started by visionary leaders who ran the organizations by the seat of their pants. This "old school" of doing business may no longer be valid. New agency leaders, many with MBAs, believe that nonprofit organizations are businesses, and the same management techniques they learned in business school are applicable to the philanthropic sector. The new school recognizes that the bottom line remains the principal concern of the agency, whether or not the bottom line is interpreted as the net revenue at the end of the year or the number of satisfied clients served. The old school agency executive is often skeptical, if not fearful, of strategic planning. Perhaps his or her vision of the agency has never been challenged, and a formal process to evaluate the agency from top to bottom, from the mission statement on down, is a threat to executive autonomy. In some cases, that skepticism is justified.

Once a new generation assumes the mantle of leadership, there is motivation to rebuild the agency from the ground up, starting with the mission statement and proceeding, in some extreme cases, to changing the model of the copying machine. A strategic plan is often the vehicle for the new leadership to assert its authority and provide a mechanism for a higher level of executive accountability.

Agency Trauma. More often than not, it is an organizational crisis that triggers the decision for a strategic plan when an agency has no regular process to prepare one. The resignation or firing of a CEO is a traumatic event for any nonprofit. Sometimes, this event has occurred because of underlying unresolved issues and problems that may have developed and been inadequately addressed over many years. In the case of the involuntary separation, the organization's leadership has the opportunity to reshape the organization before a new executive takes over and molds the direction of the agency. Other traumatic events that may trigger the initiation of a strategic plan are the loss of a major funder; the establishment of competition from another nonprofit or for-profit; major damage to, or aging of, the agency's physical plant; liability suits; or quantum advances in technology that call into question the future demand for services by the agency.

Benefits of Strategic Planning

1. **It permits discussion of issues in a proactive rather than reactive mode.** Usually developed in an atmosphere that encourages creativity and brainstorming, the strategic plan may not only include concrete directions, but also provide an institutional set of core values. In a typical board meeting, there is simply no time to engage in a meaningful discussion about the long-term future of an agency, unless the board governance model recommended by Gerry Kaufman in Chapter 7 is followed. Many nonprofits are operating on the edge of financial chaos, often one failed grant application away from having to lay off staff or fold entirely.

2. **It requires an action plan to solve real problems faced by an agency.** The action plan is a template that the staff can use to implement the policies and desires of the board. Many CEOs complain that the board helps with solving problems, but fails to provide direction on the core values of the agency. A strategic plan explicitly includes those core values, and assists the CEO in creative strategies for solving current problems and anticipating future ones.

3. **It provides a formal mandate for the reallocation of resources to respond to changing conditions, and the means to obtain additional resources if required.** A successful strategic planning process that develops an aggressive plan to attack problems often energizes a moribund board.

4. **It builds inter-board relationships that might not otherwise exist, and creates a partnership among the board chairperson, board members, staff, funders, and other stakeholders.** Each has a role that is defined in the plan and, if bought into, the added responsibilities increase the available resources of the agency. The social contact that occurs at many board retreats, particularly those designed in bucolic settings away from the hustle and bustle of the agency, cement personal relationships among participants. This improves the bond between the agency and its leadership.

5. **It provides a mechanism for the board, staff, and agency stakeholders to become more informed about the activities and problems faced by the agency.** It promotes, in many cases, a frank discussion by the agency executive of problems that might not be shared within the context of a conventional board meeting. Many CEOs welcome the process in that it takes a burden off their shoulders and shares it with the agency's "owners" and constituents.

6. **It provides an opportunity to focus on the forest rather than the trees.** It is easy for a CEO to become lost in the mundane issues of personnel, budgeting, office management, board relations, and public relations, and virtually ignore issues relating to the actual purpose and mission of the nonprofit.

Costs of Strategic Planning

1. **Money.** Serious strategic planning costs money, a scarce resource for most nonprofits. Many nonprofits recognize that it is useful to have a trained, dispassionate consultant to assist in the planning process. There are costs to schedule planning meetings and travel to those meetings. Many organizations recognize the value of eliminating outside distractions to aid brainstorming, and thus schedule planning meetings at staff retreats held at attractive, isolated campgrounds, conference centers, business resorts, or hotels. There are costs of photocopying and printing all of the planning documents. There are opportunity costs, as well, because staff and board resources are diverted from other duties.

2. **Time.** Any realistic strategic planning process requires the allocation of precious staff and board resources. Meeting preparation, meeting attendance, minutes, preparation of draft and final strategic plans, and hiring a consultant all take time. It is not uncommon for a strategic planning process to take more than a year.

3. **Potential bad will.** As with any process, things can go wrong. Bad group dynamics can result in painful meetings and destructive outcomes. A group may spend an entire four-hour meeting arguing over trivial words in a mission statement. This can be frustrating for committee members who are more interested in developing an action plan to solve agency problems. Strategic planning may bring board factions into collision, and meetings can degenerate into a test of wills. This may be healthy in the context of a committee rather than having a drag-out fight at a board meeting, but it means that to have a constructive planning process, personal baggage must be dealt with first. If the final

strategic plan is not implemented, board members who participated may feel that the agency wasted their time, and may not be as likely to participate in future efforts, or even may resign from the board. Current staff members may feel threatened that their jobs are at risk, and may look for other employment.

4. **Loss of Agency Initiative.** A formal strategic plan may diminish an executive's initiative and quick response to changing conditions, because the preferred course of action is not in the strategic plan. The strategic plan may become outdated quickly and stifle a more appropriate response to changing conditions that were not anticipated in the plan. In addition, strategic planning often involves the board not just in setting objectives and outcomes, but also in determining the methods that should be used to achieve those objectives and outcomes. Many feel that this is the role of staff, not the board, and making it the role of the board takes away the flexibility necessary for executive staff to function effectively.

A Sample Strategic Planning Model

This chapter gives a cursory review of what a strategic plan is, its costs and benefits, some advantages and disadvantages, and some issues that often arise when nonprofits consider initiating a strategic plan. It is recommended that other specific resources be consulted when exploring the need for a strategic planning process, and several excellent sources are included in the bibliography. The following is one model for developing a strategic plan and is a hybrid put together from several theoretical models.

Step 1. Decide whether to develop a strategic plan.

Consider the costs and benefits mentioned earlier in this chapter, and also the following questions:

- Is there enough time and money to allocate for this planning process now?
- Is the agency prepared to implement whatever plan eventually is approved, or will it sit on the shelf?
- Do we have a commitment from the agency's executive director, board chairperson, board members, and other stakeholders to develop a plan, or will we just be going through the motions?
- Are the agency's short-term problems so overwhelming that the agency is wasting time planning for the future when its continued existence is seriously threatened by current problems?

Step 2. Build the infrastructure necessary to develop a plan.

- **Appoint a planning committee of the board.** Include creative board members, funders, the CEO, chief financial officer, clients, and opinion makers from the community. Consider that any committee of more than 10 can become unmanageable. Some strategic planners recommend that the entire board serve on the committee.

- **Compile and distribute articles and related material on strategic planning to the entire board.** (For information on reprints or rights to photocopy this chapter or other copyrighted materials, contact the publisher of the material.)

- **Decide on whether the facilitator/consultant will be a board member or a private paid or volunteer consultant.** A board member already knows a lot about the organization, its strengths and weaknesses, its personnel, and all other members of the committee. On the other hand, that board member brings with him or her prejudices about colleagues and staff, and often has a point of view or hidden agenda that is not held at arm's length. A private strategic planning consultant has the experience to keep the discussion focused and follow the agenda. There are many consultants who have experience working with nonprofit agencies in designing the planning process itself, participating in orientation sessions for the planning committee, serving as a referee for dispute resolution, helping the committee reach consensus when that is desired, neutralizing oppositional or disruptive participants, and providing technical assistance.

A good consultant can organize the process and provide logistical support so that the agency board and staff will not be absorbed by the planning process mechanics. On the other hand, a bad consultant may influence the process beyond what is desirable, and constrain the participation of committee members. One must be careful to assure that the plan, if written by a consultant, is not a tepid re-write of the plan the consultant developed for a previous client, which may have only minimal relevance to the current client.

It is a good idea to informally survey comparable organizations to check out potential strategic planning consultants. Statewide associations may also be helpful in identifying consultants. Of course, it is vital that any contract between the organization and the consultant spell out exactly what services are required, the timetable, and the level of participation required by the consultant.

Step 3. Decide how many years the strategic plan will cover.

In general, small nonprofits choose a shorter time frame than larger nonprofits, perhaps two-four years for smaller agencies, compared to larger institutions, which prepare five-year plans.

Step 4. Put in writing the timetable and the process.

This includes the steps that are required and who is responsible for accomplishing each task. Among the tasks are:

- appointing the committee
- hiring a consultant or facilitator
- leading the orientation of the planning committee
- choosing the meeting site
- scheduling the meetings
- writing the first draft of the plan
- providing the procedures to review and revise the draft
- writing the final plan
- developing the process for the planning committee to approve the final plan
- formulating the review and the process for the full board's approval of the final plan.

Step 5. Prepare a memo on what is expected of the strategic planning process.

This memo to the planning committee should highlight the major problems that are to be resolved by the strategic plan, such as how to review and update the mission statement, how to respond to potential cuts in government funding, how to respond to the new location of a for-profit competitor, how to deal with a change in the demographics of the people in the area served by the agency, and so on. The memo should note whether the planning report should be a consensus document (which does not mean that everyone must agree to its contents) or if majority rules after all points of view are heard.

Step 6. Have the agency board endorse the planning process, and allocate funds necessary for it to proceed.

Step 7. Appoint the committee, appoint or hire the facilitator/consultant, send out orientation materials, and schedule the first meeting.

The first meeting

The first meeting is usually an orientation session, which includes some of the following components:

1. A review of the purpose of the committee, the timetable, future meeting schedule, and meeting the facilitator.

2. A review of the agency's current mission, history, short-term problems, long-term threats, staff resources, programs, activities, strengths and weaknesses, major successes and failures, core values of the organization, financial status, and future commitments. The agency's CEO and CFO should be present to answer questions from the planning committee and to ask questions of the facilitator to establish ground rules for the planning process.

3. An analysis of the needs of the stakeholders, including those currently receiving service, and scenarios about how those needs may change. For example, is the population served by the agency changing demographically? Is government funding likely to drop? Is the community becoming poorer, limiting future fee-for-service revenue and requiring more non-fee revenue?

4. An analysis of institutional limits: population served by geography, age group, and income level.

5. An identification of what in the above can be changed by the organization as a result of strategic planning and what is the result of forces beyond the control of the agency.

The second meeting

The second meeting begins the brainstorming of the committee. This meeting examines the mission statement and reviews potential changes to that statement which—in some cases— might have been unrevised for decades. The facilitator may list various problems on the horizon of the agency, with the planning committee serving as a focus group—such as funding problems, changes in markets, competitors, outside threats from changing social, economic, political, or technological conditions, or demand for services. The planning committee is given a homework assignment to come to the third meeting with suggestions for solving these problems.

The third meeting

The third meeting consists of brainstorming on action strategies that will solve the problems identified at the first and second meetings. The facilitator lists each strategy and includes a table with the costs and benefits of each, the probability of success, and the pros and cons. Each strategy for each problem may be ranked based on the committee's assessment as to the value of the strategy.

The fourth meeting

The committee develops an action plan, with a timetable for implementation that includes coming up with the resources necessary to implement the action plan. The plan also includes a procedure to review the progress made in implementing the plan.

In the above model, a draft strategic plan can be accomplished with four three-hour meetings.

In *Managing a Nonprofit Organization,* Thomas Wolff outlines six levels in the linear model of strategic planning. In the linear model, the planning committee considers one level before proceeding to the next. This contrasts with the integrated planning model, which provides for many of these levels to be considered simultaneously, recognizing that the end result is interdependent upon each of the earlier levels.

Level 1. The planners consider the mission statement, which describes the purpose the organization is trying to achieve.

Level 2. Agency goals are developed, providing the general direction in which the organization intends to go.

Level 3. Objectives and targets are set, indicating the outcomes the organization hopes to achieve.

Level 4. Strategies are formulated to meet the objectives and targets. These are the methods and ways the organization plans to achieve those outcomes.

Level 5. An action plan is developed to implement the strategies.

Level 6. An evaluation is performed after implementation, to review whether the outcomes were achieved and whether the strategies were successful.

For example, a hypothetical nursing home might have a planning document that, in an abridged form, is as follows:

Level 1. To provide quality long-term care services to the aging population of Anytown, for the purpose of improving the quality of life for those who need institutional care.

Level 2. To reduce the operating deficit and become the long-term care institution of choice in the community by improving quality of care.

Level 3. Increase non-fee revenue by 50%, and improve the cash-flow situation by taking advantage of accounting productivity. Improve government reimbursement by 25% within three years.

Increase the number of private pay residents from 30% to 50% within the next five years.

Level 4. Hire a development staff member.

Hire a lobbyist to assist the statewide association to advocate for continuing the Medicaid intergovernmental transfer program.

Hire a marketing associate to place advertisements in publications read by active, upscale, middle-aged persons whose parents may be in need of long-term care services.

Level 5. Investigate the feasibility of marketing charitable gift annuities, and hire a consultant by July 15 to develop a program for residents and their families.

Aggressively go after accounts receivable, delay accounts payable for an additional 30 days, eliminate programs that are not profitable, increase fee-for-service revenues; increase fundraising; become entrepreneurial by selling clothing and health care equipment on the organization's Web site.

Place a classified advertisement in the newsletter of the state chapter of the Society of Association Executives newsletter for a registered lobbyist.

Hire a marketing associate by June 15, and use endowment funds for seed money, and assume the new staff member will generate at least enough income to finance his or her salary.

Level 6. One year after final approval of this report, require the executive director to prepare a progress report on whether the goals outlined in level 2 are being achieved, and what mid-course corrections to Level 5 are required to meet the targets of Level 3.

The process of planning each level can be discussed and refined for two hours or nine months. The parameters differ, obviously, for a hospital with a half-billion dollars in gross revenue, compared to a charity with $50,000 in gross revenue.

The actual plan may be written by the facilitator, the chairperson of the planning committee, or staff in consultation with the board and facilitator. In every case, the planning committee should review a draft of the plan before submitting its final version to the board. The board reserves the power to approve, disapprove, approve with changes, or send the plan back for revision.

Some of the changes that may be recommended by a nonprofit agency strategic plan are:

1. a mission change
2. a change in the character of services provided
3. a plan to expand or downsize staff
4. a plan to expand or sell capital equipment and/or physical plant
5. a plan to expand fundraising
6. a plan to retrain staff
7. a plan to move the agency's location
8. a plan to seek a merger with similar organizations
9. a communications plan to improve or modernize the agency's public image
10. a plan to hire a lobbyist, or form a statewide association representing agencies with similar problems or uncertainties
11. a plan to establish a for-profit subsidiary
12. a plan to seek, or refuse, government grants
13. a plan to liquidate the agency
14. a plan to professionalize the agency, or deprofessionalize it—e.g., a decision by a hospital to substitute nurse aides where registered nurses had previously been used
15. a plan to change the governance of the organization—increase or decrease board

membership, change quorum requirements, change voting requirements, change committee structure, change the powers of officers
16. a plan to change the compensation structure to reward and improve productivity
17. a plan to change the agency's market niche
18. a plan to change into a for-profit
19. a plan to modernize the name of the agency
20. a plan to introduce new technology

Some components of a strategic plan may be:

1. a five-year projection of staffing patterns
2. a five-year projected budget
3. sources of revenue to implement changes stipulated by the plan
4. a marketing strategy
5. a schedule for periodically updating the strategic plan
6. a schedule for evaluating whether the plan is being implemented effectively and whether the strategies provided in the plan are successful
7. a physical plant/equipment plan
8. yearly updates to the plan.

Tips:

- **Don't let a strategic plan sit on the shelf after investing time and money developing it.**

- **Know when to let a strategic plan sit on the shelf when conditions have become so turbulent or changed that it would not make sense to follow it blindly.**

Chapter 7
A Transforming Model for Nonprofit Board Leadership

By Gerald Kaufman

Synopsis: A relatively new approach to nonprofit organization leadership encourages boards to focus on outcomes rather than means. Using this model, the board has the responsibility to govern and the staff has the responsibility to manage.

Overview

The nonprofit sector in the United States has undergone substantial changes over the past 25 years. There are many factors that are responsible for this change. The nonprofit sector itself has grown enormously over the past decade, fueled by the tremendous increase in fees and government funding. The nonprofit sector's funds are no longer predominantly from charity; only 19.9% of the revenue of the sector, excluding religion, came from philanthropy in 1997. The remainder came from fees (31.3%), government (37.5%), and other sources (11.4%).

Society now relies on the nonprofit sector to deliver health and social services, participate in economic development, build housing, feed the hungry, educate and protect children, provide art and cultural experiences, and supply many other services. The sector no longer primarily dispenses charity, but rather provides essential services to all people, regardless of their income level.

Increased government funding has brought with it all of the trappings of bureaucracy: rules and regulations regarding internal management and financial accounting; program operation manuals governing all aspects of client treatment; and a strong emphasis on reimbursement for a detailed and defined set of services, often overshadowing the organization's original mission and narrowing the vision.

Providing services to individuals, although essential, does not translate into building strong, safe communities. The rise in numbers and importance of community development corporations and the resurgence of the settlement house movement may be vehicles for some community building.

Boundaries between the nonprofit sector and government and the for-profit sectors are eroding. Many parts of the nonprofit sector are becoming quasi-government. Large corporations and nonprofits are forming partnerships to solve community problems or to enhance the corporate image. This trend challenges the responsibilities, independence, and traditional values of the nonprofit sector.

Individual nonprofit organizations have become larger and more complex, often requiring sophisticated, professional management. An increasing number of them are using the most modern technology and marketing tools to raise money, attract clients, and influence public policy. In this climate, small community-based organizations have difficulty competing.

One result of the growth in size, complexity, and importance of the nonprofit sector is increasing scrutiny by the press, the public, and governments at all levels. Public officials are raising questions about whether nonprofits are being operated in the public interest or for private gain. Challenges to tax exemptions are occurring in many jurisdictions. The IRS is increasing its auditing and oversight of nonprofit, tax-exempt organizations.

Disclosures of one well-known major charity's excessively high salary and perks for its executive director and similar scandals have led to the lessening of public confidence in the nonprofit sector, according to a Gallup poll.

Current Board Functioning

In many instances, boards of directors continue to operate as if change of this magnitude had not occurred. Too often, as one author put it, boards "... fall into trivia, short term myopia, meddling in staff work, and other failings. They do so even when composed of intelligent, experienced, caring members."

Professionally staffed, large, complex organizations tend to pursue funding without too much regard to mission. In these situations, boards often evaluate executive directors on the basis of the fund balance at the end of the year, rather than the accomplishment of the mission.

Ideally, the essential role of boards of directors is assuring that nonprofit organizations are mission-driven, governed by a board of citizens responsive to the community that they serve, based on the values of altruism, community and diversity, operated in an ethical and prudent manner, and providing citizens an opportunity to participate in the civic life of the community.

When one observes boards and board committees or reads minutes of meetings, one sees that much time is spent listening to reports. Committees meet to listen to appropriate staff members report on the subject matter under the committees' jurisdiction.

These meetings typically involve several telephone calls between the staff and the committee chairpersons, resulting in preparation of a report and an agenda by the staff. The meeting might take several hours of discussion and, as a result, some minor changes might be made to the report. The same process is repeated at board meetings, with many or all of the committees reporting. In addition to committees, the executive director and treasurer also make reports.

The line between board and staff roles and decisions is blurred. Too often, when the board is asked to take some action, it is one of a trivial nature that should have been made by the executive director, such as: what kind of computer to buy, what insurance agent to use, what color the invitations should be for the fundraising dinner, what the sign-in and -out requirements should be for employees, and on and on. Some boards get involved in more weighty administrative decisions, such as hiring staff, signing all checks, and approving grant proposals. In these instances, although much time is involved, seldom are the recommendations of the executive director not followed.

All of this activity gives many board members a sense that they are doing important work. But much of it is rubber stamping at best, or destructive interference in responsibilities of staff at worst. Others, however, frequently complain about the mind-numbing details that occupy board meeting time. As a result, board attendance is frequently low and quorums hard to assemble. What these activities largely amount to is reviewing what has already occurred, and they have little relevance to what are uniquely the board's responsibilities.

A major complaint of many executive directors is the enormous amount of staff support that these board activities require, and a feeling that much of it is meaningless. Another point of conflict often surrounds fundraising, with the executive director's expectations of the board seldom being fulfilled.

Boards also do some important work, such as composing the mission statement or engaging in strategic planning. Here, too, boards often defer to executive directors and give pro-forma approval to executive directors' efforts. However, some boards engage in strategic planning over extended periods of time, even as long as a year, involving themselves in the minute details of program operation.

Most board members receive little or no training as to their role or what is expected of them, other than being told that they "make policy," approve budgets, and have a fiduciary obligation for the fiscal integrity of the organization and for fundraising. This often translates into: routine approval of the annual plan and detailed financial reports prepared by the staff, receiving and reviewing the annual audit, and selling a few tickets to the annual fundraising event or helping to arrange a silent auction.

Another function performed by many board members is to act as volunteers in some aspect of the organization's programs. Although this is a worthwhile activity, it has nothing to do with board members as governors of the agency.

There is often tension between boards and executive directors concerning access to information. Boards spend so much time on trivia because they have not articulated what is important to them. They may look at anything and everything because they are not sure what they are looking for. Boards complain that they don't get enough information, or they get too much and don't know what to do with it. Executive directors complain that boards demand information and then they don't read it. If the nonprofit sector is to be the strong value- and mission-driven sector that the public expects and its history and role in society demand, strengthening and emphasizing the centrality of boards of directors is essential.

A New System of Board Governance

If we are to transform nonprofits into much more effective and accountable organizations, we must redefine the role of board governance. In this new world, we need a model of board governance that will ensure that nonprofit organizations will be operated with vision on behalf of the communities they serve, in an ethical and prudent manner, producing results that justify the costs.

John Carver, the father of this model of board governance, in his book, *Boards That Make A Difference*, defines board governance as follows:

> Board leadership requires, above all, that the board provide vision. To do so, the board must first have an adequate vision of its own job. That role is best conceived neither as volunteer-helper nor as watchdog but as trustee-owner. Policy Governance is an approach to the job of governing that emphasizes values, vision, empowerment of both board and staff, and the strategic ability to lead leaders.

The concept of trustee-owner is central to this new system of board governance. Every nonprofit exists for the benefit of the "moral" owners and the board functions as trustees on their behalf. The board's job is to define who those moral owners are. In the case of a legal services agency, the owners might be all low-income people living in the community that the organization serves. For a low-income housing development group, the owners might be, at one level, all of those needing decent low-income housing; but, at another level, the owners are all residents of the city, because a healthy society is one in which everyone is housed decently.

Every nonprofit exists for those who would benefit from the realization of its mission in its broadest sense. Boards of trustees operate nonprofit organizations in trust for these moral owners. The *primary* responsibility of boards then is not to support the staff, but rather to assure that the organization fulfills its fiduciary obligation to the owners.

Board members may also act as volunteer-helpers but they do so as any non-board member would, not as trustee-owners. The board has certain, defined watchdog functions, but that should not take up the majority of its time as it does now in so many organizations.

While everyone in an organization makes policy at some level, the question is what policies are the board's? Policy is defined as, "The values or perspectives that underlie actions." The following is a short summary of the four areas that define the board's job and for which written policies are required:

1. Ends or Outcomes. The board must determine how the world will be different as a result of the activities of the organization. To do that, the board must decide what human needs will be met, for whom, and at what cost. The board should formulate these ends policies starting at the broadest level—the mission statement—and continue from the next broadest formulation to a point at which they are willing to stop and delegate the balance to the executive director.

The mission statement is a statement about outcomes. Outcomes are not activities; they are the results expected from the activities of the organization. Under this model, boards are concerned with results or ends, and their obligation as owners of the organization is to assure the production of worthwhile ends.

Practices, methods, and activities are means, not ends. Boards should stay out of staff means, except to say what means are not acceptable, which will be discussed below.

A typical nonprofit mission statement might be that it provides "high-quality services to people with developmental disabilities" or "shelter and supportive services for the victims of domestic violence." These are statements about activities, not about outcomes. Boards must decide what they expect the agency to accomplish and what results are expected from these high-quality services.

An example of a results-based mission statement might be to prepare persons who are developmentally disabled for "independent living in the community." In that instance, the board might further specify that independent living includes job readiness, household maintenance, knowledge of community resources, and other skill areas that the board believes are necessary to enable the clients to live independently in the community. What means the staff put in place to achieve the ends should not be a matter of board concern.

Private and government funders often dictate staff means by requiring very specific programs, activities, and methods. Under these circumstances, if boards are clear about ends, then staff can negotiate with funders about means. If staff believes that programs prescribed by funders will not achieve the results or ends determined by the board, then the organization should refuse the grant or contract or the board should revise the ends policies.

Such an approach will counteract the seduction for nonprofit agencies to pursue whatever funding is available, whether or not the funding will help accomplish the organization's mission.

In the area of domestic violence, for example, there are studies that show that if police are trained to intervene strongly with an abuser, the repetition of domestic violence can be substantially reduced. However, most domestic violence agencies are paid to provide only shelter and treatment for the abused partner.

Under this model, boards would grapple with the question of what outcomes the organization is expected to achieve and would regularly monitor the agency on that basis. Outcomes might include reduction of abuse, independent lives for the abused away from their abusers, temporary respite, or preservation of families.

The formulation and reformulation of ends policies will occupy much of the board's time and, to perform that role, much of a board's attention will be focused outside the organization. The board will need to inform itself of community needs and how those needs are changing, whether there are other organizations it should be collaborating with, how changes in public policy are likely to affect the mission, and whether the organization should merge with other groups to better accomplish the mission.

2. Executive Limitations. These policies articulate the board's values regarding how the executive director manages the organization. Executive limitations policies are proscriptive; that is, they are expressed in negative terms and state what the board will not permit in the following areas: treatment of staff and volunteers, financial planning (budgeting), financial condition, asset protection, board awareness, and information. These are the usual areas of board concern with the means the executive director uses to manage the organization.

Under this model of board governance, boards do not get involved in the program activities as governors of the organization, other than to assure themselves that the activities are achieving the desired ends. (Board members may get involved in the activities as volunteers working under the supervision of the appropriate staff person, and in those instances, they are not acting in their board member/governor capacity.)

If boards determine the ends to be attained and then ordain the means of attaining them, it is not reasonable to hold the executive director accountable for the outcomes. Executive limitations narrow and define the board's involvement in staff means.

Under traditional board operations, boards prescribe from time to time how the executive director is to operate the organization. A typical example is the formal adoption of a set of personnel policies. At other times, board members suggest what kind of telephone system to install, how often the newsletter should go out, fundraising ideas, marketing strategies, or even how to run a staff meeting.

Board actions or suggestions are scattered through the minutes over the months and years, often forgotten. The executive director may not be sure whether the board is directing the executive director to take some action, or merely offering suggestions, and many of these ideas and suggestions just float out in limbo. On the other hand, some board members may interpret a suggestion as a board directive and later criticize the executive for not complying.

Executive limitations place the responsibility for operational details where it belongs, on the executive director, other than the values of prudence and ethics that the board has identified as important limitations on the executive's authority. These policies regarding executive limitations normally can be written in five or six pages and provide the basis for clearly defined and targeted monitoring of executive director actions.

Boards, under this approach, free themselves from the operational minutiae and the impossible and endless task of monitoring all details of programs and management. With executive limitations in place, the board will have identified what is really important to it and confine its monitoring accordingly.

Thus, instead of boards drafting or even approving personnel policies, executive limitations would state what they would not allow in the treatment of personnel. For instance, board-drafted personnel policies normally include a detailed grievance procedure for employees. Executive limitations would simply state that the executive director shall not fail to have a policy permitting employees to submit a grievance to the board.

Other examples of value-laden executive limitations are prohibiting discrimination regarding hiring or promotions, sexual harassment, and making purchases over a certain amount without competitive bids. Boards should not concern themselves with matters that do not involve their values, such as what holidays the staff has off, whether the organization has flex time, or other details of staff operation properly in the province of management.

Executive limitations policies free the board for the much more important and exciting work of defining the organizational ends, of envisioning the future. The staff, in turn, has much more time to do the work necessary to reach the vision.

3. Executive Director-Board Relationship. This set of policies describes what is expected of the executive director (achievement of ends policies and non-violation of executive limitations), and how and when the policies of the board will be monitored. The executive director is evaluated on the performance of the agency, not on individual performance.

A fundamental principle is that a board monitors only against criteria previously set. The board monitors against these pre-set criteria in one of three ways, depending on which criterion is being monitored: executive director's report regarding ends and executive limitations; external report, such as an audit; and direct inspections of documents or locations. A monitoring schedule, with times and manner of monitoring, is included in this set of policies.

4. Board Process. These policies describe how the board is going to govern itself. They include the role of the president, committees, board job description, and board internal dynamics. The board job products are linkage with the ownership, written governing policies, and assurance of executive performance. Optional products include fundraising and government relations or advocacy.

An important principle is that the board speaks with one voice and relates to one employee, the executive director. Board holism is fragmented by the use of traditional board committees, which normally concern themselves with some aspect of staff operations and, therefore, accomplish little other than rubber stamping staff recommendations or interfering with staff work. Under this model of governance, board committees are used to help the board do its job, not the staff's job.

If the board is to speak with one voice, it is not acceptable for individual board members to direct employees or the executive director to take action or produce reports, unless the whole board has spoken on the subject. This principle alone could save many organizations countless hours and substantial staff stress.

Conclusion

This approach to board governance defines the jobs of the board and executive director; gives boards leadership responsibilities to determine the mission and vision of the agency; keeps boards out of operations by focusing them on ends, not means, other than to assure themselves that the means used are prudent and ethical. The executive director is an active participant in the discussions leading to the adoption of all of the policies.

The move to this model of board leadership takes time, and it takes letting go of old habits and processes. Boards will need outside assistance in making the transition. Board meetings will be different, and those board members who like dealing with administrative and program details might be somewhat uncomfortable. The major emphasis for selecting board members will be on finding people with vision who are connected to the broader ownership.

By implementing this model of board governance, the board and staff of nonprofit organizations will be united in a common vision and mission, will have delineated clear boundaries between the board and staff concerning staff methods and activities, will be in closer touch with their "community" and other parts of the external world, and, above all, will be producing worthwhile outcomes rather than inputs.

An important consequence of this model is that many organizations will need to be much more collaborative with others to fulfill their missions and attain their ends. A "drug-free community," or similar world-changing mission, is not possible without the involvement of many other groups and organizations.

Governance is not about managing an organization, but about creating a world. Governance is about dreaming.

Gerald Kaufman, the author of this essay, serves as executive director of the Awbury Arboretum Association in Philadelphia, PA.

White Hat Communications

Chapter 8
Nonprofit Organization Ethics

by Gerald Kaufman and Gary Grobman

Synopsis: Nonprofit charities have a special obligation, both legal and moral, to uphold the highest standards of ethical practice, to be accountable to their boards and the public, to avoid conflicts of interest, and to treat their employees with dignity.

Introduction

Nonprofit organizations, especially those qualified under section 501(c)(3) of the Internal Revenue Code, occupy a special and unique place in American society. Their uniqueness has many attributes.

All such organizations are supported by the nation's taxpayers: they are exempt from federal and state income taxes; contributors, for the most part, can deduct their contributions from their federal income tax (and from their state income taxes in most states); they are eligible to have their postage subsidized by the federal government; and many are exempt from state and local sales and property taxes.

Ethics in the Nonprofit Environment

Among the general categories of ethical conflicts that are endemic to the nonprofit sector are accountability, conflict of interest, and disclosure. Specific issues of interest are relationships between board members and the staff; board members and the organization (such as business relationships); self-dealing; charitable solicitation disclosure; the degree to which donations finance fundraising costs rather than programs; the accumulation of surpluses; outside remuneration of staff; the appropriateness of salaries, benefits, and perquisites; and merit pay. For example, pay based on income received rather than mission accomplished is considered unethical. Staff members of charities are under more of an obligation not to exploit their position on staff for personal gain (such as charging a fee for outside speaking engagements on their own time) than their for-profit counterparts. Unlike their for-profit or government counterparts, charities generally are under an ethical, if not legal, obligation not to accumulate large surpluses. Salaries, benefits, and perquisites must be "reasonable," and prior to the promulgation by the IRS of regulations relating to this and other "excess benefit" transactions, the legal requirements applying to these issues were in a gray area.

The following are some issues relating to ethics that are appropriate for nonprofit boards and staff to consider:

1. Accountability

Accountability often is overlooked in discussions about ethics. Because of the unique status of 501(c)(3) organizations, they have a special obligation to the public to be accountable for the results of their activities that justify their tax exemptions and other privileges. Organizations should continually challenge themselves by asking if the outcomes produced are worth the public investment.

Nonprofit boards of directors have a special obligation to govern with integrity. Governing with integrity means that the organization recognizes that it is accountable to the public, to the people it serves, and to its funders. Accountability includes the concept that nonprofit organizations exist only to produce worthwhile results in furtherance of their missions.

In addition, accountability encompasses a core system of values and beliefs regarding the treatment of staff, clients, colleagues, and community. Yet, organizational survival needs too often undercut core values. Although everyone in the organization is responsible, it is the board's ultimate responsibility to assure that its values are not compromised, and that the activities are conducted within acceptable limits.

A more subtle issue of accountability is seldom discussed when staff will sometimes pursue grants and contracts, or engage in direct solicitation campaigns, for the primary purpose of growing. Boards sometimes ask whether the executive director "grew the organization" as the primary criterion for measuring success. Boards have an obligation to ensure that all activities support the organization's mission.

2. Conflict of Interest

A potential conflict of interest occurs any time organizational resources are directed to the private interests of a person or persons who have an influence over the decision. Examples might include the leasing of property owned by a relative of the executive director or a board member, the board awarding itself a salary, the organization hiring a board member to provide legal representation, or the executive director hiring a relative or a board member's relative.

A conflict also can occur when the person (or persons) making a decision expects something in exchange from the person in whose favor the decision is made. One example is the case in which an executive director retains a direct mail firm, and the executive director's spouse is hired by that direct mail firm shortly thereafter.

With regard to board members, the cleanest approach is to adopt a policy that does not allow any board member to profit from the organization. It is the duty of every board member to exercise independent judgment solely on behalf of the organization. For example, suppose a board member who owns a public relations business successfully argues that the nonprofit needs a public relations campaign and then is hired to conduct the campaign. The board member's self-interest in arguing for the campaign will always be subject to question.

Suppose in the above example the board member offers to do the campaign "at cost," and that is the lowest bid. It may be that even at cost, the board member's firm benefits because the campaign will pay part of the salary of some staff members or cover other overhead. It may be perfectly appropriate to accept the board member's offer, even though it is a conflict of interest. However, it is absolutely essential that the board have a procedure in place to deal with these types of issues.

Some organizations permit financial arrangements with board members, provided that the member did not vote on that decision. Given the good fellowship and personal relationships that often exist within nonprofit boards, such a rule can be more for show and without substance.

A similar problem can cause a conflict in the awarding of contracts to non-insiders. There may be personal reasons for one or more members of the board or the executive director to award contracts to particular persons, such as enhancing their personal or professional relationship with that person.

There are instances in which it is appropriate to have a contract with an insider, such as when a board member offers to sell equipment to the organization at cost, or agrees to sell other goods or services well below market value. Here, too, the organization should assure itself that these same goods or services are not available as donations.

It is essential for the board to confront and grapple with these issues and adopt a written policy to govern potential conflicts of interest, to avoid the trap of self-dealing or its appearances. Many potential abuses are not only unethical, but also illegal as a result of the Taxpayer Bill of Rights 2 (see page 77). A sample conflict of interest policy can be found at: *http://www.irs.gov/pub/irs-pdf/i1023.pdf* (see page 25 of the form).

3. Disclosures

There is much disagreement within the nonprofit sector regarding how much disclosure is required to those who donate to charitable nonprofits. The first obligation of every organization is to obey the laws and regulations governing disclosure. Nonprofits have a legal and ethical obligation to report fundraising costs accurately on their IRS Form 990, to obey the requirement regarding what portion of the cost of attending a fundraising event is deductible, and to comply with state charitable registration laws and regulations.

Nonprofits face a more difficult ethical issue when deciding how much disclosure to make that is not required by law, particularly if the organization believes that some people may not contribute if those disclosures are made.

In the for-profit corporate world, the Securities and Exchange Commission demands full, written disclosure of pertinent information, no matter how negative, when companies are offering stock to the public. There is no comparable agency that regulates charitable solicitations by nonprofits. Nonprofits must be very careful to disclose voluntarily all relevant information and to avoid the kind of hyperbole that misrepresents the agency.

Another difficult issue is whether fundraising costs should be disclosed at the point of solicitation. The costs of telemarketing campaigns or of maintaining development offices are sometimes 80%, or even more, of every dollar collected. Some argue that people wouldn't give if these costs were disclosed. Others argue that if the soliciting organization cannot justify these costs to the public (and in many cases they are not justifiable), then the organization is not deserving of support.

4. Accumulation of Surplus

If the funds of a charitable nonprofit are to be used for charitable purposes, what is a reasonable amount of surplus to accumulate? One national charitable watchdog agency, the Better Business Bureau's Wise Giving Alliance, has suggested that a charity's unrestricted net assets available for use should be no more than three times the size of the past year's expenses or three times the size of the current year's budget, whichever is higher.

Organizations should consider the circumstances under which it is appropriate to disclose to prospective donors the amount expected to be used to accumulate a surplus. Clearly, if a major purpose of the solicitation is to build a surplus, that should be disclosed.

5. Outside Remuneration

Executive directors and other staff often are offered honoraria or consulting fees for speeches, teaching, providing technical assistance, or other work. The ethical issue is whether the staff person should turn the fees over to the nonprofit employer or be able to retain them. Potential conflicts can be avoided if the policy is based on the principle that all reasonably related outside income belongs to the organization. Thus, an executive director's honorarium for speaking to a national conference as a representative of the organization or as an expert in his or her field would revert to the employer, but a fee for playing in a rock band on weekends would be his or hers to keep.

An argument against this principle is that the employees' usage of their spare time should be of no concern to the employer. The argument on the other side is that the line between the employer's and personal time is not so easy to draw. Is it ethical for an employee to exploit the knowledge and experience gained on the job for personal gain? Are we buying only the employee's time from our employees, or do we expect that we are getting the undivided professional attention of that person?

If the board or executive director is silent on this issue, the assumption is that earning outside income is a private matter. It makes sense to have a clear policy on outside income before an employee is hired.

6. Salaries, Benefits, and Perquisites

Determining an appropriate salary structure is perhaps the most difficult ethical issue in the nonprofit sector. Ethical considerations arise at both the high and low ends of the salary spectrum.

If an organization is funded by grants from foundations and corporations or by government contracts, the funders can and do provide some restraint on excessive salaries. However, if the nonprofit is funded primarily by individual donations or fees for service, such constraints (other than, perhaps, those relating to the intermediate sanctions regulations of the Internal Revenue Service—see below) are absent.

Boards fall into an ethical trap if they reward executive directors based on the amount of income received, rather than on how well the mission is accomplished. A board can consider many criteria when setting the salary of the executive director. These include the size and complexity of the organization, what others in similar agencies are earning, and whether the salary is defensible to the public. Some nonprofits include proportionality in their salary structures by limiting the highest paid to a factor of the lowest paid (e.g., the highest can be no more than three times the lowest).

As a result of enactment of the *Taxpayers Bill of Rights 2*, there are now *legal* as well as ethical restrictions about paying excessive compensation. Ethical management of employees requires that each person be treated with dignity and respect, paid a salary that can provide a decent standard of living, and given a basic level of benefits, including health coverage. A potential, critical conflict arises when a charitable organization working to spread its social values treats its staff in a way that conflicts with its organizational values.

7. Personal relationships

Nonprofit organization executives and board members must be careful to avoid sexual harassment or behavior that makes an employee feel uncomfortable at best or threatened and intimidated, at worst. Employees should be treated fairly, which among other things, means that no favoritism should be permitted with respect to work assignments. Discrimination should not be permitted even if it doesn't meet the threshold required for legal violations.

Nepotism—the hiring of family members—should be prohibited. Nonprofit executives and board members should seek to keep personal friendships from influencing professional judgment. Managers shouldn't make it difficult for employees to maintain an appropriate work-family balance. Privacy and confidentiality of workers should be respected. A diverse workforce means that cultural differences among staff should be respected to the maximum extent possible.

Standards for Excellence

In 1998, the Maryland Association of Nonprofit Organizations initiated an ethics and accountability code for the nonprofit sector entitled *Standards for Excellence.* Along with the code, the program includes educational components and a voluntary certification process whereby charities can receive certification that they meet basic ethical and accountability standards. As a result of two major grants, the program has been expanded beyond Maryland to include nine other states (Florida, Georgia, Idaho, Louisiana, North Carolina, Ohio, Oklahoma, Pennsylvania, and West Virginia). Launched in July 2004, a national institute *(http://www.standardsforexcellenceinstitute.org)* now provides nonprofit organizations access to the educational tools to support implementing the Standards. The 55 performance standards required for an organization to be certified by the program are grouped in eight areas:

- Mission and Program
- Governing Board
- Conflicts of Interest
- Human Resources
- Financial and Legal Accountability
- Openness and Disclosure
- Fundraising
- Public Policy and Public Affairs

Participating charities may demonstrate that they adhere to the standards by participating in a peer review process. They submit an application, document their compliance with the standards, and pay a fee. If the peer-review panel affirms that the organization meets the standards, the organization receives a Seal of Excellence, with the expectation that having the Seal will provide the organization with increased credibility with donors and grantmakers. The full set of standards can be found at:

http://www.standardsforexcellenceinstitute.org

Among the standards are:

1   On average, over a five-year period, a charity should assure that fundraising revenues as compared with expenses have a greater than a 3:1 ratio.

2.   Fundraisers, whether or not they are employees or independent consultants, should not be compensated based on a percentage of the amount raised or some other commission formula.

3. Nonprofit organizations should have a conflict of interest policy and a procedure to provide board, staff, and volunteers with an annual opportunity to submit a conflict-of-interest statement, to disclose actual and potential conflicts of interest.

Taxpayer Bill of Rights 2—Intermediate Sanctions

The *Taxpayer Bill of Rights 2* was signed into law by President Clinton on July 30, 1996. The principal purpose of this law is to punish individuals affiliated with charities and social welfare organizations who are participating in financial abuses, and to provide the government with a sanction other than simply revoking the charity's exemption status. The law also includes expanded public disclosure requirements for annual federal tax returns.

Previous law required charities to make their 990 tax returns available for public inspection, but did not require that copies be provided. The law was changed to require that if a person requests a copy of the 990 in person, it must be immediately provided for a reasonable copying fee. If the request is made in writing, it must be provided for a reasonable copying and postage fee within 30 days. Organizations that make these documents "widely available," such as posting them on the Internet, are exempt, although they still must make the document available for public inspection. The law expands the disclosure that must be made on the 990, adding information about excess expenditures to influence legislation, any political expenditures, any disqualified lobbying expenditures, and amounts of "excess benefit" transactions.

The law increases the fine for failure to file a timely 990 from $10 per day to $20 per day, with a maximum of $10,000. Higher fines apply to organizations with gross receipts over $1 million.

Both state and federal law have prohibitions against "private inurement"— permitting a charity's income to benefit a private shareholder or individual. Legislation at the federal level to define what constitutes a prevalent form of private inurement and to refine the definition of a private shareholder was enacted. It aims to respond to alleged financial abuses by some organizations that were perceived as providing unreasonable compensation to organization "insiders."

To curb financial abuses, the law authorizes the IRS to impose an excise tax, 25% in most cases, on certain improper financial transactions by 501(c)(3) and 501(c)(4) organizations. The tax applies to transactions that benefit a "disqualified person," defined as people in positions who exercise substantial influence over the organization, their family members, or other organizations controlled by those persons.

Disqualified persons include voting members of the board, the president or chair, the CEO, the chief operating officer, the chief financial officer, and the treasurer, among potential other officers and staff. The benefit to the disqualified person must exceed the value that the organization receives to be subject to the tax. To avoid problems, tax experts are advising organizations to treat every benefit to a director or staff person as compensation, and reflect these benefits in W-2s, 1099s, and budget documents. Seemingly innocent benefits, such as paying for the travel and lodging expenses for a spouse attending a board retreat or a health club membership for an executive director, may trigger questions about excess benefit. Luxury travel could be considered an excess benefit.

Compensation is considered reasonable if it is in an amount that would ordinarily be paid for similar services by similar organizations in similar circumstances. The term "compensation" is defined broadly, and includes severance payments, insurance, and deferred compensation.

Most of the provisions relating to intermediate sanctions apply retroactively to September 14, 1995, the date the legislation was first introduced. Steep additional excise tax penalties, up to 200% of the excess benefit plus the initial 25% excise tax, apply for excess benefit transactions that are not corrected in a reasonable amount of time. An excise tax may also be applied to organization managers (a term that is meant to include an officer, director, trustee) who approve the excess benefit transaction in an amount of 10% of the excess benefit, up to $10,000 maximum per transaction.

Although these excise taxes apply to individuals and not to the organizations themselves, there is nothing in this law that prohibits organizations from paying the tax or purchasing insurance to cover an individual's liability for the tax penalty. However, if the organization does purchase this insurance, the premium must be considered compensation to the individual. This insurance could become the basis for an excess benefit if total compensation to the individual, including this insurance, exceeds the fair market value that the person provides to the organization in exchange for the total compensation that person receives from the organization. It makes sense to consult an attorney who is knowledgeable about the *Taxpayer Bill of Rights 2* if there are any unresolved issues that would make an organization's directors and staff vulnerable to an IRS audit.

The Internal Revenue Service published draft regulations on this section of the Revenue Code in the *Federal Register* on August 4, 1998. Final regulations were published in the *Federal Register* on January 10, 2001 that were temporary. Permanent final regulations were published in the January 23, 2002 issue of the *Federal Register*.

The final regulations provide more examples of situations that might be faced by charities. One change included in the final regulations is the safe harbor for organizations to rely not only on the advice of their attorneys (as was a feature of the draft regulations), but also on the advice of other outside consultants, such as their accountants.

Codes of Ethics

Ethics in organizations are enforced through the use of codes of ethics, codes of conduct, staff ethicists, ethics committees, policies and procedures relating to ethical dilemmas, and ethics training.

As explained by Dr. Jeremy Plant of Penn State University, a code of ethics is a systematic effort to define acceptable conduct. It may be general or specific, aspirational or legalistic. The code may be a simple list of ten golden rules, or a long, detailed, codified system of procedures and ideals. In the context of an ethics code, it may have the force of law (such as a statutory ethics code for public officials), be a collection of principles that are not law but are morally binding, or simply contain a system of symbolic principles for meaningful communication.

Unlike government (which has the taxing power) and for-profit business (which generates revenue through market transactions), charities generate much of their revenue through nonmarket mechanisms such as seeking donations (in the form of contributions from the public and grants from foundations and government). This form of revenue generation is a ripe area for fraudulent practices, and many of the ethics-related principles that differentiate nonprofit organizations from their government and private sector counterparts focus on this area.

In recent years, there has been a move toward turning nonprofit management into a recognized profession, with credentialing becoming available for fundraising executives, association managers, and nonprofit organization managers. Organizations such as the Association of Fundraising Professionals (AFP), the American Society of Association Executives (ASAE), and the National Council of Nonprofit Associations—and the state and local chapters of these organizations—have sought to professionalize their memberships.

Until 2003, there had been two major ethical codes focusing on fundraising standards for charitable organizations. The first, which was developed during the late 1980s and went into effect in 1992 (National Charities Information Bureau, 2000), is the National Charities Information Bureau's (NCIB) *Standards in Philanthropy.* Almost all of these ethical standards would have been meaningless in anything other than a nonprofit context. The standards were not enforceable by law, but served as a guide to both donors and those who run the charities. The standards were grouped into nine areas:

1. Board Governance
2. Purpose
3. Programs
4. Information
5. Financial Support and Related Activities
6. Use of Funds
7. Annual Reporting
8. Accountability
9. Budget

The Council of Better Business Bureau's *Standards for Charitable Solicitations* were first published in 1974. Two revisions were made, the last being in 1981. A process was initiated in the fall of 1999 to help develop a third revision of the standards. The purpose of these standards was to "encourage fair and open solicitation practices, to promote ethical conduct by charitable organizations, and to help sustain public confidence and support of charities."

The fundamental goal of the revision effort was to create standards that were meaningful and relevant to donors, easily understood by users, and fair and not overly burdensome to charities; to instill public trust and support for philanthropy; and to be reasonable for the parent agency, the BBB, to administer.

In 2001, NCIB merged with the Foundation of the Better Business Bureau, and the new organization, the Better Business Bureau's Wise Giving Alliance, developed an updated code, published in March 2003. The 20 standards that comprise this influential ethics code can be found at: *http://www.give.org/standards/index.asp.*

Among the most controversial aspects of this code is the provision that calls for charities to allocate at least 65% of their donations for program expenses, spending no more than 35% of related contributions for fundraising. This is a higher standard than either the NCIB (60%) or the BBB's Philanthropic Advisory Service (50%) had enforced prior to the merger.

Other standards in this code provide for regular assessment of the CEO's performance, establishment of a conflict-of-interest policy, the completion of a written assessment of the charity's performance at least every two years, and standards protecting donor privacy. The new standard frowns upon accumulating unrestricted net assets available for use that exceed either three times the amount of the past year's expenses or three times the current budget, whichever is higher.

The national professional association of fundraisers also has an ethics code. The *Statement of Ethical Principles of the Association of Fundraising Professionals* (AFP) was adopted in 1991 when that organization was known as the National Society of Fund Raising Executives (NSFRE). AFP "exists to foster the development and growth of fund-raising professionals and the profession, to promote high ethical standards in the fund-raising profession and to preserve and enhance philanthropy and volunteerism." The AFP Code was amended in October 2004.

AFP's ethics code consists of a set of general ethical principles, introduced by a preamble that recognizes the stewardship of fundraisers and the rights of donors to have their funds used for the intent they expect.

Many of these principles would be appropriate for any type of organization, such as to "foster cultural diversity and pluralistic values, and treat all people with dignity and respect" and "value the privacy, freedom of choice and interests of all those affected by their actions." Some of the principles are appropriate for public organizations, such as having an obligation to "safeguard the public trust" and others are parochial to the profession, such as to "put philanthropic mission above personal gain," and "affirm, through personal giving, a commitment to philanthropy and its role in society."

One year after the adoption of the AFP principles, the organization adopted its "Standards of Professional Practice" and incorporated them into its ethics code. The standards consist of 15 "shalls" and "shall nots," one "may," and one general statement that could have been a "shall" or "shall not" with some judicious editing ("members recognize their individual boundaries of competence and are forthcoming and truthful about their professional experience and qualifications.").

A statement attached to the standards notes that violations "may subject the member to disciplinary sanctions, including expulsion, as provided by the (AFP's) Ethics Enforcement Procedures."

Some of these standards are perfunctory, such as "members shall comply with all applicable local, state, provincial, federal, civil and criminal laws." Others are general and broad, with implications that are not easily subject to interpretation, such as "Members shall not exploit any relationship with a donor, prospect, volunteer or employee to the benefit of the member or the member's organization." Among issues raised by the standards are conflicts of interest, truthfulness, privacy, and financial accountability.

Another issue raised in the principles that is of current interest in a number of professions is the standard that "Members shall not accept compensation that is based on the percentage of charitable contributions...." Some states have expressly prohibited lobbyists from signing contingency fee contracts in which they are paid only when they are successful in getting a bill or amendment passed by the legislature.

The theory is that such contracts encourage lobbyists to engage in efforts that go beyond the boundaries of acceptable behavior. On the other hand, contingency fees are routine for attorneys in civil cases. It is also not unusual for professional fundraisers to be paid a percentage of the amount they raise. Many in the field find that this practice promotes unethical solicitations (e.g., presentations that exaggerate facts, minimize disclosure, and other behaviors that intimidate and harass potential donors), and it is interesting that a major professional organization such as the AFP has taken an unequivocal position on this issue.

The standards are not enforceable by law, but serve as a guide to both donors and those who run the charities. For more information, contact:

Council of Better Business Bureaus
4200 Wilson Blvd.
Suite 800
Arlington, VA 22203
(703) 276-0100
http://www.give.org/standards/

A different set of ethical issues exists around disclosures to foundation and corporate funders. For instance, what is the obligation of disclosing changed circumstances after the proposal is submitted and before it is acted upon, such as when key staff members have announced plans to leave? If the organization knows that the changed circumstance might affect the decision, is it unethical not to disclose it?

In February 2004, Independent Sector adopted a Statement of Values and Code of Ethics for Nonprofit and Philanthropic Organizations, and recommended that it serve as a model. The statement identifies a set of values to which nonprofits may subscribe including commitment to the public good, accountability to the public, and commitment beyond the law. It also outlines broad ethical principles in the following areas: personal and professional integrity, mission, governance, legal compliance, responsible stewardship, openness and disclosure, program evaluation, inclusiveness and diversity, and fundraising. The full text can be accessed at: *http://www.independentsector.org/members/code_ethics.html*

There are many excellent publications on the subject of ethics. A few of them are:

1. A series of articles by David E. Mason in *Nonprofit World,* published by the Society for Nonprofit Organizations.

The Society For Nonprofit Organizations
5820 Canton Center Road, STE 165
Canton, MI 48187
(734) 451-3582
(734) 451-5935 (fax)
http://www.snpo.org

2. Making Ethical Decisions (33 pages, $6.95 plus $3.25 shipping and handling).

Josephson Institute of Ethics
9841 Airport Boulevard
#300
Los Angeles, CA 90045
(310) 846-4800
(310) 846-4857 (fax)
http://www.josephsoninstitute.org

3. Ethics and the Nation's Voluntary and Philanthropic Community.

Independent Sector
1200 18th Street, Suite 200
Washington, DC 20036
(202) 467-6100
(202) 467-6101 (fax)
http://www.independentsector.org

Conclusion

There are many other ethical issues that nonprofit organizations will confront on a regular basis, such as: personal use of office supplies and equipment; personal use of frequent flier mileage; the extent of staff and board diversity; and the use of private discriminatory clubs for fundraisers, board meetings, or other events. The list is endless.

What is important is that nonprofit organizations proactively engage in discussions about ethics and values on a regular basis, recognizing that the charitable nonprofit sector has a special obligation to uphold the very highest standards. Boards of directors of charitable nonprofits have an important role in this regard. Boards cannot play a more important role than assuring that nonprofits are accountable, and that they operate as mission- and value-driven organizations.

Many who choose to work in the nonprofit sector do so because the stated values of the sector and their personal values are in harmony. It is critical that such people be vigilant against the erosion of those very principles that attracted them to the work.

Only in this way can the public be assured that the charitable nonprofit sector remains worthy of its privileges and that the sector continues to occupy its special and unique place in our society.

Tips:

- **Challenge yourself and your organization to hold yourself up to the highest ethical standards, avoiding even gray areas of conflicts of interest and appearances of conflicts of interest.**

- **When in doubt, ask yourself, "How would I feel if my family and friends read about this on the front page of the daily newspaper?"**

- **Obtain salary surveys published by your state chapter of the American Society of Association Executives (ASAE), and determine whether anyone in the organization has an unreasonable salary.**

- **Demand that all business relationships with the organization be at "arm's-length," and obtain at least three bids on any work that costs at least $1,000, even if a board member claims that he/she will provide the product/service at cost.**

Chapter 9
Section 501(c)(3) Tax-Exempt Status

Synopsis: Federal 501(c)(3) tax-exempt status is valuable not only because of the tax advantages to the nonprofit corporation, but to the organization's contributors. Corporations with this status may not substantially engage in lobbying or engage in partisan political activities.

Introduction

After filing the Articles of Incorporation, achieving 501(c)(3) status should be the principal objective of virtually all nonprofits organized and operated for religious, charitable, scientific, literary, or educational purposes, testing for public safety, fostering national or international amateur sports competitions, and the prevention of cruelty to children or animals.

The federal regulation implementing Section 501(c)(3) tax-exempt status states (Reg. §1.501(c)(3)-1(d)):

> (d) Exempt purposes. (1) In general.
> (i) An organization may be exempt as an organization described in section 501(c)(3) if it is organized and operated exclusively for one or more of the following purposes:
> > (a) Religious,
> > (b) Charitable,
> > (c) Scientific,
> > (d) Testing for Public Safety,
> > (e) Literary,
> > (f) Educational, or
> > (g) Prevention of cruelty to children or animals.
>
> *(ii) An organization is not organized or operated exclusively for one or more of the purposes specified in subdivision (i) of this subparagraph unless it serves a public rather than a private interest. Thus, to meet the requirement of this subdivision, it is necessary for an organization to establish that it is not organized or operated for the benefit of private interests such as designated individuals, the creator or his family, shareholders of the organization, or persons controlled, directly or indirectly, by such private interests...*

For nonprofits whose activities are eligible, designation by the Internal Revenue Service for 501(c)(3) tax-exempt status is a major objective to be achieved as quickly as possible. This status confers several substantial benefits to the organization:

1. The nonprofit will be exempt from federal income taxes other than unrelated business income taxes (UBIT). The current rate (as of 2008) of federal corporate income tax is 15% on the first $50,000 in taxable income, 25% on the next $25,000, 34% on the next $25,000, 39% on the next $235,000, and 34% on the rest up to $10 million. While many nonprofits will not generate large amounts of net revenue, particularly in their early years, it is a major advantage to have the option to capture this net revenue for future expansion, venture capital, and covering future operating deficits.

2. Persons contributing to the nonprofit can take a deduction on their own income taxes for their contributions. Since the incremental tax rate for middle- and upper-income persons on adjusted gross income for the tax year 2007 was 10% (on income of 0-$7,825

for singles, $0-15,650 for married filing jointly), 15% (on income of $7,825-$31,850 for singles, $15,650-$63,700 for married filing jointly), 25% ($31,850-$77,100 for singles, $63,700-$128,500 for married filing jointly), 28% ($77,100-$160,850 for singles, $128,500-$195,850 for married filing jointly), 33% ($160,850-$349,700 for singles and $195,850-$349,700 for married filing jointly), and 35% ($349,700 and over for singles and married filing jointly), this represents an attractive incentive for persons to leverage their own contributions with the "tax expenditure" contributed by government.

3. Many major donors (such as United Ways and certain foundations) will not make contributions to organizations that do not have 501(c)(3) status.

4. The designation of 501(c)(3) status indicates a minimal level of accountability, policed by the Internal Revenue Service, which is a useful governmental stamp of approval of the charitable activities of the organization.

5. In some states, qualifying 501(c)(3) organizations may elect to self-insure for purposes of complying with unemployment compensation laws.

There are several disadvantages:

1. A 501(c)(3) may not engage in partisan political activity on behalf of, or in opposition to, political candidates.

2. Such organizations may not substantially engage in lobbying or propaganda.

3. Such organizations have a higher level of accountability, and must, as all 501(c) exempt organizations, make copies of their 990 tax returns available in their offices upon request (see Chapter 1).

4. There is a substantial application fee ($750 in most cases, $300 for smaller organizations), and this fee is not refunded if tax-exempt status is denied.

Although not always the case, most incorporators of nonprofits have some altruistic motive for incorporating. The motives of the incorporators cannot be for personal gain. As one might expect, the motives are usually of an "eleemosynary" nature, i.e., related to charity.

Many nonprofit corporations are formed because a person or group of persons is frustrated with the lack of government action to solve a problem that, in that person's view, should be solved by government. Congress historically has recognized that government cannot do everything for everybody, even when the cause is just. Instead, Congress provides an opportunity for citizens to form organizations to do the activities themselves. They are rewarded by having certain privileges, such as the tax-exemption, provided that the activity falls within a statutorily enumerated list of activities.

Section 501(c) of the Internal Revenue Code lists more than 20 classes of activities that can qualify a nonprofit corporation for tax-exempt status. A list of these classes is provided in this chapter. Only one of these classes, 501(c)(3), permits a tax deduction for contributions made to organizations in that class, and requires that such organizations not engage in substantial lobbying or propaganda activities, or engage in political activities that advance the cause of candidates.

501(c)(3) status is not granted pro forma. There are stringent requirements for approval. Because of this, 501(c)(3) status is prized, and it is viewed by many in the public as a stamp of approval by the federal government. The fact is that 501(c)(3) status does not necessarily imply government's endorsement of the organization's activities. In FY2006, the Internal Revenue Service granted 83,350 (c)(3) applications, denied 1,283, and took "other" action on 15,805, many of which were eventually approved after additional information was provided.

Successful application is facilitated by having certain provisions in the organization's governing documents. These provisions are discussed in Chapter 2.

How To Apply for 501(c)(3) Status

To apply, an organization needs the following forms and booklets from the Internal Revenue Service:

- Form SS-4—*Application for Employer Identification Number*
- Form 5768—*Election by an Eligible Organization to Make Expenditures to Influence Legislation*
- Package 1023—*Forms and instruction booklets for applying for 501(c)(3) tax-exempt status*
- Publication 557—*Tax-Exempt Status for Your Organization*

The above forms and booklets can be obtained at any local IRS office or online at the IRS Web site.

According to the IRS, it takes nine hours and 39 minutes to complete the basic form and several more hours to complete supplemental schedules. It also takes an additional 5.5 hours to learn about the law and how to complete the forms. It is advisable to be as careful as possible in completing the forms, since the wrong phrase can result in denial.

Some organizations are exempt from having to file the 1023. Among them are:

1. Those that will have gross receipts of less than $5,000 annually.

2. Bona fide religious institutions.

3. Certain groups affiliated with a parent organization that already has tax-exempt status and will send a letter extending its exemption to them.

The Internal Revenue Service expects that an application for 501(c)(3) status will be filed within 15 months after the end of the month in which the Articles of Incorporation are filed. If the organization files on time and the application is approved, 501(c)(3) status will be retroactive to the date of the Articles of Incorporation. There is a form to file if the 15-month deadline is not met. For more information about this option, see IRS Publication 557.

Fees

There is a $750 application fee to file Form 1023. New organizations expecting gross receipts of not more than $10,000 for each of the first four years, or existing organizations that have not had gross receipts of that amount in each of the last four years, can qualify for a reduced fee of $300. The fee must be paid by check, but a corporate check is not required.

Completing the Application

The best advice for filling out Form 1023 is to carefully read the instruction booklet and follow the directions. It sounds obvious, but many fail to do that and are surprised by delays in having their applications approved for organizations that are obviously qualified for 501(c)(3) status. Beyond that, however, there are some tips that experts offer to assist you.

1. Avoid an organizational name that would raise a red flag to an IRS examiner.

2. Have all governing documents (e.g., Articles of Incorporation and bylaws), include the language suggested in Chapter 2 with respect to corporate purposes, propaganda and lobbying, and distribution of assets upon dissolution.

3. Have an organizational conflict of interest policy that is consistent with what appears in the instruction booklet to IRS Form 1023 (or that can be found at: *http://www.irs.gov/pub/irs-pdf/i1023.pdf*)

4. Provide a three-year budget that makes sense. First, it should be consistent with the fee schedule you are seeking, i.e., should average less than $10,000 per year if you want to pay the $300 application fee rather than $750. IRS examiners know you cannot possibly predict with any precision what your revenue and expenses will be for your completely new organization three years in advance. They just want something realistic. How does one do this? Experts suggest two approaches. The first, the expense approach, is you set the organization's goals, calculate what it would cost to accomplish those goals, and then develop a plan that raises that amount of money. The second, the revenue approach, involves estimating the amount of revenue you can reasonably expect to generate for the organization, through fundraising, membership dues, sales of goods and services, and grants. Then you decide how that amount of money could be responsibly spent. A third approach is to blend these two approaches. With either approach, make sure that the source of funds is broad enough to justify exemption as a public charity. If you receive funding from only a handful of sources, you may be eligible for tax-exemption, but as a private foundation rather than as a public charity. See below for an explanation of the differences.

Differences Between Private Foundations and Public Charities

Public charities and private foundations are both granted tax-exempt status under Section 501(c)(3) of the Internal Revenue Code. However, Section 509(a) differentiates organizations that receive their income from a broad range of public sources from those organizations that receive their income principally from one, or a limited number of sources plus investment income. Private foundations pay a federal tax on net investment income, must meet a minimum annual threshold for making distributions of their assets to charities, and are flatly prohibited from lobbying. To be considered a public charity rather than a private foundation, an organization must pass a public support test enforced by the IRS. There are two such tests, one of which must be passed for the organization to be considered a public charity. The test is based on financial data for a four-year period. If one test is passed, the organization will qualify as a public charity for the following two years. For information about these tests, see: *http://members.aol.com/irsform1023/1023/compari.html*

Nonprofits that don't fit neatly into the public-serving or member-serving category are the 375,000 religious congregations, about 80% of which do not register with the IRS or file a 990 federal annual tax return because there is no requirement to do so. While these congregations exist primarily to serve their members, their tax treatment is as if they primarily serve the public. In fact, nonprofit organizations are not required by law to file for exempt status with the Internal Revenue Service provided they have a recognized creed or form of worship, are "sacerdotal" in character, carry on regular religious services, and operate for other than private gain.

There are several commercially available guides for filling out the Form 1023 in a manner that will maximize your chances for your application to be approved. Among them are:

> *How to Form your Own Non-Profit Corporation* (8th Edition) by Anthony Mancuso (Nolo Press, 950 Parker Street, Berkeley, CA 94710, July 2007, $49.95).
> Sandy DeJa's e-book: *Prepare Your Own 501(c)(3) Application,* available at: *http://www.form1023help.com*
> (see also: *http://www.501c3book.com/* for free information about filling out this form).

Timetable

You can expect a form letter from the IRS within a few weeks of its receipt of your application acknowledging that it was received. Organizations that file an application requiring minimal decision-making by the IRS or that do not require a followup letter from them are processed in six-ten weeks. This applies to about half of applications. On the average, about three-quarters of all applications are approved. Less than 2% of applications are denied. About a quarter of applications are neither approved nor disapproved, but include the granting of tax status different than the category applied for, those sent down from the IRS's Cincinnati Office (located in Covington, KY) to the IRS headquarters in Washington for more work, and those awaiting a response to inquiries for more information, among other reasons.

A Short History of Tax-Exempt Status

In ancient times, government, whether secular or non-secular, recognized that certain activities assisted the role of government and were deserving of tax exemptions. A passage in the Bible (Ezra 7:24) provides that "it shall not be lawful to impose toll, tribute, or customs" upon certain priests and their staff. Several thousand years ago, some of the best land in the Nile Valley was set aside tax-free by the Egyptian pharaoh for the priests of Osiris.

Modern tax-exemption law has its roots in England, with the passage of the Statute of Charitable Uses in 1601. According to *Unfair Competition? The Challenge to Charitable Tax Exemption,* by Harrison Wellford and Janne Gallagher, current U.S. tax-exemption law draws its roots from an 1891 court case in Britain *(Commissioners of Income Tax v. Pemsel)* that provided a judicial definition of charity strikingly similar to the American legal standard.

The modern federal tax-exemption can be traced to 1863, when the income of religious organizations was exempted from a corporate tax enacted to finance the Civil War. The first general U.S. corporate income tax, enacted in 1894, imposed a 2% flat tax and statutorily exempted charitable income. Section 32 of this Act extended this exemption to charitable, religious, educational, fraternal, and some savings and loan institutions. The 1894 Income Tax Act was eventually declared unconstitutional and subsequently repealed. Yet it served as the precedent for exempting organizations that were for "charitable, religious, or educational purposes."

A 1924 Supreme Court case, *Trinidad v. Sagrada*, decided that for purposes of tax-exempt status, the destination of the funds, rather than the source, was the key determinant. This case involved a religious order that sold food, wine, and other goods to support its school, mission, church, and other operations. Thus, tax-exempt organizations were permitted to run profit-making enterprises provided that the net profits were funneled to tax-exempt purposes. This policy was revised by Congressional enactment of an "unrelated business income tax" (UBIT) in 1950. The rationale for this was that charities were seen as competing unfairly with for-profit enterprises, the most celebrated case of which was New York University's ownership of a macaroni factory.

From 1909 to the present, many other categories of tax-exempt status were added by federal statute (see below), including labor, horticultural and agriculture organizations (1909), business leagues, chambers of commerce, scientific organizations, and mutual cemetery companies (1913), public utilities, social clubs, land banks, title holding companies, and farming associations (1916), societies for the prevention of cruelty to animals (1918), foundations and community chests (1921), and homeowner associations, fishing associations, and organizations that promote national and international sporting competitions (1976).

Following a 1917 tax increase to finance World War I, the Congress permitted a deduction for contributions made by individuals to exempt charities.

Tax-Exempt Status Other than 501(c)(3)

The Internal Revenue Code provides more than 20 other categories of tax-exempt status besides 501(c)(3). Those who wish to file for tax-exempt status under section 501(c) for other than 501(c)(3) need to request Package 1024 from the IRS.(Download at: http://www.irs.gov/pub/irs-pdf/k1024.pdf)

Among the other categories are:

> 501(c)(4)—civic leagues, social welfare organizations
> 501(c)(5)—labor, agricultural, or horticultural organizations
> 501(c)(6)—business leagues, chambers of commerce, trade associations
> 501(c)(7)—social clubs
> 501(c)(8)—fraternal beneficiary societies
> 501(c)(9)—voluntary employee beneficiary associations
> 501(c)(10)—domestic fraternal societies and orders that do not provide life, sick, or health benefits
> 501(c)(11)—teacher retirement fund associations
> 501(c)(12)—benevolent life insurance associations and other mutual businesses
> 501(c)(13)—cemeteries and crematoria
> 501(c)(14)—credit unions
> 501(c)(15)—mutual insurance companies
> 501(c)(16)—farmers' co-ops
> 501(c)(17)—unemployment compensation benefit trusts
> 501(c)(20)—prepaid group legal services organizations
> 501(c)(25)—title holding corporations or trusts.

With limited exceptions, these organizations have the same federal tax benefits as a 501(c)(3). One major difference is that with few exceptions, contributors cannot deduct the amount of their contribution from their personal income tax payments. For many of these organizations, there is no limitation against lobbying activities, and most are permitted to engage in partisan political activity (although there may be a substantial federal excise tax associated with political expenditures).

Tips:

- Before filing an application for exempt status, review Chapter 2 for provisions that should be in your organization's governing documents.

- Make sure you are not eligible for the discounted filing fees available to smaller organizations before sending a $750 check to the IRS ($300 if gross receipts for the first four years will average less than $10,000 annually).

- Consider developing a conflict of interest statement (see Chapter 8) and providing it to the IRS with other organization documents. There has been anecdotal evidence recently that some IRS application examiners, but not all, are requiring such a statement.

Chapter 10
Liability, Risk Management, and Insurance

> **Synopsis:** Nonprofit organizations, like all others, are exposed to risk in a variety of areas. Staff members, volunteers, clients, and members of the general public may suffer injuries while participating in or attending an organization's activities. The nonprofit may be sued for a variety of alleged wrongful acts, from unemployment discrimination to negligent supervision to breach of fiduciary duty. Every nonprofit organization should consider how it will minimize its risks, even though state and federal laws provide some protection to nonprofit organizations.

General Liability Concerns of Nonprofit Corporations

Murphy's Law has many variations and corollaries. In its simplest form, it states, "If something can go wrong, it will." No one can foresee catastrophic events, and even if one could, it is virtually impossible to protect an organization against all possible eventualities.

A nonprofit corporation, like a business corporation, should take reasonable steps to prevent foreseeable, downside risks. A nonprofit should also examine ways to minimize the effect of losses that occur despite the organization's best efforts. A nonprofit, like any other business, could suffer personal injury or property damage claims caused by floods, fire, theft, earthquake, wind damage, building collapse, and slips and falls, just to name a few possibilities. Even when a claimant seeks a small amount, the effect on the nonprofit can be devastating in terms of resources that must be used to defend the case. These claims do not happen very often, but when they do, the results can be disastrous for the organization and its leadership.

Nonprofits are exposed to legal risks in many other areas. Many nonprofits engage in typical business transactions on a routine basis. They arrange for conventions, seminars, and other meetings. They publish newsletters. They are employers with the attendant risk that hiring, advancement, or firing decisions may be challenged based on contract rights, discrimination, or fraud.

A nonprofit corporation could be exposed to the antitrust laws if its membership has a competitive advantage. Nonprofit associations conduct a variety of programs that permit their members to self-regulate, such as by business or professional codes, product standards and certification, or professional or academic credentialing, to use but a few examples. These decisions are open to challenge by parties who feel aggrieved.

Liability of Officers, Directors, and Other Volunteers

Nonprofit volunteers are exposed to the same potential liability for actions in performance of their duties as individuals involved with business corporations. Volunteer officers and directors of nonprofit corporations are bound by the same basic principles governing their conduct as directors and officers of profit-making business corporations.

Nonprofit boards' legal duties include the duty of care, the duty of loyalty, and the duty of obedience. They owe a fiduciary duty of reasonable care and the duty to act in the corporation's and its members' best interest. This involves a duty of loyalty or good faith in managing the affairs of the corporation. These duties require individuals to use due care in the performance of their duties for the organization, to act in good faith in a manner that serves the mission of the nonprofit, and to put the interests of the nonprofit above their own personal interests when acting as a board member for the organization.

Although there are no statistical data available on whether lawsuits against nonprofits are increasing, the perception exists that this is true. Several factors may contribute to increasing liability exposure for nonprofit organizations. First, federal and state laws adopted during the past 20 years, such as the 1988 *Drug-Free Workplace Act* and the 1990 *Americans With Disabilities Act,* have fueled an increase in lawsuits against organizations. Second, the increased use of technology by nonprofits has resulted in new techniques for the collection and dissemination of personal and/or confidential information. Many feel that the techniques for preserving privacy and security in the nonprofit organization environment are not keeping pace with the technology for collecting and storing information, making organizations vulnerable. Third, nonprofits are engaging in business activities to an increasing degree to fund their programs. These activities, such as the sale of mailing lists, engaging in e-commerce, and publishing documents and selling them on the Web, may expose organizations to increased liability. And fourth, related to each of these three, nonprofit organizations are increasing partnering with for-profit organizations, making agreements by contract and delegating some of their authority to third parties that may not have the same interest in preserving the integrity of the nonprofit's "brand name" as that nonprofit.

Civil and Criminal Liability

Nonprofit organizations have two types of liability to consider. The first category is civil liability, which includes tort actions and contract actions. A tort is a civil cause of action, other than a breach of contract, for which the law provides damages. The damage may have been intentional or unintentional, but the action that caused the damage usually, but not always, does not fall to the level of being a crime. An example might be in subjecting a potential employee to employment discrimination. If the aggrieved person can prove in court that he or she was not hired because of unlawful discrimination, the trier of fact (a judge or jury) may find in the plaintiff's favor and award monetary damages.

A second type of liability is criminal liability. An organization's treasurer who embezzles funds may be charged with a crime and prosecuted in the criminal courts. In contrast to a civil trial that has a standard of "preponderance of the evidence," the criminal trial has a standard of "beyond a reasonable doubt." In contrast to a civil judgment, punishment for those found guilty of a crime may include a prison sentence and/or restitution.

Strategies to Minimize Exposure to Lawsuits

What can a nonprofit do to minimize its exposure to lawsuits? Among the strategies that can be considered are:

1. *Don't offer programs and activities that impose too high a risk on the organization.* This may be the strategy of choice if your organization does not have the funds to adequately train and supervise workers or if you typically hire low-salary, entry-level workers rather than those with experience who require higher salaries. Can you afford state-of-the-art safety equipment and are you willing to make this investment? When the nature of the service you want to deliver is simply "an accident waiting to happen," it may be best simply to avoid sticking your neck out. (I would

be remiss if I didn't mention that many nonprofits make society better for all of us *because* they are willing to stick their necks out and provide a needed service when neither government nor the private sector is willing to do so.)

2. *Change the activity or the procedures involved to reduce your organization's exposure.* This may take the form of doing background checks on potential employees. It may include periodically certifying that your workers are capable of performing their jobs and providing continuing education and training. Or it may simply be reducing the chances of criminal activity against one of the program participants by changing the time or venue of an event, or by providing additional security personnel.

3. *Finance the risk by transferring some portion of financial responsibility for loss to an insurance company.* It is important to keep in mind that not all exposures are insurable, and a nonprofit may not be able to purchase coverage for all of its risks.

4. *Share the risk with another organization that is better prepared or more appropriately positioned to deal with the exposure.* For example, an organization may choose to outsource client transportation to a provider that already has sufficient insurance to cover potential losses, and has experienced, licensed, and trained personnel (e.g., professional drivers, rather than your organization's volunteers).

Regardless of the strategy you choose, you should consider basic general liability insurance to cover personal injury and property damage claims. Consideration should also be given to purchasing directors' and officers' (D&O) insurance to protect volunteer leadership from personal legal claims. Finally, a similar but broader type of insurance policy dealing with general professional liability protects not only officers and directors, but all association volunteers and staff, as well. Fortunately, federal and state laws have been enacted to limit the liability exposure to those who volunteer for nonprofit organizations.

Volunteer Protection Act

The *Volunteer Protection Act* (VPA) was signed into law by President Clinton in July of 1997, with an effective date of September 16, 1997. The intent of the law is to provide limited legal immunity for the volunteers of charities under certain circumstances. The VPA provides some protection, but there are some limitations to its applicability. Among these limitations are—

- protection applies only to volunteers—those who do not receive compensation for their services other than reasonable reimbursement of their expenses. Directors and officers are covered if their compensation is $500 annually or less.

- protection applies only in cases in which the volunteer was acting within the scope of his or her volunteer responsibilities at the time of the incident.

- the liability limitation does not apply if the volunteer was required to be licensed or certified to perform an activity, and that volunteer lacked such certification or licensing.

- the liability limit does not apply if the person intentionally caused harm to others or showed flagrant indifference to the safety of those who were injured.

The immunity does not extend to harm caused by the operation of a motor vehicle, crimes of violence, activities not authorized by the charity, or to hate crimes, civil rights violations, damage resulting from the use of alcohol or drugs, or sexual offenses. It encourages states to grant liability immunity to nonprofit organization volunteers who are acting in good faith and within the scope of their official duties.

Nothing in the law provides immunity or protection for the nonprofit itself. Furthermore, the Act does not protect volunteers against large categories of claims to which volunteers are exposed, such as those alleging violations of civil rights laws (often involving employment cases), those alleging intentional harm, and suits involving the use of an automobile.

Insurance for Nonprofits and Nonprofit Personnel

There are various forms of coverage that nonprofits may consider as they look for ways to finance insurable risks. The Nonprofit Risk Management Center has published a comprehensive guide on insurance for nonprofits and provides detailed information on a wide range of coverages available to and purchased by nonprofits. The Guide, *Coverage, Claims and Consequences: An Insurance Handbook for Nonprofits*, is available at: *http://www.nonprofitrisk.org*. The most commonly purchased coverages are discussed below:

Commercial general liability insurance—Commercial general liability or CGL policies cover liability exposures that are common to all organizations. The policy actually includes a combination of three separate coverages, each with its own insuring agreement and exclusions: Coverage A (general liability), Coverage B (personal injury and advertising injury liability) and Coverage C (medical payments). The most common CGL claims against nonprofits are third party claims alleging bodily injury or property damage. While most CGL policies are based on standard wording available from the Insurance Services Office (ISO), there are dozens of different policies available to nonprofits and many more exclusions, endorsements, and other provisions that add or delete coverages. For example, one nonprofit may purchase a CGL policy that provides coverage for its special events, while another nonprofit may choose a policy that includes protection against suits alleging sexual abuse.

Commercial property insurance—Property insurance covers risk of loss to an organization's buildings or personal property. Coverage usually includes buildings, personal property of the insured, personal property of others on site and in the insured's possession.

Crime coverage—Many nonprofits purchase crime coverage, typically a package of policies that protect an organization against intentional theft by insiders, as well as theft of assets by third parties. Crime coverage generally includes a fidelity bond (also called employee dishonesty coverage) plus a basic menu of other coverages.

Directors' & officers' liability insurance—D&O insurance provides coverage against *wrongful acts* which might include actual or alleged errors, omissions, misleading statements, and neglect or breach of duty on the part of the board of directors and other insured persons and entities. Many D&O policies include employment practices liability coverage, protecting a nonprofit against claims alleging improper or illegal employment practices.

Professional liability insurance—Also known as *malpractice coverage* or *errors and omissions* (E&O) coverage, professional liability insurance protects against claims alleging negligence in the delivery of (or failure to deliver) professional services, such as medical services, counseling, legal services and more.

Workers' compensation and employers' liability insurance—Workers compensation coverage covers expenses an employer is mandated to pay by state statute to cover specific benefits for employee injuries. Employers' liability insurance protects employers from employee-related suits that are separate from WC claims.

Unemployment Compensation Insurance

The state unemployment compensation program is a job insurance program. Its purpose is to provide some limited protection against loss of income for workers who lose their jobs through no fault of their own. Contact your state Department of Labor or equivalent to learn about the requirements for participating in this program.

Risk Management

The term "risk management" refers to management strategies your organization can utilize to protect its assets from erosion or loss. Every nonprofit has a wide range of assets, including personnel, property (real estate and personal property), income, and reputation. Risk management involves giving consideration to the risks an organization faces and deciding how the organization will respond to those exposures. Among the steps of a typical planning process are the following:

1. Identify potential exposure and risk to the organization's personnel, property, clients, funding, and reputation.

2. Evaluate and prioritize potential risks.

3. Develop strategies to address these risks.

4. Periodically evaluate and update your risk management plan.

The Nonprofit Risk Management Center offers a wide range of free and affordable services designed to help nonprofits cope with risk. These resources include free technical assistance, free online tutorials (including one on basic risk management), a large library of publications for sale, online and in-person conferences, and risk assessment software. Another online program helps nonprofits develop a customized risk management plan. Information on all of these resources can be found at:

http://www.nonprofitrisk.org

Tips:

- **This chapter provides an introduction to some of the liability concerns facing nonprofits. Seek legal counsel before making any organizational decisions with respect to changing policy that could affect your exposure to liability, or about any liability suits and claims.**

- **Be certain you have an up-to-date personnel policy manual and that it includes a sexual harassment policy. Take steps to enforce these policies. While the** policies should be customized to the needs of your organization, templates can be found in inexpensive computer files you can purchase from a general office supply store.

- Provide detailed job descriptions even for volunteers. Some provisions of the federal immunity law apply only in cases in which volunteers are engaged in activities within the scope of their duties.

- Make sure that all volunteers are certified or licensed if they engage in activities that require certification or licensing for paid staff.

- If your organization transports clients, verify that volunteers have vehicle insurance and that all insurance policies for vehicles owned by the organization will cover damages caused by volunteers while driving those vehicles.

- If you serve on a board and disagree with a board decision being made at a board meeting that you feel may result in unreasonable increased liability exposure to you or your organization, ask that your objections be recorded in the minutes.

- Shop around for directors' and officers' insurance. Check to see if any policy you are considering will insure directors and officers for more than civil lawsuits.

- Make sure that those who hire employees are familiar with the questions they can and cannot legally ask (see Chapter 13).

Chapter 11
Financial Management

> **Synopsis:** All nonprofit corporations must keep certain financial records and create reports of their financial condition. There are three standards of financial verification used by accountants to verify financial data—audit, review, and compilation, with the audit being the highest level of scrutiny. *Line-item* and *program* budgets are the two major forms of budgeting utilized by nonprofit corporations. Nonprofit organizations must institute financial management systems to assure they will operate efficiently and effectively, and to minimize waste, fraud, and abuse.

The Importance of Financial Management to Nonprofits

Some of the most critically important duties of an organization's board and staff are to take steps to pay its obligations, invest its money, and plan for its financial future. Imagine the consequences that may occur if an otherwise "perfect," respected organization finds itself unable to meet its payroll because a large check anticipated from a funder failed to arrive in time. An organizational culture that condones stealing—whether in the form of allowing office supplies to be requisitioned for personal use, using credit cards to make personal purchases, or even not penalizing the use of long distance calling cards and cell phones for personal use—may experience a hemorrhage of organizational resources that could be fatal during tough economic times. Buyers who steer purchases to their relatives and friends rather than make dispassionate business decisions that are in the organization's best interest are subjecting the organization to a hidden "tax." Both board and staff leadership have a fiduciary duty to act in the best interests of the organization rather than in their own personal interest, and to manage the financial affairs of the organization prudently. To do otherwise is not only dangerous to the long-term health of the organization, but is both unethical and illegal, as well.

An organization's board and staff leadership are not the only sources of pressure to make its operations more "business-like," and to assure that each dollar expended is necessary and used effectively to further the organization's mission. Government and private funders are increasingly demanding efficiency, cost effectiveness, and outcomes that demonstrate real, measurable progress toward achieving program goals. The press has perhaps become more vigilant about monitoring the voluntary sector since high profile scandals involving respected institutions such as American University, the United Way of New York City, the Association for Volunteer Administration, and the American Red Cross have made recent headlines.

Nonprofit organizations are increasingly operating in a competitive environment not dissimilar to their for-profit counterparts. They compete for grants and donations, for board members, contracts, volunteers, media coverage, and qualified staff. Failure to manage the financial affairs of an organization can be catastrophic, resulting in bankruptcy, cutbacks of services, layoffs, involuntary merger/takeovers, and dissolution.

Where the transfer of money is involved, there are always ethics and accountability issues of which to be aware. As a result of high profile financial scandals in the nonprofit sector, the elimination of waste, fraud, and abuse in nonprofit organizations is not simply a public relations problem. In 2004, the Finance Committee of the U. S. Senate launched a new initiative focusing on devising changes to laws that affect how the sector will develop, whether its historical tax exemptions will be secure, and what disclosure will be required to assure the highest level of ethics and accountability of these organizations that are ostensibly formed for the public good rather than any individual pecuniary interest. Obviously, the financial management practices of the sector are among the prominent areas under scrutiny.

As this is being written, there is a climate of increased demand for human services and fewer resources to pay for them from all levels of government (see Chapter 36). Competent financial management is the glue that can hold a nonprofit organization together during tough times.

How Nonprofit Financial Management Differs From the Private Sector

The private sector's general goal is to make a profit for the organization with the highest return on investment (ROI), and it uses financial management as a tool for that purpose. In contrast, a nonprofit organization uses financial management to make the optimal use of resources to achieve its mission(s) and accomplish its goals. Rather than trying to maximize profit, a nonprofit organization seeks to maximize the production and delivery of goods and services, consistent with demand, to those who for one reason or another, cannot receive those goods and services from either government or the marketplace. It may be that this is because they cannot afford the market cost of the services. Or it could be that the organization provides collective goods that the government either chooses not to provide, or chooses to subsidize nonprofit organizations that will. (See Chapter 35 for a discussion of why these organizations exist.) Nonprofit organizations also advocate for various causes, knowing that they will never generate any direct income from providing advocacy services.

Generally, nonprofit organizations experience more of a political process in virtually every aspect of financial management compared to a private sector organization. And those involved in that political process are typically more diverse demographically and are not always on the same page with respect to the principal goal of the organization. In theory, the goal of for-profit organizations is to make as much profit as possible. A nonprofit organization may have many competing goals, some of which may be in conflict with each other. For example, a nursing home may want to increase its share of private-pay patients compared to those whose care is financed by Medicaid, but want to become the institution of choice for those who need care for Alzheimer's disease.

Because of the public benefits granted to nonprofit organizations, particularly those with 501(c)(3) tax-exempt status, the degree of accountability for funds is somewhat higher than for for-profit organizations. And because such organizations are entrusted with the care of people, many of whom are vulnerable and who have not voluntarily chosen that organization to receive services in the marketplace, there is an implicit acceptance by the public and government agencies that ethical standards are higher for such organizations than would apply to their for-profit counter-parts (although many would argue that all organizations should have equally high ethical standards, regardless of their sector). Even with this being the case, there is no federal government regulatory authority over the financial management of nonprofit organizations comparable to that which the Security and Exchange Commission (SEC) has over stock-issuing corporations. If it did exist, such an agency might "impose uniform accounting standards on public charities, disseminate information on the financial conditions of organizations, and create channels through which donors, volunteers, clients, and community members could access and use this information" (Frumkin, 2002, p. 159).

Components of Financial Management

Among the activities encompassed by financial management are a sequence of related activities, including planning, programming, budgeting, financing, controlling, and evaluating (McKinney, 2004).

Planning involves assessing the organization's current and likely future situation, surveying its strengths and weaknesses, setting out its goals and objectives, and developing a roadmap to achieve them. See Chapter 6 for an in-depth discussion of strategic planning. There are financial implications to changes in market conditions, new competitors, new laws and regulations, additional paperwork requirements (such as might be required by a new government or foundation funder), and an increase in the demand for services—both an increase in the number of clients and an increase in the level of services required by each client—resulting from changing social, economic, or political conditions.

Programming is the scheduling of the activities the organization needs to engage in to make its goals become a reality. In this phase, the organization creates distinct programs. A program is defined as "a collection of organizational resources that is geared to accomplish a certain major goal or set of goals" (McNamara, 2003). Prudent financial management requires that financial data be segregated by program, so that the performance of each program can be independently evaluated. This is particularly important to nonprofit organizations, as funders—and to an increasing degree, donors as well—want their grants and donations used for a particular purpose that may be only one small part of the overall operations of the organization.

The "program" is intended to achieve a particular outcome. Resources are sought from government, foundations, and the public to finance any net loss that the agency would incur by conducting that program, whether or not fees are charged to those who benefit directly from program services.

Budgeting is the process for allocating expenditures to each program. A budget is defined as an itemized summary of estimated or intended expenditures for a given period, often for a given fiscal year. A "fiscal year" is a one-year period at the end of which all accounts are reconciled, and for which the one-year budget applies. It does not necessarily coincide with a calendar year. For example, the federal government's fiscal year begins on October 1. Many states begin their fiscal year on July 1.

Typically, an organization's budget is not only a document to control the activities of subordinates, but it is also a political document. A budget, either directly or indirectly, indicates the priorities of the organization. Annual budget documents in all three sectors usually indicate what was spent during the previous fiscal year, what is being spent during the current year, and what is proposed to be spent for the next fiscal year. Stakeholders reading the budget get a sense of the direction the organization is heading with respect to each of its programs, whether it is growing or declining, from where it is planning to get its funds, and its general financial health. One gets a sense from the budget about whether the organization is more comfortable outsourcing or performing tasks with its own personnel. Those who prepare an organization's budget should look at it in its entirety and think about what message it is sending. For more details about budgeting, see pages 109-111.

Financing includes the activities necessary to obtain the resources needed in the budget. It may include borrowing from financial institutions to start new entrepreneurial ventures, or perhaps using endowment funds to serve as startup capital. It typically involves managing cash flow to assure that the organization has enough funds to pay its obligations, and policies relating to managing its cash and other assets. Fundraising, investment of surplus revenues, management of endowment funds, and use of funds generated by for-profit subsidiaries are among the activities that are included in the financing phase of the financial management cycle.

Controlling includes the development of a system that assures that the programs envisioned in the plans are being carried out appropriately. It also provides for feedback to warn when a program does not measure up to its expectations so that mid-course corrections can be implemented to get it back on track. Included in this phase of operations are policies to assure that the organization's assets—such as equipment and supplies, inventory of goods, and cash—are protected from inappropriate use or distribution. Most importantly, this includes systems that are designed to measure whether the implementation of programs is consistent with budget plans and projections, and to have procedures in place to expand, contract, or otherwise modify program operations when their performance differs from what was anticipated by the budget and planning documents. The basic accounting system; expense account policies; policies designed to minimize waste, fraud, and abuse; and the general Management Information System (MIS), if the organization has one, are among the systems that fall under this phase.

According to McLaughlin (2002), there are six elements of an internal control system.

1. *Control Cues.* This involves management and leadership sending signals, both overt and covert, of proper ethical behavior, and training staff in appropriate control policies that promote accountability.
2. *Policy Communication.* This entails having written policies and procedures for issues relating to accountability and ethics when you can, but in the absence of that, being able to communicate to employees what is acceptable and what is not by e-mail, fax, interoffice memo, or voice mail.
3. *Segregation of Duties.* This involves breaking up work duties so that one person does not have total dominance over a portion of the financial system. For example, it might make sense for the person ordering the good or service, filling out the purchase order, writing the check, signing the check, mailing the check, and receiving the ordered goods to be different people within the organization. This becomes a challenge for organizations with only a few employees, but even for a one-person office, a system of checks and balances needs to be developed.
4. *Record-keeping.* This relates to documentation and recording of all financial transactions. Among ways nonprofits try to minimize their vulnerability to internal fraud and abuse is by using a reliable payroll service, contracting out accounts receivable, and taking advantage of those financial institutions willing to do cash management for organizations. Of course, doing so increases the organization's vulnerability to external fraud and abuse.
5. *Budgets.* The budget is perhaps the best strategy to control behavior, since if there are no funds in the budget, it is difficult for spending to occur that has not been preauthorized and planned for.
6. *Reporting.* McLaughlin's view is that "you only need five financial reports to control the average nonprofit corporation" (p. 207): the balance sheet, revenue and expenses, aged accounts receivables, cash flow projection, and utilization reporting (which generally refers to how many people are using the organization's services, and to what extent). By looking at these reports periodically, a manager ostensibly can see trouble spots.

Evaluation (see Chapter 32) provides data on whether the programs are accomplishing what they set out to do. It involves validating the efforts of what is working and providing enough information to eliminate components of programs, or entire programs, when it is determined that they are not working. Many funders require the independent evaluation of the specific programs they fund as a condition of the grant. Since the popularity of the "reinventing government" movement and outcome-based management, nonprofit organizations are under increasing pressure to evaluate programs based on outcomes rather than the more easily measured outputs (see Chapter 31 for more on this topic) . Regardless, systems to collect data that facilitate evaluation that are in place at the beginning before a program starts operating make evaluation easier than having to start from scratch after the program has been operating.

Generally, it is considered more efficient if all of the functions described in this financial management cycle are administered by one person. In smaller organizations, the executive director is responsible for all of the tasks involved that are described above. Larger organizations, however, will have one person (typically with the title of Chief Operating Officer or Chief Financial Officer) who will have these duties. In the case of the latter, as some high-profile criminal and civil cases have shown with respect to the for-profit sector, it is expected that there will be sufficient communication between the CEO and the CFO or equivalent. The CEO is ultimately responsible for the health of the organization, and simple ethics require that the CEO maintain a close watch over the financial affairs of the organization, even if a subordinate staff member maintains day-to-day control over the financial operation of the organization.

Controls for Waste, Fraud, and Abuse

There are two general classifications of systems that are used to control waste, fraud, and abuse in nonprofit organizations. The first is to discourage these before they occur. The second is to assist in discovering them after they have occurred.

The traditional method of thwarting waste, fraud, and abuse *before* they occur consists of—

1. *The independent auditor's annual audit and the annual management letter.* The management letter is an opportunity by the auditor(s) to point out any deficiencies seen in the operations of the organization that affect financial accountability and ethical concerns directly to the board. When you get a management letter that cites chapter and verse with respect to internal control problems, you need to deal with it (and quickly!). This requires a plan of corrective action that is approved by the board before implementation.

2. *Internal controls of the organization.* This consists of a system of checks and balances to assure that no one person (or perhaps even more than one) can control assets without appropriate accountability. This involves the requirement that expenditures be preauthorized by a responsible organization official in accordance with predetermined policies affecting disbursements. All expenditures are recorded by the accountant/bookkeeper, with appropriate documentation for the expenditure becoming part of the file. That financial officer has the responsibility to raise any questions about the expenditure. Oversight might include pre-audit checks of all purchase orders and vouchers, and review by someone other than the person requesting them before a payment is made, and separating those who order goods and services for the organization from those who receive the goods and services. It also might include spot checks of credit card transactions, long distance telephone bills, and cell phone accounts to assure that no personal expenses are charged to the organization.

3. *Policies requiring large orders of goods and services to be put out for bid.* This includes related policies that discourage purchasers from dividing up orders into small increments to undermine this policy. This does not necessarily mean that the organization must prepare a formal *Request for Proposal* (RFP) for every large purchase. But it should mean that quotes should be obtained from several qualified vendors and contractors for large purchases.

4. *Ethics policies that apply to organization resources are distributed to individuals.* These policies might apply to credit cards, telephones, Internet accounts, cell phones, and organization vehicles, for example. These ethics policies would also include what is acceptable with respect to receiving gifts. For example, those who authorize company purchases would be prohibited from accepting gifts from suppliers other than *de minimus* gifts such as calendars. More substantial gifts, such as a box of cookies, would have to be

shared with everyone in the organization. (The free vacation to Las Vegas as a thanks from the vendor to the organization's purchaser would have to be declined.) An ethics policy should also cover the issue of gifts made to staff members from those who receive services. All ethics policies should be reviewed at least once annually and updated as appropriate.

5. *Training all employees on how to deal with the elimination of waste, fraud, and abuse.* The philosophy inherent in this method is that it is difficult to deal with a "bad" behavior when an individual might not have a clear sense as to what that might be in every case. The training should include procedures for staff to report suspected cases of fraud.

6. *Severe penalties for violating the public trust.* This involves written policies that require those found to have stolen from the organization to be fired and referred to criminal authorities, or otherwise appropriately sanctioned by reprimand or suspension if the violation is in a gray area.

7. *Record keeping about all assets and taking a periodic inventory.* This is important so that when something is missing (such as a lap-top computer), an investigation can commence quickly.

8. *Electronic protection of records.* The purpose of maintaining backups is so have an electronic trail, if not a paper trail, in the event of a fire or flood that destroys paper records.

Methods used to find occurrences *after* they have occurred include—

1. Determining when an employee has suddenly adopted a high lifestyle beyond his/her known income.

2. Investigating when it becomes suspected that purchasers are funneling purchases to personal friends or relatives, or receiving expensive gifts from suppliers.

3. Taking swift action when there appears to be missing documentation, "lost" organization checks, or an increased backlog in recording transactions.

4. Randomly reviewing credit card transactions and organization telephone bills for personal expenses charged to the organization's account.

5. Determining which expenses seem too high compared to what they have been historically, particularly when it is difficult to account for this with a reasonable explanation.

Basic Financial Statements

For a sample, actual document that summarizes the financial position of a nonprofit, the Association for Research on Nonprofit Organizations and Voluntary Action (ARNOVA), see Appendix C. There are three basic financial statements that are prepared by the organization's accountant:

1. *Balance sheet (Statement of Financial Position).* The purpose of the balance sheet is to demonstrate the financial position of the organization at a certain point, typically the end of a fiscal year, by comparing its assets (what the organization owns) to liabilities (what the organization owes). Current assets consist of the monetary value of what is owned by the organization other than long-term assets, including the cash in the checking account and cash equivalents, such as certificates of deposit; accounts receivable (minus the value of those receivables that are not likely to be collected, called "bad debts"); pledges receivable; grants receivable; the current value of investments (stocks, bonds, and other marketable financial assets); inventories of goods; and prepaid expenses and other deferred charges (such as, for example, a fully-paid life insurance policy that covers more than one fiscal year). Fixed assets (including the value of land, buildings, and equipment owned by the organization that has a life of more than a year) are those that

are not likely to be converted into cash at any time in the near future, such as stocks and bonds or real property owned by the organization.

Liabilities are debts that the organization owes to those outside of the organization. Current short-term liabilities include accounts payable, grants payable (for those nonprofits that make such grants), taxes owed but not yet paid (such as sales taxes collected and UBIT—unrelated business income taxes— that apply even to those organizations that are tax-exempt), and current loans. Long-term liabilities include long term loans, bonds, and mortgages. The report is called a balance sheet because assets and liabilities are brought into balance in the "bottom line" as a result of merging liabilities with the "net assets," also referred to as "fund balance"—the net value, the net worth, or the equity of the organization at that point in time.

2. *Income Statement.* Income statements consist of three parts, showing revenues, expenses, and the net difference between these two (positive if there is a profit, negative if there is a loss). That net difference can be distorted when an organization is on a cash basis of accounting, and there are either expenses or revenue paid out (or taken in, as the case may be), in a different accounting period. The accrual method of accounting overcomes this flaw (see page 106). Categories of income may include grants; donations; income from fees for services; income from for-profit subsidiaries; and sales of land, buildings, and equipment. Expense categories may include salaries, supplies, depreciation on buildings and equipment, administrative, general and fundraising expenses, and other expenses. The statement usually includes a line at the bottom comparing the net profit of the current year to the previous year, and the amount of this profit that has aggregated over time (called the "fund balance").

3. *Statement of Changes in Financial Position.* This statement typically includes the amount of cash from revenues; the amount of cash expenditures (and the difference between the two as net revenue or net loss); expenses from purchases of land, equipment, and income from the sale of these; and income from loans and bonds. The "bottom line" on this statement shows the net profit or loss and the cash balance, as well as how that cash balance compares to the previous year.

4. *Form 990—Return of Organization Exempt From Income Tax.* This annual information form has been required by the Internal Revenue Service since the 1940s, and was substantially revised in December 2007. It applies to most federally tax-exempt organizations with gross revenues of $25,000 or more. Organizations with gross revenues of less than $100,000 and total assets of less than $250,000 may elect to file the short version of the form, 990-EZ. The filing deadline is four and a half months following the end of the organization's fiscal year. Organizations are required by law to provide a copy of their Form 990 to anyone who requests it, although organizations that make their returns "widely available," such as by posting their 990s online, are exempt from this requirement. The organization may charge a reasonable copying fee (none if the requester provides his or her own copying equipment on site) and actual postage costs. Form 990 requires detailed disclosure relating to Revenue, Expenses, Changes in Net Assets or Fund Balances (Part 1); Statement of Functional Expenses (Part 2); Statement of Program Service Accomplishments (Part 3); Balance Sheets (Part 4); a list of officers, directors, trustees and key employees that includes salary information (Part 5); and "Other" information that includes information about lobbying, fundraising, unrelated business income, in-kind donations, among other issues (Part 6). The fine for not filing this return is $20 per day, not to exceed the lesser of $10,000 or 5% of the gross receipts of the

organization for the year. For large organizations (those with annual gross receipts exceeding $1 million), the penalty is $100 per day up to $50,000.

Fund Accounting

Separate accounting records are maintained for each fund of a nonprofit organization. The nonprofit establishes each of these funds to meet a specified purpose. A small-sized nonprofit may only have a single fund, called the general fund, operating fund, or unrestricted fund. Larger nonprofits may have several funds in addition to this general fund. Among the most common are—

Endowment Fund. A permanent endowment fund assumes that the financial principal remains unspent, but that the interest earned on this fund may be spent for either any purpose or a restricted, specified purpose.

Fixed Asset Fund. This fund includes the fixed assets of the organization and liabilities associated with the physical plant (both purchase and maintenance). Pledges to construct new facilities are included in this fund.

Restricted Funds. It is not unusual for donors to specify how their donations must be used. If the board does not have the power to use donations for any purpose it chooses, the donations are placed in a restricted fund and reported in a separate accounting statement of Income, Expenses, and Changes in Net Assets. Some nonprofits have funds established for each major donor.

Accounting rules tend to get somewhat complex and legalistic. Some donations have conditions attached before they can be counted on by the charity. Two examples of these are bequests and matching pledges. Rather than being included as assets in fund accounting, these donations are often disclosed as footnotes in the financial reports.

Cash-Flow Analysis

Nonprofit organizations, as with other organizations, benefit from performing a cash flow analysis. The analysis is designed to answer the questions of how much cash the organization needs to pay its obligations at each point in time, and when and from where is it coming at each such point in time. This analysis is necessary because revenue, such as that coming from grants, is not always received before expenses need to be paid. A year-long grant may be paid in monthly installments. But for organizations that write paychecks every two weeks, there are three payrolls rather than two every third month.

Utility bills (such as for heating in the winter and cooling in the summer), may be seasonal. The organization's annual fundraiser may create a spike in donations in May, a month or so before the end of the fiscal year. In short, a budget may balance appropriately based on a year of revenue and expenses. But if the expenses are incurred mostly before the income is received, the organization may find itself unable to pay its obligations. A cash-flow analysis will look at how revenues and expenses project each month, and determines whether there is a problem with having enough cash in the bank to write checks for obligations when they need to be written. When a problem is identified, there are often strategies for dealing with it. Some payments can be made in installments. Purchases can be put on a credit card until enough cash comes in. Accounts payable could be delayed a month or so to catch up, or the organization could seek a loan.

What is the FASB?

The Financial Accounting Standards Board is a private-sector organization founded in 1973 with the mission "to establish and improve standards of financial accounting and reporting for the guidance and education of the public, including issuers, auditors and users of financial information" (FASB, 2005). Its accounting standards are promulgated with an open, participatory process, and are recognized by government agencies with statutory authority to enforce organizational accountability, including the Securities and Exchange Commission, and professional associations such as the *American Institute of Certified Public Accountants.* Indeed, while the board is independent of all government and professional associations, it consists of fifteen representatives from eight membership associations with an interest in financial reporting.

There are two important standards issued by the FASB that apply to nonprofit organizations.

FASB Statement 116 and Statement 117 were issued in June 1993, and apply to all charities with at least $5 million in assets and $1 million in annual expenses. They are generally required to be adopted for financial statements for fiscal years beginning after December 15, 1995. Statement 116 sets standards with respect to accounting for contributions made and received. Among changes in policy made by this statement is that donor pledges that are unconditional are counted as assets even though no actual payment on the pledges has been received (Shim and Siegel, 1997). For a summary, see: *http://www.fasb.org/st/summary/stsum116.shtml*

FASB Statement117 establishes standards for financial statements of nonprofit organizations. It requires, among other standards, that nonprofit organizations provide a statement of financial position, a statement of activities, and a cash-flow statement. Organizations must report total assets, liabilities, and net assets in a statement of financial position; report the change in an organization's net assets in a statement of activities; and report the change in cash and cash equivalents in a statement of cash flows. The main theme of FASB 117 is to take into account the presence or absence of donor restrictions and to group an organization's funds into three categories: permanently restricted, temporarily restricted, and unrestricted, applicable only to the organization's net assets (McLaughlin, 2002). For a summary, see: *http://www.fasb.org/st/summary/stsum117.shtml*

Sarbanes-Oxley

The *American Competitiveness and Corporate Accountability Act,* commonly known as the Sarbanes-Oxley Act, was enacted by the Congress in 2002 as a response to corporate financial scandals, such as those at Enron, Arthur Anderson, and Global Crossing (Silk, 2004). Generally, this act does not apply to nonprofit corporations, although two provisions—those relating to protecting whistle-blowers and the destruction of litigation-related documents—do apply to both for-profit and nonprofit corporations (Board Source & Independent Sector, 2003). See Chapter 36 for more on efforts by the Congress and state legislatures to apply more provisions of this law to nonprofit organizations.

Bookkeeping

Both state and federal law require corporations to record all expenses and income in an organized format. This can be done manually or by using one of many popular computer programs.

Several basic decisions must be made with respect to record-keeping. First, the corporation must decide on the period of its fiscal year. Because federal law requires the Form 990 nonprofit tax return to be filed within four-and-a-half months after the end of the fiscal year (technically, by the 15th day of the fifth month after the end of the fiscal year), that alone can determine when to begin the fiscal year. Other factors to consider are the fiscal years or the announcement dates of grants of major funding sources, using a calendar year for simplicity, or beginning the fiscal year as soon as the first corporate income has been received.

A second issue is to decide whether the bookkeeping system will be on a "cash" or "accrual" basis. Cash basis financial reporting recognizes a transaction the date income was actually received and deposited and when expenditures were made. The "accrual" method recognizes a transaction when it is made, i.e., when supplies are ordered, not when they are received. The "accrual" method factors in "accounts payable" (when the organization owes someone money, but has not actually sent them a payment) and "accounts receivable" (when there is a legal obligation to pay the organization something in the future, but the organization hasn't yet received payment). Most novices find the cash basis easier and simpler. The accrual method, on the other hand, gives a more realistic picture of the actual financial situation of the organization, and thus complies with generally accepted accounting principles.

The "cash" vs. "accrual" decision should be discussed with the organization's accountant, or whoever is likely to prepare the tax returns and annual financial report. The accrual method is the method of choice for all but the smallest of organizations. This is the time when the foresight of placing a certified public accountant or two on the board of directors can pay dividends.

Some funding agencies may have their own unique financial reporting requirements that must be complied with to qualify for grants.

Levels of Financial Verification

There are three levels of financial verification. In descending levels of scope and scrutiny, they are audits, reviews, and compilations. The level of financial verification required is often determined by the nature and source of funding for the organization. Many government grants explicitly require a minimum level of financial verification in their contracts. Such a contract may be a "pass-through" of funds from another source, and the original source may need to be tracked down to determine whether it has its own requirements. For example, a nonprofit organization may receive a grant from a United Way, but the funding is provided by a state government. As a result, the United Way may require financial reports from the nonprofit organization that will permit it to comply with its own reporting requirements to that state government grantor.

It is wise to request all financial reporting information, in writing, from any contracting agency that provides the organization with grant funds.

All of the three financial verification levels require that all organizational funds be kept segregated by the appropriate organizational accounts (and, of course, from the accounts of other organizations) and all transactions be accounted for. Thus, it is never good organizational policy to sign over an incoming check payment to a third party. Instead, deposit the check into the organization's account and then write a new check to the third party. While ignoring this advice may save the time of making a deposit and writing a check, it will result in a loss of "paper trail" necessary to determine who paid what to whom, when, and for what.

In the absence of an overriding requirement in a contract, federal, state, and local governments require an audit report when the funds in the contract are $100,000 or more in any single year.

State and local governments generally require a review if funding is between $25,000 and $100,000 annually. If funding is less than $25,000, a compilation report is usually acceptable.

Audit Report

The highest level of financial verification, an audit, is a complete arm's-length verification of the accuracy and reliability of account statements and financial reports. Records are systematically examined and checked to determine how they adhere to generally accepted accounting principles, management policies, and other stated policies. The purpose of independent audits is to eliminate bias, self-interest, fraud, and unintentional errors.

What does the auditor do? The auditor will request information from individuals and institutions to confirm bank balances, contribution amounts, conditions and restrictions, contractual obligations, and monies owed to and by your organization. The auditor will review physical assets, journals and ledgers, and board minutes to ensure that all activity with significant financial implications is adequately disclosed in the financial statements. In addition, the auditor will select a sample of financial transactions to determine whether there is proper documentation and whether the transaction was posted correctly into the books. In addition, the auditor will interview key personnel and read the procedures manual, if one exists, to determine whether or not the organization's internal accounting control system is adequate. The auditor usually spends several days at the organization's office looking over records and checking for completeness (CompassPoint, 2006).

While an auditor can never obtain *absolute* proof of the representations made in a financial statement, the standard used is that of a "reasonable man" (or woman) who has "adequate technical training and proficiency as an auditor," according to the American Institute of Certified Public Accountants. Auditors have a professional code of ethics to ensure their independence from the management of the nonprofit organization they are auditing. Although they are paid a fee by the corporation, they are considered to be responsible to the public rather than to their corporate clients.

Many government agencies have audit requirements for recipients of their grants, as do many foundations and other umbrella fundraising organizations, such as United Ways and Jewish federations. Audits are often required by major umbrella fundraising organizations unless the revenues are relatively small.

The American Institute of Certified Public Accountants (AICPA) has prepared a comprehensive publication entitled *Audit and Accounting Guide: Not for Profit Organization*, published July 2007, specifically to assist nonprofit corporations in preparing for their annual audits. This *Guide* can be purchased for $86.25 in paper and $68 on CD-ROM (discounts available for AICPA members), plus $9.25 for postage and handling from:

American Institute of Certified Public Accountants
Service Center
220 Leigh Farm Road
Durham, NC 27707
(888) 777-7077 (option 1)
http://www.cpa2biz.com

SAS 112 Auditing Rule of AICPA

A new auditing rule issued by the Auditing Standards Board of the American Institute of Certified Public Accountants (AICPA) issued in July 2007 is expected to make major changes in how auditors do their work with nonprofit organizations. The title of the rule is "Communicating Internal Control Related Matters Identified in an Audit" (SAS 112). SAS 112 requires auditors to not only identify the organization's internal control weaknesses or deficiencies, but to tell the board or governance committee about them in writing. The rule defines three internal control problems—"control deficiency," "significant deficiency," and "material weakness," and generally lowers the standard by which one of these is considered a problem that needs to be remedied.

SAS 112 defines a "control deficiency" as "when the design or operation of a control does not allow management or employees, in the normal course of performing their assigned functions, to prevent or detect misstatements on a timely basis."

The term "significant deficiency" is defined as "a control deficiency, or combination of control deficiencies, that adversely affects the entity's ability to initiate, authorize, record, process, or report financial data reliably in accordance with GAAP, such that there is *more than a remote likelihood* that a *misstatement of the entity's financial statements that is more than inconsequential* will not be prevented or detected.

A "material weakness" means "a significant deficiency, or combination of significant deficiencies, that results in *more than a remote likelihood* that a *material misstatement of the financial statements* will not be prevented or detected.

This development is considered to be potentially problematic to many small and medium nonprofit organizations for several reasons. First, it lowers the bar for what is considered a problem. Second, grantors, donors, regulators, and financial agencies may start routinely requesting these letters and make funding decisions based on them. Third, many smaller organizations may not have the capacity to respond effectively to the recommendations of one of these letters when deficiencies are found. And fourth, the rule is expected to disproportionately affect small nonprofits, because they may be required to have an audit because of state fundraising regulatory requirements while for-profits of similar size would not have such a requirement.

The rule applies to auditing periods ending on or after December 15, 2006, although earlier implementation is permitted.

To review the rule, see: *http://www.aicpa.org/download/members/div/auditstd/AU-00325.pdf*

Review

A second standard of financial verification, called a "review," is the application of analytical procedures by the accountant to the financial data supplied by the corporation. It is substantially narrower in scope than an audit. Much of the information supplied by the corporation is accepted at face value, although there may be a spot check to see if there are any glaring errors or inconsistencies between expenses recorded and the checks that are written. The examination of internal control and the proper allocation of income and expenses is similar to that of an audit report. Unlike an audit, the review will not include a formal auditor's "opinion" as to the compliance with generally accepted accounting principles.

Compilation

The third level of financial reporting/verification, a "compilation," calls only for the proper classification of assets, liabilities, fund balances, income, and expenses, from information supplied by management. Third-party verification of assets and liabilities is not required, although internal supporting documents may be used in their place. "Spot checks" are employed only when the accountant is aware of inconsistencies in other areas of the examination. As in a review, the accountant will not render an "opinion" on the accuracy of the report.

In the absence of legal requirements, it is good policy for nonprofits that expend more than a few thousand dollars to have at least a review. Many nonprofits have certified public accountants on their boards who may be willing to arrange for a review of the corporation on a *pro bono* basis.

Budgeting

Some nonprofits can exist for years using volunteer labor, donations of stamps, in-kind printing and other services, and have no need to raise money or make any expenditures. Others are more likely to have some staff and pay office rent or, if not, still have expenditures for workshops, postage, printing, telephone, and other typical corporate expenses.

The annual budget document is the blueprint for both spending and income. A poorly conceived budget can lead to the corporation's demise. On the other hand, a well-conceived, realistic budget can be the catalyst for program planning that provides a corporate life for many fruitful years.

Line-item and program budgets are the two major types of budgeting used by nonprofit corporations. Each has its advantages and disadvantages.

Line-Item Budget

The line-item budget is as it says—a list of various categories and the amount the corporation expects to spend for each category. Corporations, from the largest to the smallest, have some of the same categories in a line-item budget. Among the most common are:

1. salaries
2. consulting services
3. professional services
4. taxes
5. fringe benefits
6. telephone
7. postage
8. printing and photocopying
9. travel
10. workshops and conferences
11. bank fees
12. dues
13. subscriptions and publications
14. data processing
15. equipment
16. equipment maintenance and repair
17. legal services
18. insurance
19. rent
20. office supplies
21. maintenance and repairs
22. security services
23. utilities
24. bookkeeping and payroll services

25.   Web hosting services
26.   miscellaneous

As an expense is incurred, its amount is entered in a journal prepared for this purpose, coded by its expense category. At the end of each month, the amounts of each category are aggregated on a ledger sheet called a "monthly summary." The monthly totals should be compared with the budget for each category to determine whether spending patterns are consistent with the budget. For example, an organization can have "annual conference" as a program, and include all expenses associated with it included, such as printing, postage, travel, consulting, and so on. Or as an alternative, the individual expenses of the conference for printing and postage could be included in the organization's regular printing and postage line-items.

The advantage of a line-item budget is the ease of assigning every expenditure. A dollar spent on paper clips is an expense for "supplies," and a dollar spent on Web hosting is an expense for "Web hosting." The disadvantage is that it is not always clear how much can be saved by eliminating any particular program of an organization, because the expenses of that program are subsumed within many different line-items, such as would be the case with the example of an annual conference.

Program Budget

The second type of budget is called a program budget. The program budget also contains various line-items, but the difference is that each program of a nonprofit, such as conferences, newsletter, membership, or publications, has its own budget within it.

For example, if the organization is having a conference, then the conference itself has a budget. Printing, postage, and telephone costs are attributed to the conference. Printing and postage costs may be associated with another program, as well, such as a newsletter.

The advantage of the program budget is that one can quickly determine the incremental savings that will accrue to the organization if a particular program is eliminated. The disadvantage is that it is not easy to allocate overhead costs—such as the CEO's salary and rent—to various programs.

It is not unusual for nonprofits to combine the two types of budgeting—to have a general line-item budget, but to allocate some spending in all categories to certain programs. For small nonprofits, line-item budgets are the easiest to prepare and follow, but program budgets provide better information.

The Budget Process

Each organization is likely to develop its own budgeting process, which evolves over time based on the personalities of its staff and board, the stability of its funding streams, the needs of outside stakeholders, and other factors. The following is one possible model.

Step 1. Begin the budgeting process at least three months before the start of the organization's fiscal year, allowing enough time for the board to approve the final budget after having the opportunity to provide feedback.

Step 2. Review all programs and management achievements. Compile a comparison of estimated costs to actual costs, which is called a "variance."

Step 3. Make estimates of expenses for commitments made for the upcoming year (in salaries, new programs, capital expenses) that did not require funding for the current year, such as new programs and the expansion of existing programs approved in the organization's strategic plan.

Step 4. Make estimates of expenditure increases resulting from predictable budget items, such as salary inflation adjustments and merit increases, rent, utilities, insurance, and other categories that grow as a result of inflation rather than expansion of services or programs.

Step 5. Make estimates of income—including estimated contributions, grants, fees, the sale of goods and services, and investment income.

Step 6. Adjust spending and income based on the organization's ability to build surpluses or incur deficits, but avoid making adjustments in income based on the need to balance a budget. The reason is that spending is more likely to be controllable compared to income.

Step 7. Submit the budget to the board for approval.

Step 8. Periodically adjust the organization's budget and resubmit changes to the board as new information is received.

Expense Reimbursement

Organizations incur expenses. Many of these can be paid conveniently by corporate check. Many others can be paid by corporate credit card, which is particularly useful for travel expenses. For reasons of good financial management, it is not atypical for newly formed organizations to require two signatures on checks. This is not unreasonable for recurring expenses that can be processed well in advance, such as paychecks, federal withholding, rent, major equipment purchases, and taxes.

However, requiring two signatures does present problems when making small, but reasonable, on-the-spot purchases. An expense reimbursement system should be designed to provide protection against one person making unilateral, capricious decisions on spending, but needs to be flexible enough to keep the organization from being hamstrung when trying to pay $25 for office supplies.

One suggestion is to set up an "imprest account" to pay routine office expenses, requiring only one signature. The authorized person (such as the executive director) has a reasonable sum to disburse from this checking account, which is entirely separate from the "master" checking account. The imprest account is replenished from the master checking account using a check that requires the usual two signatures, only upon a review by the chairperson or treasurer (or both) of what was expended—including supporting documentation, such as receipts. This account should provide an amount needed not only to pay reasonable expenses for the month, but enough to cover expenses for part of the following month, since several days or weeks may elapse during the processing of the expense report.

The organization's leadership should provide general guidelines as to what types of expenses are acceptable for reimbursement and what expenses should be absorbed by the staff. For example, hotel accommodations in any city can range from $30-$300. A dinner can be purchased for $4 or $75. Many organizations refuse to make decisions concerning what is appropriate, and instead provide a per diem allowance—a flat payment that is expected to pay reasonable travel expenses for each one-day period. The staff member then must absorb costs that go beyond this amount.

Many other expense issues arise that require board policies. How much should staff be reimbursed for mileage? What if a spouse attends a conference with a staff member and shares a room, resulting in an incremental cost increase? How will expenses be reimbursed that cannot be directly documented with a receipt, such as tips or parking meter expenses?

All of these issues can be resolved on an ad hoc basis, but it is useful to think about the nature of expense reimbursement before it creates problems. Many organizations have failed because their budgets were depleted by discretionary spending in the absence of an expense policy.

Fiscal Sponsorship

Social entrepreneurs often face a difficult dilemma once they decide to run with an idea to improve the quality of life for their communities. If they create a formal organization, they face spending countless hours building its infrastructure and complying with all of the legal requirements described in Chapters 2 and 3. Yet, if they choose to go it alone, they suffer the consequences of not being able to accomplish as much as they could by having a formal organization, and face the reluctance of donors to make donations to them. Grantors seldom are willing or able to fund individuals, and donors are often wary of making donations to organizations that do not qualify as 501(c)(3)s and permit those donations to be tax-deductible.

There is a third way beyond these two alternatives that is increasingly attractive, but relatively obscure—finding a fiscal sponsor. Perhaps this is not as obscure at first glance. Perhaps the majority of scientific research is carried out by individuals who are affiliated with universities. The grantor makes a tax-deductible check out to the university, and the university passes along most of the grant to the individual researcher and handles all of the administration.

This model can be, and has been, adapted for social entrepreneurship. A social entrepreneur, instead of creating his or her own 501(c)(3) tax-exempt organization, approaches an existing tax-exempt organization to serve as the fiscal sponsor. The entrepreneur becomes in effect an employee of that fiscal sponsor. The sponsor receives the grants and donations on behalf of the program being carried out by the entrepreneur, provides a salary and benefits, handles all financial transactions, and provides financial oversight over the program. The donors receive their tax benefits, and the entrepreneur is free to devote his or her energies to the program rather than administration.

One barrier to doing this is finding a willing fiscal sponsor. Among those that might be considered are those with an interest in supporting the mission of the program you plan to pursue. This might include foundations, United Ways or similar umbrella fundraising organizations, institutions of higher learning, professional societies, museums, health agencies, labor unions, religious institutions, and arts organizations.

Of course, if you choose this route, you must be willing to relinquish some control over the organization. Technically, you would be an employee of the fiscal sponsor, and the board of the fiscal sponsor is the de facto "ruler" of your organization rather than yourself. The agreement between your organization and the fiscal sponsor needs to be in writing and quite clear as to the responsibilities of each party. You will want everything spelled out about what control you will have, and whether you will have the ability to spin off your organization as a separate, independent organization in the future, should you desire to do so.

For a comprehensive online guide to considering whether to structure your organization via the fiscal sponsorship model, see the Foundation Center's tutorial at: *http://foundationcenter.org/getstarted/tutorials/fiscal/*

Tips:

- **Before choosing either a cash or accrual basis of accounting, verify that your organization is not required to adopt the accrual method because of government or funder requirements.**

- **If you are not the individual performing the accounting, yet are legally responsible for its accuracy, periodically examine the organization's books to see if there are any inconsistencies, or whether they are being kept sloppily.**

- **Have clear, written policies that inform staff of the need to avoid diverting organizational resources for personal use and the penalties for doing so.**

- **Keep duplicate paper and electronic copies of important financial records, and store them at an alternative physical site.**

Online Resources to Explore

Business Owner's Toolkit: Small Business Guide
http://www.toolkit.cch.com/

Guidestar—Nonprofit Resources
http://www.guidestar.org/npo/

Carter McNamara's Basic Guide to Non-Profit Financial Management
http://www.managementhelp.org/finance/np_fnce/np_fnce.htm

Nonprofit Good Practice Guide
http://www.npgoodpractice.org/

Idealist.org's Nonprofit FAQ—General Management
http://www.idealist.org/if/i/en/npofaq

Board Source/Independent Sector: The Sarbanes-Oxley Act and Implications for Nonprofit Organizations
http://www.boardsource.org/clientfiles/Sarbanes-Oxley.pdf

References

Board Source & Independent Sector. (2003). *The Sarbanes-Oxley and implications for nonprofit organizations.* p.2. Author. Retrieved online at: http://www.boardsource.org/clientfiles/Sarbanes-Oxley.pdf

CompassPoint. (2006). *What does an auditor do?* Nonprofit Genie (FAQ). January 17, 2006. Retrieved online at: http://www.compasspoint.org/askgenie/details.php?id=70

FASB. (2005). Facts about FASB. Retrieved online at: http://www.fasb.org/facts/index.shtml

Frumkin, P. (2002). *On being nonprofit: A primer.* Cambridge, MA: Harvard University Press.

McNamara, C. (1999). *Program planning and management.* Retrieved online at:http://www.mapnp.org/library/prog_mng/prog_mng.htm#anchor1676854

McLaughlin, T. (2002). *Streetsmart financial basics for nonprofit managers.* New York: Wiley and Sons.

McKinney, J. (2004). *Effective financial management in public and nonprofit agencies* (3rd Edition). Westport, CT: Praeger Publishing.

Shim, J. A. & Siegel, J. G. (1997). *Financial management for nonprofits: The complete guide to maximizing resources and managing assets.* New York: McGraw-Hill.

Silk, T. (2004). Ten emerging principals of governance of nonprofit corporations. *The Exempt Organization Tax Review.* 43(1), pp. 35-39, January 2004.

Chapter 12
Personnel

> **Synopsis:** Nonprofit corporations with staff should have a written personnel policy. There are a number of state and federal laws that apply to nonprofit operations and many standard forms that must be filed to comply with these laws.

Introduction

Whether a nonprofit corporation has one salaried employee or hundreds, a written personnel policy can prevent disputes that, in some cases, can destroy an organization even before it gets off the ground. Obviously, a personnel policy for a small organization will be less complex than that of a large one. It is advisable to review personnel policies of several organizations of similar scope and choose among the provisions that are most sensitive to your organization's needs. It is not necessary to reinvent the wheel, but *having* a wheel is important.

Qualified and trained personnel are an organization's most prized assets. Staff members need to feel that the organization is flexible enough to respond to their individual needs. Conversely, the organization must have the ability to operate efficiently, effectively, and economically, and to treat all employees fairly and equally. A balance must be attained, and each organization can best determine for itself where the balance lies.

Before hiring the first employee, among the issues to consider and for which to develop policies are:

- Should staff be paid employees of the corporation, or should the corporation hire a consultant? (see Chapter 13)
- What will be included in staff job descriptions?
- How much should each staff member be compensated? Should a staff person be paid on a salaried basis or by the hour?
- If an office is established, what should the office hours be, and where should the office be located?

It may be advisable for the organization to have a personnel committee. Its role is to study the issues raised in this section; develop a personnel policy for ratification by the board, if appropriate; and serve as the adjudicating body to resolve grievances by employees.

After a decision is made to hire employees, some of the issues to consider for inclusion in a personnel policy are the following:

1. Hiring policies—How should job vacancies be advertised? Will there be affirmative action to recruit minorities? Should the search be national, statewide, regional, or local? Should current employees be given preference in hiring for vacant positions?

2. Firing policies—What are the conditions that permit dismissal without appeal, such as "for cause"? Will there be severance pay? Will placement services be provided? Will notice be given of unsatisfactory job performance before dismissal?

3. Probationary periods of employment—Should there be a period of probation during which an employee can be terminated without access to any grievance procedure or without receiving benefits, including leave?

4. Sick leave and vacation—How many days will be allowed? Can they be accumulated, and if so, how? Will a doctor's note verifying a sickness be required?

5. Holidays—Which holidays are paid holidays and which are optional? What is the policy with respect to the observance of religious holidays?

6. Personal days—How many personal days will be permitted, and will they be accumulated? If not taken, will they carry over? Can they be "cashed in" upon retirement?

7. Overtime policies—Which classes of employees are eligible for overtime pay? Is overtime mandatory if requested by the corporation? Will overtime be compensated in salary or compensatory time?

8. Compensatory ("Comp") time—Should comp time be granted in lieu of overtime pay? Should surplus comp time be required to be used for routine doctor and dentist appointments rather than sick leave?

9. Full-time vs. part-time status—How many hours per week qualify the employee for benefits?

10. Health insurance—Is there a group plan? Will gross salary be increased if an employee is covered by the health insurance policy of a spouse and desires not to be covered by the organization?

11. Pension—How long does it take for an employee to be vested? What is the employer and employee contribution required?

12. Life insurance, disability insurance, long term care insurance, and other insurance benefits—Is there a menu from which to choose?

13. Employee evaluation—Who performs the evaluation? How often will the evaluation be performed? Under what conditions may employees exercise their legal rights to examine their files? Who has access to personnel files?

14. Merit salary increases; cost-of-living increases—What are the criteria used for salary increases, and how often and by whom are salaries reviewed?

15. Continuing education benefits—Are they offered? Who has authority to approve requests? What are the time and cost limitations? When do employees become eligible?

16. Staff training/orientation—Is a pre- or post-employment physical or other examination required? Is there a formal review for new employees concerning staff personnel policies? What type of training will be provided and who will provide it?

17. Maternity leave—What documentation is required? What is the maximum leave the employee may take without losing her job?

18. Bereavement leave—How long will such leave be, and which relatives will be included in the policy?

19. Family and medical leave—For what purposes will this leave be granted, what documentation is required to accompany a leave request, will the leave be paid or unpaid, and what will the effect be on unused sick leave and vacation (see #17)?

20. Pay for jury duty, military leave—What is the organization's policy?

21. Sabbatical leave—After how many years will employees qualify, for how long, and will this be paid or unpaid leave?

22. Expense reimbursement documentation—How will expenses be filed and what expenses are eligible? Is there a flat per diem rate for out-of-town travel or reimbursement? What amount will be reimbursed for mileage?

23. Notice required for resignation—What is the minimum notice required, and what are the sanctions for not complying?

24. System for resolution of employee grievances—May employees appeal to the board of directors? Is there a committee for this purpose?

25. Disciplinary sanctions for rule-breaking—Is there provision for suspension with or without pay?

26. Prohibition against secondary employment—What types of outside earned income are prohibited or permitted?

27. Telephone policy—What is the organization's policy with respect to personal calls at work, including reimbursement by the employee for toll calls?

28. Payroll—Will salary be provided weekly, every other week, or monthly?

29. Use of the Internet—What is the organization's policy for using the organization's Internet account for personal use, during working hours, and after working hours?

30. Use of organization cell phone—What is the policy with respect to using the cell phone issued by the organization for personal use?

While the issues may seem overwhelming, a small organization may only need basic policies such as hours of operation, vacation and sick leave policy, benefits provided, and holidays. The rest can be determined on an ad hoc basis by the executive director, in consultation with the board's chairperson and/or the personnel committee, if there is one.

Major Federal Laws Affecting Employers

Taxpayer Bill of Rights 2 (P. L. 104-168)
This law was enacted on July 30, 1996, but its provisions relating to excessive income are retroactive to September 1995. It includes "intermediate sanctions" provisions that authorize the Internal Revenue Service to levy excise taxes on excessive compensation paid out by 501(c)(3)

and (c)(4) organizations, and to penalize nonprofit managers who authorize such compensation. The law also provides for increased public disclosure of financial documents.

Fair Labor Standards Act of 1938 (52 Stat. 1060, 29 §201 et seq.)
Enacted in 1938, the law provides for a minimum wage, controls child labor, and requires premium pay for overtime.

Equal Pay Act of 1963 (P.L. 88-38, 29 § 206)
Requires that men and women performing equal work be paid equally.

Civil Rights Act of 1964 (P.L. 88-352, 28 §1447, 42 §1971, 1975a-1975-d, 2000 et seq.)
Prohibits discrimination, including employment discrimination, on the basis of race, color, religion, sex or national origin. Includes prohibition of certain questions being asked by prospective employers at job interviews.

Equal Employment Opportunity Act of 1972 (P.L. 92-2615 §5108, 5314-5316, 42 §2000e)
Amends the Civil Rights Act by expanding anti-discrimination protection.

Age Discrimination in Employment Act of 1967 (P.L. 90-202, 29 §621 et seq.)
Prohibits discrimination against persons age 40-70, as revised by the 1978 amendments.

Immigration Reform and Control Act of 1986 (P.L. 99-603, 7 §2025 and other references)
Requires employers to certify that their workers are not illegal aliens, and prevents discrimination on the basis of national origin.

Employee Retirement Income Security Act of 1974 (ERISA) (P.L. 93-406, 26 § 37 et seq., 29 §1001 et seq., and other references)
Requires accountability and reporting related to employer pension plans.

National Labor Relations Act of 1935 (49 Stat 449, 29 §151 et seq.)
Authorizes workers to form unions and other collective bargaining units.

Pregnancy Discrimination Act of 1978 (P.L. 95-555, 42 §2000e(k))
Amends the Civil Rights Act (which prohibits discrimination on the basis of sex) to change the definition of "sex" to include "because of or on the basis of pregnancy, childbirth, or related medical conditions."

Drug-Free Workplace Act of 1988 (P.L. 100-690, 41 §701 et seq.)
Requires organizations receiving federal contracts valued at $25,000 or more to certify that they will provide a drug-free workplace, notify their employees of actions taken against those who violate drug laws, and establish a drug-free awareness program.

Americans With Disabilities Act of 1990 (P.L. 101-336, 29 §706, 42 §12101 et seq., 47 §152, 221, 225, 611)
Prohibits employers with 15 or more workers from discriminating on the basis of disability.

Family and Medical Leave Act (P.L. 103-3, 29§2601 et seq.)
Requires businesses with 50 or more employees to provide certain workers with up to 12 weeks annually of family or medical leave to care for a sick spouse, child, or parent, or to care for a new child.

Uniformed Services Employment and Re-Employment Rights Act of 1994 (P.L. 103-353, 38§4301-4304).
Protects the job rights of individuals who voluntarily or involuntarily leave employment positions to undertake military service and prohibits employers from discriminating against past and present members of the uniformed services and applicants to the uniformed services.

Sample State Laws Affecting Nonprofit Employers (examples from Pennsylvania)

Solicitation of Funds for Charitable Purposes Act (10 §161.1 et seq.)
Provides for regulation and disclosure of organizations that raise funds from the public for charitable purposes.

Child Labor Law (43 §41 et seq.)
Prohibits the employment of persons under 16 with limited exceptions, and provides labor standards for the employment of persons 16-18.

Corporation Not-for-Profit Code (Nonprofit Corporation Law of 1972 and Nonprofit Corporation Law of 1988—15 Pa. C.S.A. §7101 et seq.; §7301 et seq.; and 15 Pa. C.S.A. §5101 et seq.)
Contains codified statutes that apply to all nonprofit corporations in Pennsylvania.

Directors' Liability Act (42 §8361 et seq.)
Reduces the liability for directors of nonprofit corporations.

Equal Pay Law (43 §336.1 et seq.)
Requires employers to provide fair wages for women and persons 16-21, and to keep records of hours worked and wages paid to their employees.

Pennsylvania Labor Relations Act (43 §211.1 et seq.)
Protects the right of employees to organize and bargain collectively.

Human Relations Act (43 §951 et seq.)
Prohibits discrimination because of race, color, religious creed, ancestry, age, or national origin.

Employee Records Inspection Law (43 §1321)
Requires employers to make employee records with respect to qualifications for employment, promotion, additional compensation, termination, or disciplinary action available for inspection by the employee or his or her agent during business hours, and permits the employer to require that the inspection take place during the employee's or agent's free time, as the case may be.

Pennsylvania Lobbying Disclosure Law (Act 134 of 2006)
Requires persons receiving compensation to advocate the passage or defeat of legislation to register with the State, and to disclose certain expenditures and contacts.

Minimum Wage Act (43 §333.101 et seq.)
Sets the Pennsylvania minimum wage.

Pennsylvania Workmen's Compensation Act (77 §1 et seq.)
Provides for a worker's compensation program.

Unemployment Compensation Law (43 §751 et seq.)
Provides for unemployment compensation to workers who lose their jobs through no fault of their own.

Standard Paperwork for Corporations with Employees

Federal Forms

1. Form SS-4, Application for Employer Identification Number (revised 7/07)—This is the first federal form to be filed when starting a corporation. Once this form is filed, the Internal Revenue Service will establish an account for the organization and assign a federal tax number (EIN). This number will be the organization's account for paying taxes and is requested by other government authorities for tax purposes. It is requested by most foundations and grant makers, as well. This form should be filed at least a month before the number is needed. To obtain this form, call the IRS toll-free at 1-800-829-3676, or download it at: *http://www.irs.gov* (click on "Form SS-4" from the menu at the top, left).

2. Form W-4—Employee's Withholding Allowance Certificate—Each employee must file with the employer a copy of form W-4, which documents the number of exemptions and additional federal withholding requested. The information in the W-4 enables the employer to calculate how much should be withheld from gross salary (not including state and local withholding).

3. Circular E—Employer's Tax Guide—Employers need to obtain a copy of this publication (also known as Publication 15) for the current year (call toll-free 1-800-829-3676 to request this guide), to calculate the amount of federal income tax withholding, Social Security withholding (for calendar year 2008 set at 6.2% of gross wages up to $102,000), and Medicare withholding (for calendar year 2008 set at 1.45% of gross wages, without any ceiling). The amount of wages needed to earn a Social Security credit is $1,050 in 2008. So, workers will need to earn $4,200 in 2008 to earn the maximum four credits for the year. Most workers need 40 credits to be eligible for retirement benefits.

4. Form 8109 Federal Tax Deposit Coupon Book—These are coupons the corporation sends with payment for the federal withholding described above and the required federal payroll taxes. The employer is required to match the employee's contribution to Social Security and Medicare. Thus, a check should be made out for the total of federal income tax withholding plus 15.3% (the rate in effect for 2008) of gross wages and salaries of all employees, consistent with the ceilings noted above on Social Security and Medicare.

Form 8109 is also used for the payment of other taxes, including Unrelated Business Income Tax (UBIT) and Federal Unemployment Tax (FUTA). These tax payments are due by the end of the month following the month in which the payments are withheld. Most corporations file their tax deposits with a local bank, making the check payable to the bank. A bank that accepts federal tax deposits can provide information on the procedures for filing correctly. Note: Organizations with tax deposits exceeding $200,000 annually are required to file electronically, and it is optional for others. See: *http://www.eftps.gov for more information about electronic filing.*

5. Form 941—Employer's Quarterly Federal Tax Return—Each quarter, the IRS will send a form for reconciling federal tax payments that were deposited for the previous quarter. The final line will indicate if the corporation owes any payments to the IRS.

6. Form 940—Employer's Annual Federal Unemployment (FUTA) Tax Return— Nonprofit organizations other than those with 501(c)(3) status are subject to FUTA taxes. This form must be filed if more than $1,500 was paid in wages during any calendar quarter or if the organization had one or more employees at any time in each of 20 calendar weeks during the previous two calendar years. The tax rate for 2008 is expected to be 6.0% of the first $7,000 paid to each employee, a decrease from the 6.2% rate for 2007. Businesses receive a credit on the amount of unemployment taxes paid to their state. Quarterly tax deposits may be necessary, depending on the amount owed. These deposits are made in the same way as federal quarterly withholding deposits.

7. Form W-2—Wage and Tax Statement—This statement is given to all employees on or before January 31. It details their gross salary and amounts withheld in federal, state, and local taxes during the previous year. Employees file a copy with their Form 1040 personal income tax filing.

8. Form W-3—Transmittal of Income and Tax Statement—This return looks like a Master W-2, and aggregates information for all employees. It is filed with the Social Security Administration, accompanied by one copy of each employee's W-2.

9. Form 990—This is the tax-exempt nonprofit corporation's tax return, and has been substantially changed for the 2008 tax year (returns filed in 2009).

10. Form 990-T—This is a supplement to the tax-exempt nonprofit corporation's 990 tax return that reports gross income of $1,000 or more from unrelated business income during the fiscal year. See Publication 598 for more details. Note: A 2007 ruling by the IRS requires organizations to make their 990-T returns public beginning with the 2008 tax year, even if the organization is not required to make their 990 returns public. This requirement applies to organizations that have revenues less than the $25,000 income threshold that applies to 990 return public disclosure requirements, as well as places of religious worship.

11. Form I-9—This form is kept by the employer for each worker to certify that all workers are citizens, nationals, or aliens legally authorized to work in the United States.

12. Form 1099 MISC—This form must be filed if the organization pays more than $600 in the calendar year to those who are not direct employees, such as independent contractors. One copy is given to the individual on or before January 31. The other is sent with similar forms to the IRS on or before February 28, using **Form 1096** as a transmittal form.

Tips:

- **Don't ever be "too busy" to comply with the law and fill out all of the paperwork.**
- **Make a copy of your organization's Form 990 Annual Tax Return available on your Web site to avoid having to make copies for members of the public who request their own personal copies.**
- **Check with your state's Department of Labor to see if posters are available that explain state and federal legal requirements that apply to employees.**

Chapter 13
Hiring, Evaluation, and Firing

> **Synopsis:** Nonprofits have options for staffing their agencies. A planning process is necessary when hiring and firing employees, and there are legal requirements for doing so. A regular evaluation process for staff and the executive director is recommended. There is a continuum for disciplining employees short of termination.

Introduction

Few can argue with the view that a nonprofit's human capital is its most important resource. The executive director influences the direction, morale, image, and financial stability of an organization. Yet, even the least senior employee can have a significant impact, negative or positive, on the organization. Employees can be creative, nurturing, versatile, ingenious, inspiring, and team building. And they can be disruptive, destructive, infecting morale, and creating scandal that can ruin the reputation of a charity that took decades to foster.

The 1992 scandal involving the United Way of America's CEO is just one example of how a single individual can stain an entire sector. The shock waves from the New Era Philanthropy scandal are continuing to be felt. The forced resignation of the American Red Cross's chief executive in 2001, blamed in part on an alleged policy of deceptive fundraising, was front page news. And so was the forced resignation of the organization's 5th CEO in six years in November 2007 for alleged inappropriate behavior toward a staff member.

As our society becomes more litigious, poor performance by an employee can have disastrous consequences. Many human services nonprofits that work closely with aging populations, children, and people with disabilities have experience with defending the actions of their employees in court, and they are at risk for damage suits in the millions of dollars. In some cases, poor performance may be a matter of life and death for at-risk clients. The responsibility for choosing staff in a nonprofit should not be taken lightly.

Each hired employee is an investment by a nonprofit not only in the salary paid to him or her. The chemistry of an organization is changed by a new hire, and bad hiring decisions can haunt a nonprofit for many years or destroy it completely.

In recent years, nonprofits have lost the stereotype of having certain characteristics compared to their for-profit counterparts. That stereotype often viewed nonprofits as—

- less hierarchically structured
- less willing or able to fire non-productive employees
- more informally managed
- paying less and providing fewer benefits for longer hours
- more altruistically managed, with less emphasis on the bottom line
- more interested in their employees' personal satisfaction

This stereotype may no longer be valid, or it is at least becoming frayed at the edges. Nonprofits today face many of the same competitive and financial pressures to succeed as their for-profit counterparts. Nonprofits are becoming more comfortable hiring MBAs and those with for-profit business experience to manage their enterprises, whereas once social work degrees were the educational pedigree of choice.

Many of the jobs available in the nonprofit sector are equally available in the for-profit sector. For example, both often require a CEO, accountants, legal staff, supervisors, receptionists, Webmasters, government relations personnel, public relations officers, administrative assistants, and secretaries. For many of these jobs, the actual tasks performed by nonprofit employees are indistinguishable from those performed by for-profit employees.

Regardless, it is important to recognize that those who apply for jobs offered by nonprofits may retain the stereotypical image. It is useful to consider whether a prospective employee may have an unreasonable expectation of working for a nonprofit. This can be assessed during the job interview.

Hiring requires a positive attitude, which is often missing on the part of the hirer. First, if the hiring is being done to replace a fired employee, or resigned employee, the hirer often is distracted by the disruption caused by the separation. The hirer often is in a position of having to perform a task that is not pleasant—putting aside current responsibilities to perform the job search and interview. Few, if any, managers enjoy this process.

Before embarking on hiring a new employee, it is useful to do some planning that considers:

1. What are the tasks and duties the new employee will perform?
2. Are these tasks absolutely necessary?
3. Could someone already in the organization perform these tasks? Do these tasks require special education, professional credentials, and/or experience that are currently lacking?
4. Can we obtain these services through means other than hiring an employee?
5. How long will it take to hire a new employee, and will these duties still be required at that time?
6. How will these tasks change over time?
7. What can we expect in productivity of this new hire?
8. What support services will this person require? For example, will we also have to hire a secretary or administrative assistant?

Options—Advantages, Disadvantages, Legal Considerations

Hired Staff—The Sunday paper classifieds are usually filled with hundreds of job openings from nonprofit organizations that have decided to hire full-time staff.

Advantages: Employees have the most stake in the organization; they tend to be loyal, may work additional hours, and can be flexible in doing tasks not included in the job description when necessary.

Disadvantages: Employees must be paid even when work is not required, require payroll taxes and expensive benefits, are paid for vacations and when sick, possibly disrupting work flow.

Paid Contractor—private for-profit companies and individuals market their services to nonprofits to perform tasks that are intended to obviate the need for hiring full-time workers. Among the most popular services that are outsourced by nonprofit organizations are payroll and accounting. Other services that are often outsourced to private companies are web services, newsletter production and distribution, order fulfillment for goods and services, and fundraising.

Advantages: The nonprofit does not have to withhold income, Social Security, Medicare, state and local taxes, or pay unemployment and Social Security taxes. Contractors can be hired for short-term or long-term projects and can be terminated easily, do not require year-round benefits (although the equivalent is often built into the contract price), and do not obligate payment by the nonprofit unless the job is completed successfully. The contractor may have skills and resources that the nonprofit would not otherwise be able to afford, except on a temporary basis.

Disadvantages: Hiring independent contractors may be legal only under certain limited circumstances. The Internal Revenue Service Publication 15-A *(Employer's Supplemental Tax Guide)* provides details on the factors that indicate whether an individual is considered an employee or an independent contractor. This publication can be accessed at: *http://www.irs.gov/pub/irs-pdf/p15a.pdf*

Independent contractors sometimes charge steeply to cover overhead and marketing, as well as make a profit.

Volunteers—unsalaried workers, some of whom may be there not solely because they are altruistic and want to help, but because they may be fulfilling educational requirements, or disciplinary requirements ordered by a court (see Chapter 14).

Advantages: They do not require a salary, and they are there not for a paycheck but, with rare exceptions, because they want to be.

Disadvantages: They do not have the paycheck as motivation, generally work fewer hours than employees, and may leave the organization on short notice.

Temporary Hires—hiring people for short-term employment without a promise that the employment will continue beyond a certain date.

Advantages: They permit the organization to respond to seasonal fluctuations in workload.

Disadvantages: The recruitment and administrative burden of temp workers can be substantial.

Process in Hiring

Search Process. Many nonprofits, through their personnel committees, develop a procedure for hiring new employees. Search committees are often authorized by the board to develop job descriptions, prepare job notices, cull through résumés to identify several candidates to interview, and recommend a candidate to the board. Others entirely delegate the process to the executive director (unless, of course, it is a search for an executive director). In either case, the basic steps remain the same:

1. **Prepare a job description.** The job description is a useful planning document for the organization. It also allows prospective employees to decide if they are interested in, and capable of, performing the duties expected of them.

2. **Prepare a job notice.** The job notice provides standard information, such as job title, description of the job, education and/or work experience required, salary range, deadline for application, and the person to contact. Decide whether the notice will request applicants to send résumés or file applications provided by the organization.

3. **Advertise the job.** Jobs may be advertised in daily newspapers, trade journals and publications, the newsletter of a state association, through the State Job Service, with educational institutions, online through the Internet, and, most importantly, internally. There are job boards that target nonprofit sector employment, such as Idealist *(http://www.idealist.org)*, the Chronicle of Philanthropy *(http://philanthropy.org)*, the Foundation Center *(http://foundationcenter.org/pnd/jobs)*, and Nonprofit Oyster *(http://www.nonprofitoyster.com)*. Many nonprofit organizations also include a current job opportunities listing on their own Web sites, as well.

4. **Review the applications.** Develop a process for reviewing and ranking for the purpose of deciding who will be invited for interviews. Remember to send a letter to those not interviewed, informing them that they were not successful.

5. **Interview candidates.** The interview should be a dialogue, not a monologue by the interviewer. Let the candidate talk, so the interviewer can make judgments about how articulate the candidate is. It is useful to be friendly, ask a few softball questions first, and perhaps make a comment about something interesting on the résumé, such as a hobby, professional association membership, or award. Ask about any years that appear to be missing from the résumé.

There are questions that should be asked by the interviewers, and questions that by law cannot be asked. Among the questions that may be asked are:

• What background and experience make you feel you would be suitable for this particular position?

• What is your educational background, and how has that prepared you for this position?

• What has attracted you to apply for a position with this organization?

• What experience, education, or background prepares you for this position that would separate you from other applicants?

• What former employers or teachers may be consulted concerning your abilities?

• What are your long-term professional goals?

• What are the two or three things that are most important to you in a new professional setting?

• What motivates you to perform? How do you motivate those who work with you or for you?

• What are some of your most important accomplishments in your previous position, and what did you do that was special to achieve them?

• Describe a situation in which you had a conflict with another individual, and explain what you did to resolve it.

• Are you more comfortable working with a team on a group assignment, or by yourself?

• What are your significant strengths and weaknesses?

- Why are you shifting direction in employment?

- Where do you see yourself professionally in five years?

- How do you feel about your current/previous employer(s)?

Among questions that you may *not* ask are:

- questions relating to an applicant's race, sex, sexual orientation, national origin, religion, or age

- questions relating to the applicant's physical and mental condition that are unrelated to performing the job

- questions that provide an indication of the above, such as the number of children, the applicant's maiden name, child care arrangements, height/weight, whether the applicant is pregnant or planning to have children, the date the applicant graduated from high school, and whether the applicant is a Sabbath observer

- whether the applicant has ever been arrested or convicted of a crime, without proof of business necessity for asking.

6. **Select the best-qualified candidate.** This is different from selecting the best candidate. The best candidate within the pool of applicants may be identified easily, but if that person is not quite up to the task, it is a mistake to hire him or her. It is better to begin the search again, or try to find another way to have those duties performed without taking a chance that a bad hiring decision will harm the organization, perhaps irreparably.

7. **Verify information from the résumé and interviews; investigate references.** Under laws in some states, you may not refuse to hire an employee based on a prior criminal conviction, unless that conviction specifically relates to the prospective employee's suitability for employment. Even in that case, the applicant must be informed in writing of a decision based on that, in whole or in part. For some nonprofit jobs, particularly those involving children, state law requires a State Police background check.

   It is not unusual for job candidates desperate to make their résumés stand out to embellish their educational or professional qualifications. A few telephone calls can ferret out many of these. This is a wise investment; someone who is dishonest enough to falsify qualifications on a résumé is likely to be just as dishonest when it comes to other professional issues. Investigating references can often turn up reasons for not hiring someone. It is good practice to request permission from the applicant to check references and to contact previous employers. While a candidate may refuse for personal reasons to permit contact with a previous employer, it is sometimes, but not always, an indication of a flawed relationship. It is also advisable to perform a Google search on the candidate's name. This will likely give you some idea about the candidate's background and interests.

Among the questions that are appropriate when contacting prior employers are:

- How long did the applicant work for you?

- What was the quality of this applicant's work?

- What level of responsibility was the applicant given?

- How did the applicant get along with coworkers?

- Did the applicant show initiative and creativity? In what ways?

- Was the applicant a self-starter, or did he/she require constant supervision and direction?

- Was the applicant punctual?

- Is there anything you can tell me that would be relevant to my decision to hire or not hire the applicant?

8. **Make an offer to the candidate and negotiate salary, benefits, and other terms of the offer.**

9. **Put the offer in writing once the offer is successful.** Use a contract, if necessary or desirable. Once the contract is signed or the offer is otherwise accepted, notify other candidates that they were not successful, and arrange an orientation session for the successful candidate.

Evaluation

Periodic staff evaluations are an important tool for executive directors and human resource managers to communicate important information to staff and obtain valuable feedback. One principal purpose of these evaluations is for the executive director to convey to the employee, in a measurable way, how well that employee is performing with respect to each of several areas of the position. This process is useful to both parties. Most employees want to do as well as they can, and the staff evaluation is an opportunity for the executive director to share potential shortcomings that might otherwise have been difficult to communicate.

The staff evaluation is an opportunity to focus on both strengths and weaknesses. Weaknesses are not necessarily the fault of the employee. In areas where improvement is needed, the executive director can suggest strategies, such as on-the-job training, mentoring, continuing education, and additional supervision, which can assist an employee in improving performance. Many nonprofit executives are reticent about approaching the subject of poor employee performance, and many employees are unaware that their managers feel that improvement is necessary. A regular staff evaluation can put in motion a series of positive steps that assist the employee in addressing shortcomings that might otherwise fail to be communicated. For problem employees, the staff evaluation is an opportunity to formally point out shortcomings in advance of disciplinary action or firing.

Staff evaluations are generally an annual affair, often scheduled a few weeks into a new calendar or fiscal year, or a month before or after the Annual Meeting.

In a typical staff evaluation process, certain questions are addressed, regardless of whether the evaluation is a simple 15-minute, informal meeting between the manager and employee or a formal process that involves filling out survey instruments that become a part of the employee's permanent personnel record and are the basis for merit salary increases.

There are many different formats, but many organizations have a formal personnel policy that requires all staff members to be evaluated (typically by the executive director, if the organization is small enough), with a written memo summarizing the results of an evaluation interview. The memo is shared with the employee, who signs it, acknowledging that it has been read, but not necessarily agreeing to the content. In many evaluation processes, the employee is provided an opportunity to respond in writing to any of the criticisms included in the evaluation, and this is included with any evaluation that is placed in that employee's personnel file.

Issues to be addressed should include:

- What goals were the employee expected to accomplish, and how successful was the employee in accomplishing these goals?
- What could have been done by the organization to help the employee accomplish more toward meeting these goals?
- What were the areas that the evaluator found to be the employee's strongest and weakest areas?
- What can the employee suggest to assist him/her to improve in those weak areas?
- What goals are expected to be accomplished before the next employee evaluation?
- How well has the employee gotten along personally with colleagues?
- How well has the employee worked with colleagues as a team to accomplish organizational goals?
- Has the employee shown loyalty to the organization by cheerfully taking on tasks when needed that may not have been in the job description?
- Has the employee favorably represented the organization outside of work?
- Has the employee demonstrated professional work habits by arriving on time, taking reasonable lunch and break time, and not being unnecessarily absent?
- What can the employee share about organization policies, procedures, and work processes that could be improved?

Evaluation of the Executive Director

The task of evaluating the Executive Director is relegated to the Board of Directors. A formal process to evaluate the executive director is appropriate annually. It can be performed by the Chairman, the Personnel Committee, or a group designated by the Board that could consist of an ad hoc committee of board members. While an interview with the executive director is a major component, an evaluation of the executive director should also include feedback from staff members, grantors and other contributors, organization clients, and other stakeholders.

Some of the areas that may be evaluated include:

- Success of the executive director in furthering the stated mission and vision of the organization and implementing the organization's strategic plan
- Financial management, including adherence to board-approved budgets, fundraising, and maintenance of financial viability of the organization
- Ability to maintain and improve staff morale and teamwork
- Ability to communicate with the board, staff, clients, donors, lawmakers and regulators, and the public

- Success in maintaining and improving public trust in the organization
- Success in collaborating with other organizations
- Maintaining a highly ethical, credible, organization.

Firing

The loss of one's job is often the most stressful and traumatic event in a worker's life, with the exceptions of the death of a close family member or divorce. For most managers, having to fire someone is unpleasant at best, and it can be traumatic. In many cases, it represents a failure not just by the affected worker but also by the organization.

Managers must be careful about how the firing is done; employee lawsuits over firings are becoming more common. When a nonprofit is unionized, even firings for the most egregious offenses may be challenged. It is also important to make sure that there is the authority to fire. For example, the board chairperson may not fire the executive director without authority from the board, unless the bylaws provide for that. The executive director may not fire the communications director, for example, unless the organization's bylaws and/or job description of the executive director make it clear that he/she has this authority.

Planning Issues

Before firing an employee, it is important to do some advance planning. Among the issues to consider are how to deal with the workload performed by the fired employee, the effective date of the termination, what to tell coworkers about the action, how to ensure that the employee will not take away sensitive files and other materials, what to tell the employee about health and life insurance continuity and pension benefits, how to deal with separating personal property and organization property, how and when to terminate e-mail addresses and passwords, how much severance pay and other benefits to offer, and whether any letter of recommendation will be provided.

When to Fire

It is usually appropriate to summarily (without warning) fire an employee for gross misconduct that threatens the organization. Examples of this are drinking on the job, being convicted of a serious criminal offense, the willful destruction of agency property, stealing from the agency, or causing harm to others (such as clients or other employees). Most unacceptable behaviors that eventually result in dismissal are not as abrupt, and it is only after the manager has attempted a series of mitigation efforts that have failed that the employee is told to leave. Among these behaviors are unexplained absences, chronic tardiness, insubordination, laziness, and general poor job performance. Many nonprofit managers are close to their employees and shy away from taking appropriate disciplinary action. They need to realize that the health of the organization requires discipline and that they are getting paid to ensure that the organization functions. Problem employees inhibit otherwise productive coworkers.

Discipline Short of Firing

Poor performance on the job may be the result of many factors. These might include personal problems of the employee, miscommunication by the manager, or skills required to perform the task that—for whatever reason—the employee does not have. Each of these has a remedy and, if the manager is flexible, dismissal can be avoided. For example, the birth of a child or serious illness of a spouse or other close family member can leave a valued employee temporarily unable to perform job duties. Some time off, flextime, counseling, or temporarily decreasing duties can all help. Continuing education can improve job skills. Improving communication from the manager, either "coaching" on how to do the job better, or at least providing some feedback on what is going wrong, can avoid the necessity of terminating an employee. Most employees want to do well, and many believe they are doing well but are never told that their professional work is actually considered poor by those who evaluate and manage them. For some employees, however, discipline is required.

Discipline Continuum

1. **Verbal communication.** Short of the gross misconduct referred to in the beginning of this section, this should always take the form of informal communication by the manager. It should be verbal, and one-on-one—definitely not in front of coworkers. The manager should explain the problem and seek an explanation from the employee of what the manager can do to help improve the worker's ability to perform. In many cases, this will be enough. Make a notation in your records when this communication was provided and what was said, and whether the employee acknowledged the problem and agreed to improve his or her performance.

2. **Written warning.** If there is no appropriate response to the verbal communication (e.g., the employee continues to show up to work late or misses reasonable deadlines), a written memo outlining the problem should be shared with the employee. It should not be accusatory, but should state that the employee is engaging in behavior that is unacceptable, needs to be changed, and that this memo follows up on a verbal communication.

3. **Written formal warning.** This involves a formal memo to the employee from his or her immediate supervisor, similar to the written warning, but notes that this new memo will become a part of the employee's permanent personnel file. The memo should make it clear that the person's job may be in jeopardy unless there is significant progress measured by a certain date, and that this progress will be evaluated on or shortly after that date.

4. **Suspension without pay.** Some employees just won't comprehend the seriousness of being late or being disruptive unless there is a real financial penalty attached. A one-day suspension, without pay, makes it clear that the manager has authority to take action and that permanent suspension (i.e., firing) is possible.

5. **Firing.** This is the last resort. In the larger nonprofit, this may actually have a beneficial effect on other employees if they feel that this troublemaker is hurting the organization. In the smaller organization, firing is rarely beneficial in the short term; a poor employee is often much more productive than no employee at all. In the nonprofit organization, firing should always be for cause. It is not appropriate to fire your administrative assistant who has been faithful, loyal, and productive for 10 years just because the daughter of your college professor moved to town and needs a job, even if the administrative assistant has a contract that provides for employment "at will." Even if there is no avenue for the fired employee to appeal, a nonprofit manager should be convinced that the firing is justified and could be defended in a court of law, if necessary. Some may have to defend the firing in court or before a grievance panel of some kind, such as a human relations commission. In recent years, courts have considered "wrongful discharge" suits and have awarded

damages to fired employees who were dismissed unfairly. If in doubt that the firing is both legal and appropriate, consult an attorney.

How to Fire

1. It is common courtesy to make sure that the fired employee is the first to know, other than those up the chain of command who must know or be consulted first to obtain dismissal authority.

2. Fire the person in private, in a one-on-one situation, or with another supervisor present, as appropriate.

3. Explain to the person why he or she is being fired, and point out the previous attempts to reach accommodation. Don't turn the meeting into a debate or let the person plead for his or her job. By this time, it is counterproductive to rescind the decision. Explain that the purpose of the meeting, in addition to letting the person know about the firing, is to share productive information about procedures and benefits.

4. Explain applicable organization procedures, and benefits, such as severance pay, outplacement services, the effective date of the firing, when to turn over keys and files, and COBRA benefits. COBRA (the Consolidated Omnibus Budget Reconciliation Act of 1985) permits employees who retire, are laid off, who quit, or who are fired for reasons other than gross misconduct to continue to qualify for group health coverage for up to 18 months after termination, provided they pay the premiums. The manager may make suggestions about other jobs.

5. If appropriate, arrange for an exit interview, permitting the employee the opportunity to share information about the organization, job description, coworkers, job function, and so on. While this exit interview may not always be pleasant, the information provided may be invaluable.

Tips:

- **Make sure your policy is clear on what is permitted with respect to using the computer and Internet service provided by the organization, both on organization time and personal time while in the office. For example, use of the computer to retrieve, store, or disseminate pornography should be expressly prohibited. Other policies should address other prohibited uses, such as visits to gambling sites, playing games, looking for other jobs, forwarding copyrighted material, hacking into the system, or using the organization hardware and/or software for other illegal purposes.**

- **Consult an attorney to resolve particularly sticky personnel matters.**

- **Keep good records of employee misconduct and what you did at every step to address the problem.**

- **Treat all employees as you would like to be treated if you were in the same position.**

- **Keep calm, even if the employee you are disciplining starts yelling, screaming, or crying.**

- **Consider the advance of technology on your personnel policies. Revisit your formal document at least annually.**

Chapter 14
Volunteers

> **Synopsis:** Volunteers are a crucial strength for nonprofits. They can be highly motivated and can save organizational resources. There are significant disadvantages, as well. Managing volunteers requires many of the responsibilities of managing paid staff.

Introduction

Nonprofit organizations rely on volunteers to perform organizational functions from receptionist to board chairperson. Indeed, the term "voluntary sector" is a working synonym for "nonprofit charities."

Nonprofit organization budgets rarely permit salaries for all needed employees. During times of economic uncertainty, nonprofit organizations are particularly vulnerable to budget cutbacks, ironically at the very same time that the demand for their services increases. Using volunteers is an effective way to stretch limited organizational resources, build community support, improve communications, and tap hard-to-get skills.

The changing demographics in recent decades—more single-parent households, more two-parent working families, more women in the workforce, an increasing incentive to continue working to maintain income rather than retiring—demand that volunteer recruitment, training, support, and recognition change to meet new realities.

National statistics provided by Independent Sector validate the view that volunteering continues to be popular. According to statistics compiled by that organization, 83.9 million (44% of U.S. adults) provided volunteer service in 2000. This compares to 45.3% in 1987. The monetary value of this service was $239 billion in 2000, based on 15.5 billion hours of volunteer work. The average volunteer donated 3.6 hours/week. A 1998 survey commissioned by Independent Sector indicates that the plurality of volunteer work assignments are "informal" (14.6%). The second leading category of beneficiary agencies is churches, synagogues, and other religious organizations (13.7%); followed by youth development (10.5%); education (10.4%); human services (9.5%); health (6.5%); work-related (6.2%); environmental (5.5%); adult recreation (5.2%); arts, culture and humanities (5.2%); public/societal benefit (4.7%); arts (4.1%); political (2.8%); and international/foreign organizations (1.5%).

Volunteerism is alive and well in the United States, despite data from a study published in February 2007 by the Department of Labor's Bureau of Labor Statistics that suggests the number of volunteers is on the decline, dropping from 65.4 million to 61.2 million from 2005 to 2006. New public-private sector initiatives are strengthening the institutions that promote volunteerism. Partnerships are developing in schools, colleges, religious institutions, and the private sector. Successful volunteer programs tap "non-traditional" sources of volunteer strength. Increasingly, these partnerships are being directly encouraged by government.

Federal legislation enacted on September 21, 1993, the *National and Community Service Trust Act* (P.L. 103-82), provides incentives to promote volunteerism among the young and not-so-young, and to pay them living and educational stipends, as well. The federal budget request for FY 2001-2002 for this program was $733 million. By February 2004, the Administration's request grew to $1.018 billion, an $82 million increase over the funds provided in FY 2004, and enough funding for 75,000 AmeriCorps members, 600,000 senior volunteers, and 1.5 million who participate in service learning activities. The appropriation funds three programs—AmeriCorps, Learn and Serve America, and the National Senior Service Corps. In a speech on November 8, 2001, President George W. Bush spoke to the nation about changes to the federal budget he would propose in the wake of the September 11th terrorism. Included would be expansion of the AmeriCorps programs for public safety and public health. In his January 29, 2002 State of the Union address, the President proposed establishing a new "US Freedom Corps," which would also expand volunteer opportunities. The Corps was established that day by executive order, as both an Interagency Council chaired by the President and as a separate White House office.

The President's FY2008 budget request was $828.6 million, enough to support 75,000 AmeriCorps participants, 500,000 Senior Corps workers, and 1.3 million Learn and Serve America students. On December 26, 2007, President Bush signed H.R. 2764, the *Consolidated Appropriations Act for Fiscal 2008*. This "omnibus" measure provides $856,331,000 for the Corporation and its programs for Fiscal 2008, including a 1.747 percent across-the-board rescission.

Interested organizations should monitor local newspapers and the *Federal Register* for RFP announcements, regulations, and briefings about the AmeriCorps program.

Benefits and Considerations of Volunteers

Among the benefits of using volunteers are:

1. They do not require salaries or fringe benefits. While this is the most obvious advantage, there may be other financial savings, as well.

2. They are often highly motivated. Volunteers are there because they want to be, not because it is their livelihood. If it was "just a job," volunteers might be somewhere else.

3. They can speak their minds without fear of loss of a livelihood. Volunteers can often be a useful sounding board. They are often less shy about speaking out than a paid employee might be.

4. They may bring skills to the organization that it may not otherwise be able to find or afford.

5. They may have a network of community contacts who may be a source of contributions, expertise, prospective staff, or additional volunteers.

Other considerations are:

1. Just because volunteers are not on the payroll does not mean that the organization incurs no costs. Volunteers need telephones, work space, equipment, supplies, desks, and virtually everything else besides a paycheck. Training and orientation costs may be just as high as for salaried workers.

2. Volunteer retention is often a problem. Paid employment elsewhere may replace volunteering. Family commitments or other duties may intervene. A volunteer can be easily captured by competing interests.

3. Volunteers, just like paid staff, dislike dull, repetitive, uninteresting work. They are more likely to do something about it quickly than would paid staff.

4. Volunteers are generally available for fewer hours per day and have a higher turnover than salaried employees. Many, such as students, volunteer for specific time periods and for short terms. They often require more hours of training and supervision per hour of productive work than employees.

Nonprofit Organization Volunteer Policy

To maximize the effectiveness of volunteer help, a carefully planned strategy is recommended.

Volunteer Job Description

Individuals are more likely to volunteer to assist an organization if they have specific information about the tasks they are being asked to perform. Before requesting volunteer assistance, develop a detailed job description that includes at least the following information:

- Examples of duties to be performed
- Specific skills or training needed
- The location where the duties will be performed
- The hours per week required
- The time period (e.g., weeks, months) the duties will be performed
- The supervision or assistance that will be provided
- The training that will be provided.

Volunteer Recruitment

Active recruiting is required to maintain a dedicated volunteer pool. The following are some ideas for generating volunteers:

1. Pass around a sign-up sheet at community speaking engagements where potential volunteers can indicate their interest. Be sure to provide space for addresses, telephone numbers, and e-mail addresses, as well as space to indicate specific skills or interests.

2. Include information about volunteer opportunities in any public relations brochures, media stories, newsletters, and public service announcements. Many local newspapers have a regular column devoted to nonprofit organization volunteer opportunities.

3. Ask users of the organization's services if they would like to volunteer, if this is appropriate.

4. Target solicitation of potential volunteers to groups in the community that are likely to have time to share. Retired people, schoolchildren, and religious groups are excellent sources for volunteers.

5. Post volunteer opportunities on your Web site and on general sites that permit the posting of volunteer opportunities, such as IdeaList (see page 139).

Interview potential volunteers as you would potential employees. Be sure their interests are compatible with the organization's. Find out what their motivation is for volunteering. Is it to perform a service or advance a cause? Is it to develop marketable job skills and make contacts? Is it to have a place to "hang out" and have access to a telephone? A volunteer can have the same organizational impact, negative or positive, as a paid staff member. The fact that a person is willing to work for free does not automatically make him or her the best candidate for the "job." The organization should not lower its standards in any way. Be sure that expectations are clear and performance is reviewed.

Tell potential volunteers about the organization and obtain basic information about them, such as their skills, training, and interests. Ask about their time availability. Once satisfied that the right volunteer is matched with the right job, review the volunteer job descriptions with them and ask them if they are ready to volunteer for specific assignments.

Orientation

Make certain that each volunteer receives a complete orientation before starting to work. In some instances, a group of volunteers may participate in a formal volunteer orientation program. In other situations, a one-on-one orientation at the work site is appropriate. It is important to include the following:

1. Overview of the organization's mission.
2. Description of the specific task to be performed.
3. Confirmation of the hours required.
4. Statement of whom to contact if help is needed.
5. Individual to contact if an assignment will not be completed as scheduled.

Rewards

While volunteers don't receive a paycheck for their services, they should receive other types of payment. Remember to thank them for the work they perform. Both informal thanks and periodic formal award ceremonies to thank volunteers are appropriate. Encourage volunteers to attend training programs to update their skills. Include them in agency social events. Remember that extra "payments" to volunteers will pay off in effective service to the organization.

Virtual Volunteering

A growing number of organizations are harnessing a new source of volunteers—those unable or unwilling to work on site, but who are eager to participate in volunteering for their favorite cause by working from their home or work computer. Virtual volunteering has obvious advantages for those who are elderly, disabled, caretakers, or who otherwise are restricted in their mobility or willingness to travel to a volunteer site. For many others who are too busy or otherwise unable to commit to a specific time and place for their volunteering, this non-traditional method opens up opportunities.

Virtual volunteers are being used to design and update Web sites, prepare newsletters, respond to requests for information, research reports, and prepare advocacy materials. Virtual volunteering has appeal to those who are too busy to make a commitment, but have the ability to fit in volunteer work from home on an ad hoc basis—provided they have a computer and a modem. While there are some limitations involved in virtual volunteering (such as no hands-on supervision or the lack of face-to-face interaction), advances in technology are providing opportunities for people who otherwise would not make a commitment to volunteer. An eye-opening feature on virtual volunteering first appeared in the April 17, 1997, issue of *The Chronicle of Philanthropy,* with a second article on January 26, 2006 about this innovative strategy to exploit this resource. For more information, see: *http://www.volunteermatch.org/virtual*

Impact Online, an organization founded in 1994, administers a Virtual Volunteering Project. You can find information about how to begin, and you can even locate volunteers at this site, which can be found at: *http://www.volunteermatch.org/*. As of my last visit in September 2007, the site listed more than 50,000 organizations that were registered, offering a total of 45,785 volunteer opportunities.

Web Resources

IdeaList
http://www.idealist.org/

This site, sponsored by the New York-based Action Without Borders, is an excellent online resource for nonprofits. It boasts the participation of more than 41,700 organizations in 165 countries. Nonprofit organizations can join for free, although a donation is gratefully accepted. Member organizations may post information about their address, mission, contact person, telephone number, Web site URL, and e-mail address. The organizations are categorized by 46 types to facilitate searches by the public. Organizations post information about volunteer opportunities available, a job description, what skills are requested, and the dates that the volunteer is needed. There is an application form for posting organizations that is used to verify the information. At the time of this review in September 2007, 8,170 jobs and 11,392 volunteer opportunities were posted.

Nonprofit Genie
http://www.compasspoint.org/askgenie/index.php

Click on "volunteer mgt" from the FAQ menu for the current FAQs relating to volunteer management. Use the Nonprofit Web Directory search engine for sites on "Volunteer Management and Recruitment." This site is an excellent resource.

ServiceLeader
http://www.serviceleader.org

Service Leader is a project of the RGK Center for Philanthropy and Community Service of the LBJ School of Public Affairs (University of Texas at Austin).While there is some original material on this site, its primary value is having hundreds of links in one place devoted to volunteer management. These links are organized in categories such as *Volunteers in Schools* and *For Volunteer Managers*. Included on this site is the Virtual Volunteering Project, which includes a Frequently Asked Questions page, manuals, and other resources for use by agencies setting up a virtual volunteering program, and material useful to virtual volunteers. Click on *Documents* from the home page for *The Virtual Volunteering Guidebook* in PDF format, *The Future of Volunteering: Children Under the Age of 14 as Volunteers,* and other useful publications.

Carter McNamara's Managing Volunteer Programs
http://www.mapnp.org/library/staffing/outsrcng/volnteer/volnteer.htm

This area of Dr. McNamara's comprehensive site of nonprofit organization resources has excellent material on volunteer management, virtual volunteering, risk management relating to volunteers, and contributions to the *Nonprofit FAQ* that relate to volunteering. The material on volunteer job/task descriptions is particularly helpful.

SERVEnet.org
http://www.servenet.org

ServeNet.org, a project of Youth Service America, bills itself as "the premier site for service and volunteering." The site claims more than 10,000 registered nonprofits, offering thousands of service projects. Here potential volunteers can enter their volunteer interests and be matched with nonprofit organizations that seek volunteers. The site primarily serves 501(c)(3) organizations, but other organizations may apply for an account with permission. Click on *Help for Nonprofits* and then *Tip Sheets for Nonprofits* to access ideas on how to increase volunteer opportunities, including *100 Ways to Make a Difference in Your Community* and *Engaging Youth With Disabilities in Service.*

Tips:

- Interview all prospective volunteers.

- Make sure you clearly define duties and expectations, and review their performance.

- Have a policy for volunteer termination or reassignment, just as you would for paid employees.

- Consider having a formal awards ceremony for volunteers.

- Perform an "exit interview" with volunteers who leave or are terminated.

Chapter 15
Charitable Solicitation Registration

Synopsis: Most states require charities to file registration forms before engaging in fundraising solicitations. A Unified Registration Statement is available, which is accepted by 35 states and the District of Columbia, to streamline submissions.

Introduction

All but 11 states (Hawaii, Idaho, Indiana, Iowa, Montana, Nebraska, Nevada, South Dakota, Texas, Vermont and Wyoming) regulate charitable fundraising. State laws requiring charities to register and to provide information about their fundraising activities to the government is not a recent development—for example, the Pennsylvania General Assembly enacted a law to regulate fundraising back in 1919.

Many states during the 1980s and 1990s enacted tough laws regulating charitable solicitation. This trend had been motivated by abuses in virtually every state in which unscrupulous organizations posed as charities. Engaging in deceptive practices, these organizations generated contributions from the public that were intended for charitable purposes. Some of these organizations took names similar to those of reputable charities and diverted most, if not all, of the proceeds of their solicitation to line their own pockets. Other abuses involved professional fundraising organizations that would solicit business from bona fide charities, offering to raise funds in exchange for an unreasonably large percentage of the contributions received. Even if the charity received a minuscule percentage of what was raised and the charity benefited—it was at the expense of an unwary public.

Abuses such as these continue to this day. But state laws have made it tougher for deceptive practices to occur, and have given law enforcement officials new authority to take action to enjoin illegal or deceptive fundraising activities. Perhaps as important, these laws have provided the public (and the media) with easy access, often a toll-free telephone call or mouse click on a Web site away, to information about charities, their leadership, and how much of the money contributed is actually being funneled to the charity and used for charitable purposes. The State Directory of this book that begins on page 375 summarizes the charitable solicitation statutes in each of the 50 states and the District of Columbia.

From the perspective of most bona fide charities, these laws are a positive development—despite the prospect of costly and burdensome reporting requirements. The public, generous with charitable giving, was becoming more cynical with each fundraising scandal. As one mainstream charitable association (United Way of Pennsylvania) explained in its newsletter on why it testified in support of the 1990 Pennsylvania charitable solicitation law:

> *United Ways and hundreds of other legitimate charities, which are "squeaky clean," are adversely affected and risk loss of public credibility and confidence as a result of a small but growing number of "charitable" fundraising efforts which raise money solely or primarily for personal gain under the guise of charity.*

While most of these laws are weak in prescribing a minimum threshold on the percentage of donations required to be actually put to use for charitable purposes (rather than paying the expenses of professional fundraisers), the public policy philosophy is more along the lines of "a little sunlight is the best antiseptic."

While one can find similar patterns, each state that regulates charitable solicitation has its own law, regulations, and forms for registration, registration renewal, and expense/fundraising reporting. Many states also require registration and reporting for professional solicitors and fundraising counsels, and they require those who make their living in this manner to post a bond with the state.

For charities that raise funds in more than one state (on the Internet or by direct mail, for example), complying with the requirements of each state can be problematic, expensive, and time-consuming. While the information provided in the State Directory is helpful, the requirements change without warning in some states. For several years, national and regional charities have legitimately complained about the impracticality of keeping up with the legal requirements for solicitation law compliance. An innovative project, the Unified Registration Statement, has addressed this concern.

The Unified Registration Statement

The National Association of Attorneys General and the National Association of State Charities Officials have developed the Unified Registration Statement (URS). This document can be downloaded from the Internet *(http://www.multistatefiling.org/contact.php)* in PDF file format. This format requires the use of Adobe Reader, which can be downloaded for free at: *http://www.adobe.com/products/acrobat/readermain.html.*

Although each state regulating charitable solicitation maintains the practice of providing its own individual registration form, 35 states and the District of Columbia accept the URS for registration purposes—all but four of the states (Alaska, Arizona, Colorado, Florida) that require registration. Nine of the 36 jurisdictions that accept the URS (Arkansas, District of Columbia, Georgia, Mississippi, North Dakota, Tennessee, Utah, Washington, and West Virginia) also require a supplemental filing. These supplemental forms are not extensive and are available on the Internet as an appendix to the URS forms.

Charities may print out the PDF file directly from the Internet (or save it to disk for printing out later), fill in the information, and file it with each participating state. Instructions are provided at the Web site for printing or saving the file. A version of the form in HTML can be found on the Web site to review, but this version is not acceptable for printing out and submitting to state regulatory offices.

The URS is continually being updated and improved in response to comments provided by the charities and state regulators that participate. As this book went to press, the latest version of the form was v3.1, which was made public in October 2007. You should verify that the most current form is being used by checking with the Web site:

http://www.multistatefiling.org

As of October 2007, the District of Columbia and the following states accept the URS for registration:

Alabama	Kentucky	New Hampshire	Rhode Island
Alaska	Louisiana	New Jersey	South Carolina
Arizona	Maine	New Mexico	Tennessee
Arkansas	Maryland	New York	Utah
California	Massachusetts	North Carolina	Virginia
Connecticut	Michigan	North Dakota	Washington
Georgia	Minnesota	Ohio	West Virginia
Illinois	Mississippi	Oregon	Wisconsin
Kansas	Missouri	Pennsylvania	

Each state has individual exemptions and exclusions from registration requirements (based on, for example, the type of organization or the amount of fundraising conducted annually). Also, each state requires different supporting documents to accompany the URS and charges an individual registration fee. Charities may still submit the state's individual registration form, but most charities soliciting in several states that accept the URS find it much more convenient to submit the standardized form.

The general Unified Registration Statement, version 3.1, consists of 22 questions on three pages. It requests:

- general information about the charity
- whether there was a previous legal name used
- information about misconduct by the organization's officers, directors, employees, or fundraisers
- a list of states where the charity is registered and the dates and type of solicitation conducted
- information about the organization's federal tax status
- methods of solicitation
- information about the purposes and programs of the organization for which funds are being solicited
- the names, titles, addresses, and telephone numbers of officers, directors, trustees, and principal salaried executives
- information that describes relationships (such as financial interest or relationship by blood, marriage, or adoption) between organizational leaders and professional fundraising organizations, suppliers, or vendors
- information about felonies or misdemeanors committed by the organization's leaders
- the names of those who are responsible for custody and/or distribution of funds, fundraising, financial records, and those authorized to sign checks
- banks where funds are deposited, along with the account numbers and bank telephone numbers
- the name and address of the accountant/auditor
- the name and address of the person authorized to receive service of process
- whether the organization receives financial support from other nonprofit organizations, shares revenue with other nonprofits, whether anyone owns an interest of 10% or greater in the organization, and whether the organization owns a 10% or greater interest in any other organization (and explanations for all of these)
- whether the organization uses volunteers or professionals to solicit directly to the public
- a list of professional fundraisers, solicitors, fundraising counsels, or commercial co-venturers accompanied by information about their services, compensation arrangements, contract dates, dates of the campaign, and whether these persons/organizations have custody or control of donations
- the amount paid to these persons during the previous year.

It also requests financial information about the charity, including:

- contributions received in the previous year, fundraising costs from the previous year, management and general costs

- fundraising costs as a percentage of funds raised
- fundraising costs plus management and general costs as a percentage of funds raised.

Note that the URS can be used only for registration and registration renewal, not for the annual financial reporting required by almost all states that regulate charitable solicitation. A standardized reporting form for annual financial reporting is being developed.

Tips:

- **If you know that your organization is not in compliance with charitable solicitation regulations, consider "turning yourself in" rather than being "caught red-handed." Most state regulators are more interested in bringing nonprofit organizations into compliance than punishing them. Your organization's penalty, if any, is more likely to be reduced if you make a good faith effort to correct past abuses or noncompliance.**

- **Take advantage of the Uniform Registration Statement if you are able to do so.**

Chapter 16
Fundraising

Synopsis: The basic rule of fundraising is to ask—ask the right people at the right time in the right way. There are many conventional and creative ways to raise funds for a nonprofit organization.

ASK.

The rest of what is needed to know about fundraising—the amount to ask, whom to ask, when to ask—are technical details that will be expanded upon in this chapter. However, the simple task of asking for funds for an organization is the major point of this chapter, since it is rare, but not unheard of, that funds are sent to an organization unsolicited.

Most states require organizations to register *before* they raise funds for charitable purposes. Before launching a formal fundraising campaign, refer to Chapter 15 and the State Directory at the back of this book to ensure compliance with current state law.

How Much to Fundraise

There are enormous differences in fundraising techniques if you're trying to raise $10 million for a new hospital wing or $891 to finance the costs of filing Articles of Incorporation, 501(c)(3) application, and a roll of stamps. There also are many similarities.

First, the organization must start with a reasonable budget plan. How much is needed to finance the organization's first-year activities? Will it have paid staff? Staff salaries, benefits, and payroll taxes generally are the largest line-items in any budget. The next decision that determines the magnitude of an organization's budget is whether it will have an office, which requires paying rent, telephone, furniture, equipment, and supplies.

A good practice is to prepare three budgets:

1. A "low-end" budget, which assumes a minimum level to get the organization off the ground. The organization would cease to function if revenue did not cover expenses in this budget.

2. A "middle-end" budget, which is as realistic as possible and considers the likely availability of funds for the year, and

3. A "high-end" budget, which is optimistic enough to assume the organization can pay for almost anything it seeks to do.

In asking for money, one should tailor the "pitch" to the demographics of the contributors. It helps to understand the motivation of the contributors, as well. People give money for a reason. It may be they share the organization's motivation for starting up. It may be they feel guilty because otherwise they would not be doing anything to address a problem. It may be they desire power in the organization that they can get only by being contributors. Givers may also be looking for ways to get a tax deduction, align themselves with a popular cause, or seek immortality (such as by contributing an endowed chair or building wing that would have their name on it). They may be contributing to an organization because they want a particular organizational leader to be their friend or to contribute to their own favorite cause.

The most successful fundraising is done by requesting contributions from people who have money to give away, who both know and respect the organization (or someone on its board or staff), and who are given reasons for contributing that are sensitive to their private motivations.

It is a good idea to select some board or advisory committee members based on their ability to tap funds from their friends and associates. Many of their well-heeled friends will write a check to virtually any cause solely because that influential board member picked up the telephone and asked them to do it.

The donations of board members are often an important source of revenues for new organizations. Many organizations will identify members of the community to serve on their boards because of their willingness and ability to make substantial financial contributions rather than having governance expertise.

Board members are usually—but not always—delighted to donate when asked, recognizing that the organization, to be successful, does need some start-up funding, and it would make them look foolish if the organization is stillborn as a result of lack of seed money.

It is not unusual for external funding sources to consider the extent to which board members make contributions. Therefore, the participation percentage of board member contributions may be as important, or more so, as the dollar amount raised from them.

Always suggest an amount when asking for a donation. Of course, the solicitor should consider the ability of the person to give that amount. The solicitor also should give examples of how that specific amount will be used to benefit the organization (e.g., "Your $2,000 donation will purchase the computer system the office needs...").

IRS Substantiation Rules

The federal *Omnibus Budget Reconciliation Act* (OBRA), enacted in 1993, imposed new restrictions on charities and donors with respect to the substantiation of donations made beginning with the 1994 tax year. The law requires charities to provide a contemporaneously written acknowledgment of contributions of $250 or more when requested by a donor; the donor may not take a charitable tax deduction without having such a written acknowledgment.

The practical effect is that charities are sending these statements routinely to their donors as a part of a "thank you" letter. The written acknowledgment must include the amount of cash paid or a description of property transferred by the donor, a statement of whether the donor received goods or services in exchange for the donation, and a good-faith estimate of the value of such goods and services, if any.

If the donation is in excess of $75, federal law requires charities that provide goods or services in exchange for the donation to provide a written statement to the donor. The statement must disclose that the deductibility of the donation is limited to the excess of the amount donated over and above the value of the goods and services provided, and an estimate of the value of the goods and services provided by the charity. For example, if your 501(c)(3) organization holds a fundraising dinner and you estimate that your costs for catering and entertainment are $45 per person and you charge $100 per ticket, you must disclose to ticket holders that they can deduct the contribution of $55 per ticket purchased. IRS Revenue Ruling 67-246, 1967-2 C.B. 104 provides examples of fact situations that require this disclosure.

Final regulations issued in December 1996 by the IRS provide some guidance to charities on several issues. First, charities may ignore benefits provided to members that can be used "frequently," such as gift shop discounts, free or discounted parking, or free or discounted admission to the organization's facilities or events. Second, there are safe harbors (examples you can follow and avoid violating the law) for benefits provided that are of minimal value. The first safe harbor permits the donor to deduct the entire value of the contribution if the benefit received has a value less than 2% of the contribution or $95, whichever is less. For example, a $1,000 contributor may receive a t-shirt and mug as a thank you gift without tax penalty to the donor, provided these gifts have a value of under $20. A second safe harbor applies in the case of small contributions, and when the benefit received is relatively small. This applies to contributions of at least $45.50 when the value of the benefit provided to the contributor is less than $9.10. These thresholds are for calendar year 2008. Each year, the IRS adjusts these numbers (referred to as the "de minimis threshold amounts") for inflation. To obtain the latest thresholds, call 1-877-829-5500 (toll-free).

Charities must provide written substantiation of a donation to volunteers who wish to claim as a deduction the cost of unreimbursed expenses of $250 or more. The regulations also require that institutions such as colleges that raise money by offering their alumni the right to purchase hard-to-get athletic tickets must consider 20% of the payment for the tickets as the fair market value for the right to purchase them. This amount may not be deducted.

There are many gray areas with respect to substantiation issues. For more information, consult IRS Publication 1771, *Charitable Contributions—Substantiation and Disclosure Requirements,* which can be found at: *http://www.irs.gov/pub/irs-pdf/p1771.pdf*

 It makes sense to consult an attorney familiar with this issue if there is any question about whether your organization is in compliance with IRS requirements.

Sources of Funding

Among potential sources for funding are:

1. **Umbrella Fundraising Groups** (e.g., United Ways, Jewish Federations, Catholic Charities, Junior Leagues, and similar service organizations)

   In addition to providing an important source of funding, membership in a federated fundraising organization provides added visibility and community endorsement. This is especially important for agencies that lack name recognition. Membership in a federated fundraising organization carries no iron-clad guarantee that funding levels will be sustained or increased (especially in a recessionary and highly competitive fundraising environment). However, member organizations fulfilling priority needs of umbrella groups can count on relatively stable funding.

   Although members sometimes chafe at accountability, program, and fundraising requirements imposed by umbrella organizations, few would trade their federated funding for total independence. While it sometimes appears that existing member agencies have a total lock on funding, the trend in recent years has been toward funding "cutting-edge" programs that are highly responsive to critical community needs.

2. Foundations

Major foundations usually require written proposals, many of which can be time-consuming to prepare. There is also a time lag between when the application is submitted—and, perhaps, a response to questions from the foundation on issues that were not adequately covered by the application—and when the "check is in the mail."

Many smaller foundations are managed by the philanthropists themselves who establish the foundations for tax purposes. The benefactor may write a check as soon as the request for funds is received.

Most foundation proposals can be prepared by someone without special training or education. The trick is to research the kinds of organizations and activities of interest to the foundation and tailor the grant application to that information. It is also vitally important to tailor it to the application guidelines of the foundation, since many proposals are rejected on technical grounds even before they are judged on their substance.

Many local libraries have sections devoted to foundation fundraising, including research materials with the names, addresses, and type of funding provided by each foundation.

According to *The Art of Fund Raising* by Irving R. Warner, foundations are responsible for just five percent of philanthropy. However, the individual gift may be quite substantial, and the awarding of a major gift by a name foundation can have benefits beyond the financial reward. It can serve as a catalyst for other grants and give the beneficiary organization increased credibility.

3. Direct Mail

The key to direct mail fundraising is a mailing list of people who are likely to consider making a contribution. Professional services sell mailing lists categorized by various interests and demographics. Organizations may wish to send a few newsletters to such a list, and then follow up with a direct mail appeal. If an organization is a membership organization, its members are among the first who should receive an appeal for voluntary contributions. After all, they have already indicated their interest in the organization's activities and are most likely to know what the organization is doing and how its funds are being spent.

Others to include on solicitation lists are—

- Persons who benefit from the service provided by the organization and families of such persons, if this is appropriate
- Individuals who are in attendance at your speaking engagements
- Persons who make contributions to similar organizations.

A fundraising letter should appeal to some basic instinct that will make the reader have an irresistible urge to run to his or her checkbook and write a check to the organization. Appeals that honestly portray the needs of the organization and the importance of the services it provides are a basic component of direct mail letters. Among the most popular appeals are those that generate:

- *Guilt.* Make people feel guilty that they are not participating in solving some urgent problem.

- *Affiliation.* Appeal to the need to belong to an organization that is doing something worthwhile.

- *Self-interest.* Find some way to show that by helping the organization, donors' own lives will be improved in some way.

- *Ego.* Make prospective donors feel they are wonderful people only if they make a contribution.

- *Idealism.* Appeal to the idea that the world or community will be a better place for everyone and that only a chosen few selfless people will help this cause.

- *Religious obligation to give to charity.* Religious organizations have relied on this for years, but many secular organizations find this line of appeal equally effective for certain target audiences.

4. Businesses

Many organizations receive operating funds and in-kind contributions of services, equipment, and supplies from businesses in their communities. These businesses may include—

- Employers of board members

- Suppliers of goods and services to the organization

- Businesses that make contributions to other nonprofit organizations in the community

- Businesses that sell goods and services to board members, members, or clients

- Major employers in the community.

Rather than visiting a business "cold," it is effective to involve representatives of businesses in the organization's program before asking them for funds. Among ways to do this are:

- Have business representation on the board.

- Establish a "business advisory committee" consisting of local businesspeople.

- Invite business representatives to an "open house" to see the organization in action.

- Place business representatives on the organization's mailing list. Send them the newsletter and newspaper clippings about the organization's accomplishments.

- Invite business representatives to speak to the organization's board or membership about their products and services.

Many business corporations have established foundations that are specifically staffed to consider funding requests from charities.

5. Telephone Solicitation

Similar to direct mail, telephone solicitation is effective if done with the right list of names and correct telephone numbers. A college making calls to its alumni using student volunteers will certainly have a much better response than if it makes calls at random. Similarly, an organization is well served if it can tailor calls to those with a likely interest in its purpose. Note that charities are exempt from the federal "do not call" law.

6. Government Grants

During the 1980s, federal government grants to nonprofits, particularly for social services, plummeted. Yet there are millions of dollars in federal and state grants to nonprofits that still go begging for takers. The trick is to identify the source of funds and determine eligibility. The *Catalog of Federal Domestic Assistance* is available in many libraries. It can also be found on the Internet, in searchable format, at *http://12.46.245.173/cfda/cfda.html.* This document provides a summary of available federal grants and the qualifications and conditions for applying. Using the site at *http://www.grants.gov,* you can identify and apply for federal government grants entirely online (see page 153).

Government grants usually are accompanied by lots of paperwork and operational requirements, some of which may be inconsistent with the manner in which an organization intends to operate. The Istook Amendment, actually a series of amendments placing curbs on public advocacy and lobbying by organizations that receive federal grants, was successfully added by Rep. Ernest Istook (R-OK) in 1995 to appropriations legislation. An amendment by Rep. Istook to the conference report of H.R. 2673, the $373 billion Consolidated Appropriations Act, considered December 2003, prohibits transit agencies receiving federal funds from displaying advertising from groups that want to decriminalize marijuana and other Schedule I substances for medical or other purposes. It would not be unexpected for the Congress to approve additional curbs on advocacy by nonprofit organizations that receive federal funds. In 2006, language was attached to H.R. 1461, the *Federal Housing Finance Reform Act,* that would have placed similar restrictions on nonprofit organization advocacy. As passed by the House, the bill would have disqualified nonprofit organizations from receiving grants under a new Affordable Housing Fund if they engage in partisan or nonpartisan voter engagement activities, certain grassroots advocacy, or lobbying at any point from one year before applying through the grant period. It did not become law, however.

If you are applying for government grants, learn about any additional requirements to be in compliance with the law.

7. Revenue-Generation Other Than Voluntary Contributions

The following are strategies used by nonprofits to increase income:

- Newsletter subscriptions
- Newsletter advertising
- Annual fundraising dinner
- Reception for a famous person or someone well known in the field of expertise of the organization/testimonial dinner
- Sale of publications
- Fees for services to clients

- Sale or rental of mailing lists (make sure the buyer will use the list in a manner consistent with the organization's goals and it will not resell the list to others)
- Small games of chance (provided they comply with state regulatory laws)
- Wills, bequests, charitable gift annuities, and other planned giving strategies
- Social events (e.g., bus trips to sporting events)
- Newspaper advertising to request contributions
- In-kind donations
- Card calling (using board and organizational members to do peer one-on-one solicitation)
- Fees from workshops and conferences
- Sale of exhibit space at workshops and conferences
- Special fundraising events such as bake sales, flea markets, house tours, walk-a-thons, and running races
- Auctions of donated items (including those from celebrities) at a special event or one conducted over the Internet.

Searching for Funding Sources Online

Government agencies at all levels, foundations, and corporations have billions of dollars to give away each year to support the missions of worthy charitable organizations. Some of these grants come with substantial strings attached, and others can be used for almost any reasonable purpose. What they have in common is that information about these funding sources is usually posted on the Web sites of the funders, in addition to being available in databases that are often searchable by categories that will help you target your search.

It wasn't too long ago that nonprofit organizations were comfortable with budgeting thousands of dollars for thick directories of these funding opportunities. Now, many of these directories are available for a reasonable fee on CD-ROM, by subscription on the Internet, or for free at scores of Web sites. If you are looking for funding from such grantors, you need to know about these sites, which will save you countless hours of search for the funds you need.

Of the almost three hundred billion dollars raised annually by charities, perhaps only 15% or so comes from sources other than individual donors, such as foundations run by individuals, families and corporations, community foundations, and corporate giving programs. Yet, there remains a certain caché to having a grant come from a prestigious foundation, providing your organization with instant credibility. The Internet has made it much easier to identify potential funders, using online directories and databases that are searchable by the funder's program priorities, geography, and type of support. Today, almost all major foundations have a Web site, as do many of the smaller ones. Among typical documents posted are mission and values statements, annual reports, newsletters, grant opportunities, biographies of staff and leadership, funding priorities, guidelines and deadlines, information about previous grants made (including amounts of funding awarded), and, to an increasing degree, application forms that can be submitted electronically.

Identify most likely funding sources

The first objective in a search for funding sources is identifying potential grantmakers that have a history of awarding grants in your charity's area of interest in your geographical area. Among the obvious targets are—

- private foundations—non-governmental organizations with an endowment derived principally from a single source (individual, family, or corporation) that makes grants for charitable purposes
- corporate giving programs—grant-making programs within a for-profit business
- public foundations—charities that make grants to unrelated organizations and individuals
- community foundations—charities that make grants to organizations within a specific locality or region
- government—federal, state, regional, and local governments

Identify foundation funding

Many nonprofit organizations depend on foundation support to maintain their programs. But with all the progress offered by the Internet, foundations will not come to your site to give. Despite that, grant writers were among the first to benefit from the access the Internet provided them to look for and approach foundations whose objectives match their missions and to manage the process of applying for grants.

Through the Foundation Center's Web site *(http://foundationcenter.org)*, grantseekers can find a particular foundation or research those most likely to be attracted to their programs by areas of interest, type of funding, or the geographical region they support. The Foundation Directory, long a vital resource for fundraisers, is available online here.

Fundraisers can read a foundation's guidelines on its Web site and learn how to apply. Many allow proposals to be sent online or by e-mail. The Internet provides a convenient way to ensure that you are sending the best possible proposal, and it helps foundation staff, as they have to answer fewer questions. Fundraisers should always consult a foundation's Web site before contacting a program officer with questions. It is wise to become intimately familiar with a foundation by reading through its site before and during the process of applying.

Foundation staff frequently complain when charities call with questions that were clearly answered on their Web site. Demonstrate to them the courtesy of looking there first. At the same time, while it has become increasingly possible to find a grant and apply for it entirely online, we caution against this. Make "personal" contact with the grantmaker before applying. Tell the staff if you found useful information at the site. We recommend that this be done by telephone or letter. However, follow-up e-mail requests for information or responses to questions are perfectly acceptable.

Some of the information you can find at a foundation's Web site includes announcements about grants the funder has already made, contact information, strategic plans, annual reports, and other documents you will find useful in crafting your proposal. You can often find useful information from the grantmaker's federal tax return (usually a 990 or 990PF) at such sites as Guidestar *(http://www.guidestar.org)* or Charity Navigator *(http://www.charitynavigator.org)*. The searchable GrantSmart database has more than 300,000 federal tax returns from more than 85,000 private foundations and charitable trusts. You can also use popular search engines such as Google *(http://www.google.com)* to find general information about the grantmaker, those that have received funding from it, and the grantmaker staff.

Thank and acknowledge support

Cultivate a strong relationship by publicly acknowledging foundation support on your organization's Web site. Do this in much the same way as you might your individual donors, through donor listings, or even a dedicated page or online press release announcing the gift and describing the foundation's history and matching objectives. If you have done this, be sure to let the foundation know how you have acknowledged its support.

Access free and low-cost databases

Want to search community foundations by state? Point your browser to: *http://www.tgci.com/ funding/community.asp* to tap into the Grantsmanship Center's database. You can find grant sources organized by topic (e.g., children and youth, recreation, arts & cultural activities, and the aged) at *http://www.lib.msu/harris23/grants/2sgalpha.htm.*

Visit the Foundation Center *(http://foundationcenter.org*—see "finding funders") for searchable databases that help identify potential funding sources. Here you can find basic information about thousands of private and community foundations, including their assets, amount of grants, contact information, and Web site address.

The Chronicle of Philanthropy has a subscription-based database that includes information about all foundation and corporate grants published in that publication since 1995. If you are a subscriber to the print version (a must read for all who need to, or want to, follow what is happening in the nonprofit sector), you can use the search engine free for searches involving the last two issues.

Government Grants

The Catalog of Federal Domestic Assistance *(http://12.46.245.173/cfda/cfda.html)* has been available free online in a searchable format since the mid-1990s. The latest version of this Web site has much more useful information for grantseekers than was available a decade ago, including a "top 10%" page that lists information about the top 10% of items in the catalog by number of "hits." Women's Business Ownership Assistance, administered by the Small Business Administration, was number one at the time I looked at this in January 2008.

Consider government grant sites

Grants.gov, launched in October 2003, takes the online search for federal government funding to a higher level. The objective of this site is to level the playing field so all eligible organizations, regardless of their size or grantsmanship sophistication, can have a fair opportunity to receive federal grants. The site directs grant seekers to funding programs offered by 26 grant-making federal agencies that aggregately award over $400 billion annually to state and local governments, academia, not-for-profits, and other organizations. It not only makes it easier for organizations to find grants of interest, but also streamlines the paperwork needed to apply for them and permits the entire process to be conducted online. All application forms, financial report data in support of agency audit and performance measurement activities, grant management procedures, and information about grant programs have been standardized across these participating agencies.

The site hosts everything an organization needs to find, apply, and manage a federal grant. Even grant notifications are made electronically. Site visitors download forms, work on them offline, and then submit completed applications electronically, saving hours of time and money. The site is divided into sections that help you engage in a six-step process, consisting of finding grant opportunities of interest, downloading the grant application package, registering with a Central Contract Registry, registering with a credentials provider, registering with grants.gov to submit grant applications, and logging on. There is even a toll-free number to use to request assistance. This site is the first place to go if you have any interest in federal grant funds.

Other places to look for information about federal government grants include—

http://www.fundsnetservices.com/gov01.htm
http://www.usa.gov/Business/Nonprofit.shtml

Don't forget that many states, counties, and individual municipalities also make grants to nonprofit organizations. They often have searchable Web sites that can help in identifying funding opportunities.

Finding Corporate Support

Corporate funding sources that are not foundations do not file a 990. However, there are databases, some free and some subscription, which permit you to check them out as well. Among them are EDGAR *(http://www.sec.gov/edgar/searchedgar/webusers.htm)* and Hoover's *(http://www.hoovers.com)*. Edgar includes all filings of publicly-traded companies with the SEC since 1994. The annual filing, form 10-K, includes a lot of basic financial information, some of which may be of use to fundraisers. Hoover's includes information on both public and private companies. Some of the basic information can be viewed for free, but more detailed documents and databases require a subscription. There are other, less well known, sources for information about corporations of use to grantseekers, such as David Lamb's Prospect Research Page *(http://www.lambresearch.com/CorpsExecs.htm)*, which has plenty of links to corporate information. You can also find corporation information at Yahoo! (see *http://biz.yahoo.com*).

Of course, you will want to visit the corporation's Web site and learn more about its products and services, financial information, annual reports, newsletters that may provide details about how the organization is involved in its community, and biographies of key leadership.

Find in-kind donations

One thing that distinguishes corporate giving from its non-business counterparts is the willingness to make in-kind donations of company-produced products. Corporations give a staggering amount of products to charity. According to a survey of 150 of the largest corporations conducted by the *Chronicle of Philanthropy,* as much as 30% of total giving by these organizations consisted of in-kind gifts, more than $1 billion in 1999. The same survey conducted five years later found that two individual companies, Pfizer and Merck, have each reached or exceeded this amount in in-kind donations. Among other companies that achieved in-kind donation totals annually reaching nine figures were Johnson and Johnson, Safeway, Time-Warner, Microsoft, Bristol-Myers Squibb, and IBM.

Several intermediary Web sites have sprung up to find matches between corporations willing to provide such in-kind donations and charities that can put the products to good use. In 2007, Gifts-in-Kind *(http://www.giftsinkind.org)* alone distributed an estimated $900 million worth of goods, partnering with firms such as Office Depot, Gillette, IBM, Avon, and General Motors (each of which was honored with a "Light of Hope" Award for its efforts). According to Gifts-in-Kind, more than 150,000 charities benefited from these donations. The Web site provides an easy way for 501(c)(3) organizations to register, and there is an annual registration fee (the 2008 fee ranges from $150-$300, depending on the size of the annual budget of the organization, with a $125 fee for national charity local affiliates), as well as shipping and handling costs to receive goods.

Many organizations depend on corporate support. Corporate investment in nonprofits is based on entirely different motivations from individual philanthropy. Corporations are looking for mutual benefits. Some corporations support programs in their communities hoping that community building activity will strengthen and support their workforce. Others seek marketing benefits and value associations with organizations whose cause and good name will encourage consumers to purchase their products or services. Corporate fundraisers need to be skilled and knowledgeable in both building good relationships with corporations and helping their organizations think creatively about how they can benefit commercial enterprises.

Design your Web site to facilitate corporate support

Perhaps the Internet's primary value for corporate philanthropy is in visitor traffic. The fundraiser's Internet strategy must touch on both the organization's Web site and the corporation's. Banner ad space or recognition of corporate sponsors on an organization's Web site is important. Conversely, allowing companies to use your logo and name on their site will have a similar beneficial value, spreading the name of your organization and information about its mission to the company's stakeholders.

Some organizations develop a corporate sponsors page, typically linking logos to the corporation's Web site. These can link specifically to pages at the company's site that talk about your work, creating a "two-way street" for Web surfers. The company page might focus on the link between the particular product or service and the organization's mission. For example, a company selling baby care products might wish to be identified with an organization providing services related to infant health or child welfare.

These relationships tend to be active partnerships. Therefore, a Web strategy should be particularly dynamic—relating perhaps the regular progress toward the organization's goals with the success of the fundraising relationship.

Employee giving programs

Another form of corporate giving is the employee giving program. Companies with large numbers of employees may encourage them to support a particular organization with which they have a relationship. Employees may give individually or participate in fundraising events. Large nonprofits may also seek support from their own employees.

Because workplace giving operates as a special campaign, it may be worth creating a separate Web page for this, including integrating the option to give online and reporting progress to date toward a particular goal.

Hiring a Consultant

There are hundreds of honest, hard-working, professional fundraising consultants who will, for a fee, provide an organization with fundraising advice or even handle all of its fundraising. There also are hundreds who are not reputable. Most states regulate this industry, and there are opportunities to obtain information about them before making a hiring commitment. Your state association of nonprofit organizations may be able to help you identify candidates for this duty. Since most states require these consultants to register, you can look at these records (some states post reports online) or contact organizations that have hired them to see if they are pleased with the services being provided.

Tips:

- Review other organizations' solicitation materials and use effective presentations as a model for solicitation.

- Keep a file of newspaper clippings about benefactors in the community and others who would have a potential interest in the work of your organization. A few well-placed and well-timed telephone calls can be effective in reaching these influential people.

- Involve everyone in the organization in the fundraising effort. It is not prudent to isolate fundraising from the programs the organization funds.

- Always thank each donor, regardless of the amount received. A $2 check from an individual may have required as much personal sacrifice as a $1,000 check from a wealthier contributor.

Chapter 17
Writing Effective Grant Proposals

by Michael A. Sand

> **Synopsis:** Grant applicants should research the grantor before applying. They should not deviate from the format of the grant application except with express permission. There is a formula to follow for effective grant applications that, among other components, emphasizes the needs of the community, not those of the applicant.

Introduction

Competition for government, corporate, and foundation grants is increasing. At the same time, funding from government sources for human services is shrinking, and the demand for human services is skyrocketing.

In response, charities are becoming more sophisticated in the ways they seek alternative sources of funding. Many are hiring development staff with specialized training and experience in obtaining grants. Others without the resources to make such a major investment are forced to do what they can. The purpose of this chapter is to provide a framework for the preparation of proposals for those without substantial grantsmanship experience.

It is often useful for grant seekers to develop the attitude that the relationship between them and the grantors is collaborative. True, all of the wonderful plans you have in mind will never come to fruition without the funds. However, the grantor needs the creativity, dedication, staff resources, and vision provided by the grant recipient. A grant proposal that is seen as simple begging is not as likely to be as successful as one that encourages the grantor to become a partner in an effort that will have substantial benefits to the community.

Before embarking on a costly and time-consuming search for grants, verify that the purpose of the grant is consistent with the organization's mission. Some organizations apply for grants simply because the money is available and obtainable, and they have a plan to win it. However, a successful grant application may result in the organization losing its focus if the grant is inconsistent with its direction.

Even if the grant's purpose is consistent with the mission, consider whether the project is viewed as constructive by the organization's stakeholders, such as members of the board, clients, and staff. It may be useful to convene a focus group to gauge whether the grant would truly be beneficial to the organization and its clients.

In addition, organizations should consider cash-flow issues, grant eligibility, the politics of the grant, and the source of the grant. The check from the funder may arrive months after the organization has committed itself to hiring staff and paying other project costs. Is a source of funds available until the grant funds are received? Are there laws or other grant requirements that must be adhered to that, for any reason, you are unable or unwilling to honor? Have the grants for which you are applying been promised informally in advance to other organizations? Does the grantor have a reputation for making unreasonable demands on the organizations it funds?

Researching the Grantor

Once you believe a funding source may have funds available, do not begin to write the grant application until you have tried to find the answer to several questions. Try to obtain an interview with a representative of the funder before beginning to fill in the funding application. In any case, you should have the following information before beginning the proposal-writing stage:

1. The application format

Why write a 30-page application when a three-page application would have been funded? Why write a three-page application and not get funded when a 10-page proposal would have been accepted? Many government agencies will send you a *Request for Proposal* (RFP) that will outline exactly what should be included in the application. Many larger foundations will provide specific instructions.

If you are given written instructions by a funding source, do not deviate from these instructions without permission. One major reason grants do not get funded is that the writer does not follow the instructions to the letter. Even minor deviations can make the proposal ineligible. If you believe a particular instruction does not apply to your situation, request written permission from the funder to make changes.

2. Motivation of the funding source

Many funding sources specialize in awarding grants for specific purposes. An organization will not receive a grant from such a funder unless the proposal clearly is responsive to the vision and mission of the funding organization. When applying for a government grant, for example, obtain and study the legislative history that led to a funding appropriation. When applying for foundation funds, be sure to obtain the donor's funding instructions. Many corporate and family foundations have a priority listing of the types of programs they fund and will be glad to share this information.

3. The amount of funds awarded by the grantor per award, and the amount of total funds awarded

This will be extremely helpful information if you can obtain it. In many instances, a government agency has a specific allocation of funds for a particular program. Large foundations set specific priority areas and make general allocations in the priority area. Foundation directories provide information about the priority areas of grantors and are available in most public libraries. It just makes no sense to develop a grant application if the funds awarded by the source are too small for the organization's program needs.

4. Successful applications that were funded in previous funding cycles

Perhaps the best indicator of the types of funding applications that will be successful is a review of actual applications that have been funded. A strong argument can be made that government agencies have an obligation to provide you (as a taxpayer) with copies of funded applications. While you may have to review the applications at the agency's headquarters or pay for duplication, you should be able to review past grants.

Many foundations will provide a list of the previous year's grants and the total of each. You can contact a funded organization and ask for a copy of its application. While lists of past grants are often difficult to obtain from businesses, many annual reports and business newsletters include a list of grants that have been awarded and their sources.

5. The names of individuals making the funding decisions and their backgrounds

When writing a grant application, it is important to know who will be reviewing it. If the reviewers have extensive expertise in your field, you will not have to define every term. In many instances, however, a foundation trustee or a business official on the allocations committee will not have any knowledge of your particular field. You will then have to carefully explain your services in layman's terms, spell out every abbreviation, and define each technical term you use.

6. The criteria used in making the grant selection

Knowing the selection criteria can be crucial in determining how to write a grant. Many grantor agencies have limited amounts of funds and will give preference to smaller grants. Others will make the selection based on non-cost factors and then negotiate the cost of the proposal. Knowing whether it will be helpful or harmful to have political officials contact the grantor agency is important information.

Sections of a Grant Application

1. Cover Letter

Many grant applications specifically request a cover letter and define what information should be included. If this is not expressly prohibited by the grant application format, write a short cover letter on the organization's stationery that:

- Is addressed to the appropriate individual at the grantor agency, making sure the name, title, agency name, and address are absolutely correct.

- Contains a one-sentence description of the proposal.

- Provides the number of participants, jobs obtained, or other units to be funded by the grant.

- Lists the total amount of funds requested.

- Provides the name, address, and telephone number of the individual at the requesting organization the grantor can contact to request additional information.

2. Executive Summary

Include in this section a succinct summary of the entire proposal.

3. Introduction

Provide important information that may not otherwise appear anywhere else in the grant application. Items you might include are—

- Your organization's mission
- How long you have been providing the type of service included in this program
- Brief history of your organization
- Major indicators that you are capable of operating programs efficiently and effectively
- If there are eligibility requirements in the proposal, a statement that you are eligible to receive the funds
- IRS Section 501(c) tax-exempt status determination letter
- Outline of letters of support from past clients, representatives of cooperating agencies, and legislative officials (The letters themselves should be included as appendices to the application.)
- Statement of how you will obtain funding for the program at the end of the grant period.

4. Need

For a grant to be funded, the organization must demonstrate the need of individuals in the community for the service to be provided. What is the extent of the need and how is the need documented? The need described should be the need of the individuals in the community for the services, not the need of the organization. Rather than stating, "We need a counselor because our organization doesn't have one," or "The funds for the one we had were cut back by the government," estimate the number of individuals who need counseling services. The need should be the need in your coverage area. While national or statewide figures might be given, if you serve a particular county, the estimate of need for that county should be provided.

The need should be the need for the particular service you are providing. If you provide services for victims of domestic violence, for example, the estimated number of victims of domestic violence should be provided, rather than unemployment figures or other available statistics. The need should be quantified. How many individuals do you believe are eligible for the particular service you provide in your coverage area?

Common sources of data are—

a. **Census Data**—Make certain you are using data from the most recent census. In most cases, earlier data are outdated.

b. **County Planning Departments**—Call the office of your county government to find the telephone number for your county's planning department.

c. **State Agencies**—The Departments of Education, Health, Labor, and Human Services, or their equivalents, are all excellent sources of data.

d. **Local Governments**—Local police departments are excellent sources of crime data, and local school districts can provide educational information.

e. **Self-generated data**—In many cases, you can provide the data from sources within your organization. Sources might include—

- Waiting lists
- Letters from potential clients requesting a service
- Letters complaining that a particular service is not in existence

- Testimony at public hearings
- Information obtained from questionnaires administered to present clients asking them to list other services they might like
- Community surveys.

5. Objectives

Objectives are the proposed results of the project. Objectives should have the following characteristics:

- They are measurable. How many individuals do you estimate will participate in your program?

- They are time-based. How many individuals do you estimate will participate in your program in the next three months? In the next year?

- They are realistic.

The information needed to measure objectives can be obtained as part of the program funded by the grant. Do not list objectives in your proposal that are impossible to measure.

6. Project Description

Here is where you will outline your program. An easy way to remember what to include are the 6 W's of program writing:

a. **Who?** Who are the clients? How are they selected? What are the restrictions (e.g., age, income, geographic)? Who are the staff members?

If you are asking the funding source to pay for new staff members, include a job description and a qualifications statement that lists the education, experience, and other job requirements. If you are applying for funds to continue existing staff, include a résumé and a biographical statement for each staff member.

b. **What?** What services will be provided? What will be the benefits of this program? What are the expected outcomes? For educational programs, include a course outline. You may include relevant sections of an operations manual. For other programs, a narrative outlining the services would be appropriate. Still others might provide a "day in the life of a client." What outreach efforts will be made?

c. **Where?** Where will the services be provided? Give the addresses of all main and field offices. If you will be obtaining new space with the program funds, what type of space are you seeking?

d. **When?** What are the hours that services will be provided? On which days during the year will services be provided? It is also useful to provide a timetable for project implementation.

e. **With whom?** What other agencies are participating with you in the provision of services? For example, include agencies referring clients to you. Outline the agencies to which you refer clients. It is important to obtain letters from the other agencies confirming any relationships you describe.

f. **Why?** Why are you providing these services rather than alternatives? Are you utilizing any unique approaches to the provision of services?

7. Budget

If it is not clear from the grant application forms, ask the funding source how much financial detail is required. Many businesses, for example, may only require the total amount you are going to spend. On the other hand, most government agencies require a line-item budget that includes a detailed estimate of all funds to be spent. Such a budget might be set up to include the following:

a. Personnel costs (salaries, fringe benefits, consultant and contract services)

b. Non-personnel costs (travel, office space, equipment, consumable supplies, and other costs such as telephone, postage, and indirect costs)

Some grantors may require your organization to contribute a matching share. If you are permitted to include in-kind or non-cash expenditures, use the same budget categories as above. In the personnel category, for example, you would list the worth of the time volunteers are contributing to your program. In the non-personnel category, you would include the market value of the equipment donated to your program.

8. Evaluation (see Chapter 32)

Inform the funding source that you will be conducting an evaluation of the services you are providing.

a. **Detail who will participate in the evaluation process.** Outline the participation of board members, staff members, clients, experts in the substantive field, and representatives of the community in the evaluation process. Some grantors require an independent evaluator.

b. **Explain what will be evaluated.** List some of the issues the evaluation team will consider. For example, the evaluators will review whether the need was reduced as a result of providing the services. Were the objectives met? Were the services provided as outlined in the Project Description section? Will the budget be audited by an outside firm and, if not, who will review the receipts and expenditures?

c. **Specify what type of evaluation will be provided.** Provide in as much detail as you can how the program will be evaluated. If formal classes are provided, include the pre- and post-test you will use to evaluate them.

If a client questionnaire will be used, attach a copy to the application. Describe how the program data will be reviewed in the evaluation process. Include a description of the audit or the process you will use to review the budget items.

9. Conclusion

In no more than two or three paragraphs, summarize the proposal's main points and the reasons the community will be improved as a result of successful completion of the project.

When you have finished writing your grant application, ask yourself the following questions before you send it to the funding source:

- Is the application free of the jargon of your field?
- Are all abbreviations spelled out the first time you use them?
- Have you followed all of the instructions in the Request for Proposal (RFP)?
- Are all words spelled correctly? Remember that your computer's spell-checker only tells you that the words you use are spelled correctly and in English, not that they are the correct words for the context.
- Is your application interesting to read?
- If you were the grantor agency, would you fund it?

Finally, get the application in the hands of the grantor well before the deadline. The fundraising field is replete with horror stories about multi-million dollar proposals that were not even considered because someone put the application in the mail and it didn't arrive until well after the deadline. Make sure there is enough postage if the application is mailed. It is highly recommended that applications be either hand-delivered or sent by a trackable, overnight courier, such as UPS, Federal Express, or Airborne Express. Make several office copies before submitting the original, and be sure that you provide the number of copies requested by the grantor.

Tips:

- **Double check your proposal for spelling and grammar, that all pages are included in the proposal (i.e., the last page was not left in the copy machine as a result of making a copy of the submission for your files), that the correct number of copies is provided, and that all attachments are included.**

- **Hand deliver your grant proposal, or use a trackable, reliable delivery service. Track the package to see if it has arrived prior to the deadline. This is not the time to save a few dollars by putting your proposal in the mail.**

- **Even if your proposal is rejected, send a short thank you letter to the funder for the opportunity to submit the proposal, and expressing a willingness to maintain a relationship with respect to future funding opportunities.**

- **Be careful what you wish for; you might get it. Begin thinking about how to administer a grant even before you apply for it. You may decide that the stress of winning a particular grant might be too much on your organization.**

White Hat Communications

Chapter 18
Lobbying

Synopsis: Lobbying by nonprofit corporations is not only legal, but should be encouraged. There are effective strategies for communicating with legislators in person, by letter, or by telephone. All states require lobbyists to be registered and report expenditures.

Lobbying is the time-honored tradition of communicating with elected or appointed officials for the purpose of influencing legislation and other public policy. The word itself derives from the outer room of the legislative chambers where paid professionals congregated, seeking to button-hole legislators before they cast their votes. In recent years, the term has developed a pejorative connotation as the public, justified or not, perceives special interest lobbyists as using their influence to work against the public interest.

Organized lobbying is an effective way to communicate an organization's views on a pending issue, to promote a favorable climate for those served, and to directly influence the outcome of government decision-making. Lobbyists are employed by organizations who view themselves as working in the public interest—speaking for the poor and disenfranchised, improving the environment, establishing programs to serve the disabled, or expanding government support for vital human service and community needs.

Whether referred to as "advocacy," "government relations," or "lobbying," it is a right afforded by the First Amendment to the U.S. Constitution relating to freedom of speech, as well as the right to petition to redress grievances. Many of the public policy decisions made in Washington, state capitals, and cities and towns across America have a direct effect on nonprofit organizations and the interests and clients they serve.

Many nonprofits are expressly created to advance one cause or another whose fate is considered by a government body.

Legal Requirements for Lobbying

Federal Requirements

The *Lobbying Disclosure Act*, PL 104-65, was enacted on December 19, 1995, and provides major changes in registration and reporting requirements for lobbying the Congress and the Executive Branch. The bill also includes a provision (Section 18) that places restrictions on the lobbying by nonprofit civic leagues and social welfare organizations, among others, which receive federal funds. The effective date of the act was January 1, 1996. Minor changes were made by the *Lobbying Disclosure Technical Amendments Act of 1998*. On September 14, 2007, President George Bush signed into law the *Honest Leadership and Open Government Act,* which made substantive reforms affecting lobbying, a response to a major scandal. The new law makes major changes in lobbying reporting requirements, gift disclosure, and travel financed by lobbyists. Of particular importance are the following:

- Lobbying disclosure forms are now required to be filed quarterly rather than semi-annually.
- Thresholds for reporting lobbying expenses have been reduced.
- Information requirements for reporting and disclosure have been expanded.

- New reports are required relating to political contributions made by, or transferred to politicians by, lobbyists
- With some exceptions, gifts to members of Congress and their staff from lobbyists are prohibited
- With some exceptions, lobbyists, or organizations that employ them, may not pay for the private travel of members of Congress or their staff
- Lobbyists may not participate in privately funded Congressional travel.

The *Lobbying Disclosure Act* defines "lobbying contact" as—

> *any oral or written communication (including an electronic communication) to a covered executive branch official or a covered legislative branch official that is made on behalf of a client with regard to—*
>
> *(i) the formulation, modification, or adoption of Federal legislation (including legislative proposals);*
> *(ii) the formulation, modification, or adoption of a Federal rule, regulation, Executive order, or any other program, policy, or position of the United States Government;*
> *(iii) the administration or execution of a Federal program or policy (including the negotiation, award, or administration of a Federal contract, grant, loan, permit, or license); or*
> *(iv) the nomination or confirmation of a person for a position subject to confirmation by the Senate.*

It defines "lobbyist" as—

> *any individual who is employed or retained by a client for financial or other compensation for services that include more than one lobbying contact, other than an individual whose lobbying activities constitute less than 20 percent of the time engaged in the services provided by such individual to that client over a six month period.*

A packet of materials, including a copy of the *Lobbying Disclosure Act*, registration and expense reporting forms, instruction booklets for filling out the forms, and answers to frequently asked questions, can be obtained by contacting—

> Secretary of the Senate
> Office of Public Records
> 232 Hart Senate Office Building
> Washington, D.C. 20510
> (202) 224-0758

Unless they are self-employed, individual lobbyists do not register with the House and Senate. The law requires registration by lobbying firms, defined as entities with one or more employees who act as lobbyists for outside clients. A separate registration is required for each client. A typical nonprofit that has one or more employees who engage in lobbying activities is required to register, provided that its expenses attributable to lobbying exceed $10,000 in a semi-annual period (either January 1-June 30 or July 1-December 31). Registration is required no later than 45 days after a lobbyist first makes a lobbying contact or is employed to do so, whichever comes earlier. To register, the organization must electronically file a Form LD-1 in duplicate with the Secretary of the Senate and the Clerk of the House:

Secretary of the Senate
Office of Public Records
232 Hart Senate Office Building
Washington, D.C. 20510
(202) 224-0758

Clerk of the House
Legislative Resource Center
B106   Cannon House Office Building
Washington, D.C. 20515
(202) 226-5200

Registration discloses general information, a description of the registrant's business or activities (e.g., social welfare organization), and a list of employees who act or are expected to act as lobbyists (an employee is not considered to be a lobbyist if he/she spends less than 20% of his or her time lobbying). Also disclosed are an indication of the issues to be lobbied (selected from a list of 74 general categories, such as "welfare"), and the specific issues to be addressed, including specific bill numbers or executive branch activities.

Online forms and instructions can be found at: *http://lobbyingdisclosure.house.gov/*.

Expense Reporting Requirements

Registered organizations are required to file four quarterly reports each year. The reports are due 20 days after each quarter. One copy each must be filed with the Secretary of the Senate and the Clerk of the House. Organizations employing lobbyists must report whether their lobbying expenses were less than $5,000, or more. If lobbying expenses were more than $5,000, the organization must make a good-faith estimate, rounded to the nearest $10,000, of its lobbying expenses during the reporting period.

Organizations must also file a separate sheet on each general lobbying issue that was engaged, specific information about each bill or executive branch action, houses of Congress and federal agencies contacted, and the name and title of each employee who acted as a lobbyist. Online forms and instructions can be found at: *http://lobbyingdisclosure.house.gov/lda.html*

State Requirements

Every state has individual registration and reporting requirements for lobbyists. Consult the state directory in the back of this book for the requirements in your state. Don't rely on this book for the legal requirements, as they may have changed since this book went to press. Always contact the office that administers this state law for reliable information.

Effective Strategies for Lobbying and Advocacy

- Know Your Legislators—Give them the information they need to help your nonprofit organization meet its objectives.

- Identify Key Contacts—Survey your organization's network to discover who has a personal or professional relationship with key public policy decision-makers, and who contributes to political campaigns.

- Target Decision-Makers—Pay special attention to legislative leadership, the majority and minority chairpersons of relevant committees, and their staffs.

- Use Local Resources—Identify constituents connected to the organization, and match them up with their legislators so that they can engage in advocacy contacts.

- Schedule Lobby Days—Many nonprofit organizations and other groups schedule a Capitol Lobby Day. Such events typically include a briefing on an important pending issue by the organization's executive director, a rally and/or press conference in the Capitol, scheduled office visits to local legislators and legislative leadership, and a closing session conducted by staff to exchange information gleaned from those visited.

- Schedule Press Conferences—Non-governmental organizations can hold press conferences in the Capitol or on the steps of the Capitol.

- Circulate Petitions—While viewed as one of the least effective forms of lobbying, the presentation to a legislator or government official of a petition signed by thousands of persons is a worthy "photo opportunity" and may get some coverage.

- Present Awards—Many nonprofit organizations present a "Legislator of the Year" or similar award to recognize key legislators for their interest in the issues of concern to them. These awards further cement a positive relationship and ensure continued access to that legislator.

- Arrange Speaking Engagements—Most legislators are delighted to receive invitations to address groups of their constituents. Such gatherings provide opportunities to educate the legislator on issues of interest to the organization.

- Provide Contributions—Money is still considered to be the mother's milk of politics. While corporations, by law, cannot make contributions themselves, individuals and corporation-affiliated Political Action Committees (PACs) may and do. Those who make contributions find their access to public policy makers is vastly improved. As a general rule, the more an organization's activities are perceived to be in the public interest, the less need there is to rely on making political contributions to develop access and to deliver the organization's message.

  Note: Organizations exempt under Section 501(c)(3) may not establish political action committees. Other exempt organizations may do so and pay administrative and other indirect expenses of their affiliated PACs. A 1998 publication of the Alliance for Justice, *The Connection: Strategies for Creating and Operating 501(c)(3)s, 501(c)(4)s, and PACs* is available for $25, including shipping and handling *(http://www.afj.org)*. It is an excellent guide for charities and social welfare organizations that want to influence the political process without violating federal laws and regulations.

- Request Public Hearings—Public hearings held by a legislative committee provide an opportunity for media coverage, a forum for an organization's point of view, and a way to galvanize support for an issue. Having an organization's clients fill a hearing room sends a clear message to the committee members and staff. While it is true that the suggestion by a committee chairperson to hold hearings on an issue may be a strategy to delay or kill a bill, public hearings can nevertheless be utilized by the organization to focus attention on an issue. A hearing can generate public and media support. It can provide a forum for improving the proposal, thereby minimizing opposition to the legislation.

501(h) Election

The U.S. Congress in 1976 enacted a law that expanded the rights of nonprofits to lobby. However, it was not until August 30, 1990, that the IRS and Treasury Department promulgated final regulations to implement this law. In the preceding 14 years, there had been a pitched battle between nonprofits and the Congress. Nonprofits fought diligently to preserve their rights to lobby under the Constitution and the 1976 law. Some in the executive branch also sought to deny those rights. The principal issue is the definition of the term "substantial," since the law prohibits 501(c)(3) nonprofits from carrying on "substantial" lobbying activities.

The regulations permit electing organizations to spend on lobbying, on a sliding scale, up to 20% of their first $500,000 in expenditures, and up to 5% of expenditures over $1.5 million, with a $1 million ceiling in each year. Organizations can spend no more than a quarter of their lobbying expenses on grassroots lobbying (communications to the general public that attempt to influence legislation through changing public opinion).

These regulations exclude certain expenditures from lobbying, including—

1. Communications to members of an organization that brief them on provisions of legislation, but do not urge that they take action to change those provisions.

2. Communications to legislators on issues that directly affect the organization's own existence, such as changes to tax-exempt status law, or lobbying law.

Of major importance to nonprofits, the organization would no longer be subject to the "death penalty" (i.e., the total revoking of their tax-exempt status) for violations. There is a system of sanctions replacing that.

All 501(c)(3)s must report the amount they spend on lobbying on their Form 990 annual federal tax returns.

IRS Regulations on Lobbying

The August 1990 regulations of the Treasury Department with respect to lobbying are quite complicated. An excellent 57-page publication, *Being a Player: A Guide to the IRS Lobbying Regulations for Advocacy Charities,* is available from The Alliance for Justice, Eleven Dupont Circle, 2nd Floor, Washington, D.C. 20036 *(http://www.afj.org; 202-822-6068).* The guide explains in clear and precise terms what is permitted under these regulations, and includes many sample forms and worksheets. The cost is $15.

Contacts With Legislators

1. When Visiting a Legislator—

• Make an appointment, if at all possible.

• Arrive promptly, be warm and courteous, smile, and speak for five minutes or less on a single issue.

• Don't threaten or exaggerate your political influence. If you are really influential, the legislator will already know.

• Listen carefully to the legislator's response and take notes; be polite, but keep the legislator on the subject.

- Leave the legislator with something in writing on the issue, if possible.

- Request that the legislator do something to respond to the organization's position—vote in a specific way, take action on a problem, or send a letter to legislative leadership requesting action.

- Follow up the meeting with a thank-you note, taking advantage of this second opportunity to reinforce the organization's views and remind the legislator of the action requested.

- Do not feel slighted if referred to a staff member—legislators often have last-minute important meetings or unscheduled votes. Staff members are valued advisors who, in some cases, have as much influence as the legislator in the process and may have more time to help.

2. When Writing to a Legislator—

- Restrict letters to one issue; be brief and concise.

- Clearly indicate the issue of concern, the organization's position on it, and the bill number, if known.

- Write the letter in a manner that will require a written response and include a return address.

- Use facts to support positions, and explain how the issue affects the organization, its members, and the community.

- Use professional letterhead, if appropriate; type the letter, if possible, or write neatly and legibly.

- Try not to indicate that the letter may be a form letter sent to scores of other legislators.

- Make the letter positive—don't threaten the loss of votes or campaign contributions.

- Follow up after the vote on the issue to indicate to the legislator that the organization is following his or her actions with interest and that it appreciated or was disappointed by that vote.

3. When Telephoning a Legislator—

- Speak clearly and slowly.

- Make sure that callers identify themselves in a way that will permit the legislator to reach them or the organization by letter or telephone.

- Follow the guidelines listed above for writing and visiting that are equally appropriate for telephoning.

Tips:

- Those who expect to spend a substantial amount of time in legislators' offices should register as lobbyists, even if they feel the law may not require them to do so. The judge of whether a person doing advocacy is in compliance with lobbying laws will not be that advocate.

- Comply with all state and federal reporting requirements.

- If the nonprofit corporation is a human service provider, invite local legislators to tour the facility and observe the services being provided.

- If the organization has members, invite local legislators to speak to the membership.

- Read the comprehensive, 158-page second edition of *The Nonprofit Lobbying Guide* that can be downloaded free at: http://www.independentsector.org/programs/gr/lobbyguide.html

  Other useful publications can be ordered or downloaded from the Alliance for Justice, (http://www.afj.org) including *E-Advocacy for Nonprofits* (2000, 82 pages, free download), *Worry-Free Lobbying for Nonprofits* (1999, 12 pages, free); and *Being a Player* (1995, 57 pages, $15).

- Consider an e-mail advocacy campaign. Many organization members are more comfortable sending an e-mail to a legislator based on a sample provided on an organizational Web site than they would be writing a conventional letter.

Chapter 19
Political Activity by Nonprofits

Synopsis: Charities are proscribed by law from engaging in electioneering. However, many political activities, such as candidate forums, questionnaires, awards, and compiling voting records, are not only permissible but are constructive activities for charities and other nonprofit organizations.

Introduction

Volunteer leaders and executives of nonprofit organizations are, generally, key opinion makers and play an important role, both in their organizations and in their personal lives, in shaping public policy. Many elected officials got their first taste of community service by serving as nonprofit board volunteers. Many elected officials continue to serve on nonprofit boards, and their expertise and political influence are often of great value.

Yet, there has been a historic concern that nonprofits, particularly nonprofit charities, may be using taxpayer-financed subsidies to unduly influence the outcome of elections. This concern has been codified in federal and state law that, in general, prohibits 501(c)(3) organizations from helping candidates for public office and places severe restrictions on other tax-exempt organizations. Some state laws mimic federal law, prohibiting corporations and unincorporated associations, other than political action committees (PACs) and other organizations formed solely for political activity, from making contributions or expenditures in connection with the election of a candidate.

By federal law, a 501(c)(3) organization explicitly may "not participate in, or intervene in (including the publishing or distributing of statements), any political campaign on behalf of, or in opposition to, any candidate for public office." No corporation, nonprofit or for-profit, may make campaign contributions. Moreover, any expenditures by a charity, for or against a candidate, can result in the loss of the organization's tax-exempt status, the assessment of a large excise tax, and potential fines against the charity's executives and volunteers. Charities may not endorse candidates or oppose candidates for public office. Generally, a person is considered to be a candidate for public office when he or she makes a public announcement to that effect, or files a statement with the elections commission of an intention to run.

Department of Treasury regulation §*1.501(c)(4)-I(a)(2)(ii)*, as amended in 1990, expressly forbids 501(c)(4) organizations from engaging in direct or indirect participation in political campaigns on "behalf of, or in opposition to, any candidate for public office" as part of its definition of "social welfare." However, a subsequent IRS Ruling (Rev. Rul. 81-95, 1981-1 C. B. 332) has interpreted that this regulation does not impose a total ban on political activity by 501(c)(4)s. The level of political activity that is permitted by 501(c)(4)s without jeopardizing their tax exemptions is still unclear. What is clear is that the political activity by the organization must not be a substantial part of its activities, and the activity must be consistent with the organization's social welfare mission, according to the May 1992 *Harvard Law Review* (p. 1675), which provides substantial guidance and applicable case law on this complicated legal issue. Other classes of exempt organizations, including those that are exempt under Section 501(c)(5), (c)(6), (c)(7), and (c)(8), also are permitted to engage in political activity, provided it is secondary to their primary purpose.

Among the types of expenditures that may be considered political activity are candidate travel expenses, fundraising expenses, polls, surveys, candidate position papers, advertising and publicity, and money paid to the candidate for speeches or other services. Expenses relating to non-partisan voter registration drives are not considered political expenses.

Individuals who are associated with an exempt organization (or any other type of organization) may form an organization that is exempt under Section 527 of the Internal Revenue Code. Organizations exempt under this section are political action committees (PACs). These organizations have as their primary purpose engaging in political activity. They pay no federal tax on their operating income, but their investment income is subject to tax. Contributions made to them are not tax deductible. The excise tax that applies to political expenditures of social welfare organizations, exempt under Section 501(c)(4) of the Internal Revenue Code, does not apply to PACs.

These 527 organizations are coming under a lot of scrutiny. They are perceived as taking advantage of a loophole in the law that permits them to engage in "advocacy" activities that target the election or defeat of political candidates without any of the accountability and fundraising limits that apply to traditional political action committees. They are regulated by the IRS rather than the Federal Elections Commission (FEC). In August 2004, the IRS announced it would beef up its enforcement of public disclosure requirements that apply to these organizations, but the FEC had indicated that it would not take any action on enforcement until after the 2004 elections.

Examples, such as the Leadership Forum, America Coming Together, and Move On, raised tens of millions of dollars to influence the outcome of the 2004 Presidential election, all of it "soft money," without the traditional reporting requirements and contribution limits that applied to traditional political action committees under the McCain-Feingold campaign finance reform that went into effect in November 2002.

A 501(c)(3) organization cannot have its own PAC, but other exempt organizations are permitted to form one. Individuals associated with a 501(c)(3) may set up a "nonconnected political action committee," provided it receives no funds from the 501(c)(3), the individuals forming it do not imply any connection between the 501(c)(3) and the PAC, and the PAC is not controlled by the governing body of the 501(c)(3). For more details on this option, see FEC Advisory Opinion 1984-12.

Individual Political Activities

The Federal Election Campaign Act of 1971, as amended, prohibits all corporations, regardless of whether they are for-profit or nonprofit, from getting directly involved in federal political campaigns, with few exceptions. However, volunteers and agency staff of charities have the same First Amendment rights as anyone else. There is no prohibition against such persons making political contributions, volunteering to work on a campaign, signing letters of support (provided any reference to their charitable organization affiliation clearly indicates that the reference is for identification purposes only), and issuing statements on a candidate's behalf. Moreover, the resources of the charity cannot be used for electioneering. Charitable organization leadership and staff should not write letters on a charity's stationery in support of a candidate. They should not turn the offices into a *de facto* campaign office for the candidate, using the telephone, copy machine, computer, and other resources, even during non-business hours.

Penalties

Beyond the sanctions of loss of tax exemption authorized by the 1954 Revenue Act, the Revenue Act of 1987 increased the sanctions available to the IRS in enforcing the prohibition against political activities. It also provided the IRS with the authority to seek an injunction to bring about an immediate cessation of violations that are deemed to be "flagrant." Most political campaign expenditures by 501(c)(3)s and 501(c)(4)s are now subject to a 10% excise tax applied to the organizations and a 2.5% excise tax (up to $5,000) applied to each of the managers of the organization who knew that a political expenditure was being made. This tax only applies if the expenditures were willful, flagrant, and not due to reasonable cause. If the illegal expenditure is not corrected, an additional 100% tax is imposed on the organization and 50% (up to an additional $10,000) on each manager who knew of the violation. Correcting the violation means that the managers tried to recover the contribution and took steps necessary to stop future violations.

While this area of law has a substantial gray area, there are several important general rules to be understood in guiding an agency's quasi-political activity. Each case decided by the IRS is fact-specific, and its rulings provide only general guidelines. The best advice for charitable organization leadership and staff is to provide a wide margin for error when contemplating involvement in political activities and not to engage in any activity that would even raise the specter of being improper, even if such an activity falls within the legal framework provided by current case law.

Quasi-Political Activities

Among the most common issues raised by charities are the following examples of borderline, quasi-political activities:

1. **Influencing Ballot Questions.** Federal law only prohibits organizations exempt under Section 501(c)(3) from engaging in political activity for or against a candidate for public office. Nothing in the law prevents efforts to influence ballot measures, such as constitutional changes, ballot initiatives, and referenda. These efforts, of course, must be insubstantial compared to the organization's activities in support of its primary purpose.

2. **Get Out the Vote Campaigns.** 501(c)(3) organizations may engage in nonpartisan get out the vote campaigns, but may not demonstrate any bias for or against any candidate or political party.

3. **Voting Records.** There is nothing illegal about a charity annually publishing a compilation of voting records of the Congress or the General Assembly. Some guidelines to follow are that the compilation should not be released only before an election and should list the voting records of all of the public officials or those in a relevant region (rather than in selecting only those who are up for re-election or who are targeted by the organization because they consistently vote for or against the organization's public policy positions). It should also involve a wide range of subjects, not imply organizational approval or disapproval of the public officials, and should not be disseminated beyond the membership or mailing list of the organization (i.e., the general public).

4. **Questionnaires.** It is not only permissible but advisable for charities to communicate with candidates, informing them of the organization's positions on issues and requesting their views. When candidates run for office, it is a vulnerable time for the shaping of their

public policy positions. Many regret the positions they have taken during the election in response to a seemingly innocuous questionnaire. However, the use of these responses by an organization can be troublesome.

The IRS has ruled (Rev. Ruling 78-248) that it is permissible for charities to send a questionnaire to candidates and publish the answers in a voter's guide. However, the charities should make an effort not to demonstrate obvious bias in the questions, or to favor one candidate over another by making editorial comment. Organizations with a narrow range of interest, such as a pro-life or pro-choice group, are more in jeopardy by publishing the results of a questionnaire than groups with a broader range of interests, such as the League of Women Voters. If viewed by the IRS as a back door method to influence how your constituency votes, then questionnaires could place an organization's exemption in jeopardy.

5. **Public Forums.** Many 501(c)(3) organizations have a Candidates' Night to permit their volunteers and staffs to meet the candidates and question them about issues. This is not illegal, and it is expressly permitted by the IRS, provided it ensures "fair and impartial" treatment of the candidates (Rev. Rul. 86-95). However, such programs should be conducted with common sense. The moderator should be someone who can be impartial. All *bona fide* candidates should be invited, although it is not a prerequisite that they all accept the invitation for the event to be scheduled. Organizational leaders should refrain from making editorial comments about the positions of the candidates. Any account of the event in the organization's newsletter or other publication should be unbiased and should refrain from making editorial comment in favor of, or in opposition to, a candidate's views.

6. **Mailing lists.** The mailing list of a charity may be a valuable asset in the hands of a candidate. Many organizations get substantial revenue from selling or renting their mailing lists. There is no prohibition against selling a mailing list to a candidate for public office. However, giving a mailing list to a candidate is tantamount to making a political contribution. Also, all candidates must be given the same opportunity to purchase or rent the mailing list; no favoritism is permitted. As noted elsewhere in this publication, the sale or rental income from organizational mailing lists is potentially subject to federal unrelated business income tax, despite court rulings that decided they are not.

7. **Awards.** Many charities give "Legislator of the Year" or "Public Citizen of the Year" awards or similar citations to elected officials. However, making such an award just prior to an election in which the awardee is a candidate may be considered improper electioneering. From a practical viewpoint, even if this is done without any intention to help that candidate, a charitable organization's volunteers or contributors who may not like that particular candidate could view it as a disguised attempt at electioneering. It is a good policy to avoid providing awards to candidates during election periods.

Note: The above analysis is not intended to serve as legal advice about any particular set of facts, but only as a review of currently available reference materials on this issue. Consult a lawyer for a definitive answer to any particular legal situation.

Tips:

- **If you as a nonprofit executive are a "political animal" who *must* get involved in partisan political activity, find another entity, such as a PAC or a political party committee, to channel those energies. Never use your organization's stationery for political purposes.**

- Seek experienced and competent legal counsel before engaging in any political activity that falls into a gray area.

- Use permissible political activities to the advantage of the organization, such as candidate forums, candidate questionnaires, and awards to public officials.

- Note that each state also has laws that apply to political action committees. While they are typically similar to federal laws with respect to tax treatment, there is some variation in tax and accountability requirements.

- Review *The Rules of the Game: An Election Year Legal Guide for Nonprofit Organizations* published in 1996 by the Alliance for Justice (http://www.afj.org). The cost is $20 per copy, including shipping.

- Encourage members to make individual political contributions. It is good advice not to get involved in partisan politics, particularly if the organization has 501(c)(3) status. Those who do choose to participate in partisan politics should be scrupulous about separating personal political activities from those of the organization and not using organizational resources for partisan political activities.

Chapter 20
Communications and Public Relations

Synopsis: Organizations need to communicate their objectives, activities, and accomplishments effectively to attract funding, participation, and public support. Publications, media contacts, and workshops are among the methods used to do this.

Introduction

A well-planned public relations/communications strategy is important for two reasons. First, the organizational leadership has made a major investment in forming a nonprofit corporation, and a solid public relations effort will promote the organization's purposes. Second, few newly formed nonprofits begin with a silver spoon in their mouths. The first few years are often a fight for survival financially. Sound organizational communications and building a solid public image through a public relations strategy are instrumental in building and maintaining a donor base and attracting grants and contracts.

But there is often a "Catch-22" at work here. New organizations must quickly accomplish something useful to obtain the credibility necessary to attract financial assistance. Yet the organizations often need this financial assistance to accomplish something useful.

Public relations serves an important function. It puts the organization in a positive light and generates the essential public support needed to perpetuate it. An organization may be quietly successful in changing public opinion, advancing a legislative agenda, or providing vital services to worthy clients and its members. But if the right people—the board, funders, and potential funders and leadership—are unaware of the organization's successes, then its continued existence may be at risk.

There are thousands of creative ways to get the name of an organization in front of the public in a positive context.

Menu of Nonprofit Communication Tools

Among the conventional communications techniques nonprofits use are—

1. Organizational Brochure

Each nonprofit organization, from the largest to the smallest, should have a brochure. The brochure should clearly include the organization's name, address, telephone number, e-mail address, and Web site address; its mission, its purposes and principal interests, its affiliations (if any); its federal tax-exempt status, and ways to make contributions; the names of its board members, advisory committee, and key staff people; and its major accomplishments. The organization's logo should appear on the brochure. If the organization is a membership organization, the brochure should provide information on dues and how to join.

The brochure should be distributed with all major fundraising solicitations. It should be a standard component of press packets, and should be distributed at speaking engagements made on behalf of the organization. All board members should have a supply of brochures to distribute to their friends and colleagues who may be interested in joining, contributing, volunteering, or assisting in other ways.

2. Print and Electronic Newsletter

On at least a quarterly basis, the organization should publish a newsletter and distribute it free to all board members, all dues-paying members, significant opinion leaders on the issue(s) of interest to the organization, political leadership (such as members of the state legislature, local members of Congress, and local elected officials), the media, current and potential funders, and colleagues in the field.

Among the items the newsletter may contain are—

- Recent board decisions
- The organization's "wish list" of in-kind donations
- Legislative action in Washington, the state capital, and municipal government of interest to the membership and clients
- Planned giving information
- Schedules of upcoming meetings, workshops, conferences, and training sessions
- Messages from the executive director and/or board president
- Articles contributed by experts on the board or the membership about issues of interest to the readership
- Articles about organizational accomplishments, such as grants received, advocacy accomplished, coalitions joined, and letters of commendation received
- Profiles of people involved in the organization
- General information about the status of issues of interest to the organization
- New features of the organization's Web site, including podcasts, blogs, and Webcasts
- Names of new donors
- A list of all board members and staff
- A form to join the organization, volunteer, or make a donation
- Information on services and publications available from the organization.

The newsletter need not be fancy, but it should be as current as possible. It is advisable to select a creative and descriptive name for the publication and establish a master layout, so that subsequent issues will have the continuity of similar design.

The newsletter is often the only contact hundreds of influential people will have with an organization. As such, it is vitally important to present a professional, accurate, and eye-pleasing format. The newsletter should be carefully proofread and *all* typographical and grammatical errors eliminated. Make sure articles on one page continue correctly on subsequent pages.

Headlines should help busy readers find their way through the newsletter. Tricky headlines can be annoying. Double-check all headlines for appropriateness. Double check all names, telephone numbers, addresses, and Web site references.

3. News Releases

The media annually provide millions of dollars in free publicity to nonprofit organizations. The typical mode of communicating with the media is through the mailing, faxing, or e-mailing of a standard news release.

The news release is a pre-written "news" article that includes the name, organization, and work telephone number of the key organizational contact person at the top. If the release is *really* important, include the home telephone number or cell phone number, as well. The release should be dated, along with "For Immediate Release" or "Embargoed Until (insert date/time)" as appropriate.

Examples of topics for news releases are—

- The initial formation of an organization

- An organization's official comment on a new law, legislative proposal, new regulation, or court decision affecting the organization's clients or members

- An accomplishment of an organization

- The release of a study or survey commissioned by an organization

- The hiring or promotion of a staff member, or change of leadership within an organization

- Awards given by or to an organization.

News releases are distributed to those who are most likely to print or broadcast them. A news release to a TV or radio station should be no more than six or seven sentences, and no more than two double-spaced pages for the print media. Most news releases will be edited before final publication or broadcast, although many neighborhood newspapers will print news releases word-for-word.

The basic style of the body of a press release is—

- Precede the text with a catchy, descriptive headline.

- Put the most important sentence first.

- Place subsequent facts in descending order of importance.

- Include suitable quotes from organizational leadership when appropriate. The quotes should express a view/opinion, rather than providing a fact that could appear in the release narrative.

- Make sure the text answers the basic questions of "who," "what," "where," "when," "why," and "how."

4. Press Conferences

Organizations with a story of major interest to the public may want to consider holding a press conference. To do so, a media advisory is distributed in the same manner as a news release, telling the press where and when the press conference will be held, the subject, and speakers. It may be helpful to make follow-up calls to the news desks of local newspapers and broadcast stations.

At the press conference, written materials (a press packet consisting of a copy of a written statement, the organization's brochure, and materials relating to the topic of the press conference) should be distributed.

Another good idea is to arrange for a black-and-white photo of the organizational representative speaking at the press conference. The photograph may be accompanied by a picture caption and sent in a press packet to media outlets not covering the press conference. Take into account that 1-hour commercial photo developers may require several days to develop black-and-white film.

Digital cameras have eliminated some of the frustration of having to wait for a picture to be developed commercially. The files of these pictures can be sent conveniently through the Internet as e-mail attachments to newspapers on deadline, or can be posted on the organization's Web site. The camera's resolution should be set high enough for good print quality.

A banner with the organization's logo, draped in front of the podium, creates a photograph that is useful for future annual reports, newsletters, and related publicity.

5. Public Service Announcements

Many TV and radio broadcasters regularly broadcast public service announcements (PSAs) for nonprofit organizations free-of-charge. PSAs are an excellent and cost-effective way to get an organization's message and its name across to thousands of viewers and listeners.

The last line of such an announcement can be: "This message is brought to you by (the name of the organization) and this station as a public service." The rest of the announcement can be a 30-second sound bite of information of interest to people—how to obtain a free service, how to avoid health and safety risks, or even how to join or volunteer for the organization while accomplishing some vital objective in the public interest.

Before preparing a PSA, check with a potential broadcaster for the technical specifications for the form and format of the announcement. Some stations may be willing to produce your announcement without charge, as well as broadcast it.

6. Conferences and Workshops

Well-planned conferences and workshops can serve a useful public relations function. A one-day conference can bring together interested lay leadership and professionals in a shared field of interest, introduce them to the organization, increase networking among the participants, and advance the organization's interests. The charge for the workshop can be set to cover all anticipated costs, or even generate net revenue—provided it is planned well in advance and the plan is executed properly.

There are scores of major decisions to make in running a conference, such as choosing speakers who will generate attendance and excitement, preparing and distributing the conference brochure, selecting the site for the conference, and arranging for exhibit space and advertising. There are hundreds of minor decisions that need to be made as well, such as choosing the type of name tag to use, deciding who staffs the registration table, and choosing the luncheon menu. There are many sources of advice on how to run a successful conference, many of which can be borrowed from the local library.

7. Intraorganizational Communication

Board and key contacts need to know what is happening beyond what they read in the organization's newsletter. Periodically, it is useful to send out "Action Alerts" or "Background Briefings" by mail or e-mail that describe the status of a problem and what they can do to participate in its resolution.

Some organizations have specially printed stationery for these messages. A sample letter may be included if the organization is encouraging its constituency to write advocacy letters. However, the organization should urge recipients of these communications to use their own words rather than copy the sample exactly. The address, telephone number, and/or e-mail address of the person who is the target of the advocacy should always be included.

8. Annual Report

Among the typical publications produced by nonprofit organizations is the annual report. Many nonprofits use this opportunity to supplement the financial information provided to stakeholders with a report on the operations of the nonprofit during the fiscal year.

The annual report can be professionally designed with a fancy layout, fonts, charts, graphics, and color pictures, which imply progress and success in meeting organizational goals and objectives. It can also be a word-processed report photocopied on plain paper. In either case, the annual report offers the opportunity to communicate what the organization has been doing on behalf of its board and membership, clients, funders, and the public, as well as its goals and plans.

9. Other Publications

Many nonprofits publish small booklets about various issues of concern, which are disseminated to their constituents and other interested parties. This is one more way to get the name of the organization in front of additional people, and it is another effective way to communicate the organization's views to those whose opinions count. Subjects of such publications include—

- The latest developments on issues of interest
- How to contact government offices
- How to lobby on behalf of the organization's issues
- Information about the state legislature, and who serves on committees of interest to the organization.

These publications can also be considered the written equivalent of the public service announcement. Many institutions, such as hospitals, community centers, nursing homes, day-care providers, and libraries, will distribute these public relations booklets free of charge to the organization's target audience.

10. Membership/Board Surveys

Membership and board surveys can be, but may not always be, a useful tool to obtain information and feedback. The target of the survey may feel a sense of connection to the organization, and the survey will provide useful input from the membership.

Member surveys can be tailored to suit the needs of the organization. For example, many advocacy nonprofits periodically survey their boards and/or membership to determine who among the board and membership has influence or personal relationships with key public policy decision-makers. Surveys can be used to gauge the effectiveness of organizational programs and activities.

Free or low-cost software is available to administer online surveys. There are also free and low-cost commercial services that provide high-quality surveys, but may include advertising. Among the services to investigate (features change quickly in the dot-com environment) are Free Online Surveys *(http://www.freeonlinesurveys.com)*, SurveyMonkey *(http://www.surveymonkey.com)*, and Vovici *(http://www.vovici.com)*.

11. Speakers' Bureaus

Many groups, such as men's and women's clubs, fraternal organizations, educational organizations, membership organizations, and places of worship, have speakers at their regular meetings. Organizational leaders may wish to proactively seek invitations to discuss the activities of their organizations with these groups.

Such meetings may be the source of volunteers, donations, ideas, or simply good will and public support. Local newspapers (don't forget the "Shopper" newspapers) list many of these club meetings and their leaders. Addresses can be found in the telephone book, if they are not listed in the newspaper announcement. Members of the board can be deputized to speak on behalf of the organization. Many of them have associations with other organizations and clubs that would be delighted to host a speaker.

12. Newspaper Op-Ed Articles

Virtually all newspapers print feature-length opinion articles on their Opinion/Editorial (Op-Ed) pages. Many will include a picture and a line of biographical material about the author. The Op-Ed page is usually the page most widely read by a newspaper's readership, along with the Letters to the Editor page. It is an excellent forum to share an organization's ideas on an issue and bring attention to the organization.

There are many cases in which a thoughtful Op-Ed article resulted in legislation being enacted by Congress or the state legislature to address the issue raised by the Op-Ed piece.

13. Letters to the Editor

Letters to the Editor are an effective way to "talk back" to a newspaper when the organization believes an article or editorial unfairly and erroneously shapes an issue. They can also be an effective medium to reinforce a position and permit the writer to expand on that position from the perspective of the organization.

The general guidelines for writing letters to the editor vary from paper to paper, but they usually provide for writing on a single issue, being concise (no more than three paragraphs), using non-threatening language, and providing information that might not be available to the readers from any other source.

14. Web Sites

Thousands of nonprofit organizations are establishing sites on the Web (see Chapter 21). Web pages communicate information about donations; volunteer opportunities; products, services, and publications; and general facts about the organization. Web sites can be prepared and maintained for very little cost and permit the general public to access information by computer from the privacy of their own homes and offices. You can increase traffic to your site by adding emerging Web-based communication tools, such as webcasts, blogs, and podcasts.

15. Coalitions

There is strength in numbers. Two heads are better than one. Whatever the cliché, many organizations find a benefit in pooling their resources to accomplish an objective. One strategy is to form a coalition with other organizations to address an issue of critical importance (see Chapter 24).

Tips:

- Use the power of the Internet to reach a global audience to foster relationships between your organization and potential future stakeholders. Review Chapters 21, 22, and 23 of this book for more ideas.

- Don't hold a press conference unless you feel that the information being shared is truly newsworthy. Be prepared for every reasonable question (and perhaps unreasonable ones, as well) from reporters that may not have any direct relationship to the subject matter discussed at the conference.

Chapter 21
The Internet for Nonprofits

Synopsis: Nonprofits have an exciting, versatile resource in the Internet. Once connected, organizations can share information inexpensively and quickly, and they can use search engines and directories to find information. Nonprofits can set up their own pages on the Web, and generate donations and other revenue.

Introduction

The recent explosion of useful resources for nonprofits on the Internet is perhaps the most exciting positive development for this sector in years. Thousands of nonprofit institutions whose leadership had barely heard of the Internet a decade ago are not only connected, but have their own Web sites, post videos on YouTube, create podcasts and blogs, develop wikis, and create online communities to build organizational support.

Nonprofit executives have taken advantage of this revolution in communications by using the Internet to seek donations, lobby members of Congress, advertise job openings, purchase office equipment and supplies, and hold online meetings and information sessions. They market their services, check references of prospective consultants, distribute board documents, reserve library books, generate grass-roots advocacy letters to government officials, research new laws and regulations, and download the latest Supreme Court decisions, all without leaving their offices.

Need a 990 tax return form? Download it from the IRS web site *(http://www.irs.gov)*. Need driving directions to your board meeting? Have a computer generate not only the directions but even a map, and e-mail them *(http://www.mapblast.com)* to your board members.

In previous years, if you wanted to distribute a document to a board, you had to photocopy the document, collate it, stuff it in envelopes, put correct postage and mailing labels on the envelopes, and mail it. The recipient would receive it two or three days later. Time could be saved by faxing the document, or broadcast-faxing it, to the list of recipients, but the cost of long-distance charges could be substantial. Via the Internet, the same operation results in almost immediate delivery of the documents to every person on the list, for the price of a local telephone call. The Internet has revolutionized the way all businesses operate, and the benefits to the for-profit world are just as applicable to the nonprofit sector.

 Saving money, while of prime concern to nonprofits, is only one advantage of utilizing the Internet. Perhaps the most exciting aspect is that nonprofit executives can communicate inexpensively and efficiently with like-minded counterparts who may be in an office next door or on another continent. The culture of the Internet has made it easy for people who have something in common and information to share to find each other. It is also easy to begin a one-on-one or one-on-ten-thousand dialogue without having to laboriously screen out the other hundreds of millions of people who also are participating.

Many nonprofit executives report that attending a national conference results in serendipitous contacts with previously unknown colleagues who generate new ideas, new strategies for solving problems, interchanges that promote innovation, collaboration opportunities among people otherwise separated by geography, and useful social contacts. The Internet has become all this and more. The speed of communication among people has made a quantum leap as a result of the Internet. Nonprofits that don't take advantage of the opportunities afforded by this technology to save money, expand markets, and promote themselves may be left in the dust by competitors that do.

Practical Applications of the Internet

Among the most popular services and applications of the Internet are e-mail, the World Wide Web, chat, newsgroups, mailing lists, podcasts, blogs, and wikis.

E-mail: Most of the information transmitted over the Internet is in the form of electronic mail. These are text and graphics communications that are sent from one person to another. E-mail is a "store and forward" system that permits someone to send a message to someone else for later retrieval. Each Internet user is given an Internet address that is used to send and receive e-mail. E-mail messages also can have files attached to them. Using e-mail, one can avoid playing "telephone tag."

Mailing Lists: Mailing lists are a form of e-mail. Users who subscribe to a particular list may send a message on a topic of interest to that list. That message is automatically distributed as e-mail to every subscriber on the list. Every subscriber will see that message as e-mail. Some mailing lists generate hundreds of messages a day. Others publish one each day, or arrive even less frequently. If you are paying a server for each message, or have limited storage space for e-mail messages, it may be important to you to limit the number of lists to which you subscribe.

Subscriptions to almost all electronic mailing lists are free. To subscribe to a mailing list, the subscriber generally sends an e-mail message to an administrative address (in this case, nonprofit-request@rain.org) in a standard format that automatically processes the request. The administrative address is different from the address to which messages are sent that are intended for the entire distribution list (in this case, posts are sent to: nonprofit@rain.org).

Newsgroups: A newsgroup is another form of Internet communication that provides for group discussion of a narrow topic. It is like a bulletin board in the supermarket, where you have to take action to see the messages posted there and read them. You have the opportunity to post a reply for others to see. Sending a message to a newsgroup results in each subscriber of the newsgroup having the capability of seeing the message without receiving it as an e-mail. Typically, someone makes a comment on a newsgroup, another person responds to the comment, and so on until there is a string of related messages on a topic. Simultaneously, others online will start another string of messages. All the messages are stored, often chronologically, and given a title, and viewers can pick and choose, using a newsgroup reader (specialized software to facilitate reviewing newsgroups) to decide which messages to look at. According to Wikipedia, there are 20,000 newsgroups still active among more than 100,000 that exist, but many have been abandoned, replaced by blogs.

Chat: Chat is the Internet equivalent of ham radio. Using chat software, you can have a "conversation" with someone by using the computer keyboard, all in real time. What you type and the response of the other participant(s) appears on your screen simultaneously. It is possible to have a nonprofit board meeting entirely by chat. Most commercial providers provide for privacy among those who participate. More popular, however, are informal chats among those who just happen to frequent a chat room. More and more, these chat rooms are becoming specialized, so participants have something in common. Many Web sites, including those of nonprofit groups, use software, often provided free by commercial providers, that permits visitors to participate in chats. In return for the use of free chat rooms, the visitors often see advertising messages controlled by the software provider, not under the control of the organization that is sponsoring the individual chat room.

Wikis. A wiki is a feature of a Web site that facilitates collaboration and participatory contribution among its users, who can add, remove, or edit content quickly and easily. Following the Hurricane Katrina disaster, a wiki was established permitting the public to create a master database of messages from those who were seeking information about missing friends and relatives, consolidating the message boards of dozens of those established by media outlets, disaster relief organizations, and others. Hundreds of volunteers, including this author, participated in the project, and were delighted by the convenient opportunity to respond to the tragedy in a more tangible way than by simply donating money. Wikis can be public or password-protected, and software supporting this feature can be accessed for free or at minimal cost. For more details, read the *Exploring the World of Wikis* article at: The Tech Soup Learning Center *(http:// www.techsoup.com/learningcenter/index.cfm)*.

The World Wide Web

The World Wide Web (generally referred now to the "Web") permits Internet users to link to resources on other computers, even if those computers are on the other side of the world. Web resources are reportedly expanding at the rate of 20% each month. The *Google.com* search engine site boasts that it has access to more than eight billion unique Web pages, and this is only a fraction of those available. The Web supports not only text, but graphics, photographs, full-motion videos, and sounds. Web pages are often formatted to give the appearance of an on-screen magazine, but there is one major difference. Web pages are formatted using computerized codes, called HTML (hypertext markup language), which permit the user to use a mouse or other pointer device to click on one part of the screen and be connected to a totally different Web page. For example, a Web page relating to libraries can be coded with links to libraries in hundreds of places. By clicking on one of these links, the computer's browser transports the user to the Web page of that library. To see Web pages and navigate through these links, "browser" software is required, such as Microsoft's Internet Explorer or Mozilla's Firefox.

The Web contains information made available by people and organizations. No one is in charge of maintaining or organizing the Web, so what you see is only what someone else saw fit to make available. So far, most of the content on the Web is free, but more and more sites are charging for access. It is not unusual for organizations to provide limited access to a site free to the public, and restrict access to certain pages to their members or those who pay a fee.

How to Find Resources on the Web

One of the complaints about the Internet in its early years was that one could find a plethora of fascinating databases, files, and information, but it was almost impossible to find something one was actually seeking in advance. Commercial companies offered services to assist researchers in finding Internet resources, and they often charged handsomely. That has changed dramatically with the development of powerful search tools, all of which can be accessed free of charge.

Among the more popular search engines are Google *(http://www.google.com)* and Yahoo! *(http:// www.yahoo.com,* which between them account for almost three-quarters of all Internet searches, according to the Neilson Netratings Search EngineRatings. Users access the search engine by connecting to its address, and then fill out an online form with the term or terms to search. For example, typing the term "nonprofit" in the Google search engine generates, within a second or two, more than 40 million related links. Clicking on any one of these links transports you to the referenced page.

Directories

A directory is analogous to a library card catalog. It organizes information on the Internet by preselected categories. You may find directories useful when looking for a specific Internet site if you know the site exists. For example, if you are looking for the site of Penn State University, using a search engine will likely provide a response of thousands of related possibilities. The site you are seeking may be listed first or buried among many others. However, by using the Yahoo! Directory *(http://www.yahoo.com),* you can find the main category *Education* and work your way down through categories to find exactly the page you want (i.e., by clicking serially on the following: *Universities, United States, Public by State,* and *Pennsylvania* until you reach *Penn State University@).*

A directory is particularly useful if you are looking for many Web sites that are similar, such as "public universities in Pennsylvania." It is usually more efficient to find a specific organizational Web site by using a search engine. More often than not, typing in the name of the organization on the Google.com search form and clicking on the "I'm feeling Lucky!" button will take you directly to that organization's home page.

Domain Names

A domain name is the part of the e-mail after the "@" sign or the part of a Web address after the "www." For example, the personal e-mail address of the author of this book is: gary.grobman@paonline.com. Paonline is his Internet Service Provider (ISP), and "com" indicates that it is a commercial provider. *Paonline.com* is the domain name.

How To Register a Domain Name

Registering a domain name is a simple and straightforward process. It only takes a few minutes to claim an identity on the Internet.

Step 1—Choose a Registrar

More choices exist now than ever before. In the early days of the Web, all domain names were registered through Internic/Network Solutions. You can still register through Network Solutions at *http://www.networksolutions.com* for $15-35/year per domain name registered, depending on the period of registration (1-10 years). Discounts apply for registering for more than one year at a time and/or for registering multiple domains, in some cases. There are also other companies that serve as domain registrars. Some examples are *http://www.register.com* and *http://www.register4less.com.* Many of these companies offer domain registration at discounted prices, so it is wise to comparison shop.

Step 2—Choose a Name

Go to the registrar's site and do a search for the domain name you want. Most will have a simple form where you can type the domain name and click "enter" to find out if the name is available for registration. If someone else has already registered the name, you will get an "unavailable" answer. Depending on the registrar, you may get a listing of suggested domain names, related to your first choice, that are available. If the name is not available, you can do a "whois" search (try: *http://www.networksolutions.com/whois/index.jsp* to find out who currently has the name registered). This information may be of use to you now or in the future. If the name is available, you are ready to register.

Step 3—Register the Name

If you have found a domain name that you like and it is available, you are ready to register it. Simply go to the registrar's registration form and fill in the requested information. This will include the domain name, your name, the organization's name, address, phone number, e-mail address, and other pertinent information. If you already have a Web host, you will be asked for the host's DNS information. Otherwise, most registrars will "park" your domain name with a "Coming Soon" page until you have a host and are ready to publish your site. The registration process also requires that you pay for the domain registration, usually via secure online credit card payment. Have your credit card information ready.

Step 4—Wait for the Name to Take Effect

Once you have completed and submitted the online registration for your domain name, it may take a short time for the name to show up in the "root" registry, making your Web site accessible to all Web users around the world.

If the Domain Name You Want Is Not Available

If your first choice of domain name is not available, keep searching until you find a suitable alternative that is. In the meantime, you can do a "whois" search to find out who the current registrant is for your desired name, and when the registration expires. If it is to expire soon, you can keep checking back to see if the registrant renewed it, or if he or she let it expire. Be aware that there is typically a "grace period" after expiration during which a domain name is still not available for registration. During that time (possibly two to three months), the former registrant can still renew it. Once the registrar releases it and makes it available for registration, anyone (including you) can register it.

Developing Your Own Web Page

There are thousands of commercial services offering to design and administer Web sites for a fee. With a minimum of technical background, you can do it yourself. Open source Web content management software (Joomla comes to mind as one of the better ones that is available free) is available that converts documents into HTML language and puts your Web pages in a pleasing format. The latest versions of the most popular word-processing programs can save documents as HTML files suitable for posting on your Web site.

Once you know the HTML codes to insert, you can even prepare a Web page entirely in Windows Notepad or other programs that create ASCII files, the simple files that consist entirely of text characters. Among the types of information that can be found on typical Web sites of nonprofits are:

> newsletter, annual report, press releases, brochure, how to contribute or volunteer, financial data, action alerts, job openings, information about board and staff members, publications, upcoming conferences and seminars, product catalogs and order forms, a way to e-mail the organization, and links to other organizations and government-based sites related to the mission and purpose of the organization

Simply having a Web site is clearly not enough to bring your organization fame, friends, and fortune. The "build it and they will come" philosophy may work well for Hollywood baseball movies, but you need to take proactive steps to build a base of loyal visitors and keep them returning.

Encouraging First-Time Visitors

Building a Web site that encourages first-time visitors has become an art form. Page design, load time, color schemes, pictures, animations, graphics, and how content is linked from one page to another based on your visitors' needs have become important issues for Web page designers.

> *Unique content is the key*

Of primary importance to nonprofit organization Web sites, of course, is the content itself. You can safely assume that a visitor is not likely to be visiting your site to be entertained, as there are thousands of commercial sites that do that quite well. In most cases, visitors will be pointing their browsers to your organization's site because they have an interest in the organization's cause and the information is not available anywhere else, or because they were directed there by some other source.

Take advantage of that knowledge, and put content on your site that will meet the specific information needs of your visitors. If you can do this in a pleasing format, fine, but don't sacrifice the unique content only you can provide—backed by the credibility of your organization's reputation—in exchange for "bells and whistles." A simply designed site with good content can be quite effective.

I offer additional advice for driving new traffic to your site:

Put a "Refer to a Friend" button on your home page. Part of what has become known as a "viral marketing" strategy, this allows visitors to send an e-mail to someone he or she knows. The automated format of this e-mail includes information about your site, including a link to it. Because the receiver of this message gets it from a friend and is likely to be interested in your site, that person is likely to visit it, and, perhaps, tell more friends. It is an electronic way to tell about your site using "word of mouth," or "word of mouse." You can find the code to incorporate this feature on your site at, among other places, http://send-a-link.com.

Use metatags in your Web pages. Registering with search engines and directories doesn't guarantee that the person looking for information will find your organization in the search results instead of hundreds of others with similar information. Type the words "animal shelter" in the Google search engine, and it responds with two million "hits." Viewers are not likely to browse through more than a few of these pages. You want to take steps to help the search engine give you high placement compared to competing Web pages. One way to do this is using metatags— key words and descriptions that appear in your Web page source code and are used by search engines to rank the likelihood that your particular page will be useful to the searcher. Each search engine uses a different process to calculate the placement of search results. There are sites that are helpful in explaining all of the technical details about submitting to search engines and directories, and inserting the right metatags. Among the most popular free ones are Stepforth *(http://news.stepforth.com/2003-news/ten-minute-optimization.shtml)* and Digital Web Magazine *(http://www.digital-web.com/articles/designing_for_search_engines_and_stars/).*

Maximize links to your Web site from other organizations. Develop a link strategy to get the message out about your site. One popular strategy is to identify Web sites that appeal to the same audiences as yours. You can do this by using search engines to search key words. Then e-mail the Webmaster for these organizations and offer to exchange links. You can have a separate "links" page on your site, with one-sentence descriptions. In this way, visitors to those sites who may not know about yours have the opportunity to visit with a simple click of the mouse.

Another form of exchanging links is participating in a Web ring. These are cooperative linkages of Web sites that have a common theme or topic. Each ring is administered by an individual Web site owner who screens requests to join the ring. For example, there are at least 23 Web rings on the topic of breast cancer. If your organization has a mission related to this topic and receives permission to join one of these rings, you will receive the appropriate code to place on your Web site. A visitor to your site and others that are members of the ring sees graphics and buttons that permit him or her to visit each site that is a member of the ring by clicking on them. This drives targeted traffic to your site from those who are visiting the sites of other members of the ring. For more information, check out *http://dir.webring.com/rw* and *http://www.ringsurf.com.*

Promote your Web site address on all organization materials. A final suggestion is to add your organization's Web site address to all of your organization's promotional items, brochures, newsletters, and conference/workshop materials. Put your site's address on your e-mail signature, your business cards, letterhead, and all of your advertisements—both print and online. It doesn't cost any more to do so, and this free advertising gets the word out.

Encouraging Repeat Web Site Visits

Changing the content often is the most important step toward keeping loyal visitors returning. This requires a commitment that consists of two parts. First, content relating to your organization's activities, upcoming events, public policy and advocacy briefings, staff responsibilities, newsletter postings, and other information should be updated at least every week—more frequently if you are able to do this. Second, you need a strategy to let everyone know when there is updated information on your site.

Many Web-savvy organizations routinely keep focused on what needs to be updated on their sites by publishing weekly newsletters that are distributed by e-mail to stakeholders who request them (see page 196). You can archive back issues on your site and use the content of each newsletter as your reminder to systematically keep your conventional Web site content current.

Let Visitors Know About Your Site

Now that you've updated your site, you need to let visitors know about it. Your electronic newsletter can be the vehicle for informing your stakeholders and other site visitors of updates and new material added to your site. You can design your site with a "What's New" link that will make it easy for visitors to see what has been added recently. This can also be accomplished by putting a "NEW!" or "UPDATED!" icon beside a link to a page that was recently added or updated. It is also useful to add a line at the bottom of your home page divulging the date when the page was last updated. Doing this may even provide an incentive for you to update your site more often, so as to avoid the embarrassment of having too many days pass before any material was changed on your site. You can send an e-mail or press release to the publishers of electronic and print newsletters and electronic mailing lists informing them about the availability of new files and features on your Web site. Take advantage of all of the free promotional resources you can!

Add Features to Attract Visitors

Experienced Webmasters know that simply adding new content and telling people about it is not always enough to encourage repeat visitors. They use a variety of techniques. For example, offer something free, such as an electronic newsletter, contests (with prizes), surveys, or a downloadable screensaver with your organization's logo and URL. If your organization sells goods and services or charges for events (see the book *Fundraising Online: Using the Internet to Raise Serious Money for Your Nonprofit Organization* for ideas—an order form can be found in the back of this book), provide a printable coupon on your site that will give visitors a discount.

Add useful services such as a job bank, blogs, chat room, message board, or a library of informative issue papers that will encourage visitors to return again and again. Chat rooms and message boards are among the best techniques for building an online community—the ultimate goal you should have for promoting repeat visits. It is from building such an online community that an organization can substantially increase its pool of volunteers (virtual and otherwise), donors, advocates, and loyal supporters.

Use your Web site to conduct an auction of donated goods and services (see Chapter 23). This not only increases Web site traffic, but can generate supplemental revenue, as well.

Ask visitors to bookmark the site, using a custom-designed bookmark icon. Bookmarking provides a convenient way for a Web browser to "remember" your site's Web address. It may not be obvious, but having your Web site in a person's "favorites list" is one of the best strategies to generate repeat visits.

How do you add these tools to your site without busting your budget? See an online article on bookmarks by Dr. Ralph Wilson, which can be found at: *http://wilsonweb.com/wmta/bookmark.htm*. Visit sites such as BraveNet *(http://www.bravenet.com/)* and Media Builder *(http://www.mediabuilder.com)*. Keep in mind that some free services may require advertising messages from the sponsor, and you may not wish to have these appear on your site. Some may offer these services/tools without advertising, for a fee.

Your Web site should not be a stagnant pond. Rather, it needs to be a vibrant river—flourishing, animated, dynamic, and zippy—making a measurable, positive contribution to your organization's communications and public relations efforts. An investment in some time and effort in building traffic to your Web site will help you in reaching your organization's goals.

Blogs

Blogging is sweeping the online communications world. Short for "Web Log," the blog has changed the way individuals and organizations communicate to a degree rivaling the impact of Web sites. According to Lee Rainie, director of the Pew Internet & American Life Project, there are at least ten million of them, with a total readership of more than 35 million Americans. More than a hundred thousand new blogs are added each week. Technorati *(http://www.technorati.com)* now boasts that its blog search engine can find 17.5 million blogs. To compete, Google launched a new search engine in September 2005 specifically tailored to this emerging medium *(http://blogsearch.google.com)*.

The nonprofit sector, with limited exceptions, appears to be on the sidelines, missing an opportunity to take advantage of what blogging has to offer. For fundraisers, the blog offers an opportunity to share with donors and potential donors information with a "human touch" that they would not likely get from any other source, even from the traditional Web pages of the organization, with an opportunity to provide feedback in the form of comments, criticisms, suggestions, and other interaction. Nonprofit blogs are not just informative; they are entertaining to those who are interested in what staff are thinking.

What blogs are

A blog is a Web page that consists of a frequently updated journal or diary by an individual. The style of commentary is typically informal and personal, usually including links to additional online resources embedded within the content. Each entry is in reverse chronological order—the latest entry is placed on top. Each dated entry has its own Web address (called a "permalink"), making it easy for other blogs and search engines to link to any particular entry (rather than to the entire blog). Previous entries are archived on the blogger's site. There is a process that permits viewers to add their comments to each entry, which can be seen by all viewers. Many blogs have an RSS (for *Really Simple Syndication*) feed, a software application that lets viewers subscribe to blog updates by using an RSS reader, thus eliminating the requirement to visit each blog site individually to obtain access to updates of their favorites.

Blog content can be personal

In the nonprofit context, a blog might include the daily musings of an executive director of an advocacy agency, sharing her thoughts on a news development of the day, adding links to online articles that have come across her computer screen about that news, commenting on how her organization's stakeholders will be affected, providing some insight into some of the internal debate within her agency about how to deal with it, and perhaps observing how thrilled she is that her two-year-old has finally been potty-trained. Included might be vacation pictures and links to the blogs of her friends and colleagues. It is this glimpse into the staff member's personal life that gives the organizational blog its special charm, although divulging such personal information is certainly not a requirement and in some cases may be inappropriate.

Blogs are perhaps a reflection of a change in popular online culture as much as an advance in online technology. In one form or another, blogs have been around since Web sites began. What is different is the informality of posts, and the willingness of individuals to "let their hair down" and show their vulnerability.

For the nonprofit community, blogs provide another mechanism to improve interaction with an organization's stakeholders, enhance the bond with donors, and create a dialogue with outsiders while giving them an inside look at what the organization is trying to accomplish. The technical tools are easily accessible, and we encourage you to at least take a blog for a test drive and verify that the benefits to you and your organization are substantial.

Nonprofits should consider blogging

Blogs serve many purposes for a nonprofit organization. If they are interesting or provocative, they draw readership—not only from the general public, but from the media and political leadership, as well. And these site visits often translate to new and more productive current donors, volunteers, advocates, and friends. They often give more of a sense of a vibrant, active, dynamic, and HUMAN organizational life than a print newsletter/annual report or a Web page that is more like a sterile brochure than an organic, flourishing online community. Because of the ability for viewers to comment, the feedback is often invaluable to bloggers. And, according to a September 2005 study sponsored by America Online (AOL), nearly half of bloggers do so because they find it to be "therapeutic"!

Cautions about blogging

Of course, there are some disadvantages. The advice I always give to "never put anything in an e-mail that would make you uncomfortable seeing on the front page of the *New York Times*" applies to blogs, as well. To date, hundreds of employees have been fired for what they have written in blogs, for anything from bad-mouthing their organizations to disclosing confidential or proprietary information, or to writing denigrating comments about coworkers. One instructor at Boston University was canned for blogging about a "distractingly attractive student," according to one press report. Many organizations have formal, written blogging policies, spelling out what types of posts are inappropriate. Many other organizations have simply banned them.

Bloggers need to vigilantly monitor all comments, routinely deleting "comment spam" and inappropriate comments.

Examples of nonprofit organization blogs

Among those to check out for ideas on how the blog concept works and might add value to your own organization's Web site are—

Common Cause: *http://www.commonblog.com*
Vermont Nonprofit CommunIT: *http://cvnp.typepad.com/blog/*
Michael Gilbert's Nonprofit Online News: *http://news.gilbert.org/*

Tools for blogging

Setting up a blog is remarkably simple and inexpensive. The method that requires the least technical proficiency is using an application service provider such as Typepad *(http://www.typepad.com)*. As of January 2008, Typepad, one of the most popular services, offers a 14-day free trial with a fee starting at less than $50/year. There are many competitors from which to choose. Each service has its advantages and disadvantages.

You can install blogging software (e.g., using WordPress, *http://www.wordpress.org* or Radio UserLand, *http://radio.userland.com),* and there are distinct advantages and disadvantages to each of these. WordPress is open source software, which means it is free and can be customized by your organization. Radio Userland can be licensed for under $40/year and offers a 30-day free trial.

For a discussion of server-installed choices, visit Blog Software Breakdown at: *http://www.asymptomatic.net/blogbreakdown.htm*

Electronic Newsletters

An electronic newsletter, sent by e-mail to those who have voluntarily requested to become subscribers, is becoming the model of choice for fundraising and friendraising. Unlike indiscriminately sent direct e-mail, this model of indirect fundraising appears to be both ethical and effective, and is considered a useful service by recipients. The electronic newsletter is a periodic e-mail that includes content that would be appropriate for an organization's print newsletter. The advantages are that compared to a print newsletter, there are no printing costs, no postage costs, no labels to be printed out and affixed, and minimal time-lag between the time the material is written and the time it goes to "press." Direct and indirect fundraising solicitations can be embedded within the newsletter, along with advocacy alerts, information about organization successes, upcoming fundraising events, calls for volunteers, notices concerning fee-based services, details about new laws and regulations that affect the organization's constituency, information about new Web sites of interest to stakeholders, jobs that may be available within your organization or similar ones, new features of the organization's Web site, and so on.

Some organizations solicit advertising for their electronic newsletters, or embed simple links or a clickable link logo of a business partner who has agreed to pay a sponsor fee.

Unlike telephone and direct mail, an e-mail newsletter comes with little or no price tag other than staff time. It provides a valuable service to your donors and friends, and many look forward to receiving these regular communications in their in-box. We can't think of any downside to it. Typically, your organization's Web site will have a simple form that permits viewers to enter their e-mail address to subscribe to the newsletter.

It is technically possible to maintain your electronic newsletter using your e-mail software. But doing so is cumbersome at best, and it uses up the available bandwidth your Internet Service Provider (ISP) permits. Many ISPs impose limits on the number of e-mails that can be sent with the identical message.

Consider third parties to administer electronic mail lists

Fortunately, free and low cost software packages (such as Dada Mail) are available on the Web that permit administration of electronic mailing lists. Many Web site hosts will permit you to send out thousands of e-mails to those who have opted in to receive them. If your host limits your use of e-mail, there are for-profit providers that will send your newsletter out for you using their own servers. In the event that you do not wish to tie up your own Web server, these third party services may be a good investment.

Here is some advice for planning your electronic newsletter:

- Provide the newsletter only to those who opt in by taking a positive step to subscribe, such as clicking on a button on your Web site. Sending out these e-mails to those who have not opted in is considered spam. At best, it is annoying. At worst, it could result in your ISP taking away your service, as well as infuriating your donors and other stakeholders.

- Advertise the availability of the newsletter on all organization materials.

- Make sure the electronic newsletter provides value to the readership, so subscribers won't automatically delete it or unsubscribe.

- Provide information in each newsletter on how to unsubscribe, preferably with a link to do so, and honor each unsubscribe request.

- Don't sell, rent, or give away your list of e-mail addresses.

- While it is acceptable to include advertising in your newsletter, use it sparingly. If you are using a third-party mailing list service, be willing to pay a few dollars more to purchase the "premium" version rather than using the free version that includes advertising solicited by the application service provider. Some of the ads accepted by the application service provider may be considered inappropriate by your readership and reflect poorly on your organization.

- Provide an opportunity for subscribers to donate to your organization if they choose to, such as by providing a link to your Web site's donation form, publicizing a specific "wish list" of items that could be donated or financed, and including information about planned giving opportunities.

Some issues to consider when choosing whether to administer your mailing list on your ISP's or Web host's server or through an application service provider are:

- *The amount of bandwidth required.* If your newsletter is simple text and is sent out to only a few subscribers, your requirements will be less than if your newsletter contains high-resolution pictures in an HTML format and is sent to tens of thousands.

- *Constraints of your application service provider.* You may be unable to send out your newsletter using your current Web host because of technical limitations.

- *How your subscribers will subscribe and unsubscribe.* This can be opt-in, opt-out, or even better, double opt-in, which means that subscribers who have hit the subscribe button receive an e-mail asking them to confirm that they want to subscribe before their e-mail address is entered into the subscriber database.

- *How bounced messages will be handled.* This includes addresses from those whose e-mail inbox is full or who no longer have an active e-mail address.

- *How you will deal with advertising.* Advertising, if you will permit it, can be solicited by your own organization, or inserted by an application service provider in exchange for the use of free newsletter administration software.

- *Who on the staff will be responsible for newsletter content and mailing list management.* There is work involved in creating the newsletter, soliciting advertisements and sponsorships, and dealing with bounced addresses.

HTML-Formatted E-Mail and Newsletters

Most people despise spam e-mails. But we sometimes are impressed by the design of some of these, utilizing slick fonts, graphics, backgrounds, pictures, and catchy special effects. While there are advantages in keeping an electronic newsletter simple by keeping it text-only, an eye-catching electronic newsletter can have the same appeal as a well-designed print newsletter. Sending your newsletter in HTML format also provides you with the option of personalizing the messages, not only in the header, but in the body of the message, as well.

Standard e-mail programs such as Outlook and Eudora permit limited formatting, such as using different typefaces, font sizes, bold, italics, and indenting. More sophisticated software, such as Dreamweaver, permits you to insert backgrounds, tables, and graphics. Another option is to use software that is specifically designed for sending out bulk HTML-formatted e-mail. Among the more reasonably priced programs are Enewsletter Manager, Group Mail, and World Merge. If you still feel clueless, you can simply hire an application service provider with experience in setting up HTML e-mails—there are scores of them.

There are some technical issues to resolve if you do decide to send out HTML-based newsletters and e-mail. First, what you send will look different depending on the browser being used to view it. Some recipients may not be able to see it at all, depending on their e-mail program. You need to pre-test it using all of the most popular viewers, such as Outlook, AOL, and Hotmail. For more practical advice, you can visit the Techsoup Web site *(http://www.techsoup.org)* for articles about electronic newsletters and e-mail.

Podcasts

As I write this, the podcast craze is now sweeping the nation. It is adding another arrow in the quiver for charities that want to send a targeted audio or video message to stakeholders in a timely, convenient, and most importantly, cost-effective way.

Back in the 1980s and 1990s when I was the CEO of a statewide association, I would get occasional requests to appear on a "live on tape" radio or TV show to discuss public policy issues that my organization was dealing with. I would dutifully spend precious time preparing to be interviewed, drive to the station, and wait what seemed like hours for the interview to start. Almost without fail, the shows would broadcast at a time when it was quite unlikely that anyone would ever listen to what I had to say. It was rare that I ever heard from anyone who had actually listened to the program I was on.

Podcasting changes all of this. It makes *you* the producer of a radio show (or TV show), and gives you the ability to reach your target audience when they are most perceptive to hearing what you want to say about your charity.

Examples of podcasting by nonprofit organizations

The Royal Society for the Protection of Birds, a UK-based charity founded in 1889, podcasts regularly with the sounds of birds and other wildlife. To hear an example, point your browser to: *http://www.rspb.org.uk/birdwatch/getready/podcast.asp*

Reverend Nancy McDonald Ladd of the Bull Run Unitarian Universalists in Manassas, Virginia, offers her weekly sermons by podcast, attracting an audience of members who live too far away to conveniently attend services, and the congregants' children who are away at college. And a growing segment of the audience appears to be those who attend the Sunday service and want to hear the sermon again when it becomes available by RSS (Really Simple Syndication, the protocol that supports subscriptions of podcast and blog broadcasts) feed on Tuesday. According to national church leaders, Bull Run is just one of 25 Unitarian churches around the nation that podcast all or some of their weekly services.

Florida public radio station WXEL has been one of the pioneers in podcasting its radio programs. If you visit the station's podcast page *(http://www.wxelpodcasts.org)*, scroll down to programs in April through June 2007. Here you can find podcasts of Dr. Stephen Goldstein's radio show "Fundraising Success" and seven programs in which I was a guest on the program on the topic of online fundraising. Did you catch this program when it was broadcast "live on tape" on Sunday evenings at 9 p.m.? Probably not. But you could listen to it now if you desired, or when you are working out at the gym. This capability makes it a very powerful communications tool.

The Collective Heritage Institute, also known as "Bioneers," is a nonprofit organization that promotes practical environmental solutions and innovative social strategies for restoring the Earth and communities. If you point your Web browser to *http://www.podcast.net,* you can find a directory of Bioneer's podcasts of 27 shows the nonprofit organization produced for public radio. You can hear them with the click of a mouse—a lot simpler than waiting for a radio broadcast.

On December 1, 2005, the Campaign to Make Poverty History joined with Gcast.com to launch the first ONE podcast. The World AIDS Day ONEcast featured former President of South Africa Nelson Mandela, Bono (U2 lead singer and co-founder of DATA—Debt, AIDS, Trade for Africa), and Chris Martin of Coldplay, along with members of the faith community and other ONE supporters. That month, Bono's charity ONE: The Campaign To Make Poverty History launched a monthly podcast focusing on AIDS, hunger in Africa, and other social issues.

What is podcasting?

Podcasting refers to the creation of audio files and uploading them to the Internet, using a process that enables the subscriber of the broadcast to be notified that this audio program is available to be downloaded to the subscriber's audio player or computer. These files are typically in MP3 format and 5 to 60 minutes in duration, making them suitable for hearing on the subscriber's computer or personal audio player, such as an iPOD or other MP3 player.

Advantages and disadvantages

What makes podcasting an incredibly powerful means of communication is that anyone in the world with an Internet connection can listen to podcasts at any time he or she chooses. This contrasts to cable TV and radio shows, which are on at a specific time and require action on the part of the viewer/listener to first know that there is a program of interest and then take steps to either listen to it in real time or record it. With podcasting, the subscriber is in complete control using the technology, deciding what content to subscribe to, and when to hear it. Podcasting affords the capability of listening to the program over and over again, having the ability to store it indefinitely, rewinding it, pausing it, deleting it, transferring the program to other media such as a CD-ROM, and distributing the files freely to others. Usually, there is no advertising to listen to, although there is no law against a charity making a subtle plea for donations to support its mission.

To hear your program, all subscribers need is a media player, preferably portable, and an Internet connection. The broadcaster's costs for equipment are negligible, and the subscriber pays nothing for the service. Even if subscribers don't have an iPOD or equivalent, the broadcaster's Web site can be designed to permit visitors to listen while they sit in front of the computer screen, with the capacity to download the file for future use.

How to podcast

The basic equipment needed to create a podcast consists of a microphone that connects to your computer, headphones, a computer, and an Internet connection. You can find detailed instructions on how to set up a podcast at sites such as Webmonkey *http://www.webmonkey.com* (search on the term "podcast") and Podcast411 *(http://www.podcast411.com/howto_1.html)*. The basic steps required are:

1. *Create your content.* This is accomplished by speaking into a microphone connected to your computer, or other devices that can create audio files. The content can be whatever you might include if the organization were producing its own radio show: highlights of the organization's accomplishments, pending public policy issues and advocacy efforts that listeners can participate in, details about a new general fundraising or capital campaign, new programs and services offered by the organization, or new features of the organization's Web site. Editing software can easily blend in music (make sure you have permission to use it) to open and close the program. Record directly into the computer using programs

such as Audacity for Windows/Mac or GarageBand for Mac. While it is not required, a good quality microphone and a room in which the sound isn't bouncing off the walls are of benefit.

2. *Save your content as MP3 files.* Use software such as RiverPast Audio Converter for Windows ($29.95 at *http://www.popularshareware.com/vc-rate.html)* and a free version of Audio Hijack for MAC *(http://www.rogueamoeba.com/audiohijack/download.php).*

3. *Edit your files.* Among popular editing software titles for this purpose are *Audacity (http:// www.topdrawerdownloads.com/showdownload.php?company=Audacity&title=Audacity);* GarageBand *(http://www.apple.com/ilife/garageband/),* Adobe Audition *(http:// www.download.com/Adobe-Audition/3000-2170_4-10324430.html),* and SoundStudio *(http:// www.freeverse.com/soundstudio/).*

4. *Publish your podcast.* You have a choice of publishing it on your Web site or a site that serves as a catalog of podcasts (or both). Among the popular ones are:

OurMedia.org *(http://www.ourmedia.org)*
Itunes Music Store *(http://www.itunes.com/podcasts)*
Podcast Alley *(http://www.podcastalley.com/)*
Podcasting News *(http://www.podcastingnews.com/)*
Podcast.net *(http://www.podcast.net)*

5. *Syndicate your podcast.* This entails sending it to subscribers. for details, see: *http://www. ehow.com/how_203188_syndicate-my-podcast.html*

Why podcasting is the future

I remember a few decades ago when personal stereo headphones such as the Walkman became popular. Today, if you see someone walking down the street without talking into a cell phone, he or she is likely to have an earpiece connected to one of the 100 million iPODs sold by Apple between November 2001 and April 2007 (April 19th, to be precise, according to a company press release). And this doesn't count the millions of iPOD clones with the capability of downloading and storing MP3 files. In a massive shift in popular culture, demand responsiveness is how people want their information, and podcasting fits this perfectly.

For charities, podcasting is a natural fit, providing a forum to reach major givers with "insider" briefings about the organization, updates about programs funded by donations, details about a capital campaign, and opportunities to advocate on behalf of a public policy issue of importance to the organization.

Online Communities

An online community is any Web site that attracts people who have something in common, and allows them to contribute to content or discussions at the site. The types of services that are typically available are real time chat, forums or message boards, member directories, instant messaging (such as AOL's "buddy" program), job/career information, shopping, and news and information. What members of the site have in common can be anything: their age, their social status, their profession, their religion, their politics, some health concern, or interest in a particular public policy issue.

What distinguishes online communities from other Web sites is that much of the content is contributed by visitors. This content may be moderated by the Web site administrator, although in many cases, it is not.

Challenges of Online Communities

1. Creating and maintaining an online community requires substantial time and effort.

2. Some visitors post inappropriate content, such as putting slanderous or libelous messages on the message board, posting commercial messages, violating confidentiality, or infringing on a copyright.

3. Some words used in real-time posting may be offensive, requiring the use of filtering software. It is difficult to choose which words to censor.

4. Online communities need an effective Code of Conduct.

Even when an online community is free, most require members to register and to select a user name and password. Doing so ensures that the organization has at least minimal control and can deny access to those who consistently violate the site's Code of Conduct. There are also marketing reasons to have a password-protected site, such as having access to information about those who visit.

Internet Etiquette (a.k.a., Netiquette)

As millions of new users have joined in, the culture of the Internet has developed over a short period of time and has changed. Most servers have written rules about proper use of their service. There are general written and unwritten rules regarding the Internet. Among some of the more useful are:

- Don't type entirely in capital letters. This is considered the computer keyboard equivalent of "shouting," and can result in being flamed (being sent a threatening or denigrating unsolicited message).

- Don't put a message on a blog, mailing list, or even personal e-mail that you would be embarrassed to have circulated to thousands of people. It just might happen.

- Don't post copyrighted material to a blog or mailing list without permission from the copyright holder.

- Spend time "lurking" (the equivalent of listening quietly) on a blog or mailing list before diving in by posting messages. Many groups and lists have a Frequently Asked Questions (FAQ) page. Read it before posting your first message.

- Don't post clearly commercial messages on a newsgroup or mailing list. Announcements about new products are fine; sales pitches are strictly verboten and usually result in flame messages.

Problems With the Internet

The Internet is not without its problems. Consumer fraud exists, just as it does in the non-virtual world. Although newly developed software has improved the security of communications (particularly important, since financial information, including credit card numbers, is routinely sent through e-mail), it is not fool-proof. In general, most e-mail is plain text, which is virus-proof, but viruses can be transmitted through attached binary files.

Copyright issues relating to electronic communication still are unresolved. Finally, the Internet has opened up an entire new world for exploration, and studies indicate that for some people, it may be psychologically addictive.

Useful Internet Resources for Nonprofits

Thousands of charities and other nonprofits have their own Web sites. There are scores of interesting and handy gateways to them and other sites that have substantial resources of interest to nonprofit organizations. Perhaps the best thing about accessing these Web sites is they are free-of-charge to visit (other than the fee to your service provider for Internet access). Among them are:

1. The Internet Nonprofit Center
http://www.nonprofits.org

This site, first put online in 1994, is sponsored by the Evergreen State Society of Seattle, WA. The site is home to the popular Nonprofit FAQ, a searchable library of frequently asked questions (and answers) on nonprofit management, fundraising, technology, legal requirements, and almost every other practical facet of running a nonprofit organization. Bulletins are posted on the site with articles and late-breaking news of interest to the sector, and you can sign up to be notified by e-mail about newly available issues.

2. The Foundation Center
http://foundationcenter.org/

The Foundation Center is an independent nonprofit information clearinghouse established in 1956. The Center operates five libraries and provides materials to hundreds of public libraries. The mission of the organization is to foster public understanding of the foundation field by collecting, organizing, analyzing, and disseminating information on foundations, corporate giving, and related subjects. The site has a searchable archives, an excellent reference on how to prepare grant applications *(A Proposal Writing Short Course,* accessible from the *Learning Lab* menu on the home page) and standardized grant application forms. There is access to an online librarian who will answer your questions about where to find resources and basic information of interest to nonprofits. Just fill out the online form with your question.

3. GuideStar
http://www.guidestar.org

GuideStar is administered by Williamsburg, VA-based Philanthropic Research, Inc., a 501(c)(3), and publishes comprehensive reports about individual American charities. Its purpose is "to bring the actors in the philanthropic and nonprofit communities closer together through the use of information and communication technologies. GuideStar collects and analyzes operating and financial data from the IRS Form 990 and from voluntary submissions from the charities themselves." The database consists of more than 850,000 reports on individual charities, and the site is colorful, accessible, and well-designed. The database can be searched at no charge by any number of parameters, such as name, location, or type of charity. This is simply the best site on the Internet for finding financial information about charities. Charities can provide their reports and update them online at no charge. The site also includes links of interest to charities and essays about philanthropy in its *Nonprofit Resources* and *Donor Resources* sections.

4. Nonprofit Managers' Library
http://www.mapnp.org/library/index.html

While much of this site is targeted to the needs of Minnesota nonprofits (such as local grant information), it is an excellent resource for all. The site boasts updated files on ethics, fundraising, communications skills, marketing, organizational change, risk management, strategic planning, and much more, sorted by more than 70 categories and indexed with 675 topics. There are numerous useful links to outside organizations that make this site an excellent resource for those interested in grants, foundations, government information, and general information useful to nonprofits. The site also hosts a free Nonprofit Organization and Management Development Program (a.k.a., *Free Nonprofit Micro-eMBA*).

5. Philanthropy Journal Online
http://www.pnnonline.org

This online newspaper, based in North Carolina, is a service of Philanthropy News Network, a 501(c)(3). It posts breaking news stories of interest to the nonprofit community. The home page menu sorts these news stories (and feature stories, as well) by categories such as technology, volunteers, fundraising, and corporate giving. You can subscribe to the biweekly e-mail version for free.

6. The Nonprofit GENIE
http://www.compasspoint.org/askgenie/index.php

This site is a project of the California Management Assistance Partnership. Here you can find book reviews of nonprofit management books, plus more than 135 entries in a comprehensive Frequently Asked Questions (FAQ) for nonprofit managers, organized in nine general categories, such as insurance and strategic planning. There are plenty of interesting links to nonprofit resources, as well.

7. The Chronicle of Philanthropy
http://www.philanthropy.com

The site provides highlights from this print publication, which is the trade journal for America's charitable community. The tabloid-format biweekly is the number one source for charity leaders, fundraisers, and grant makers, and the Web site provides more than just a taste of what its subscribers receive in snail mail every two weeks. The site is updated every other week at 9 a.m. on the Monday before the issue date, and job announcements are updated on the Monday following that. You can sign up for a free weekly e-mail update of news and new features of the site, plus breaking news when it occurs. The principal categories of this site are gifts and grants, fundraising, managing nonprofit groups, and technology. Each of these headings is further divided by a news summary, workshops and seminars, and deadlines. Also on the site are front-page news stories, a news summary, conferences, Internet resources, products and services, and jobs. Most of the articles consist of one-sentence summaries but are still useful, particularly if you don't have the $72 in your budget to subscribe to the publication for a year. The "Jobs" link transports you to a searchable database of hundreds of positions available. In some respects, this searchability makes the Internet version of the *Chronicle* more useful than the conventional version. There is also a directory of "Products and Services." If you are a subscriber, you will have access to a handy, searchable database of archived issues.

8. The Nonprofit Times

http://www.nptimes.com

This is the online version of the monthly tabloid newspaper. It has full-text articles from the latest issue, as well as classified advertisements. The Resource Directory, accessible from the home page, links to a database of vendors, consultants, and other professionals who serve the nonprofit community.

9. Independent Sector

http://www.independentsector.org

Independent Sector is the leading advocacy coalition in Washington that serves the nonprofit sector. This site is the first place to go for definitive statistics of interest about the nonprofit sector (click on *Nonprofit Information Center*). It also has files on ethics, advocacy, accountability, and leadership issues. There is current information about new laws and regulations affecting charities, as well as public policy advocacy updates.

10. HandsNet

http://www.handsnet.org

Founded in 1987, HandsNet links more than 5,000 public interest and human services organizations using the Internet to promote collaboration, advocacy, and information-sharing by the sector. The public pages are updated daily, and the members-only pages are considered to be the most valuable around for nonprofits that engage in advocacy. The site's Action Alerts provide numerous government links, state-of-the-art information on current issues (most of which is provided by member organizations whose niche includes that particular public policy issue), capsule summaries, sources to find more information about the issue, sample advocacy letters, and information about new legislation. While a generous sample of content is provided free, organizations are encouraged to join a fee-based *Web Clipper* service, which provides full access. A trial membership is free.

11. FirstGov.gov

http://www.firstgov.gov/Business/Business_Gateway.shtml

This site's strength lies in its convenient and user-friendly links to federal departments and agencies—executive, legislative, and judicial—and an easy-to-use guide to access publications of importance to nonprofits, such as the *Federal Register,* the *Catalog of Federal Domestic Assistance,* and access to the General Services Administration. It has a grid of federal agencies that permits easy access to each agency's home page, and a page on grants. Its search page can find information from more than a million government Web pages.

12. Volunteer Match/Impact Online

http://www.volunteermatch.org

This site provides a posting area for nonprofits to advertise volunteer opportunities that can be performed online, and it has excellent resources relating to "virtual volunteering." From the home page, click on "Virtual" for cutting-edge information about harnessing the power of those who are homebound, those who are unable to commit to a specific time and place to volunteer, or those who are simply too busy—but who have valuable skills they are willing to share. The "Volunteer Match" may help you find suitable volunteers for your organization who can transcend the limitations of geographical inaccessibility, as well as general volunteering resources.

13. Tech Soup
http://www.techsoup.org

TechSoup *(http://www.techsoup.org)*, originally conceived by CompuMentor, a San Francisco-based nonprofit, has developed a reputation as being *the* place for nonprofits to visit for answers to questions about hardware and software, building Web sites, and taking advantage of all that technology can offer to help nonprofits achieve their vital missions. The content is all free and worthy of repeat visits. A service of TechSoup, DiscounTech is a partnership of America Online, Novell, Microsoft, CNET, and several national and community foundations and other computer-related for-profits. For more than a decade, CompuMentor has distributed donated Microsoft and other name-brand products. The strings attached to receiving donated software through this program are minimal: Eligible organizations are nonprofits and schools with valid 501(c)(3) status. Microsoft does not permit K-12 schools, political organizations, or religious organizations to participate in this program, or nonprofits from Washington State. Additional restrictions apply to those purchasing server products. Lotus products may not be purchased by organizations that advocate, support, or practice discrimination based on race, religion, age, national origin, sex, sexual orientation, or physical handicap. Overall, this is one of the best sites on the Internet for information about nonprofit technology issues, including hardware, software, connecting to the Internet, and finding discounts on products and services offered to nonprofit organizations.

14. Network For Good
http://www.networkforgood.org

Network for Good is a charity portal founded in November 2001 by AOL-Time Warner, Cisco Systems, and Yahoo!. Charities large and small can find extensive resources here to assist in their online fundraising efforts. Even more valuable is the service it provides to charities that register, enabling them to place a "donate here" link on their own Web pages to permit donors to make secure, online contributions without the charity needing its own merchant account. By 2007, Network for Good delivered more than $100 million to more than 20,000 charities. I applaud the sponsors for their vision in helping small charities build an infrastructure to accept real-time credit card donations and help even the smallest charity benefit from this service.

15. Grants.Gov
http://www.grants.gov

While the searchable Catalog of Federal Domestic Assistance *(http://www.cfda.gov)* has been available free online in a searchable format since the mid-1990s, this site, launched in October 2003, takes the online search for federal government funding to a higher level. The objective of this site is to level the playing field so that all eligible organizations, regardless of their size or grantsmanship sophistication, can have a fair opportunity to receive federal grants. The site directs grant seekers to funding programs offered by 26 grant-making federal agencies that aggregately award over $360 billion annually to state and local governments, academia, nonprofits, and other organizations. It not only makes it easier for organizations to find grants of interest; it streamlines the paperwork needed to apply for them and permits the entire process to be conducted online. All application forms, financial report data in support of agency audit and performance measurement activities, grant management procedures, and information about grant programs have been standardized across these participating agencies. The site hosts everything an organization needs to find, apply, and manage a federal grant. Even grant notifications are made electronically. Site visitors download forms, work on them offline, and then submit completed applications electronically, saving hours of time and money. The site is divided into sections that help you engage in a six-step process, consisting of finding grant opportunities of interest, downloading the grant application package, registering with a Central Contract Registry, registering with a credentials provider, registering with grants.gov to submit grant applications, and logging on. There is a toll-free number to use to request assistance. This site is the first place to go if you have any interest in federal grant funds.

16. Nonprofit Good Practice Guide
http://www.nonprofitbasics.org/

This site is a project of The Dorothy A. Johnson Center for Philanthropy & Nonprofit Leadership at Grand Valley State University. The searchable site is organized by ten topic areas, including "Fundraising and Financial Sustainability" and "Technology." You can find links to more than 3,000 articles, online courses (many of which are free), research papers, booklets, and case studies, all organized by topic. While the strength of this site is in its organization of links to online resources found on other Web sites, it does have substantial useful content of its own. The Guide has a unique way of integrating both types of resources in a pleasing format that is both fun to browse and almost guaranteed to uncover some useful nugget that is worthwhile to print and save. Clicking on each topic area takes you to a page that opens with a list of "preferred practices" and "pitfalls"—in short, a list of "do's" and "don'ts." While many of these initial offerings have been seeded by the center's seasoned executive director, Joel Orosz, Ph.D., there is a link that permits visitors to add to the lists and to submit information about new resources. Thus, the site is organic and is likely to become one of the leading sources nonprofit staff and board members can turn to for advice, once folks know it is available and it reaches the critical mass necessary to sustain itself as an online community. Another useful feature is a glossary, accessible from the home page menu. It defines more than 2,500 terms of interest to nonprofit organizations, some with hyperlinks that point your browser to supplemental information. All in all, this is one of the best new resources on the Internet for nonprofit organizations.

Tips:

- **Subscribe to a general nonprofit electronic mailing list to keep current with what your colleagues in the field are thinking and discussing.**

- **Use popular search engines and search on your own organization's name. Take steps to ensure that what you find is accurate and up to date.**

- **Protect your domain names by keeping your fees paid.**

- **For details about using the Internet to raise funds and sell goods and services, see Chapters 22 and 23 respectively.**

Chapter 22
Fundraising on the Internet

by Gary Grobman and Gary Grant

Synopsis: The Internet assists, but does not replace, traditional fundraising efforts. While not without its problems, there are many creative ways to mount a successful online fundraising campaign. The Internet is a useful tool for development staff for use in prospect research, direct marketing, major gifts, corporate and foundation relations, and special events.

Introduction

On December 26, 2004, a massive undersea earthquake struck in the Indian Ocean. Initial reports were that several thousand people were killed by the tsunami waves that swept through coastal communities in South Asia and Africa. It took several days before the global community recognized that these reports failed to measure the cataclysmic devastation in Indonesia, Sri Lanka, and nearly a dozen other countries. The loss of life was eventually counted in the hundreds of thousands, and entire communities were swept out to sea without a trace.

To many Americans, these communities were simply places on a map on the other side of the world. Yet something in this tragedy touched a chord with millions of Americans, and they responded by making hundreds of millions of dollars in donations to help. And to an astounding degree, much of this occurred via the Internet.

Of the $173 million raised by the International Red Cross within the first few weeks after the disaster, $73 million was donated via the organization's Web site, exceeding the total donated online after the September 11th terrorist attack. More than 45% of Catholic Relief Service's donations in response to the tragedy came online, almost $12 million. International relief organizations such as CARE, Save the Children, and Direct Relief International were all swamped with online donations.

Doctors Without Borders/Médecins Sans Frontières (MSF), recipient of the 1999 Nobel Peace Prize, took what is believed to be an unprecedented step in January 2005 and raised almost $20 million for its tsunami relief efforts—and then decided that further fundraising would be counterproductive. According to a posting on the organization's Web site within about ten days after the disaster, the organization was inundated by donations, largely via its Web site's secure form. MSF noted that "at this time, MSF estimates that we have received sufficient funds for our currently foreseen emergency response in South Asia." MSF directed donors to donate either to the organization's general fund or to other international relief organizations.

In August 2005, hurricanes Katrina and Rita in the gulf coast of the U.S. resulted in 24-hour coverage by the news networks, followed by an almost constant appeal during commercial breaks to make cash contributions. As we write this, an amount in excess of a billion dollars appears to have been contributed online to the American Red Cross. In the first two weeks after Katrina, the Red Cross raised $439.5 million for relief efforts, and $227 million of that came in through the Internet—according to the September 15, 2005 article about it in the *Chronicle of Philanthropy*. Impressive!

The spike in online giving during 2004 and 2005 was documented in a survey conducted by the Pew Internet & American Life Project. According to this study, conducted in September and October of 2005, 26 million people had made at least one donation online, with nearly half of them contributing to Katrina relief. This translates to about 18% of Internet users, a growth from the 10% estimated to have done so in a comparable survey conducted in October 2001, just after the terrorist attacks.

When we co-wrote the book *The Wilder Nonprofit Field Guide to Fundraising on the Internet* in 1999, our enthusiastic endorsement of using the Internet for fundraising was met with some healthy skepticism from the nonprofit community. There were lingering questions about security of data, privacy, and the cost—in both time and money—of buying and maintaining the hardware and software necessary to take advantage of this new medium for attracting donations. There were also cultural barriers to overcome—such as the level of comfort donors would have to share their credit card information online and the virulent reaction most of us have to unsolicited e-mail solicitations, often considered to be "spam." Adding to the confusion was a lack of clarity with respect to how state regulators viewed charitable contributions solicited via the Internet.

Additionally, there were trust factors with which to grapple, such as whether to authorize third-party, for-profit providers to manage technology issues for nonprofit organizations. Doing so would permit leadership and staff of nonprofit organizations to focus on their primary missions. But it would also entail trusting outside organizations, which may or may not share the nonprofit's values, with both charitable contributions and sensitive data. A damaging scandal in 2003 involving PipeVine, one such third party provider—ironically a nonprofit itself— profoundly affected how we view relationships between charities and outside vendors with respect to being the steward for charitable donations. PipeVine, a donation processing application service provider, was forced to shut down operations in 2003 after it failed to deliver an estimated $19.1 million in contributions it collected, most of which were on behalf of California's Bay Area United Way. It could be years before nonprofit organizations recover from the fallout of the PipeVine scandal and again become comfortable working with outside organizations in managing online fundraising efforts.

Now, as we survey the landscape and chronicle the successes and failures of online fundraising, we have to report that many of these same issues—security, privacy, cultural adjustment, trust, and government regulation—have yet to be completely resolved to our satisfaction.

We continue to urge caution regarding these issues, but our earlier strong endorsement of using the Internet for fundraising has proven warranted as it has clearly become a vital part of the operations of virtually every nonprofit organization. We saw a glimpse of the power of online fundraising after the September 11th terrorist attacks, and more of this was unveiled during the series of devastating hurricanes that hit the southeastern United States during the 2005 storm season. Today, the online donations generated by the December 2004 tsunami and Hurricane Katrina have validated that the Internet is quickly becoming the method of choice for donors who want to respond immediately to do something tangible to help those in need, whether they live next door or on the other side of the globe.

The actual experiences of charities that look to the Internet for donations continue to be mostly positive. "Online Donations Surge" is the title of a June 10, 2004, cover story in *The Chronicle of Philanthropy* about its annual survey of online giving. That year's survey documented a 48% increase over the previous year in online gifts overall for the 157 charities that responded. Although the spike in post-September 11th online giving experienced by the American Red Cross was not sustainable in the following fiscal year, two large charities—Heifer International and the

United Way of Metropolitan Atlanta—reported raising more than 15% of their total revenue online.

According to Kintera, a full-service fundraising application service provider founded in 2001, about 1% of 2004 charitable fundraising was generated by the Internet, but this percentage is increasing geometrically, thanks to the successes of the post-tsunami and Katrina appeals. A Network for Good study published in 2004 before the tsunami hit found that online giving grew by 50% compared to the previous year, to a total of $2 billion.

"The Internet has gone from being one of several channels used by nonprofits for fundraising to being – in some cases – the primary vehicle being used to generate donations," says Dr. Harry Gruber, founder and CEO of Kintera. "Key reasons for this explosion in Internet fundraising are efficiency for the organization and convenience for supporters. Donors are realizing that it's much easier to make a difference immediately with an online gift than by mailing a check."

Internet fundraising has become much more than simply having a "donate here" button linked to a page that can process credit card transactions. Online donations to charities made through third-party online charity portals, such as Network for Good and JustGive.org, have skyrocketed; both recorded a doubling of the number of people making gifts in this manner between 2002 and 2003. Network for Good boasted in a December 17, 2005, press release that it had distributed $76 million from more than 300,000 donors to 20,000 charities in the previous four years. Within days of the tsunami disaster, the charity portal recorded at least $10 million in online donations made to tsunami relief organizations. Over $1 million was donated by credit card on a single day, December 29. Donations for Katrina relief exceeded this record several-fold in August 2005.

A description of the success of the Web site Moveon (http://www.moveon.org), in the April 17, 2003, issue of the *Chronicle of Philanthropy* provides a snapshot of the future of nonprofit advocacy and fundraising. In March 2003, this online advocacy group founded in 1998 sent a short e-mail to its two million-member e-mail list requesting donations to Oxfam America. More than 8,400 responded with online donations totaling more than $640,000 in six days. A previous appeal to raise $27,000 for an anti-war advertisement in the *New York Times* generated nearly $400,000.

Politicians from all political persuasions are scrambling to emulate the blitzkrieg fundraising success of Howard Dean's campaign for the 2004 Democratic presidential nomination. Although he ultimately didn't win his party's nomination, Governor Dean attracted thousands of supporters, mostly found through his staff's imaginative online grassroots campaign. According to news reports, this campaign started small. In the early spring of 2003, 432 supporters each pledged to find one more person to support and contribute to the Dean campaign. Within nine months, the campaign was communicating with 650,000 contributors by e-mail, with more than $50 million being raised and an average contribution of just $77. The campaign's success in mobilizing grassroots fundraising raised the bar for all political campaigns. The eventual Democratic nominee, John Kerry, reported raising $56 million on the Internet of the slightly more than $180 million the campaign raised prior to July 2004. Republican Presidential candidate Ron Paul raised $6.2 million in a single day, December 16, 2007, over the Internet, and presidential candidates from both parties aggressively were trying to emulate his success in 2008.

The direct appeal by charities to give money is only one strategy available via the Internet. New models, assisted by sophisticated advances in technology, are providing innovative ways for charities to generate donor dollars.

According to The Hunger Site *(http://www.thehungersite.com)*, visitor clicks on a button embedded on the site's Web page resulted in 49.6 million cups of food being donated in 2007 for distribution to groups such as Mercy Corps and America's Second Harvest. A "blogathon" in which participants stayed up all night posting Web logs (a.k.a. "blogs") raised $20,000 for charity when the first was organized by Cat Conner in 2001, and subsequent annual blogs are doubling the amount raised each year and are becoming a world-wide phenomenon.

Much has changed in the ways charities use the Internet to raise funds in the eight years since we first collaborated on a book about Internet fundraising. One conclusion we have drawn from watching this online communications revolution is that online fundraising is not likely to replace its conventional, off-line counterparts any time soon. We certainly do not recommend that organizations drop their direct mail programs, telephone solicitation, charitable auctions, and face-to-face appeals because of the availability of raising funds via the Internet. But we do see using the Internet for fundraising as another tool in the fundraiser's toolbox, with its distinctive advantages and disadvantages, and as an attractive strategy to pursue.

With the advance of technology and creative business models advanced by third-party providers, even the smallest nonprofit can build and display a Web-based fundraising "public face" that will generate both funds and public support. The "playing field" has been leveled on the Internet. Even the smallest nonprofit can create a sophisticated Web site with e-philanthropy and e-commerce functions that has the look and feel of the largest nonprofits with full-time Webmasters. The price of entry into building a highly attractive, professional Web site for the typical nonprofit is a few dollars a month for a host and some sweat equity. There are many Web hosting services that will even provide free Web space for nonprofits. Free and moderately priced content management software makes Web site design and content updating a breeze for the expert and novice alike.

If you are not taking advantage of the Internet to raise funds for your organization, you are missing out on an opportunity to take your organization to the next level. It is not as hard to raise funds on the Internet as you might think.

In putting together an online fundraising strategy, it is helpful to consider what makes online fundraising different from more conventional methods, such as direct mail, telephone solicitation, face-to-face meetings, and fundraising events. Doing so will permit you to take advantage of the strengths offered by online fundraising, and address how you will take into account its limitations.

Advantages of Internet Fundraising

Among the advantages are—

1. *The Internet has a systemized culture that offers potential donors an invitation to find your organization.*

   Traditionally, nonprofit organizations reach out to potential donors by purchasing targeted mailing lists, advertising in print publications, and culling newspaper articles for information about those with substantial wealth for future follow-up communication. Through the use of links from other Web sites, search engines, online and print directories, and even word of mouth, potential donors will find your organization even if you have not found a way to contact them directly. Your organization can enhance this possibility by publicizing its Web site through news releases and other organizational communications and publications. See Chapter 21 for practical advice on attracting new visitors to your organization's Web site and keeping your visitors returning. The best such efforts lead donors to bookmark your site or link it to their personal home pages and blogs.

2. *There is almost universal access to the Internet and increasing comfort with online transactions.*

According to Neilson NetRatings, 69.7% of Americans have Internet access, as of May 2007. Access in the office workplace has become almost universal with more than 50 million Americans—37% of the total workforce—online at work, according to a report from eMarketer and *The Wall Street Journal*. Even those without their own computers have access to the Internet through their local schools and libraries, and free e-mail accounts are available to everyone with the motivation to sign up for one. People who only a few years ago didn't have an e-mail account eagerly participate in eBay auctions, purchase airline tickets and hotel rooms online, buy and sell securities, and examine PDF-format 990s online before they consider making a donation.

3. *Potential donors can make "contact" with your organization 24 hours a day, seven days a week from anywhere in the world for virtually no incremental cost on their part.*

Donors can find your Web site's "donate here" button at any time of the day or night from any computer that has Internet access. Free or inexpensive software makes it practical for online forms to capture and process identifying information, payment information, and acknowledge a gift in the blink of an eye, providing the donor the instant gratification that is unavailable through many conventional fundraising methods. Compare making an online donation to the hassles of writing a check, filling out a paper form, finding a stamp and envelope, and taking the envelope to the post office. Or waiting for the organization's office to open in the morning to call in a pledge. By that time, your donor may have gone back to sleep and forgotten that he or she even wanted to make a donation.

4. *In many cases, raising money online is cheaper and faster than traditional fundraising methods.*

Compare making a change in a direct mail fundraising brochure to making the same change to the online brochure. Solicitation materials can be modified electronically at any time at virtually no cost, with no extra charges for color. Full-color, glossy, print brochures are often thrown away without having been read and are costly to update. Online fundraising messages can incorporate animations, scrolling messages, and flashing screens that make Web pages more dynamic than their print counterparts. These flashy bells and whistles can be added at no additional cost. In (almost) a blink of an eye and at virtually no cost, your computer can transmit thousands of electronic newsletters, each containing information of interest to your organization's supporters, as well as a subtle request for funds to finance a new service or program. There are no long distance charges, such as are incurred by a broadcast fax. Your telephones are not tied up if you use a Web-based service for this task. Responses (in the form of online donations) can literally come in within seconds, compared to the weeks required just to lay out and publish a print version of an organization's newsletter or fundraising brochure.

5. *The Internet is less intrusive and less annoying than many conventional methods of fundraising.*

Direct mail and telephone solicitation appeals too often annoy and alienate. Both are getting less efficient: sending charitable bulk mail is getting more costly.

Telephone appeals are not as simple as in the past as a result of the popularity of "do-not-call" lists, caller ID, and other methods that potential donors use to screen calls from sources they do not know. To generate one donation from such a call, the organization must contact many individuals, most of whom will view your organization's contact as annoying.

Your fundraising message can be delivered by e-mail and read at a time that is convenient for the reader, who actually has signed up to receive it (along with other communications). While you won't want to send "spam" messages to ask for funds, there are several techniques you can use (see Chapters 21 and 22) that ethically and appropriately rely on e-mail to raise funds.

6. *Internet fundraising can easily be integrated with other marketing and promotional materials and programs.*

Solicitations for donations can be coordinated with other features of an organization's Web site, such as being included in an electronic newsletter, posted on donor recognition Web pages, on links to an organization's sales of goods and services, and with testimonials about the organization that indirectly enhance opportunities for giving. Individuals will visit your Web site for many reasons other than to make a donation. A functional Web site can plant the seeds of future giving and make it convenient for those who make spur-of-the-moment gifts based on what they see on your site.

7. *There are decreased transaction costs for Internet-based donation processing and donor outreach efforts.*

New business models make it easy to partner with third parties to streamline the online donation process and reach donors who otherwise might never have heard of the organization. Computers using sophisticated software automate many processes, such as accounting, database management, donor acknowledgment, and contact management, which previously relied on time-consuming work by staff. Many of these useful software packages can be purchased off the shelf, obviating the need to rely on third party providers.

8. *There are increased opportunities to build positive relationships with the business community.*

Many for-profit businesses are willing to sponsor the Web sites of charities, usually with no more than a "thank you" or a link (typically in the form of the sponsor's logo) from your site to the sponsor's own Web site. Internet models such as "click-to-give," online shopping malls, and charity portals are innovatively harnessing the power of the Internet to cement relationships between the business community and nonprofits that can carry over to relationships involving non-Internet collaborations.

Disadvantages of Internet Fundraising

Using the Internet for fundraising has its disadvantages, as well.

1. *The online medium can be impersonal compared to face-to-face fundraising.*

Online fundraising, with rare exceptions—such as when using real-time conferencing—is not face-to-face. The personal, human contact, with the ability to read, interpret, and respond to body language and other non-text cues, is an important component of fundraising, particularly when soliciting large gifts. There are limitations in relying on only what can be viewed on a computer screen to communicate.

2. Government regulation of online fundraising is unsettled.

There are unresolved legal and regulatory issues that have surfaced as a result of online fundraising. Among them are the degree to which the states regulate it, and what the roles are of third party for-profit dot-coms that agree to serve as intermediaries between donors and charities.

3. There are vulnerabilities as a result of having to rely on for-profit third parties.

Many charities are unwilling or unable to build the infrastructure to seek and process online donations. For-profit providers are available to offer these services (see Chapters 22 and 23). Many of them have no track record for reliability, ethical conduct, or financial stability. In addition, new business models have been created that involve partnerships and affiliation agreements with for-profits. The need for clear agreements between charities and these third parties raises issues of the transaction costs of creating contracts, motivation, opportunities for outright fraud, privacy with respect to sensitive donor and charity data, and the potential inability of a charity to control a third party's use of that charity's logo. Abuse by third party providers in the name of a charity can stain a reputation that took years to build. As we mentioned in our introduction, the PipeVine scandal of 2003 has placed a pall over relationships between charities and those who wish to help them raise funds. That said, there are scores of reputable for-profit application service providers (ASPs) that have exemplary relationships with their nonprofit clients.

Most charities are recognizing that, in almost every case, the advantages of using the Internet to supplement traditional fundraising far outweigh the disadvantages. Almost every major charity in the United States has reported raising significant revenues utilizing the Internet. In the next sections, we will describe some of the techniques charities are using to harness the power of the Internet, including use of e-mail, electronic newsletters, Web sites, online auctions, partnering with application service providers, networking with colleagues, online communities, using the Internet for prospect research, and finding funding sources on the Web.

Most organizations do not dedicate staff solely to Internet fundraising. Instead, most development teams are integrating Internet approaches into their existing fundraising programs. So the question for these organizations is not necessarily, "How can I raise support online?" The more particular question may be, "How can the Internet enhance our annual appeals, our major gift program, our fundraising events, and our capital campaigns?"

Direct Marketing

Organizations of all types utilize basic direct marketing to reach the broadest possible public for support. Through mailing campaigns, these organizations strive to gain vital revenue to maintain their operations. The goals of a direct marketing effort are to build a mailing list as large as possible, as engaged as possible, and abundant with the names and addresses of those who support loyally, often in unrestricted dollars.

The challenges posed by direct marketing are ideally addressed by Web-based efforts. First, the Web provides a cost-effective way to help the public know about the organization. For large national organizations, a Web presence is absolutely vital and most likely to result in people seeking and finding their way to the organization. But even on the local level, a Web presence will lead to results.

The Community Food Bank (CFB) in Tucson, Arizona *(http://www.communityfoodbank.org/)* set up its Web site hoping that the local community would learn about what it was trying to do and support its efforts. In only six months, the organization began seeing donations coming in every day through its Web site. A year later, donations of up to $1,000 were given regularly online.

Attract new donors

Direct marketing online may also attract a different kind of donor. The Community Food Bank was used to receiving support primarily from those over 50 giving through traditional direct marketing efforts. A survey of the organization's new online constituency demonstrated a dramatic increase in donors who were in their 30s and 40s. This younger contributor was being engaged for the first time thanks simply to an Internet marketing approach.

Build the giving "habit"

Web sites as a form of direct marketing are also credited for larger and repeated giving. Consider that most donors who respond to annual solicitations or direct marketing appeals give according to their income level. This contrasts with major donors, who give based on their assets. The size of an annual gift is based on disposable funds after meeting one's spending and saving needs at the time. When a gift is made only once each year, then the organization may only receive the contribution the person can afford in the particular month when the gift is made. Donors who give monthly will therefore tend to give larger gifts than those who give once in a year. Most donors do not save their disposable income each month to preserve their ability to give the largest contribution over the course of the year.

Promote monthly giving habits

For this reason, many organizations are seeing the value in promoting monthly giving habits. Donors who click to give often develop such habits. This is likely to be an especially effective mechanism for churches and temples to which contributions are often made in the form of monthly or weekly gifts. An online appeal may make it easier, especially for individuals who miss attending services in a given week. Any organization, however, that hopes to increase repeat giving will be served well by offering Web site giving options consistent with this approach.

Although monthly giving helps individuals maximize their philanthropy to organizations they care about, it is inconvenient to write a check that often. It requires time, stamps, and envelopes, and if any one of those is missing when the donor is ready to give, then the donor may not send the gift at all that month. Some organizations attempt to encourage frequent giving by mailing more often or soliciting pledges to be paid monthly and providing the materials to make the gift, but this is costly and may not appeal to all donors who are already inundated by mail.

Giving online addresses all of these concerns. It allows monthly giving habits to form without the inconveniences. Increasingly, people are getting used to paying their monthly bills online. Many donors are willing to support organizations in the same manner. Giving donors the option to automate giving or to give monthly shows that the organization is service oriented.

Cultivate a community of donors

Another aspect of Web-based direct marketing is the opportunity to cultivate a relationship with a large constituency. Direct marketers know that engagement is necessary to maintain their constituency's support over time. At a minimum, organizations need to communicate with donors and engage them in a participatory way. Personalization is important as organizations seek to build a real relationship with their donor public.

Conveying information can be a challenge if carried out primarily through direct marketing appeals. Letters and brochures convey only so much information. As a result, most are drafted to the needs of the largest segment of the donor public. A shotgun approach is necessary for effective fundraising. Thus, for example, if an environmental organization expects that the majority of its donors are more moved by hearing about its latest advocacy efforts than they are by learning about environmental impact research, then its appeals will likely focus on the former and neglect the latter. It's simply impractical to appeal to the smaller segments of the organization's constituency. A Web site, however, allows visitors to go to whatever topic interests (and moves) them, and these visitors can be invited to contribute while there.

Make giving easy

Several direct marketing fundraisers shared that online fundraising reduced barriers to giving. They advised us to **make sure the option to give is pervasive on your site.** The button to make a donation should exist on every page. Donors should not be required to leave what they are reading to navigate your site to find the place where a gift can be made. When possible, fundraisers can also relate the value of giving right at that point. How would $50 help advance the advocacy efforts of the organization? How would the same gift affect vital research supporting the cause?

Integrate and reinforce traditional direct appeals

Another helpful technique is to integrate mailings, phone appeals, and print ad forms of direct marketing with the organization's Web site. Repetition is often valuable in direct marketing. One message is easily missed. A letter can be tossed out because it is received at an inconvenient time. The Web site is a place where the same message can be viewed just because it's available when the donor wants to read it—even if that's at 3 a.m. Repetition helps to ensure that the message is seen.

Repetition may also strengthen the message. Seeing an image online that was previously seen in a magazine ad or reading a story that was heard in a phone call reinforces the message. The organization looks well organized and lively when something received in another medium is carried through online. This can demonstrate that the Web site is being maintained daily, consistently with other communications. Not everyone reads the "last updated" line to determine this.

One organization we spoke with tracks the relationship between its traditional media approaches and the Web site. A mailing, for example, will often refer the donor public to a particular place within the organization's Web site. The resulting traffic to that page can be tracked as another way to test the reaction to the mailing. From there, similar tracking can be done to determine if donors are then going to the donations page and making a gift. Over time, such research can be essential to perfecting a direct marketing approach to fundraising.

Engage donors in the organization

Communicating effectively with donors will help increase giving, but actively engaging donors can truly raise the bar on contributions. In an e-mail newsletter, the Brookfield Zoo offered recipients the chance to name the latest zoo baby. This kind of participation encourages individuals to click from the e-mail to the Web site and feel as if they are actively participating in the life of the organization.

The zoo's engagement, however, began earlier when individuals first opted to receive the e-mail newsletter (see Chapter 21). Giving people the chance to opt in is a major tool for direct marketing fundraisers. By opting in, the subscriber gives an organization permission to write (and to solicit). This is familiar to many membership organizations, universities, and clubs. Such organizations have long benefited from the bond their constituency has agreed to accept from the start. Other organizations have been disadvantaged by inherently temporary, arms-length, one-sided relationships. If donors send checks in response to a direct mail appeal, they are not necessarily going to view themselves as a part of that organization in the long term. But if they ask to receive communications online, they may do so—especially if the organization takes the opportunity to create a personalized and welcoming environment.

Establish a bond with discussion forums

Donor discussion forums are another form of engagement. They can help a constituency establish a bond with the organization and a relationship for appeals that feel more individualized.

Dads and Daughters *(http://www.dadsanddaughters.org/),* for example, is an organization that has grown around an opt-in discussion forum. DADS seeks to help fathers be successful parents for their daughters and engages them in addressing cultural and commercial messages that may negatively affect girls or damage their self-esteem. From the first page, visitors are encouraged to sign up for the electronic mailing list. The e-mail discussions are two-way. Participants can raise everyday parenting challenges and get input from other members. E-mail action alerts are sent to the list, as well as requests for support—from financial to in-kind needs. This works because each person has opted in and feels sufficiently engaged, so the requests for support are viewed as appropriate, even welcomed as convenient.

This approach is obviously more challenging for larger, well-established organizations, but any degree of engagement of one's donor public can enhance the level of giving, the frequency, and donor loyalty.

Even the simple act of registering at a site can create some level of engagement. Some organizations will encourage Web site visitors to register. Then when they return and "sign in," they get a degree of personalization from the site itself. Beginning with a "welcome back Mary" sign, the site can also be made to recognize various preferences or past activities. Online message boards, for example, may show what has been read and what has not.

Password protect the site

Having a password into a Web site encourages visitors to bookmark the site. By registering visitors, an organization can also request information. Visitors may voluntarily share a range of data on their interests, their contact information, including phone number, and even wealth information. Some organizations will retain credit card information with confidentiality. This can be done to make it even easier to give regularly. Donors don't even have to take their cards from their wallet or purse.

Prospect Research

Prospect research includes finding information not only on individuals, but also on corporate and private foundations and government agencies that will provide funds. It encompasses collecting and analyzing information to help fundraisers find out the ability and inclination of prospective donors to donate, and obtaining clues to the best strategy to assist donors in providing the largest gift that would feel comfortable to them. Good prospect research cannot guarantee successful "asks," but it can provide critical information about the background, needs, style, financial capacity, approachability, and interests of someone who can make or break your fundraising campaign. Before the Internet revolution, prospect researchers used newspapers and magazines, real estate records, data and mailing lists purchased from private companies or other charities, annual reports from businesses, industry association directories, and biographical directories (such as *Who's Who in America)* to cull for juicy leads. Today, there is a plethora of electronic sources, many free, dwarfing those available a decade ago.

Treat $50 donors today as if they will be $50 million donors tomorrow

One cannot ever know when any particular $50 donor today may become a potential $50 million donor tomorrow, and thus it is important to treat every donor and potential donor as if his or her donation is the most important the organization will ever receive. Yet the mathematics are that a single $5 million donation has as much purchasing power as 100,000 donations of $50 each, and with a lot less transaction cost. No wonder charities are willing to make substantial investments in prospect research.

Find prospects using free online databases

When Gary Grobman speaks at conferences making his PowerPoint presentations on the subject of online fundraising, one prospect research technique never fails to leave his audience ooohing and aaahing. He points his Web browser to *http://www.melissadata.com/lookups.* Then he clicks on "Campaign Contributors." Then he asks a fundraiser in the audience to provide him with a 5-digit ZIP-code of an upscale neighborhood in the area of his or her charity. When Gary submits that into the online form, it returns information about individuals who made contributions of at least $200 to a federal election campaign. Inevitably, the list is a "who's who" of philanthropists. It doesn't take much imagination to think about how such a database can be of use to fundraisers. Other sites that are favorites of professional prospect researchers include Edgar Online People *(http://www.edgar-online.com/default.asp),* Hoover's Online *(http://hoovweb.hoovers.com/free/),* Forbes.com *(http://www.forbes.com/),* and David Lamb's Prospect Research Page *(http://www.lambresearch.com/).* Some of these sites are free; others require a subscription.

Identify interests, motivations, backgrounds, and financial capacity

In 2003, Jerold Panas wrote a riveting two-part column in *Contributions* Magazine about his harrowing, semi-successful experience in making a $50 million "ask" on behalf of a university fundraising campaign. Obviously, the preparation required for such an endeavor is more than, let's say, seeking a $50 donation, because the stakes are so much higher. Veteran fundraiser and *Washington Post* columnist Bob Levey often tells the story of a neophyte fundraiser who approached the legendary philanthropist and *Washington Post* owner Katherine Graham seeking a major gift for a worthy cause, only to be immediately shown the door after calling her "Katie."

Major gift officers and other high-level fundraising and executive staff want to know their prospects. They want to understand their potential so they can make realistic assessments for future solicitations. They want to understand their personalities so they can approach them in the right way. They want to learn their motivations so they can focus on what appeals to each particular individual and avoid pitfalls that might turn them off to the organization. They want ideas for making initial introductions.

The Internet offers an efficient tool to access lots of publicly available information about individuals. Careful online research can answer many questions about potential donors.

Major Gifts

Major gift fundraisers work closely with a small set of an organization's top donors. Their donors contrast with annual supporters in making "stop and think" contributions ranging from once every few years to once in a lifetime. Major gifts tend to be given for special purposes—often restricted to projects with specific measurable outcomes. How do the Internet and the organization's Web site and electronic communications assist the major gifts team?

Don't use the Internet as a crutch

Fundraisers often view the Internet with great hope for finding the key information and insight they feel they need. The reality is that the Internet can be useful, but ought not be used as a crutch. For the most part, prospect research should be left to prospect researchers (if your organization has them), particularly for determining giving capacity. While many cannot help but "Google" a prospect before a visit or while planning an initial contact, fundraisers should be careful not to rely too heavily on cursory research or believe that they can truly understand the person from whatever they find. Major gift work still requires the traditional emphasis on face-to-face interactions for getting to know one's prospects and building a real relationship.

In addition to aiding in prospect research, the Internet can be a valuable aid in all aspects of major gift fundraising, including identifying new donors, cultivating relationships, solicitation, and stewardship.

Find hidden potential donors using the Internet

Identifying major gifts donors is one of a fundraiser's greatest challenges. Few donor prospects contact an organization requesting to have their relationships with the organization managed by a major gifts officer. Instead, they are often initially hidden. They may be hidden in the public at large, interested in the mission of your organization, but not yet connected. Or they may be hidden among the current annual donors. Some of the wealthiest individuals still give $25 or $50 gifts in response to direct mail appeals.

Sharing philanthropic news within your organization can also be an effective way to help encourage those who support far below their capacity to perhaps step forward and give more. Major gift stories provide a wonderful opportunity to communicate not only about the programs of the organization, but about the exciting support and endorsement a major gift demonstrates. To the extent possible, major gifts fundraisers want these stories to be shared broadly to set the highest possible bar on generous giving and to build a stronger culture of philanthropy throughout their donor constituency.

As you identify major donor prospects, the next step is to begin building a stronger affinity with the organization. This can mean several things, each of which may be enhanced through Internet tools.

Educate major donors about the organization

Potential major donors need to get to know the organization and its mission over time. There is an education process that must happen. While the most important efforts will be face-to-face, you can enhance these interactions and develop a closer connection through e-mail communications and referring donors to specific parts of your Web site. E-mail takes on a very different nature when the recipient knows the sender. If you are managing the fundraising for a political campaign, for example, and you tell a particular donor that the candidate will e-mail directly with some information, this is quite different from getting a general letter from the candidate to a larger number of people.

In short, e-mail can be a convenient form of communication but also extremely personal if it is combined with other one-on-one approaches. A fundraiser might send a note referencing a particular topic or article on your Web site for which they know the donor has interest. Fundraisers can facilitate communications with board members, leaders, and others as they help the donor understand how they operate and work to accomplish their goals. You might even have a program beneficiary write to a prospective donor to share information about the impact the organization has had.

If your organization has developed good case materials, you may want to adopt the common practice among successful fundraising programs of including case statements online in PDF format. You can see numerous samples of these simply by entering "case statement" into any popular search engine, or check the samples posted at:

http://dukehealth1.org/childrens_services/case_statement_p2.asp
and
http://www.capitalcampaigns.com/sampcasehosp1.html

In addition to educating donors about their organizations, fundraisers need to listen to major gift prospects and understand their needs, interests, and motivations. Again, the addition of Internet communication into the traditional mix can help escalate input both ways.

Keep track of the relationship between donors and the organization

Similarly, major gift donors and prospects often need to develop a relationship with leadership and trust in their ability to guide the organization successfully. Enhancing face-to-face relationships through online communications can increase the leadership's ability to engage with prospects. Your organization's leader can interact with higher quality communications as well as with a greater quantity of donors. Major gifts fundraisers should actively recommend, draft, and track e-mail conversations between leadership and top prospects.

Leadership should also remember to share valuable discussions with individuals who are supporting the organization. Remember to send a blind copy to relevant staff. Private conversations should be respected, but when appropriate, sharing information can avoid duplication of efforts or wasted time later.

Include contact information on the Web site

Although you may have given a donor prospect your card, it is common for anyone to misplace a number and seek you out through your Web site. Web sites that lack simple staff directories can create frustrations, and visitors may feel that you have failed to focus on helping them navigate your organization. With a staff directory, a donor will gain a more positive impression. Being able to "see" the staff they are trying to find will help make the communications seem more personal, warm, and friendly.

Ultimately, major gifts work leads to solicitations. Here your Web site can again support your efforts, beginning by detailing your organization's giving opportunities. Whether or not you have a case statement online, you should also detail major gift projects that can be funded. Because major donors tend to need specificity, it may be wise to give substantial details. Rather than just mentioning the organization's top giving levels, you can provide a description of how the organization can use gifts of $25,000 or $100,000 or $1 million. Your description can provide the impact, the visibility to the donor, and the reason why these opportunities are so high a priority.

Develop Web pages that encourage major gifts

While it may be unlikely that a donor will randomly visit your site and contact you interested in one of your top giving opportunities, the presence of these at the Web site can support gift discussions. Keeping these online reaffirms for donors that they authentically do represent the organization's top priorities. And you never know when your organization will receive a donation windfall as a result.

Planned Giving

In addition to presenting top gift opportunities online, you should also detail giving vehicles. Many organizations provide some information about planned giving options, estate gifts, and instructions for giving stock gifts or mutual funds. Such practical information can help donors as they consider making major contributions. Try to ensure that your site has all the details a donor would need and up-to-date contact information in case they have questions.

Here are some examples of planned giving pages:

> *American Red Cross* (http://www.redcrosslegacy.org)
> *National Foundation for Infectious Diseases* (http://www.nfid.org/donations/planned.html)
> *Harvard Alumni* (http://www.haa.harvard.edu/pgo/)

In presenting both giving opportunities and giving vehicles, what can be particularly helpful are actual donor demonstrations. If donors are willing, you can share their stories as models for others. Major donors often are pleased to do this, because it ensures that their leadership gift is actually leading. Suppose you wish to show what a charitable gift annuity can do for a donor. While you probably don't want to share the exact financial details of any individual donor's gift annuity, you can still articulate and quote a donor to demonstrate why such gifts can be mutually advantageous.

The same can be done for giving options—adding a personal touch to your list of giving opportunities. In this way, you gain the endorsement of past donors to promote new major gift philanthropy. Donors might be asked to share what motivated them to make the gift. They can share their appreciation for the visibility or the chance a gift gave them to remember a loved one. They can articulate the impact they have seen their gift have and how that made them feel. All of this can make a significant difference to a new donor. It will also add value and interesting reading to the giving opportunities section, so you may have better reason to direct donors there.

Post donor recognition pages

Once you have secured a major gift, stewardship and recognition come into play. Here there are many options, and organizations may want to think through it carefully. There is no substantial research on the risks/benefits of recognizing gifts online. Some fundraisers are hesitant. Even if donors approve, they may worry about getting unwanted attention by being put online for their major gift. Organizations may worry that other organizations will fish for the recognition pages and immediately try to "steal away" their donors.

Others are more optimistic and see more value in the gains that publicizing a gift online can have. As we review these options, we leave it to the reader to weigh the pros and cons.

One method of recognizing gifts is to create an online donor board. Many organizations provide donor boards in their buildings, especially museums, universities, theaters, and other places that have high visitor traffic. Donors appreciate donor boards, because they provide visible recognition. Organizations enjoy the opportunity to encourage other gifts. Because Web sites often attract substantial visibility, an online board may be desirable. We may even see more of these in the future, in particular from organizations that do not have a suitable or sufficiently visible location for a traditional donor board.

Consider posting virtual donor plaques

If an organization is concerned that listing donor names on a donor board may lead to other competing organizations tapping into their donor constituency, it may consider using graphical donor "plaques" instead of a text list. A graphical plaque is even more attractive. It would mean that you put the donor's name on an image that appears like a real-life plaque. As an image, it cannot be found by regular search engine methods, provided that the donor's name is not used as the name of the image file.

A more detailed possibility for donor recognition is to build pages dedicated to donors. These can contain some combination of background on individuals and their families, and the programs they are funding. Such pages can be done in combination with a donor board, allowing individuals to click on the name for more information. Donor boards and donor pages offer the possibility for greater visibility and may make donors feel a greater sense of how they are creating a legacy for the organization.

A variation on this is the online press release. Oftentimes, donors hope for a press release in response to their gifts. Unfortunately, most newspapers and media outlets are not interested in pure philanthropic stories, short of the mega-gifts that happen from time to time. But a formal press release can be posted online and made visible to those visiting the Web site. While perhaps not as exciting as being in the *New York Times,* such visibility can at least be a practical compromise solution.

Again—be very careful to communicate with every donor as you do anything with his or her name online. Even seemingly harmless forms of recognition, such as attaching a name to a professorship or a program detailed online may upset a donor. Communicating in advance is necessary.

Special Events

A museum organizes an annual gala event. A health organization holds an annual bike-a-thon. A university seeks class gifts in preparation for its big reunion weekend. A political campaign organizes "meet up" events to raise money. A church group plans a concert to raise support.

Events, although all very different, are a mainstay in the fundraising menu of most every kind of nonprofit organization. But what does this have to do with the Internet? How can the Internet enhance such programs? How can it help them have a bigger impact? How can it help them grow over time? How can it help them attract larger numbers of people? How can it help increase their visibility?

Most special events fundraisers see their role as two-fold. First, they want to raise significant support for their organization while controlling costs. The second objective of special events is to create awareness and visibility for the organization. For this reason, gala events may be lavish affairs.

Increase visibility for your special event

Visibility as an objective serves multiple purposes. Walks, galas, and other high profile events, for example, have helped to educate and make the public more aware of devastating diseases, to move the government to support programs for the poor, and to build excitement about cultural events. Such events have direct mission benefits.

In addition, visibility can serve other fundraising goals. Fundraising events can help to identify new major gift donors or to recognize existing ones. They offer a special visible option for recognizing corporate philanthropy. They provide an opportunity to address a larger donor constituency and to build their knowledge of and commitment to the organization.

Attract corporate sponsorship with similar markets

Understanding the complex goals of a special event fundraiser, we can begin to look at how the Internet might be helpful. Let's focus first on corporate event sponsorship. Highly visible special events provide an opportunity to link corporations to philanthropy in a context that is often particularly valued by the company. If a company has a market that is similar to your organization's beneficiary public, then it may be particularly attracted to event sponsorship.

Events covered by the media often acknowledge such philanthropy in a way they never would otherwise. Outright major gifts almost never get major publicity, unless they are extremely large, i.e., in excess of $25 million. But the news will often show a corporate check presentation as small as $10,000, if it is done in the context of a public event of interest.

Develop a page for your special event

As fundraisers look for and approach potential event sponsors, the more visibility they can offer them, the more appealing their proposal will be. Using the organization's Web site to show how the sponsor's name will be featured is one valuable part of that package, particularly for organizations with heavy traffic. This can be done on a special page dedicated to the event, but linked from the organization's home page. Doing the same in mass e-mail communication to the organization's constituency about the event can be another aspect of this.

Is there value to a special page dedicated to an event like a gala? The short answer is "absolutely!" A page (or section) on a major event gives a fundraiser a chance to create an ongoing album for the event. It should contain photos of the most recent event, as well as substantive information about what the event is accomplishing. Over time, archived pages can be kept at the site, so visitors can look back to years past. A section of the Web site dedicated to a signature event can be a great point of pride for an organization and for its constituency as the program grows.

First time attendees will have a sense of the event if they visit the page. Individuals may encourage others to purchase seats or tables and may point friends to your site for this information. Previous attendees will enjoy seeing their own pictures there. Donors and sponsors may link to this part of your site.

Over the long run, an Internet presence for a major gala event can enhance the program. It can create loyalty in those who have attended in the past and help to broaden the appeal of the event significantly. The gala page can celebrate the visibility achieved each year—linking to news coverage it received.

Put the gala program booklet online

Ultimately, this will all serve to help raise the fundraising for a gala style event. Donors can give through the gala site. Individuals who cannot attend the event might especially enjoy being part of the fundraising action in this way. Some organizations may wish to put their program booklet online and raise the price for a page by adding an Internet version of the space in addition to the printed version. Auction items not purchased at the event can be auctioned off after the event, via the Web site.

In short, the Internet gala page can bring a major event to life *before* and help keep the excitement going *after* the actual event itself. As participants feel a part of the site through the images and perhaps the words they add there, they will feel more closely bonded to your organization. These feelings of connection to the event and the organization may help plant the seeds for budding major donor relationships.

Create a life-long bond

It is not enough for an organization to have donors merely invest in their mission itself. Investments are made at arms length and may be impersonal. Organizations want donors to develop an emotional and life-long bond—to become part of their family. Similarly, organizations should want their galas to be more than just wonderful parties that people attend because they are fun and for a good cause. It is better if they become family celebrations and gatherings that represent keystone moments on a shared journey to accomplish a vital public interest objective.

Universities and many private high schools and other educational programs know this, as they have long focused on the life-long bond alumni relationships can create. These are celebrated and funds are raised around special class years during reunions. Reunion weekends have organically spawned tremendous innovation and creativity through their Web presence.

The reunion site

All the elements described for galas are regular features of many reunion Web sites. These sites are graphic intense with pictures of alumni, faculty, and students. These pages are also highly interactive, encouraging visitors to be involved through the site for a year or even more before the actual event. They serve, in this way, to build excitement. Any high school reunion today is likely to have some activity develop through commercial sites such as Classmates.com, Facebook, or similar resources. By the time the event happens, classmates have already connected and begun talking and sharing with one another.

A typical university reunion site will provide the schedule of events (why should anyone depend on the printed version, which is so easily lost?). It will include a listing of the reunion committee members with e-mail addresses, so that everyone can provide input for the event early on. It will have a photo gallery, a full class list, and a variety of links to help graduates get caught up on information about the school today. It will have a section devoted to finding "lost" classmates who have moved away and for whom the event committee has no contact information.

Add a giving section

Of course, it will also have a giving section. These may describe special projects the class members have decided to join together to fund, or it could describe a variety of giving options. Reunion classes enjoy seeing how much they have raised, so a total to date is likely to be included. And just to further enhance the excitement of giving, there may be a friendly competition for the most dollars among different class years.

Many fundraisers feel that the purpose of special reunion fundraising efforts is to "bump up" giving over the alumni donor's lifetime. So while donors may give $25 each year their first few years out, perhaps by their 5th reunion, they will leap to $100 and may remain at about that level until their 10th or 25th, by which time they may leap to being $500 or $1,000 donors. In addition, reunions are events in which major gift giving becomes a special focus for fundraising. The reunion site is designed to help bolster these efforts. If their popularity is any sign, then they are succeeding. Just one of many enjoyable examples can be found in the online press release of a recent $5 million class gift from Denison University's 50th reunion *(http://www.denison.edu/ offices/publicaffairs/pressreleases/reunion_2004.html)*.

Sometimes reunion sites are predominantly managed by volunteers. The organization might give over some control over the design so that volunteers rather than staff can develop the site. This can be a good idea for any school or organization that is concerned with the staff time it might take to manage a reunion site.

One of the conveniences of a reunion Web site is the ability for participants to register and pay for their participation in the event. Online registering, however, is turning out to be much more than just a convenience. It's turning out to be a boon for fundraising.

Special events that require registration

Today's walk-a-thon, bike-a-thon, and similar public fundraising events are benefiting hugely from organized online registration and fundraising. These kinds of fundraising events succeed when they are heavily attended. While a gala has limited seating and reunions are limited only to alumni graduates, walks can become enormous events in which hundreds or thousands participate. The sheer number of participants helps achieve the media coverage and visibility sought and the giving, because it's smaller on average, benefits by larger and larger attendance totals.

In years past, a family that was dealing with a devastating illness might join in a walk-a-thon to raise money for that cause. In the weeks before the event, they would take gifts and pledges through their personal solicitation of friends and family. They would call, write, or visit the individuals they were asking. It takes a significant commitment of time to do this.

Organize teams online

Today, most major walks organize their teams online. Commercial resources make this relatively simple to do. Typically, a person connected to the organization signs up online to be a team captain. The event's site will automatically allow a high degree of personalization. The volunteer can add personal pictures, personalize the message, and set his or her personal goals.

The sites then automate much of the fundraising (see *Personal Fundraising Pages* in this chapter). The volunteer just adds the names and addresses of those he or she knows (they can transcribe them all right from their e-mail address book) and decide if they want the pre-written solicitation or if they would like to make it their own. Their friends and family can click right from the e-mail message they get, give the gift by credit card (secured communications, of course), and then appear soon after on a scrolling banner of donors.

The volunteer's donors can return as needed to check on the progress toward the fundraising goal. They may even see the progress in a traditional fundraiser's "thermometer" and might decide to give a bit more to put the team over the top. The volunteer can get regular reports on progress. It's almost like giving them their own fundraising staff.

Generate financial support from nonparticipants

Many elements contribute to making this approach successful. It saves volunteers a lot of time, effort, and money, so they can be more active solicitors. Volunteer fundraisers can reach out to friends and family globally, yet personally. Because it is easier, it engages fundraising from those who may not be quite as focused or dedicated to the organization at this point. In the past, walk teams were comprised mostly of the diehard loyal donors and volunteers. Online fundraising broadens the participation. Many participants may not even attend the walk at all—but are happy to have helped raise the level of philanthropic support for something they do indeed care about.

In addition, donors report that fundraising in this way is simply fun. For many, asking for annual support from friends and family is an excuse to contact them. They may personalize their message for each one to catch up. How many of us need that excuse to contact Uncle Jack or our best friend from high school? The beneficiaries of this are the nonprofit organizations who are gaining greater support and more awareness and visibility for themselves and their missions.

This kind of approach recently has caught fire in political fundraising. Popularized by Howard Dean's primary campaign for the Democratic Party's 2004 presidential nomination, online fundraising has become a mainstay in all major campaigns. Again, Web sites automate a personalized fundraising campaign by individuals. They can do much the same work that walk fundraisers are doing online. A popular addition to these is encouraging such volunteer fundraisers to organize "house parties" or "meet ups" (see *http://www.meetup.com*) to bring like-minded individuals together to raise support. Unlike the walk efforts online, these events use the Internet to connect neighbors who do not know each other. Geographic proximity and a common interest in a candidate or cause is what connects the participants. They value finding one another and possibly staying connected socially. And they value supporting the cause for which they gathered.

Use automation and volunteers

In essence, this online fundraising technique is creating a mini-gala model, letting volunteers take over everything—providing a place for the event, food, invitations, and so on. All that the organization needs to do is to receive the check and use it wisely. Of course, to be very successful, the organization needs to support these efforts, providing the volunteers with good materials, both videos and printed, to make the event worthwhile for the participants. The most successful house party efforts may involve a phone-in period during which the candidate addresses multiple events simultaneously.

Innovative new and cutting-edge efforts such as these are in their early stages, but there are good signs that they represent how the Internet is creating a more diverse set of fundraising practices under the broad net of special events. They appeal particularly to a younger new generation of fundraising volunteer—individuals comfortable with utilizing technology to build grassroots efforts.

Many of these first generation efforts still have a rough feel to them. In the future, we will see them become more elegant and much more common, perhaps in other fundraising venues. How long will it be before we see a neighborhood food pantry or a church group using the Internet to support its fundraising in some of these ways and with some of these tools?

Make online fundraising event administration routine

We will also continue to see the Internet change special event fundraising in more dramatic ways. Organizations are already exploring the idea of using the Internet to actually be "at" a live event. Through video broadcasts over the Internet, it is now possible for individuals to attend seminars and hear speeches online. The Internet has become a common venue for certain fundraising events.

To sum up, the Internet's benefit for special events includes a number of very basic ideas, such as using a Web site to publicize and draw in more participants and even gifts before and after the event. It includes some important broader concepts, as well, such as employing the Internet to help build a different kind of connection to the organization, one that is more participatory and intimate while also more convenient.

Capital Campaigns

The capital campaign has become a way of life for many organizations, especially universities, public radio and television stations, and religious institutions. Not long ago, capital campaigns were held only occasionally and usually for a special need. Today, the planning for the next often begins as soon as the previous one ends. Capital campaigns build public excitement around fundraising. They serve to identify a set of needs and priorities, and in so doing make an organization's strategic plans a little more accessible to the organization's donor constituency. Capital campaigns also help make larger solicitations easier, creating urgency and the motivation of achieving a goal.

As capital campaigns have become more popular, they have given birth to the campaign Web site. As suggested above, the primary goals of a campaign Web site are to present the fundraising priorities and to generate excitement around giving.

Typical campaign sites include many or all of the following features:

1. *A goal stated on the first page.* This can take the form of a graph or "thermometer" showing progress toward the goal. It will also include stories of key leadership gifts in the campaign.

2. *Messages from the campaign chair or others about the effort.* Often these are presented in video or audio clips, as well as text, especially if high profile individuals or celebrities are helping to lead the campaign.

3. *A case statement in PDF format.* The traditional case statement provides donors with a well-designed printed piece that explains the needs and attempts to motivate philanthropy toward them.

4. *Detailed information about the institution.* Even institutions with complete Web sites will often reorganize and re-present their factual data, organizational structure, and history. Many campaign Web sites have a completely separate look from the main Web site of the organization. The purposes of doing this are to deliberately contrast with what the donors are used to on the site and thus grab their attention, or to create a more polished and prestigious look to appeal to high-scale donors. An organization with an extremely well branded look may simply want to draw greater attention by adopting a new campaign logo with different color schemes and page designs. The University of Chicago did this with its campaign Web site at *http://chicagoinitiative.uchicago.edu/*. Here even the URL is unique. You can see the logo and color scheme versus the university's home page at: *http://www.uchicago.edu*. If the capital campaign is sufficiently large, then sub-branding or branding differently may be a good strategy. It may not be worth doing for smaller campaigns.

5. *A list of needs and complete detail on them, as well as recognition levels.* These may be replicated in the case statement, but don't count on everyone printing out that document.

6. *Pictures.* Appropriate pictures here are of people, program beneficiaries, and model construction planned. Some will include video feeds, allowing visitors to monitor 24 hours/day building projects under construction.

7. *Current news.* News stories may help ensure that the site looks lively and up-to-date. The campaign Web site can be viewed as a secondary portal into the organization.

   Market to donors rather than to the public

In essence, capital campaign Web sites recast the organization's online presence and market the organization very specifically to donors rather than the public at large. While the main gateway to the organization typically is focused on its mission, with philanthropy carefully and appropriately woven in, the campaign Web site can be unabashed in its drive for dollars. In a role reversal, fundraising becomes the highest priority on these pages, and the mission is woven in to show how essential fundraising is to meeting the organization's objectives.

Capital campaigns also often take place at large complex institutions and can serve an ancillary role of unifying multiple fundraising efforts. In a university, they bring together all of the college, graduate, and professional schools toward a common goal. They may connect geographically separate campuses, or organizations with separate chapters. The new Web portal can be a place to reflect that unity and to demonstrate the interconnectedness of an organization with multiple parts.

Online Fundraising Strategies

E-mail

E-mail is still considered the "killer application" of the Internet, and with good reason. For charities that abuse it, it may well, indeed, earn its name. A charity that purchases a disk with 20 million e-mail names on it and then indiscriminately e-mails a fundraising solicitation to the list is *likely* to make a name for itself. That name will be spelled "M-U-D." There is a consensus that using such a strategy is about as injudicious as one can get in using e-mail for fundraising. Our culture accepts the "cost" of wading through junk snail mail, most of it from tax-exempt organizations seeking contributions. Perhaps there is a feeling that the sender at least made some effort to weed out duplicates and, at least, is trying to target the mailing because even the charitable bulk mail postage rate is getting fairly steep these days. Printing fundraising letters, return envelopes, and the "free gift inside" of personalized mailing labels, calendars, or greeting cards must cost something, let alone the cost of designing and sending out the mailing.

Avoiding spamming

We do not (and should not!) as yet feel the same way about unsolicited e-mail. Pornographers, scam artists, crooks "phishing" for personal financial information, and purveyors of illegal drugs send a high percentage of the "spam" mail we all receive. Sending "spam" mail may associate an organization with these types of unsavory operations. No organization should want that.

The culture of participation in the Internet community is still evolving. What is not totally clear is what types of e-mail solicitation are acceptable, and what types are the most effective. Communicating organizational needs by e-mail to stakeholders who already have some relationship with the organization, such as donors, board members, and those served by the organization, is usually appropriate. Sending out online newsletters to an organization's stakeholders who have opted in to receive them is even better.

Using e-mail to interact with stakeholders

One legitimate use of direct e-mail is to simply interact with your stakeholders and provide them with information and services that bring them closer to your organization. E-mail is a cost-effective means for increasing direct communication between your organization's actual and potential donors. Because of the convenience of the "reply" button available within all e-mail programs, it also provides a convenient way for getting feedback. Sharing timely and informative news about what your organization is doing, and plans to do in the future, can keep your organization on the minds of your donors and maintain your visibility. Among information that can be shared with broadcast e-mails are the following:

- new features added to the organization's Web site
- requests for volunteers to help the organization with a program or service
- calls to action, such as to send letters or e-mails to public officials concerning an important, emerging public policy issue
- directions on how to participate in an online or offline survey
- information about an upcoming fundraiser
- details about an upcoming meeting or program (with driving directions)

Of course, even those who have expressed interest in your organization in the past may no longer maintain that enthusiasm. We recommend that you place instructions at the bottom of any mass-distributed e-mail on how to be deleted from the list for future e-mails.

Collecting e-mail addresses

Almost universally, online fundraising advocates agree that seeking a donor's e-mail address is a positive strategy, even if there are no current plans to communicate with those donors online. Plans can change. E-mail remains the fastest and cheapest way an organization can communicate, even if it may not be the most appropriate way in every circumstance. But simply having the capacity to contact every stakeholder quickly by e-mail is considered to be a top objective by those of us who give advice about online fundraising.

There are obvious strategies that will increase the percentage of donors who will give your organization their e-mail addresses. Organizations should routinely include "e-mail address" as a field in their donation forms and other forms (such as those used to request additional information from the organization). The online newsletter subscription is also a good method used to harvest e-mail addresses from donors and supporters. Some organizations require Web visitors to register with their e-mail addresses and other identifying information if they want to have access to some features of the site, such as the online community.

Turn your web site into a catcher's mitt

The organization's Web site offers lots of opportunities to obtain e-mail addresses, such as through electronic newsletter subscriptions, online surveys, information requests, e-mail feedback to the organization, and similar online transactions in which the e-mail address is routinely needed to respond. As Mathew Emery, of the application service provider Kintera, explained at a 2004 workshop on e-philanthropy sponsored by the Pennsylvania Association of Nonprofit Organizations, "The Web site has been (typically) treated like it's a brochure, but it's really a catcher's mitt. You want something on every single page where you can find something about the visitor." According to Emery, even if a donor doesn't make an online donation, online communications have a positive effect on direct mail. His organization found that there was a 10% increase in donations made as a result of a direct mail fundraising piece when an e-mail was sent to donors prior to sending out the direct mail.

"E-Mail to a Friend" strategies

Another fundraising strategy that appears to be effective is the online version of getting organization supporters to write personal letters to those they know, including friends and neighbors, appealing for donations. In the offline version, a charity might make a call to a past donor. Rather than requesting a direct donation, the charity requests that the donor send a note to ten or twenty neighbors requesting a donation. If the donor agrees, the charity provides the names of those it desires to solicit, perhaps a sample letter, and if appropriate, other support.

In the online version of this technique, donors are asked to e-mail their friends and relatives with a donor appeal. The solicitations are not considered spam, because they are coming from personal friends and relatives. Recipients of the solicitations see the communication coming from someone they know, rather than an organization, and are more likely to open the e-mail and respond.

There is increasing evidence that this type of e-mail solicitation is effective. One application service provider, Kintera, has developed software to facilitate such online volunteer fundraising, called "Friends Asking Friends®." Kintera reports that its 3,352 campaigns utilizing this software raised $192 million in the 12 months ending in March 2004, $48 million of which was donated online. This approach is particularly effective for specific fundraising events, in which an organization's supporters e-mail their online contacts about an upcoming charity auction, race/walk, or benefit concert. The Kintera software package has integrated links providing information and the ability to donate or register for the event, and tracks donations and responses (see *Personal Fundraising Pages* in this chapter).

In addition to the obvious "donate here" link on your organization's Web site, there are new business models that facilitate online fundraising. Among them are creating partnerships with businesses who will provide the charity with funds in exchange for marketing opportunities, holding online charitable auctions, soliciting tribute gifts, creating online shopping malls, and engaging in search engine marketing—which involves placing advertisements on search engine Web sites that will appear on the search engine query results of those searching on a term related to the organization's mission. For each of these, there are for-profit application service providers (ASPs) to whom organizations can outsource all of the work. Many charities that engage in these strategies do this work in-house.

"Donate Here" Buttons

One obvious way charities have raised funds is by placing a "donate here" link on their Web site's pages. Clicking on the button links the donor to a secure page (i.e., where the information sent by the donor is encrypted). The page will have an online form that permits the donor to make a contribution and pay by credit card or through PayPal. It will typically also have information about other methods for making donations, such as a form that can be mailed or faxed to the organization, a telephone number to call during business hours to make donations, and information about planned giving. It may also have an offer for a modest "thank you" gift for donors, such as a mug with the organization's logo, a calendar, or a t-shirt.

The page should provide the donor information you need to process the donation, such as payment information, address, telephone number, and e-mail address. The page should also include information such as the organization's address and telephone number, which the donor needs to mail in a check or call in a donation. Even for those donors who do not choose to take advantage of making an online donation, it is useful to request those donors' e-mail addresses on the donation form.

Even for those organizations without merchant accounts to process credit cards or an application service provider who will (see Chapters 22 and 23), a clearly visible "donate here" button can link to a page that can be printed out and mailed with a check.

Cause-Related Marketing (CRM)

In her 1999 book, *Cause Related Marketing—Who Cares Wins*, Sue Adkins defined cause-related marketing as "commercial activity by which a business with a product, service or image to market builds a relationship with a cause or a number of causes for mutual benefit." While the term is relatively new, cause-related marketing efforts are often traced back to the 1960s, when the Insurance Company of America offered to make a donation to CARE for every insurance policy it sold. It reached prominence, however, by virtue of a well-publicized effort of American Express begun in 1983, when it pledged to donate a penny to the Statue of Liberty restoration fund for each time its card was used to make a purchase. According to press reports, this strategy was successful in increasing card use by 28% in a single year while raising substantial funds for the Statue of Liberty restoration project.

Since then, scores of mainstream charities have partnered with for-profits to exploit their brand names and raise funds. CRM is not without controversy. A joke continues to circulate about this exploitation: Some see it as "tainted" money, while others see it as " 't ain't enough." Regardless, CRM collaborations are raising millions of dollars for charities, including the American Lung Association, the American Cancer Society, and our personal favorite—the recipients of the $.10 General Mills donates to our kids' schools when we buy their cereal with the "Box Tops for Education" coupons on the top.

Involve celebrities in cause marketing efforts

In some cases, cause-related marketing can involve three partners—the organization, the corporation, and a celebrity spokesperson. The fundraiser is looking for a good synergy that may influence everyone. A celebrity may want to help a good cause, but may also appreciate positive publicity and a boost to his or her public image. The corporation is seeking increased revenues, brand loyalty, and a positive corporate image. The charity is looking for revenues and increased awareness among the general public.

Relationships built around cause related marketing can be long-term. A good Internet strategy can help cement and maintain the relationship over time. Via e-mail, Web pages, and electronic newsletters, charities can communicate with their stakeholders about these cause-related marketing opportunities.

Tribute Gifts

Tributes are memorial gifts given in the name of a loved one, usually shortly after they die. Tribute gifts encourage family and friends to join together, and sometimes hundreds participate. Most fundraising offices do not have staff dedicated solely to tributes. Instead, they are folded into the work of other fundraisers, either in major gifts, direct marketing, special events, or other specialist or generalist fundraisers.

We mention tributes here because they often provide a particular challenge. Managing tribute gifts can be highly labor intensive. Often, the size of the tribute is not proportional to the amount of work it requires. Gifts need to be meticulously tracked and recorded. Communications need to be sent to the donors and to the family, keeping them apprised of each contributor and the total.

Soliciting tribute gifts requires sensitivity

While tributes are always highly valued and appreciated, fundraisers can see them as difficult to manage and distracting to the more proactive fundraising they are charged with doing. Smoothly managing tribute funds often goes unpraised, while the slightest error draws unwelcome attention and consequences. What manager wants to hear a complaint from a family at this deeply emotional time of their lives?

Furthermore, fundraisers have long sensed the potential to increase fundraising around tributes, but struggle with how to sensitively make an approach. Many of the largest gifts honor a lost loved one, but tribute gifts happen when a family isn't focused on philanthropy. The timing for discussing what the family could do is the worst possible, usually taking place around the funeral of a loved one. And often the connection, if there was any, was with the deceased, making it hard to re-engage with family members after enough time has passed. So, too often, the family and the organization part ways after a tribute fund is established, despite the possibility of greater support.

One new approach by Our Lasting Tribute *(http://ourlastingtribute.com)* seems interesting to us and may represent a creative way to use the Internet to increase giving through a culture shift in traditional philanthropy. Although this company utilizes written materials in its approach, as well as the Internet, we will focus on the role of the Internet here.

Imagine that a family wishing to establish a tribute did so through the creation of a mini-campaign online. Automated technology can allow a donor to set up a Web page connected to your organization's. At this Web site, the family can put pictures and details about their loved one and why they have designated your organization as their charity of choice. Others visiting could add their own thoughts, poems, prayers, and memories, and at the same time pledge their support to the fund.

Set up an online tribute page

An online tribute page can alleviate many of the managerial headaches of tribute funds while maximizing their potential and respecting the needs of the family at a difficult time. Visitors automatically know the exact fundraising total. Family members can be informed of gifts through e-mail, and while some paper acknowledgment and receipt is still needed, e-mail versions can help cut down significantly on problems, perceived or real, and in doing so, reduce the number of complaints. Because this Internet approach encourages families to come back to the question of philanthropy later, after the most difficult and immediate emotionally absorbing event, it can help resolve some of the timing and appropriateness issues associated with fundraising for tributes.

In short, the Internet may hold a key to helping to unlock the untapped potential in tribute funds. It can help to empower families to do more and to take greater satisfaction in the impact they are having in the name of a loved one. This may in turn lead to more substantial relationships with such families, and in some cases may even transform them into lifelong supporters or major donors.

Personal Fundraising Pages

Donors, be they casual or wealthy philanthropists, are more likely to give when asked by someone they know, or to whom they have some connection. Colleges and universities ask current students to volunteer to solicit alumni. Charities provide their supporters with donor materials, and ask that they mail solicitations to their neighbors with a personalized appeal. Organizations hold galas and other special events and encourage the well-heeled to invite their friends to attend, or to make a contribution if they cannot be there in person.

The technology revolution has added new wrinkles to many existing fundraising techniques, eliminating some labor-intensive aspects, and streamlining invitations, donor processing, acknowledgment and substantiation, and collections. Technology has also spurred the development of new, creative fundraising models. Among them are charity malls, online auctions, "click-to-give," and electronic tribute gifts. Some of these models take advantage of using "personal" appeals of individuals to their friends, neighbors, and relatives, despite the fact that these appeals are highly automated and involve minimal labor on the part of either the charity or the solicitor.

One such model, the personal fundraising page, is rapidly catching on as an effective fundraising technique for charities on the cutting edge. It was successful recently in generating a donation from one of us, Gary Grobman, to a charity that he had not previously supported, the Leukemia and Lymphoma Society. Here's how it occurred.

ASPs can manage personal fundraising pages

In January 2005, Gary Grobman received an e-mail from a casual friend and neighbor, Shalom Staub of Harrisburg, PA. The message, not particularly long or detailed, said Shalom was participating in a 100-mile bike ride around Lake Tahoe in June to raise millions of dollars for this particular charity, and he was committed to raising $3,800 himself. He asked for Gary's participation by clicking on a link embedded in his e-mail. The link was to Shalom's personal fundraising page on Active.com. Gary complied, making a small donation online. Within minutes, he received two e-mails, one from the local chapter of the charity thanking him for his gift, and a receipt from the application service provider, Active.com. Apparently, scores of others responded to the appeal. In July, Gary received another "custom" e-mail from his cyclist friend saying that more than 1,900 bike riders raised $7 million, and that he more than met his fundraising goal. Attached to the e-mail were pictures of the event.

Active.com is a site managed by Active Giving Solutions, one of many application service providers who have developed software applications for personal fundraising pages. "We chose Active Giving Solutions for its customized technology and ability to integrate with our internal systems," said Richard J. Geswell, executive vice president, marketing and revenue generation for the Leukemia & Lymphoma Society, in a June 2005 press release. "We needed an easy tool to encourage and expand online fundraising by our participants. With Active's history of managing online transactions for participatory sports and its ties to the active lifestyle community, we're also looking forward to the additional exposure we gain through the partnership."

Perhaps the leader in the personal fundraising page model is Justgiving.com, with more than a million online donations received for its 1,200 nonprofit organization clients in the United States and Great Britain in its first five years of operations. A March 2005 survey of more than 1,000 Justgiving users validated the company's claim that making donations via this method is convenient, secure, and provides many other advantages over conventional methods of solicitation. One satisfied customer, Nathaniel Tilton, was diagnosed with Multiple Sclerosis in 2002. Rather than being impeded by his debilitating disease, he set a goal of running the Boston Marathon. Setting up his personal fundraising page on Justgiving.com, he raised more than $10,000 for his charity and finished the race in a respectable 4:43 on a hot day and challenging course (and likely passed Gary Grobman somewhere after Heartbreak Hill).

To Shalom Staub, this automated service relieved much of the anxiety and time involved in fundraising.

"Some people who were distant to me, or who only knew of me through a friend or family member, donated quite generously," he told Gary in an e-mail. "Others who are closer friends of mine, failed to, which was frustrating. The point is, you just never know who might feel a personal connection to your cause and who might be willing to make a contribution—so don't be afraid to ask!"

The technology made his plea for support painless at every step. The cost to charities is reasonable, with typical transaction fees being 5% or less of donations made through the Justgiving platform. From the home page *(http://www.justgiving.com)*, you can find the personal fundraising pages of some of the top fundraisers who use the service, and the names and comments of their donors.

Also started in 1999, CharityFocus *(http://www.charityfocus.org)* is a California-based 501(c)(3) that is run completely by volunteers. Its basic services, including setting up personal fundraising pages (see: *http://www.pledgepage.org),* are free, although there may be charges for any third-party costs the organization incurs on your behalf.

Third party application service providers are becoming more sophisticated in meeting the customized needs of charities that want to encourage their donors to set up personal fundraising pages. Typically, these pages permit the participant to upload pictures, provide progress reports on the amount of donations received, and have colorful graphics that illustrate how close the participant is to meeting his or her fundraising goal. Anecdotal evidence is strong that charities, participants, and donors alike appreciate the convenience of this online giving option. And it is another effective strategy charities can use to add to their donor lists and publicize the important mission they have, even among those who may not be interested in making a donation.

Tips:

- Purchase keywords from major search engines to attract donors to your Web site. Some organizations even purchase common misspellings of keywords!

- E-mail communications have a different tone than conventional letters. As one Direct Marketing manager shared, Web sites are all about the organization. The tone is focused on "we." Mail appeals, however, tend to start with "you," the donor. They bring the donor into the heart of the organization and reinforce the idea that the recipient is being asked to support "their" mission through "their" organization. Communications by e-mail, whether solicitations or not, should similarly focus on the donor.

- An element that may help in cultivating prospect relationships is to have a staff directory at your Web site, preferably including pictures. For one thing, just as major gift officers want to be able to read something about their donors and prospects, donors may want to investigate your leadership. Giving a bio online can help them do this.

- Make sure the option to give is pervasive in your site. The button to make a donation should exist on every page. Donors should not be required to leave what they are reading to navigate your site to find the place where a gift can be made.

Chapter 23
Nonprofit E-Commerce

Synopsis: Nonprofit organizations can effectively utilize the power of the Internet to sell goods and services and raise donations. Those who take advantage of this must consider issues such as privacy, security, customer service, order fulfillment, and payment processing. Many for-profit providers have developed online shopping malls, charity auction services, and other innovative business models. They are seeking partnerships with nonprofit organizations.

Introduction

The main focus of the previous chapter is how to use the Internet for fundraising, but I would be remiss if I did not cover a related topic that goes hand-in-hand with online philanthropy—the online marketing of an organization's goods and services. Many of the same techniques and strategies that are effective in generating donations online are equally effective in such marketing. And many of the tools are the same: a Web site, a merchant account to process payments, and a list of e-mail addresses of stakeholders, among others.

Nonprofits that don't take advantage of the natural marriage between e-philanthropy and e-commerce are missing out on an opportunity to generate income. And, after all, that is what fundraising is all about. Few organizations would engage in it if they didn't need revenue, and e-commerce offers opportunities to reduce the need for conventional fundraising.

The term *e-commerce* refers to business that is conducted electronically. It includes the marketing of goods and services, using the Internet to join an organization or subscribe to a publication, and automated customer service.

Technically, using the telephone to place an order also qualifies as e-commerce. So would using your debit card to make a purchase at your local convenience store. This chapter uses a narrower definition, becoming increasingly common in books and articles, to describe business conducted over the Internet. It focuses on how nonprofit organizations can use the Internet to increase membership, market products and services, and respond to customer inquiries and complaints.

Customer service? Marketing? Products? Why does any of this have anything to do with the nonprofit sector? Many of us lose sight of the fact that a nonprofit organization is a form of business. Nonprofits and for-profits have many things in common. Both need capital to launch their operations; cash flow to pay their bills in a timely manner; and revenues to pay for staff, supplies, utilities, rent, equipment, printing, and other goods and services. Charities typically receive revenues beyond what is gratuitously donated by the public, the business community, or foundations. For example, they sell services. It is typical that a third or more of the revenue from a social service agency comes from user fees. While many agencies charge on a sliding scale based on income, it is not unusual for them to charge a market rate to those who can afford to pay and use the surplus so generated to cross-subsidize those who cannot afford to pay the full costs of services.

The for-profit world has embraced e-commerce, recognizing that it is the future of how business-to-business (B2B) and business-to-consumer (B2C) purchasing will be conducted by millions, if not billions, of participants. As mentioned previously,, the Internet is becoming a convenient way for consumers to make retail purchases. According to the Goldman, Sachs & Co., Nielsen/

NetRatings and Harris Interactive's Holiday eSpending Report, holiday shoppers in the U.S. alone spent over $30 billion online during the 2006 holiday shopping season. Some of the spending was on goods offered by nonprofits, which recognize that shoppers feel good about sending presents that benefit a favorite charity. Overall, online retail sales reached $102.1 billion, a 24% increase over 2005, according to a report by the market research firm ComScore Networking. And I think we have just scratched the surface of online commerce's potential.

The business models and strategies used by for-profits can be adapted by nonprofits to generate revenue that will finance the expansion of nonprofit organizational programs and activities. At the very least, these techniques make it a bit easier to raise funds and thus reduce what must be one of the leading causes of stress and burnout among nonprofit executives and staff—the constant battle to raise dollars to balance organizational budgets.

For years, charities have generated income through a variety of programs and activities, such as selling newsletter subscriptions and other publications, collecting fees at conferences and workshops, operating thrift shops, conducting flea markets and running races, renting mailing lists, having auctions, scheduling fundraising dinners, and selling group outings to sporting events or theater performances.

The Web has made all of this easier, at least for many organizations, in two significant ways. First, it has provided organizations with a way to reach almost everyone, and to do this quickly and inexpensively. Using a combination of strategies, such as conventional mail, telephone, and media advertising, along with Web postings, mailing list postings, broadcast e-mail, and Web advertising, an organization can reach its target market and expand its reach. Second, organizations can utilize homebound volunteers (at one end of the scale) and pricey, professional "back end" providers (at the other end of the scale) to do much of the work.

As a result of e-mail, the Web, electronic mailing lists, and real-time chat, the velocity of business transactions has made a quantum leap. The Internet has salient advantages over conventional sales marketing, such as—

- Overall marketing and order processing costs are lower using the Web.
- Organizations can reach a global, targeted market virtually instantaneously.
- A Web-based "store" is open 24 hours/day, seven days/week, and always has free parking.
- The playing field is leveled between small organizations and those with many more resources.
- Business transactions can be consummated electronically without the need for expensive labor or intermediaries, such as brokers.
- Internet search engines and directories bring potential customers to organizations without unreasonably expensive marketing efforts.
- Customer service can be almost completely automated.
- "Back office" for-profit organizations with substantial expertise, labor, and sophisticated software will do the necessary work and make it appear to customers that the nonprofit organization is performing the work.

Build, Buy, or Rent

An organization's Web site is the most visible ingredient of its e-commerce strategy. Organizations have three basic choices in deciding which direction to go. Making the choice depends on factors such as—

- The amount of financial investment they are prepared to make
- The amount of staff time they are willing to devote to building, maintaining, and troubleshooting
- Whether they are comfortable with "off the rack" features or want a site that is state-of-the-art and custom-made
- Their comfort level with outside vendors having access to their financial transactions
- Whether they want to have complete control over their Web sites so, for example, they don't have to depend on private companies to update files when they have the time
- Whether they are comfortable with paying an outside firm based on the amount of revenue that is transacted on their sites
- The importance to them of having all visitors stay on their sites rather than being routed to a private vendor who may subject the visitor to advertising that the nonprofit organization cannot control, or may be inconsistent with the organization's values.

Build: Almost all of the tools a nonprofit needs to build a credible e-commerce site can be found using the links at sites such as *http://www.webmasterengine.com/* and *http://www.applytools.com/*. At these sites, you can find shopping carts, security software, domain name services, bank card services, associate programs, auction software, and Web site promotional services. Much of the software can be downloaded for free.

Buy: If an organization is as well-heeled as the Metropolitan Museum of Art *(http://www.metmuseum.org)*, it can afford to buy the very best. From the appearance of this site, one can expect this organization's investment in hiring a private firm to custom-design a Web site will result in financial dividends over the long run. This site was custom-designed by a locally-based firm, Icon Nicholson *(http://www.nny.com/nny/)*. Everything about this site is, pardon the pun, state of the art. Icon Nicholson is one of many commercial firms an organization can use if it chooses to "buy" a Web-based, e-commerce solution.

Rent: Application Service Providers (ASPs) are sprouting up and are advertising in the nonprofit national media about the availability of their services. In this context, renting involves purchasing services from a firm that will, for a monthly or annual fee, "rent" nonprofit organizations a customized e-commerce (and donation processing) site based on a template. The pages usually reside on the server of the ASP.

Setting Up an Online Store

If your organization sells products and services, you can enhance these sales by adding a secure online store to your organization's Web site. Before opening your store, think about costs, how you will handle online transactions, customer service issues, receipts and invoices, tax issues, and shipping.

Costs

What will an e-commerce-enabled Web site cost you? Surprisingly, less than you would think in terms of money (but likely more than you think in time). Here are some typical costs.

Web site hosting. Hosting services can be free for nonprofit organizations. A typical charge is $10/month. If you plan to take credit card information over the Internet, make sure that your Web host has the capability of supporting secure forms for this purpose. Secure online store hosting can be found for, perhaps, $30-$40 per month.

Domain Name Registration. This costs up to $35 annually, although there are discounts for pre-payment, and some registrars such as Go Daddy *(http://www.GoDaddy.com)* and Register.com *(http://www.register.com)* will register a name for $10 or even less.

Software. Web page construction software such as Microsoft's *FrontPage,* which includes templates for professionally designed pages, can be purchased for under $100 from discount software companies. Some software can be downloaded from the Internet for free. The latest versions of standard word processing programs are capable of saving files in HTML format. An HTML page can be constructed entirely by using Windows Notepad. Shopping carts can be free (often including advertising that may be unwanted or inappropriate) or cost thousands of dollars. Many accessories that are great on a Web site, such as counters, "send to a friend" forms, and language translators, are available for free. One emerging development is the availability of "open source" software, free for downloading in many cases, with hundreds of commercial and volunteer developers creating customized add-ons that are geared to the needs of charities (see Chapter 25).

Content. Most nonprofit organizations create their own Web site content. It is not unusual to make a purchase or two of graphics or photographs suitable for the Web, but there are many sources that provide these items for free.

Site Maintenance. It takes time to update Web sites and respond to feedback from visitors. Some organizations are large enough to hire full-time Webmasters to design and maintain sites, and some have the executive director or a technically savvy volunteer do this.

Hardware. If you have a remote virtual Web site host, you don't need anything more than your standard office computer and monitor, which you can buy for perhaps $1,000 for an entire system, including CPU with modem, monitor, and color printer.

SSL Certificate. This ensures that the customers' credit cards and other personal information is secure (see page 252)

Marketing. This can be your largest cost. Advertising the site through print publications, postcards, press releases, banner advertising on other sites, and similar strategies can bring more visitors, but can be expensive.

You can spend as little or as much as you want, but it is possible to obtain everything you need to set up an online store on your existing Web site for no cost. If you do not yet have a site (or even a computer), it is possible to buy everything you need for a one-time investment of $1,000, and a monthly payment of under $50.

Handling Online Financial Transactions

Qualifying for merchant status to accept popular credit cards such as Visa, MasterCard, American Express, and Discover is often routine. An organization typically approaches its bank to set up a merchant account. One can find hundreds, if not thousands, of financial institutions willing to establish merchant accounts on the Web. One way to find them is to search under the terms "credit cards" and "merchant accounts."

Startup fees, account maintenance fees, per transaction fees, and the bank's percentage of sales fee for processing each transaction varies by financial institution and may be negotiable.

Organizations will also need a system for transmitting the information about the transaction to the financial institution for processing—typically a terminal sold or leased by the financial institution—or computer software. The financial institution, within a few business days, credits the organization's account for the amount of the sale after deducting transaction charges. The card number, expiration date, and sales information is entered into the terminal or software (or transmitted through a real-time process, using an online ordering system), and the system verifies that the card is bona fide and the purchaser has not exceeded his or her credit limit. There is some paperwork involved, and occasionally a purchaser will challenge a charge, which can result in a loss of time and revenue, even if the charge is legitimate. On the other hand, entrepreneurial nonprofit organizations may lose out on revenue opportunities unless they satisfy the expectations of their customers by offering online credit card purchases.

An alternative to setting up a merchant account for credit cards is to utilize the services of a third-party payment processor that will accept credit cards for you using a secure, online platform. One such popular provider, PayPal *(https://www.paypal.com)*, not only provides this service but also gives access to tools that you can use to build your online store, such as shopping carts, invoices, and shipping/tracking management services. From the home page, click on *Merchant Tools* for details about these services. There are no setup fees to establish an account as a merchant. PayPal charges a fee of from 2.2% to 2.9% (depending on sales volume) plus 30 cents per transaction. There are additional fees for foreign currency transactions. More than 155 million individuals have PayPal accounts. The company was purchased by eBay in 2002 and is quickly becoming the standard for making and receiving online payments.

In June 2005, PayPal established a new system, Website Payments Pro, to accept credit cards directly on your site without having a traditional merchant account. Using PayPal's Web site, you can input credit card information securely and obtain approvals, with funds transferred from the purchaser to your PayPal account. The transaction appears to be a routine credit card transaction to the customer. As someone who has utilized this "virtual terminal" in my own business, I can attest that it compares favorably to more traditional payment services.

Customer Service

Depending on what products and services are offered, many of the issues relating to customer service will be the same for a nonprofit as for a for-profit organization. Organizations will need to have policies for, and routines for, processing returns, exchanges, refunds, and shipping.

One obvious disadvantage of shopping over the Internet is that shoppers cannot touch and feel the product, or try it on or try it out. People are more willing to make purchases over the Internet when they feel that they can return the products if they are not completely satisfied. A refunds and returns policy should be posted on your site, and it should be a more liberal policy than one would expect to find at the local mall. This is good business practice; nonprofits certainly don't want to alienate a customer who is also a donor or potential donor. Among the issues that should be addressed are:

1. Will refunds be given in cash or credit for a future purchase?
2. How much time is permitted to elapse before returns will not be accepted?
3. Can returns be made unconditionally, or only for defective products?
4. Is there a restocking fee?
5. Must the product be returned in salable condition in the original packaging?
6. Will shipping and handling also be refunded, or only the product purchase price?
7. Will the organization pay for shipping back returns?
8. Will certain products not be returnable (such as publications, electronics, or jewelry)?

Receipts and Invoices

Products should be shipped with a receipt if pre-paid, or an invoice if payment is due. If they were not prepaid, the invoice should state the terms of payment, such as when the bill is due, and the percentage added to the bill per month for any outstanding balance. The receipt should include the name of the purchaser, the name of the organization, the description of the product(s), the price of each purchase, and the amount of tax, shipping, and handling. Generic accounting software such as Quickbooks, Quicken, MYOB Accounting, or Peachtree provides forms for standard invoices and receipts.

Collecting Taxes

Only the states of Alaska, Delaware, Montana, New Hampshire, and Oregon do not have a state sales and use tax. The sales tax applies to sales made within a state to a purchaser from that same state. The use tax applies to sales of products bought in one state and taken into another. The use tax is intended to be paid by the purchaser and goes to the purchaser's state treasury, although this requirement is rarely, if ever, enforced. Generally, organizations are obligated to collect sales and use taxes on sales they make to customers within their own states.

In November 2004, the Congress extended its moratorium against Internet sales taxes for an additional three years. Sales taxes still must be collected for intrastate purchases in states with sales taxes, although enforcement of this requirement is spotty. Even if an organization is tax exempt, most states still require nonprofit organizations to collect sales taxes on sales they make to customers within the state.

Typically, states require organizations to obtain a sales tax license, and to transmit the collected taxes to the state using a provided form. It is advisable to check with a reputable local business organization, such as the Chamber of Commerce, to find out what the requirements are for collecting and transmitting state sales taxes in a particular state before engaging in the sale of goods and services there.

Shipping and Handling

Organizations need to decide how much they will charge for shipping and handling and display that information prominently on the site. Some shopping cart software provides for letting the customer decide how the product is to be shipped—automatically adjusting the amount for shipping and handling (such as by using a database provided by UPS or other shippers), based on how much the organization wants to add over the actual cost. They can charge a flat fee for shipping, charge by weight, charge by the number of products ordered, or provide for free shipping if the order exceeds a certain amount. Organizations should also consider policies with respect to out-of-country sales, which raise issues with respect to payment, shipping, and customs duties.

Online Auctions

With only a modest investment, substantial funds can be raised by offering goods and services to the public using online auction software, or using the services of a provider that administers online auctions. Charities can often obtain items, such as donated artifacts from celebrities, that are valuable to millions who may never have heard of the charity or may not specifically care about its mission. They will make a bid because of their interest in the items themselves.

Here are some online charity auction successes:

- A September 2007 online charity auction sponsored by Singapore Airlines raised $1.3 million, with the proceeds divided up among four charities, including Doctors Without Borders. The airline auctioned off trips on its new Airbus.

- Frederick's of Hollywood sponsored a November 2005 online auction of corsets designed and autographed by celebrities, with proceeds benefiting the Tuberous Sclerosis Alliance.

- In October 2005, the U.S. computer and video game industry raised a record $1 million to support organizations that improve the welfare of America's children from a combination of its annual black-tie dinner and an online auction.

- An X-Files online fan club raised more than $100,000 for charity. The Gillian Anderson Web Site *(http://www.gilliananderson.ws)* scheduled its eighth annual online auction in 2005, raising $23,000 (read an account of the auction at: *http://www.nfinc.org/ nfinkSumFall05.pdf)*. Its previous auctions raised a total of $600,000 for Anderson's favorite charity, Neurofibromatosis, Inc.

- TV personality Ellen DeGeneres raised $25,000 for Peace Games by auctioning off a customized Vespa.

- General Motors raised more than $137,000 for the SAE Foundation for Science and Technology Education by auctioning the second Chevy SSR off its production line.

- The *Today Show* raised $83,000 for Project A.L.S. by selling its *Green Room Book* on eBay.

- The National Hockey League Players' Association and National Hockey League online jersey auction raised more than $335,000 in November 2005 to support those affected by Hurricane Katrina. Among the jerseys bid on were those of Pittsburgh Penguins rookie phenom Sidney Crosby, worn in Crosby's second NHL game, which fetched almost $20,000.

You can find a listing of some current charitable online auctions at: *http://www01.charityfolks.com*

Simply searching on the term "online charity auction" using the Google search engine returns almost 100,000 hits.

There are a number of advantages of having an online auction compared to conducting an auction in real time.

- You can auction off an almost infinite number of items.
- The auction can last for hours or months.
- Everyone can participate, even if they would not have found the time convenient for a conventional auction.
- People can participate from all over the world.
- The design and administration of the online auction can be performed online, providing home-bound volunteers, or those busy during traditional business or meeting hours, with an opportunity to volunteer their services.
- Turnkey operations (see below) abound to assist you in startup.

Consider ASPs to manage the "backoffice"

Scores of "Dot Com" for-profit companies are competing for the right to host charitable auctions, and many provide these services free-of-charge to charities. Each for-profit host is different, and charities should be choosy and informed about the advantages and disadvantages of each. Some hosts, such as Yahoo!, provide their "backoffice" services transparently, so donors can visit the charity's Web site and access all the information they need to participate. This requires the charity to actively generate traffic to its auction site, arrange item categories, and make sure the items auctioned get to where they need to be. Other hosts can provide a soup-to-nuts menu of services, but generate Web hits for the commercial partner (and its advertisers) rather than the charity.

Consider MissionFish to set up your online charity auction

One application service provider that is gaining a reputation as the leader in online charity auctions is MissionFish (http://www.missionfish.com). MissionFish, formed in 2000, is a program of the Points of Light Foundation. Charities can register and run a charity auction using the tools on this site in the same way that members of the public do.

In November 2003, MissionFish launched a program that permits the more than 135 million eBay users to donate from 10-100% of their proceeds from items sold on eBay to a favorite 501(c)(3) organization. The charity must register to be eligible to receive these donations, but registration is free. According to the Web site, more than 2,700 nonprofits have registered to benefit. As of the end of 2005, MissionFish charged a processing fee of about $3 per donation plus a 2.9% fee for credit card processing. The fee is waived up to an annual aggregate of $2 million annually for certain transactions when the seller agrees to submit at least 90% of the purchase price to a designated charity.

Participating charities have online tools to review the types of goods being auctioned off. Why is this a useful feature? As one MissionFish press release points out, a charity that is dedicated to the protection of animals wouldn't want to be the beneficiary of an auction of fur coats! Charities benefit not only from the donation, but also from the exposure of having their names listed at the auction site. There are administrative fees involved for processing, but it is possible for a charity to encourage its stakeholders to participate in this form of auction, which requires no work for the charity other than cashing the checks.

Reading some of the online testimonials (http://www.missionfish.org/About/ aboutwhatpeoplesay.jsp) provides some ideas for charities that want to take advantage of this service. One charity executive writes that some in kind gifts were actually "unkind gifts," and MissionFish converted these unwanted goods into cash. A thrift store operator found that the revenue from the sale of one particular good online was scores of times more than what would have been received from a store sale.

Charity auction tips

What does it cost to run an online charity auction? With a bit of ingenuity, a charity auction can be administered using eBay for just a few dollars.

Here are some of our suggestions for running an online charity auction through a commercial provider.

- If you have the expertise, keep the portal for your organization's charity auction on your own Web site, creating an online community and keeping hits from potential donors on your site, not that of a commercial provider.

- Take pictures of the items you have for auction and post these online.

- Don't restrict publicity of your auction to online notices, electronic mailing lists, and e-mail. Use PSAs, newsletters, your local newspapers, snail mail postcards, and conventional publicity flyers.

- Send e-mail thank-yous to those who are the successful bidders. Mail out the items to successful bidders promptly, along with the required substantiation letter.

- If you are contracting out your charity auction to an online commercial service, ask lots of questions. Know exactly what your commitments and responsibilities are with respect to the agreement or contract. Direct your questions not only to the auction staff, but to other charities that have used the commercial host.

- Don't commit your organization to pay anything for participating unless you are sure that such payments are appropriate and reasonable. Many host companies do not charge anything up front to the charity, instead making their profit on a commission based on the proceeds of the auction. You will have to expend some resources to change your organization's Web site to accommodate the auction and send out promotional materials. If up front fees are charged, make sure these services are not typically provided elsewhere for free.

- Understand how and when your organization will receive its payments from successful bidders.

In summary, charity auctions are a great strategy for generating significant donations and getting people involved in a charity and educated about its mission and focus. But it takes some work and creativity.

Online Shopping Malls

Just imagine. Instead of going to their favorite mall to purchase a national brand product, your charity's friends and supporters go online and visit a Web site that charges them the customary (and often discounted) price, and funnels a percentage of the purchase price directly to your charity. Their purchases from retailers and discounters such as Toys R Us, Amazon.com, and Sharper Image are delivered on their doorstep within a day or two, and your charity receives a check aggregating all of these donations, no strings attached.

This is not the future.

This scenario is occurring thousands of times each day on scores of Web sites, and the number of such transactions is expanding exponentially. Online retailing accounted for just .5% of purchases made in 1998, but climbed to 1.2% in one year. David Schatsky, senior vice president of research at JupiterResearch, reported that for 2005, U.S. online retail sales would reach $79 billion, versus $66 billion in 2004.

Online shopping malls compete

Intense competition is just beginning among for-profit entrepreneurs who seek to obtain the cooperation of charities in directing traffic to their sites. We think that this development is very positive for both charities and consumers, although both need to be aware of limitations and potential problems associated with this trend.

Many in the charitable community have had a love-hate relationship with the private sector. We benefit from the generosity of grants and donations from capitalist enterprises, while at the same time we denigrate the exploitation and lack of altruism inherent in rampant commercialism and consumerism. After all, many charities (and government programs, as well) were initiated because of the failure of the market to address many human needs.

Some of the entrepreneurs who have initiated these collaborative programs with charities have a genuine desire to parlay their commercial success into socially responsible activities that benefit society. And others, no doubt, cynically recognize that they can generate revenue by serving as middlemen and reaching a new market of consumers attracted by the incentive of helping their favorite charity. Regardless of the reasons motivating these "dot-com" companies, the advent of e-commerce has seen a proliferation of for-profit Web sites geared toward combining the joys of shopping with the imperative of helping the less fortunate. They are probably here to stay.

Among the prominent charity-shopper sites are (in alphabetical order):

Benevolink *(http://www.benevolink.com/)*
Charitymall.com *(http://www.charitymall.com)*
GreaterGood.com *(http://www.greatergood.com)*
iGive.com *(http://www.igive.com)*
Mycause.com *(http://www.mycause.com)*

Search Engine Marketing (SEM)

Studies show that 80-85% of initial visits to a Web site begin with a query to a search engine. This astounding statistic illustrates how important it is for charities to build and develop a successful search engine marketing and optimization campaign, which includes placing metatags in HTML to enhance search engine results placement, purchasing paid ads from search engines based on keywords you select, having lots of links to your site (which can affect search engine ranking), and adding new content to increase traffic to your site as much as possible.

In March 2003, there was an interesting article in the *Chronicle of Philanthropy* about a partnership between the international aid organization, Childreach, and the producer of the movie *About Schmidt*. The movie was about a retired insurance executive who "sponsored" a seven-year-old child from Tanzania with his donations to Childreach. The article documented some of the steps taken by the charity to exploit the publicity generated by the movie to increase its fundraising—including signing a contract with the producers that provided benefits to both parties.

Buried deep in the article is a lesson that every charity should consider when developing its Internet marketing plan. While Childreach engaged in substantial direct mail and telephone soliciting coordinated with the message in this Oscar-winning movie, a competing charity found a way to reach potential donors who had an interest in the movie. Children International purchased Google AdWords on the popular search engine. When people searched on the term "About Schmidt," the search engine provided a link to Children International, urging them to "make a difference" by sponsoring a child.

For-profit businesses have been engaging in search engine marketing (SEM) strategies routinely for several years. But it has been only recently that charities have recognized the return on their investment provided by establishing partnerships with companies such as Google *(http:// www.google.com)*, Yahoo! Search Marketing *(http://searchmarketing.yahoo.com/index.php)* and Enhance *(http://www.enhance.com)*.

> *Even common misspellings pay dividends*

The December 26, 2004 tsunami disaster mobilized scores of international relief organizations to implement strategies to take advantage of the outpouring of donors and potential donors to do something fast to help. Within hours of the disaster, using Google to search on the term "Tsunami" resulted in user screens showing paid links to organizations such as World Vision, UNICEF-USA, Save the Children, and the American Red Cross. We even found paid advertisements for Direct Relief and MercyCorps when we intentionally put the misspelled word "sunami" into the search engine form.

What are the results? Rick Christ of NPAdvisors.com, an online fundraising consulting group, reports that—

"One of our clients got to work with us Sunday, Dec. 26 (2004), even though they were also being hit with a one-foot snowstorm near them. They authorized a keyword buy and began working on an e-mail to sponsors. The keywords produced over 34,000 visits to their tsunami relief page between December 27 and January 18 and together with the e-mail they have raised about ten times their normal December amount online, mostly in the last few days of the month. The keywords have helped generate over 600 new online donors to their cause."

How do you start an SEM campaign? Here are three basic steps.

Step 1: Research the sites that offer this service. While Google and YAHOO! Search Marketing dominate this industry, competing programs are offered by Enhance *(http://www.enhance.com/)*, Kanoodle *(http://www.kanoodle.com)*, and FindWhat *(http://www.findwhat.com)*. There is minimal standardization on how these programs work. Google, for example, lets you set what you are willing to pay based on a daily budget and a maximum cost per click (CPC)— the cost the advertiser pays to the site publisher each time a visitor clicks on the advertiser's ad—and partners with AOL, CompuServe, and other high-traffic search engines.

Yahoo! Search Marketing requires a monthly budget and allows you to place a bid on any keyword, but sets a minimum price of ten cents/click-through—defined as when a Web page visitor clicks on an ad and that visitor's browser exits the page on which the ad appeared and enters the Web site linked to in the ad—and also sets a maximum bid price. You can use a tool on the site to search on a prospective keyword and see what the current bid is. Its main search engine clients are its parent company, YAHOO!, Lycos, and Alta Vista.

Step 2: *Identify the keywords that are the most likely to help search engines find you.* These are for use in metatags—which are hidden HTML tags containing the page's title, description, and keywords that are used by search engines to index pages but don't appear on the Web page—and the keywords that will help those who use search engines find your site. Your brainstorming needs to focus on the most likely words people will use in their search engine submission, considering that they may not have heard of your organization, and their initial search may not be particularly targeted to finding you, but rather some general information about something directly or indirectly related to your organization's mission.

Step 3. *Do the preliminary work required before making the purchase.* This includes preparing a budget, identifying the keywords to purchase, redesigning your site, if necessary, and making sure the pages linked to by the ad are consistent with the advertising copy in the ads.

Step 4: *Make the purchase.* Major SEM sites provide clear instructions, making it easy to begin your marketing effort virtually instantaneously, provided you have a major credit card.

Can't afford to buy an ad? Google has established a program called "Google Grants" to provide free AdWords to 501(c)(3) tax-exempt organizations that share Google's values, particularly those with missions in the areas of science and technology, education, global public health, environment, youth advocacy, and the arts. Google Grants makes its awards to about 300 organizations each quarter, and each receives at least three months of this in-kind donation. To apply, you can fill out an online form available at: *http://www.google.com/grants*. Organizations will need to provide sample keywords, ad copy, and a statement of how they will benefit from their participation. Organizations already participating in the Google AdSense program are ineligible. Is this an effective strategy? According to the Google Grants site *(http://www.google.com/grants)*, The U.S. Fund for UNICEF's e-commerce site increased its sales 43% a year after receiving one of these grants.

Search engine marketing is only one of many emerging, innovative strategies to increase your organization's reach to potential donors. While it does, in most cases, require some up front investment, the ROI is among the best of any that can be found in the toolbox of the online fundraiser.

Affiliate Marketing

New business models have emerged that permit nonprofit organizations to take advantage of technology and raise funds that would not have come their way otherwise. Even if your organization does not sell products or services of its own, you can generate revenue by marketing products and services of others through "affiliate" or "associate" programs.

The "affiliate" model was pioneered by Amazon.com. The Seattle-based company simply announced to the world that by placing specially coded links on your Web site, you can earn a commission on purchases of books, CDs, DVDs, videos, electronics, software, video games, toys, or home improvement items that are generated by those links.

Joining the Amazon Associates program involves visiting the Amazon.com site, clicking on the "Join Associates" link at the bottom of the home page, electronically submitting a form provided on the site (after reading and agreeing to the operating agreement), and using tools provided on the site to set up your links to Amazon.com and promote products. Each link has your Associate ID code embedded in it, so when someone buys something from Amazon.com through a link on your site, your organization gets a commission, which is paid monthly by Amazon.com.

More than 1,000,000 Web sites have become Amazon.com associates. For nonprofits and for-profits alike, this simple, yet revolutionary, business model is generating valuable revenue without the need for any investment or exposure to risk.

Similarly, affiliate programs exist for many other online retailers and online services. Your organization can become an affiliate of eBay, Buy.com, allPosters.com, or CareerBuilder.com, for example. Typically, if a site offers an affiliate program, there will be a link for it somewhere near the bottom of the page, leading to an explanation of how to join and how the program works.

When considering joining an affiliate marketing program, think about how the site you will be affiliating with fits with your organization's mission, as well as how you will incorporate the affiliate program into your own site. For example, if you are joining an affiliate program of an online bookstore (such as Amazon.com), will you place reviews and links to carefully selected books that are in line with your mission, or will you set up a complete store where your site's visitors can buy anything that is available in the affiliated store, encouraging your visitors to do all their shopping through your site, as a way of supporting your organization? Each of these approaches has its pros and cons.

Let's say your organization is an animal shelter. Using the first approach, you can create links to (and perhaps reviews of) books on animal care. This will keep the focus on your mission and promote products that your site's visitors are likely to be interested in. You can target these links to the visitor's interests, so a person who is reading an article about German shepherds will see a link on that page to a book on German shepherds. The conversion rate (from seeing the link to clicking on it to purchasing the item) on such links will be higher than that for random links that are unrelated to your site's content. You will need to monitor the links to make sure that they are up-to-date and the items are still available for purchase.

Using the second approach, you can build a store on your site using an automated data feed (if one is provided), and then "educate" your visitors to "support this site" by shopping there. If your visitors get in the habit of going through your site to make their purchases, you can do well with this method. They may buy animal care books, or they may buy office products, or both—either way, you will earn the commission. However, keep in mind that you do not have complete control over the items that are shown through the data feed, and some items may not be in keeping with the mission or character of your organization.

Advertising

Another way you can generate revenue from your organization's Web site is to allow advertisements to be placed on it. The quickest and easiest way to earn money through advertising is to join Google Adsense (or one of its competitors, such as Yahoo! Publisher Network). Once you join, you will be able to log in to Google's Adsense site and generate HTML code to put on your site. Then ads will begin to appear on your site that correspond with key words in the content of your site. Google will send you a monthly check for a portion of the advertising revenue from these ads.

One downside to this is that you do not have complete control over the content of the ads that appear on your site. You can filter the ads to a certain extent, but it will take some staff or volunteer time to monitor the ads to make sure they are appropriate.

Instead of or in addition to this approach, your organization may decide to sell classified and/or banner advertising directly on your site. You will need to develop a policy stating what types of ads you will accept, your advertising rates, and so forth. And you will need to develop a "media kit" telling advertisers the benefits to them of advertising on your site, the procedure for placing an ad, and how to make payment. If your site is a popular one that is getting a significant amount of traffic in your niche, this can be an excellent way to use your site to generate revenue.

Miscellaneous Issues

Privacy

Despite a global reputation for having an entrepreneurial spirit, our culture in North America also is one that fosters a strong and vibrant voluntary sector, compared to our friends in Europe, Africa, and Asia. As a people, we also value our privacy.

The advance of technology has placed privacy issues front and center on the public policy agenda. Nonprofit organizations are using the Internet to sell goods and services and seek donations. This involves the exchange of credit card information and other data, such as private telephone numbers and addresses, and standard demographic data.

Organizational memberships are solicited online, and the data collected via electronic forms can often be aggregated in databases that are easily shared. Organizations are being asked to collect more and more data to share with funders to justify the value of grants and donations. It is not unusual for charities to be approached by political campaigns, telemarketers, and direct mail solicitors offering to buy organizational mailing lists for a lucrative fee.

Consumers are wary about sharing personal information on the Web, even with trusted organizations. They should be; information shared with a nonprofit organization with which they have a relationship could be inappropriately shared with another organization and be subject to abuse. It is not unusual for savvy consumers with privacy concerns to look on a Web site for the organization's privacy policy, and many sophisticated providers of Web content place their privacy policy on the site in a prominent place.

One feature of the Internet that has contributed to fears about privacy violation is the cookie. The cookie feature was created by Netscape as part of its browser. Cookies are ASCII files (plain text) that can be created and accessed by a Web site visited by the browser. The file is resident in the browser directory, so if the Web site visitor decides to use another browser, the cookie won't be readable by the originating Web site. The visitor can also delete cookies or disable the browser feature that creates them. The benefit of the feature is that the cookie file lets the site being visited know something about visitors and their interests by accessing it, and it permits the site to provide custom-designed information based on the cookie file. Having a cookie can save a lot of time and keystrokes, because the site will "recognize" the visitor as a repeat visitor and "remember" what he or she did on previous visits. The downside is that the visitor may not wish to share this information and may not even know that cookie files are being created.

Many see the Internet culture as a threat to privacy concerns. Obviously, nonprofits and for-profit organizations alike accrue substantial benefit in collecting and sharing data about their Web site visitors. But is the cost to society of unfettered data collection and dissemination too high? Should the responsibility for regulating privacy on the Internet fall chiefly to state governments or the federal government? Is self-regulation by the industry a reasonable alternative to legislation? Should Web sites require that visitors prospectively "opt-in" by expressly pre-authorizing the site to collect data, or merely to "opt-out" to prohibit data from being collected (with the "default" decision being that permission is assumed to be granted)?

Regulators at the state and federal levels are wrestling with how to strike a balance between the legitimate needs of organizations to collect data and forestalling unwarranted intrusion into our personal lives. Nonprofit organizations have a stake in the outcome of this debate. On one hand, our sector benefits from collecting and sharing data. On the other hand, we are often the only organized advocate for vulnerable and exploited populations.

It is not yet clear the direction the online privacy debate is headed. But the trend is for those who collect information from Web site visitors, including nonprofit organizations, to develop and publish a policy stating how this information is used. If you are using your Web site to collect information of any kind from your site's visitors, a written, formal privacy policy is becoming a necessity, if only to protect your organization from potential legal liability.

A Web site privacy policy generally includes—

1. *What information provided by Web site visitors will be shared with others, and under what circumstances.* For example, many organizations sell or rent their mailing lists and databases.

2. *What information will not be shared with others.* For example, a telephone number may be required for credit card verification. While many business organizations will request the telephone number for that purpose (or to communicate with the customer in the event there is a problem with the transaction), they will not release the customer's telephone number to outsiders.

3. *What customers can do to keep their names, addresses, and other data confidential.* This may entail simply checking a box on an electronic form.

4. *What information is being collected without the direct knowledge of the Web site visitor.* The use of cookies has become a standard practice, and a privacy policy should explain how cookies will be used.

   Examples of privacy policies

Almost all of the reputable nonprofit organizations on the Web have a privacy policy. For example, you can examine the policy of the Metropolitan Museum of New York (*http://www.metmuseum.org*). From the home page, click on "Met Store." From the menu on the left of the screen, near the bottom, click on "customer service." Then click on "online privacy" from the menu in the middle of the screen. Then click on "privacy policy" on the middle of the screen. This policy is comprehensive and will provide you with plenty of issues to think about when designing your online privacy policy.

For an example of a privacy policy for a membership organization's Web site, and one that is more accessible from the home page, surf to the site of the National Association of Attorneys General (NAAG): *http://www.naag.org*. Click on "privacy policy" from the menu at the bottom of the page. This organization has formulated a draft set of principles on Internet privacy, and thus would be expected to have a privacy policy that is based on those principles. As you might imagine, the draft NAAG principles are not supported by prominent members of the Online Privacy Alliance, a coalition that includes Microsoft, IBM, AOL Time Warner, and scores of other associations and individual companies (see the Alliance's own privacy policy at: *http://www.privacyalliance.org/ resources/ppguidelines.shtml*)

   Protection of Customer Data

Virtually every survey has demonstrated the pervasive fear consumers have with respect to providing their credit card numbers over the Internet. The concern that unscrupulous merchants (or those who pretend to be merchants) will abuse the credit card information is mostly unfounded; even if this happened (and it does occasionally), there are limits on the amount of loss the consumer sustains (typically $50), and there is typically no exposure to loss if the problem is reported promptly. The principal concern tends to be that hackers will somehow tap into the transaction and steal the credit card data. It is probably a more likely occurrence that credit card data is stolen simply as a result of people, both merchants and consumers, being careless with the paper records of these transactions. Nonetheless, a lot of effort has gone into making financial transactions over the Internet safe by encrypting (that is, disguising) the data so that only the intended sender and receiver can read it.

While there are several protocols for encryption, the industry standard for e-commerce has become Secure Sockets Layer, or SSL. It uses what's known as a public and private key system and the use of a digital certificate.

Without having both the public and private keys, a message that is encrypted looks like gobbledygook. Each person has his or her own private key, which is kept very secret, and a public key, which is shared with everyone. The messages cannot be read without having both. Thus, if you send an encrypted message to someone and use their public key, you cannot even read the encrypted message yourself because you don't have access to their private key.

Certification/Authentication

If you are serious about accepting credit cards on your Web site, you should obtain an SSL certificate from a certifying authority to assure donors that you are who you say you are and your server is secure. A donor can see a lock icon on the browser that indicates that the page is encrypted. Most people will refuse to send their credit card information over the Internet unless you have a valid certificate. Server certificates are available commercially from many different companies, and the cost varies.

The most widely used authority in the United States is VeriSign *(http://www.verisign.com/)*. Competing companies include Thawte Consulting *(http://www.thawte.com)*, and Entrust *(http://www.entrust.com)*. One recurring problem is that the certificates may not work on all browsers, so make sure to inquire about this.

You can have all of the sophisticated encryption systems in place, but it won't do any good if you keep the printouts of credit card numbers on your desk, or put them in an accessible file on your computer that is not password-protected. Take reasonable precautions to keep your customer data protected.

Firewalls

Firewall is a term that describes Internet security software that controls access between two or more computer networks (e.g., your organization's computer network and the Internet), allowing approved traffic in and out through a secure gateway. Firewall software can be downloaded free from the Internet or can be obtained for thousands of dollars. See *http://www.interhack.net/pubs/fwfaq/* for a complete guide to firewalls.

Tips

- Read ***Fundraising Online: Using the Internet to Raise Serious Money for Your Nonprofit Organization*** **(White Hat Communications, $29.95) for a** comprehensive guide to using the Internet for fundraising and selling goods and services.

- Look at the Web sites of similar organizations to see how they are harnessing the power of the Internet.

- Make sure you are comfortable with the legal ramifications of e-commerce applications, such as privacy, security, copyright, and tax collection, before launching an e-commerce initiative.

Chapter 24
Forming and Running A Coalition

Synopsis: Many nonprofit organizations form and participate in coalitions to accomplish objectives that would be difficult to achieve by themselves. There are significant advantages and considerations to forming a coalition, and the fact that they flourish is indicative of their value. This chapter discusses the pros and cons of creating and/or participating in coalitions.

Introduction

The tapestry of advocacy efforts at the international, national, state, and local levels is replete with collaborative initiatives that bring together diverse interests to accomplish a common goal. As a nonprofit organization seeks to accomplish its mission, its leadership often finds the value of creating formal and informal partnerships among like-minded organizations. As in any endeavor, there are traps and pitfalls in creating and running a coalition.

While it is often said that "two heads are better than one," it is equally rejoined that "too many cooks spoil the broth." Both of these clichés are often equally valid when applied to a coalition, and it is important for an organizational leader to be able to assess which one applies predominantly before embarking on coalition-forming.

The Coalition

A coalition is a group of diverse organizations that join together to accomplish a specific objective that is likely to be achieved more quickly and effectively than if the organizations acted independently. There are many types of coalitions, and the structure is often dictated by political as well as financial considerations. The prototypical coalition involving state government issues starts with a convener coalition partner who has identified an issue, usually of direct importance to the convener's organizational membership.

The convener then "rounds up the usual suspects" by soliciting membership in the coalition from constituencies that will participate in the coalition. He or she schedules periodic meetings of the coalition at which members share information about the issue and develop a strategy to accomplish a specific goal of the coalition that, as is often the case, is the passage of legislation to solve the problem. It is not unusual for the coalition to continue even after the legislation it focused upon is enacted into law.

Structures of Coalitions

- *Formal organization.* Some coalitions structure formally, creating a distinct nonprofit corporate structure, such as a 501(c)(3), which will permit the coalition to hire staff, seek tax-deductible contributions from the public, rent office space, and have a system of governance that parallels, in many respects, the constituent organizations that comprise the coalition. Obviously, one would not seek to create such a complex legal entity if the objective of the coalition was to be achieved in the short term. It is not atypical for a new 501(c)(3) coalition staff to spend much of its efforts raising funds to keep it in business rather than focusing on the actual mission of the coalition. Even if funding is stable, many formal coalitions spend an inordinate amount of time on intra-organizational issues, compared to achieving their stated purposes.

- *Semi-formal coalition.* These coalitions consist of organizations that have some financial resources themselves and are able to fund the activities of the coalition. While not incorporated as separate legal entities, these coalitions nevertheless may have office space and staff. The office space may be provided as an in-kind contribution from one of the coalition members, and the staff may or may not be employees of one of the member organizations.

- *Informal coalition.* Most coalitions are informal, with a convener organizational leader, but with no dedicated organizational staff or budget, or separate bank account. The convener organization convenes the coalition, sends out meeting notices, holds the meeting in the convener's office, and staffs the coalition as a part of its routine organizational duties. Costs can be shared among coalition members, and the convener duty can be rotated among members. In general, member organizations are not bound by the positions taken by the coalition.

- *Group networks.* A group network is a type of informal coalition that has been formed to serve an information-sharing function with less emphasis on coordinated action. These networks have no staff, no budget, take no positions, and are useful in raising the consciousness of participants about a particular issue or set of issues. These networks also are valuable in bringing people together to "network," and to build trust among organizational leadership. While efforts to coordinate action on an issue are often the result of a network-based coalition, the network itself often does not take a formal role in the coordination; rather, the discussions among the participants in and after the meeting result in the synergistic effects of the network.

Advantages of Forming a Coalition

- Coalitions focus attention among the media, opinion leaders, and those with advocacy resources on a specific issue. Any organization, no matter how large and powerful, has a limited ability to get its message across to the public, government officials, and the media. Building a coalition is an effective strategy to call attention to an issue, since messages not perceived to be important when heard from one organization may be considered important from another.

- Coalitions bring together experts on a particular issue. A convener of a coalition often has a burning desire to solve a particular public-policy problem and has well-developed organizational skills, but may lack the technical expertise to develop the solution. Creating a coalition is a strategy to bring together experts in the field who collegially can participate in developing a solution.

- Coalitions provide a forum to resolve turf issues and to limit destructive competition. Very few important public policy issues are so narrow that a single organization is the only one with a direct interest in their resolution. Virtually any public policy issue, particularly one that influences human services, affects a broad range of advocacy organizations, whether it impinges on children, schools, the environment, business, the disabled, or the aged. Trying to solve a problem without the "buying in" of key decision-makers is a recipe for disaster. Coalitions provide the framework for obtaining the cooperation of opinion makers who otherwise would be threatened by any effort to change public policy that violates their political turf.

- Coalitions provide credibility to an issue and to the convener organization. One obvious application of this principle is the effort, often unsuccessful, of various extremist organizations not accepted in society, such as the KKK, to try to form or participate in coalitions that have a goal consistent with a community consensus. Another principle is that organizational messages viewed as self-interest are viewed negatively. When coalitions include organizations that are viewed to be acting in the public interest (such as those affiliated with the religious community or the League of Women Voters), it is more beneficial to have the organization's message delivered by a coalition.

- Coalitions permit resources to be shared. Coalitions benefit by the resources of their membership, including money, volunteers, staff, office equipment, and meeting space. It is more cost-effective for an organization to form a coalition to permit resources to be shared, rather than having to pay the entire bill itself.

- Coalitions provide a path to inform new constituencies about an emerging issue. For example, the religious-based advocacy community's constituency may not have access to detailed information about a specific state budget problem, other than seeing an occasional newspaper article. It is one thing for welfare recipients to write to their legislators requesting a grant increase, and another for middle-class taxpayers to write advocating for an increase based on economic justice, not self-interest. Coalitions provide a framework for expanding constituencies beyond those of the convener.

- Coalitions result in positive public relations for a convener coalition-builder. New organizations build respect by forming and running a successful coalition. While the "credit" for a success achieved single-handedly can be savored, achieving that success is often much more difficult than with help from a coalition. By bringing other organizations together and working for a common goal, those organizations learn to work with the convener, to build trust, to get visibility for the new organization, and to make it more likely that the convening organization will be invited to participate in other coalitions.

Disadvantages of Coalitions

- It is often difficult for members of a coalition to focus on an issue that is usually not the priority issue for any member of the coalition other than the convener.

- Coalition members who are not the convener often have an agenda that differs from that of the convener. They may seek to exploit the coalition for their own goals in a manner that may be inconsistent with the purpose for which the coalition was formed.

- Coalitions usually reach agreement on issues by consensus, which is sometimes difficult to achieve. When it is achieved, the result is often the lowest common denominator and dilutes the aggressiveness that might have been necessary to solve a problem.

- Coalitions require considerably more time to make decisions than would be required by the convener acting alone. Many coalition members require major decisions to be discussed by their own boards. There is a lag time between when a decision is requested and when a decision can be made by a coalition, compared with an individual organization. Even scheduling a coalition meeting to discuss when a coalition consensus can be developed can be extremely difficult at times.

- Many important coalition partners have organizational difficulties that make them used to working independently rather than in coalition.

- Coalitions can require substantial organizational work, such as preparing agendas, mailing materials, and coordinating meeting times.

To Form a Coalition or Not

There are many questions that should be answered, and an honest assessment made, in determining whether forming a coalition to solve a problem is constructive. Among them are:

- What is the outcome I wish to achieve with this coalition? Is it realistic to achieve it by myself? Are the chances for success improved with a coalition?

- Whose turf am I treading on by trying to solve this issue alone? Is there a more appropriate organization to form this coalition?

- Are there constituencies in my own organization that will react negatively if I form this coalition?

- How much will a coalition cost me in terms of money, time, and focus?

- Who should be invited to participate; who should not be invited?

- Will I have better access to outside experts if I form a coalition?

- Will my prospective coalition participants get along?

- How will the coalition dissolve after my goals are achieved?

- What kind of commitment do I need from participants, and is it realistic to expect to receive these commitments?

How to Form a Coalition

- Make sure that there are no irreconcilable major differences between coalition participants, either as a result of ideology or personal enmities.

- Identify all organizations that have a direct or indirect interest in the issue.

- Invite, if appropriate, organizations that would increase the credibility of the coalition.

- Make sure that the effort is not perceived to be partisan.

- Invite outside experts to either serve on the coalition or speak to it.

- Consider business, labor, education, religious advocacy, good government citizen groups, health, local government, state government, federal government, beneficiaries of success of the coalition's objective, provider associations, lobbyists, experts on the issue, community leaders, foundation and other grantmaker representatives, charities, and religious leaders as coalition members.

Tips:

- **Remember that if the objective of the coalition were the most central focus of all members of the coalition, they would have formed it first.**

- **Respect the fact that your coalition is perhaps one of many, and keep meetings short with the agenda focused. Encourage all in attendance to participate, but don't dominate the discussion yourself or let any other participant dominate. Reach consensus as quickly as possible, and then move on.**

- **Delegate the work of the coalition to participants (such as by forming committees when necessary to develop a consensus).**

- **Make the meeting pleasant by being hospitable (such as providing soft drinks or lunch).**

Chapter 25
Miscellaneous Administrative Issues

Synopsis: The offices of nonprofit corporations require computers, filing systems, and office equipment that are sensitive to organizational needs. The Postal Service offers discounted postage rates to organizations that prepare bulk mailings in a manner consistent with its format and regulations.

Office Equipment

Many small nonprofit corporations are headquartered in the residences of their incorporators. There are obvious limitations to that, particularly if the corporation needs to expand its "shoebox" existence. For those who rent or own office space, some basic equipment items to consider (and budget for) are—

1. File cabinets (legal or letter size)
2. Postage meter, postage scales
3. Copy machine
4. Fax machine
5. Telephone system, including cell phone
6. Telephone answering machine or voice mail service
7. Computer, printer, monitor, and peripherals, such as modem, scanner, mouse, flash drives
8. Electronic printing calculators
9. Office furniture (including desks, bookcases, supply shelves, cabinets, chairs, lamps, end tables, coat racks, umbrella stand).

Staffing Patterns

Thousands of registered nonprofits operate effectively with no paid staff, while others, such as colleges and hospitals, may have staff in the thousands. Salaries are, by far, the largest budget expenditure for organizations with paid staff. A typical "one man band" staff configuration has an executive director or director who performs all of the operations of the organization. There may be the need for some part-time assistance to do bookkeeping or help with a special project on occasion, but it is not impossible for one versatile person to run a highly successful organization. More typical is a two-person office—an executive/administrator and a secretary/clerk who performs the routine office management functions.

Nonprofits that can afford additional staff may have an assistant director, who may be responsible for publications, membership, or development (a euphemism for fundraising). Other typical generic staff positions of nonprofits are government relations representative, program director, publications specialist/newsletter editor, administrative assistant, public relations/community relations specialist, librarian, office manager, Webmaster, and data processor. Many nonprofits provide specific services that require staff with some particular educational credentials or training. Hospitals will hire doctors, nurses, social workers, and lab technicians. Colleges will hire professors and deans. The organization's mission may determine the types of specialists hired (see Chapter 13).

Many nonprofits choose to start small—hiring one staff member—and then expand with experience and fundraising, so there is a reasonable expectation that the budget can be supported in the long run. If a nonprofit is too ambitious at first, the staff may end up spending most of its time raising funds to support salaries, rather than accomplishing the mission of the agency.

Stationery/Logo

Every nonprofit corporation needs to have letterhead stationery to provide a professional first impression. This stationery need not be fancy or expensive, although it is generally a good practice to print stationery on bond paper with some cotton content, which is heavier than the 20-lb. stock used in the copy machine. Most corporate stationery has a graphic (also known as a "logo") that is descriptive of the corporation. This graphic can also be used on the masthead of a corporate newsletter; on the Web site; on mailing labels, brochures, and press packets, and other promotional literature. Paying an artist to draw a distinctive and creative logo is usually a good investment, although it is often possible to make one by using some of the popular "clip art" or graphics software programs. If you don't have a scanner, a computer store may be willing to scan logo art work, so it can be printed out in various sizes or "imported" into computer-generated publications as needed.

The letterhead should also include the organization's name, address, e-mail address, and Web site address. Most organizations also list their board members, officers, and key staff members, as well.

Filing Systems

The filing systems of nonprofit corporations usually evolve over several years and are as individual as each corporation. Several factors should be considered in setting up a filing system.

Keep files of the corporation's internal operations separate from other files. For example, keep the files relating to tax-exempt status, corporation budget, office leases, insurance, taxes, Articles of Incorporation, membership, mailing lists, lobbying, and charitable registration in a different place from files about general political and public policy issues. A corporation should have correspondence files—one for "outgoing" and another for "incoming." One nonprofit always makes three copies of all outgoing correspondence—one for the "outgoing" file, one for the "incoming file" stapled to the incoming letter that generated the outgoing letter, and one for the subject file that relates to the issue of the letter. "External" files can be subject matter relating to the mission of the corporation. However, "internal" files will be similar from nonprofit to nonprofit. Among typical internal files are:

> allocations, annual report, Articles of Incorporation, bank statements, board meeting agendas, board minutes, board meeting packets, bookkeeping, brochure, budget, bylaws, computer, dues structure, expenses, financial reports, grass-roots alerts, insurance, mailing lists, newsletters, office equipment, office leases, payroll, personnel, photographs, planning, postal service, press mailing list, press clippings, press releases, printing, grants, publications, speeches and testimony, special projects, tax-exempt status, taxes, and Web site. Some of these files will have sub-categories (e.g., newsletter—previous, newsletter—current), and others will be categorized by year.

Computer

Perhaps there remain a handful of nonprofit executives who are quite satisfied replying to correspondence the old-fashioned way by either writing replies using pen and paper, or banging out an answer on the same trusty Remington typewriter they used when they were in college back in the 1970s. Many of them are satisfied with what they have—and don't begin to question this primordial existence until they are faced with having to type out 3,000 "personal" letters asking for funds to save their jobs or tire of personally addressing 6,000 newsletters each month. The computer is, with good reason, a fixture in the modern nonprofit office.

The good news is that in the hands of a knowledgeable operator, a computer can do a variety of tasks and save thousands of expensive staff hours. The bad news is that it can be expensive and complicated to learn, may be vulnerable to computer viruses and other cyberterrorism, and can "crash" at the most inopportune times.

Hardware/Software

This handbook provides only the most cursory review of basic computer buying decisions. It is geared to the small nonprofit interested in the advantages and disadvantages of purchasing a personal computer and the basic options.

Among many issues to consider when purchasing a computer system are:

1. Who will be using the system, and will they be sufficiently trained?

2. Is software available that is compatible with your hardware, and will this software be capable of providing the output you need?

3. Are you paying for features or capacity you are unlikely to ever need?

4. Is there sufficient follow-up support to answer questions, troubleshoot problems, and provide maintenance?

Basic Hardware Decision: Apple or IBM-Compatible

In the old days, these two types of computers were as incompatible as Beta format and VHS for VCRs. What were once uncrossable boundaries between these two hardware systems are now being crossed and integrated. Basically, the Apple-based Macintosh ("Mac") computers are considered to be more "user-friendly," and employ a pointing device ("mouse") to choose among various options on a monitor. The operating system is usually a "graphical user interface" (GUI) that doesn't require the user to memorize all sorts of esoteric commands. On the other hand, IBM and IBM "clones" are generally less expensive and have more programs that are compatible, but require more knowledge on the part of the user. IBM and its imitators have developed software that imitates the user-friendliness of the Mac. Increasingly, the Mac-based hardware is permitting the use of files created using IBM-compatible software. Each system has those who swear by it and swear at it. The state-of-the-art is advancing so swiftly that this decision may become moot in the near future.

Typical Software for Nonprofits

There are thousands of programs available that are being used by various nonprofits. In general, several families of programs exist that are useful in a typical computer-based nonprofit office. Among them are:

1. Word Processing—Corel WordPerfect, Lotus Word Pro, and Microsoft Word are among the most popular word processing packages. An advantage of word processing programs is that an entire document does not have to be retyped to make corrections or multiple copies. This is a major productivity enhancement if an organization desires to send a "personal" letter to 50,000 potential contributors.

2. Spreadsheet—Lotus 1-2-3 and Microsoft Excel are among the most popular spreadsheet programs. In simple terms, the objective of a spreadsheet is to perform operations and calculations on numbers and automatically adjust a total when one number in a sum is changed. Spreadsheets are indispensable for bookkeeping, budgeting, and similar documents. Many spreadsheets contain graphics capability that permits numerical data to be displayed in pleasing and informative formats.

3. Database—Approach, dBase, Paradox, and Access are among the most popular database programs. The objective of a database is to sort data into various fields, which can then be used to generate mailing lists, store information that can be sorted, and perform other similar tasks.

4. Desktop Publishing (DTP)—Adobe InDesign, Microsoft Publisher, and Quark Xpress are among the most popular DTP or page layout programs. These programs "import" graphics and output from word processing programs and can manipulate the result on the screen in an eye-catching format. Text can be printed out in a variety of type faces and sizes, giving documents the appearance of having been professionally designed and typeset.

5. Presentation Software—Microsoft PowerPoint, Lotus Freelance Graphics, Adobe Persuasion, and Harvard Graphics are among the most popular presentation software programs. These are used with LED screens to project speaker presentations of short bites of text and graphics for large audiences, and can be coordinated with music and video files.

There are software "suite" packages that provide the above types of programs all-in-one and are designed to work with each other. Some of the most popular are Microsoft Office, Corel Word Perfect Suite, IBM's Lotus SmartSuite, and OpenOffice.org (formerly known as "Star Office"). Before purchasing any software (which can be obtained for free from computer bulletin boards or cost thousands of dollars), it is best to seek advice of those who are knowledgeable about the advantages and disadvantages of each program.

Nonprofits affiliated with a state or national association should check with the staff of that organization to ascertain what software packages are used. Often, these organizations share data among their affiliates in only one format. While software is available to make conversions between formats and hardware configurations, substantial time, energy, and money can be saved by having compatible computer systems.

Open Source Software

Open source software is quickly becoming the choice of thousands of charities for applications including operating systems (Linux), productivity office suite packages (OpenOffice), browsers

(Firefox), databases (MySQL) and Web site design (Joomla). The term refers to software whose source code is public. Often, the software is licensed to users using a standardized form that sets rules for changing it and using it—but for the most part, there is no charge for using open source software. The open source software model is intended to encourage collaboration for the purpose of making a software product better for every user, rather than making money for the developer. Among the advantages are that you don't have to pay for periodic updates, you can put the software on as many computers as you like, and there is a community of software developers who collaborate to improve the product and eliminate bugs. However, keep in mind that there may not be stable technical support, quality control may be "iffy," and the software may not run on all operating systems. Generally, open source software tends to be high quality, and worthy for charities to consider.

Computer Communications/Internet

Computers with modems provide a gateway to communications with millions of other computers and their databases and bulletin boards, and they permit you to send letters, computer files, and simple messages (i.e. e-mail) through the telephone wires. Commercial online services such as CompuServe and America Online provide news, weather, and other information valuable to nonprofits. According to Clickz.com, as many as 150 million people in the U.S. have connections to the Internet at home, affording virtually instantaneous communications among those connected. Millions more have access through their schools, libraries, and workplaces. Using a commercial service permits communications between your personal computer and a computer on the other side of the world for the cost of a local telephone call. "Conversations" and "meetings" can be held in "real time" with each participant typing questions and responses on the keyboard.

Computer-assisted communication is revolutionizing how business is conducted by nonprofits, and staff should be prepared to harness advances in technology to their advantage. See Chapter 21 for more information on how nonprofits use the Internet.

Credit Card Sales

Nonprofit organizations are businesses and have many aspects in common with for-profit businesses. They sell products and services, such as memberships, publications, counseling, and tickets to events. They also solicit donations from the public, and it is not unusual for many contributors to be comfortable making these donations by credit card, either through secure forms on the Internet or, more conventionally, through the mail. Inexorably, we are becoming a cashless society, and the public increasingly relies on credit cards for financial transactions. Nonprofit organizations should consider whether having "merchant status" is advantageous. For more information about how to obtain this status, see Chapter 23.

Postal Service Issues

Nonprofit corporations typically generate a large volume of mail in the course of sending out annual reports, newsletters, program brochures, fundraising solicitations, surveys, grass-roots action alerts, and meeting notices. As a result of U.S. Postal Service advances in technology, mass mailings have become more complicated. Because of recent reforms that substantially change the way both organizations that qualify for nonprofit mailing status and others must prepare bulk mail, the USPS has expanded its outreach by providing educational programs.

The Postal Service offers free training on how to process bulk mailings. Call the U.S. Postal Service's regional bulk mail center to get information on the next scheduled workshop.

General Postage Rates

The U.S. Postal Service publishes the *Postal Bulletin,* which details the latest rates, fees, and changes in regulations. Subscriptions to this bi-weekly publication are available for $183/year. You can download back issues for free at:
http://www.usps.com/cpim/ftp/bulletin/pb.htm

A more comprehensive publication, *Domestic Mail Manual,* is published twice annually, and is available for $60 or electronically at *http://pe.usps.gov.* Copies of the latest edition (2007) are also available from main post offices or from the Government Printing Office.

Postage Meters

Postage meters permit organizations to affix exact postage to letters and packages without the inconvenience of purchasing stamps of varying denominations. The postage is printed by the meter, and the organization pays in advance for the postage used. Most new postage meter systems permit postage accounts in the machine to be replenished by telephone/modem. Postage machines are not sold but, in accordance with federal law, are rented by commercial companies. A license is required from the Postal Service, but the paperwork is handled by the vendor. Pitney-Bowes is the firm that developed the system and is the leader in the field. Competing companies can be found in the Yellow Pages under "Mailing Machines and Equipment." The cost of renting a machine is about $20 per month and up, including a postage scale, depending on the system's sophistication.

Stamps.com and other competitors allow for a similar service that is Internet-based. Postage is provided by establishing an online account and printing out postage from your computer.

Bulk Mail Permit Procedures

The USPS has a terrific online tutorial for those who wish to set up a bulk mail operation. From the USPS home page *(http://www.usps.com),* click on *Grow Your Business.* Then click on *Business Mail 101.*

Organizations that desire to participate in the bulk mailing program must first obtain an imprint authorization from the Postal Service using Form 3615. The one-time-only imprint fee of $175 is good for both first and standard class (formerly known as "third class") mailing. Mailing permits must be renewed annually, and there is a $175 fee for first class and $175 for standard class. Organizations seeking nonprofit mailing status should file Form 3624. Forms are available online at: *http://www.usps.com/forms.* The Postal Service automatically forwards the correct form when it is time to renew the permits.

Having such an imprint entitles the organization to pay the postage in advance without having to affix postage to each individual piece of mail. The permit also provides a discount, provided there are at least 200 pieces or 50 pounds in the bulk mailing and the mailing is sorted and processed in accordance with post office regulations. Each piece must be correctly ZIP-Coded or it will not be accepted.

Once in receipt of the imprint permit, the organization can affix the imprint to mail pieces using a rubber stamp, or they can print it directly on the piece.

The bulk mail discount can be large. The rate for a first-class letter rose to 41 cents per ounce (17 cents for each additional ounce) on May 14, 2007. A comparable piece of mail sent standard-class bulk rate can be sent for less than half of that amount, depending on how it was prepared. There are also substantial discounts to encourage barcoding of bulk mailings.

501(c)(3)s (or organizations that have the characteristics of such organizations) may qualify for the U.S. Postal Service's Special Bulk Rate. Organizations that may apply for this discount rate are agricultural, educational, fraternal, labor, philanthropic, religious, scientific, and veterans' nonprofit organizations. Organizations that are not eligible are auto clubs, business leagues, chambers of commerce, citizens and civic improvement organizations, mutual insurance associations, most political organizations, services clubs (such as Lions clubs and Rotary clubs), social and hobby groups, and trade associations. To apply, you need to file a PS 3624 form, which is available from any post office. The application will require you to submit your Articles of Incorporation, proof that your organization fits one of the eligible categories, a list of activities, a financial statement, and documents that show how your organization operates, such as brochures, newsletters, and board minutes. The Post Office reviewers pay close attention to any advertising you may have in your newsletter. For more details on this benefit to nonprofits, consult *Quick Service Guide 670* published by the U.S. Postal Service.

As of 2007, the basic nonprofit rate for letters under 3.3 ounces was 16.4 cents (25.5 cents for other than nonprofit rate). This basic rate can be reduced further, depending on the nature of the presort and the destination. Use the online calculator at: *http://dbcalc.usps.gov* to calculate your bulk rate postage.

For all rates, publications, and rate calculators, visit: *http://pe.usps.gov*

Automation

Bulk mail postage rates are substantially lower for mail that can be handled by automated equipment. Computer software is available at reasonable cost that will automatically place a U.S. Postal Service-compatible barcode on each label generated by your computer. Even if you do not have barcoding capability, providing enough space for the Postal Service's equipment to optically read the address on each label and place its own barcode, while not reducing your postage rate, will qualify you for time-saving reductions in bulk mail preparation. Consult the U.S.P.S. for more information about this "upgradeable mail."

The entire system for presorting to comply with Postal Service regulations is too complicated to be described briefly. It has changed substantially since the last edition of this book. A thumbnail sketch of this system is provided below.

Size of Standard-Class Letter Mail

The dimensions of letter-size bulk mail are limited to the following:

length: 5 inches - 11 1/2 inches
width: 3 1/2 inches - 6 1/8 inches
thickness: .009 inches - .25 inches (enough to send a 20-page newsletter of 20-lb. paper, folded once)
aspect ratio (length divided by height): must be 1.3 inches - 2.5 inches

Standard Mail Sorting

To obtain bulk mail discount postage rates, mail must not only meet certain criteria to be considered "machinable" such as those relating to length, width, thickness, and aspect ratio, but must be delivered to the Post Office's business mail entry unit in trays sorted by ZIP Code. Note that trays are provided free by the USPS Business Mail Entry Unit. The following is a short version of how the mail should be placed in these trays:

Step 1: Make up a tray or trays of mail going to your Post Office's origin ZIP-Codes. Each bulk mail processing center has a list of such ZIP-Codes, and these Sectional Center Facility (SCF) letters qualify for a reduced rate. They should be in ZIP-Code order.

Step 2. Make up a tray or trays of letters going to the same Automated Area Distribution Center (AADC). These should be in ZIP-Code order. You can obtain a list of which Zip Codes comprise each AADC from your Post Office (ask for Labeling List L801, AADCs—Letter-Size Mailings).

Step 3. Make up a tray or trays of the remaining letters.

Tray Requirements

Trays should be at least 85% full. If not, skip the step that created that tray. The USPS wants you to provide them with full trays. "Full" is defined as at least 85% full, so choose either a one-foot tray or two-foot tray to comply with this requirement.

Trays must be enclosed by a tray sleeve and bound with polyethylene strapping. Strapping material can be purchased from a commercial office supply house. The trays must be labeled appropriately to reach the correct destination. The Postal Service can provide correct tray labeling information.

The applicable postage must be deposited in the organization's postage account if the current balance is not enough to cover the postage for the mailing. A mailing statement provided by the Postal Service that identifies the organization, its bulk mail account, and the number of pieces being mailed for each standard-class category, must accompany each mailing.

The bulk mail operation is performed successfully by hundreds of for-profits and nonprofits alike every day. It can save thousands of dollars in postage compared with mailing every piece first class. It also saves the bother of affixing individual postage stamps. While it may appear intimidating at first, it becomes routine with practice.

In general, the Postal Service attempts to deliver standard class mail within ten days of receipt. Often, this mail is delivered just as expeditiously as first-class mail, although a four- or five-day time period for processing is not unusual. As a general rule, nonprofits should think twice before mailing anything standard class that absolutely *must* be received within 12 days after the organization delivers the mailing to the Business Mail Entry Unit.

Only certain U.S. Postal Service branches are equipped to process bulk mail. There are commercial services that specialize in processing bulk mailings. Some volunteer organizations will offer to help nonprofit organizations do bulk mail, as well.

Tips:

- **When creating a mailing list, it is useful to have the list in ZIP-Code order or to be capable of sorting it in ZIP-Code order. Otherwise, letters must be sorted by hand to take advantage of the bulk mail discounts.**

- Most of the popular word processing programs will perform a ZIP-Code sort operation and create mailing labels, and all of the database programs do. Many are capable of automatically inserting a barcode, which further reduces postage rates if printed in accordance with postal service regulations.

- Contact the U.S. Postal Service for help with bulk mail preparation or rates. A useful telephone number is:

    1-800-238-3150—National Customer Support Center
    USPS Web site: *http://www.usps.com*

Chapter 26
Nonprofits and Small Business Competition

Synopsis: Some small business advocates have charged that nonprofits have unfair advantages when they compete in the sale of goods and services. Legislation and regulations to remove these advantages are a clear threat to the ability of the nonprofit sector to function effectively.

Introduction

An issue has emerged on the agenda of small business advocates that could jeopardize the ability of many nonprofits to perform their vital missions. Tracing its beginning to the early 1980s, the issue of alleged unfair competition between nonprofits and small business earned its first stamp of legitimacy when the U.S. Small Business Administration issued a report in late 1983 entitled *Unfair Competition by Nonprofit Organizations with Small Business: An Issue for the 1980's.*

Small businesses had, until then, complained with muted voices that nonprofit corporations possessed advantages in the marketplace that hindered the ability of small businesses to compete. Among these advantages were said to be—

- Tax exemptions—the most tangible benefit of nonprofits
- Reduced postage rates
- Tax deductions for those who contribute goods and services to nonprofit organizations
- Use of venture capital—the ability to use contributions and non-taxable surpluses for expansion, state-of-the-art equipment, and seed money for new activities that may compete with private enterprise
- "Captured referrals"— "sweetheart deal" arrangements between affiliated nonprofits that eliminate competition from non-affiliated businesses
- Use of plant, staff, supplies, and equipment donated or funded by grants to spur unrelated business enterprises that may compete with small business
- "Halo effect"—referring to the willingness of the public to do business with a nonprofit because of the perception that the organization is serving the public good rather than being operated for a private profit motive.

During the 1970s, nonprofit corporations were becoming increasingly sophisticated in their efforts to generate revenue. These efforts accelerated during the 1980s, when many social service nonprofits were hit by the loss of government funding during the retrenchment of domestic spending under the Reagan Administration. Nonprofit hospitals were a particular target of small business owners, who resented the establishment of laundry and pharmaceutical services that competed with them. Small business advocates continue to complain that state government has no effective mechanism to track funds that may be channeled between a nonprofit agency and its for-profit affiliates.

Also targeted nationally were YMCAs and their Jewish counterpart JCCs. Some of the YMCAs and JCCs began marketing their lucrative health club services to an "upscale" market segment to generate revenues to cross-subsidize services provided to their needier clients. Such facilities were caught in a "Catch 22." If they charged less than the market rates, they were accused of undercutting small business by taking advantage of their tax exemptions and other advantages. If they charged the same or more than the private health clubs, they were accused of operating just as any other business and thus, not deserving of any tax exemption. Private health clubs across the nation, through the guidance of their associations, participated in legal actions against several YMCAs and instigated reviews by local taxing authorities designed to challenge the historical tax-exempt status of these facilities. An effort by nine private health clubs in the Pittsburgh area to challenge the tax exemption of the Golden Triangle YMCA in Pittsburgh was partially successful.

Colleges and universities garnered the wrath of small business owners who objected to college bookstores selling television sets and refrigerators, marketing surplus computer time, operating testing services, establishing travel agencies, or otherwise entering markets in direct competition with small business.

These small business owners found a voice in the Small Business Administration. On July 27, 1983, the Small Business Administration's Office of Advocacy held a one-day symposium on this issue, and followed up the conference with a November report entitled *Unfair Competition by Nonprofit Organizations With Small Business: An Issue for the 1980's.* This report charged that "traditional 'donative' nonprofits, such as the Red Cross and the Salvation Army, which rely primarily on gifts and contributions for their operating revenue, are being replaced by 'commercial nonprofits'... which derive all or nearly all of their income from the sales of goods or services they produce." The report charged some of the nonprofit sector with creating an oversupply of goods, and charging significantly less than the prevailing market rates as a result of exemptions from laws and regulations. The report concluded:

It is the responsibility of the Congress and the Executive Branch to make a systematic inquiry into whether these exemptions are still justified in light of the emergence of the commercial nonprofit sector.

Among other recommendations, the report called for:

- A higher tax or outright prohibition on unrelated business activities by nonprofits

- Defining "substantially related" more clearly and narrowly for purposes of what constitutes an unrelated business

- Establishing a threshold above which a nonprofit engaging in unrelated business activities would lose its tax exemption

- Eliminating the "convenience" exception for the payment of unrelated business income taxes.

Soon after the report was released, approximately 20 national business associations, many of which participated in drafting the 1983 SBA report, formed the "Coalition for Fair Business Competition" to lobby on behalf of business interests on this issue.

The issue of nonprofit competition with small business was among the most compelling of the issues reported by small business owners at the 1986 White House Conference on Small Business. Conference delegates designated it the number three issue on a list of 40 major concerns culled from a list of 2,232 proposed by small business owners nationwide. Legislation was introduced in several states in response to this conference.

Federal Unrelated Business Income Tax (UBIT)

Federal law stipulates that nonprofit corporations pay federal taxes on unrelated business income. Corporations with at least $1,000 of such income are required to file a 990-T annually. Income is defined as "unrelated" if it is derived from a trade or business, is regularly carried on, and is substantially unrelated to the exempt purpose of the corporation. Income clearly exempt from UBIT includes that generated from activities performed by volunteers, from selling merchandise received as gifts or contributions, and dividends, interest, royalties, and capital gains. Also exempt is income from business operations conducted for the "convenience" of an organization's members, students, patients, and staff, such as a hospital cafeteria or college bookstore.

The Internal Revenue Service reports that $884.68 million in UBIT was collected from nonprofit organizations for the 2006 fiscal year.

Both the Congress and the Internal Revenue Service have been skeptical about whether charities should have a broad exemption from paying taxes on business income. The House Ways and Means Committee's Oversight Committee held a series of hearings in June 1987 on the issue of changing federal policy on unrelated business income taxes. The subcommittee followed up on its hearings by issuing a press release on March 31, 1988, describing policy options on changes to UBIT, many of which caused concern in the nonprofit sector. The options included suggestions to narrow the "substantially related" test for exempting organizations from UBIT, repeal the "convenience" exception (which, for example, permits college bookstores and cafeterias to be tax exempt), apply UBIT to fitness/health clubs unless the program is "available to a reasonable cross section of the general public such as by scholarship or by fees based on community affordability," and apply UBIT to advertising income and allow deductions from UBIT only on direct advertising costs (a major concern to exempt nonprofits whose publications accept commercial advertising to defray expenses of the parent organization).

In March 1990, a revised report leaked from the subcommittee entitled *Summary of Main Issues in Possible Modification of Oversight Committee UBIT Options.* The draft proposal eliminated many of the controversial proposals that caused so much concern to nonprofits. While the "substantially related" test was retained in the proposal, the "convenience" exception was repealed. Most indirect and overhead expenses relating to advertising income would be deductible, but such expenses could not reduce net income by more than 80%. The subcommittee membership was unable to reach a consensus on UBIT proposals.

The Internal Revenue Service has aggressively audited some charities focusing on UBIT issues, and has taken charities to court to promote its policy of restricting UBIT exemptions. During the 1990s, the Internal Revenue Service expanded its attention to enforcement of UBIT and developed policies with respect to some of the borderline areas that were problematic to charities. Some cases involving the interpretation of what constitutes unrelated income were litigated. Several relatively recent decisions on generic UBIT issues have been decided in favor of charities. Three examples have been cases involving mailing list rental income, affinity credit card income, and income from bingo games.

A case decided in August 1996 in U.S. District Court involving the American Academy of Family Physicians determined that the organization's income from a group insurance plan offered to its members underwritten by a private insurance carrier was not subject to UBIT. Again, the facts of this case may not be typical of conventional agreements between an insurance carrier and an exempt organization, but the opinion of the court on the issue was a favorable development.

Differences Between Nonprofits and For-Profits

There are clear and fundamental differences between the operations and motivations of nonprofits and for-profits. The buildings of some types of nonprofit charities and their for-profit counterparts may, in some cases, be similar. For-profit and nonprofit hospitals, nursing homes, day care centers, and recreational/youth service facilities may have the same equipment and physical plants, and they may provide some of the same services. Yet, these similarities often are exaggerated in an effort by some overzealous small business advocates to discredit the tax exemptions of those they perceive as competitors. The YMCAs in a growing number of communities particularly have endured vicious attacks from some private health club owners. In specific cases around the nation, these attacks have been given a credibility unsupported by the facts and have resulted in the loss of tax-exempt status.

Among the differences between nonprofit charitable organizations and for-profits are the following:

1. A nonprofit charity is driven by its service mission philosophy rather than by the profit motive.

2. A nonprofit charity serves those who cannot afford to pay full costs.

3. Any excess revenue over expenditures is funneled back into the institution to further its exempt purpose.

4. The charitable institution likely will remain in the community even if it suffers financial losses.

5. The nonprofit charity is more accountable to its board for public service.

6. The nonprofit charity often will proactively look for ways to respond to community needs without regard to any profit motive.

7. A nonprofit charity may not compensate its employees higher than "reasonable" rates, as is evident from the successful prosecution of several television religious broadcasters who were paid exorbitant salaries and benefits.

8. A nonprofit charity's board of directors is typically comprised of unpaid community leaders motivated by public service and serving the unmet needs of the community rather than making a profit.

9. A nonprofit charity, because of its legal mission to serve rather than to make profits, often attracts thousands of hours of volunteer time and philanthropic contributions that further its purposes.

Tips:

- **Don't publicly advertise products and services in a manner that underscores price competition with the for-profit sector.**

- Refrain from entering markets that are not substantially related to the mission of your organization, and be prepared to pay unrelated business income taxes (UBIT) on income derived from activities not "directly" related.

- Review all activities that could be construed as commercial, and identify all those that require the filing of a 990-T and payment of UBIT.

- In exploring options for generating new agency revenue, be sensitive to meeting needs that are unmet by the for-profit sector, rather than relying on undercutting the price of goods and services already being offered in the marketplace.

- Support efforts to improve disclosure and accountability of the voluntary sector. Cooperate with expanded enforcement of laws governing this sector, so that the few nonprofits that are abusing the law do not stain the reputation of the entire sector.

- Periodically review the organization's bylaws and tax-exempt status purposes, and update these documents to reflect changing conditions.

Chapter 27
State and Local Tax Exemptions

> **Synopsis:** Every state authorizes tax exemptions for charitable organizations, although in some jurisdictions, this principle is being challenged. Taxes, payments in-lieu-of taxes, or user charges all have the same effect—draining charities of resources that are better used for providing free and reduced-cost services. The tax exemption for charities is justified and should continue.

Sales and Use Tax Exemptions

All but five states (Alaska, Delaware, Montana, New Hampshire, and Oregon) levy a sales and use tax or equivalent on purchases of goods and/or services made by the public. (For state rates, see: *http://www.taxadmin.org/fta/rate/sales.html.*) With few exceptions, charities are eligible for exemption from paying this tax. Consult the State Directory of this book for more details on which states levy the tax and the requirements and procedures for exemption.

In many jurisdictions around the nation, exemptions from sales taxes, and local property taxes as well, are under scrutiny by those eager to increase revenues at a time when the demand for government services is increasing and revenues are not. Some government entities have sought to impose payments in lieu of taxes or user charges on tax-exempt organizations, or have tried to eliminate the exemptions entirely.

Why User Charges May Not Be the Answer

There are no reasonable ways to measure the public services that are directly utilized by charitable nonprofits.

Property taxes, by themselves or disguised as "user charges," neglect the factors by which these institutions have earned their tax exemptions in the first place. They are, for the most part, created to provide benefits to the community. The tax exemption provided to these organizations is a benefit that is returned to the communities many times over.

The amount of financial support accruing to municipalities by taxing charities is generally not believed to be substantial. At least one study done in Wisconsin showed that 67% of the state's tax-exempt property belonged to government, and that an additional 10% was owned by religious organizations. There is no profit that is distributed into private pockets. Thus, the payment of taxes would result in a limited set of options for charitable nonprofits, all of which are injurious.

The first option is that charities can decide that they are unable to continue operations, since the property tax payment required could be substantial in comparison to their total budgets. A second available option is to reduce services. A third option is to increase the cost of their services, but doing so often makes the services inaccessible to those who most need them.

In every one of these cases, the cost of reducing the activities of these charities is eventually borne by the community. That is why these organizations were granted tax-exempt status in the first place—to assure that their total resources are dedicated to meeting community needs.

Even with tax-exempt status, times are tough for these institutions. Government support for many nonprofit charitable activities has substantially declined since 1981. Demographic trends—including the aging of our population; the increase in homelessness, drug abuse, single-parent families, domestic violence, and children living in poverty; and the increasing economic necessity of two parents in the family who must work to make ends meet—have resulted in the demand for more free and subsidized services. Private enterprise has, in recent years, invaded the traditional turf of nonprofit human service agencies. In virtually every case, the for-profit business has marketed its services to garner the most lucrative market segment, siphoning away clients who generated incremental revenue that was used by the nonprofit charities to cross-subsidize services for the needy. By skimming off this market share, private enterprise has placed an additional burden on the charitable nonprofit sector.

Finally, economic instability has had an impact not only on an increase in service demand but a decrease in the revenue depended upon by charities, including fees for service and charitable contributions.

Justification For the Charitable Tax Exemption

The experience of charities with the Colorado ballot question of November 5, 1996, in which an unsuccessful attempt was made to repeal the property tax exemption for many traditionally tax-exempt charities, served as a wake-up call that the charitable exemption may no longer be taken for granted. In Pennsylvania, thousands of charities have had their exemptions challenged as a result of misinterpretation of the state Constitution and several unfavorable court interpretations. Charities in other states have also been challenged. The principle of exemption for bona fide charities deserves to be protected and continued.

Some of the reasons are:

1. Charitable nonprofits augment and, in some cases, replace the role of government in responding to and preventing society's problems. Tax-exempt status is an acknowledgment that these organizations have been deputized to act in the public interest and to improve societal conditions, rather than to serve any private interest. As a result, such tax-exempt organizations have a special responsibility to ensure that their programs and activities are consistent with these principles and that the level of accountability is on par with the government's.

2. Nonprofit charities have many advantages in responding to societal problems that are not available to government. Among them are:

   • Nonprofit charities can be galvanized to attack a problem much more quickly than can government. Those who disagree with this need only consider how long it took for government to respond to problems such as AIDS, homelessness, and drug abuse compared with individual nonprofit charities. Clearly, nonprofits can respond to problems before a political consensus is developed by either the public at large or a legislative body. Charitable nonprofits can, in many cases, direct resources toward solving the problem without the typical government bureaucracy and lag time between the identification of a problem and the approval of a statute, budget, regulation, request-for-proposal (RFP), and the actual expenditure of funds to solve the problem.

   • Nonprofits can effectively and efficiently respond to and solve problems that are localized in nature. This is a politically difficult task to accomplish under our present governmental system. Our political system often requires that a problem be universal in nature before resources are allocated to it. Also, politics make it more likely that government will be unable to target resources to solve a problem because there is often a cost to obtaining the necessary votes to pass a law.

- Nonprofits attract volunteers. Volunteers, both on boards and doing the actual work of the agency, include many who would not be attracted to government service and the constraints of government-affiliated organizations.

- Nonprofits can provide services when government programs, because of a limit on tax revenues, cannot expand. Charitable nonprofits often fill the void between what government provides to those who are destitute and what the for-profit sector provides to those who can afford the market rate for services. These charities provide services to those caught in the middle, who are not "poor enough" for government entitlement programs, but yet would be denied services by the for-profit sector. By charging fees for services on a sliding scale, these nonprofits are able to serve many who would otherwise not be served. This permits government to concentrate on serving only the neediest, while private business serves those who can afford to pay market rates.

The entire public benefits from the improvement of society resulting from the activities of these organizations. The tax exemption provided to charities is a cost to the entire public, but is only a small fraction of the public benefit accruing from these activities. Beyond the monetary benefit of this exemption, which permits these charities to commit *all* of their resources to the mission of the organizations, there is a principle involved. The tax exemption is an acknowledgment that the public values this type of altruistic activity and has foregone the collecting of taxes. It makes a statement that these organizations play an important role in strengthening the safety net that the government alone cannot offer.

It is in the public interest to promote the health of these charitable organizations, because government could not perform their missions as creatively, efficiently, or as cost-effectively.

Tips:

- **To protect tax-exempt status, serve clients who cannot afford to pay the full cost of services and make services accessible to some clients who cannot afford to pay at all.**

- **Periodically quantify the dollar amount of free and subsidized services provided to the organization's clients and to the public at large.**

- **If state and local tax-exempt status is desired, develop a careful and honest outline of how the organization complies with state and local criteria. If staff members feel that compliance with these criteria is problematic, then consider changing operations to reasonably meet them.**

Chapter 28
Property Tax Challenges: How To Respond

by Pam Leland, Ph.D.

Synopsis: This chapter outlines the steps a nonprofit organization can take to be prepared should its tax-exempt status be challenged.

Efforts across the nation to challenge nonprofits' property tax-exempt status have produced a great deal of anxiety within the nonprofit community. Rumors abound; questions are raised; organizations are challenged; exempt status may or may not be retained.

The reasons behind these challenges are many and complex and, thus, are not likely to be addressed easily or quickly. It must be assumed that, for the moment, local governments and school districts will continue their attempts to obtain revenue from the nonprofit community. Nonprofit organizations must be prepared to respond. Organizations may choose from a number of responses: pay the tax bill (accept the loss of property tax-exempt status), negotiate a voluntary payment (retain exempt status), or fight to retain their full exemption. Though there is no single, easy or quick answer that can be offered in response to a challenge to tax-exempt status, there are a number of things organizations can do to ensure that the appropriate response is chosen—whether the choice is to negotiate a settlement or fight the challenge in court. Each organization must determine for itself how to respond to such a challenge.

Ultimately, the nonprofit organization must be able to articulate its charitable nature through the provision of evidence that leaves no doubt as to its charitable status. Even a choice to negotiate a voluntary contribution is based upon the legitimacy of tax-exempt status. Should the charitable status of the nonprofit organization be overturned, responsibility for the entire tax burden is no longer at issue.

The evidence needed to prove the legitimacy of exempt status can be generated through a process that involves five components: education, planning, documentation, communication, and collaboration. Each will be discussed below. After a brief summary, key questions that must be considered as part of each component are listed.

Education

The first step in preparing an appropriate response to a challenge to property tax-exempt status is to gather the knowledge to make the correct decision. Nonprofit organizations must educate themselves about this issue before a challenge is presented. Through training and discussion, both board and staff must understand the implications of the challenge for their own particular organization. For example, it is no longer enough to assume the mantle of "educational" or "health care" institution. Organizations must be able to articulate for themselves the reason their nonprofit health care organization is different from a for-profit health care organization. Another example might be: Why is a nonprofit day care center deserving of an exemption when a for-profit day care center is not?

This process of education is only accomplished through introspection, training, and dialogue. Boards of directors and staff must involve themselves in a broad-based conversation in which every member and group understands the issue and its implications. Through this dialogue, the following kinds of questions need to be answered:

1. What has happened in our geographic area regarding tax exemption and nonprofits? What efforts have the taxing authorities initiated? What taxing bodies are actively involved?
2. Which organizations have been formally or informally challenged? How did they respond?
3. What decisions or outcomes have occurred thus far? Are any decisions pending or in appeal?
4. Why does our organization deserve continued exemption? What is our expressed rationale for tax-exempt status?
5. Is there consensus among the board and staff as to these issues?

Planning

A natural outcome of knowledge is the ability to plan a response. As an organization understands the issues and their implications, decisions can be made as to appropriate strategies. The position of strength for a nonprofit organization is to be prepared for a challenge should one emerge. The goal in a planning process is to have necessary policies and procedures in place so that the normal difficulties associated with a tax challenge will not be exacerbated by indecision, bickering, and in-fighting among and between board and staff. To have the time to make reasoned, deliberate decisions is critical; planning allows for this.

Some of the planning questions that need to be answered include:

1. If challenged, what would we do? Would we negotiate? Would we go to court? Who makes this decision?

2. How is the board's position expressed? Is there a policy or stated position?

3. Which board members are involved on a day-to-day basis? At what point does the full board need to be consulted?

4. Which staff would be involved? Who would have direct responsibility for this issue?

5. What legal services would we need? What do we have available?

6. What financial resources would be needed? Where will we get dollars?

Documentation

Critical to any organization's successful response to a property tax challenge is the ability to provide both quantitative and qualitative information as to its charitable nature. It is not enough to simply say, "We serve poor people," or "We do good things for children." Everything an organization says about itself or its services must be proven.

Some of the questions that need to be answered include:

1. Who are our clients? Who is our constituency? How many do we serve?

2. Who uses our services? What are their ages, their incomes?

3. How many donors do we have? Who are they? How much money do they give us?

4. Who are our volunteers? How much time do they give us? What is the dollar value of their time?

5. Are our services responsive to the needs of the community? How do we know this? What information can we provide that shows our organization is responsive to changing needs?

6. Who receives which services? Who uses our programs, our community screenings, our educational programs?

7. If fees are charged, how are levels of payment determined? Is anyone turned away for lack of resources?

8. What levels of subsidy are available? How many people are subsidized? Where do the subsidies come from?

9. What is our policy regarding ability to pay? How do we communicate these policies?

10. If local taxpayers are not the direct receivers of our services, how do they benefit?

11. How is *local* government relieved of a burden?

Communication

Research has revealed the discrepancy between the community's perception of nonprofit organizations and their financial realities. Yet, "perception" can be argued to be "reality" in that what people believe to be true drives behavior and interactions. Therefore, effective communication between the nonprofit organization and its community is critical.

Questions to be considered include:

1. What messages do we, as an organization, communicate to the community?

2. Do our publications and advertising promote an image of inclusivity or exclusivity? Are we communicating, in written form, our charitable nature and mission?

3. Do we communicate issues of reduced fees, subsidies, scholarships? Would members of the community know of these policies?

4. If asked, would the community be able to express the benefits our presence offers? Would they agree that our organization deserves tax exemption? Would they agree that they are the direct or indirect recipients of our services and presence? How do we assess community perception?

Collaboration

The lack of collaboration among nonprofit organizations is viewed as a weakness in potential responses to a property tax challenge. There is tremendous power in the nonprofit sector; choosing to separate oneself from other nonprofit organizations because of some perceived uniqueness can be destructive to that power. This is not to argue that nonprofit organizations should create a single, unified response. Sharing of information and ideas, and efforts to collaborate, however, can be positive for several reasons.

First, collaboration engenders a sense of community across diverse nonprofit organizations. Second, it empowers a group that could easily become fragmented and divisive. Third, it increases knowledge and experience of younger, smaller organizations. Fourth, it communicates to local units of government the strength that can be mustered should nonprofit organizations become united on issues. Fifth, it fosters creativity and innovation within the nonprofit sector. Finally, it creates a knowledge base about this issue. Much of what we know thus far about these challenges to property tax status is anecdotal. More good data is needed to create effective, responsible policy. The nonprofit sector should be proactive in the creation of this data, not reactive. Good information helps to assure a position of power.

Questions to be considered include:

1. What are the issues that unite us across fields of activity, across dimensions of size and geography?

2. What do we as a sector gain through collaboration? What do we lose if we are divided?

3. In what kinds of activities, unrelated to tax exemption, might we collaborate?

4. How can we ensure the adoption of appropriate and effective legislation? What kinds of legislation will strengthen our position as nonprofit organizations?

5. Are there existing structures or organizations in which we can participate and join others on this issue?

Discussion

Many nonprofit organizations will find the questions listed above difficult to answer. Some organizations may find that they are not currently in a position to answer them adequately. For these organizations, this process of self-examination and discussion becomes critical—not only as a means to improve existing services and operations, but also as a means of preparation should exempt status be challenged. Yet, any organization can benefit from this process of self-examination.

In considering *how* to respond to a property tax challenge, the most difficult part may be the removal of "blinders" and acknowledging that, warranted or not, the status of your organization may be challenged. Research has shown that many executives are not really interested in this issue until directly confronted with a tax bill. Chief executives often are surprised and dismayed by a challenge; they wonder how anyone could question their charitable status. Realizing that there are people and groups in your community who do question your charitable status can be a shock. For the smaller, more traditional charities, this may be especially true.

This is a hurdle that must be overcome. Nonprofit organizations and their boards of directors must understand that whether or not they are directly challenged, they will be affected. The manner in which all nonprofit organizations operate in the future will change as a result of these challenges.

To avoid the issue—to *not* plan a response—is the worst tactic an organization can choose. Through a process of discussion and education, planning, effective documentation and communication, and collaboration, a nonprofit organization can be well prepared for a challenge. It is these organizations that will be in a position of strength when questioned by a local unit of government. It is these organizations that will be successful in defending their exempt status.

Yet, more than being successful in a direct challenge to tax-exempt status, organizations may rediscover the "essence" of the nonprofit sector. Nonprofit sector scholar Jon Van Til (1993) writes,

> *... we might discover that the reason we exist is not to be "nonprofit," but rather to profit our communities and society in ways that families, governments, and corporations cannot. We might, in other words, discover the soul of a sector that has been lost by many contemporary nonprofits, blinded as they are by their quest to be both "business-like" and "tax-free."*

Tips:

- **Hire legal counsel with experience handling tax-exemption challenge cases.**

- **If challenged, consider not only appealing the exemption challenge, but appealing the amount of the assessment on the property.**

- **Keep up to date with relevant legislation, case law, and regulations on exempt status, since any judgments involving the feasibility and desirability of making a settlement with a local government will be colored by inaccurate or non-current information.**

NOTE: The strategies suggested in this chapter are based upon conclusions drawn from a research project conducted during the spring of 1994. Information presented here is a slightly modified version of the third chapter of a larger document summarizing this research entitled, Responding to a Property Tax Challenge: Lessons Learned in Pennsylvania. Copyright, Pamela J. Leland, Ph.D., ©1994. All rights reserved. Reprinted with permission.

Chapter 29
Mergers and Consolidations

Synopsis: Mergers involving nonprofit organizations are increasingly common and require planning. There are steps that should be taken when planning for a merger between nonprofit organizations to meet legal requirements and promote a successful transition.

It wasn't too long ago that many nonprofit boards considered liquidation to be a preferable alternative to mergers. Considering the loss of identity was just too painful, and the term "merger" conjured up a vision of a corporate shark gobbling up weaker entities. Since then, mergers and consolidations among nonprofit organizations have become increasingly common, spurred in part by cost-containment pressures that have been affecting the delivery of social services for several decades now, particularly in the healthcare industry.

Managed care, cuts in Medicare and Medicaid, DRG payments, and increased competition have been among the factors that have induced hundreds of nonprofit mergers among hospitals. There are increasing incentives for all nonprofit organizations to improve their efficiency and effectiveness. With the entry of for-profit organizations into providing services historically provided by nonprofits, competition for service dollars has increased. To create new sources of revenue, even staid nonprofits have become entrepreneurial and are offering services that may only be indirectly related to their core mission. Unwittingly, they may be siphoning off revenue from colleague agencies.

Factors That Trigger Merger Consideration

Among the events that trigger consideration of nonprofit mergers are:

- Organizations that deliver similar services recognize that economies of scale can be achieved.

- Organizations that are struggling financially seek a partner to stave off bankruptcy and liquidation.

- National organizations may place restrictions on local affiliates, such as having a minimum asset level, technology capability, and service menu, which cannot be met without combining with another local affiliate.

- Two nearby agencies find themselves engaging in destructive competition.

- Changes in leadership capability, both of staff and within the board, may trigger a strategic plan that recognizes an organization's inability to continue with the status quo.

- Scandal or other ethical challenges might surface in which merger or consolidation is seen as an alternative to liquidation.

- Changes in the outside regulatory environment or economic environment (e.g., managed care) may make it more attractive to increase economic power to maintain a viable market niche.

- A loss of membership may make it difficult or unfeasible to continue.

- The agency's mission has been accomplished successfully.

Generally, the reasons for suggesting a merger can be divided into three categories.

Economic reasons: A merger will help the organization become more efficient, take advantage of economies of scale, increase its access to members and/or clients, help it raise more donations and grants, and contain costs. The nonrenewal of a major grant that provided overhead expenses to the agency can threaten its continued existence. There is no longer the cash flow necessary to continue the operation.

Programmatic reasons: Agencies recognize that a strong synergy can be created by combining each agency's expertise to create new programs or offer a streamlined menu of existing services to a common population, permitting clients to avoid having to negotiate two or more organizational systems and venues to access services.

Strategic reasons: Strategic reasons include—

- An agency may be in a precarious state either economically or programmatically.
- Competition from for-profits or other nonprofits is becoming destructive, and funders are complaining.
- The board might be losing interest.
- A long-term CEO may be retiring, and there is no one to take his or her place with the vision necessary to lead the organization.
- The staff is demoralized because of an ineffective CEO who cannot be removed for political reasons.
- The public or funders have lost confidence in the agency as a result of ethical lapses or a reputation for poor quality.
- An agency in the outside environment is identified that, if a merger occurred, would create a strong collaboration.

How to Begin

At a 1997 workshop session on nonprofit mergers sponsored by the Pennsylvania Association of Nonprofit Organizations, William Morgan of Performance Industries and Paul Mattaini of Barley, Snyder, Senft & Cohen distributed a list of areas to consider when contemplating a merger.

Among the issues they raised were—

- The importance of infusing key leadership with the view that merging is a viable option

- Whether the CEO will find a way to sabotage the merger because of ego

- Whether the merger will fit into the organization's mission

- Finding the right candidate to merge with, and finding the right staff (such as an attorney, accountant, and consultant)

- Bringing together the two organizational cultures

- Handling the public relations and community relations aspects.

Steps to Merger

1. Each participating board should adopt a resolution in favor of the general principle of merging.

2. Each board should appoint a merger committee of board members and staff.

3. An outside, experienced merger consultant should be jointly hired to structure negotiations, with the cost shared by the participating organizations.

4. Meetings should be scheduled among the parties to discuss the goals of the merger, determine whether merging is feasible and makes sense for all parties, and negotiate, over time, the details, such as the change in the mission and values, new name, staffing, logo, merger budget, board selection, bylaws, personnel policies, location, and what happens to staff who are no longer needed.

Budgeting

Mergers cost money. There are likely to be legal fees, consultant fees, audit fees, personnel costs relating to layoffs, moving costs, costs relating to covering the liabilities of the non-surviving corporation (which may be substantial, and responsible for triggering the merger idea in the first place), and even providing new building signs, printing new stationery and business cards, and designing a new logo.

As David La Piana writes in *Nonprofit Mergers: The Board's Responsibility to Consider the Unthinkable,*

> *Although it is unlikely that the financial position of two merging organizations will immediately improve as a result of a merger, well-conceived and -implemented mergers can raise staff morale, better focus the organization's activities, and increase overall energy levels—that will help the new group tackle difficult problems. Thus, a successful merger can offer relief and renewed hope for nonprofit boards, staff, and donors, and, most importantly, benefit clients because of the greater energy, increased funding, and better management possible with a more stable organization. In contrast, poorly conceived mergers may simply bring together two weak organizations that compound each other's problems.*

Obstacles to Merger

Virtually every article about the difficulty of merging two or more organizations refers to the two scourges that often scuttle the best laid plans: "turf" and "ego." Many, if not most, mergers of nonprofit organizations involve a financially strong organization merging with an organization that is merging to stave off bankruptcy or liquidation. The surviving organization will have one chief executive, and it is often a traumatic and, at times, potentially humiliating experience for the chief executive of the non-surviving organization to hand over the reins of decision-making.

It is not unusual for an otherwise "routine" merger to be derailed by petty squabbling over the name of the combined agency, the logo, or the office space that will be provided to the staff of the non-surviving agency.

Legal Requirements

The legal procedures for mergers and consolidations that involve nonprofit corporations can be found in state law. Obviously, experienced, professional legal advice is necessary to carry out a successful merger.

Tips:

- **Merging organizations is not a "do it yourself" task. Always consult qualified professionals.**

- **If you are unable to assure employees that their jobs will not be in jeopardy as a result of a merger, plan to offer outplacement services.**

- **Don't take advantage of a merger situation by humiliating a party to a merger by flexing your power. The Golden Rule makes perfect sense in this situation.**

Chapter 30
Quality Issues

Synopsis: Quality is as important to nonprofit organizations as it is to for-profit businesses, if not more so. Nonprofits need quality programs to compete for donations, clients, board members, workers, and political support.

Introduction

Those who govern and manage nonprofit organizations are increasingly finding them subject to many of the same economic pressures as their for-profit counterparts. Their operations often resemble their for-profit competitors in both organizational structure and corporate culture. They are increasingly led by those trained in business rather than social work, and their mentality and administrative style often reflect this. Stereotypically, they often make the "bottom line" paramount above the needs of clients.

One nonprofit CEO with whom I spoke recognized the inconsistency of trying to run a human service organization and retain his "humaneness," while at the same time being forced to make rational business decisions that could mean the firing of "nice" people who were hurting the performance of his organization. He commented to me that his management credo was to be "ruthlessly altruistic."

In many cases, the products and services once provided solely by nonprofit, charitable organizations are now being provided by for-profits. One can often find health clubs, hospitals, schools, nursing homes, and day care centers—both for-profit and nonprofit—competing for clients on an equal basis within communities. When there is this direct competition, particularly in the delivery of human and educational services, cost is just one factor in a customer's decision. Quality of service is often even more important, and nonprofits that offer high-quality products and services obviously have a competitive edge. Those that can't offer quality may find themselves out of business.

Many thousands of other nonprofit organizations don't have direct economic competition from others providing the same service. There is only one United Way affiliate in each community, one Arts Council, one Arthritis Foundation, one AARP affiliate, and one Special Olympics affiliate. Except under unusual circumstances, it is unlikely that another organization will sprout up to directly challenge one of these. It would be easy to jump to the conclusion that having a monopoly of this nature would mean that quality and performance are not as important as they are to those with direct, head-to-head competition for providing a particular product or service. That conclusion would be flawed.

Why Quality is Important to Nonprofit Organizations

Quality is important to all nonprofit organizations. None is immune from the consequences of neglecting it. Charities rely on loyal customer support. Even if a nonprofit is not involved in direct economic competition, there is substantial competition for things that indirectly affect the viability of organizations. Among them are—

1. **Competition for government and foundation grants.** Most charitable nonprofits depend on grants to supplement any client fees they receive. Foundations are acutely aware of

organizations that have poor reputations with respect to skimping on service quality. No one wants to be associated with such an organization. It is no wonder that first-class organizations often have little trouble attracting funding, because everyone wants to be associated with them.

2. **Competition for private donations**. Would you make a donation to a charity that had a reputation of treating its clients like animals? Unless that organization is the Society for Prevention of Cruelty to Animals (SPCA), you are more likely to look elsewhere for a charity worthy of your donation.

3. **Competition for board members.** Why would anyone want to serve on the board of a second-class nonprofit and risk being condemned or otherwise embarrassed by the media, the political hierarchy, and clients? There are only so many skilled, committed civic leaders in each community who are willing to donate their time and expertise to serve on nonprofit boards, and it is clearly not attractive to serve on the board of a charity with a reputation for poor quality.

4. **Competition for volunteers.** What can be said for board members goes double for service delivery and other volunteers. No one wants to be associated with an organization with a reputation for poor quality. Many volunteers see their volunteer work as a springboard for a career, and volunteering for a pariah in the community does not serve their interests.

5. **Competition for media.** The media play an important role in helping a nonprofit charity promote its fundraising, encourage clients to utilize its services, and improve employee morale. Poor quality can result in the media ignoring an organization or, worse, highlighting its shortcomings for the entire world to see.

6. **Competition for legislative and other political support.** Nonprofit charities have benefited from the support of political leaders—directly through the provision of government grants, and indirectly through the provision of favors such as cutting government red tape and legislation to help solve problems of the organization and those of its clients. Political leaders are certainly not going to be responsive to an organization if they receive letters of complaint about the organization's poor quality.

7. **Competition for qualified employees.** Particularly during times of low unemployment, quality nonprofits have less employee turnover and find it easier to attract employees to fill vacancies and for expansion.

The consequences of poor quality, or the reputation (public perception) of poor quality, can result in the board of directors throwing up its hands and deciding to liquidate the organization. Or, in extreme cases, a state government agency may step in and liquidate the organization. Imagine the aftermath of a child care agency that failed to perform a quality background check on an employee who was later found to be a child abuser. A hospital that failed to adequately verify whether a staff member it had hired was adequately board-certified could be exposed to a major stain on its reputation, in addition to potential legal liability.

As pointed out by Dr. John McNutt of the University of Delaware, most, if not all, states look at the community benefit provided by a nonprofit organization in considering whether it is eligible for nonprofit status in the first place. Quality and community benefit are inextricably linked.

In 1998, a scandal affected international agencies that raise funds for child welfare. Who knows how many millions of dollars will not be contributed to these agencies because some agency official did not feel it was important to inform donor sponsors that their sponsored child had died several years earlier?

The Cost of Poor Quality

The cost to organizations with poor quality standards can be substantial. Just read the newspapers and you can find many examples. Owners of assisted living homes have failed to see the value of installing sprinkler systems and, as a result, have seen the loss of life and of their properties. Doctors have mistakenly removed the wrong kidney from a patient. Hospital maternity ward staff members have given the wrong newborn to the wrong parents. The ramifications far exceed the financial loss and loss of prestige to the organization—human suffering for the clients and potentially huge, successful lawsuits against the nonprofit organization as a result of a preventable lapse in quality-related policies.

An Associated Press article on the January 8, 2002 front page of my home town newspaper reported that the American Red Cross disposed of 49,000 pints of blood collected after the September 11th disaster because of a lack of storage space. Many will think twice before responding to an urgent call from that organization for blood donations, despite the obvious need to continually replenish the nation's blood reserves.

Quality in the Nonprofit Organizational Context

For the typical nonprofit that doesn't deliver client services, quality should mean much more than the ability to answer the telephone on the first ring. It means having a newsletter without typographical errors. It means having an attractive, periodically updated Web site. It means spelling the names of donors correctly in substantiation letters. It means delivering on promises made to legislators for follow-up materials. It means having conferences at which participants feel they get their money's worth. It means ensuring that each board member has the necessary and appropriate information to make governing decisions. It means that volunteers know in advance what is expected of them.

For those who deliver direct human services, it means, among other things:

- treating each client with the dignity he or she deserves
- respecting confidentiality
- respecting client privacy
- providing on-time services
- providing timely resolution to legitimate complaints
- providing services in a safe and secure setting
- providing services in a facility that is accessible, clean, and functional
- delivering services provided by competent, trained personnel
- ensuring that services meet high standards and respond to the clients' needs
- obtaining informed consent from clients before services are provided
- seeking constant feedback from clients to improve the delivery of services
- using advances in technology to improve communication between the organization and its clients.

Tips:

- Consider providing all organization staff with training that focuses on improving quality.

- Make it organizational policy to promote "continuous quality improvement" of every program, activity, and work process.

- Continually seek feedback from organization funders, clients, and staff to identify problems before they evolve into serious quality deficits.

Chapter 31
Change Management

> **Synopsis:** Change management strategies, such as Total Quality Management, Business Process Reengineering, Benchmarking, Outcome-Based Management, and Large Group Intervention, are potential ways to improve nonprofit organizational quality and performance.

In the context of this chapter, "change management" does not refer to a prescription for getting rid of the people who run the organization. Rather, it is a menu of management strategies to change the philosophy of management to accomplish an objective or set of objectives such as, for example, improving efficiency and competitiveness, motivating employees and increasing their job satisfaction, or reducing absenteeism. In this sense, "change" is used as a noun rather than a verb.

There is general agreement among scholars, practitioners, and management experts that organizations must adapt to changing conditions if they are to survive. Technology advances, markets change, the requirements and expectations of customers evolve, the needs of workers are altered as a result of demographics, economic conditions, and changes in culture, among other things.

Businesses, both for-profit and nonprofit, go out of existence every day. This is attributable to many causes. There may be an organizational scandal that causes the public to lose confidence or the government to take action. There may be quality lapses. The services provided by an organization may no longer be needed, or a competitor skims off a lucrative market share. The organization's operations may be too economically inefficient to support it. Government funding priorities or regulatory requirements may shift, leaving an organization in the lurch. The list of possible causes is endless.

For years, the for-profit business community has utilized formal change management strategies to improve operations and keep organizations competitive and vibrant, improve efficiency, generate loyalty, and maintain or expand support from customers. It has only been recently that the nonprofit community, with health care institutions leading the way, started implementing some of these strategies. The material appearing here is based on my book, *Improving Quality and Performance in Your Non-Profit Organization,* which was published in January 1999.

Among the most popular change management strategies being considered by nonprofit organizations are Total Quality Management (TQM), Business Process Reengineering (BPR), Benchmarking, Outcome-Based Management (OBM), and Large Group Intervention (LGI).

Total Quality Management (TQM)

TQM is an innovative, humanistic, general approach to management that seeks to improve quality, reduce costs, and increase customer satisfaction by restructuring traditional management practices. It requires a continuous and systematic approach to gathering, evaluating, and acting on data about what is occurring in an organization. The TQM management philosophy includes the following:

1. It asserts that the primary objective of an organization is to meet the needs of its "customers" by providing quality goods and services, and to continually improve them. In the nonprofit organization context, customers include not only the direct recipients of services, such as clients, but the organization's board, elected and appointed government officials, the media, and the general public.

2. It instills in all organization members an *esprit de corps* that ensures them that *having quality* as the number one goal is an important tenet. *Every* organizational member is responsible for quality, even if it is related to an issue beyond the scope of his or her job. Eliminating the "It's not my job" mentality becomes an achievable organizational objective.

3. It continuously searches for ways to improve every activity, program, and process. It does so by constantly seeking feedback from the organization's customers and promoting suggestions from all sources, both external and internal, on how to improve.

4. It rewards quality, not only internally, but from its suppliers. It recognizes that poor quality from its collaborators, be they suppliers or other organizations, affects its own quality.

5. It recognizes that staff must receive continuous training to improve their work performance.

6. It encourages all components of the organization to work as a team to solve problems and meet customer needs rather than compete against each other.

7. It empowers workers at every level. It permits them to be actively engaged in decisions that affect the organization and to constantly look for ways to improve it.

8. It permits employees the opportunity to have pride in what they produce for the organization and to see the fruits of their labor measured in the quality of the service they provide, rather than just receiving a paycheck.

9. It promotes a planning process geared toward continuously improving quality in *everything* the organization does.

TQM principles are finding their way into nonprofit settings other than healthcare, such as community centers, arts organizations, and human services agencies. Focusing on the needs of the "customer" rather than on the "bottom line" is a value with which the nonprofit sector should feel comfortable compared with its for-profit counterparts. When a nonprofit organization's leadership becomes excited about TQM, this excitement can become contagious, provided that the behaviors of the leaders are consistent with their words. When it "happens," those in a TQM environment notice the difference, whether they work there or benefit from the organization's services. Workers feel empowered. Clients notice a positive difference in staff attitudes. Everyone associated with the organization feels good about it.

Business Process Reengineering (BPR)

If your heart stops beating and you keel over breathlessly, a professionally trained medical professional can often revive you by administering CPR. But if it's your *organization's* heart that fails, BPR, administered by professionally trained consultants or by those within an organization, is increasingly becoming the TLA ("three-letter acronym") of choice for cutting-edge managers. BPR is a successor to TQM as the latest management bromide for reviving comatose organizations.

Business Process Reengineering is defined by Michael Hammer, BPR's leading guru, as "the fundamental rethinking and radical redesign of business processes to achieve dramatic improvements in critical measures of performance (cost, quality, capital, service and speed)."

Fanatical interest in Total Quality Management peaked in the 1980s, but its once-pervasive influence seems to have waned in recent years. One of the reasons often given for TQM's apparent decline in the United States is that the philosophy of slow, incremental, and continuous improvement is generally inconsistent with American culture. Perhaps this is so; American organizational leaders are perceived as more impatient to see the tangible results of their business management interventions compared with their Asian, African, and European counterparts. They want to see quantum leaps of measurable improvement rather than the tortoise-paced improvement promised by TQM advocates. The tenure of many organizational leaders is short; several CEOs may come and go before TQM is fully implemented and shows results.

A major strategy involved with BPR efforts is to look at a business process involving many tasks that have been performed by several specialists. Then, the specialists are replaced with generalists (or the specialists are retrained to become generalists) who can handle all the tasks of the process and have access to all of the information they need to do it.

BPR requires a new way of thinking. Unlike TQM, which requires the involvement of everyone in the organization, BPR is necessarily implemented from the top. It is the zero-based budgeting of business processes, contending that, at least theoretically, the past should have no bearing on what is planned for the future. It makes the assumption that organizations have evolved incrementally, reflecting a history of culture, tradition, technology, and customer needs that may not be particularly relevant today. BPR suggests that managers step out of the constraints of their current physical plant, work processes, organizational charts, and procedures and rules, and look at how the work would be performed if they were starting from scratch.

BPR requires an organizational leader to step back and answer the question: If I were building this organization today from scratch, knew what I know now, had the technology and human resources that I have now, and knew the customer needs that I know now, would I still be doing things the same way? More often than not, the answer is a resounding "No!" In the nonprofit environment, this might mean redesigning data collection and reporting, client intake, billing, purchasing, and every other process.

In many cases, new and more efficient technology is available. For example, a human service agency may receive a telephone call from a client requesting even a minimal change in service as a result of some change in circumstances. The person answering the telephone may have to put the person on hold and call the client's caseworker, who has the client's case file. The caseworker may have to put the person on hold and check with the supervisor for a decision on whether to waive a rule, and the supervisor may have to meet with the caseworker to make the decision.

After a BPR implementation, the person answering the telephone for the agency may be able to pull up the case file on a computer screen and be preauthorized to approve a change in services within a constraint programmed into the computer by the agency. Or the person answering the telephone may be able to give the caller technical advice on how to solve a problem by searching a "frequently asked questions" file on a computer screen, instead of transferring the call to a technical specialist.

Another way of looking at this is that everyone in the organization is conventionally functioning solely as his or her part of a process rather than on the overall objective of the organization. The receptionist answers the telephone. The case manager holds the file for a particular set of clients. The supervisor makes decisions authorizing variances from agency rules. BPR permits a work process to change so that the true objective of the process—responding to the client's needs—does not require the intervention of several people in the organization. The revolutionary advances in information technology permit this.

With the use of networked computers and an educated labor force, it is possible for a single person to process and troubleshoot an entire order that previously may have required being passed serially from person to person in the organization, taking many days to complete. And the more hands involved, the higher the probability of an error.

Among the major principles of BPR are:

1. Use modern technology to redesign work processes rather than work tasks, concentrating on permitting a single person to achieve a desired outcome/objective.

2. Let the worker who uses the output of a process also perform the process. For example, instead of having a purchasing department make purchases of pencils and paper clips for the accounting department and other departments, the accounting department orders its own pencils and paper clips and other "inexpensive and nonstrategic" purchases.

3. Let those in the organization who collect information be the ones who process it. For example, when the public relations department wants to send out its newsletter to a mailing list, it should be able to generate the mailing labels itself rather than having to make a request to a data processing department.

4. Treat decentralized organizational resources as centralized, utilizing information technology to bring them together. A college with several satellite campuses, for example, could link its bursars so that a student making a payment at either the main office or a satellite campus would have the payment show up in the records of the registrars of all of the campuses.

5. Electronically link disparate parts of an organization to promote coordination.

6. Let those who perform the work make the decisions, thereby flattening the pyramidal management layers and eliminating the bureaucracy and delay that slow down a decision-making process.

7. Use relational databases and other technology to collect and store information only once, eliminating both redundancy and error.

Generally, BPR often enables a single person to perform all of the steps in a process by using information technology. One byproduct of BPR is that the need for many employees may be eliminated. This saves a lot of money for organizations. One downside is that BPR may have the effect of terrorizing a work force.

Benchmarking

Benchmarking refers to the process by which organizations study how organizations similar to theirs perform their business processes and learn how to adapt those that are most efficient, innovative, and successful. Obviously, no two organizations are alike, and there is no guarantee that copying something from another organization will automatically work well in your own. But certainly there is value in exploring how other organizations perform some of the tasks your organization does, and discussing what efficiencies they may have found that would improve your business operations. For-profit organizations have been doing this in a formalized way for many years. Nonprofit organizations are just recently recognizing the value of benchmarking.

There are two types of benchmarking that nonprofit organizations might wish to consider. The first, internal benchmarking, looks at your organization and projects future goals, including a process by which employees are encouraged to meet performance targets. External benchmarking, on the other hand, tries to determine the "best practices" of similar organizations. Rather than reinventing the wheel, external benchmarking permits you to allocate minimal resources to finding how others have solved a problem, or have exponentially increased productivity with respect to some process, rather than having to discover that on your own.

Many nonprofit organizations are not only willing to share this information, but are quite proud to do so. The fact that competition among nonprofit organizations is almost always either friendly or nonexistent promotes benchmarking in a manner that avoids some of the troublesome potential conflicts and ethical dilemmas in the for-profit context.

Jason Saul, writing in a chapter on benchmarking in *Improving Quality and Performance in Your Non-Profit Organization*, says that nonprofits should typically consider benchmarking in three general categories: A **process** (such as screening job applicants or organizing inventory in a food bank), a **policy** (such as a salary structure or incentive plan), or a **program** (such as welfare-to-work or educational incentives).

Three approaches taken to benchmarking include:

- *technical approach* (using computer models, statistics, spreadsheets, and other quantitative methods)

- *committee approach* (bringing in a team of experts from outside your organization to gather data and make judgments about which changes would be beneficial to the organization)

- *survey approach* (combining the above two models by creating a team of individuals from within the organization to identify which processes should be benchmarked, define the measures and organizational performance, obtain "best practices" information, and implement these practices).

Saul, who is the co-founder of The Center for What Works, a Chicago-based clearinghouse for those studying solutions to social problems, recommends a seven-step process for benchmarking. It includes self-assessment, measuring performance, assembling the team, data collection, evaluating practices, translating best practices, and continuously repeating the process.

Outcome-Based Management (OBM)

To improve quality in a larger organization, simply adopting a progressive management philosophy such as TQM or BPR is not going to suffice in today's modern competitive business climate. As an organization grows, there are more pressures for accountability, not only internally from a board of directors, but externally from elected officials, government funders, foundation funders, individual donors and volunteers, and the public. Leaders of large organizations generally do not have the ability to visualize every aspect of their organization's operations and assess what is going on just by looking out their office windows, or by engaging in informal conversations with their staff and clients. The proverbial "one-minute manager" is an ideal construct that is not particularly well suited to crystallizing the information a CEO needs to make judgments on how to allocate precious resources.

To accomplish the important task of determining what is really going on within a large organization, most organizations have a Management Information System (MIS), which permits the aggregation of data in a form that can be analyzed by a manager, enabling him or her to see trouble spots and make adjustments in operations and to generate reports required by the government, funders, auditors, and the board of directors.

For many larger nonprofits, particularly those that depend on government and foundation grants rather than private donations, the objective of "meeting clients' needs" has become a more formalized process. Times have changed within just the last decade or so. Traditionally, measures of organizational performance for human service organizations were based on a model more appropriate for industrial processes, where raw materials were turned into finished products. In the language of industrial systems analysis, inputs (the raw material) were processed into outputs (the finished product).

In adopting an analogous frame of reference to industry, the conventional thinking was that human service agencies took in unserved clients (input), provided services (process), and changed them into served clients (output). In this way of thinking, organizations improved their output by increasing the number of clients served.

An exciting new way of looking at the output of an agency is called outcome-based management (OBM) or "results-oriented accountability" (ROA). Most recently, results-oriented management and accountability (ROMA) has become the buzzword describing this general tool. OBM focuses on program outcomes rather than simply quantifying services delivered. Program outcomes can be defined as "benefits or changes for participants during or after their involvement with a program" (from *Measuring Program Outcomes: A Practical Approach, United Way of America*).

For example, an organization with a mission of reducing drug abuse may have a stellar record of attracting clients through a flashy outreach program. It may be exemplary in convincing doctors in the community to donate thousands of hours of free services to the program, thereby reducing unit costs per client. It may have few complaints from the clients, who feel the staff are competent and treat them with dignity. An analysis of conventional data might indicate that there is little room for improvement. But, perhaps, data are not collected on whether those treated for drug abuse by the organization are successfully able to become independent, avoid future interactions with the criminal justice system, and abstain from drug use for an extended period of time—all measurable outcomes for a successful substance abuse program. If most of these clients are back on the street abusing drugs, is that organization providing successful treatment, even if drug abuse services are being provided? Are funders and taxpayers getting a fair return on their investment?

In the outcome-based management model, the number of clients served is an input. The outcome is considered to be a measurement of the change in the condition of the clients after receiving the services. For example, if thousands of clients are served, but the condition of the clients has not improved, then the outcome is zero, even if the services were provided 100% on time, every client received a satisfactory number of hours of services, and there were no client complaints. It is no longer indicative of the effectiveness and value of an organization to only collect data on how many clients sought services, how many of these were accepted into the client stream rather than being referred or turned down, how many hours of service were provided, and how much each service cost and was reimbursed. Outcome data, together with the above process data, are needed to measure the effectiveness and value of an organization.

In addition to a significant change in attitude about the accountability of the private nonprofit sector, the passage in 1993 of the *Government Performance and Results Act,* PL 103-62, changed the way federal agencies plan, budget, evaluate, and account for federal spending. The intent of the act is to improve public confidence in federal agency performance by holding agencies accountable for program results and improving congressional decision-making. The act seeks to accomplish this by clarifying and stating program performance goals, measures, and costs "up front." These changes were implemented beginning in September 1997.

For some organizations, the shift to outcome-based management will have modest cost implications. It may mean more data being collected from clients during intake. It may mean follow-up surveys to see what happens to clients after they have availed themselves of the organization's services. When this information is available, it is of extraordinary value to those who design, administer, and deliver those services.

What makes outcome-based management an easy sell to the human services sector is that it is common sense. What is the point of investing thousands, if not millions, of dollars of an agency's resources if the end result is not accomplishing what is intended by the investment—improving the lives of the agency's clients?

Our human service organizations have been established to make people's lives better. When our organizations change their focus to concentrate on doing what it takes to make people's lives better, as opposed to simply providing human services, it is much more likely that this worthy goal can be accomplished successfully. Such a philosophy is compatible with the values of most in the sector, who often make financial sacrifices to make a difference in the lives of those who need human services.

In cases in which the data show that an agency is successfully providing services, but those services are not having the intended effect on the clients, the agency leadership should be the first to recognize that it is wasteful to continue business as usual. Outcome-based management is a powerful tool that allows organizations to allocate their precious resources to do the most good. If successfully implemented, it also can provide the ammunition to fight the increasing public cynicism about what is often perceived to be a poor return on investment of tax dollars, and provide a competitive edge to organizations that adopt it.

Large Group Intervention (LGI)

Large Group Intervention (LGI) is the generic name given to a family of formal change management strategies that involve placing large parts of an organization, or even the entire organization, in simultaneous contact with one another to plan how the organization is going to change. Proponents and users of LGIs believe these methods are particularly well suited to organizations seeking to establish a shared vision of their future and to build a road to get there. Some LGI models are designed specifically for organizations seeking to change the way their work is done (e.g., through reengineering or business process redesign).

Although many different LGI models have been developed and are in current use, they generally have common origins and are rooted in similar principles. Among these principles are getting the "whole system" into interactive discussion, using a carefully designed mixture of communication elements and processes designed to make effective use of participants' emotions as well as thoughts, and facilitating effective dialogue while validating differing perspectives.

Large Group Interventions are usually staged in a setting away from the workplace, where participants can focus on the objective at hand without the distractions of the normal work environment. Artificial boundaries within organizations, such as functional departments, are routinely and intentionally fractured to facilitate communication and participation. These boundaries often get in the way of addressing important needs of organizations.

Strategies such as TQM and BPR, as well as strategic planning itself, demand that each member of the organization think about the needs of the entire organization rather than his or her piece of it. "Democratic," participatory efforts by organizations may facilitate their members to see beyond the borders of their individual organizational niche and develop the spirit required to make TQM not simply a "program" but a working philosophy.

The general philosophy inherent in planning change is recognizing that there is resistance to change within organizations. Change is more likely to be successfully implemented when people affected can participate in the process, influence the process, and prepare for its consequences.

Much more than a device for overcoming psychological resistance, LGI is an effective approach to substantially improve the planned change and achieve more desirable results for the organization. One dimension of additional benefits is more effective communication about the planned changes. Plans become far less distorted when everyone affected is hearing the same message at the same time, rather than having it communicated through the grapevine, through regular hierarchical channels, or not at all.

Another advantage of LGI is that those affected by the changes can provide invaluable input. It is rare that a few layers of management (or a subset of the full breadth of functions) within an organization can have an adequately detailed grasp of the whole. In most change management strategies, those at the bottom of the hierarchy, who are usually the most aware of the "nuts and bolts" of current reality, are often frozen out of the planning process. Most LGI models bring in a broad base of stakeholders to brainstorm together and to weed out problems and unintended consequences that often are otherwise built into initial designs for change, because they are invisible to the unrepresentative group of staff traditionally involved in planning.

A third advantage of LGI is that it builds a diverse and broad base of support for planned changes. Useful in all cases, this advantage becomes particularly powerful when circumstances alter, planned changes need to be modified, and time is of the essence. Circumstances that otherwise could be expected to derail well-laid plans can be addressed by a robust and already engaged subset of the organization. Plans are far more open to effective alteration midstream when developed via an LGI approach.

LGIs tend to bring together people from various hierarchical levels within the organization, who otherwise may have minimal direct interaction. Many organizational development experts believe that bringing large groups of organizational members together pays an additional dividend of creating positive social linkages among organizational members that would otherwise not have been created. Large Group Interventions create a new and different organizational bonding, which increases networks of informal communication within an organization and makes for more robust capabilities.

All of this can occur in a three-day period, significantly curtailing the process time of conventional change management planning.

Permitting workers affected by planning to participate in the planning process is one strategy to erode resistance to organizational change, in addition to generating fresh ideas from people who have expertise as a result of doing their jobs every day. They may have shied away from making valid, responsible suggestions, not only because "no one ever asked us," but because they may feel that their views are not important, or that management does not have an interest in listening to them.

Among the most popular models for LGIs are the Search Conference, Future Search Conference, and Real-Time Strategic Change. For additional details about these interventions, consult the book *Improving Quality and Performance in Your Non-Profit Organization*.

Tips:

- **Don't fall into the "goal displacement" trap by concentrating more on the paperwork involved in making a TQM program run than on the actual change in culture and staff attitudes that make TQM an attractive change management strategy.**

- **Consider the steps that might be necessary to undo a change management strategy in the event that it simply doesn't work for one reason or another.**

- **Avoid the undesirable outcome of making your organization more streamlined, efficient, and effective, but with employees who can't stand to be there anymore.**

- **Incorporate useful concepts in this chapter, such as benchmarking and outcome-based management, into your strategic planning process in the event your organization engages in such planning.**

Chapter 32
Organization and Program Evaluation

Synopsis: A formal program evaluation process is often a requirement of funders, but is otherwise an important exercise to determine whether nonprofit organizations and programs are effective. There are two major types of evaluations—formative and summative. Evaluations may be performed by in-house staff or outside consultants, and each has its advantages and disadvantages. Regardless of who performs an evaluation, organizations should engage in a thorough planning process.

Introduction

In the opening to his seminal book *Utilization Focused Evaluation,* the required textbook in the graduate school course on program evaluation that I took at Penn State, Michael Quinn Patton relates the following parable:

> *In the beginning, God created the heaven and the earth.*
> *And God saw everything that He made. "Behold," God said, "it is very good." And the evening and the morning were the sixth day.*
> *And on the seventh day God rested from all His work. His archangel came then unto Him asking, "God, how do you know that what you have created is 'very good'? What are your criteria? On what data do you base your judgment? Just exactly what results were you expecting to attain? And aren't you a little close to the situation to make a fair and unbiased evaluation?"*
> *God thought about these questions all that day and His rest was greatly disturbed. On the eighth day God said, "Lucifer, go to hell."*
> *Thus was evaluation born in a blaze of glory....(Patton, 1997, p.1)*

I love this story for many reasons, but I think it crystallizes in my mind some of the dilemmas of program evaluation in a humorous way. To those who run programs, an evaluation is often perceived as a way outsiders find fault with how they operate their programs and make decisions. To the evaluators, they often find that staff are not forthcoming because of a fear that blame for any shortcomings will fall on them. Yet, it clearly makes no sense for those who run and fund programs not to step back occasionally and determine whether what they are doing is really working as they expect, and how their programs could be improved.

Evaluation is a general term that describes determining whether an existing organization or a particular program of an organization is fulfilling its purposes, goals, and objectives, and if it is achieving results from its efforts and allocation of resources. The term is also used in the context of determining how well an organization's employees are functioning, and this topic is discussed in Chapter 13.

Organizations are increasingly being asked to engage in formal evaluation exercises by stakeholders, including the organization's own board, government grantors, private foundations, and donors. Many subsectors within the nonprofit sector, such as hospitals, universities, and nursing homes, are required to have periodic formal evaluations by the private agencies that have been formed to provide accreditation. Virtually every government or foundation grant includes a requirement for an evaluation of the program being funded at the end of the grant period. And, as described in Chapter 31, the scope of evaluations has ratcheted upward with a movement to focus on program outcomes, evaluating not simply whether an agency is doing the work that it says it is doing—such as providing so many hours of counseling—but determining whether those who are receiving the agency's services are actually having their lives and the community in which they live changed for the better as a result of having received those services. The *Government Performance and Results Act of 1993* was enacted "to shift the focus of government decisionmaking and accountability away from a preoccupation with the activities that are undertaken—such as grants dispensed or inspections made—to a focus on the results of those activities, such as real gains in employability, safety, responsiveness, or program quality" (Government Accountability Office, 2007). The United Way of America displayed leadership in adopting an outcome-based approach and advocating for its implementation by nonprofit organizations funded by its affiliate umbrella fundraising charities.

Program evaluation has in recent years become a routine requirement, as nonprofit organizations are increasingly being asked to be accountable for the dollars being spent to further their missions. And this is a good thing, generally. It certainly doesn't make much sense to spend government tax dollars and funds gratuitously donated by foundations, corporations, and the public on programs that are not accomplishing much. Even the fact that there will be an evaluation of a program can serve as motivation to continue to improve its operation, so as to avoid the consequences of a poor evaluation. Evaluations often uncover flaws in program management that might not otherwise be discovered, thus improving the delivery of services to those who need them and making programs both more efficient and effective. For the leadership of nonprofit organizations, this is valuable information.

One downside is that those involved in programs being evaluated often view evaluations as something that is being done *to* them rather than *with* them, and there can be a real fear that a poor evaluation, regardless of whether this is performed by an outside consultant or in-house staff, could result in a program being terminated, putting their jobs at risk. Evaluations cost money and other scarce resources, and they often require staff to put aside their work of providing services to participate in the data collection process.

The intent of formal program evaluations is to provide objective assessments of what is going on in an organization and/or its programs. Ideally, the evaluation should be carried out by someone experienced in the tools and techniques of program evaluation, and who has no bias with respect to judging the program and its staff. This is easier said than done. It is quite clear that it is much more subjective and a clear conflict of interest for the staff of an organization's programs to be the ones who evaluate their own organization or program. Yet, evaluations performed by outside consultants can be expensive, and such consultants often do not have the background and know the staff well enough to reach conclusions about what might improve a program.

Regardless of who carries out the evaluation, the more "objective" the evaluator can be, the more likely the evaluation will address program shortcomings in a fair way. Evaluations should be focused on making programs better in the future rather than pointing the finger of blame, and crafted in language that provides a clear roadmap for implementing constructive changes.

What is Program Evaluation?

Program evaluation is a form of research. It involves data collection and analysis of that data. Program evaluation is a process that involves the systematic collection of information about an organization to determine how well the organization or its individual programs are working, and what might be done to improve performance. Information that is collected might include the program's activities; program outputs; program outcomes; program work processes and policies; data about program quality; how stakeholders, including clients, perceive the program; and judgments about ways the organization's program could improve to reach its stated goals.

There are two general forms of a program evaluation. A *summative evaluation* is one that focuses primarily on the effectiveness of a particular program. Typically, a summative evaluation is conducted after a program is completed, and its purpose is to determine whether the program is effective enough to continue. This is the type of evaluation most requested by funders, who need to determine whether to continue funding the program for future years. A *formative evaluation* is one that is used to determine how a program might be improved. Formative evaluations look at a program's strengths and weaknesses, problems that exist with implementation and how they might be addressed, changes in the program that are being suggested by stakeholders, unintended consequences of program implementation, and new ideas that might be tested to improve performance. Stakeholders are staff and board of the organization, its funders, those who directly benefit from its services (*clients, patients,* and *consumers* are among the terms used by organizations to describe recipients of their services, and each one has a connotation that can be viewed as positive or negative, depending on the organization's culture), community leaders, government leaders, and the public at large.

The distinction between the two is that *summative* implies a final judgment about the program; *formative* does not. As related in Patton's book, Bob Stake, an evaluation theorist at the University of Illinois, came up with an apt metaphor to describe the difference:

"When the cook tastes the soup, that is formative; when the guests taste the soup, that's summative"! (Patton, 1997, p. 69).

Why Program Evaluation is Performed

The most common reason why program evaluation is performed is somewhat obvious—it is required by an organization's stakeholder with power to require it (such as an accreditation body), or a grantor (such as the government or a foundation). Yet there are clear benefits for an organization's board or CEO to insist that a program or the entire agency be periodically evaluated.

Benefits include—

1. Evaluations uncover flaws in a program, which can lead to corrective action, improving service delivery, outcomes of clients, and more efficient use of scarce organizational resources.

2. They can help determine whether a program is really doing what it was designed to do.

3. They validate that a "good" program is really a "good" program by having this determined by an objective third party, rather than the organization itself.

4. They help program staff step back and reflect on what they can do to improve efficiency and effectiveness of a program. Staff can brainstorm and communicate ideas to someone trained in looking for patterns, and who may have experience in working with other organizations that have responded to the same type of problems. Program staff may otherwise be too engrossed in providing the services and have little time to consider how the delivery of these services could be improved, or communicate about program policies that they feel are barriers to overcoming problems.

Who Performs a Program Evaluation

There are generally three options in deciding who will perform a program evaluation: using an outside consultant, using staff from the organization itself, or using a combination of an outside consultant and staff. For example, an outside consultant may design and direct the evaluation with organization staff performing a major role in collecting and analyzing the data. (Thomas, 1997). Outside evaluators are often found in research think tanks and educational institutions. There are also many private consultants who offer this service.

Each option has its own advantages and disadvantages:

Outside Consultants:

Advantages

- Outside consultants typically have special training in how to perform formal program evaluations.
- They can be more objective than an in-house staff evaluator, as they have no direct stake in the findings of the evaluation.
- They have experience working with other organizations and can provide a perspective that in-house evaluators do not have.
- They can do much of the work of an evaluation, freeing the organization's staff from tasks that would otherwise disrupt their routines.

Disadvantages

- Outside consultants are expensive compared to in-house evaluators.
- They are likely to not have too much background about the organization.
- They are likely to not have as much background about the program's recipients.
- They may be unable to get close enough to the program to understand what is really going on.
- They may be willing to provide an organization with a more "positive" evaluation than warranted by the facts, knowing that this may enhance their potential for obtaining future evaluation contracts from the organization

In-House Staff

Advantages

- In-house staff are likely to be less expensive than outside consultants.
- They are more likely to understand the program's objectives.
- They are more likely to understand the programs themselves, their target populations, and their other stakeholders.
- They are more likely to understand and be sensitive to the internal politics of the organization and already know the staff, organization structure, and culture.

Disadvantages

- In-house staff are more likely to be perceived as being less objective than an outside consultant.

- They are less likely to know how other, similar organizations are dealing with work processes.
- They may be too busy doing their other tasks for the organization to do a good job evaluating.

Combination of the Two Models

Some organizations use an evaluation method that combines these two models. An outside consultant can direct the evaluation, develop the methodology, and analyze the data, while staff can do the leg work and collect the appropriate data. Or a staff member can direct the evaluation and a consultant can make sure the data collection and analysis are both appropriate and valid. This assures that there is some outside technical expertise that can be accessed, but that staff feel more buy-in to the results if they have a major role in participating in the evaluation.

Obviously, whatever model is chosen must be consistent with the practices and standards of the stakeholder requiring the evaluation.

Planning for Program Evaluation

The planning for program evaluation begins at the point at which a program is conceived, often at a point before funding is obtained to implement it. First, each program needs to be associated with a concrete, measurable set of goals and objectives. What must be measured are aspects of the program that relate to how well the organization is providing its services. This is typically done by compiling a set of outputs and outcomes that are hoped to be achieved before a program is started. A list of these benchmarks is typically provided to a funding agency in advance of funding, as part of the grant application. Although it seems to be common sense, organizations don't always design their management information systems to capture this data, even though doing so saves a lot of time and effort when it is time to perform an evaluation.

For example, let's consider a program to assist homeless people in a community not to engage in using illegal substances and alcohol. In applying for grant funds for such a program, an organization would likely provide data on how many people in the community are homeless and how many of them use illegal drugs and alcohol. The organization would carefully document the lack of other programs that sufficiently provide these services, to demonstrate that this new program would not be duplicative and would fill a need. The organization that received a grant to provide such a program would have intake of homeless clients with a drug or alcohol problem, provide treatment, and then attempt to keep track of these clients over time and measure whether they still use illegal drugs and alcohol after completing the program. Of course, this is not so simple; homeless people tend to be transient. It may not be possible to know whether someone is using drugs and alcohol (although it may be possible to know that clients are being admitted to other programs in the area for treatment, or are entering the criminal justice system for drug- and alcohol-related crimes—data that could serve as a surrogate for other data that would be much harder to collect). But the point is that data should be routinely collected that will help evaluators determine whether a program is being effective, and it makes sense to have a system in place that has this data collected *before* it is required for an evaluation rather than after.

An excellent model for planning an evaluation can be found at:

http://www.managementhelp.org/evaluatn/fnl_eval.htm#anchor4294569952

Another useful document is provided by the Office of Planning, Research & Evaluation of the Department of Health and Human Services' Administration for Children and Families (OPRE). In Chapter 6 of this free, online, evaluation guide, the Office recommends that organizations consider scores of issues when designing their program evaluation. Among them are recommendations to—

1. *Designate the evaluation framework.* This includes the program objectives; evaluation questions; evaluation time frame; and a discussion of the context for the evaluation, particularly the aspects of the agency, program staff, and participants that may affect the evaluation.

2. *Consider procedures and methods.* These include those that will be used to obtain the evaluation data and answer the evaluation questions. Organizations need to decide where the data will come from (e.g., client records, staff interviews, observations by evaluators of clients receiving services, data already collected by the MIS system), whether the data will consist of samples or comprise the entire population being studied, what types of survey instruments will be used (such as e-mail questionnaires, telephone interview questions, focus groups), how to keep the information collected confidential and secure while respecting the privacy of respondents, how to design consent forms permitting the release of data from individuals, who will administer the instruments or otherwise collect the data, and the methods that will be used to analyze the data.

3. *Select your evaluation design.* The design should allow you to assess whether participation in the program is *really* responsible for making a difference seen in the recipients or is perhaps caused by some other factor(s). This gets to the issue of causality. For example, let's assume that you run a drug treatment center that provides services to individuals. Your data show that those who received services used illegal drugs less after one year in the program. One interpretation is that the program was effective in reducing drug use. But there are other possible explanations: Perhaps the price of drugs increased beyond the ability of these individuals to afford them. Or, perhaps new laws and increased drug law enforcement put drug pushers in jail, so that users no longer had easy access to drugs. Or perhaps these individuals simply "grew up" and no longer felt the need to use illegal drugs.

Evaluators often use scientific procedures to eliminate threats to validity, as they are called, that call the explanation of results of a study into question.

For example, there are a lot of threats to validity when evaluators rely on a simple pre-test/post-test design of an evaluation. That is, the evaluator measures some variable that is considered important (e.g., drug use) before services are delivered, and measures the same variable in the individuals after the services are delivered.

Many threats to validity are eliminated by using a control group. The evaluator may randomly assign two groups of individuals, one group receiving the treatment and the other not receiving any treatment, and then do pre-test/post tests to determine if there are any differences between the two groups. There are problems with this procedure, as well, as it may be unethical for an organization to deny services to those who need them simply because of an evaluation experimental design. But putting ethical considerations aside, using a control group with random assignment is much preferable to a simple pre-test/post-test research design in determining whether the program itself is the cause of improvement in program recipients. Many nonprofit organizations can ethically use control groups in their evaluations, because the demand is so great for their services that there is often a large waiting list of unserved clients.

But the bottom line remains. As the OPRE document summarizes, evaluations are designed to answer basic questions such as:

- Did program participants demonstrate changes in knowledge, attitudes, behaviors, or awareness?
- Were the changes the result of the program's interventions? (OPRE, 2007)

Those who are trained in administering evaluations have a lot of research and statistical tools, including effective experimental designs, at their disposal to get valid answers to these questions.

4. *Manage and monitor the evaluation.* This involves how staff will be trained and monitored with respect to working on the evaluation, making sure the survey instruments are culturally appropriate and clear, making sure staff are informed about what is going on and their responsibilities to cooperate with the evaluation, and validating that the evaluation will answer the right questions.

The full text of the OPRE document can be accessed at:

http://www.acf.hhs.gov/programs/opre/other_resrch/pm_guide_eval/reports/pmguide/chapter_1_pmguide.html

Conclusion

Many nonprofit executives have a fear of program evaluation, but in most cases, this fear is unfounded. For those who are committed in the sector to serving the needs of the most vulnerable in our society, program evaluation is one of the most useful tools available to improve the management of nonprofit organizations. A nonprofit organization's board and staff leadership have a stake in identifying what is working and not working in their programs. They have an obligation to document to funders and the public that their dollars are being used wisely, and that the organization is accountable for the trust placed in it to provide services that are appropriate and high quality. In many cases, an evaluation provides the evidence that the agency is meeting its obligations and worthy of being funded. As more and more evaluations of organizations occur, the knowledge base of what works and what doesn't is expanding, and society is the main beneficiary of this effort.

References

Government Accountability Office (2007). Reports on the Government Performance and Results Act. Accessed at: http://www.gao.gov/new.items/gpra/gpra.htm

Brun, Carl F. (2005). *A Practical Guide to Social Service Evaluation.* Chicago, IL: Lyceum.

McNamara, Carter (2007). Basic Guide to Program Evaluation. The Nonprofit Management Library. Accessed at: *http://www.managementhelp.org/evaluatn/fnl_eval.htm#anchor4294569952*

Office of Planning, Research & Evaluation, Administration for Children and Families, U.S. Dept. of Health and Human Services (2006). The Program Manager's Guide to Evaluation. Washington, DC:

Author. Accessed at: *http://www.acf.hhs.gov/programs/opre/other_resrch/pm_guide_eval/reports/pmguide/chapter_1_pmguide.html*

Patton, Michael Q. (1997). *Utilization-Focused Evaluation* (3rd Ed.). Thousand Oaks, CA: Sage.

Thomas, John Clayton (2004). Outcome Assessment and Program Evaluation. in *The Jossey Bass Handbook of Leadership and Nonprofit Management*, Robert D. Herman and Associates (Ed.), San Francisco, CA: Jossey Bass. pp. 391-415.

Wadsworth, Yoland (1997). Everyday Evaluation on the Run. St. Leonards, Australia: Allen and Unwin.

Part II

A Student Guide to Nonprofit Organizations

Author's Note: This section of *The Nonprofit Handbook*, *A Student Guide to Nonprofit Organizations,* was added beginning with the Third Edition in recognition of the fact that previous editions of this publication have been used as a textbook in nonprofit management courses. I have been delighted by this, and I wanted to add material that would make it more useful to students without changing the focus of the principal purpose, which is to provide an accessible handbook for practitioners.

The material in this section is divided into four chapters covering the definition and scope of the sector, a history, theory relating to it, and its future. The source of the first three chapters of this material was my doctoral dissertation. The source of the chapter on the future of the sector is an academic paper I presented at the 2004 annual meeting of the Association for Research on Nonprofit Organizations and Voluntary Action (ARNOVA). The intent of these chapters is to increase the book's value for students, educators, and practitioners in obtaining a better understanding of the sector and the role it plays in civil society.

In 2004, I created a textbook version of *The Nonprofit Handbook,* called *Introduction to the Nonprofit Sector: A Practical Approach for the 21st Century.* This book includes discussion questions and activities in each chapter, and eliminates material from *The Nonprofit Handbook* that is of limited use to students. In 2007, White Hat Communications published a second edition of this textbook.

I welcome your comments and criticisms, which you can send to me at: *gary.grobman@paonline.com*

Chapter 33
Defining and Describing the Nonprofit Sector

Synopsis: The nonprofit sector is a significant part of our national economy and social fabric. There are significant differences between nonprofit and for-profit organizations, although both are forms of businesses. Nonprofits are mission-driven rather than profit- or power-driven, despite the fact that revenues come more from fees and dues than from contributions from private sources. The assets of U.S. nonprofit organizations exceed $3 trillion.

Nonprofit organizations take many forms and have been collectively referred to in many ways, including "nonprofits," "not-for-profits" (Brinckerhoff, 1994), "non-governmental organizations," (Najam, 1999), voluntary sector (Smith, 1972, Van Til, 1988), the "Third Sector" (Gidron, Kramer, and Salamon, 1992), the "philanthropic sector" (Hansmann, 1989), "voluntary agencies" (Kramer, 1987), the "independent sector" (Independent Sector), the "social sector" (Drucker, 2003), and "the charitable sector" (Osborne and Hems, 1995). To that list, economist Burton Weisbrod adds "collective" and "nonmarket" organizations (Weisbrod, 1975).

Nonprofit organizations are included in the construct "mediating structures," defined as those institutions that serve as a bridge between the individual and government, including families, neighborhoods, institutions of worship, and voluntary associations, and that are the value-generating and value-maintaining society structures (Berger and Neuhaus, 1977).

In recent years, the term "civil society" has been used to describe this broader social infrastructure of organizations and associations, although there appears to be no clear agreement on what is encompassed by the term. The term "hollow state" (Milward, et al., 1993) has been applied to organizations that perform the duties of government through contracts, including the nonprofit sector.

From hospitals, day care centers, cemeteries, and museums to youth organizations, community centers, schools, and religious institutions, nonprofit organizations have a pervasive influence on everyday life.

Certainly, this is clearly true in the United States. Of the 27.7 million organizations of all types in the United States in 1998, 1.626 million, or 5.8%, were federally tax-exempt. By 2005, the sector accounted for 5.2% of the U.S. economy and paid 8.3% of all U.S. wages, according to a report of the Urban Institute's National Center for Charitable Statistics. In 2004, nonprofits reported to the IRS a total revenue of $1.4 trillion in revenue and $3 trillion in assets (Urban Institute, 2007).

Because of the sector's diversity, some writers suggest that there is reason to question whether nonprofits constitute a distinctive sector at all, although these writers acknowledge that this uncertainty is just as applicable to the business sector (Gidron, Kramer, and Salamon, 1992).

Definition of Nonprofit Organizations

What distinguishes nonprofit organizations from their for-profit counterparts is that nonprofits have no outside equity interests. That is, they are not privately owned, but rather are controlled by a self-perpetuating board of directors with constraints on their activities, as provided in their articles of incorporation (or corporate charter document). Although the United States Congress has chartered some nonprofits, most are either incorporated or structured in other ways under state law (Hopkins, 1992).

Being a nonprofit does not preclude the organization from making a profit (often called "net revenue"), but these profits must be used to further the purpose of the organization rather than be distributed. It is this "private inurement doctrine" that is the essential difference between nonprofit organizations and their for-profit counterparts (Hopkins, 1992).

There are other distinctions between nonprofits and for-profits. Among them are the principal purpose (i.e., accomplishing a particular mission, compared with making money), governance structure (members of the community with diverse backgrounds compared to businesspersons), level of public accountability (substantial for nonprofits compared to minimal for for-profits), and destination of net revenue (required to further the purposes of a nonprofit organization rather than go into the pockets of the owners). Charities benefit from donations made to them by businesses and individuals who support their missions and purposes. The nonprofit sector also relies on the generous support of the half of American adults who volunteer on behalf of nonprofits.

An academic definition of a nonprofit organization is provided by Salamon and Anheier (1996). According to this definition, nonprofit organizations have five things in common:

1. They are formally constituted.
2. They are organized separately from government.
3. They are non-profit-seeking.
4. They are self-governing.
5. They are voluntary to some significant degree.

In a subsequent book, Salamon adds "of public benefit" to this list (Salamon, in Ott, 2001). While this is certainly true of charities, many nonprofits are formed to serve the interests of a broad class of membership, and are "of mutual benefit" rather than being "of public benefit."

I offer the following distinctions between nonprofits and for-profits:

1. Nonprofits are privately governed, but the benefits of what the organization produces accrue no more to the organization's governors than to other members of society or the organization's beneficiaries.

2. The principal purpose of the nonprofit organization is to promote a collective goal that is perceived to increase the benefit to the collective (defined as a constituency) much greater in number than the organization's board, such as a group with a common interest, a neighborhood, community, city, state, nation, or globe, rather than to generate profits.

3. The nonprofit organization makes "business" decisions designed to increase the benefits to that constituency rather than to maximize profits, and it is not viewed as making a "bad" business decision if it implements a strategy that advances the interests of its constituency resulting in financial loss. As Ott (2001, p. 1) points out, "Revenues are resources, not the end purpose."

4. Because of these first three factors, people feel that their contributions to the nonprofit organization, in time and money, will benefit that constituency rather than any private

interest, and are thus willing to volunteer their time and donate their money to the organization.

Despite these differences, nonprofits have much in common with commercial businesses.

> *Tax-exempt nonprofit corporations can, and do, operate in all other particulars like any other sort of business. They have bank accounts; own productive assets of all kinds; receive income from sales and other forms of activity, including donations and grants if they are successful at finding that sort of support; make and hold passive invest-ments; employ staff; enter into contracts of all sorts; etc. (McNamara, 2000).*

Nonprofits and for-profits share many aspects in common. Both need capital to launch their operations; both need cash flow to pay their bills in a timely manner; and both need revenues to pay for staff, supplies, utilities, rent, equipment, printing, and other goods and services. Charities typically generate revenue beyond that which is donated by the public, the business community, or foundations. For example, they sell services. It is typical that a third or more of the revenue from a charity that provides social services comes from user fees. While many agencies charge on a sliding scale based on income, it is not unusual for them to charge a market rate to those who can afford to pay and use the surplus so generated to cross-subsidize those who cannot afford to pay the full costs of services.

Models of Nonprofit Organizations

There is no monolithic model of the direction a nonprofit organization's activities may take to alleviate a societal problem. Advocates for the nonprofit sector are fond of relating the following illustration:

> *A person taking a stroll along a riverbank sees children floating down the river, all of them in obvious distress: one strategy the person can use to alleviate this distress is to jump in and rescue them one at a time. Another strategy is to trace their path upstream and see what is causing the children to fall into the river and fix that. A third strategy is to leave the scene and mobilize others to help pull children out of the water. And a fourth strategy is to raise funds to support organizations that will perform one or all of these strategies.*

Each strategy, translated to the establishment of an organization, has its place in nonprofit organization purposes and activities.

For example, during the spring and summer of 2001, the nation's attention focused on the case of a missing Capitol Hill intern, Chandra Levy. Government at all levels participated in the search for the missing woman. Voluntary sector organizations were created as a result of this case, including a foundation established by the parents of the missing woman. An organization using the first model described above might create a database of missing persons, and provide support and counseling to the families of victims. An organization using the second model might fund research to find out the core reasons for people to become missing and what preventive steps might work to mitigate this. An organization using the third model might create an advocacy organization to increase public awareness about the degree to which finding missing persons is high or low on the law enforcement agenda, and increase its visibility so as to encourage the devotion of more resources to finding missing children. An organization using the fourth model would provide grants to law enforcement agencies, advocacy organizations, or direct service providers that follow one of the other three models.

Classification of Nonprofit Organizations

Salamon (1999) divides the nonprofit sector into two broad categories: those that primarily serve the public and those that primarily serve the organization's members.

Public-Serving Organizations

A subclass of public-serving nonprofit organizations provides direct service, such as day care services, hospitals, nursing homes, mental health services, shelter to the homeless, and arts and music organizations. About 40% of known nonprofits fit in this category, and they account for about 80% of nonprofit organization employment. The bulk of nonprofit organization revenue is captured by health-related organizations (see Figure 1).

A second subclass is comprised of those organizations whose principal mission is to mobilize others to engage in activities that promote the public good. To do this, the organizations will be involved in substantial direct lobbying of legislative bodies to promote the passage or defeat of legislation, and/or engage in substantial grass-roots lobbying and public education efforts to change public attitudes. They include political action organizations that are primarily concerned with influencing the political process. These organizations may apply for federal tax-exempt status under Section 501(c)(4) of the Internal Revenue Code.

By law, nonprofits that are 501(c)(3) organizations may engage in lobbying efforts provided this activity is not "substantial," but they are prohibited from participating in partisan political activity in support of, or opposition to, any candidate for public office. Organizations exempt under Section 501(c)(4) of the Internal Revenue Code, on the other hand, may (and do) engage in substantial lobbying activities—often this is their sole purpose—but their donors are not eligible for tax deductions on donations to these organizations.

A third subclass of public-serving nonprofit organizations consists of educational and research organizations, such as the Brookings Institution, the Urban Institute, and the Heritage Foundation. These organizations are eligible for federal tax exemption under Section 501(c)(3) of the Internal Revenue Code.

Figure 1: Categories of Charitable Organizations (2001)

	# of Tax Returns	Revenue (in millions)
Arts, Culture, & Humanities	26,006	22,743
Education	41,153	157,307
Environment, Animals	9,413	9,019
Health	32,195	509,017
Human Services	91,131	135,846
International/For'n Affairs	3,360	10,494
Mutual Membership/Benefit	583	1,667
Public/Societal Benefit	21,537	43,666
Religious	14,989	7,163
Other or Unknown	202	52

Source: Internal Revenue Service: Figure D. Charities and Other Tax-Exempt Organizations, 2001 by Paul Arnsberger, Retrieved from: http://www.irs.gov/pub/irs-soi/01eochin.pdf

---

A fourth subclass of public-serving organizations is comprised of "funding intermediaries," or "umbrella" fundraising organizations—those whose principal mission is to channel financial support to other nonprofit organizations" (Salamon, 2001). The role of these intermediaries is to "help generate...private funding, to manage it once it is accumulated, and to make it available for use by other organizations in the sector" (Salamon, in Ott, 2001, p. 26). Included in the roster of funding intermediaries are foundations and federated funders, such as United Way and Jewish federations.

The number of foundations of all types is growing (see Figure 2). In 2006, the 79,765 foundations that provided reports to the IRS in the United States had assets of $472.7 billion and made grants totalling $36.4 billion (Lawrence, Austin & Mukai, 2007). The remaining 10% of the foundations are corporate foundations, community foundations, and operating foundations. Operating foundations are classified by the IRS as private foundations but function as both grantmakers and operators of charitable programs, particularly research, social welfare, or other charitable programs (Foundation Directory, 2006).

Figure 2: Number and Type of Foundations, 2003, 2004 and 2005

	2003	2004	2005
Total #	66,398	67,736	71,095
Independent	58,991	60,031	63,059
Corporate	2,549	2,596	2,607
Community	699	700	707
Operating	4,159	4,409	4,722

Source: Foundation Growth and Giving Estimates: Current Outlook, 2007 Edition, Foundation Center. p. 4.

The amount of assets of the largest foundations is impressive (see Figure 3). In 2005, corporate foundations controlled 4% of foundation assets—$17.8 billion—and provided $4 billion in grants. Community foundations controlled 6% of total foundation assets—$44.6 billion— and provided $3.2 billion in grants (Lawrence, Austin, & Mukai, 2007).

A second group of funding intermediaries consists of organizations such as United Way. These organizations typically solicit contributions from corporations and individuals with the promise

Figure 3: Top 10 Foundations in the United States as of October 2007

1.	Bill & Melinda Gates Foundation (WA)	$33,120,381,000
2.	The Ford Foundation (NY)	12,252,645,528
3.	J. Paul Getty Trust (CA)	10,133,371,844
4.	The Robert Wood Johnson Foundation (NJ)	9,367,614,774
5.	The William and Flora Hewlett Foundation (CA)	8,520,765,000
6.	W. K. Kellogg Foundation (MI)	7,799,270,734
7.	Lilly Endowment Inc. (IN)	7,601,664,181
8.	The David and Lucile Packard Foundation (CA)	6,350,664,410
9.	The Andrew W. Mellon Foundation (NY)	6,130,848,000
10.	John D. and Catherine T. MacArthur Foundation (IL)	5,492,269,240

Source: The Foundation Center (http://foundationcenter.org)

to allocate the bulk of these donations to member charities, all of which are required to be accountable to the intermediary through financial reports and community-based planning.

Member-Serving Organizations

Part of this class are business leagues that are granted federal tax-exempt status under Section 501(c)(6) of the Internal Revenue Code. The most common form of business league is the trade association, "a nonprofit, cooperative, voluntarily-joined, organization of business competitors designed to assist members and its industry in dealing with mutual business problems" (Hopkins, p. 582). The IRS defines a business league as "an association of persons having some common business interest, the purpose of which is to promote that common interest and not to engage in a regular business of a kind ordinarily carried on for profit. Trade associations and professional associations are considered business leagues" (Internal Revenue Service, 2003). They include Chambers of Commerce, boards of trade, real estate boards, and other organizations formed to promote business interests and "devoted to the improvement of business conditions of one or more lines of business as distinguished from the performance of particular services for individual persons" (Internal Revenue Service, 2003). The number of organizations exempt under Section 501(c)(6) of the Internal Revenue Code during FY 2005 was 86,563 (IRS, 2007).

Other types of member-serving organizations include social and recreational clubs (exempt under Section 501(c)(7)), labor and agricultural organizations (exempt under Section 501(c)(5)), benevolent life insurance associations (exempt under Section 501(c)(12)), and political organizations—both political action committees and political parties.

Differences Between Private Foundations and Public Charities

Public charities and private foundations are both granted tax-exempt status under Section 501(c)(3) of the Internal Revenue Code. However, Section 509(a) differentiates organizations that receive their income from a broad range of public sources from those organizations that receive their income principally from one, or a limited number of sources plus investment income (Kramer and Sykes, 2001). Private foundations pay a federal tax on net investment income, must meet a minimum annual threshold for making distributions of their assets to charities, and are flatly prohibited from lobbying. To be considered a public charity rather than a private foundation, an organization must pass a public support test enforced by the IRS. There are two such tests, one of which must be passed for the organization to be considered a public charity. The test is based on financial data for a four-year period. If one test is passed, the organization will qualify as a public charity for the following two years. For information about these tests, see: *http://members.aol.com/irsform1023/1023/compari.html* (Deja, 2002).

Nonprofits that don't fit neatly into the public-serving or member-serving category are the 375,000 religious congregations, about 80% of which do not register with the IRS or file a 990 federal annual tax return because there is no requirement to do so (Ott, 2001, p. 35, notes). As Salamon (1999) points out, while these congregations exist primarily to serve their members, their tax treatment is as if they primarily serve the public. In fact, nonprofit organizations are not required by law to file for exempt status with the Internal Revenue Service provided they have a recognized creed or form of worship, are "sacerdotal" in character, carry on regular religious services, and operate for other than private gain (Salamon, 1999).

Henry Hansmann (1987) has typologized nonprofits into four types, depending on their primary source of income (from either sales or donations) and their governing structure (a board consisting of members who do, or don't, directly benefit from the organization's services any more than anyone else in the community). The four types are: *donative and mutual, donative and entrepreneurial, commercial and mutual,* and *commercial and entrepreneurial.*

Organizations that generate most of their income from sales of goods and services are "commercial" nonprofits. Those that generate most of their revenue from donations are "donative" nonprofits. Those whose members directly benefit from the services provided by the organization are "mutual" nonprofits. And those whose members benefit no more from the organization than others in the community are "entrepreneurial" nonprofits. Examples are:

> **Donative and Mutual:** Common Cause, National Audubon Society, political clubs
> **Donative and Entrepreneurial:** CARE, March of Dimes, art museums
> **Commercial and Mutual:** American Automobile Association, Consumers Union, country clubs
> **Commercial and Entrepreneurial:** National Geographic Society, Educational Testing Service, hospitals and nursing homes (Handsmann, 1987).

Michael O'Neill has proposed differentiating the nonprofit sector into nine subsectors: religious, private education and research, health care, arts and culture, social services, advocacy and legal services, international assistance, foundations and corporate funders, and mutual benefit organizations (in Ott, 2001, p. 5). These functional categories are not necessarily mutually exclusive (e.g., a health care organization provides social services, and an international assistance organization might provide services related to one or more of the other eight categories), but this provides a useful framework for distinguishing a "field of interest."

How Organizations Are Funded

The source of nonprofit organization revenue is a function of many factors, including asset size (see Figure 4). According to a 2007 report published jointly by Independent Sector and the Urban Institute, *The New Nonprofit Almanac & Desk Reference,* total revenues of U.S. public charities totaled more than $1 trillion in 2005. Private contributions accounted for just 12.5% of this amount. The rest came from dues, fees, and charges (70.9%); government grants (9%); and other revenue, such as investments (7.6%). See Chapters 16 and 22 for a discussion on practical organizational fundraising strategies.

Figure 4: Source of Charitable Organization Revenue by Asset Size (FY 2001)

Total Assets (in dollars)	<100,000	100k-500k	500k-1m	1-10 M	10-50M	>50M
% from Contributions	55	53	45	44	29	15
% from Program Service Revenue	32	35	46	50	65	70
% from Investment Income	<1	1	1	2	2	3
% from Other	13	11	8	5	4	2

Source: Internal Revenue Service: Figure C. Charities and Other Tax-Exempt Organizations, 2001 by Paul Arnsberger, Retrieved from: http://www.irs.gov/pub/irs-soi/01eochin.pdf

---

Legal Definition of Tax-Exempt Charitable Organizations

Nonprofit status is conferred by individual states through incorporation procedures. It is federal law, however, that authorizes federal tax exempt status for nonprofit organizations that meet certain criteria. Such status has influence in many states on whether an organization will qualify for state and local sales, income, and property tax exemptions.

Section 501(c) of the Internal Revenue Code grants tax-exempt status to 25 categories of nonprofit organizations, including charities, business and trade associations, fraternal organizations, cemeteries, and credit unions (see Chapter 9). With limited exceptions, only one category, nonprofits exempt under Section (c)(3), provides that donations made by the public to such organizations are tax-deductible. These organizations are forbidden from engaging in substantial lobbying or propaganda activities, or engaging in political activities that advance the cause of any candidate for public office (Internal Revenue Service, 2001).

Size and Growth of the Voluntary Nonprofit Sector

The growth of the sector registered with the Internal Revenue Service in recent years has been significant (see Figure 5). Between 1989 and 1994, the population in the United States increased by 1.1%, while the number of reporting public charities increased by 6.3% (Stevenson, Pollack, and Lampton, 1997).

As pointed out by Lester Salamon, "under American law organizations are not required to incorporate, or even to seek formal recognition by the tax authorities, to function as tax-exempt nonprofit organizations. This organizational fluidity is, in fact, one of the prized features of this sector, enabling groups of people to meet together to pursue common purposes without having to seek official approval or even acknowledgment" (Salamon, 2001, p. 23). Yet federal tax-exempt status is highly prized, and only 501(c)(3) organizations, those that operate "exclusively for religious, charitable, scientific, literary, or educational purposes," are eligible to receive tax deductible donations from individuals and corporations. A standard justification for this policy is that "the organizations are serving purposes that are public in character and that government might otherwise have to support through tax revenues" (Salamon, 1999, p. 24).

According to the Internal Revenue Service (2006), there were 1.726 million nonprofit organizations with 501(c) status in FY 2006. This compares to 87,000 units of federal, state, and local government (University of California at Berkeley, 2003) and 22.2 million private, for-profit business firms in 2002 (Small Business Administration, 2003). The estimate does not include religious organizations, which are not required to register.

The sector employs more than 12.5 million people and encompasses about 9% of total employment (Independent Sector, 2001). Employment in the sector is more racially diverse than the other sectors and provides more employment for women. In 1994, 68% of employees were women and 15% were African-American, compared to 44% women and 10% African–American for the other sectors (Hodgkinson and Weitzman, 1996).

Between 1977 and 1994, the nonprofit sector expanded at a faster rate than the rest of the economy, with a 3.7% growth rate (which includes the assigned value of volunteer time) compared with 2.1% for the for-profit sector and 2.3% for the government sector. During this period, the annual increase in total employment in the nonprofit sector was 3.3% compared to 1.9% for for-profits and 1.4% for government (Hodgkinson and Weitzman, 1996). The authors attribute much

Figure 5: Growth of 501(c) Tax-Exempt Organizations, FY 2002-2006

Fiscal Year	# of Applications	Approved	Denied	Neither Approved or Denied
FY 2002	79,379	64,188	531	4,660
FY 2003	83,843	66,580	1,094	16,169
FY 2004	80,601	64,545	1,027	15,079
FY 2005	77,539	63,402	765	13,372
FY 2006	83,350	66,262	1,283	15,805

Source: Internal Revenue Service, IRS Databook, Publication 55b—Tax-Exempt Organizations and Other Entities Listed on the Exempt Organization Business Master File, by Type of Organization and Internal Revenue Code Section for fiscal year 2002, 2003, 2004, 2005, and 2006

of this growth to federal policies that funded Medicaid and Medicare, education grants, housing, job training, and other social welfare programs, which spurred the expansion of the nonprofit sector. By 1994, there were 1.03 million nonprofit entities (4.2% of all entities), generating 6.5% of national income, employing 9.7 million full- and part-time workers, and an additional 5.5 million full-time equivalent employee volunteers.

Nonprofit Taxonomies

There are several classification systems that provide a taxonomy of nonprofit organizations. The National Taxonomy of Exempt Entities (NTEE) is used by the Internal Revenue Service as part of its Master List of Exempt Organizations. There are approximately 645 different subcategories, with major categories including arts, education, environment, health, human services, public/ societal benefit, international, religious, and mutual/membership benefit (Barber, 2000). An updated version of the NTEE-CC is available at: *http://nccsdataweb.urban.org/FAQ/index.php?category=73*

A broader classification system—the North American Industrial Classification System (NAICS)— is used by the Census Bureau and for purposes of compliance with the North American Free Trade Agreement (NAFTA). It includes 1,170 categories of organizations. Nonprofit organizations are included in the Standard Industrial Codes (SIC) taxonomy first published in the 1930s by the Central Statistical Board of the United States. Major SIC classifications include "health services," "educational services," "social services," and "museums, botanical & zoological gardens," each with subcategories. The NAICS replaced SICs in 1999.

Section 501(c) of the Internal Revenue Code provides a taxonomy of various categories of nonprofit organizations that are eligible for tax-exempt status (see Chapter 9).

Assets of the Sector

One early estimate of $600 billion in total sector assets appears in the literature (Bakal, 1979). Gaul and Borowski estimated that nonprofit organizations control property, cash, and investments valued at $850 billion, a figure that they consider "conservative" (Gaul and Borowski, 1993, p. 3) because it doesn't take into account wealth controlled by churches or small nonprofits that are not required to file federal Form 990 tax returns. They estimated that the "true figure probably exceeds $1 trillion" (p. 3). These estimates of real estate value are considered flawed for two reasons. First, nonprofit property is typically not subject to regular appraisal. And second, it is

Figure 6: Total Assets and Net Worth of U.S. Charities Filing Annual Tax Returns (in $Millions)

	FY 2000	FY 2001	FY 2002
# of Organizations Filing Returns	230,159	240,569	251,676
Total Assets	1,562,536	1,631,719	1,733,852
Total Liabilities	539,367	611,390	693,576
Net Worth	1,023,169	1,020,329	1,040,275
Total Revenue	866,208	896,974	955,267
Contribtions, Gifts & Grants	199,076	212,427	214,484
Investment Income	29,136	23,678	20,518
Total Expenses	796,434	862,721	934,672

Source: Internal Revenue Service: Figure D. Charities and Other Tax-Exempt Organizations, FY 2002, 2001, and 2000 by Paul Arnsberger, Retrieved online from: http://www.irs.gov/pub/irs-soi/02eochin.pdf, http://www.irs.gov/pub/irs-soi/01eochin.pdf, and http://www.irs.gov/pub/irs-soi/00eochin.pdf, respectively.

difficult to appraise property of tax-exempt institutions under standards that apply to residential or business property because the value of a property is based on the profit it can generate (Simon, 1987).

Government estimates of sector assets are considerably higher. The Internal Revenue Service, using data from annual tax returns (see Figure 6), reported that assets of the sector increased from $899 billion in 1975 to $1.9 trillion in 1995 (Meckstroth and Arnsberger, 1998). This more than tripling of assets during the period contrasts with a 74% increase in gross domestic product during the same period.

A current estimate from the National Center for Charitable Statistics and the Bureau of Labor Statistics is that public charities in 2005 had $1.819 trillion in assets, private foundations had $455 billion, and other nonprofit organizations had $692 billion (Urban Institute, 2007).This compares to $777 billion in assets that public charities controlled in 1994. According to this study, most of these assets in 2005 were controlled by educational institutions ($534.44 billion) and health care institutions ($748.34 billion).

Boundaries of the Sector

As pointed out by Ott (2001), many nonprofit organizations that started out as voluntary associations have evolved into organizations that resemble large business organizations. Examples are Blue Cross/Blue Shield, credit unions, and the American Association for Retired Persons (AARP). Many large nonprofit hospitals, financial services companies, and mutual benefit companies also fit into this hybrid category of what he calls "corporatized nonprofits" (Ott, 2001, p. 5).

Added to this list are nonprofits that depend so heavily on government contracts that they have become almost indistinguishable from the government agencies that fund them. Some governmental instrumentalities form nonprofit organizations to avoid the managerial constraints they would have if a program or function were to be directly carried out by government.

Ott considers these organizations to be nonprofit organizations because they satisfy the legal definitions of this type of organization. But including them in the sector for this reason is not "uplifting," and if they are indeed part of the sector, they are on its outer fringes.

Differences Among the Sectors

Among some of the more salient differences described in the literature, both academic and other, are the following:

1. *Distribution of output differences.* The nonprofit can provide for individual choice that could not otherwise be provided by the private sector. The private sector has incentives to provide a uniform service to stay economically competitive (Ferris and Graddy, 1989). In general, nonprofits provide their output to the most needy, while for-profits provide their output to those who pay the most. Burton Weisbrod points out one interesting manifestation of this. Nonprofit organizations often have waiting lists for the services they provide. Weisbrod notes that profit-maximizing firms have little incentive to keep a waiting list because if there is an excess of demand for their services, they will increase their price (although there may be a waiting list to deal with uncertainties of unpredictable demand). Since the nonprofit is mission-driven and its goals are not to maximize profit, but rather to distribute its services to the most needy (under financial constraints that often result in the nonprofit engaging in cross-subsidization), waiting lists are appropriate (Weisbrod, 1988).

2. *Dissemination of information differences.* Studies by Weisbrod (1988) of facilities for long-term nursing care, long-term psychiatric care, and long-term care for the mentally handicapped showed that nonprofits were more willing than their for-profit counterparts to share information. Weisbrod attributes this willingness to the fact that nonprofit organizations do not gain an advantage by covering up information or otherwise taking advantage of the consumer.

3. *Willingness of people to volunteer.* People do not generally volunteer for for-profit organizations. Volunteering for government organizations, such as by student interns, is not uncommon, but it is not visible to the extent to which American adults volunteer in nonprofit organizations. Volunteering for nonprofit organizations is ingrained in our culture.

4. *Governance by a diverse volunteer board of community members.* Typical nonprofit organizations have volunteer, diverse board members, who make collective decisions and have a fiduciary responsibility for the affairs of the organization. This contrasts to boards of for-profit corporations, who frequently receive lucrative fees, are relatively homogeneous, and often receive direct benefit from the decisions they make (through the ownership of stock in the organization, for example).

5. *Mission-driven rather than profit-driven (or by a quest for political power or votes).* The voluntary sector has traditionally had a distinct role compared to the public and private sector, such as pioneering service delivery, promoting volunteerism, and advocacy (Kramer, 1981). Because "mission" is the driving force for nonprofits, rather than profits, nonprofits are more likely to respond to the heterogeneity of public demand, rather than simply providing a one-size-fits-all product. An example would be the programming of a public radio station compared to a top 40 station that lives or dies on ratings.

At least in theory, decisions regarding what services to provide and to whom to provide them are based not on profit-maximization considerations but rather whether doing so is consistent with the mission of the organization, given financial constraints. The incentive to maximize profits is at least reduced, if not eliminated, because any profits cannot by law inure to the benefit of the organization's board or trustees. The compensation of its employees must be reasonable and not based on the amount of net revenue. This constraint is enforced by the 1996 *Taxpayer Bill of Rights 2* law, final regulations of which were published by the Internal Revenue Service in the *Federal Register* in January 2001 (see Chapter 9).

Some nonprofits also seek to maximize profits. They create health care conglomerates, for-profit subsidiaries, partnerships, and mergers, although by law, the profit may not inure to the benefit of private persons. It is fashionable, consistent with New Public Management, for units of government to seek to "make a profit" by entrepreneurship, finding creative ways to generate revenue to respond to the burgeoning recession-induced deficits of the late 1980s and early 1990s (Osborne and Gaebler, 1992). But a case can be made that people (including employees, volunteers, and donors) are attracted to a nonprofit more because of the values it seeks to instill in society rather than its thirst for either power or profits (Van Hook, 1998).

6. *Accountability to the public, not stockholders.* Because nonprofits do not have stockholders who seek a return on their investment, the boards of directors of nonprofits do not have accountability to private seekers of profit. Rather, these organizations are authorized to exist by the state for limited purposes and, to qualify for their tax exemptions and other benefits, must not have a private profit motive.

Unlike most for-profit businesses, nonprofits must register and file public reports with various agencies of the federal and state government about their finances. Many states authorize the state attorney general to intervene in the affairs of the organization if there are allegations that decisions made by the board are not in the public interest. For example, decisions by a board to convert a nonprofit hospital to a for-profit hospital are typically subject to state review.

Specialized tax rules and accounting practices apply to nonprofit corporations. Larger organizations are required to disclose many details to the general public and to state regulators and watchdog agencies. They are required to file an annual tax return, Form 990, showing any salaries paid to officers or directors and to the five highest-paid employees (McNamara, 2000).

Organizations that raise at least $25,000 in donations from the public in Pennsylvania (most other states have similar reporting and registration requirements) must register and file reports with the Pennsylvania Department of State's Bureau of Charitable Organizations. The Attorney General has the power to review asset transfers of nonprofit organizations, and to make recommendations to a court about any questionable transfer. These may include a transaction that is not at arm's length, when fair market value is not obtained, or when one of the board members of an organization receives some financial benefit from the transaction.

7. *An ethical framework and a set of values that is geared to the benefit of society and the collective rather than to any single individual.* Lohmann (1992) writes that the nonprofit sector serves as the "commons" in which people voluntarily form communities with shared visions and values.

An ethical framework is primary to the nonprofit, compared to being only secondary within the government or business milieu.

The ethical frame can be shifted by the exigencies of organizational life in the government or private sectors. Government and business utilize ethical frames only as secondary mechanisms by which to measure performance. The rightness or wrongness of an act may be modified by whether it makes a profit for the firm or supports a government's appropriate need to control. However, for a non-profit organization the ethical frame is primary. Thus the very existence of a non-profit organization depends on its moral standing, its integrity, and its virtue (van Hook, 1998, p. 798).

8. *Depends on donations for some of its revenue, and may be directly subsidized by government grants and indirectly subsidized by tax laws that encourage the public to make these donations.*

As Professor Hansmann points out, a donor to a public radio station, symphony, or theater company can be reasonably assured that the donation will be used to enhance the service provided by the nonprofit organization. If the donation were made to a profit-making institution, there would be no reasonable expectation that the donation would go to improving the product rather than simply being added to profits. An overwhelming majority of donors of these organizations also attend performances. Donations, therefore, provide a form of voluntary differential pricing based on ability to pay (Hansmann, 1996).

9. *Depends for its existence on people behaving in ways not necessarily to increase their personal benefit but rather to increase the benefit to society.* This is the case, whether it be at the level of a neighborhood, community, city, state, country, species, or any one of thousands of subcategories such as an ethnic group, those who appreciate a particular form of music, those who wish to cure a particular disease, or those who want to save a particular animal from extinction. This is in contrast to government, which can invoke coercive power of law and imprison those who do not submit to it, or business, which depends on using the market for voluntary compliance with quid pro quo transactions.

As pointed out by Douglas (1987, in Ott, 2001, p. 206), "The problem arises when the benefits from a transaction cannot be confined to those who have contributed to the exchange and there is nothing to stop non-contributors from taking a free ride on the backs of the contributors."

It is this "free rider" problem that is of intense interest to economists and others who study nonprofits. When WITF, the local public radio station in Harrisburg, Pennsylvania, asks listeners for their annual membership contributions, the listeners probably assume that the station will continue broadcasting even if they choose not to contribute. The listener who pays membership dues will benefit from the station to approximately the same degree as his or her neighbor who may also listen to the station but chooses not to become a member. But these individuals make contributions, anyway. This is an aspect of nonprofit organizations that makes them unique.

Online Resources to Explore

Independent Sector
http://www.independentsector.org

National Center for Charitable Statistics
http://nccsdataweb.urban.org/FAQ/index.php?category=31

Nonprofit Genie
http://www.compasspoint.org/askgenie/index.php

Council on Foundations
http://www.cof.org/Council/?ItemNumber=4009

The National Council of Nonprofit Organizations
http://www.ncna.org/

References

Bakal, C. (1979). *Charity U.S.A.* New York: Times Books.

Barber, P. (2000). *Nonprofit faq (Frequently asked questions).* Retrieved February 10, 2002, from http://www.nonprofits.org/npofaq/16/27.html

Berger, P. L., & Neuhaus, R. J. (1977). *To empower people: The role of mediating structures in public policy.* Washington, DC: American Enterprise Institute.

Brinckerhoff, P. C. (1994). *Mission-based management: Leading your not-for-profit into the 21ˢᵗ century.* New York: Wiley and Sons.

University of California at Berkeley (2003). *Public Affairs Report.* v43, n4., Winter 2002-2003.

Deja, S. (2002). *Comparison of 509(a)(1)/ 170(b)(1)(A)(vi) & 509(a)(2) public charities www.form1023help.com.* Retrieved June 7, 2003, from http://members.aol.com/irsform1023/1023/compari.html

Douglas, J. (1987). Political theories of nonprofit organizations. In J. S. Ott (Ed.). *The nature of the nonprofit sector.* Boulder, CO: Westview Press.

Drucker, P. (2003). *About the Drucker foundation.* Retrieved June 7, 2003, from http://www.pfdf.org/about

Ferris, J. M., & Graddy, E. (1989). Fading distinctions among the nonprofit, government and for-profit sectors. In V. Hodgkinson, R. W. Lymen & Associates (Eds.). *The future of the nonprofit sector* (pp. 129-139). San Francisco: Jossey-Bass.

Foundation Directory. (2006). *Glossary of terms.* Retrieved online: *http://foundationcenter.org/getstarted/tutorials/gfr/glossary.html*

Gaul, G., & Borowski, N. (1993). *Free ride: The tax-exempt economy.* Kansas City, MO: Andrews and McMeel.

Gidron, B., Kramer, R. M., & Salamon, L. M. (Eds.). (1992). *Government and the third sector.* San Francisco: Jossey-Bass.

Hansmann, H. (1987). Economic theories of nonprofit organizations. In W. W. Powell (Ed.). *The nonprofit sector: A research handbook* (pp. 28-42). New Haven, CT: Yale University Press.

Hansmann, H. (1989). The two nonprofit sectors: Fee for service versus donative organizations. In V. A. Hodgkinson, R. W. Lyman & Associates (Eds.), *The future of the nonprofit sector* (pp. 91-102). San Francisco: Jossey-Bass.

Hansmann, H. (1996). *The ownership of enterprise.* Cambridge, MA: Harvard University Press.

Hodgkinson, V., Weitzman, M., & Abrahams, J.. (Eds.). *Nonprofit almanac (1996-97): Dimensions of the independent sector.* San Francisco: Jossey-Bass.

Hopkins, B. R. (1992). *The law of tax-exempt organizations* (6th Edition). New York: John Wiley and Sons.

Independent Sector. (2001). *The new nonprofit almanac in brief: Facts and figures on the independent sector 2001.* Washington, DC: Author.

Internal Revenue Service. (2001). *Tax-exempt status for your organization (Publication 557).* Washington, DC: U.S. Treasury Department.

Internal Revenue Service. (2003). *Tax exempt/Employee plans statistics—exempt organizations.*

Internal Revenue Service (2006). Publication 55b Table 22—Tax-Exempt Organizations and Other Entities Listed on the Exempt Organization Business Master File, by Type of Organization and Internal Revenue Code Section, Fiscal Years 2002-2005. Washington, DC: Author.

Internal Revenue Service (2007). *Publication 55b Table 25—Tax-Exempt Organizations and Nonexempt Charitable Trusts, Fiscal Years 2003-2006.* Washington, DC: Author.

Kerkman, L. (2003). Foundation giving in 2003 likely to drop, report says. *Chronicle of Philanthropy.* v15 n21. August 21, 2003, p. 10.

Kramer, D., & Sykes, V. (2001). *The guide for nonprofit organizations.* Dresher, PA: Nonprofit Issues.

Kramer, R. M. (1981). *Voluntary agencies in the welfare state.* Berkeley, CA: University of California Press.

Kramer, R. M. (1987). Voluntary agencies and the personal social services. In W. W. Powell (Ed.). *The nonprofit sector: A research handbook* (pp. 240-257). New Haven, CT: Yale University Press.

Lawrence, S.; Austin, A.; & Mukai, R. (2007). *Foundation Growth and Giving Estimates.* New York: The Foundation Center.

Lohmann, R. (1992). The theory of the commons. In J. S. Ott (Ed.). *The nature of the nonprofit sector* (pp. 89-95). Boulder, CO: Westview Press.

McNamara, C. (2000). *Two basic types of U.S. business organizations: For-profit and nonprofit.* Retrieved June 8, 2003, from http://www.mapnp.org/library/org_thry/types.htm#anchor1387675

Meckstroth, A. & Arnsberger, P. (1998). *A 20-year review of the nonprofit sector, 1975-1995.* Washington, DC: Internal Revenue Service.

Milward, H. B., Provan, K. G., & Else, B. (1993). The nongovernmental provision of public services to the mentally ill: What does the hollow state look like? In B. Bozeman (Ed.). *Research on public management* (pp. 309-322). San Francisco: Jossey-Bass.

Najam, A. (1999). Review of the book *Non-governments: NGOs and the political development of the third world*. *Nonprofit and voluntary sector quarterly, 3*, 364-367.

Osborne, David & Gaebler, Ted. (1992). *Reinventing government: How the entrepreneurial spirit Is transforming the public sector.* Reading, MA: Addison-Wesley.

Osborne, S., & Hems, L. (1995). *The economic structure of the charitable sector in the United Kingdom* (Abstract). Retrieved February 10, 2002, from http://poverty.worldbank.org/library/view.php?topic=4294&id=6228

Ott, J. S. (Ed.) (2001). *The nature of the nonprofit sector.* Boulder, CO: Westview.

Salamon, L. (1999). *America's nonprofit sector: A primer* (Second Edition). Washington, DC: The Foundation Center.

Salamon, L., & Anheier, H. K. (1996). *The emerging nonprofit sector.* New York: Manchester University Press.

Simon, J. G. (1987). *The tax treatment of nonprofit organizations: A review of federal and state policies.* In W. W. Powell (Ed.). *The nonprofit sector: A research handbook* (pp. 67-98). New Haven, CT: Yale University.

Small Business Administration. (2004). *2003 state small business profile: United States.* Retrieved online: http://www.sba.gov/advo/research/profiles/

Smith, D. H. (Ed.). (1972). *Voluntary action research: 1972.* Lexington, MA: Lexington Books.

Stephenson, D. R., Pollack, T. H., & Lampkin, L. M. (1997). *State nonprofit almanac.* Washington, DC: The Urban Institute and Independent Sector.

Urban Institute. (2007). *The nonprofit sector in brief: Facts and figures from the nonprofit almanac.* Washington, DC: Author.

Van Hook, P. J. (1998). Ethics in non-profit organizations. In *The international encyclopedia of public policy and administration.* Boulder, CO: Westview.

Van Til, J. (1988). *Mapping the third sector: Voluntarism in a changing social economy.* New York: The Foundation Center.

Weisbrod, B. A. (1975). Toward a theory of the voluntary nonprofit sector in a three-sector economy. In S. Rose-Ackerman (Ed.). *The economics of nonprofit institutions* (pp. 21-44). New York: Oxford University Press.

Weisbrod, B. A. (1988). *The nonprofit economy.* Cambridge, MA: Harvard University Press.

Chapter 34
A Brief History of the Nonprofit Sector

Synopsis: Religious tradition sustained the nonprofit sector in the United States. The growth of secular organizations is a relatively recent phenomenon. Modern nonprofit law has its roots in England. Government policies have encouraged the nonprofit sector to flourish. Organizations advocating for the nonprofit sector have been established in recent decades.

Introduction

Voluntary "associations" first formed about 10,000 years ago, during the Neolithic Period. Villages developed complex linkages that were not totally integrated into the local political and economic system (Anderson, 1973). "For pragmatic reasons, primitive societies were the first to develop and exhibit the concept of charity or philanthropy" (Bakal, 1979). In these early societies, the welfare and preservation of individuals and families required the community to share in the tasks of food gathering, hunting, and providing shelter (Block, 2001, in Ott, p. 98). Religious associations were among the first voluntary associations of civilization and were "often of a secret nature, playing important roles in conserving traditions, building bonds and alliances across family and tribal structures" (Scott, 1998 in Ott, 2001, p. 40).

The values inherent in the work of nonprofit organizations are deeply ingrained in American culture, having evolved out of a religious tradition of serving community needs. Their roots go back to the Torah, New Testament, Koran, and other holy books written thousands of years ago. The religious tradition motivating the formation of nonprofit organizations continues to this day as perhaps the most potent factor (James, 1987). That motivation occurs not only proactively as a way to proselytize, but also as a defensive reaction to enforce and maintain traditional values, such as providing an alternative to public schools when secular ideology is inconsistent with that of the religious ideology of a particular constituency (James, 1987).

A concept of philanthropy existed in ancient Egypt as far back as 2,300 B.C.E. (Block, 2001) with Egyptian aristocrats being buried with records of their gifts to the poor and needy. During the reign of Ramses III, as much as 15% of the cultivatable land was tax-exempt. Religious leaders were granted exemption for their temples, slaves, and other personal property (Columbo and Hall, 1995).

In contrast, the ancient Greek philanthropy consisted more of charitable giving designed to make the community stronger, such as gifts of theaters and stadiums, rather than targeted to help the poor (Block, 2001). The Code of Hammurabi (1780 B.C.E.), who ruled Babylonia from 1795-1755 B.C.E., instructed his subjects to protect their community's vulnerable and serves as an example of one of the first secular references to charity (Horne, 2001, Block, in Ott, 2001, p. 98; Harper, 1904 in Ott, 2001, p. 98).

> *That the strong might not injure the weak, in order to protect the widows and orphans, I have in Babylon the city where Anu and Bel raise high their head, in E-Sagil, the Temple, whose foundations stand firm as heaven and earth, in order to declare justice in the land, to settle all disputes, and heal all injuries, set up these my precious words, written upon my memorial stone, before the image of me, as king of righteousness* (Hammurabi, in Hooker, 1996).

The Rosetta Stone, famous for helping archeologists find the keys to translating Egyptian hieroglyphics, was carved by a group of priests in Egypt in 196 B.C.E. to document all of the good works of the King Ptolemy, including providing revenues for the operation of temples and providing tax benefits to the priests (Dull, 2001).

Beginning in the 11th and 12th centuries, merchant associations were formed in Greece, China, Rome, and Egypt, augmented by organized craft guilds (The Columbia Encyclopedia, 2001a). Guilds played an important role during this period.

In the 14th century, William Langland wrote a poem, *The Vision of Piers Plowman,* which listed the type of activities that would be supported by a wealthy businessman to save his soul:

> *...and therewith repair hospitals*
> *help sick people*
> *mend bad roads*
> *build up bridges that had been broken down*
> *help maidens to marry or to make them nuns*
> *find food for prisoners and poor people*
> *put scholars to school or some other crafts*
> *help religious orders, and*
> *ameliorate rents or taxes (in Wellford and Gallagher, 1988, p. 117)*

By the 18th century, more competitive trade practices and early industrial expansion eroded the guilds' practical power over their trades, but guilds retained their roles as administrators of trusts and benefactors of educational institutions (The Columbia Encyclopedia, 2001b).

The activities we associate with nonprofit organizations, such as health care, religion, the arts, and social welfare activities, were organized and administered by non-secular bodies. It was only after the Reformation that civil law, rather than canon law, prevailed (Douglas, 1987, in Ott, p. 205).

Modern Roots of American Charitable Law and Organizations

The laws granting tax exemptions in the United States, which are similar to the charitable activities described in the poem by Langland, have their roots in laws passed by the British Parliament starting in 1601. The first of these laws, *The Statute of Charitable Uses,* was accepted by Queen Elizabeth I just before the end of her reign. It was intended to create a new relationship between the secular and non-secular institutions of Elizabethan England.

These laws had a long shelf life, maintaining their effect long after the American Revolution (Hammack, 1998). The statute, among other provisions, set out a list of legitimate objects of charity, and established a procedure for accountability for charitable fraud. It authorized an investigation by a bishop of the Church of England concerning allegations against charitable boards, even if the allegations were against church-based charities of religious dissenters, such as Quakers, Baptists, or Presbyterians (Hammack, 2001).

The Elizabethan Poor Laws of 1597 and 1601 required churches to care for the poor, and made local communities responsible for their care in the event charitable gifts were not able to do so—although the gifts were, for the most part, sufficient to forestall any government intervention (Wellford and Gallagher, 1988).

As in England, the tradition in the colonies was for government to establish religion. One notable exception was Pennsylvania, established by William Penn, a Quaker with a personal aversion to government-sponsored religion. The earliest "charitable" organizations in the New World were Harvard College, established in 1636, and locally based hospital societies (Scott, 1998). With its tax exemption under attack, Harvard president Charles Elliot convinced the Massachusetts General Assembly that the general public benefited by the organization. It responded by expanding the range of institutions eligible for exempt status, and other states adopted this model (Scott, 1998).

Benjamin Franklin created a voluntary association to defend Pennsylvania. Soon thereafter, he created voluntary associations for the Free Library Company, the Philadelphia Hospital, and the University of Pennsylvania, all of which were independent of government, although some government funds subsidized these efforts (Hammack, 2001). *The Autobiography of Ben Franklin* provides a practical example of Weisbrod's public goods theory (see Chapter 35) Many activities of government first began as activities of voluntary associations, and later became acceptable to "the median voter." An example:

> *Our city, tho' laid out with a beautiful regularity, the streets large, strait, and crossing each other at right angles, had the disgrace of suffering those streets to remain long unpav'd, and in wet weather, the wheels of heavy carriages plough'd them into a quagmire, so that it was difficult to cross them; and in dry weather the dust was offensive...After some inquiry, I found a poor, industrious man, who was willing to undertake keeping the pavement clean, by sweeping it twice a week, carrying off the dirt from before all the neighbors' doors for the sum of sixpence per month, to be paid by each house...I then wrote and printed a paper setting forth the advantage to the neighborhood that might be obtain'd by this small expense...I sent one of these papers to each house, and in a day or two went round to see who would subscribe an agreement to pay these sixpences; it was unanimously signed...and this rais'd a general desire to have all the streets paved, and made people more willing to submit to a tax for that purpose* (Franklin, 1964, p. 202-203).

Despite the efforts of Franklin, who was a pioneer in establishing nonprofit organizations, there were few corporations in the colonies before 1780. This emanated from hostility toward corruption of the Stuart monarchy and the Church of England (Hall, 1987). Although there were a few colonial associations, the Church of England was established with a "near-monopoly of legal authority" (Hammack, 2001, p. 157) in Georgia, the Carolinas, Virginia, Maryland, New Jersey and New York. The Church provided educational, social, and religious services, and churches not associated with the Church of England, such as those founded by the Puritans, provided similar services.

Following the American Revolution, the established governments in the former colonies, now states, adopted a new doctrine of not funding religious institutions. Private organizations were created to provide services funded through donations and purchases of service rather than through direct and indirect grants from government (Hammack, 2001).

In Europe, social welfare for the needy was originally provided for by the nobility, then by cities and local provincial bodies. Later, this authority was assumed by centralized national governments. In contrast, it is often illustrated by the writings of Alexis de Tocqueville (1835/1956), who compared the United States of the early 19th century to his French homeland, voluntary associations sprung up in the New World to meet community needs that were routinely addressed by national governments in Western Europe (Ott, 2001, p. 91).

In a landmark case decided by the United States Supreme Court, Daniel Webster argued on behalf of Dartmouth College that nonprofit organization trustees, on behalf of their institutions, had property rights (Hammack, 2001). The State of New Hampshire wanted to alter the charter of the institution against the will of its trustees. The opinion by Chief Justice Marshall set an important legal precedent that protected nonprofit corporations from arbitrary government interference.

By the 1830s, foreign visitors were describing voluntary organizations supported by private contributions as the prototypical American contribution to the democratic idea (Hall, 1992).

It was not until 1844 that nonprofit organizations had a firm legal footing under federal law, as a result of the case decided by the U.S. Supreme Court involving the will of Philadelphia philanthropist Stephen Girard, which enforced the charitable trust he established with $7 million for a school for orphans (Hall, 1987).

During the civil war, the federal government outsourced medical care services for soldiers to religious-based nonprofits. Other services, such as vice law enforcement and Native American education, also were provided by these nonprofits (Hammack, 2001).

In 1894, the Congress enacted the first federal income tax, and provided an exemption for "corporations, companies or associations organized and conducted solely for charitable, religious or educational purposes" without any substantive debate on this exemption (Colombo and Hall, 1995, p. 15). This exemption was extended with every subsequent income tax law (Colombo and Hall, 1995).

The number of nonprofit organizations grew dramatically between the end of the Civil War and 1920 (Bremner, 1960), as corporate America and private wealth, along with religious congregations, financed the growth of universities, libraries, hospitals, professional organizations, and private clubs (Hall, 1987). Some of this effort was fueled by the views of business leaders who were against using government to solve societal problems (Hall, 1987).

Many wealthy industrialists established foundations that were granted tax advantages, and that funded operating charities. The early part of the 20th century was called "The Golden Age of Philanthropy" (Scott, 1998) as industrialists such as Andrew Carnegie and John D. Rockefeller donated millions of dollars to create libraries and fund universities.

Supplementing the philanthropy of affluent individuals was the flourishing of the settlement house movement. Modeled after the Toynbee House settlement in England, social activists such as Jane Addams, founder of the social work profession, created institutions in poor neighborhoods to help the poor improve their social conditions by offering social and educational services, such as day care, playgrounds, counseling, places to meet, and advocacy (Block, 1990, in Ott, 2001).

A second philanthropic movement, also secularly based, called the Charity Organization Society, took a rational approach to providing charity, seeking and ruling on applications for charitable assistance from service providers and coordinating services through planning. These organizations predated federated fundraising campaigns such as Jewish Federations and United Ways.

The earliest estimate of charitable giving, for 1922, amounted to .6% of GNP (Hammack, 2001). Indications are that charitable giving, through churches and other private charities, was "measurable, if meager" (Hammack, 2001, p. 161) between 1900 and 1930—increasing to about 1% of GNP in 1930, a fraction of giving estimated for all later years. This percentage doubled during the next 30 years, and has stabilized at about 2% (Hammack, 2001). Traditional values of limited government, church-state separation, and low taxes encouraged growth of the private nonprofit sector, which grew to 2.5-3% of the total labor force by 1960 (Hammack, 2001).

Gidron, Kramer, and Salamon write that the relationship between government and the voluntary sector has been a zero-sum game in that the growth of the welfare state in the half-century since the Depression occurred at the expense of the voluntary sector, conjuring up the statement they attribute to President Reagan in 1981 that "We have let government take away those things that were once ours to do voluntarily" (in Gidron, Kramer and Salamon, 1992, p. 5). In direct contradiction, Hall (1987) writes that "Overall, the growth of the welfare state after 1936 appears to have stimulated rather than discouraged the growth of the nonprofit sector, but the direction of its growth changed markedly (Hall, 1987, p. 17). According to Hall (1994), more than 90% of existing nonprofits were founded since World War II (in Scott, 1998).

Hall's perspective is validated by Lester Salamon, who writes that the Great Depression of the 1930s laid the foundation for the welfare system that exists today in the United States (Salamon, 1999). Salamon writes that local governments and private charitable groups maintained the responsibility for responding to poverty and other social needs that emanated from urbanization and industrialization. The federal role took center stage only after President Franklin Roosevelt responded to need that far outstripped the ability of local governments and private organizations.

Despite landmark federal legislation that provided programs for old age pensions, unemployment insurance, and income maintenance, coverage under these programs was "patchy" (Salamon, 1999, p. 59). Cash assistance payments were held artificially low so as not to compete with salaries paid for agricultural and household jobs.

Hammack (2001) writes that several government policies contributed to the growth of the nonprofit sector in the early to mid 20th century. First, some government decision makers, notably Herbert Hoover, gave preference to business associations to coordinate economic and social activity. This was accomplished by permitting professional associations and private standard-setting bodies (such as the Educational Testing Service) to "regulate" rather than relying on government agencies. Nonprofit sector growth was limited in the 1930s, because the devastated American economy made it difficult for the public to pay for services provided by the sector (Hammack, 2001). One intent of the New Deal was to beef up the voluntary sector through government initiatives, but the U.S. Supreme Court rejected Roosevelt's approach (Hammack, 2001).

It was not until the 1960s that increasing poverty and urban riots spurred a quantum increase in government social welfare spending. Rather than replacing nonprofit organizations as providers of services, the expanded government role in social welfare "promoted, rather than displaced" the nonprofit sector (Salamon, 1999, p. 62). The primary reason was the federal government chose to fund these services using local governments and private organizations, including the nonprofit sector, rather than delivering the services itself.

Despite federal policies that encouraged the growth of the sector during this period, state restrictions reined in some of the potential growth. Hammack (2001) points out that many African-Americans were simply denied their rights to form associations prior to the passage of civil rights laws, and dissident groups also were denied legal status. In some states, judges had the right to approve nonprofit charters, and could, and did, arbitrarily deny applications based on sexism, racism, or xenophobia.

A 1982 economic analysis by Lester Salamon and Alan Abramson made it clear that the large increase in the nonprofit sector after 1940 "was in large part funded by government, which depended on private-sector organizations to implement its policies" (Hall, 1992, p. 18). The nonprofit sector, particularly private foundations, was put under increased political scrutiny in the years leading up to the United States' entry into World War II (Hall, 1992). Some political leaders who were committed to keeping the United States on the sidelines perceived a threat from some private foundations and other tax-exempt organizations that were supportive of American intervention.

After the war, the anti-Communist hysteria, fueled by the demagoguery of Sen. Joseph McCarthy, targeted foundations and other exempt organizations to determine if they were using their resources for the purposes for which they were established. The implication was that instead, they were diverting these resources for subversion. In 1952, the 82nd Congress approved H. Res. 561 to launch this investigation. The final report of the Select Committee to Investigate Tax-Exempt Foundations and Comparable Organizations was benign to the sector, but did recommend better public reporting by these organizations. A follow-up investigation in 1954 raised the issue that unchecked power by unregulated foundations could become a threat to democratic values (Hall, 1992, in Ott, 2001).

These and subsequent political challenges to foundations and other tax-exempt organizations culminated in the sector launching an effort to organize and respond to the Congress. The Council on Foundations was established in 1949 (initially under another name), as well as the Foundation Library Center. As the Congress focused on legislation that would affect nonprofits, the nonprofit sector needed to be able to defend itself with professional and technical responses. As Hall writes, "Quite clearly, quoting Tocqueville to Congress would no longer serve as an effective defense. Future efforts would have to rely on technical language of law and economics that had come to frame the creation of tax policy by the late 1960s" (Hall, 1992).

During the 1970s, scholarly research on the nonprofit sector increased substantially, as public awareness of the sector increased. The Commission on Private Philanthropy and Public Needs, chaired by insurance industry executive John Filer, provided a stimulus for research of the sector (Powell, 1987). This effort was commissioned by John D. Rockefeller in 1973 to respond to a perception that the Nixon Administration was hostile to nonprofits. Some of this alleged hostility was attributed to the fact that President Nixon and his allies felt that staff at nonprofit institutions, such as think tanks and universities, were outspoken critics of the President's Vietnam War policies (Ott, 2001). This seven-volume report detailed the importance of the sector as employers, as a provider of important social services, and as a force in the political life of the nation (Hall, 1987).

Filer summarized the commission's findings in four broad observations:

1. "The voluntary sector is a large and vital part of American society, more important today than ever…

2. "Giving in America involves an immense amount of time and money, is the fundamental underpinning of the voluntary sector, encompasses a wide diversity of relationships between donor, donations, and donee, and is not keeping pace.

3. "Decreasing levels of private giving, increasing costs of non-profit activity and broadening expectations for health, education and welfare services as basic entitlements of citizenship have led to the government's becoming a principal provider of programs and revenues in many areas once dominated by private philanthropy…

4. "Our society has long encouraged 'charitable' nonprofit activity by excluding it from certain tax obligations. But the principal tax encouragement of giving to nonprofit organizations—the charitable deduction in personal income taxes—has been both challenged in some quarters in recent years on grounds of equity and eroded by expansion of the standard deduction (Van Til, 1988, p. 23)."

The report recommended retaining the charitable deduction; expanding it to permit those who take the standard deduction to also deduct charitable contributions; allowing those with incomes under $15,000 to deduct twice their charitable contributions and those with incomes of $15,000-$30,000 to deduct 150% of their contributions; and setting a goal that corporations should give 2% of their pretax net income to charity. The report further recommended requiring all larger charities other than churches to prepare and make available detailed annual reports on their finances, programs, and priorities; requiring all tax-exempt organizations to maintain "arms-length" business relationships with for-profits; delegating to the state governments the duty to regulate intrastate charitable solicitation and establishing a federal system to regulate inter-state charitable solicitation; permitting nonprofits other than charities to have the same right to lobby as business organizations; and establishing a permanent national commission on the nonprofit sector (Filer, 1975).

> Most importantly, the work gave substance to what, up to then, had been only an idea: that charitable tax-exempt organizations composed a coherent and cohesive 'sector' of American political, economic, and social life. This unified conception of nonprofits as part of a 'third,' 'independent,' or 'nonprofit'—or, as the commission preferred to call it, 'voluntary'—sector lay the groundwork for establishing organizations that could give its common interests unified expression (Hall, 1992).

There has been little literature addressing nonprofit institutions as a distinct sector; most of the literature has examined particular fields, such as education, health care, and social welfare (Hall, 1987). Although the Filer Commission has sought to show the nonprofit sector as having some autonomy, the government funding cuts of the Reagan era demonstrated the interdependence of the voluntary sector (Hall, 1987).

Much of the current literature on nonprofit organizations is generated by members of the Association for Research on Nonprofit Organizations and Voluntary Action (ARNOVA), an international, interdisciplinary network of scholars and nonprofit leaders formed in 1971 (initially as the Association of Nonprofit Scholars) to foster the creation, application, and dissemination of research relating to the nonprofit sector on voluntary action.

In 1976, Yale University initiated an interdisciplinary research program based at the Institution for Social and Policy Studies to study the role, character, organization, and impact of the nonprofit sector (Powell, 1987).

The Carter Administration resisted a recommendation of the Filer Commission to create a quasi-governmental agency in the Treasury Department to formulate public policy that would apply to the nonprofit sector. The reason for this resistance was, ostensibly, to keep public policy on the sector from being too highly influenced by the political process.

Almost simultaneously with the election of Ronald Reagan, the nonprofit sector established a major national trade association, Independent Sector, to represent its divergent political interests. Independent Sector was formed in 1980 with a formal mission statement: "To promote, strengthen, and advance the nonprofit and philanthropic community to foster private initiative for the public good" (Independent Sector, 2001a). Today, it serves as the chief nexus for advocacy on behalf of the sector, and describes itself as "a nonprofit, nonpartisan coalition of more than 700 national organizations, foundations, and corporate philanthropy programs, collectively representing tens of thousands of charitable groups in every state across the nation" (Independent Sector, 2002b).

As pointed out previously, there is a direct link between government spending for social welfare and revenues received by nonprofit organizations as a result of public policy favoring limited government. By the end of the 1970s, increasing federal deficits spurred selective cuts in domestic spending, translating into braking a decade and a half of accelerated federal social welfare spending (Salamon, 1999).

In 1980, federal government support of nonprofit organizations had reached $40.4 billion. State and local governments also made sizable contributions to nonprofit organization revenues (Salamon, 1999).

The election of President Reagan launched "a much more basic assault" (Salamon, 1999, p. 64) on this spending. Putting aside health and pension expenditures, federal social welfare spending declined by 17% (adjusted for inflation), and state and local government social welfare spending declined by 10% during 1977-1982. The Reagan Administration justified some of the reductions on the basis that nonprofit organizations would have more opportunities to meet human needs and that private donations could fill any gaps left by government retrenchment.

Research studies summarized by Salamon (1999) indicate that the nonprofit sector did undergo a rapid expansion during the 1977-1996 period, but that this expansion was not fueled by increases in charitable donations. Rather, the increase in revenues by social service organizations came from commercial income, such as from fees, investment income, and sales of products. Despite the changing character of nonprofits during this period, the sector expanded at a rate much faster than the nation's economy. The GDP of the United States increased by 62% from 1977-1996. In comparison, total nonprofit sector revenues increased by 96%.

Increasing American affluence is certainly one key explanation of the nonprofit expansion. An increasingly wealthy American population buys more nonprofit services than ever; revenues from fees and charges now account for about half of all nonprofit income (Hammack, 2001).

Hammack points out that increasing affluence resulted in more services being purchased. Since these organizations provided services rather than goods generally, the fact that the share of services comprising GDP increased from just over 8% in 1950 to nearly 20% in 1990 translated to more business for the sector. When compounded by the increase in services purchased by government, the result was a tripling of the nonprofit share of the U.S. economy between 1945 and 1990.

In 1992, the administration of President George Herbert Walker Bush participated in a bipartisan effort to create the National Civilian Community Corps "as a demonstration program to explore the possibility of using post-Cold War resources to help solve problems here at home" (Corporation for National Service, 2001).

On September 21, 1993, President Clinton signed into law the *National and Community Service Trust Act.* This legislation created the Corporation for National Service, which administers the AmeriCorps and several other programs. These programs promote service-learning and national service.

Faith-Based Initiatives

Beginning with the Clinton Administration, serious proposals came from the White House to expand the ability of religious-based social service organizations to receive federal funding. A so-called "Charitable Choice" provision was included in Section 104 of the 1996 welfare reform legislation, *Personal Responsibility and Work Opportunity Act of 1996*. The section permitted faith-based organizations to be eligible to receive government funds for social services, and prohibited states from placing constraints on these organizations with respect to the display of religious arts, icons, scripture or other symbols as a condition for receiving a federal contract (Lindner, 2003).

The proposed *Charitable Choice Act of 1999* provided that faith-based organizations accepting government funds would not be required to change their religious character, systems of internal governance, or requirements that employees follow religious teachings. President Clinton's antipoverty proposals, dubbed the New Markets/Renewal Communities Agreement, also included charitable choice provisions. He proposed opening a percentage of program funding to competitive bidding for faith-based organizations (Wilson, 2001).

Nine days after his swearing in, President George W. Bush signed an executive order creating the Centers for Faith-Based and Community Initiatives in the Departments of Health and Human Services, Housing and Urban Development, Labor, Justice, and Education. The President signed two other executive orders related to this initiative. The first created the White House Office of Faith-Based and Community Initiatives. The order authorized the head of this office to report directly to the President. The purpose of the second executive order was to clear bureaucratic barriers "that make private groups hesitate to work with government" (The White House, 2001). In his official remarks launching the proposal, the President said:

> *It is one of the great goals of my administration to invigorate the spirit of involvement and citizenship. We will encourage faith-based and community programs without changing their mission. We will help all in their work to change hearts while keeping a commitment to pluralism* (The White House, 2001).

In his 2002 State of the Union address, months after the September 11 terrorist attacks, President Bush called on each American to dedicate at least 4,000 hours of service during his or her lifetime to community service. He launched the USA Freedom Corps, charged with building "a culture of service, responsibility, and citizenship" (USA Freedom Corps, 2003).

In April 2003, the Senate passed some proposals of President Bush's Faith-Based Initiative as part of the *Charity Aid, Recovery, and Empowerment* (CARE) *Act* (The White House, 2003), but did not approve two key elements supported by the President—to allow the government to directly fund the social service programs of houses of worship and allow these institutions to conduct taxpayer-funded social service programs in locations inundated with religious icons, texts, and sacred scriptures (The Interfaith Alliance, 2003). The intent of the legislation is to promote, chiefly through tax incentives, a healthy increase in charitable giving to both secular and nonsecular institutions.

In his final State of the Union address on January 28, 2008, President Bush called on Congress to enact legislation to make his administrative changes, relating to permitting faith-based charities to compete for federal grants, permanent.

In June and July 2004, the Senate Finance Committee, chaired by Sen. Charles Grassley (R-IA), held hearings beginning a national debate on the role of the federal government in regulating and monitoring philanthropy, and to curb abuses in the sector. Senate committee staff prepared more than 200 potential reforms (Wolverton, 2004). Among the committee chairman's targets of criticism during the following two years included the entire hospital industry, the American Red Cross, and American University. With the takeover of the Senate by Democrats following the 2006 elections, the Committee, chaired by Sen. Max Baucus (D-Montana), made the issue of targeting abuses by tax-exempt organizations much less of a priority.

In October 2004, the Congress enacted legislation that authorizes the National Institute of Standards and Technology (NIST) to expand the Malcolm Baldrige National Quality Award Program to include nonprofit and government organizations. The program is soliciting applications from nonprofit organizations in 2006 for a pilot program with the first awards to be granted for applications made in 2007.

In 2006, the National Council of Nonprofit Associations (NCNA) began organizing The Nonprofit Congress for the purpose of bringing together nonprofit leaders to "forge a common identity based on shared values, to develop a unified vision and message, and exercise a collective voice. Almost 400 nonprofit delegates were gathered in Washington October 16-17, 2006, to create a policy platform for the sector and strategize for outreach and united action (Nonprofit Congress, 2006, Perry 2006). Rather than adopt a national strategy for starting a nonprofit-power movement, the conferees instead focused on effecting change at the state level. A follow-up conference was tentatively scheduled for spring 2008.

In July 2007, aides to Sen. Grassley unveiled a proposal to revoke the tax-exemptions of nonprofit hospitals that do not spend at least 5% of their budgets on charity care, citing their research that the tax exemption of these hospitals costs the federal government approximately $40 billion annually in tax revenues (Panepento, 2007).

References

Anderson, R. (1973). Voluntary associations in history: From paleolithic to present times. In D. H. Smith (Ed.). *Voluntary action research: 1973* (pp. 9-28). Lexington, MA: Lexington Books.

Bakal, C. (1979). *Charity U.S.A.* New York: Times Books.

Block, S. R. (1990). A history of the discipline. In J. Ott (Ed.). *The nature of the nonprofit sector* (pp. 152-156). Boulder, CO: Westview Press.

The Columbia Encyclopedia. (2001a). *Livery companies.* New York: Columbia University Press. Retrieved June, 8, 2003, from http://www.bartleby.com/65/li/liveryco.html

The Columbia Encyclopedia. (2001b). *Guilds.* New York: Columbia University Press. Retrieved June 10, 2003, from http://www.bartleby.com/65/gu/guilds.html

Columbo, J. D., & Hall, M. A. (1995). *The charitable tax exemption.* Boulder, CO: Westview Press.

Corporation for National Service. (2001). *About us:* Retrieved July 21, 2006, from http://www.nationalservice.gov/home/site_map/index.asp

Douglas, J. (1987). Political theories of nonprofit organizations. In J. S. Ott (Ed.). *The Nature of the Nonprofit Sector.* Boulder, CO: Westview Press.

Dull, D. (2001). *Text of the rosetta stone.* Retrieved February 10, 2002, from http://pw1.netcom.com/~qkstart/rosetta.html.

Filer, J. H. (1975). The Filer commission report—Giving in America: Toward a stronger voluntary sector. In J. S. Ott (Ed.). *The nature of the nonprofit sector.* Boulder, CO: Westview Press.

Franklin, B. (1964). *The autobiography of Benjamin Franklin.* New Haven, CT: Yale University Press.

Gidron, B., Kramer, R. M., & Salamon, L. (Eds.). (1992). *Government and the third sector.* San Francisco: Jossey-Bass.

Hall, P. D. (1987). A historical overview of the private nonprofit sector. In W. Powell (Ed.). *The nonprofit sector: A research handbook.* New Haven, CT: Yale University Press.

Hall, P. D. (1992). Inventing the nonprofit sector: 1950-1990. In J. S. Ott (Ed.). T*he Nature of the Nonprofit Sector.* Boulder, CO: Westview Press.

Hammack, D. C. (2001). Introduction: Growth, transformation, and quiet revolution in the nonprofit sector over two centuries. *Nonprofit and Voluntary Sector Quarterly, 2,* 157-173.

Hooker, R. (1996). *World civilizations: An internet classroom and anthology.* Retrieved February 10, 2002, from http://www.wsu.edu/~dee/MESO/CODE.HTM

Horne, C. F. (2001). *The code of Hammurabi: Introduction.* Retrieved February 10, 2002, from http://www.fordham.edu/halsall/ancient/hamcode.html

Independent Sector. (2002a). *About us: Independent Sector's mission, vision, and statement of values.* Retrieved February 10, 2002, from http://www.independentsector.org/about/vision.html

Independent Sector. (2002b). *Survey by Independent Sector and Cisco Systems finds technology boosts nonprofits' effectiveness.* Retrieved February 10, 2002, from http://www.independentsector.org/media/media.html

The Interfaith Alliance. (2003). *Senate rejects president's controversial faith-based provisions; The Interfaith Alliance commends compromise bill.* Retrieved June 12, 2003, from http://www.interfaithalliance.org/News/News.cfm?ID=4826&c=37

James, E. (1987). The nonprofit sector in comparative perspective. In W. Powell (Ed.). *The nonprofit sector: A research handbook* (pp. 397-415). New Haven, CT: Yale University Press.

Lindner, E. W. (2001) Considering charitable choice. In *The yearbook of American and Canadian churches.* Retrieved June 11, 2003, from http://216.239.57.100/search?q=cache:xo78JVdIxXEJ:www.electronicchurch.org/2001/Considering%2520Charitable%2520Choice.pdf+%22Charitable+Choice%22+1996&hl=en&ie=UTF-8

Nonprofit Congress (2006). *Nonprofit Congress: Many missions, one voice.* Retrieved online: http://www.nonprofitcongress.org

Ott, J. S. (2001). *The nature of the nonprofit sector.* Boulder, CO: Westview Press.

Panepento, P. (2007). Nonprofit hospitals could face new rules under proposal. *Chronicle of Philanthopy,* July 19, 2007; Retrieved online: http://philanthropy.com/news/updates/2709/nonprofit-hospitals-could-face-new-rules-under-proposal

Perry, Suzanne (2006). Nonprofit Leaders Map Plan to Influence Public Policy. *Chronicle of Philanthropy*, v19 n2.

Powell, W. (Ed.) (1987). *The nonprofit sector: A research handbook.* New Haven, CT: Yale University Press.

Salamon, L. (1999). *America's nonprofit sector: A primer.* (Second Edition). Washington, DC: The Foundation Center.

Scott, J. T. (1998). Voluntary sector. In J. S. Ott (Ed.). *The nature of the nonprofit sector.* Boulder, CO: Westview Press.

Tocqueville, A. de. (1835/1956). *Democracy in America* (R.D. Heffner, Ed.). New York: Penguin Books.

USA Freedom Corps (2003). *Bush administration announces comprehensive national study of America's nonprofit sector.* Retrieved July 28, 2006 from: http://www.usafreedomcorps.gov/about_usafc/newsroom/announcements_archive.asp

Van Til, J. (1988). *Mapping the third sector: Volunteerism in a changing social economy.* New York: The Foundation Center.

Wellford, W. H., & Gallagher, J. (1988). *Unfair competition? The challenge to charitable tax exemption.* Washington, DC: The National Assembly of Voluntary Health and Social Welfare Organizations.

The White House. (2001, January 29). *Remarks by the president in announcement of the faith-based initiative.* Retrieved June 12, 2003, from http://www.whitehouse.gov/news/releases/20010129-5.html

The White House. (2003). *President commends senate passage of faith-based legislation.* Retrieved June 8, 2003, from http://www.whitehouse.gov/news/releases/2003/04/20030409-2.html

Wilson, S. (2001). *Election year proposals affecting charities: A prelude to future legislation?* Retrieved online July 21, 2006, from http://www.urban.org/publications/310255.html

Wolverton, B. (2004). Rethinking Charity Rules. *Chronicle of Philanthropy*, v16 i19, July 22, 2004, p. 31. Retrieved online: http://www.philanthropy.com/premium/articles/v16/i19/19003101.htm

Chapter 35
Theory of the Nonprofit Sector

Synopsis: Economic models of nonprofit organization formation and behavior dominate current thinking. These models have serious flaws and drawbacks. Among the leading theories explaining the existence of nonprofits are government failure, market failure, contract failure, and externality theory. Pluralistic theory and the Theory of the Commons are alternatives to these economic theories.

Theories relating to nonprofit organizations have tended to focus on two phenomena—how they are created and how they behave once they are created. They can be further differentiated by whether they are economic, i.e., based on economic self-interest, or non-economic theories.

One economic model explains the existence of the sector as a response to the failure of government. The Weisbrod Model (see below under "Public Goods Theory") falls in this category. A competing economic theory explains the existence of the sector as a response to information differences between the buyer and seller (referred to in the literature as information asymmetries) and transaction costs in the for-profit sector. Henry Hansmann's theories fit into this category.

Another economic model theorizes that individual entrepreneurs take advantage of the special treatment afforded to nonprofit organizations (such as tax treatment, the halo effect, cheaper postage rates, and perceived lack of direct competition) as a way to further their individual goals and agendas. The research by Dennis Young and Estelle James looks at the personal characteristics of nonprofit executives and attempts to draw some distinctions between their motivations and those of executives who work in other sectors. Among non-economic theories are those that relate to pluralism, mediating structures, and the "Theory of the Commons."

Some of the leading organizational theories relating to the formation of nonprofit organizations are presented in this chapter.

Economic Theories

1. Public Goods Theory

This economic theory, proposed by Burton Weisbrod, suggests that nonprofit organizations are formed because of "government failure." Government fails to provide enough public goods because of the structure of the democratic process that is tied to the needs of the median voter. This process leaves many voters dissatisfied with the output of government and/or the level of taxation. They address this dissatisfaction in four ways:

- *migration* ("vote with your feet")—This strategy has a high transaction cost (i.e., moving costs, finding employment in another locality, and finding a new house), but people do leave a jurisdiction because of high taxes or the lack of adequate services (such as a substandard school system).

- *formation of a lower level of government*—Voters may take action to break away from a jurisdiction and form their own municipal government, or address the lack of services provided by a state government by convincing a local government to provide them (such as may be the case with a park or library).

- *seek private market alternatives*—An example is hiring private security guards to patrol a housing development if public police protection is considered inadequate, or to install fences, better locks, and alarms. In many cases, Weisbrod points out that there are private alternatives to collective goods (also called public goods, defined as goods that are provided by government and which cannot be practically excluded from one citizen without withholding them from all citizens), even though these may be economically inefficient to produce.

- *create voluntary organizations to provide collective goods*—Weisbrod theorizes that public demand for a collective good will first be fulfilled by a voluntary agency, until the demand increases to the extent that the service is demanded by the median voter, at which point the government will consider providing it. He points to the fact that services provided by voluntary organizations in 16th century England included schools, hospitals, fire-fighting apparatus, parks, bridges, dikes, libraries, care of prisoners in jails, and charity to the poor (Weisbrod, 1975, in Rose-Ackerman, 1986).

This process can be facilitated when subgroups, such as those of a particular religion or culture, desire goods that the government is unwilling or unable to provide.

The Weisbrod theory of government failure predicts that the nonprofit sector will be most active where citizen populations are most diverse, and that nonprofit organizations are important for satisfying the service needs of political minorities (Douglas, 1987).

2. Market Failure Theory

Nonprofit organizations may form as a result of market failure. Burton Weisbrod and Henry Hansmann are among those who have written extensively on market failure explanations of nonprofit organization formation. Market failure occurs when the private market demand for a good or service is too low to encourage private firms to provide it— because they would fail to make a profit (or the opportunity cost for investing in the provision of a high-demand good or service would be higher). If the good or service is provided by a nonprofit, that organization can have access to private donations and be exempt from taxes that a for-profit would have to pay.

Thus, a nonprofit organization might form to pay for a meals-on-wheels service, leveraging government grants, private donations, and minimal fees from homebound elderly who use the service. Such a service would not otherwise be economically efficient for a for-profit provider to offer.

3. Market Failure And High Transaction Costs

The United States has adopted a European pattern of responding to the private market's failure to provide for collective goods by first regulating the private sector, and then taking over the function when that doesn't work. However, there are problems that arise that involve both market failure and the government being unwilling or unable to take over the function. Rather than being an intermediate step between private regulation and government takeover, nonprofit intervention is a generic alternative (Wellford and Gallagher, 1988, p. 11).

According to this model, government is too bureaucratic, and takes too long to solve a problem, and lacks the ability to respond to local problems. Government's transaction costs are too high compared with the nonprofit sector—such as the time it takes to build a political consensus, enact authorizing legislation, provide appropriations and develop regulations, issue and distribute checks, provide for fiscal accountability of the program, evaluate the program, and so on.

Furthermore, according to this model, government could not politically afford to move too quickly, because it would run the risk of compelling citizens to pay taxes for services of which they don't approve. Thus, nonprofit organizations can effectively fill this void. Wellford and Gallagher have written extensively about this theory.

4. Externality Theory

One way of looking at the formation and role of some nonprofit organizations is to view them in the context of externalities. This term is used by economists to describe the costs and benefits of a market transaction that accrue to those who are not direct parties to the transaction. For example, a battery maker charges a price for its batteries, which is approximately the same regardless of the consumer's geographical location. However, the people who live near the battery plant experience both positive and negative externalities from the plant.

Negative externalities might include the increased healthcare costs of breathing in pollutants emitted from the plant, decreased property values as a result of the pollution, loss of recreational opportunities because fish in the streams have high levels of mercury, higher stress levels from noise made by the plant, and higher commuting times during rush hour as hundreds of workers drive to and from the plant. Positive externalities might include lower costs of searching for employment, financial support for local community organizations, leadership of community organizations provided by executives who have relocated to work at the plant and better schools as a result of property tax payments made by the plant's owners, and increased advocacy for schools from those who work at the plant.

Many nonprofit organizations are formed for the purpose of addressing externality issues, both positive and negative. For example, a nonprofit organization might be formed by residents in a community who object to a proposal to build a Wal-Mart or a McDonald's in their neighborhood. The fear is that while the benefits of having a Wal-Mart will mean profits to that company, externalities—such as putting "Main Street" businesses out of business, creating traffic tie-ups, and contributing to suburban sprawl—will have negative consequences.

Other nonprofit organizations are formed to promote positive externalities. For example, organizations that form to provide recreational activities to at-risk youth, such as midnight basketball, have as one objective the improvement of the quality of life for these youngsters. But an equally compelling objective is to keep youngsters off the streets during high-crime hours. In this case, all businesses and homeowners in the area benefit from the program.

5. Contract Failure Theory

This theory of Henry Hansmann suggests that in cases in which consumers are unable to adequately evaluate the quality or quantity of a service, a nonprofit organization is more likely to be chosen to provide the service. The reason is that the consumer is likely to feel that the nonprofit will not have an incentive to shortchange the customer, because excess revenues will not be distributed to the organization's "owners." In contrast, the for-profit firm has both the incentive and the opportunity to exploit the customer.

In some respects, this theory has its origins in principal-agent theory, which is based upon information imbalances between two parties. The theory is used to explain how to get the employee or contractor (agent) to act in the best interests of the principal—the employer—when the employee or contractor has an informational advantage over the principal and different interests from the principal. Principal-agent theory assumes that parties providing services—the agents—will shirk their responsibilities unless policed, such as by tightly drafted contracts, supervision, or quality control by those purchasing the services—the principals.

Researchers who studied nonprofit and for-profit day care centers found that parents had more trust in nonprofit day care centers. These parents felt that nonprofit centers did not have the incentives to take advantage of them despite the fact that they lacked sufficient information to judge the quality of the centers.

Dennis Young writes of three cases of information asymmetry, imbalances of the amount of information available to two parties. The first occurs when the good or service is too complex or technical for the consumer to judge, such as is the case with health care or higher education. The second occurs when the consumer as an individual is not competent to evaluate the good or service, such as might be the case with seeking care in an assisted living arrangement. The third case occurs when the purchaser of the service is not the ultimate consumer, or is not in close contact with the place where the service or goods will be provided—such as when a person seeks to obtain long-term care for an elderly parent located in a distant city, or when a donor seeks to provide disaster relief funds in response to a flood in another part of the country.

As Young points out (in Ott, 2001), there are alternatives to using nonprofit organizations to provide services when there are information dissymmetries, such as government regulation, professional standards for practitioners, accreditation bodies, or using third-party experts—such as insurance claims adjusters, or doctors who work for the health insurer—to reduce the information dissymmetry.

Young suggests that nonprofits are trustworthy not so much because the profits do not accrue to the benefit of the individuals, but rather because leaders of nonprofit organizations are intrinsically different from those of profit-making organizations. They are much more motivated to act in the public interest rather than feathering their own nests or seeking power.

Another factor that explains why the behavior of nonprofits is more trustworthy than those of for-profits, or at least, is perceived as such by consumers, is that their governing structure is more pluralistic and has more direct influence by those who have an interest in the organization behaving honorably, such as donors, consumers of the services, and community leaders. The existence of this so-called "halo effect" of nonprofits has been verified by empirical research.

Colombo and Hall (1995) suggest that charities deserve tax exemptions because of market failure and government failure. Market failure results from the fact that capitalism meets individual needs well, but is not as well-suited to meet collective needs. This is because of "free riders"—those who make no effort to donate money or volunteer time for public goods. Government failure occurs because of the inefficiencies of the political process in allocating goods and services to those who need it.

The nonprofit producer, like its for-profit counterpart, has the capacity to raise prices and cut quality in such cases without much fear of customer reprisal; however, it lacks the incentive to do so because those in charge are barred from taking home any resulting profits (Hansmann, 1980). However, this perspective has been challenged by Bennett and DiLorenzo (1989). They write:

> A fatal flaw in the "contract failure" rationale ...is the assumption that CNE (commercial nonprofit enterprise) managers cannot benefit from the organization's profits and so will devote all of the organization's resources to improvements in service quality....Managers, board members and others involved with CNE operations can and do personally benefit from the profits. In fact, since competitive pressures are weaker in the nonprofit sector, a strong case can be made that CNE managers are even more prone than private sector managers to use their organization's resources for personal benefit rather than improving service quality (Bennett and DiLorenzo, 1989, p. 63).

Bennett and DiLorenzo acknowledge that there are generally four rationales for the granting of subsidies to nonprofit organizations—*thin markets* (the demand for goods is too small for private enterprise to make a profit), *public goods* (the goods provided will not be provided by private firms), *contract failure* (consumers cannot judge a product's quality before purchasing it, such as in health care), and the *promotion of equity* (such as serving vulnerable populations)—although they suggest that none of these situations occurs to any great extent.

6. Subsidy Theories

This theory posits that initiation of nonprofits in some fields is encouraged because of the government subsidies that are available to them, such as direct government funding for services, the tax exemption, lower postage rates, the ability to issue tax-exempt bonds, and favorable personnel regulations.

7. Consumer Control Theory

This theory explains why social clubs and cooperatives form nonprofit organizations rather than for-profits. Incorporating as a nonprofit helps patrons maintain control of an organization. Otherwise, the owners of a firm could maintain monopolistic control of a service.

Non-Economic Theories

1. Pluralistic Theory

A theory related to Weisbrod's government failure theories, also attributable to a form of "government failure" (albeit less related to economics), applies even to the case in which government does have the political support to begin providing a collective good. Private, nonprofit organizations may still be called upon to deliver a service when the public perceives that governmental provision of these services would be less politically expensive (even if government could deliver the services with higher economic efficiency). This occurs, as Lester Salamon points out, "because of the cumbersomeness, unresponsiveness, and bureaucratization that often accompanies governmental action" or because of cultural resistance to expanding government.

One example might be the rejection of former President Clinton's plan to increase the federal role for financing health care, with opponents of the plan exploiting the public's skepticism about government expansion while concurrently holding views favorable about Social Security and Medicare. Nonprofit organizations have a history of both being entrepreneurial and responsive to many societal interests when government has, for one reason or another, not been responsive. The social value of freedom and pluralism is highly valued in American society, and the political system is designed to encourage the formation of organizations that can meet a variety of interests. Atkinson (1997) terms this feature of the nonprofit sector a "meta-benefit" that serves as an additional justification for government subsidization beyond the direct benefits provided to the collective.

Lester Salamon's view is that nonprofit organizations are perceived as encouraging individual action for the public good in the same way that business corporations encourage individual action for private gain. Unlike the cookie-cutter approach of government, this theory takes the view that the independence of nonprofit organizations from government fosters values of freedom and pluralism.

> *Even if it were the case that government was far more efficient than the nonprofit sector in responding to citizen needs, Americans would still insist on a vibrant nonprofit sector as a guarantor of their liberties and a mechanism to ensure a degree of pluralism* (Salamon, in Ott, 2001, p. 165).

2. Mediating Structures

Peter Berger and Richard John Newhaus (1977), in *To Empower People: The Role of Mediating Structures in Public Policy,* defined the term "mediating structures" to include those organizations that come between the individual and megastructures, such as large capitalist conglomerates, labor unions, and government. These mediating structures, such as families, neighborhoods, religious institutions, and voluntary associations, help shape cultural values in a positive way, and thus should be encouraged by government public policy.

Through mediating structures, people are drawn to seeking the well-being of others. This contrasts with many other popular theories that emphasize self-interest. "Meaning and purpose is found in individual private life, while public life is impersonal, unsatisfying, and ultimately seems illegitimate. Mediating structures are a means of overcoming this" (Pennings, 2003).

3. Theory of the Commons

Roger Lohmann (1992) defines the "commons" as "an economic, political, and social space outside the market, households, and state in which associative communities create and reproduce social worlds"—which are defined as "the images, meanings and sense of reality shared by autonomous, self-defining collectivities of voluntarily associating individuals." In the commons, transactions are governed by a basic norm of fairness rather than by a quid pro quo norm of the marketplace or equity in democratic governments (in Ott, p. 172).

Those in the commons share a common language, common training/education, and a common culture that transcends the marketplace dominated by maximizing individual utility.

In contrast to virtually all other nonprofit theories, Lohmann limits his Theory of the Commons to exclude those nonprofit organizations, formal or not, that are engaged in "unproductive or volunteer labor." This is regardless of whether they are incorporated, have employees, or are included in national data about the voluntary sector. The term "unproductive labor" can be traced to Adam Smith's *Wealth of Nations,* first published in 1776, which was meant to refer to labor that didn't add value to "the subject upon which (it) is bestowed."

The common goods produced in the "commons" include religious worship, contemplation, scientific inquiry, helping and charity, artistic expression, play, and many other desirable projects of voluntary-action groups (Lohmann, 1992). The goods produced in the commons are distinguishable from both private goods and public goods in that they are produced for purposes that benefit individuals or groups other than the producer. Lohmann bases his theory on nine initial premises and assumptions:

1. *Social Action.* These organizations engage in social action to which the participant attaches some subjective meaning, ignoring or rejecting a profit orientation in favor of doing something for the good of others.

2. *Affluence.* The participants in these organizations are not primarily concerned with their own self-interest. As a result, it is assumed that the participants are "affluent," Lohmann's term to describe those who do not face any immediate threats to their own safety, security, health, or well-being and thus have the luxury of choosing to engage in behavior that is not self-serving.

3. *Authenticity.* This is an enforced norm in the sector; that is, those who are perceived to be acting in their own self-interest rather than having altruistic motivations are sanctioned by their peers (by, perhaps, being expelled from the organization) or by the state (such as by enforcement of charity fraud laws).

4. *Continuity.* The organizations in the sector engage in rituals and ceremonies, have norms and folkways, and conduct other activities that link the past, the present, and the future.

5. *Rationality.* These organizations make rational decisions—setting goals and objectives and obtaining the resources necessary to meet those goals.

6. *Near–universality.* Most, if not all, human cultures engage in collective action in which individuals voluntarily associate to pursue common objectives outside of markets, households, and government.

7. *Autonomy.* Participants in these organizations exercise both individual and group self-control and create their own autonomous social worlds.

8. *Intrinsic valuation.* The proper way to evaluate these organizations is on the basis of their values, rather than on conventional measures such as, among others, efficiency or effectiveness.

9. *Clarity.* The theory must be stated in language that participants in the sector can understand.

Are Nonprofits Altruistic or Self-Maximizing?

The academic literature is split with respect to the motivations for forming nonprofit organizations and the ways they and those who form them behave. Dennis Young writes:

> *In particular, the rationales for nonprofits offered by Weisbrod (1979), Douglas (1979), and others have a selfless, public-spirited quality to them. Nonprofits are seen as providers of semi-public goods, or as agents of trust for consumers whose abilities to discern quality differences are impaired. Yet those who have developed explicit models*

of behavior of nonprofit organizations set quite a different tone. Scholars such as James (1978), Pauly and Redisch (1973), Niskanen (1971), Feigenbaum (1979), Tullock (1966), and Rose-Ackerman (1979) have basically assumed revenue enhancing or other self-seeking objectives on the part of management of various types of nonprofit organizations—universities, hospitals, and charities among them (Young, in White, 1981, p. 135).

Young suggests that these two competing views of nonprofits may not be inconsistent. The nonprofit may very well have been established for altruistic reasons, but once in operation and the beneficiary of grants, tax advantages, and a monopoly over the delivery of some collective good, some participants "severely test the imposed constraints and manipulate them toward selfish ends" (Young, 1981, p. 136).

References

Atkinson, R. (1997). Nonprofit symposium: Theories of the federal income tax exemption for charities: Thesis, antithesis, and synthesis. *Stetson Law Review.* 27 Stetson L. Rev. 395. Fall, 1997. 395-431.

Bennett, J., & DiLorenzo, T. (1989). *Unfair competition: The profits of nonprofits.* Lanham, MD: Hamilton Press.

Berger, P., & Neuhaus, R. (1977). *To empower people: The role of mediating structures in public policy.* Washington, DC: American Enterprise Institute for Public Policy Research.

Colombo, J. D., & Hall, M. A. (1995). *The charitable tax exemption.* Boulder, CO: Westview Press.

Douglas, J. (1987). Political theories of nonprofit organizations. In J. S. Ott (Ed.). *The nature of the nonprofit sector* (pp. 179-189). Boulder, CO: Westview Press.

Lohmann, R. (1992). The theory of the commons. In J. S. Ott (Ed.). *The nature of the nonprofit sector* (pp. 89-95). Boulder, CO: Westview Press.

Ott, J. S. (Ed.). (2001). *The nature of the nonprofit sector,* Boulder, CO: Westview Press.

Pennings, R. (2003). *Kuyper's sphere sovereignty and modern economic institutions.* Retrieved June 10, 2003, from http://wrf.ca/comment/issue/03wi/essay1

Salamon, L. (1999). *America's nonprofit sector: A primer* (Second Edition). Washington, DC: The Foundation Center.

Weisbrod, B. A. (1975). Toward a theory of the voluntary nonprofit sector in a three-sector economy. In S. Rose-Ackerman (Ed.). *The economics of nonprofit institutions* (pp. 21-44). New York: Oxford University Press.

Wellford, W. H., & Gallagher, J. (1988). *Unfair competition? The challenge to charitable tax exemption.* Washington, DC: The National Assembly of Voluntary Health and Social Welfare Organizations.

Young, D. R. (1981). Entrepreneurship and the behavior of nonprofit organizations. In S. Rose-Ackerman (Ed.). *The economics of nonprofit institutions: Studies in structure and policy* (pp. 161-184). New York: Oxford University Press.

Chapter 36
The Future of the Nonprofit Sector

Synopsis: The nonprofit sector is facing transformational challenges. Among the trends identified to watch are the threat of terrorism, changing demographics, advancing technology, increased government scrutiny, government cutbacks, donor attitude changes, the blurring of the sectors, and increasing professionalism of the sector.

Introduction

Serious challenges currently face the nonprofit sector. Yet when has there been a time when this was not so? Those who lead nonprofit organizations have always been on the front lines of the battle to improve the human condition. If there were no problems that people couldn't adequately address themselves or with the help of government alone, then the sector may well have dissolved by itself. That being said, many feel, including myself, that the nonprofit sector is undergoing a revolutionary transformation, the result of massive changes in society with respect to demographics, economic instability, technology advancement, cultural and attitudinal shifts, and increasing competition for shrinking resources.

The purpose of this chapter is to focus not on these generic challenges particularly, but to look at what transformational trends, both for good and for bad, point to potential major restructuring of the sector from the standpoint of how it is perceived by contractors, government regulators, donors, and the public. In this chapter, I will discuss eight major trends that have the potential to transform the sector.

Trend 1: Terrorism and the Fear of Terrorism is affecting the way charities do business.

At this very moment, scores, if not hundreds, of well-financed and well-trained terrorists are dedicating their lives, both literally and figuratively, to attacking America, its citizens and institutions, and bringing an end to our way of life. It is not a question of whether they would do the unthinkable—kill as many of us as they can with weapons of mass destruction. It is understood that the limitation is not motivation, but rather the means and ability to do so. As the September 11th terrorist attacks demonstrated, none of us is immune. And it is not as if we did not have any warning, since the previous attack on the World Trade Center was intended to have the same result.

Since September 11, we have seen a public reaction ranging from acceptance to panic. Duct tape and plastic sheeting sales skyrocketed in the weeks after 9-11 (Isidore, 2003; Reaves, 2003). Potassium iodide tablets were being distributed by local governments, including my own municipality of Harrisburg, Pennsylvania, just ten miles from the Three Mile Island (TMI) nuclear plant (Pennsylvania Department of Health, 2002).

Cyber-terrorism, defined as "an assault on electronic communications networks (Webster's, 2004) is a related issue that affects the behavior of the public. In 2000, the "I Love You" virus caused an estimated $5 billion loss in data (Malphrus, 2002). Dan Verton, a former intelligence officer and a *ComputerWorld* senior staff writer, writes that our computer systems are not only vulnerable, but are already being targeted by hackers with the ability to cause physical death and destruction—such as by flooding 911 call centers with phantom calls, disabling power grids, wreaking havoc with the distribution of food supplies, and disrupting communications of first responders (Verton, 2003).

Overall, computer crime—including viruses, spyware, and PC theft—costs U.S. organizations $67.2 billion annually, according to the Federal Bureau of Investigation, affecting 2.8 million organizations. The most costly expenses were responding to viruses and Trojan horses (Evers, 2006).

How will terrorism and the fear of terrorism affect the nonprofit sector in the long term? Here are some mini-trends:

First, there will likely be less travel outside of the home and less large group aggregation. After a high profile terrorist incident or during a time of high terrorism alert—which can be a weekend or last for months—we could expect that there will be a hesitation to travel outside one's home except for essential purposes in the immediate hours following such an attack. We saw this phenomenon immediately after the September 11th attacks when airline travel plummeted. Airports and airplanes now have increased security, and we now have reports that potential targets of terrorists include "softer" targets such as ports, shopping malls, hotels, apartment buildings, and train stations. The bombing of trains in Madrid on March 11, 2004 highlighted the vulnerability of our own passenger rail system. At a time of high terrorism alert (or in the wake of an attack), it would seem logical that simply staying in one's own home would decrease the exposure to risking personal safety. People would be more likely to stay connected via the telephone, radio, cable television, and the Internet rather than by meeting together. This could hamper group activities relied upon by the nonprofit community, such as face-to-face board meetings, holding group fundraising events at a centralized site, organizing advocacy days in the state and national capitals, scheduling conferences and annual meetings, and other activities that bring people together to support the work of a nonprofit organization. In response, nonprofits are likely to utilize new technologies to permit people to "come together" while safely in their own homes (see Trend #3).

A second area related to terrorism and the fear of terrorism that should concern officials of nonprofits is a potential decline in charitable giving, based on a belief that the future is uncertain and unstable. Americans were quite generous following the 9-11 attacks, responding with almost $3 billion to help (Hill, 2003). When trading on the New York stock exchange resumed on September 17, the DOW Industrial Average recorded a drop of 684 points, the largest point decline of the Dow in history (Brancaccio, 2001). Are Americans less likely to share their wealth if they believe that the wealth they feel they have, and need to provide security for themselves and their families, could "disappear" in the wake of another attack that some predict could dwarf the 9-11 tragedy? While some of this can be attributed to a flagging economy, some attribute the flagging economy to the after-effects of 9-11. According to the Giving USA Foundation, Americans donated $295.0 billion to charities in 2006. While this was 1% more than was raised the previous year when adjusted for inflation, the record-setting amount is skewed by some major gifts, including a $1.9 billion payment by Warren Buffett. This compares to $260.3 billion in 2005, $248 billion in 2004, $241 billion in 2003, $234 billion in 2002, and $212 billion in 2001—a year that saw 9-11 and that recorded about a half-percent increase in contributions from 2000 (Giving USA, 2004). Giving in America is barely keeping pace with inflation, and much of the 2005 increase of 6.1% was targeted for disaster relief, such as the Asian tsunami, Pakistan earthquake, and the Katrina/Rita hurricane disasters in the United States. For the first time since 1998, contributions declined for arts, culture, and humanities charities in 2005. The increase in giving for 2006 was disappointing to many, considering that the stock market rose 10% that year.

Third, when the equity markets collapsed post 9-11, it was not only individual investors and corporations that suffered. Foundations and nonprofit organization endowments also were devastated, reducing the capital that was available for investing in charitable organizations.

Fourth, nonprofit organizations will be urged to devote more of their resources for security and emergency-preparedness. They will need to make sure that those who access physical and virtual facilities are who they say they are and do not have weapons. More funds will need to be budgeted and spent for building security, computer security, emergency planning and equipment (such as generators, emergency kits), backup for sensitive electronic data, training, and the staff to manage these issues. In 2004, the Senate passed the *High Risk Nonprofit Security Enhancement Act* (S. 2275) to authorize up to $100 million for security improvements at buildings owned by nonprofits, including places of religious worship, although the measure never became law. Organizations can expect to experience disruptions resulting from computer worms and viruses, spend time and money backing up data, printing out hard copies to ensure that data are available in the event of electronic disruptions, storing vital records in protected environments, and other tasks that have increased the transaction costs of running an organization in an environment where there is an enhanced fear of terrorism and cyber-terrorism.

Trend 2: The Demographics of the United States population is changing.

While America has always had the reputation of being a "melting pot," it has become increasingly popular to celebrate ethnic and religious diversity. It is obvious that older people have different needs and attitudes compared to the "X" or @ generations. Language differences result in more communication problems, and these can be accentuated when cultural differences are magnified. Older donors tend to have different views about charity than younger donors. These are some of the reasons nonprofit sector futurists keep a close eye on demographic trends.

What are some important demographic trends worth watching?

a. *The nonprofit workforce, already more diverse in many respects than the general workforce, is becoming much more diverse.* According to the U.S. Census, the non-Hispanic white population will be falling steadily, from 74% in 1995 to 72% in 2000, to 64% in 2020 and 53% in 2050 (U.S. Census Bureau, 1996). This trend identified a decade ago was not quite confirmed by the 2000 census—of a total population of 281.4 million, 211.5 million, 75%, were white (U.S. Census Bureau, 2001a). Evidence is mounting that this was simply a delay in the inevitable. Among the implications are that nonprofit organization managers must be more sensitive to cultural differences among those they manage and take steps to ensure that their staff will be culturally competent. In the same way, the population being served by nonprofit organizations is becoming more diverse. Fundraisers can benefit by being sensitive to cultural differences among those they approach for gifts, taking into account the increasing ability of minorities to make donations (Anft, 2001).

b. *The U.S. population is aging.* Census data confirm that Americans are growing older; the median age in the U.S. increased from 32.9 in 1990 to 35.3 in 2000 (U.S. Census Bureau, 2001b). The U.S. Census Bureau predicts that the number of Americans aged 65 and older will increase from 13% in 1995 to 20% in 2030, even though the percentage actually decreased from 12.4% in the 2000 census to 12.6% in 1990. However, millions of baby-boomers are beginning to reach the age of 65, and that will rapidly increase the percentage of those 65 and older. The 2000 census did confirm that the fastest growing cohort of the aged was the group of those 85 and older, growing from 9.9 % of the older population in 1990 to 12.2% in 2000 (U.S. Census Bureau, 2001b). In 1995, the Census

Bureau projected the number of Americans aged 85 and over will double by 2025 and increase five-fold by 2050.

Older Americans need more health care. Some of this will be provided by their children, who might otherwise have volunteered and donated to charities. According to the Families and Work Institute study, 35% of workers reported that they had provided care for a relative or in-law 65 years of age or older within the past year (Bond, et al., 2002). On the other side of this ledger, even conservative estimates are that $41 trillion will be transferred among the generations over the next 50 years with $12 trillion transferred by 2020 (Schervish, 1999; Community Foundation R&D Incubator, 2002).

Nonprofits themselves are facing a potential internal leadership crisis as a result of the aging of our population. A study conducted by the School of Public Affairs of Baruch College, commissioned by the United Way of New York City, found that nearly half of all of the City's nonprofit executives planned to retire within five years. Little or nothing was being done to plan for their succession or train the next generation of leadership (Gardyn, 2003).

c. *There are more women in the workforce and more dual-earner couples.* According to a report of the Families and Work Institute (Bond, et al. 2002), the gap between the percentage of men and women in the wage and salaried workforce has almost completely closed, with women now comprising 49%. The proportion of these men and women who are dual-earning couples increased from 66% in 1977 to 78% in 2002. The study highlights the fact that as a result, men are spending more time doing household chores by an average of 42 minutes over that 25-year time span, and that the time these couples spend caring for and doing things with their children on workdays actually increased by almost 20%. Precious little time (an average of 1.3 hours for dads and .9 hours for moms) is spent on themselves each workday. Left unsaid in the report is that there is a strain on leisure time that can be devoted to volunteer service with the voluntary sector.

d. *There are more single-parent families.* In 1970, the number of single-parent families with children under the age of 18 was 3.8 million. By 1990, the number had more than doubled to 9.7 million (Kirby, 1995). There are approximately 12 million single-parent families in the U.S., about ten million of them headed by the mother. Of these, 34% of incomes fall below the poverty level (Bosak, 2003). While studies that show children from such families lagging behind on indicators such as achievement, intellectual development, and behavior have been challenged on methodological grounds, mother-only families are more likely to be poor. The median annual income for female-headed households with children under six years old is roughly one-fourth that of two-parent families (Kirby, 1995). This has been attributable to the lower earning capacity of women, inadequate public assistance and child care subsidies, and lack of enforced child support from nonresidential fathers (Kirby, 1995). As the number of nontraditional families increases, nonprofit organizations that provide human services must make adjustments. Many banks are open on weekends, unthinkable a decade or two ago, but a reflection of that industry's willingness to adjust to the times.

e. *The number of Americans who report a disability is increasing.* According to the U.S. government (U.S. Census Bureau, 2003), 49.7 million Americans have some type of long-lasting condition or disability, 19.3% of the 257.2 million civilians aged five and over who were not living in prisons, nursing homes, or other institutions. Nonprofit organizations must ensure that their offices are accessible to those who are disabled, that their Web sites are accessible to those who are vision-impaired, and that their staffs are trained to accommodate the special needs people with disabilities.

Trend 3: Most nonprofits are taking advantage of the technology revolution, but a digital divide threatens to divide the sector into "haves" and "have nots."

The nonprofit sector has been transformed by advances in technology. Obviously, nonprofits are benefiting by technology much more than their increasing use of the Internet. Cell phones, scanners, relational databases, bar codes, high-speed copiers, fax machines, and PDAs are just some examples of technological advances that are helping make the sector more efficient. Here, I will focus on some aspects of the Internet that are revolutionizing how nonprofit staff are doing their jobs.

Republican Presidential candidate Ron Paul raised $6.2 million in a single day, December 16, 2007, over the Internet (Bowman, 2007). Nonprofits use their own Web sites and specialized sites such as Nonprofit Oyster (nonprofitoyster.com) and VolunteerMatch (VolunteerMatch.org) to hire staff and find volunteers. Prospect research may still involve going through dusty newspapers in libraries, but a few simple clicks using search engines such as Google *(google.com)* and online databases such as Melissa Data Corporation Lookups *(http://www.melissadata.com/Lookups/ index.htm)* and Hoover's *(http://www.hoovers.com)* turn up more information about more potential prospects. A simple broadcast e-mail can instantly mobilize thousands of advocates for or against an important legislative bill or amendment. Millions of dollars of additional revenue are being raised online through the sale of goods and services, holding charity auctions, and partnering with for-profit retailers (Grobman, 2001; Grobman and Grant, 2006). Nonprofits instantly research and apply for government grants online, using sites such as grants.gov. Universities (and other types of nonprofits, as well) use the Internet for training, workshops, courses, and virtual meetings.

Here are some mini-trends:

a. *Online fundraising is skyrocketing.* The American Red Cross reported raising $157.7 million online in 2005 compared to $33 million in 2004, an almost 4,000% increase (Wallace, 2006). Network for Good boasted in a 2007 press release that it had distributed more than $100 million from more than 300,000 donors to 25,000 charities in the previous six years. Within days of the December 2004 tsunami disaster, the charity portal recorded at least $10 million in online donations made to tsunami relief organizations. Over $1 million was donated by credit card on a single day, December 29. Donations for Katrina relief exceeded this record several-fold in August 2005 (Grobman and Grant, 2006). According to Kintera, a full-service fundraising application service provider, online donations rose from $1.9 billion in 2003 to more than $3 billion in 2004 (Gruber, 2004). Estimates for 2008 are likely to be in the $5 billion-$10 billion range and continue to grow.

b. *Advocacy efforts are harnessing the full power of technology.* A description of the success of the Web site MoveOn.org *(http://www.moveon.org)*, a group founded in 1998, in the April 17, 2003 issue of the *Chronicle of Philanthropy* provides a snapshot of the future of nonprofit advocacy (and, perhaps, fundraising as well). More than 550,000 people signed an online petition directed to the United Nations concerning the Iraq situation in less than two days, and eventually, the total number of signers of the petition exceeded one million. In March 2003, this online advocacy group sent a short e-mail to its 1.3 million-member e-mail list requesting donations to Oxfam America. More than 8,400 responded with donations totaling more than $600,000 (Raymond, 2003). A previous appeal to raise $27,000 for an anti-war advertisement in the *New York Times* generated nearly $400,000 (Williams, 2003). Currently, MoveOn.org boasts of more than 3.3 million members who participate in organized advocacy on progressive public policy issues, such as ending the war in Iraq, protecting online privacy, ending tax loopholes, and increasing media accountability.

Online advocacy efforts are resulting in much more than "virtual" advocacy that generates e-mail, petitions, telephone calls, and letters to public policy decision-makers. The Internet is being used to mobilize people to physically attend political demonstrations.

c. *The "digital divide" will become more pronounced with respect to nonprofit organizations.* The mainstream media has focused attention on the so-called "digital divide." The term is typically used to describe the disparity of technology access not only among races and income levels, but also communities, regions, and countries. The generalized fear is that we are quickly becoming a society of two classes—those who have access to, and proficiency with, technology, and those who do not. Race, socio-economic status, and education level may soon take a backseat to whether or not each of us has the ability to download files from the Internet, use a laptop, or submit a résumé electronically.

There is continuing evidence that the digital divide between the rich and poor is also applicable to the comparison of for-profit organizations and their nonprofit counterparts, as well as within the nonprofit sector itself (Greene, 2001).

Trend 4: The nonprofit sector should expect increased government scrutiny, as well as more regulation and accountability requirements.

We should expect that increased regulation of charities is more likely in the future as a result of real and perceived abuses by charities. Among areas of regulation likely to be the focus of future curbs include reform relating to engaging in political activity, paying excessive fees to board members, and expanding financial accountability requirements.

The following summarizes some of the areas of nonprofit regulation that are ripe for reform:

a. *Financial accountability in the nonprofit sector.* The *American Competitiveness and Corporate Accountability Act,* commonly known as the Sarbanes-Oxley Act, was enacted by the Congress in 2002 as a response to corporate financial scandals, such as those at Enron, Arthur Anderson, and Global Crossing (Silk, 2004). Generally, this act does not apply to nonprofit corporations, although two provisions—those relating to protecting whistle-blowers and the destruction of litigation-related documents—do apply to both for-profit and nonprofit corporations. Despite this, many of the requirements of the act could apply to nonprofit organizations. In September 2004, the California legislature enacted the *Nonprofit Integrity Act of 2004*, extending many of the Sarbanes-Oxley provisions to California's nonprofit organizations. New York and Massachusetts are other states considering whether to do this. Among other provisions, Sarbanes-Oxley requires an independent and competent audit committee, requires the lead and reviewing partner of the firm providing the audit to rotate off at least every five years, prohibits the auditing firm from providing non-auditing services to an organization concurrent with an audit, requires the CEO and the CFO to certify the appropriateness of financial statements and to verify that these statements fairly represent the financial condition of the company, prohibits loans to executives and directors, and increases financial disclosure requirements.

b. *Payments to board members.* A survey of 238 foundations conducted in 2003 disclosed that more than two-thirds paid their trustees, and such fees in 1998 amounted to $31.1 million to individual board members and $13.8 million to bank trustees (Lipman, 2003). Studies such as this, and scandals involving questionable payments and loans (Lipman and Williams, 2004a; Lipman and Williams, 2004b) by some foundations to their governance and management leadership, have focused the attention of state and federal regulators on changing the way foundations calculate the minimum 5% payout rate threshold (Kramer, 2003).

c. *Advocating for public policy positions.* Most of us take it for granted that part of the civic responsibility of nonprofit organizations is to advocate for changes in public policy that will support our important missions. This imperative is not necessarily accepted by some conservative members of Congress. The Istook Amendment, actually a series of amendments placing curbs on public advocacy and lobbying by organizations that receive federal grants, was successfully added by Rep. Ernest Istook (R-OK) in 1995 to appropriations legislation (Maskell, 1998). There was a lot of sympathy in Congress for the Congressman's view that charities, subsidized by federal tax exemptions, were using their funds for public advocacy, often advocating for policy changes that were out of the mainstream. The nonprofit advocacy community mobilized, and the amendments were never enacted. More recently, Rep. Istook was offended by an advertisement that appeared on District of Columbia-area Metro bus and subway system vehicles and facilities that suggested that marijuana should be legalized and taxed. An amendment by Rep. Istook to the conference report of H.R. 2673, the $373 billion Consolidated Appropriations Act, considered December 2003, proposed to prohibit transit agencies receiving federal funds from running advertising from groups that want to decriminalize marijuana and other Schedule I substances for medical or other purposes (OMB Watch, 2003; U.S. House of Representatives, 2003). In 2005, Rep. Istook added language to the proposed Federal Housing Finance Reform Act (H.R. 1461) that would have disqualified nonprofits from participating in the grant program envisioned by the legislation if they engaged in voter registration and other nonpartisan voter activities within 12 months of applying for the grant. It should be expected that nonprofits will need to remain vigilant against continuing attempts to muzzle their legitimate right (and duty) to advocate public policy changes. And it would not be unexpected if the Congress enacts some, perhaps mild, curbs on the advocacy rights of nonprofit organizations.

d. *Churches and political activity.* Current law proscribes tax-exempt organizations from participating in partisan political activity, including taking action in support of, or opposition to, any candidate. The IRS has a history of not enforcing this prohibition with any great diligence. In 1994, churches in Virginia that allowed candidates for the U.S. Senate to address political remarks to their congregations from the pulpit received an IRS warning to not do this again (Dye, 2002). Courts have upheld a ruling by the IRS to revoke the exemption of a New York church that purchased a newspaper advertisement containing negative references to a candidate during a campaign (Dye, 2002). Allen A.M.E. Church in Queens, NY, was warned that it could lose its tax exemption after the pastor turned a service into a political rally for Al Gore in 2000 when the candidate visited (Algar, 2001). In February 2006, the IRS released a report that concluded that of the 110 churches it studied after accusations that they were illegally politicking, 59 of them were indeed violating the law and that 28 of the cases were still being reviewed. According to the IRS, it was seeking to revoke the tax-exemptions of three of these churches, was fining one other, and was sending a letter to the others requesting that the violations cease (Lenkowsky, 2006). In July 2006, the IRS sent 15,000 notices to tax-exempt organizations, including churches, to warn them that improper campaigning could put their tax exemptions at risk (Brunskill, 2006). Despite this warning, the IRS recorded 237 public complaints alleging illegal campaign activities by tax-exempt organizations during the 2006 election cycle (Panepento, 2007). An IRS audit of campaign finance reports found nearly $345,000 in illegal direct contributions to candidates from 269 organizations. In June 2007, the IRS initiated investigations of more than 350 nonprofit organizations for illegal political activity and began gearing up to monitor charities for the 2008 election cycle (Panepento, 2007).

Trend 5: Government funding for nonprofits is drying up at a time when demand for services will be increasing.

U.S. public benefit charities relied on government funding to provide about 31% of organization income in 1997, nearly twice the revenue these organizations receive from private contributions (Urban Institute, 2002). Almost a trillion dollars was spent by federal, state, and local governments that year on "social welfare services," about 53% of all government spending and almost a fifth of the entire U.S. gross domestic product, with about 59% of that total provided by the federal government (Salamon, 1999). Increasing percentages of these services are provided by the voluntary sector, and even when not, charities are often called upon to pick up the slack when people fall through the cracks and do not receive the government services to which they are entitled. The obvious implication is that the partnership between government and the nonprofit sector is vital.

As Lester Salamon points out, government growth in spending for social programs grew rapidly for a decade and a half prior to the inauguration of President Ronald Reagan. During the Reagan years, most of the cuts in federal domestic spending during the Reagan years were targeted to programs for the poor (Salamon, 1999). Some of the cuts were motivated by ideology that expressed the view that "government is not the solution to our problem, government is the problem" (Reagan, 1981) and that individual initiative and the nonprofit sector can do a better job than government in improving the lives of the needy. But the budget cuts were also justified by the Congress and the Administration by the arithmetic of budgeting. Major increases in defense spending and a massive tax cut led to federal budget deficits. Entitlement spending and interest payments on the debt left little else to attack other than domestic spending, much of which was spent on programs that political conservatives found unpalatable anyway.

Today, some of the same dynamics are at work that militate for a repeat of the disastrous 1980s, which saw attempts to poke holes in the "safety net" that protects the needy. The September 11th attacks justified a quantum increase in expenditures for defense and homeland security. The war in Iraq created tens of billions of dollars in federal spending. A large tax cut was enacted for the purpose of pump-priming the moribund American economy, slashing government revenues. And huge budget deficits were incurred despite the fact that just months before, surpluses were predicted for the coming decades.

The Nonprofit Sector and the Federal Budget, an April 2006 report of the Nonprofit Sector Research Fund of the Aspen Institute, concluded that federal grants to charities could decline by more than 11 percent over the next five years, and many other government-spending reductions are likely to harm nonprofit groups at the same time. The report, based on the President's FY 2007 budget proposal, found that Federal grants to charities, an estimated $42.2-billion in FY 2006 excluding Medicaid and Medicare funding, would decline by $14.3-billion over the following five years (Abramson, Salamon, & Russell, 2006).

The "voodoo economics" that were discredited no less than by their prime architect, Reagan budget director David Stockman (Greider, 1981), are being repeated: tax cuts skewed to benefit the wealthy, massive increases in the defense budget, and record-breaking budget deficits. According to an October 11, 2007 White House press release, the federal deficit for FY 2007 was $163 billion (White House, 2007), increasing the federal debt to more than $9 trillion (U.S. National Debt Clock, 2007).

At the same time that the government is threatening to withdraw funding for important domestic programs, there are signs that additional challenges in the demand for services are on the horizon. A report released by the Aspen Foundation in April 2006 documents the threat of federal spending cuts to social welfare programs on nonprofit organizations. According to the report, Congress enacted two-thirds of the spending reductions proposed by President Bush for FY 2006. This amounted to cuts of 2.8% below FY 2005 levels after adjusting for inflation, including a 7.3% cut in programs providing social services, employment and training, and community development. Overall, the report estimated that federal discretionary appropriations for FY 2006 of interest to nonprofit organizations (including funding for social welfare, education, health services, income assistance, international aid, arts and culture, and environment) will be $4.6 billion less than the $162.9 billion appropriated for FY 2005 (Abramson, Salamon, & Russell, 2006). An estimated $1 billion of this amount would have gone directly to nonprofit organizations.

Brinckerhoff (1995) suggests that "demand will grow irrevocably, irreversibly, and faster than you anticipate, in almost every service area" for several reasons. First, society has steadily turned to nonprofits over the last 30 years. Second, the chronic underfunding of social services results in many homeless and "underclass" citizens seeking help. Third, the trend of relocation of some nonprofits (such as inner-city hospitals) to market their services to a more lucrative market leaves many unserved or underserved.

But these are far from the only reasons. New social problems surface, and government has always been slow to respond. The terrorist attacks of 2001 and natural disasters here and abroad in 2005 created a demand for billions of charitable dollars. Americans responded generously, but many charities without missions related to helping the victims suffered a fundraising decrease, some of which was attributable to the declining economy, but certainly not all (Association of Fundraising Professionals, 2002). The number of families and individuals without health insurance has been steadily increasing. According to the Census Bureau, the percentage of children without health insurance rose from 8.2 million to 10.6 million from 1987 to 1996, a period of relative prosperity (U.S. Census Bureau, 1998). According to the U.S. Census Bureau, an estimated 15.8% of the population (47 million) had no health insurance coverage during all of 2006, an increase from 15.3% for the previous year (U.S. Census Bureau, 2007).

Census data released August 26, 2005 show that poverty was increasing, with the poverty rate rising from 11.7% to 12.1% in 2002, to 12.55% in 2003 and to 12.7% in 2004. There were three million more poor people in the United States in 2002 than in 2000, an additional 1.3 million in 2003, and an additional 1.1 million in 2004, reflecting a steady increase during that period in the unemployment rate. In 2007, census data showed that the number of persons living in poverty in 2006 was about the same as the number in 2005, and that as a result of a net population increase, this meant that the poverty rate had dropped slightly during the period from 12.6% to 12.3%.(U.S. Census Bureau, 2007).

Global warming, AIDs, and teenage pregnancy are among emerging issues that demand help from the voluntary sector, because some of the political leadership in the U.S. does not accept that global warming is actually occurring, and believes that barely little more that telling people to refrain from having sex is required to solve the other two problems. The same ideology supports keeping a high unemployment rate because of the fear that the economy would overheat and result in unacceptable inflation levels, and to keep the minimum wage rate too low to permit workers to be independent. It is the role of the voluntary sector, in partnership with government, to provide a safety net, and it can be expected that if current policy continues, lack of resources and a burgeoning demand for services will once again be the rule rather than the exception.

Trend 6: Donor attitude changes will profoundly affect how charities raise funds.

A November 2002 article in the *Washington Post* explored what may be a new attitude by donors toward nonprofit organizations. According to fundraisers interviewed for the article, donors are taking an "ask questions now, send money later" attitude (Salmon, 2002, p. H01). The trend seems to have started several years back with large donors, and now has filtered down to the point that even average donors are asking lots of questions before writing checks. The new attitude manifested itself just about the time that contributions overall were reported to drop slightly in real terms, influenced by a flat or declining economy, a lack of confidence in the management of charities as a result of scandal and mismanagement, and uncertainty about the future.

Whether called "the new donor," the "high tech donor," the "social entrepreneur," "venture philanthropist," or "high engagement philanthropists," they have something in common—they use the skills of entrepreneurs and apply them to the organizations they support. These skills include pursuing opportunities in innovative ways, leveraging new resources, assuming some risk, engaging in strategic thinking, and taking a hands-on approach to the organizations in which they invest (Wagner, 2002). Rather than simply writing a check, they do considerable research, participate in the organization's decision-making, require accountability, and expect measurable, positive results. As Wagner points out, these new philanthropists are success-oriented, achievement focused, mostly under 40, make decisions quickly, and often are willing to devote an extraordinary amount of time to ensure that their "investment" in a charity is not wasted. Although there has been criticism about the applicability of the venture capitalist model to the voluntary sector (see Wagner, 2002; Kramer, 1999), the point is that billions of dollars in assets are accessible to the charitable community, with decisions being made by those who are adherents of this model of philanthropy. Because they are mostly young, it is not likely that this perspective will die any time soon.

In response to "customer demand," the United Way in the 1990s began permitting its donors to designate charitable donations made to the United Way to particular member agencies, and, in some cases, agencies not part of the United Way. Five million donors have stopped giving to the United Way as a result, but simply use the organization as the administrative arm to distribute their gifts (Murphy, 2003). There are alternative explanations for this phenomenon, but one is that many donors want to target their donations based on their personal preferences rather than to deputize a United Way allocation committee to make the decisions for them.

There appears to be a growing trend of donors changing their attitudes in the way they view charities. In the past, it was typical for donors to give to a charity based on its reputation, whether its mission was consistent with the donor's values, and (typically) left it to the charity's board to decide how the funds would be utilized. Today, donors are becoming much more involved in how their donations are being used. The world's two wealthiest individuals, Bill Gates and Warren Buffett, joined forces in 2006 to combine their philanthropy. They do not simply funnel money to existing charities, but rather have created their own programs, emphasizing accountability, outcomes, and results. To an increasing degree, donors are not only spelling out detailed requirements for how their donations are being used, but they are requiring charities to sign enforceable contracts that even permit the donor to sue if the funds are not used exactly in accordance with the donor's wishes.

In a March 2002 cover story, the *Chronicle of Philanthropy* (Blum, 2002) explored this trend, often tied to requirements that programs financed by these grants be evaluated to determine how much good is being done. Blum offers three explanations. Some see this trend as an extension of strategic philanthropy, the practice of concentrating dollars in a specific area and measuring the results. Others see it as a nonprofit sector application of venture capitalism, in which charity is an "investment" rather than a donation, and is expected to bring a "return on investment." A third explanation is simply that charitable giving is becoming more corporatized as a result of more professionals supervising how funds are donated (Blum, 2002). In any case, many donors seem to have changed their attitudes with respect to their donations, and if this trend continues, nonprofit governors will have significantly less flexibility to direct charitable dollars to the programs they feel need them the most.

Charities are being asked to justify their performance in a manner unprecedented in history, with funders requiring the collection of data on outcomes. As documented by Paul Light, the United Way of America embraced the outcomes measurement reform movement—

with gale force, issuing policy papers, authoring measurement manuals, promoting implementation, and generally cheerleading its local associates to adopt outcome measurement as its allocation tool...the United Way of America is unrelenting about its ultimate goal to convert the nonprofit sector to its image of outcomes management. The central indicator of its success will be nothing less than the adoption of outcomes measurement by every last one of its local partners, and, in turn their use of outcomes measurement to make all funding decisions (Light, 2000. p. 20-21).

Trend 7: The nonprofit, for-profit, and government sectors will continue to converge.

The convergence of the government, nonprofit, and for-profit sectors has been a subject of study and scrutiny by the academic community for more than a decade (see Saidel, 1991; Ferris, 1993; Weisbrod, 1997). As pointed out by Lester Salamon (1999), it is a myth that nonprofit organizations get most of their revenue from donations from individuals and foundations. Based on 1997 estimates from Independent Sector, fees, service charges, and other commercial income accounted for 54% of the estimated $515 billion in U.S. nonprofit service-organization revenues. Another 36% was funded by government, and only 10% by private giving. There is substantial evidence that the trend of sector convergence is not only continuing, but accelerating. A report by the Kellogg Foundation (2003) documents this, and concludes that "(T)here is no right or wrong conclusion about the value of blurring sectoral lines. It is a fact of the times. However, the blurring should be happening in the midst of a richer dialogue about the meaning and benefits of individual engagement for the common good" (p. 28).

The Kellogg report identified five "flashpoints" of change. These include the creation of hybrid organizations that are part nonprofit and part business organizations, social entrepreneurship (which means using charitable funds to provide private enterprises), the creation of private business organizations that have social missions virtually identical to their nonprofit counterparts, the formation of partnerships that involve the collaboration of the nonprofit sector and either one or both of the other two sectors, and the creation of educational and support systems that are designed to "improve the effectiveness of social entrepreneurs and business ventures that seek to benefit the common good" (Kellogg Foundation, 2003, p. 9).

Salamon (1999) points out that another factor driving sector convergence is that for-profit businesses are increasingly competing for "business" traditionally in the purview of nonprofits, such as day care, health care, and physical fitness. Using data provided by the U.S. Census, he informs us that between 1977 and 1992, for-profit firms captured 80% of the growth in day care centers and 90% of the growth in home health and clinic care.

The trend in nonprofit hospitals being bought up by for-profit hospital chains has been well-publicized, and it has been characterized by several commentators as "the largest redeployment of charitable assets in history" (Bureau of Primary Health Care, 2000; Magat, 2004). Billions of dollars in assets received from the sale of nonprofit hospitals to for-profits have been placed in so-called "conversion" foundations, signaling a go-ahead for the new profit-oriented leadership of these institutions, many of them chains with names like Columbia/HCA and Tenet, to lay off staff, raise prices, and take steps that decrease quality of care (Piccone, Chou, & Sloan, 2002). According to a Duke University think tank studying the issue, some states now have 41% of their community non-federal, short-term beds in the hands of for-profit entities (the level for the nation was 10% and growing), with 147 nonprofit hospitals converting to for-profit from 1980 to 1983 and 206 converting between 1994 and 1997 (Center for Health Policy, 1998). An additional 80 public hospitals converted to for-profit status between 1980 and 1993.

There has been an explosion in the construction of for-profit physical fitness centers competing head-to-head with YMCAs that have been around for more than 100 years.

Relatively newly chartered for-profit universities—such as the University of Phoenix, Capella University, and Walden University—provide chiefly online educational programs and compete head-to-head with their traditional, bricks and mortar counterparts, many of which are just beginning to offer online degree programs. Founded in 1976, the University of Phoenix has already become the largest private university in the United States, serving 300,000 students (Wikipedia, 2007).

Because for-profit and nonprofit service providers in the same community often must compete for the same revenue stream from the same market to survive, it is not unexpected that they will tend to make decisions in the same way, hire the same type of staff, market their products and services in a similar manner, have similar physical facilities, and start looking like each other in many aspects. The "iron law of emulation, " a term coined by Daniel Patrick Moynihan (Rogers, Jr., 1999, p. 6 footnote), suggests that organizations in conflict will tend to become similar to one another (in this case, not only be in conflict with them but fund them, regulate them, manage them, or collaborate with them).

Another driving force behind the blurring of the sectors is the increase in cause-related marketing, defined as "the public association of a for-profit company with a nonprofit organization, intended to promote the company's product or service and to raise money for the nonprofit" (Foundation Center, 2004). The term was first used by American Express in 1983, when the company pledged to donate a penny to the Statute of Liberty restoration project for each time someone used its charge card. According to American Express, the number of new card holders "soon grew by 45%, and card usage increased by 28%" (Foundation Center, 2004). Cause-marketing efforts have skyrocketed since then. An October 2003 research study found that 98% of consumers in the United States and United Kingdom were aware of at least one cause-marketing program, an increase from the 88% figure recorded in 2000. An astounding 83% of consumers reported that they had participated in at least one cause-related marketing program, compared to 68% in 2000. The study found broad support from consumers for the general concept (Business in the Community, 2004). A second study, conducted by Boston-based Cone, found that 60% of Americans said they planned to buy at least one product during the 2003 holiday season from a company that promised to allocate a percentage of the purchase price to charity, and that revenue from cause-related marketing was expected to increase by 10.3% in 2004 to a total of $921 million (Schwinn, 2003). Some critics charge that by promoting commercial products and services to attract charitable dollars, charities are becoming more like their for-profit counterparts, perhaps sacrificing their missions to serve the public good to increase their revenues.

The practical effect of the "Reinventing Government" reform movement of the early 1990s was to encourage an increase in outsourcing ("steer rather than row"), be results-oriented (require data on outcomes rather than outputs), encourage competition among the sectors, make government more "business-like," and generally blend and blur the three sectors (Osborne & Gaebler, 1992).

Trend #8: The nonprofit sector workforce is professionalizing.

A profession can be defined as a class of workers who have their own body of knowledge, ethical standards, and educational credentials. "Profession" in Latin means "bound by an oath," deriving from the requirement of tax collectors in ancient Rome for taxpayers to declare under oath what their occupation was—because the tax was based on it, a tradition that continues in modified form to this day with occupation taxes (Baker, 1999). One characteristic of a profession is that its members profess their loyalty to the profession over that of the organization that pays their salaries.

Many professions have licensing and certification requirements, continuing education require-ments, specialized degrees with standardized curriculum requirements, accreditation bodies to set standards and evaluate educational programs, their own ethics code with committees to enforce it, and associations to further the interests of the profession.

Some professions are very organized; others are more informal. For example, social workers are licensed in every state. There is "title protection" in some states, meaning that those who do the work that is typically performed by social workers cannot legally call themselves "social workers" unless they have state social worker licenses. To qualify for licensing, one must have a degree from a university program accredited by the Council on Social Work Education; pass a licensing exam; and meet supervision, continuing education, and other credentialing requirements determined by the state. Social workers who violate the Code of Ethics of the National Association of Social Workers are subject to sanctions imposed by their peers in the profession or state licensing boards.

Contrast this with the requirements of being a journalist, a government administrator, or a nonprofit manager. There are certainly bodies of specialized knowledge and ethics codes for each of these three professions. There are curricula and accredited degrees one can obtain. But anyone can "come in off the street" and take such a position. This is not the case with a medical doctor, a dentist, or attorney, as every state provides "practice protection" to these professions, which prohibits anyone from providing the services these professionals provide unless they have qualified to do so and are licensed.

But, increasingly, the nonprofit management field is becoming more professionalized. Those in the field are putting letters after their names that designate advanced degrees in nonprofit management or certification as professional fundraisers.

Education

Perhaps the first credentialed program in nonprofit management was launched by Columbia University's Institute for Not-for-Profit Management in 1977. A Masters of Public Administration degree with a concentration in nonprofit management was offered by the University of Missouri-Kansas City as early as 1981. More and more, institutions of higher learning are offering degrees specializing in nonprofit management. Seton Hall University's Nonprofit Management Education Web site (*http://tltc.shu.edu/npo*) reports that 255 colleges and universities currently offer courses in nonprofit management. 114 programs offer a graduate degree with a nonprofit management concentration, defined as requiring three or more courses.

American Humanics was first conceived in 1947 by H. Roe Bartle, a former mayor of Kansas City, MO. The mission of the program is "to prepare and certify future nonprofit professionals to work with America's youth" (A.H. History, 2005). Today, more than 80 institutions of higher learning have an affiliation with the American Humanics program, according to the organization's Web site *(http://www.humanics.org)*.

The National Association of Schools of Public Affairs and Administration (NASPAA) has looked at the issue of nonprofit management education, and in a 2000 report co-sponsored by the Nonprofit Academic Centers Council (NACC), recommended that a graduate program with a concentration in nonprofit management should consist of 36 credit hours, with at least 12 of those hours focusing on the unique aspect of the nonprofit sector (Wilson & Larson 2002).

Typical courses offered by these programs include many of the same courses one might find in a business or public administration curriculum (e.g., strategic planning, marketing and communications, organization theory/behavior, budgeting/financial management, personnel management, ethics), along with others that are unique to the sector (e.g., fundraising, grantsmanship, nonprofit law, volunteer management, board-staff relations).

Accreditation of Fundraisers

According to its Web site "About Us" page, found at *http://www.cfre.org*, CFRE International offers a certification to "fundraising professionals who demonstrate the knowledge, skills, and commitment to the highest standards of ethical and professional practice in serving the philanthropic sector." The certification requires a written application, a written examination consisting of 225 multiple choice questions, and an agreement to uphold a code of ethics and accountability standards. Certification is required every three years. There is a continuing education requirement.

An Advanced Certified Fundraising Executive credential is offered by the ACFRE Professional Certification Board to those who already have the CFRE credential. (For more information, visit the Web site of the Association of Fundraising Professionals *(http://www.afpnet.org)* and click on *Education and Career Development/Certification and Career Management)*.

Standards for Excellence

In 1998, the Maryland Association of Nonprofit Organizations initiated an ethics and accountability code for the nonprofit sector entitled Standards for Excellence (see Chapter 8). The program includes educational components and a voluntary certification process whereby charities can receive certification that they meet 55 basic ethical and accountability standards in eight areas. If the peer-review panel affirms that the organization meets the standards, the organization receives a Seal of Excellence. The full set of standards can be found at:

http://www.standardsforexcellenceinstitute.org

This credential for nonprofit organizations is another recent development that is promoting the professionalization of the nonprofit sector.

What does this trend mean for the future of the sector? Overall, this is a positive trend. Professionalization, with its emphasis on training, best practices, quality standards, ethics, and accountability, means that workers, managers, and executives will perform their jobs better. It also implies more public visibility and increased respect not only from the public, but from government and funders and those who receive services, which should improve the ability of the sector to attract qualified, committed applicants for positions.

Conclusion

It is difficult to find a time in the long and honored history of the nonprofit sector that was free of the generic challenges that it faces today. The most obvious—a difficulty in meeting legitimate and increasing needs for services as a result of limited resources—is a plague that will not likely disappear in our lifetime. As a sector that provides collective goods dependent on voluntary donations of time and money, there will be cycles of public trust and public participation. Government partnership with the nonprofit sector will also likely go through its ups and downs, influenced by the political ideology of elected officials, budget realities, and the level of confidence these officials have in the ability of the sector to deliver goods and services consonant with that ideology.

Throughout the history of the nonprofit sector, a spirit of optimism has prevailed. Many feel that people in nonprofit organizations, working collectively to better their society, can overcome whatever physical, economic, and psychological obstacles stand in their way. And it is usually the nonprofit sector that has recognized a need for collective action first—often decades before government mobilizes any action—and has devised creative solutions to respond to society's most complex and perplexing problems.

The challenges never end, and we should not expect them to. As I write this, the fear of AIDS is being replaced by a fear of avian flu and the MRSA Superbug. The fear of global nuclear war between superpowers has been supplanted by a fear of terrorism fomented by religious fundamentalists using home-made weapons of mass destruction. The scourges of air and water pollution are being eclipsed as a focus of environmental concern by global warming. And child neglect and abuse has been pushed off center stage by an obsession with dealing with kidnapped children. Obviously, AIDS, nuclear war, air and water pollution, and child abuse and neglect continue to pose serious threats to our quality of life. Whether the threats are old or new, nonprofit organizations will continue to be partners with government and the private sector in dealing with them, and will not be hesitant to go it alone when the other sectors shirk their responsibilities.

Stakeholders of these organizations (i.e., *all* of us) should expect to continue to be called upon to meet these challenges If history is any guide, the millions of committed individuals and organizations will continue to successfully develop creative and aggressive responses in a way that makes the sector an essential component of a healthy, vibrant society.

References

Abramson, Alan; Salamon, Lester; & John Russell (2006). *The Nonprofit Sector and the Federal Budget: Analysis of President Bush's FY 2007 Budget*. Washington, DC: The Aspen Institute (Nonprofit Sector Research Fund). Retrieved online at: *http://www.nonprofitresearch.org/information1524/information.htm*

Algar, Salim (2001). Church meets state in Harlem. Retrieved online: *http://www.jrn.columbia.edu/studentwork/election/2000/uptown2000/code/church1.html*

Anft, Michael. (2001). Raising money with sense and sensibility. *Chronicle of Philanthropy*. v14 n1; October 18, 2001, p. 20-21.

Association of Fundraising Professionals (2002). Charitable giving mixed following September 11th tragedies. (Survey and press release). February 7, 2002. Washington, DC: Author. Retrieved online: *http://www.afpnet.org/research_and_statistics/sept_11_aftermath*

Baker, Robert. (1999). Codes of ethics: Some history. *Perspectives on the Professions.* v19 n1; Fall 1999. Retrieved online at: http://ethics.iit.edu/perspective/pers19_1fall99_2.html

Blum, Debra E. (2002). Ties that bind: More donors specify terms for their gifts of charity. *Chronicle of Philanthropy.* v14 n11; March 21, 2002; pp. 7-9.

Bond, James, Thompson, Cindy, Galinsky, Ellen & Prottas, David (2002). Highlights of the national study of the changing workforce (Executive Summary). New York: Families and Work Institute.

Bosak, Susan V. (2004). Mother's Day Activity Kit. Retrieved online at: *http://www.tcpnow.com*

Bowman, Quinn (2007). *Paul Hauls in $6M, Setting Another 'Money Bomb' Record.* Public Broadcasting Service. Retrieved online: *http://www.pbs.org/newshour/vote2008/blog/2007/12/paul_hauls_in_6m_setting_anoth.html*

Brancaccio, David (2001). Marketplace new archives: September 17, 2001. September 17, 2001. Retrieved online: *http://marketplace.publicradio.org/shows/2001/09/17_mpp.html*

Brinckerhoff, Peter C. (1995). What the next 10 years will bring and how to get ready. *Nonprofit World.* v13 n2; pp. 19-25; March-April 1995.

Brunskill, Mark K. (2006). IRS warns tax-exempt organizations against political campaigning. *All Headline News.* July 18, 2006. Retrieved online: http://www.allheadlinenews.com/articles/7004253035.

Bureau of Primary Health Care (2000). Health care conversion foundations: Exploring the opportunities and risks. Washington, DC: U.S. Dept. of Health and Human Services, Health Resources and Services Administration, Health Care for the Homeless Information Resource CenterNewsletter. Winter 2000. Retrieved online: *http://bphc.hrsa.gov/hchirc/newsletter/oct_00_a.htm*

Business in the Community (2004). Brand benefits—Cause-related marketing. Retrieved online *at: http://www.bitc.org.uk/resources/research/research_publications/brand_benefits.html*

Center for Health Policy (1998). *A guide for communities considering hospital conversion.* Durham, NC: Duke University, Center for Health Policy, Law and Management. May 1998.

Community Foundation R&D Incubator (2002). *Family philanthropy and the intergenerational transfer of wealth.* Retrieved online at: *http://www.cmif.org/Documents/family.pdf*

Dye, Alan (2002). Political activity by clergymen. January 23, 2002. Christian Coalition of Iowa. Retrieved online: *http://www.iowachristian.com/clergymen.htm*

Evers, Joris (2006). Computer Crime Costs $67 billion, F.B.I. Says. Retrieved online at: *http://www.news.com/2100-7349-6028946.htm*

Ferris, James M. (1993). The double-edged sword of social service contracting: Public accountability versus nonprofit accountability. In *The nature of the nonprofit sector.* Ott, J. Stephen (Ed.); (2001), Boulder, CO: Westview Press. pp. 391-398.

Foundation Center (2004). Frequently asked questions: What is cause-related marketing? Retrieved online at: *http://foundationcenter.org/getstarted/faqs/html/cause_marketing.html*

Gardyn, Rebecca (2003). New York groups could face leadership gap, study finds. *Chronicle of Philanthropy*; v16 n3; November 13, 2003; p. 31.

Giving USA (2004). Americans give $241 billion to charity In 2003: 2.8 percent growth in contributions is highest rate seen since 2000. Retrieved online: *http://aafrc.org/press_releases/trustreleases/americansgive.html*

Greene, Stephen G. (2001). Astride the Digital Divide, *Chronicle of Philanthropy*, v13 i6, January 11, 2001. Retrieved from: http://www.philanthropy.com/premium/articles/v13/i06/06000101.htm

Greider, William (1981). The education of David Stockman. Atlantic Monthly. December 1981. Retrieved online at: *http://www.theatlantic.com/politics/budget/stockman.htm*

Grobman, Gary (2001). *The Nonprofit Organization's Guide to E-Commerce*. Harrisburg, PA: White Hat Communications.

Grobman, Gary & Grant, Gary (2006). *Fundraising Online: Using the Internet to Raise Serious Money for Your Organization*. Harrisburg, PA: White Hat Communications.

Gruber, Harry (2004). Kintera personal e-mail interview to Gary M. Grobman, July 1, 2004.

Hill, Michael (2003). 9/11 charity focuses on kids. Associated Press. September 11, 2003. Retrieved online: *http://www.idsnews.com/story.php?id=18109*

Isidore, Chris. (2003). U.S. stuck on duct tape: Latest terrorism preparation warning spurs sales, production of American icon—duct tape. February 13, 2003. CNNMoney. Retrieved online: *http://money.cnn.com/2003/02/12/news/companies/ducttape/*

Kellogg Foundation (2003). *Blurred boundaries and muddled motives: A world of shifting social responsibilities*. Battlecreek, MI: Author.

Kirby, Jacqueline (1995). Single parent families in poverty. Human Development and Family Life Bulletin, v1n1.Spring 1995. Retrieved online: http://www.hec.ohio-state.edu/famlife/bulletin/volume.1/bullart1.htm

Kramer, Mark R. (1999). Venture capital and philanthropy: A bad fit. *Chronicle of Philanthropy*, April 22, 1999. p. 72.

Kramer, Mark B. (2003). Members of Congress Don't understand what good grant making takes. Chronicle of Philanthropy. May 29, 2003. p. 35.

Lenkowsky, Leslie (2006). Charities and politicking: The rules get murkier. *Chronicle of Philanthropy*. March 9, 2006, p. 46.

Light, Paul (2000). Making nonprofits work: A report on the tides of nonprofit management reform. Washington, DC: Brookings Institute Press.

Lipman, Harvy (2003). Majority of private foundations pay their trustees, survey finds. *Chronicle of Philanthropy*. v15 n23; September 18, 2003. p. 11.

Lipman, Harvy & Williams, Grant (2004a). Charities bestow no-interest loans on their well-paid executives. *Chronicle of Philanthropy,* v16 n8; February 5, 2004; page 11.

Lipman, Harvy & Williams, Grant (2004b). Several states are reviewing loans charities made to their officials. *Chronicle of Philanthropy.* v16 n10. March 4, 2004, p. 34.

Magat, Richard I. (2004). Stop the looting of charitable assets. *Chronicle of Philanthropy.* v16 n13; April 15, 2004; p. 34.

Maskell, Jack (1998). 96-809: CRS report to Congress: Lobbying regulations on non-profit organizations. Washington, DC: Congressional Research Service. Updated May 19, 1998.

Malphrus, Stephen (2002). Federal Reserve Board testimony of May 18, 2002 before the Subcommittee on Financial Institutions of the Senate Banking, Housing & Urban Affairs Committee. Retrieved online at: *http://www.federalreserve.gov/BoardDocs/testimony/2000/20000518.htm*

Murphy, John (2003). State of John Murphy, Chairman and CEO, Bell Helicopter Textron before the House Armed Services Committee on the U.S. rotorcraft industrial base; March 12, 2003. Retrieved online: *http://www.house.gov/hasc/openingstatementsandpressreleases/108thcongress/03-03-12murphy.html*

OMB Watch (2003). Istook strikes back—Another attack on nonprofit speech. Retrieved online at: *http://www.ombwatch.org/article/articleprint/1968/-1/41/*

Osborne, David & Gaebler, Ted. (1992). *Reinventing government: How the entrepreneurial spirit Is transforming the public sector.* Reading, MA: Addison-Wesley.

Panepento, Peter (2007a). IRS Investigates 350 charities over charges of improper policing. *Chronicle of Philanthropy.* v19 n17., June 14, 2007.

PA Department of Health (2002). Schweiker Administration announces potassium iodide to be distributed from August 15-21: Citizens, workers and schools within 10 miles of nuclear power plants to receive KI pills. Press release. August 5, 2002. Retrieved online July 21, 2006 at: *http://www.dsf.health.state.pa.us/health/cwp/view.asp?A=190&Q=231990*

Picone, Gabriel, Chou, Shin-Yi, and Sloan, Frank (2002). Are for-profit hospital conversions harmful to patients and to Medicare? Rand Journal of Economics. v33 n3; Autumn 2002. pp. 507-523.

Raymond, Nathaniel (2003). Internet users raise over $600,000 in 6 days for Oxfam's humanitarian relief fund for Iraqi people. Press release of March 27, 2003. Retrieved online at: *http://www.oxfamamerica.org/newsandpublications/press_releases/archive2003/art4544.html*

Reagan, Ronald (1981). First Inaugural Address, January 20, 1981. Retrieved online: *http://www.bartelby.net/124/pres61.html*

Reaves, Jessica. (2003). Living with terrorism: A how-to guide. Time (Online edition). February 12, 2003. Retrieved online at: *http://www.time.com/time/nation/article/0,8599,422141,00.html*

Rodgers, William H. (1999). The most creative moments in the history of environmental law: The whos. Washburn Law Journal. Retrieved online at: *http://home.law.uiuc.edu/lrev/publications/2000s/2000/2000_1/rodgers.html*

Saidel, Judith R. (1991). The relationship between state agencies and nonprofit organizations. In *The nature of the nonprofit sector.* Ott, J. Stephen (Ed.); (2001), Boulder, CO: Westview Press, pp. 380-390.

Salamon, Lester (1999). *America's nonprofit sector: A primer* (Second Edition). Washington, DC: The Foundation Center.

Salmon, Jacqueline (2002). Given to skepticism? With charity scandals in the news and less money to give, donors are asking more questions. Washington Post. H01. November 3, 2002.

Schervish, Paul (1999). Millionaires and the Millennium: New Estimates of the Forthcoming Wealth Transfer and the Prospects for a Golden Age of Philanthropy. October 19, 1999. Chestnut Hill, MA: Social Welfare Research Institute. Retrieved online at: *http://www.bc.edu/research/swri/meta-elements/pdf/m&m.pdf*

Schwinn, Elizabeth (2003). Poll finds holiday shoppers hope to help charities. *Chronicle of Philanthropy*. v16 n4; November 27, 2003. p. 23.

Silk, Thomas (2004). Ten emerging principals of governance of nonprofit corporations. *The Exempt Organization Tax Review*. v43 n1, pp. 35-39, January 2004.

U.S. Census Bureau (1996). Population projections of the United States by age, sex, race, and Hispanic Origin: 1995-2050. Washington, DC: U.S. Department of Commerce, Economics and Statistics Administration, Bureau of the Census.

U.S. Census Bureau (1998). Children without health insurance. March 1998. Retrieved online: *http://216.239.39.104/search?q=cache:1oWseVAL6XcJ:www.census.gov/prod/3/98pubs/cenbr981.pdf+%22without+health+insurance%22+number&hl=en*

U.S. Census Bureau (2001a). American factfinder: Fact Sheet: Highlights from the 2000 demographic profiles. Retrieved online at: *http://factfinder.census.gov/servlet/SAFFacts?_sse=on*

U.S. Census Bureau (2001b). American factfinder: People: Aging. Retrieved online at: *http://factfinder.census.gov/jsp/saff/SAFFInfo.jsp?_pageId=tp2_aging*

U.S. Census Bureau (2003). American factfinder: Fact sheet: People: Disability. Retrieved online at: *http://factfinder.census.gov/jsp/saff/SAFFInfo.jsp?_pageId=tp4_disability*

U.S. Census Bureau (2004). Income stable, poverty up, numbers of Americans with and without health insurance rise, Census Bureau reports. August 26, 2004. Retrieved online at: *http://www.census.gov/Press-Release/www/releases/archives/income_wealth/002484.html*

U.S. Census Bureau (2005) Income stable, poverty rate increases, percentage of Americans without health insurance unchanged. August 30, 2005. Retrieved online at: *http://www.census.gov/Press-Release/www/releases/archives/income_wealth/005647.html*

U.S. Census Bureau (2007). Income, Poverty and Health Insurance Coverage in the United States: 2006. Retrieved online at: *http://www.census.gov/prod/2007pubs/p60-233.pdf*

U.S. House of Representatives (2003). Making appropriations for agriculture, rural development, food and drug administration. And related agencies for the fiscal year ending September 30, 2004, and for other purposes: Conference Report to accompany H.R. 2673. November 25, 2003: Retrieved online at: *http://thomas.loc.gov/cgi-bin/cpquery/T?&report=hr401&dbname=cp108&*

U.S. National Debt Clock (2007). Retrieved online at: *http://www.brillig.com/debt_clock/*

Urban Institute (2002). The new nonprofit almanac and desk reference. Independent Sector and the Urban Institute. Retrieved online at: *http://www.independentsector.org/PDFs/NaExecSum.pdf*

Verton, Dan (2003). *Black ice: The invisible threat of cyberterrorism.* Emeryville, CA: McGraw-Hill/Osborne.

Wagner, Lilya (2002). The "new" donor: Creation or evolution? *International journal of nonprofit and voluntary sector marketing;* v7 n4 November 2002. pp. 343-352.

Wallace, Nicole. (2004). Online donations surge. *Chronicle of Philanthropy;* v16 n17; June 10, 2004; pp. 25-29.

Wallace, Nicole. (2006). *Charities make faster connections. Chronicle of Philanthropy;* v18 n17, June 15, 2006. Retrieved online: http://www.philanthropy.com/premium/articles/v18/i17/17001901.htm

Webster's (2004). Definition of cyber-terrorism. Retrieved online: *http://www.webster-dictionary.org/definition/cyber-terrorism*

Weisbrod, Burton A. (1997). The future of the nonprofit sector: Its entwining with private enterprise and government. Journal of Policy Analysis and Management, 18, 541-555.

White House (2007). Fact Sheet: FY 07 results: Deficit declining toward 2012 surplus. *Retrieved online at: http://www.whitehouse.gov/news/releases/2007/10/20071011-1.html*

Wikipedia (2007). *University of Phoenix.* Author: Retrieved online at: http://en.wikipedia.org/wiki/University_of_phoenix

Williams, Grant (2003). Advocacy group's online savvy nets more than donations. *Chronicle of Philanthropy.* v15 n13, April 17, 2003, p. 23-26.

Wilson, Sam & Larson, Mark I. (2002). Nonprofit management students: Who are they and why do they enroll? Nonprofit and voluntary sector quarterly. v31 n2, pp. 259-270.

Directory of State and National Organizations
and
Publications of Interest

State Organizations

ALABAMA
Nonprofit Resource Center of Alabama
3324 Independence Dr., Suite 100
Birmingham, AL 35209
Phone: (205) 879-4712, Fax: (205) 879-4724
E-mail: george@nrca.info
Web Site: *http://www.nrca.info/*

ARIZONA
Alliance of Arizona Nonprofits
P.O. Box 16162
Phoenix, AZ 85011-6162
Phone: (602) 279-2966
Web Site: *http://www.arizonanonprofits.org*

ARKANSAS
Arkansas Coalition for Excellence
200 S. Commerce Street, Suite 100
Little Rock, AR 72201
Phone: (501) 375-1223
Fax: (501) 324-2236
Web Site: http://www.acenonprofit.org

CALIFORNIA
California Association of Nonprofits
520 South Grand Avenue
Suite 695
Los Angeles, CA 90071
Phone: (213) 347-2070, Fax: (213) 347-2080
E-mail: info@Canonprofits.org
Web Site: http://www.canonprofits.org

COLORADO
Colorado Association of Nonprofit Organizations
455 Sherman Street; STE 207
Denver, CO 80203
Phone: (303) 832-5710, Fax: (303) 894-0161
E-mail: canpo@canpo.org
Web Site: http://www.coloradononprofits.org

CONNECTICUT
Connecticut Association of Nonprofits
90 Brainard Road
Hartford, CT 06114
Phone: (860) 525-5080, Fax: (860) 525-5088
E-mail: rcretaro@ctnonprofits.org
Web Site: http://www.ctnonprofits.org

DELAWARE
Delaware Association of Nonprofit Agencies
100 West 10th Street, Suite 102
Wilmington, DE 19801
Phone: (302) 777-5500, Fax: (302) 777-5386
E-mail: dana@delawarenonprofit.org
Web Site: http://www.delawarenonprofit.org

DISTRICT OF COLUMBIA
Center for Nonprofit Advancement
1666 K Street, NW
Washington, DC 20006
Phone: (202) 457-0540, Fax: (202) 457-0549
E-mail: wca@wcanonprofits.org
Web Site: http://www.wcanonprofits.org

FLORIDA
Florida Association of Nonprofit Organizations
7480 Fairway Drive, #206
Miami Lakes, FL 33014
Phone: (305) 557-1764, Fax: (305) 821-5528
E-mail: fanoinfo@fano.org
Web Site: http://www.fano.org

GEORGIA
Nonprofit Resource Center
The Hurt Building, 50 Hurt Plaza, Suite 845
Atlanta, GA 30303
Phone: (404) 916-3000, Fax: (404) 521-0487
E-mail: info@nonprofitgeorgia.org
Web Site: http://www.nonprofitgeorgia.org

HAWAI'I
Hawai'i Alliance of Nonprofit Organizations
33 South King St., Suite 501
Honolulu, HI 96813
Phone: (808) 529-0466
Fax: (808) 529-0477
Web: http://www.hano-hawaii.org

ILLINOIS
Donors Forum of Chicago
208 South LaSalle Street, Suite 740
Chicago, IL 60604
Phone: (312) 578-0090, Fax: (312) 578-0103
E-mail: info@donorsforum.org
Web Site: http://www.donorsforum.org

INDIANA
Indiana Association of Nonprofit Organizations
1720 Market Tower
10 W. Market Street
Indianapolis, IN 46204
Phone: (317) 464-5324, Fax: (317) 464-5146
E-mail: npteam@att.net

KANSAS
Kansas Nonprofit Association
P.O. Box 47054
Topeka, KS 66647
Phone: (785) 266-6886, Fax: (785) 266-2113
E-mail: knpa@mainstreaminc.net
Web Site: http://www.ksnonprofitassoc.net

LOUISIANA
Louisiana Association of Nonprofit Organizations
P.O. Box 3808
Baton Rouge, LA 70821
Phone: (225) 343-5266, Fax: (225) 338-9470
E-mail: contactus@lano.org
Web Site: http://www.lano.org

MAINE
Maine Association of Nonprofits
565 Congress Street, Suite 301
Portland, ME 04101
Phone: (207) 871-1885, Fax: (207) 780-0346
E-mail: manp@nonprofitmaine.org
Web Site: http://www.nonprofitmaine.org

MARYLAND
Maryland Association of Nonprofit Organizations
Main Office
190 West Ostend Street, Suite 201
Baltimore, MD 21230
Phone: (410) 727-6367, Fax: (410) 727-1914
E-mail: mdnp@mdnonprofit.org
Web Site: http://www.mdnonprofit.org

MASSACHUSETTS
Massachusetts Council of Human Service Providers
250 Summer Street, Suite 237
Boston, MA 02210
Phone: (617) 428-3637, Fax: (617) 428-1533
E-mail: mweekes@providers.org
Web Site: http://www.providers.org

MICHIGAN
Michigan Nonprofit Association
1048 Pierpont, Suite 3
Lansing, MI 48911

Phone: (517) 492-2400, Fax: (517) 492-2410
E-mail: singhsam@mnaonline.org
Web Site: http://www.mnaonline.org

Michigan League for Human Services
1115 South Pennsylvania, Suite 202
Lansing, MI 48912
Phone: (517) 487-5436, Fax: (517) 371-4546
E-mail: amarston@mlan.net
Web Site: http://www.mnaonline.org

MINNESOTA
Minnesota Council of Nonprofits
2314 University Avenue West; #20
St. Paul, MN 55114
Phone: (651) 642-1904, Fax: (651) 642-1517
E-mail: info@mncn.org
Web Site: http://www.mncn.org

MISSISSIPPI
Mississippi Center for Nonprofits
700 N. Jackson Street
Jackson, MS 39202
Phone: (601) 968-0061, Fax: (601) 352-8820
E-mail: MCN@msnonprofits.org
Web Site: http://www.msnonprofits.org

MONTANA
Montana Nonprofit Association
PO Box 1744
Helena, MT 59624
Phone: (406) 449-3717, Fax: (406) 449-3718
E-mail: bmageemna@mt.net
Web site: http://www.mtnonprofit.org

NEBRASKA
Nonprofit Association of the Midlands
5002 S. 24th Street. Suite 201
Omaha, NE 68107
Phone: (402) 557-5800, Fax: (402) 557-5803
E-mail: dcatalan@mail.unomaha.edu
Web site: http://www.nonprofitam.org

NEW HAMPSHIRE
New Hampshire Center for Nonprofits
The Concord Center
10 Ferry Street, Suite 310
Concord, NH 03301
Phone: (603) 225-1947, Fax: (603) 228-5574
E-mail: info@NHnonprofits.org
Web Site: http://www.nhnonprofits.org

NEW JERSEY
Center for Non-Profit Corporations
1501 Livingston Avenue
North Brunswick, NJ 08902
Phone: (732) 227-0800, Fax: (732) 227-0087
E-mail: center@njnonprofits.org
Web Site: http://www.njnonprofits.org

NEW YORK
Council of Community Services of New York State
272 Broadway
Albany, NY 12204
Phone: (518) 434-9194, Fax: (518) 434-0392
E-mail: dsauer@ccsnys.org
Web Site: http://www.ccsnys.org

Nonprofit Coordinating Committee of New York
1350 Broadway, Suite 1801
New York, NY 10018
Phone: (212) 502-4191, Fax: (212) 502-4189
E-mail: jsmall@npccny.org
Web Site: http://www.npccny.org

NORTH CAROLINA
North Carolina Center for Nonprofits
1110 Navaho Drive, Suite 200
Raleigh, NC 27609-7322
Phone: (919) 790-1555, Fax: (919) 790-5307
E-mail: info@ncnonprofits.org
Web Site: http://www.ncnonprofits.org

NORTH DAKOTA
North Dakota Association of Nonprofit Organizations
PO Box 1091
1605 East Capital Avenue
Bismark, ND 58502
Phone: (701) 258-9101, Fax: (701) 223-2507
E-mail: ndano2@nisc.cc
Web Site: http://www.ndano.org

OHIO
Ohio Association of Nonprofit Organizations
100 E. Broad Street, Suite 2440
Columbus, OH 43215-3119
Phone: (614) 280-0233, Fax: (614) 280-0657
E-mail: info@oano.org
Web Site: http://www.ohiononprofits.org

OREGON
Nonprofit Association of Oregon
Eastbank Commerce Center
1001 SE Water Avenue, STE 490
Portland, OR 97214
Phone: (503) 239-4001, Fax: (503) 236-8313
E-mail: info@tacs.org
Web Site: http://www.ornonprofits.org

PENNSYLVANIA
Pennsylvania Association of Nonprofit Organizations
777 East Park Drive, STE 300
Harrisburg, PA 17111
Phone: (717) 236-8584, Fax: (717) 236-8767
E-mail: joe@pano.org
Web Site: http://www.pano.org

SOUTH CAROLINA
South Carolina Association of Nonprofit Organizations
910 Elmwood Avenue, STE 101
Columbia, SC 29201
Phone: (803) 929-0399, Fax: (803) 929-0173
E-mail: info@scanpo.org
Web Site: http://www.scanpo.org

TEXAS
Texas Association of Nonprofit Organizations
5930 Middle Fiskville Road
Box 51
Austin, TX 78752
Phone: (512) 223-7075
E-mail: bsilverb@austincc.edu
Web Site: http://www.tano.org

UTAH
Utah Nonprofits Association
175 South Main Street, STE 750
Salt Lake City, UT 84111
Phone: (801) 596-1800 Fax: (801) 596-1806
E-mail: dhwarsoff@utahnonprofits.org
Web Site: http://www.utahnonprofits.org

VIRGINIA
Virginia Network of Nonprofit Organizations
1108 East Main Street, Suite 1200
Richmond, VA 23219
Phone: (804) 565-9871
Fax: (804) 565-9872
Web Site: http://www.vanno.org

WASHINGTON
Executive Alliance
PO Box 22438
Seattle, WA 98122
Phone: (206) 328-3836
E-mail: jcragin@exec-alliance.org
Web Site: http://www.exec-alliance.org/

Northwest Nonprofit Resources
PO Box 9066
Spokane, WA 99209
Phone: (509) 484-6733, Fax: (509) 483-0345
E-mail: sgill@nnr.org
Web Site: *http://www.nnr.org*

National Organizations

American Society of Association Executives and the Center for Association Leadership
1575 I Street, NW
Washington, D.C. 20005-1103
phone: (202) 626-2723; fax: (202) 371-8315
E-mail: asaeservice@asaecenter.org
Web Site: http://www.asaenet.org

Association for Research on Nonprofit Organizations and Voluntary Action

340 West Michigan Street
Canal Level—Suite A
Indianapolis, IN 46202
phone: (317) 684-2120
Fax: (317) 684-2128
Web site: http://www.arnova.org

The Foundation Center
79 Fifth Avenue/16th Street
New York, NY 10003-3076
phone: (212) 620-4230; fax: (212) 691-1828
E-mail: feedback@foundationcenter.org
Web Site: http://foundationcenter.org

Independent Sector
1200 18th Street, NW
Suite 200
Washington, D.C. 20036
phone: (202) 467-6100; fax: (202) 467-6101
E-mail: info@independentsector.org
http://www.independentsector.org

Mandel Center for Nonprofit Organizations
Case Western Reserve University
10900 Euclid Avenue
Cleveland, OH 44106-7167
phone: (216) 368-2275; fax: (216) 368-8592
Web Site: http://www.cwru.edu/mandelcenter

National Council of Nonprofit Associations
1101 Vermont Avenue, NW; STE 1002
Washington, D.C. 20005
phone: (202) 962-0322; fax: (202) 962-0321
E-mail: ncna@ncna.org
Web Site: http://www.ncna.org

BoardSource
1828 L Street, NW
Suite 900
Washington, D.C. 20036
phone: (202) 452-6262; fax: (202) 452-6299
E-mail: ncnb@ncnb.org
Web Site: http://www.boardsource.org

Association of Fundraising Executives
4300 Wilson Boulevard
Suite 300
Arlington, VA 22203
phone: (703) 684-0410; fax: (703) 684-0540
E-mail: info@afpnet.org
Web Site: http://www.afpnet.org

Publications of Interest

Nonprofit Issues (monthly)
PO Box 482
Dresher, PA 19025-0482
phone: (215) 542-7547; fax: (215) 542-7548
E-Mail: info@nonprofitissues.com
Web Site: http://www.nonprofitissues.com

Nonprofit Times (monthly)
Circulation Department
201 Littleton Road
Second Floor
Morris Plains, NJ 07050
phone: (973) 401-0202; fax: (973) 401-0404
E-mail: circmngr@nptimes.com
Web Site: http://www.nptimes.com

Chronicle of Philanthropy (biweekly)
1255 23rd Street, NW
Washington, DC 20037
phone: (202) 466-1200; fax: (202) 223-6292
E-Mail: help@philanthropy.com
Web Site: http://www.philanthropy.com

Nonprofit and Voluntary Sector Quarterly
550 W. North Street
Suite 301
Indianapolis, IN 46202
phone: (317) 278-8981; fax: (317) 684-8900
E-mail: NSVA@iupui.edu
Web Site: http://www.spea.iupui.edu/nvsq/

Contributions Magazine
PO Box 338
Medfield, MA 02052
phone: (508) 359-0019; fax: (508) 359-2703
E-Mail: info@contributionsmagazine.com
Web Site: http://www.contributionsmagazine.com

State
Directory

How to Use this State Directory

The following pages provide state-specific, summary information on incorporation procedures, lobbying registration, tax-exemption eligibility, and charitable solicitation qualification for all 50 states and the District of Columbia.

The information included in this directory is a summary culled from several sources. In preparation for the first edition of this book, I wrote to each office requesting forms, statutes, instruction booklets, and policies relating to the four general issues. Most responded, although some of the responses were incomplete. The information provided was edited to fit the format for this directory. It was supplemented by information provided by the actual state statutes, which was obtained by research at the State Law Library of Pennsylvania and the Law Library of the Widener School of Law. Additional information was obtained through Internet searches and telephone calls to many of the offices that administer the laws described in the directory. In September 2007, each office received a copy of what appeared in the 4th edition with a request to make corrections and update it. Again, most, but not all responded. Information obtained in online legal databases and organizational Web sites supplemented the material provided by each office, or to fill in missing data.

First, a word of caution. The information concerning these laws and procedures changes frequently. Fees for filing documents often increase. State legislatures pass new laws. Courts sometimes rule that some laws are unconstitutional. It is not recommended that you rely solely on the information in this directory. Always consult the contact office whose name, address, and telephone number are included. If for some reason this information has changed, try the switchboard telephone number included at the top of each state page.

Almost all of this information will change over time; telephone numbers change, offices move, governmental reorganization gives and takes away administrative responsibility. And well-meaning government officials sometimes give out wrong information. An effort was made to make the information in this directory as correct and as current as possible.

A second word of caution. The information included in this directory is a condensed and edited summary. For example, a statement in the directory that corporate names "may not be the same as or deceptively similar to another without written consent" may be shorthand for what the law actually states, such as—

> *(2) Except as authorized by subsection (3) of this section, a corporate name shall be distinguishable upon the records of the secretary of state from:*
>
> *(a)   The corporate name of a corporation incorporated or authorized to transact business in the state;*
> *(b)   A corporate name reserved or registered under KRS 271B.1-300;*
> *(c)   The fictitious name adopted by a foreign corporation authorized to transact business in this state because its real name is unavailable;*
> *(d)   The corporate name of a not-for-profit corporation incorporated or authorized to transact business in this state; and*
> *(e)   A name filed with the secretary of state under KRS Chapter 362 or 365.*
>
> *(3) A corporation may apply to the secretary of state for authorization to use a name that is not distinguishable upon his records from one (1) or more of the names described in subsection (2) of this section. The secretary of state shall authorize use of the name applied for if:*

> (a) The other corporation consents to the use in writing and submits an undertaking in a form satisfactory to the secretary of state to change its name to a name that is distinguishable upon the records of the secretary of state from the name of the applying corporation; or
>
> (b) The applicant delivers to the secretary of state a certified copy of the final judgment of a court of competent jurisdiction establishing the applicant's right to use the name applied for in this state.

(excerpt from 273.177 of the Kentucky Revised Statutes)

Here's another tip: The information in this Directory will change over time. I have included a list of Web sites of government offices that correspond to the sections of information for each state that relate to incorporation, lobbying, tax exemption, and charitable solicitation. This section begins on page 482. Consider reviewing appropriate pages on these Web sites for your state. Most state offices provide forms, instruction booklets, and other useful information online. Some states will even permit you to register and pay fees online. Taking advantage of this technology will save you time and money.

Finally, some assumptions are made, and some information does not directly appear in the directory. You can assume that only one incorporator is required unless this is explicitly contradicted. If there is no provision relating to renewability of a name reservation, you can assume that it is renewable (although the statute may be silent on this issue). Almost every state provided forms required for lobbying registration and charitable solicitation registration. Many states provided blank forms for incorporation. Some states have publications concerning these four issues which, for one reason or another, were not provided to me, but may be available upon request. There are commercial publishing firms, such as West Publishing (1-800-328-4880), which, for a fee, will provide the entire corporations code for an individual state. For most offices, most of the information you need can be found on that agency's Web site.

Let me know if the format and content was useful to you in starting your organization, or if you have a suggestion for a future edition. Contact me by e-mail at: Gary.Grobman@paonline.com or write to me c/o the publisher.

Alabama

Central Switchboard: (334) 242-8000
State Web Home Page: http://www.alabama.gov

INCORPORATION

Contact:

*Office of the Secretary of State
Corporation Division
State House
11 S. Union St.; STE 207
P.O. Box 5616
Montgomery, AL 36103-5616
(334) 242-5324*

Citation: *Alabama Non-Profit Corporation Act,* Title 10, Chapter 3A, Code of Alabama.

Publications Available: The Guidelines for Articles of Incorporation can be provided by the contact office; corporate forms may be downloaded at the Web site at: http://www.alabama.gov

General Requirements: One or more persons, partnerships or corporations may act as incorporators. Articles of Incorporation must set forth the name of the corporation; duration; purposes; a statement as to whether the corporation will have members; the street address of the registered office and the name of the registered agent at that office; the names and addresses of directors (must have at least three directors); the name and address of each incorporator; and any provision for the regulation of the internal affairs of the corporation, including a provision for distribution of assets on dissolution or final liquidation. Must be signed by the incorporator.

Corporate Name: Shall not contain a word or phrase that indicates or implies that it is organized for one or more purposes other than permitted by the articles; shall not be the same as, or deceptively similar to another; shall be transliterated into letters of the English language if it is not in English.

Name Reservation: Not permitted.

How to File: The original and two copies of the Articles of Incorporation must be filed in the county where the corporation's registered office is located. The minimum Judge of Probate's filing fee is $25 and the Secretary of State's filing fee is $20.

Other Filings/reports: None required.

LOBBYING

Contact:

*Ethics Commission
RSA Union
100 N. Union; Suite 104
Montgomery, AL 36104
(334) 242-2997*

Citation: § 36-25-16 et seq.

Publications: *The Ethics Law* is provided by the contact office and available online.

Registration Required: All lobbyists must register with the Ethics Commission no later than January 31, or within 10 days of qualifying as a lobbyist. There is a $100 annual fee. Registration statement discloses general information, information about clients, the subject matter that is the target of lobbying, and a statement signed by each client authorizing lobbying on their behalf.

Forms to Use: *Lobbyist Registration Form.*

Reporting Requirements: Quarterly expense reports are due January 31, April 30, July 31, and October 31 covering the preceding quarter. The reports disclose certain expenses valued at more than $250 that are expended within a 24-hour period on a public official, public employee and members of his or her respective household, with the name of the beneficiary of the expense; the nature and date of financial transactions between the lobbyist and public officials or candidates valued in excess of $500 per quarter (not including campaign contributions); information about loans given to or promised to such persons; and a statement of any direct business relationships with such persons or members of their households.

TAX EXEMPTIONS

Contact:

> Alabama Department of Revenue
> Sales and Business Tax Division
> Room 4303 Gordon Persons Building
> 50 N. Ripley St.
> Montgomery, AL 36132
> (334) 242-1200 (income tax information)
> (334) 242-1490 (sales tax information)

Citation: §40-18-32—Corporate Income taxes; §40-23-5—Sales and Use taxes; §40-9-9 to §40-9-31—exemptions.

Requirements: Certain organizations are explicitly exempt from sales and use taxes, including Goodwill Industries, Elks Club, Diabetes Trust Fund, some veterans organizations, rescue service organizations, and volunteer nonprofit rescue units. Most nonprofits are exempt from corporate income taxes other than unrelated business income taxes.

Application Procedure: No forms are required for sales tax exemptions; show vendor the reference in the statute. No return is required for exemption from corporate income tax; send the Department a copy of the IRS determination letter.

CHARITABLE SOLICITATION

Contact:

> Office of the Attorney General
> Consumer Affairs Section
> Alabama State House
> 11 South Union Street
> Montgomery, AL 36130-2103
> (334) 242-7335

Citation: *Alabama Charitable Solicitations Act,* Code of Alabama, 13A-9-70 —13A-9-84.

Publications: Copies of the law and forms are available online at: *http://www.ago.state.al.us*

Initial Registration: Non-exempt organizations that intend to solicit charitable contributions in excess of $25,000 for each fiscal year or that pay fundraisers, must file a *Charitable Organi-*

zation Registration Statement with the contact office. The statement discloses general information about the organization. The statement must be accompanied by a copy of the organizational charter; Articles of Incorporation and bylaws; and a statement setting forth where and when the organization was legally established, the form of the organization, and its tax exemption status. The federal or state tax exemption determination letters must be attached. A fee of $25 payable to the Office of the Attorney General must be paid at the time of registration.

Annual Reports: Within 90 days of the close of the organization's fiscal year ending after the date on which it files its initial registration, it must file an annual written report. The report must include a financial statement covering the fiscal year setting forth gross income, expenses and net income; a balance sheet; a schedule of activities; and the amounts expended for those activities. An IRS 990 may be submitted in lieu of this report.

Organization Solicitation Disclosure Requirements: See below.

Paid Solicitor Requirements: Professional fundraisers must register, pay an annual fee of $100, and post a bond of at least $10,000. Those employed by professional fundraisers as professional fundraisers must also register and pay an annual filing fee of $25. The registration expires on September 30 each year. Professional solicitors must disclose their names, that they are professional solicitors, and the percentage of funds going to the charity.

Fundraising Counsel Requirements: Must register if their activities fall under the definition of Professional Fundraiser defined in the Alabama Charitable Solicitations Act.

Alaska

Central Switchboard: (907) 465-2111
State Web Home Page: http://www.state.ak.us/

INCORPORATION

Contact:

> Alaska Department of Commerce, Community and Economic Development
> Division of Banking, Securities and Corporations
> Corporations Section
> PO Box 110808
> Juneau, AK 99811-0808
> (907) 465-2530

Citation: AS Title 10, 10.20 et seq.

Publications Available: *A sample Articles of Incorporation form is provided by the contact office and is available on the Web site.*

General Requirements: Three or more natural persons at least 19 years of age may act as incorporators. The Articles must include the corporate name; the period of duration; the purpose(s); provisions relating to the internal regulation of the corporation including provisions for distribution of assets upon dissolution or final liquidation; the physical address of its initial registered office and the name of its initial registered agent; the number of directors constituting the initial board of directors; their names and addresses (must be at least three); and the name and address of each incorporator. Issues relating to whether the corporation has members shall be set forth in either the Articles or the bylaws.

Corporate Name: May not contain a word or phrase implying that the corporation is a municipality; may not imply that it is organized for a purpose other than one or more purposes contained in the Articles of Incorporation; must be distinguishable from other entities.

Name Reservation: A $25 fee is charged for reservation of corporate name. The reservation is valid for 120 days.

How to File: Submit the original and an exact copy of the Articles of Incorporation along with a $50 filing fee.

Other Filings/Reports: Biennial corporate reports must be filed with the Division. There is a filing fee of $15. The report is due every other year from the year of incorporation.

LOBBYING

Contact:

> Alaska Public Offices Commission
> PO Box 110222
> Juneau, AK 99811
> (907) 465-4864

Citation: *Regulation of Lobbying Law,* AS 24.45.

Publications: *Manual of Instructions for Lobbyists and Employers of Lobbyists* and forms are available from the contact office and on the Web site at: *http://www.state.ak.us/apoc*

Registration: Professional and representational lobbyists must register before engaging in lobbying activities. Employee or part-time lobbyists must register after lobbying for 40 hours in a 30-day period. Volunteer lobbyists are not required to register, but may do so if they choose. Lobbyists who receive a fee or salary for their lobbying activities must pay a $250 lobbyist registration fee per client or employer. If a registration is filed under a firm name, the $250 fee must be paid for each individual within the firm who is designated to lobby. Registrations must be renewed annually and expire at the end of each calendar year. Those who employ or retain lobbyists must certify the lobbyist registration, authorizing the activity.

Form to Use: APOC Form 24-1, *Lobbyist Registration Statement for Lobbyists.*

Reporting Requirements: Paid lobbyists are required to submit monthly reports (APOC Form 24-3) when the legislature is in session, and quarterly reports after adjournment. Reports must be submitted even if there is no reportable activity. Monthly reports are due on or before the last day of the month after the month that is the subject of the report; quarterly reports are due on or before the last day of the month that succeeds the quarter that is the subject of the report. Disclosure on the reports includes itemizations of gifts made to public officials valued at more than $100; an exchange of more than $100 in value of money, goods or services with any public official or member of a public official's immediate family; or an exchange of more than $100 in value with a business entity that is owned or controlled by a public official. Schedule A is a summary of income and expenditure activity. Employers of lobbyists must file APOC Form 24-4 quarterly, due on or before the last day of the month following the quarter that is the subject of the report. The reports disclose the amounts paid to lobbyists or others made to influence administrative and legislative action, and the date and nature of any gift exceeding $100 in value to a public official, as well as in-house lobbying costs.

TAX EXEMPTIONS

Contact:

Alaska Department of Revenue
333 W. Willoughby Avenue
11th Floor, Side B
PO Box 110420
Juneau, AK 99811-0420
(907) 465-2320 (Juneau)
(907) 269-6620 (Anchorage)

Citation: §10.06.845(c).

Requirements: There is no state sales tax. An exempt organization is required to file a return using federal form 990. If the organization files a federal 990T, an Alaska return (form 04-611) accompanied by a copy of the 990T must be filed.

Application Procedure: Send a copy of the organization's 990 and 990T (if applicable) to the Department of Revenue.

CHARITABLE SOLICITATION

Contact:

*Alaska Department of Law
Attorney General's Office
1031 W. 4th Avenue
Suite 200
Anchorage, AK 99501-1994
(907) 269-5100*

Citation: Chapter 68, Sec. 45.68 et seq.

Publications: Copies of the statute and forms are provided by the contact office.

Initial Registration: All organizations soliciting charitable contributions in excess of $5,000 during a fiscal year must register with the Department of Law. There is a registration fee of $40 for charitable organizations.

Annual Reports: Registration is annual, and expires on September 1 each year. Registration discloses general information about the organization; its purpose; a summary of its programs and activities; how a citizen can verify and observe these activities; names and titles of three officers or employees receiving the greatest compensation from the organization; names, addresses and telephone numbers of paid solicitors; and information about federal tax exempt status. Copies of the most recent Form 990 and/or audited financial report must be provided, or financial information must be provided on the form.

Organization Solicitation Disclosure Requirements: See below.

Paid Solicitor Requirements: Must register with the Department and pay a registration fee of $200; must have a bond of $10,000 if less than 60% of the amount raised goes to the charity; must have a written contract with the charity in an approved form. Before a solicitation, a paid solicitor shall clearly and conspicuously disclose the true name of the person making the solicitation; the true name of the charity; the true name of the paid solicitor; the name of the person who is employing and compensating the person making the solicitation; whether the person making the solicitation is being paid or is an unpaid volunteer; the name and address of the principal headquarters of the charity; a description of how the donation will be used; and that a financial statement of the charity, and a copy of the paid solicitor's contract, will be provided upon request.

Fundraising Counsel Requirements: None.

Arizona

Governor's Office: (602) 542-4331
State Web Home Page: http://www.az.gov/

INCORPORATION

Contact:

Arizona Corporation Commission
1300 West Washington
Phoenix, AZ 85007-2929
(602) 542-3026

Citation: Arizona Revised Statutes, Title 10, Chapter 24, 10-3101 et seq. (complete text can be viewed at: http://www.azleg.state.az.us).

General Requirements: Articles of Incorporation shall set forth the corporate name; a brief statement of the purpose and character of the affairs that the corporation initially intends to conduct; the name and address of the initial statutory agent; the names and addresses of the initial board of directors; a statement whether or not the corporation will have members; the name and address of each incorporator; and optional provisions relating to director liability, anti-discrimination, and other optional provisions.

Corporate Name: Shall not contain a word or phrase that indicates or implies that it is organized for one or more purposes other than permitted by the Articles; is distinguishable from another if it is not so identical to a name that in the judgment of the Commission the corporate name is likely to mislead the public.

Name Reservation: May be reserved for 120 days for a fee of $10.

How to File: Check availability of corporate name with the Commission, sign and date a Certificate of Disclosure, and deliver the original and one copy of the Articles of Incorporation to the contact office with the $40 filing fee. A copy will be returned when all requirements are satisfied. Advise the Commission in writing of the fiscal year end date adopted by the corporation, publish in three consecutive issues an approved copy of the Articles in a newspaper of general circulation in the home county within 60 days, and file an affidavit evidencing this publication.

Other Filings/Reports: An annual report is due on or before the date assigned by the Commission. There is a $10 fee. The report discloses general information; a statement of the character of the corporation's affairs; a statement that all corporate income tax returns have been filed; a statement of financial conditions; whether or not the corporation has members; and a certificate of disclosure relating to any criminal misconduct by the organization's officers, directors, trustees and incorporators. It can be filed electronically.

LOBBYING

Contact:

Office of the Secretary of State
1700 West Washington
7th Floor
Phoenix, AZ 85007-2888
(602) 542-8683

Citation: A.R.S. §§41-1232 et seq.

Publications: *Lobbyist Handbook* is available from the contact office.

Registration Required: Organizations that employ lobbyists must register within five business days after any lobbying activity. Registration must be renewed by November 30th of even-numbered years unless the organization no longer engages a lobbyist. The registration fee is $25 for each principal and is valid for a two-year period.

Forms to Use: *Principal Registration for Lobbying; Lobbyist Quarterly Expenditure Report; Principal Annual Report of Lobbying Expenditures.* For principal registration, use form PRG-1; for lobbyist registration, use form LRG-1; for principal annual report, use Form PAR-1.1; for lobbyist quarterly report, use Form LQER-1.3.

Reporting Requirements: Lobbyists file reports in January, April, July, and October covering the previous quarter, plus annual expenditure reports filed January 1-March 1 covering the previous calendar year. Lobbyists must itemize expenditures of more than $20 according to date, amount, name of state officer or employee, nature of expenditure, and name of lobbyist or other person making the expenditure on the principal annual report. The acceptance of an entertainment expense (e.g., a ticket to a sporting or cultural event) from a lobbyist is against the law. Expenditure reporting is grouped by the categories of food or beverages, entertainment, travel and lodging, flowers, and other expenditures.

TAX EXEMPTIONS

Contact:

> *Arizona Department of Revenue*
> *Taxpayer Information and Assistance*
> *PO Box 29079*
> *Phoenix, AZ 85038-9079*
> *Sales Tax: Box 29010*
> *Phoenix AZ 85038-9010*
> *(602) 255-2060 (in Phoenix or outside Arizona)*
> *(800) 843-7196 (elsewhere in Arizona)*
> *Corporate Tax: (602) 255-3381*

Citation: Arizona Revised Statutes titles 42 and 43, §43-1201; Arizona Administrative Code R15-5-182 and 183.

Publications: *Non-Profit Organizations* (publication 501) and *Arizona Sales Tax, Health Care Organizations Exempt from Sales Tax* (publication 500) are available from the contact office.

Requirements: Organizations with federal tax exemptions are generally exempt from state income tax. 501(c)(3) organizations are exempt from the transaction privilege tax (sales tax) on sales of retail items but may not be exempt from taxes on some activities, such as commercial rentals, transporting, amusements, and personal property rentals.

Nonprofit organizations are generally not exempt in making purchases from retailers other than hospitals, rehabilitation programs for the mentally and/or physically handicapped, or qualifying health care organizations. Such organizations must obtain written approval for exemption on an annual basis. Retail sales by 501(c)(3) exempt organizations are exempt.

Application Procedure: For sales tax (Transaction Privilege Tax) exemptions, submit the request to the Arizona Dept. of Revenue at least 30 days prior to the first day of the exemption period (the 12-month period beginning on the month following the issue date of the exemption letter or the

12-month period requested by the organization). Include a copy of the IRS determination letter. Exemptions may be granted retroactively for up to four prior years. See Publication 500 for details.

CHARITABLE SOLICITATION

Contact:

> *Office of the Secretary of State*
> *1700 West Washington—7th Fl.*
> *Phoenix, AZ 85007-2808*
> *(602) 542-6187*

Citation: A.R.S. § 44-6551 et seq.

Publications: A copy of the statute and forms are available from the contact office and Web site: *http://www.azsos.gov*

Initial Registration: All organizations that solicit must file with the Secretary of State's office before soliciting. The statement, filed on the charitable registration form, includes general information about the charity; its officers and directors; any paid solicitors; a general description of the methods, locations, types and amounts of solicitations; the duration of its solicitation period; a description of the purpose of the charitable organization; and financial information (either a financial statement or a 990 from a previous fiscal year). There is no registration fee.

Annual Reports: Registration and financial statement are required to be filed between September 1 through September 30 of each year.

Organization Solicitation Disclosure Requirements: See below.

Paid Solicitor Requirements: Must register, pay a $25 registration fee, and post a $25,000 bond. Registration is valid for one year and may be renewed with the application and registration fee. Contracted fundraising solicitors must disclose, at any time during the solicitation, the name of the charity and the name of the contracted fundraiser. For oral solicitations, the solicitor must provide a written confirmation within five days including the name of the charity, the name of the contracted fundraiser, that information relating to the charity is available for public inspection, and the toll-free number of the Secretary of State. Written solicitations must include all of the above.

Fundraising Counsel Requirements: None.

Arkansas

Central Switchboard: (501) 682-3000
State Web Home Page: http://www.state.ar.us/

INCORPORATION

Contact:
> Secretary of State
> Business & Commercial Services
> Suite 250, Victory Building
> 1401 West Capitol Avenue
> Little Rock, AR 72201
> (501) 682-3409

Citation: *Arkansas Non-Profit Act* (Act 1147 of 1993), Title 4, §4-33-101 et seq.

Publications Available: An Articles of Incorporation sample form is available from the contact office.

General Requirements: One or more persons may act as incorporators. Articles of Incorporation must set forth the corporate name, the type of nonprofit corporation (public benefit, mutual benefit, or religious corporation), whether the corporation will have members, how assets will be distributed upon dissolution, the street address of the corporation's initial registered office, the name of its initial registered agent at that office, and the signatures and addresses of each incorporator.

Corporate Name: Shall not contain a word or phrase that indicates or implies that it is organized for one or more purposes other than permitted by the Articles; must be distinguishable from another without written consent. Must contain the words "corporation," "incorporated," "company," "limited," or abbreviations of these.

Name Reservation: May be reserved for a non-renewable period of 120 days by filing an application with a $25 fee.

How to File: File Articles of Incorporation in duplicate with the Secretary of State along with a $50 filing fee. A filed-stamped duplicate is returned. Submit the filed-stamped copy to the county circuit court. Articles may be filed online.

Other Filings/reports: None.

LOBBYING

Contact:
> Arkansas Ethics Commission
> PO Box 1917
> Little Rock, AR 72203-1917
> (501) 324-9600

Citation: *The Disclosure Act for Lobbyists and State and Local Officials,* 21-8-401 et seq.

Publications: A copy of the statute and forms are provided by the contact office and Web site.

Registration Required: Lobbyists who either receive more than $400 per quarter for lobbying, or who spend more than $400 per quarter for lobbying, must register within five days of beginning to lobby using the *Lobbyist Registration* form. There is no fee for registration. Lobbyists who lobby public servants of state government must submit this form to the Secretary of State. The two-page form discloses information about the nature or kind of business represented by the lobbyist, the branch of government lobbied, and the address where the lobbyist's records may be inspected. Annual registration is renewed by January 15.

Reporting Requirements: Lobbyists must file a monthly activity report if the legislature is in session, and all lobbyists must file a quarterly report. The reports itemize expenditures for food, lodging, or travel; entertainment; living accommodations; advertising; printing; postage; telephone; office expenses; and other expenses for each lobbying client. Itemization is required with respect to spending on any individual public servant in excess of $40. Lobbyists must also report details concerning any direct business association with public servants they lobby. Loans or promises of money for or on behalf of any public servant over $25 must also be reported.

TAX EXEMPTIONS

Contact:

> Dept. of Finance and Administration
> PO Box 919
> Sales and Use Tax Unit
> 1816 W. 7th Street, Room 1330
> Little Rock, AR 72203
> (501) 682-4775 (income tax information)
> (501) 682-7104 (sales tax information)

Citation: 26-54-102 et seq.; 26-51-303 (income tax).

Requirements: Nonprofit corporations and those exempt from federal income tax are generally exempt from the annual corporate franchise tax. Generally, organizations with 501(c)(3) and (c)(4) federal exemptions, as well as certain fraternal organizations, cemeteries, nonprofit business leagues, and certain agricultural, labor and horticultural organizations are exempt from the corporate income tax. There are limited exemptions from the sales tax for named organizations, such as the Boy Scouts, Girl Scouts, Poet's Round Table, humane societies, 4-H Clubs, Orphan's Homes, Children's Homes, American Red Cross, Salvation Army, and boys and girls clubs.

Application Procedure: Organizations with an IRS determination letter should file a copy of that letter, a copy of pages one and two of their form 1023 or 1024, and a statement declaring Arkansas Code exemption. Organizations without an IRS determination letter should submit an Arkansas Form AR1023CT; a copy of their Articles of Incorporation, Articles of Association, or copy of Trust Indenture or Agreement; and a copy of their bylaws. Those exempt from sales tax must present a copy of the regulation to the vendor.

CHARITABLE SOLICITATION

Contact:

> Office of the Attorney General
> Consumer Protection Division
> 323 Center Street, Suite 200
> Little Rock, AR 72201-2610
> (501) 682-6150

Citation: Act 1177 of 1991. Title 4, §4-28-401 et seq.

Publications: *A Synopsis of Act 1177 of 1991* is provided by the contact office.

Initial Registration: Before engaging in fundraising activities, charitable organizations must register with the Attorney General, unless they raise less than $25,000 each year and conduct their promotions solely by volunteers without any inurement to any officer or member. Some organizations, such as hospitals and volunteer fire companies, are exempt from registration and reporting requirements but must maintain and make available information that they would otherwise be required to report. There is no fee for registration.

Annual Reports: Organizations that do not file a 990 but have received contributions in excess of $25,000 during the previous calendar year must report the gross amount of contributions pledged; the amount allocated and dedicated to the charitable purpose represented in each promotion; the aggregate amount paid for each promotion including overhead; and the aggregate amount paid to, and to be paid to, professional fundraisers and solicitors. Organizations that do file a 990 must submit a copy of it. Reports or 990s must be filed on or before May 15 of each year.

Organization Solicitation Disclosure Requirements: If asked, a solicitor must disclose what percentage of funds raised go to the charitable purpose and what percentage go to the solicitor. Before accepting funds, the solicitor must disclose the identity of the person responsible for the solicitation and whether the solicitor is being paid for his or her efforts.

Paid Solicitor Requirements: Every solicitor must register within 72 hours after accepting employment with a professional telemarketer. There is a $10 annual fee. Fundraisers must register, pay a $200 annual fee, and post a $10,000 bond. All contracts, scripts, pamphlets, handouts and other materials used by professional fundraisers and solicitors must be in writing and kept on file in the office of both the professional fundraiser and the charitable organization. Every contract between a professional fundraiser and a solicitor must be filed with the Attorney General within 3 days of the beginning of the solicitation.

Fundraising Counsel Requirements: Must register and pay a $100 fee.

California

Central Switchboard: (916) 322-9900
State Web Home Page: http://ca.gov

INCORPORATION

Contact:

> Secretary of State
> Business Programs Division
> 1500 11th Street
> Sacramento, CA 95814
> (916) 657-5448

Citation: Nonprofit Corporation Law: California Corporate Code Sections 5000 to 10841; Corporations Formed for Specific Purposes: California Corporations Code sections 12000 to 14551

Publications Available: None

General Requirements: The Articles of Incorporation for nonprofit public benefit, mutual benefit, or religious corporations must set forth the corporate name; the required purpose statement; the specific purpose, if applicable; the name and address of the corporation's initial agent for service of process; and the typed or printed name and signature of each incorporator. Refer to the California Corporations Code when incorporating organizations other than these three types, such as consumer cooperatives and societies for the prevention of cruelty to children and animals.

Corporate Name: May not have "bank," "trust," "trustee," or related words appear unless a certificate of approval of the Commissioner of Financial Institutions is attached to the Articles of Incorporation. Shall not set forth a name that is likely to mislead the public or that is the same as, or resembles so closely as to tend to deceive, the name of another corporation.

Name Reservation: May be reserved for a period of 60 days for a fee of $10, but not for two or more consecutive 60-day periods to the same applicant or for the use or benefit of the same person.

How to File: Submit the original Articles of Incorporation, four copies, and a $30 Secretary of State filing fee to the Office of Secretary of State.

Other Filings/reports: Must file a statement of information within 90 days of incorporation, and biennially thereafter during the applicable filing period. A preprinted form (Form Sl-100) is mailed to the corporation approximately three months prior to the close of the applicable filing period. The required statement may also be filed online.

LOBBYING

Contact:

> Secretary of State, Political Reform Division
> 1500 11th Street
> Room 495
> Sacramento, CA 95814-1467
> (916) 653-6224

Citation: *Political Reform Act of 1974,* as amended, Government Code §86100-86118.

Publications: *Lobbying Disclosure Information Manual* and forms are available from the contact office. A lobbyist directory is available for $19.

Registration Required: In-house lobbyists—individuals who lobby on behalf of their employer only, are compensated for their time, and spend at least one-third of that time in a calendar month in direct communication with qualifying officials— and contract lobbyists—individuals who lobby on behalf of someone other than their employer and received or are entitled to receive $2,000 in a calendar month for direct communication with qualifying officials—must file a *Lobbyist Certification Statement* (Form 604) with the Political Reform Division within 10 days of qualifying as a lobbyist; lobbying firms must register (form 601) no later than 10 days after qualifying as a lobbying firm. The registration form must include a recent head and shoulders-only photo of each lobbyist. Lobbyist employers/lobbying coalitions must register within 10 days after a partner, owner, officer, or employee qualifies as an in-house lobbyist (form 603). Lobbyist employers and lobbying coalitions that only contract with a lobbying firm are not required to register, but must complete a Form 602 authorizing the firm to lobby. Persons who do not employ an in-house lobbyist or contract with a lobbying firm, but who spend more than $5,000 in any calendar quarter to influence legislation or administrative actions are not required to register but must file disclosure reports for that calendar quarter, using Form 645. Lobbying firms, lobbyists, and lobbyist employers must renew registration for each regular session of the State Legislature. Lobbyists pay a $25 fee, and registration is valid for two years, starting in January of every odd-numbered year. Renewals are filed in November and December of even-numbered years.

Reporting Requirements: All lobbyists (Form 615), lobbying firms (Form 625), lobbyist employers and lobbying coalitions (Form 635) must file a report for each calendar quarter regardless of activities or whether expenditures have been made. The reports are due on the last day of the month following the three months that are being reported. The reports include payments made and received in connection with lobbying activity and "activity expenses" (which include gifts, honoraria, consulting fees, salaries, and other forms of compensation that benefit public officials or their immediate families) and campaign contributions of $100 or more. Lobbying firms have more extensive reporting requirements. Lobbyists are required to attend an ethics course conducted by the Senate Ethics Committee.

TAX EXEMPTIONS

Contact:

> *Franchise Tax Board* (franchise or income tax)
> *PO Box 1468*
> *Sacramento, CA 95812-1468*
> *1-800-852-5711*
> Exempt Organizations: (916) 845-4171

For information about sales and use tax exemptions, contact:

> *Board of Equalization*
> *PO Box 942879*
> *Sacramento, CA 94279-0001*
> *1-800-400-7115*

Citation: California Revenue and Taxation Code, § 23701 et seq.

Publications: An Exemption Application form (FTB 3500) and instructions are available online at *http://www.ftb.ca.gov* or may be requested from the contact office.

Requirements: An organization must be organized and operated for purposes within the provisions of the California Revenue and Taxation Code and must apply for tax-exempt status. The Franchise Tax Board must determine whether the organization qualifies for exemption. Consult the statute or the contact office for more information, or visit the Web site at: *http://www.ftb.ca.gov*

Application Procedure: Submit form FTB 3500, *Exemption Application*; Articles of Incorporation, bylaws, budget or financial statements, and information specific to section of law under which exemption is sought; and a $25 check, payable to the Franchise Tax Board. The Board will review the application package and issue a determination letter as to whether the organization qualifies for exemption.

CHARITABLE SOLICITATION

Contact:

> *Office of the Attorney General*
> *Registry of Charitable Trusts*
> *PO Box 903447*
> *Sacramento, CA 94203-4470*
> *(916) 445-2021*

Citation: §17510.1 et seq. of the Business and Prof. Code, and §12580 et seq. of the Government Code.

Publication: *Guide to Charitable Solicitation* is available at: *http://caag.state.ca.us/charities/publications/99char.pdf* or from the contact office.

Reporting Requirements: Charities with revenue or assets over $100,000 must annually file Form RRF-1 and pay a $25 filing fee not less than four-and-a-half months after the close of the organization's fiscal year. Other charities must also file, but there is no fee. The report discloses general information, conflicts of interest, misconduct, gross receipts, total assets, whether nonprofit expenditures exceeded 50% of gross revenue, and information about professional fundraisers and government funding.

Organization Solicitation Disclosure Requirements: Prior to any solicitation, the solicitor must exhibit a "Solicitation or Sale for Charitable Purposes Card." It discloses the name and address of the soliciting organization, the name of the person who signed the card, and the name and business address of the solicitor. In lieu of exhibiting the card, information must be included in the solicitor's brochure that includes, in at least 10-point type, the name and address of the organization; how the money collected will be used (if there is no organization or fund); that an audited financial statement is available; that the organization is not tax-exempt if that is the case; and information about membership and references to certain law enforcement agencies and veterans organizations, if it makes such references.

Paid Solicitor Requirements: Must pay a $200 registration fee by certified check and post a $25,000 bond or make a $25,000 cash deposit. Annual financial reports are also required to be filed. Paid solicitors must disclose prior to solicitation that the solicitation is conducted by a professional fundraiser, and the name as registered with the Attorney General. They must also disclose, if asked, information about their employer, whether the contributions are tax-deductible, and the percentage of total fundraising expense.

Fundraising Counsel Requirements: If gross compensation is more than $25,000, must register annually with the contact office by January 15th, certify that they have written contracts with their clients with a clear statement of fees, and pay a registration fee of $200.

Colorado

Central Switchboard: (303) 866-5000
State Web Home Page: http://www.colorado.gov

INCORPORATION

Contact:

> Secretary of State
> Business Division
> 1700 Broadway
> Denver, CO 80290
> (303) 894-2200, press 2

Citation: *Colorado Nonprofit Corporation Act.* 7-121-101 et seq. and 7-90-301 et seq.

Publications Available: Visit the Web site at: *http://www.sos.state.co.us* for more information.

General Requirements: One or more persons may establish a nonprofit corporation. Articles must set forth the corporate name; address of the initial registered office and the name of the registered agent at that address; the principal office address of the nonprofit corporation's initial principal office; whether the corporation will have voting members; names and addresses of incorporators, duration, and provisions regarding the distribution of assets upon dissolution. The Articles may provide for management of the business and affairs of the corporation by some other body, without the existence of a board if directors, and may provide delegation of specific duties to other persons.

Corporate Name: Must be distinguishable on the records of the Secretary of State.

Name Reservation: May be reserved for a period of 120 days. Renewals are permitted for consecutive 120-day periods.

How to File: See the Web site for the form and cover sheet. Articles of Incorporation form must be typed and filed with a filing fee ($25 for online, $125 for paper).

Other Filings/Reports: An annual report is required by the contact office. The fee is $25.

LOBBYING

Contact:

> Secretary of State
> Lobbyist Section
> 1700 Broadway
> Suite 270
> Denver, CO 80290
> (303) 894-2200 x6304

Citation: *Colorado Sunshine Law, Regulation of Lobbyists* (Title 24, Article 6, Part 3); Rule 36, Joint Rules of the Senate and House of Representatives.

Publications: *2007-2008 Colorado Laws and Rules Concerning Professional Lobbyists* is available at: *http://www.elections.colorado.gov/ WWW/default/Lobbyists/1007-2008_professional_lobbyist_manual.pdf*

Registration Required: All lobbyists must register prior to lobbying. Professional lobbyist registration begins on July 1 and ends on June 30 of every fiscal year. Professional lobbyists register with the Secretary of State's lobbying office; volunteer lobbyists register with the Chief Clerk of the House of Representatives. The fee for manual filing of a professional lobbyist registration statement is $50. The fee is $25 if done electronically and if all monthly reports for the fiscal year are filed electronically. The fee may be waived if one of the following conditions is satisfied: 1) the lobbyist derives his or her compensation solely from a nonprofit organization, or 2) the organization is operating under financial hardship or the lobbyist will have a particular interest in only one issue or bill and does not intend to lobby through the State fiscal year.

Forms to Use: Lobbyists who prefer to file paper reports can use the *Professional Lobbyist Registration Form, Lobbying Disclosure Statement, and the State Fiscal Cumulative Disclosure Statement* for registering and disclosing monthly reports. Volunteer lobbyists use a simple one-page registration form.

Reporting Requirements: Professional lobbyists disclose information itemizing income and expenditures, gifts, media expenses and the subject matter lobbied.

TAX EXEMPTIONS

Contact:

> Department of Revenue
> 1375 Sherman Street
> Denver, CO 80261
> (303) 238-7378

Citation: §39-26-114(1)(a)(II)C.R.S.—sales tax; §39-22-304(1)—corporate income tax.

Publications: *Sales Tax Exempt Status for Charitable Organizations: Application Requirements* is available from the contact office.

Requirements: Organizations that have federal 501(c)(3) tax exemptions are generally exempt from state-collected sales tax for purchases made in the conduct of their regular charitable functions and activities, but application must be made to, and approved by, the Department. Charitable organizations with both 501(c)(3) status and a Colorado exemption certificate may also be exempt from collecting sales tax during fundraising events, if sales occur for 12 days or less during a calendar year and total sales do not exceed $25,000. Corporations exempt from federal income tax are exempt from the state corporate income tax.

Application Procedure: Apply by filing an *Application for Sales Tax Exemption* for Colorado Organizations (DR 0715).

CHARITABLE SOLICITATION

Contact:

> Office of the Secretary of State
> Licensing Section
> 1700 Broadway
> Denver, CO 80290
> (303) 894-2200

Citation: *Colorado Charitable Solicitations Act,* C.R.S. 6-16-101 et seq.

Publications: Colorado Charitable Solicitations Act instructions available at: *http://www.sos.state.co.us/pubs/bingo_raffles/instructions.doc*

Initial Registration: Prior to any solicitation campaign (which must last one year or less or be newly registered annually), charities employing professional solicitors, and some that do not employ solicitors but do not have 501(c)(3) tax-exemption status, must file a *Solicitation Notice* with the contact office. The notice must include a copy of the contract between the paid solicitor and the charitable organization; the solicitor's full legal name, address, and telephone number; when the solicitation campaign will begin and end; the nature of the campaign; address where records are kept; and the charitable purposes for which the campaign is being carried out.

Annual Reports: Every charity must register annually and include a financial report for the most recent fiscal year, filed on or before the 15th day of the fifth calendar month after the close of each fiscal year. Registration information includes contact information; names, addresses, and telephone numbers of those with custody of financial records; charitable purposes; fiscal year; and IRS exemption status. A financial report must include information about contributions, government grants, program service revenue, expenses, assets, liabilities, and amounts paid to outside fundraisers. The fee is $10.

Organization Solicitation Disclosure Requirements: None.

Paid Solicitor Requirements: Paid solicitors must register annually and pay a filing fee of $175. Must disclose information about their employers, must disclose information about the tax-deductibility of contributions, and that the solicitor is being paid. A Solicitation Notice must be filed that includes a copy of the contract between the charity and the solicitor and extensive information about the solicitation campaign. The fee is $75.

Fundraising Counsel Requirements: Must register annually and pay a fee of $175.

Connecticut

Central Switchboard: (860) 566-2211
State Web Home Page: http://www.ct.gov

INCORPORATION

Contact:

> Office of the Secretary of State
> Commercial Recording Division
> 30 Trinity Street
> PO Box 150470
> Hartford, CT 06115-0470
> (860) 509-6002

Citation: *Nonstock Corporation,* Chapter 602, Sec. 33-1000, Conn. Gen. Stat.

General Requirements: The Certificate of Incorporation must set forth the name; nature of activities conducted or the purposes; a statement that it is nonprofit and shall not have or issue shares of stock or pay dividends; whether it is to have members, and, if it does, provisions relating to them; the period of duration; and optional provisions relating to internal regulation and management.

Corporate Name: Shall contain the word "corporation" or "company" or "incorporated" or shall contain the abbreviation "corp." or "co." or "inc." The initial letter may be a capital letter and shall be written in English letters or numbers; shall not describe corporate powers, purposes or authority that the corporation does not possess; shall be distinguishable from other corporations.

Name reservation: May be reserved for a period of 120 days for a $30 fee.

How to File: File Articles of Incorporation with the Secretary of State with a $65 filing fee, which includes $25 for the Organization and First Report form.

Other Filings/reports: An annual report must be filed annually along with a $25 filing fee.

LOBBYING

Contact:

> Office of State Ethics
> 18-20 Trinity Street
> Suite 205
> Hartford, CT 06106-1660
> (860) 566-4472

Citation: Chapter 10, Part II, Connecticut General Statutes.

Publications: *Guide to the Code of Ethics for Communicator Lobbyists, Guide to the Code of Ethics for Client Lobbyists,* and *Procedures Manual for Lobbyist Recordkeeping and Audit* are provided by the contact office.

Registration required: Individuals or organizations that make or agree to make expenditures, or receive or agree to receive compensation, reimbursement, or both, of more than $2,000 in a calendar year for lobbying activities must register. Registration must occur on or before January 15 or prior to the commencement of lobbying, whichever is later. Registration filed in 2007 covers both 2007 and 2008, unless terminated. The fee is $150, which covers a two-year period. Communicator lobbyists (those engaged in the business of lobbying on behalf of others) must disclose the terms of their compensation including dollar amounts and the issues on which they expect to lobby. Client lobbyists (those on whose behalf lobbying takes place and who make expenditures for lobbying) must disclose detailed expenditure information on a periodic basis, as well. Communicator lobbyists must wear a badge issued by the Office of State Ethics while lobbying.

Forms to use: Form ETH-1A, *Communicators Biennial Lobbyist Registration;* Form ETH-1B, *Client/In-House Communicator(s) Biennial Lobbyist Registration;* Form ETH-2D, *Lobbyist Financial Report for Use by Client;* Form ETH-2B, *Communicator Lobbyist Report of Unreimbursed Expenditures and Necessary Expenses;* Form ETH-2A, *Communicator Lobbyist Report of Annual Compensation, Sales Tax and Reimbursement.*

Reporting requirements: Lobbyists must report compensation, fundamental terms of contracts, reimbursements and expenditures; expenditures made for the benefit of a state employee, public official, or a member of such person's staff or immediate family; and other lobbying-related payments.

Within the first 10 days of the calendar year, communicator lobbyists must file Form ETH-2A, an annual report of compensation, sales tax and reimbursement received from each client during the previous calendar year. Lobbyists must report (on the applicable periodic lobbying financial report, i.e., ETH-2B, 2c, or 2D) within 30 days of making an unreimbursed expenditure of $10 or more for necessary expenses incurred by a public official or state employee. Communicator lobbyists must also file Form ETH-2B to report unreimbursed expenditures and necessary expenses on either a quarterly basis, a monthly basis, or within 30 days, depending on the circumstances of the filing. Client lobbyists must file detailed spending reports that include office expenses, staff time spent in furtherance of lobbying, and paid media communications, using Form ETH-2D.

TAX EXEMPTIONS

Contact:

> Department of Revenue Services
> Taxpayer Services Division
> Twenty-Five Sigourney Street
> Hartford, CT 06106
> (860) 297-5962

Citation: Conn. Gen. Stat. §12-412(8), as amended by 1995 Conn. Pub. Acts 359, §2 —sales tax; § 12-710—corporate income tax.

Requirements: Corporations that are exempt from federal income tax are generally exempt from Connecticut corporate income tax as well, but not until a determination letter is issued.

Sales Tax: The Department no longer issues exemption certificates. When making an exempt purchase, the organization must issue to retailers a completed CERT-119, *Certificate for Purchase of Tangible Personal Property and Services by Exempt Organizations* along with a copy of its exemption permit. If the organization was not issued an exemption certificate by the Department before July 1, 1995, the organization must have a federal determination letter for 501(c)(3) or (c)(13) exemption.

Application Procedure: On Form REG-1, *Application for Tax Registration Number*, check the appropriate box indicating federal income tax exemption, and provide a copy of the federal determination letter. For sales tax exemption, provide the retailer with Cert-119 form and a copy of the exemption permit.

CHARITABLE SOLICITATION

Contact:

> Department of Consumer Protection
> Public Charities Unit
> PO Box 120
> 55 Elm Street
> Hartford, CT 06141-0120
> (860) 808-5030

Citation: *Solicitation of Charitable Funds Act,* Chapter 419d, Section 21a-175 et seq.(Public Act 05-101)

Publications: *General Information for Charitable Organizations on the Connecticut Solicitation of Charitable Funds Act,* a copy of the statute, and forms are available from the contact office and at the Web site.

Initial Registration: Organizations soliciting contributions that normally receive more than $50,000 in contributions annually or that compensate any person primarily to conduct solicitations must register prior to beginning solicitation. Religious institutions, nonprofit hospitals, and government entities are generally exempt from registration. Organizations register by filing a form PCUREG-01 with a most recently filed Form 990, *Charitable Organization Registration Statement,* along with a $50 filing fee. The 990 must be completed for state purposes, even if the organization is not required to file it with the IRS. Registration is effective for one year. The renewal fee is $50.

Annual Reports: Within five months after the close of each fiscal year, organizations must file a Form CPC-60 (Annual Report Face Sheet); a copy of the organization's IRS Form 990 (which must be completed for the state even if the organization is exempt from filing it with the IRS) and an audit report if the organization's gross receipts exceed $200,000.

Organization Solicitation Disclosure Requirements: See below.

Paid Solicitor Requirements: Must register annually, pay a fee of $500, and post a bond of $20,000. Contracts must be in writing. Paid solicitors must, for oral solicitations, send a written confirmation within five days to each person who has pledged to contribute. The confirmation shall disclose the name of the solicitor, the fact that the solicitor is being paid, and the percentage of the gross proceeds that the charity will receive. Written solicitations must include the same information. Paid solicitors must file financial reports no more than 90 days after each campaign.

Fundraising Counsel Requirements: Must register and pay a $120 fee. Contracts with organizations must be in writing and filed with the Department at least 15 days before services begin.

Delaware

Central Switchboard: (302) 739-4000
State Web Home Page: http://www.delaware.gov

INCORPORATION

Contact:

> *Department of State*
> *Division of Corporations*
> *PO Box 898*
> *Dover, DE 19903*
> *(302) 739-3073*

Citation: DCA Title 8, 101 et seq.

General Requirements: Articles of Incorporation must set forth the corporate name; registered office; the registered agent; that the corporation shall be a nonprofit corporation; that it shall not have any capital stock; conditions for membership, if any; and the name and mailing address of each incorporator, and optional provisions to qualify for federal tax-exempt status.

Corporate Name: Must include one of the following words: Association, Company, Corporation, Club, Foundation, Fund, Incorporated, Institute, Society, Union, Syndicate, or Limited, or one of the abbreviations: Co., Corp., Inc., or Ltd.; must be distinguishable from the names of others without written consent; must be in English or transliterated into letters of the English alphabet.

Name Reservation: May be reserved for a renewable, 30-day period for a fee of $75.

How to File: Documents must be suitable for scanning (e.g., black ink, 8.5" by 11" with large margins). The filing fee is $89 for a one-page document, plus $9 for each additional page.

Other Filings/reports: An annual report is required. The due date is March 1. The filing fee is $20.

LOBBYING

Contact:

> *Delaware Public Integrity Commission*
> *Margaret O'Neill Building*
> *Suite 3*
> *410 Federal Street*
> *Dover, DE 19901*
> *(302) 739-2399*

Citation: 29 Del. C. §5831 et seq.

Registration Required: Lobbyists must register with the Commission within five days of qualifying as a lobbyist. Registration statement discloses general information, length of employment, and subject matter. Clients of lobbyists must provide to the lobbyist a written authorization to act on their behalf, which is filed by the lobbyist. There is no fee for registration.

Forms to Use: *Lobbyist Registration Statement; Employer's Authorization; Lobbyist Quarterly Report Form.*

Reporting Requirements: On or before the 20th day of the month following each calendar quarter, a report must be filed covering the preceding quarter itemizing total expenditures by food and refreshment, entertainment, lodging expenses, travel, recreation expenses, and gifts and contributions (excluding political contributions). The report must also disclose information about specific expenditures of more than $50 per day that benefited a member of the General Assembly, or for employees or members of any state agency.

TAX EXEMPTIONS

Contact:

Department of Finance
Division of Revenue
820 French Street, 8th Fl.
Wilmington, DE 19801
(302) 577-8205

Citation: Title 30, § 1902.

Requirements: Organizations exempt under Section 501(c) are exempt from income taxes. The state has no sales tax.

Application Procedure: Send a copy of the organization's IRS determination letter to the Division.

CHARITABLE SOLICITATION

Contact:

Department of Justice
Carvel State Building
820 N. French Street
Wilmington, DE 19801
(302) 577-8600

Citation: Chapter 25, Title 6, Subchapter IX, §2591 et seq.

Delaware has no statute requiring registration of charitable organizations or fundraisers, but such legislation has been proposed. Legislation was enacted in 1996 to protect the public against those who fraudulently solicit contributions. The act also prohibits solicitations after 9 p.m. and before 8 a.m.

Initial Registration: None.

Annual Reports: None.

Organization Solicitation Disclosure Requirements: None.

Paid Solicitor Requirements: The law also requires every professional solicitor to keep accurate fiscal records concerning its charitable/fraternal solicitations in Delaware, and to have written contracts with charities that clearly state their obligations and compensation terms. Professional solicitors must disclose their identities and that the solicitor is a paid solicitor. They must, upon request, disclose the amount/percentage of the contribution that will be turned over to the charity or a good faith estimate if that amount is not known.

Fundraising Counsel Requirements: None.

District of Columbia

Central Switchboard: (202) 727-1000
Web Home Page: http://www.dc.gov

INCORPORATION

Contact:

> Department of Consumer and Regulatory Affairs
> Corporate Division
> 941 N. Capitol Street, NE
> PO Box 92300
> Washington, DC 20090
> (202) 442-4432

Citation: *District of Columbia Nonprofit Corporation Act,* § 29-501.

General Requirements: Three or more incorporators over the age of 21 are required for incorporation. Articles of Incorporation must set forth the name of corporation; duration; purpose(s); a statement as to whether the corporation will have members; provisions relating to membership if it will have members; how directors will be elected or appointed (or that this will be provided for in the bylaws); optional provisions relating to the internal management and regulation of the corporation, including any provisions for the distribution of assets upon dissolution or final liquidation; address of the initial registered office and name of the registered agent at that office; the names and addresses of directors (must have at least three directors); the number of directors constituting the initial board of directors and their names and addresses; and the name, address, and signature of each incorporator.

Corporate Name: Shall not contain a word or phrase that indicates or implies that it is organized for any purpose other than permitted by the Articles of Incorporation; shall not be the same as, or deceptively similar to another; shall be transliterated into letters of the English language if it is not in English; and shall not indicate that the corporation is organized under an act of Congress.

Name Reservation: May be reserved for a 60-day period for a fee of $65; and may be renewed once.

How to File: File a notarized original and one copy of the Articles of Incorporation with the contact office with a filing and indexing fee of $70.

Other Filings/Reports: A two-year report is required to be filed along with a $75 filing fee. The report discloses general information, including the names and addresses of directors and officers, and a brief statement of the character of the affairs that the corporation is actually conducting. The report is due January 15.

LOBBYING

Contact:

> Office of Campaign Finance
> 2000 14th St, NW
> Suite 433
> Washington, DC 20009
> (202) 671-0547

Citation: §1-1105.01.

Registration Required: Lobbyists must register on or before January 15th each year with the Director of Campaign Finance if they receive compensation or expend $250 or more in any three consecutive calendar month period for lobbying. The registration form must be filed for each person from whom the lobbyist receives compensation. The form discloses general information, information about clients, the nature of the client's business, and information about the matters that are the target of lobbying.

Reporting Requirements: Semi-annual reports are due between July 1 and July 10 and in January covering the previous six-month period. The report discloses information on the registration form, expenses itemized by office expenses, advertising and publication, compensation to others, personal sustenance, lodging and travel, and other. Expenditures of $50 or more must be itemized by name and address of the recipient as well as political expenditures;

loans, gifts, and honoraria; and information about who has been the target of lobbying activity.

TAX EXEMPTIONS

Contact:

> Office of Tax and Revenue
> Attention—Exempt Organizations
> 941 North Capitol Street, NE
> 1st Floor
> Washington, DC 20002
> (202) 727-4TAX

Citation: Titles 47, §1802, 47-2005 and 47-1508 of the D.C. Code.

Requirements: Nonprofit organizations may be exempt from the corporation franchise tax, sales and use taxes, and personal property taxes (with a location requirement). There is no exemption from unrelated business taxes. A prerequisite for exemption is an IRS exemption from federal taxes. Other provisions apply as well. An organization may apply for exemption before the IRS makes its determination. See: *http://brc.dc.gov/nonprofit/requirementsorg/ dc_tax_exempt.asp*

Application Procedure: Submit a Form FR 164 and the following documents: the organization's IRS tax exemption determination letter, a copy of the Certificate of Authority or other governing document, and a copy of a lease or other documentation to certify the physical location requirement.

CHARITABLE SOLICITATION

Contact:

> Department of Consumer and Regulatory Affairs
> 941 N. Capitol Street, NE
> Room 7211
> Washington, DC 20001-4259
> (202) 442-4311

Citation: §44-1701.

Initial Registration: Charities must register with the Department and pay a business license fee of $208 plus a $35 application fee, plus a $10 endorsement fee. Registration renewals are due September 1. Organizations must submit a copy of bylaws and a completed financial report (BPLA-3, Form 990, or a certified financial statement). Organizations receiv-

ing less than $1,500 in gross total receipts in a calendar year with unpaid fundraisers, or organized for educational purposes, or religious corporations or churches are exempt.

Annual Reports: Financial reports are due within 30 days after the end of each licensing period. The Department issues solicitation cards that must be presented to each prospective donor. The report discloses the amount of contributions, expenses, and how the funds were used.

Organization Solicitation Disclosure Requirements: Solicitors must exhibit a solicitor information card ($3 each) and read or present it to the person being solicited. A two-year Basic Business license fee is $208 plus a $35 application fee and $10 endorsement fee.

Paid Solicitor Requirements: See above.

Fundraising Counsel Requirements: None.

Florida

Central Switchboard: (850) 488-1234
State Web Home Page: http://www.myflorida.com

INCORPORATION

Contact:

Secretary of State
Division of Corporations—Corporate Filings
PO Box 6327
Tallahassee, FL 32314
(850) 245-6052

Citation: *Florida Not-for-Profit Corporation Act;* Chapter 617, Florida Statutes, 617.01011 et seq.

Publications Available: *Florida Not-For-Profit Corporation Act,* which includes forms, laws, and instruction booklets, and other useful state and federal information, is available from the contact office.

General Requirements: Three or more directors are required. Articles of Incorporation must set forth the corporate name; principal place of business and mailing address; purposes; manner of election of directors; limitation of corporate powers; initial registered agent and street address; and the names, addresses, and signatures of each incorporator.

Corporate Name: Must be distinguishable from the names of all other entities or filings except certain fictitious name registrations. Must contain the word "corporation" or "incorporated" or the abbreviation "corp." or "inc." or words or abbreviations of like import in language as will clearly indicate that it is a corporation. May not contain the word "company" or its abbreviation "co."; may contain the word "cooperative" or "co-op" only if the resulting name is distinguishable from the name of any corporation, agricultural cooperative marketing association, or nonprofit cooperative association existing or doing business in the state; may not contain language stating or implying that it is organized for a purpose other than permitted by law or by its Articles of Incorporation; may not contain language stating or implying that it is connected with a state or federal government agency or corporation chartered under the laws of the U.S.; must be distinguishable from the names of all other entities.

Name Reservation: None.

How to File: Send completed Articles of Incorporation to the Division of Corporations with a filing fee payable to the Dept. of State of $35 plus a fee of $35 to designate the registered agent, plus optional fees of $8.75 for a certified copy of the Articles or an optional fee of $8.75 for a certificate of status.

Other Filings/Reports: An annual report must be filed by May 1 with the Secretary of State disclosing general information, including names and addresses of its directors and principal officers; the federal ID number; and other information required by the Department.

LOBBYING

Contact:

Lobbyist Registration Office
Office of Legislative Services
Claude Pepper Building
111 West Madison St.; Room G-68
Tallahassee, FL 32399-1425
(850) 922-4990

Citation: *Executive Branch Lobbying Registration Act,* Section 11.044-11.062, Florida Statutes; Joint Rule 1 of the Florida Senate and House of Representatives; Senate Rule 9; House Rule 13.

Registration Required: Registration for those who lobby the executive branch is separate from registration for those who lobby the legislature; the contact office administers both registrations. All lobbyists must register annually for each principal represented; a separate form is required for each principal. Registration forms for the Legislature disclose contact information and the extent of any direct business association or partnership the lobbyist has with any member of the Legislature. The annual fee is $25 for each House for the first principal and $10 additional for each House for each additional principal, and $25 per principal for executive branch lobbying.

Forms to Use: The *Florida Legislature Lobbyist Registration Form; Lobbyist's Expenditure Report for the Florida Legislature; Authorization to Represent the Principal; Executive Branch Lobbyist Registration.*

Reporting Requirements: Each lobbying firm shall file a compensation report with the division for each calendar quarter during any portion of which one or more of the firm's lobbyists were registered to represent a principal. The reporting statements must be filed electronically no later than 45 days after the end of each quarter. The four quarters are

January 1-March 31, April 1-June 30, July 1 - September 30, and October 1 - December 31.

TAX EXEMPTIONS

Contact:

Florida Department of Revenue
5050 West Tennessee Street
Tallahassee, FL 32399-0100
1-800-352-3671 (calls originating inside Fl)
(850) 487-4130 (calls originating outside Fl)

Citation: Chapter 220, Florida Statutes—corporate income tax; Chapter 212, Florida Statutes—sales and use tax.

Publications: Tax information and forms may be found at: *http://www.myflorida.com/dor*

Requirements: Organizations exempt from federal income taxes are generally exempt from state corporate income tax. 501(c)(3) organizations are generally exempt from sales and use tax "when such leases and purchases are used in carrying on their customary nonprofit activities" although other restrictions apply.

Application Procedure: Nonprofit organizations that are federally exempt must file with the Central Registration/Exceptions Office Form DR-5, *Application for Consumer's Certificate of Exemption* and supporting documents that vary based on the type of organization. For details, see: *http://www.myflorida.com/dor/forms/2003/dr5.pdf*.

CHARITABLE SOLICITATION

Contact:

Florida Department of Agriculture and
*   Consumer Services*
Division of Consumer Services
Solicitation of Contributions
PO Box 6700
Tallahassee, FL 32314-6700
1-800-HELPFLA
(850) 488-2221

Citation: Chapter 496, Florida Statutes, 496.401 et seq.

Publications: A copy of the statute and forms are provided by the contact office.

Initial Registration: All organizations are required to register with the Department prior to engaging in solicitation activities. The registration fee ranges from $10 (for those with less than $5,000 in contributions annually) to $400 (for those with more than $10 million annually). The registration statement must include the charity's financial report on a form prescribed by the Department or Federal 990 or, for those that are newly formed, a budget for the current fiscal year. Also included must be the name of the charity; the purpose for which it is organized; the purposes for which the contributions will be used; whether there have been certain types of misconduct by those associated with the charity; the tax-exempt status of the charity along with a copy of its IRS determination letter; and information about professional solicitors and fundraising consultants, including the terms of their compensation.

Annual Reports: Annual renewal statements are required that include updates to the information required on the initial registration statement.

Organization Solicitation Disclosure Requirements: Solicitations must disclose the name of the charity; a description of the purposes for which the solicitation is being made; upon request, the name, address, or telephone number to whom inquiries can be made; the amount of the contribution that may be deducted as a charitable contribution under federal law; and the source from which a financial statement may be obtained. The written financial report must be provided within 14 days of the request. Every printed solicitation, written confirmation, receipt or reminder about a contribution must have a disclaimer conspicuously displayed in capital letters:

A COPY OF THE OFFICIAL REGISTRATION AND FINANCIAL INFORMATION MAY BE OBTAINED FROM THE DIVISION OF CONSUMER SERVICES BY CALLING TOLL-FREE WITHIN THE STATE 1-800-HELP-FLA. REGISTRATION DOES NOT IMPLY ENDORSEMENT, APPROVAL, OR RECOMMENDATION BY THE STATE."

Paid Solicitor Requirements: Similar disclosure constraints to those detailed above apply to professional solicitors. Professional solicitors must register with the Department, pay a $300 fee, and post a $50,000 bond. Not less than 15 days before commencing a fundraising campaign, professional solicitors must file a solicitation notice, which includes detailed information, including a copy of the contract with the charity. A financial report of campaign must be filed within 90 days of the conclusion of a campaign or the one-year anniversary of the campaign.

Fundraising Counsel Requirements: Must register and pay a $300 registration fee; no bond is required.

Georgia

Central Switchboard: (404) 656-2000
State Web Home Page: http://www.georgia.gov

INCORPORATION

Contact:

Secretary of State
Corporations Division
315 West Tower
#2 Martin Luther King Jr. Drive
Atlanta, GA 30334
(404) 656-2817 (Corporations Division)

Citation: O.C.G.A. §14-3-101, Georgia Nonprofit Corporation Code.

Publications Available: *Corporation Filing Procedures, Georgia Profit or Nonprofit Corporations* (includes sample Articles of Incorporation) is available from the contact office. Instructions for filing Articles and a sample format may be downloaded from the web site.

General Requirements: Articles must set forth the corporate name; that the corporation is organized as a nonprofit; the street address of the initial registered office (must be in the state) and the initial registered agent at that address; the name and address of each incorporator; whether the corporation will have members; and the mailing address of the initial principal office. Other items required by the IRS code regarding tax exempt status and internal regulation provisions are optional.

Corporate Name: Must contain the word "corporation," "incorporated," "company," or "limited," or the abbreviation "Corp.," "Inc.," "Co.," or "Ltd." or words or abbreviations of like import in a language other than English. May not contain anything, within the reasonable judgment of the Secretary of State, that is obscene; shall not exceed 80 characters excluding spaces and punctuation; must be distinguishable from other corporations or reserved names unless there is written permission from the other entity.

Name Reservation: Names may be reserved at the Web site: *http://www.georgiacorporations.org*

or by fax to (404) 651-7842; the reservation is valid for 30 days and can be renewed. The fee is $25.

How to File: Reserve the corporate name; file BSR Form 227 (Transmittal Form) with the corporate name reservation number and Articles of Incorporation, and the filing fee of $100. Arrange for newspaper advertisement in the home county of the registered agent's address. The fee for this is $40, payable to the newspaper. The advertisement must appear weekly for two consecutive weeks in a format provided by the Georgia law.

Other Filings/Reports: An annual report must be filed with the Secretary of State with general information, including the names and addresses of the CEO, chief financial officer, and Secretary. The first report is due 90 days after incorporation, with subsequent reports due between January 1 and April 1 of each year. The fee is $30.

LOBBYING

Contact:

State Ethics Commission
200 Piedmont Avenue
Suite 1416—West Tower
Atlanta, GA 30334
(404) 463-1988

Citation: *O.C.G. 21-5-70 et seq, The Public Officials Conduct and Lobbyist Disclosure Act of 1992.*

Publications: *Lobbyist Guide* is available in person at the Commission Office, or online at: *http://www.ethics.ga.gov*

Registration Required: All lobbyists (those who meet a $250 threshold in spending in any calendar year to promote or oppose the passage of any legislation before the General Assembly) must register with the Commission before lobbying activity occurs. All registrations expire on December 31. Registration application must contain name; address; telephone number; the person or agency that employs, appoints, or authorizes the applicant to lobby on its behalf; a statement of the general business purpose of those the applicant represents; and a signed authorization statement by that person or agency. There is no fee for registration. Lobbyists must have a color photograph taken for incorporation into a lobbyist identification badge.

Forms to use: *Lobbyist Registration Application; Lobbyist PIN Application.*

Reporting requirements: All expenditure reports are submitted electronically, using a PIN number.

TAX EXEMPTIONS

Contact:

Georgia Taxpayer Services Division
Tax Exempt Organizations
PO Box 49432
Atlanta, GA 30359
(404) 417-2409
(404) 417-2409 (Sales & use Tax Division)

Citation: §48-7-25—income taxes; §48-8-3 — Sales and Use Tax.

Publications: Forms are provided by the contact office.

Requirements: Organizations with federal income tax exemptions are generally exempt from income tax other than unrelated business income tax. Exemption takes effect when the Commissioner grants an exemption using a determination letter. Certain 501(c)(3)s, including many hospitals, nursing homes, and certain educational institutions, are exempt from sales and use tax as provided by the statute. Consult the contact office or the statute for details.

Application Procedure: For income tax exemption, file form 3605 and attach a copy of the Articles of Incorporation or equivalent, bylaws, determination letter, and a copy of the certificate of registration with the Secretary of State (if a corporation). Application requires a narrative description of activities.

CHARITABLE SOLICITATION

Contact:

Secretary of State
Div. of Securities and Business. Reg.
Suite 802, West Tower
2 Martin Luther King Jr. Drive, SE
Atlanta, GA 30334
(404) 656-4910

Citation: *Georgia Charitable Solicitations Act of 1988,* as amended, O.C.G.A. Title 43, Chapter 17, 43-17-1 et seq.

Initial Registration: All organizations that solicit contributions for charitable purposes must register with the Secretary of State by submitting form C100, their IRS Form 990, and their IRS Determination Letter, unless the organization is exempt from registration. The initial registration fee is $25.

Annual Reports: Charitable organization registrations must be renewed annually by using form C101. Renewal registrations must include a financial statement in accordance with the Act, form C101, and a $10 renewal fee.

Organization Solicitation Disclosure Requirements: At the point of solicitation, every charitable organization, paid solicitor, or solicitor agent must disclose the name and location of the paid solicitor and solicitor agent, if any, and the name and location of the charitable organization for which the solicitation is being made; that a full and fair description of the charitable program and a financial statement will be made available upon request and, if the solicitation is being made by a paid solicitor or solicitor agent, that such solicitation is being made by a paid person and not by a volunteer.

Paid Solicitor Requirements: Must register using Form S100 and pay an initial $250 fee and post a $10,000 bond. The renewal fee is $100. The fee for solicitor agents is $50 for initial registration and $50 for renewals, which expire on December 31st each year.

Fundraising Counsel Requirements: None.

Hawaii

Central Switchboard: (808) 586-2211
State Web Home Page: http://www.hawaii.gov

INCORPORATION

Contact:

Dept. of Commerce and Consumer Affairs
Business Registration Division
335 Merchant Street, Room 201
Honolulu, HI 96813
or
PO Box 40
Honolulu, HI 96810
(808) 586-2727

Citation: Section 414D, Hawaii Revised Statutes.

Publications Available: *Instructions for Filing Articles of Incorporation* and sample form are available from the contact office and Web site.

General Requirements: Articles must set forth the corporate name; mailing address of the corporation's initial principal office; the street address of the corporation's initial registered office and the name of its initial registered agent at its initial registered office; the name and address of each incorporator; and whether or not the corporation will have members.

Corporate Name: Shall not be the same as, or substantially identical to, another without written consent.

Name Reservation: May be reserved for a 120-day period for a $10 fee using Form X-1.

How to File: Articles must be typewritten or printed in black ink; signatures must be in black ink; one original should be filed with the contact office along with a $25 filing fee. Include an additional fee of $10 for a certified copy, plus 25 cents/page.

Other Filings/Reports: Annual reports must be filed with the contact office within the time periods based on the calendar quarter in which the corporation was incorporated. Reports must be filed by the last day of that quarter, reflect-ing the state of the corporation's affairs as of the first day of that quarter. For example, an organization incorporated on May 20 must annually file a report by June 30 reflecting the state of affairs as of April 1. No report is required if the corporation is incorporated in the same year that an annual report is due. Information includes disclosure of general information, the names and addresses of its officers and directors (must have at least three directors), and a brief description of the nature of its activities. There is a $5 filing fee.

LOBBYING

Contact:

Hawaii State Ethics Commission
Bishop Square
1001 Bishop Street
American Savings Building Tower 970
Honolulu, HI 96813
(808) 587-0460

Citation: *The "Lobbyists" Law*—Chapter 97, Hawaii Revised Statutes.

Publications Available: *Lobbying Registration and Reporting Manual* is available from the contact office and at: *http://www.state.hi.us/ethics/noindex/lobmanual.htm*

Registration Required: Lobbyists who receive compensation are required to register with the Commission within five days of becoming a lobbyist, provided they either spend more than $750 for lobbying in any reporting period or spend more than five hours lobbying in any month of any reporting period. The registration period is from January 1 of each odd-numbered year to the following December 31 of each even-numbered year. Re-registration is required within 10 days of the opening of the odd-numbered year's legislative session. Registration forms are not automatically mailed out by the Commission. Separate registration is required for each person, organization, or business for which the lobbyist renders services. The registration provides an authorization section from the client represented, and a menu of subjects on which the lobbyist indicates a lobbying interest. There is no fee for registration.

Forms to use: *Lobbyist Registration Form (LRG), Lobbyist Expenditures Statement.*

Reporting requirements: Lobbyists, those who employ or contract for lobbyists, and those who spend $750 or more in any six-month period for lobbying, must file a *Statement of Expenditures* form with the Commission. Itemizations include preparation and distribution of lobbying materials; media advertising; telephone, telegraph, and other forms of telecommunication; compensation; fees; entertainment; food and beverages; gifts; loans; and other expenditures. The forms are due on January 31, March 31 and May 31 of each year. The January report covers the period of May 1-December 31 of the preceding calendar year. The March 31 report covers the period of January 1-February 28, and the May 31 report covers the period March 1-April 30. Lobbyists report only the expenditures made that were not reimbursed by the client.

TAX EXEMPTIONS

Contact:
> Department of Taxation
> PO Box 259
> Honolulu, HI 96809-0259
> (808) 587-4242
> 1-800-222-3229

Citation: HRS §235-2.3 —corporate income tax; HRS §237-23.

Publications: *An Introduction to the General Excise Tax, Tax Facts,* and various leaflets explaining exemptions applying to nonprofit organizations are available from the contact office.

Requirements: All organizations exempt from federal income tax are exempt from the state corporate income tax, other than those with 501(c)(12), (15), and (16) status. The state has no general sales tax. However, any taxpayer conducting business in the state is subject to the general excise tax, which is a tax on gross receipts. Certain nonprofit organizations may be exempt from the general excise tax on income that they receive, but other businesses

may pass this tax on to customers, including exempt organizations.

Application Procedure: No application is required to obtain exemption from state income tax. File Form G-6, *Application for Exemption From General Excise Taxes* or Form G-6S, *Application for Exemption From General Excise Taxes* (Short Form) along with a copy of bylaws and Charter of Incorporation, IRS determination letter, and a $20 license fee to apply for exemption from the state general excise tax.

CHARITABLE SOLICITATION

Contact:
> Department of the Attorney General
> Tax Division
> 425 Queen Street
> Honolulu, HI 96813
> (808) 586-1470

Citation: Haw. Rev. Stat. §467B

Initial Registration: None (repealed by a 1994 law).

Organization Solicitation Disclosure Requirements: None.

Paid Solicitor Requirements: Must register with the Department, post bond in the amount of $25,000, and pay a $250 fee. Registration renewals are required before July 1.

Fundraising Counsel Requirements: Must register with the Department, pay a $250 fee. A $25,000 bond is required. Registration renewals are required before July 1.

Idaho

Central Switchboard: (208) 334-2411
State Web Home Page: http://www.state.id.us/

INCORPORATION

Contact:

> *Secretary of State*
> *700 West Jefferson*
> *PO Box 83720*
> *Boise, ID 83720-0080*
> *(208) 334-2301*

Citation: *Idaho Nonprofit Corporation Act,* Title 30, §30-3-1 et seq.

Publications Available: *Idaho Nonprofit Corporation Act* is available from the contact office or online (see: *http://www.idsos.state.id.us/corp/corindex.htm)*

General Requirements: Articles of Incorporation must set forth the corporate name; purpose(s); names and addresses of initial directors (must be at least three); names and addresses of incorporators; street address of the initial registered office and name of initial registered agent at that office; name and address of each incorporator; mailing address of the corporation; whether the corporation will have members; and provisions not inconsistent with law regarding the distribution of assets upon dissolution.

Corporate Name: Shall contain the word "corporation," "incorporated" or "limited," or shall contain an abbreviation of one of such words, provided however, that if the word "company" or its abbreviation is used, it shall not be immediately preceded by the word "and" or by an abbreviation or symbol representing the word "and"; shall not contain a word or phrase that indicates or implies that it is organized for any purpose other than what is contained in its Articles; and shall be distinguishable upon the records of the Secretary of State.

Name Reservation: May be reserved for four months for a fee of $20.

How to File: File two copies of Articles of Incorporation with the contact office along with the filing fee of $30. One copy is returned.

Other Filings/reports: An annual report must be filed with the Secretary of State. The report is mailed from the Secretary of State's office directly to the mailing address indicated in the Articles of Incorporation. The annual report is due each year on the last day of the anniversary month the Articles were filed in the Office of the Secretary of State. The form is sent out two months prior to the anniversary month. Organizations have two months after the anniversary month to file the report. There is no fee.

LOBBYING

Contact:

> *Secretary of State*
> *PO Box 83720*
> *Boise, ID 83720-0080*
> *(208) 334-2852*

Citation: *The Sunshine Law for Political Funds and Lobbyist Activity Disclosure,* Title 67, Idaho Code, Chapter 66, 67-6617 et seq.

Publications: *The Sunshine Law for Political Funds and Lobbyist Law Disclosure; Reporting Manual for Registered Lobbyists* are available from the contact office. Lobbying FAQ available at: *http://www/idsos.state.id.us/elect/lobbyist/lobinfo.htm*

Registration Required: Prior to engaging in lobbying or within 30 days after being employed as a lobbyist, lobbyists must register with the Secretary of State if they receive compensation in excess of $250 during any calendar quarter for lobbying. A $10 fee is required. The registration statement discloses the lobbyist's name; permanent business address; any temporary residential and business address during the legislative session; the name, address and general nature of the occupation or business of the lobbyist's employer; whether those who pay the lobbyist employ him or her solely as a lobbyist or include other duties; the general subject(s) of legislative interest; and the name and address of the person who will have custody of the lobbyist's records. A separate notice of representation is required of the lobbyist for each client with an additional $10 fee for each.

Forms to Use: L-1 for Lobbyist Registration; L-2 for annual reports; L-3 for monthly reports.

Reporting Requirements: Annual reports are due January 31. Interim monthly periodic reports are required for each month or portion thereof that the legislature is in session. These interim reports are due by the 10th day after the end of the month that the report covers. The annual and monthly reports must contain itemized expenditures categorized by entertainment/food, living accommodations, advertising, travel, telephone, office expenses and other expenses/services; the totals of each expenditure of more than $50 for a legislator or other public official; contributions made to any legislator or on behalf of any legislator; and the subject matter, including bill numbers, that was supported or opposed by the lobbyist.

TAX EXEMPTIONS

Contact:

> Idaho State Tax Commission
> Taxpayer Service
> 800 Park Boulevard, Plaza IV
> PO Box 36
> Boise, ID 83722
> (208) 334-7660 or (800) 972-7660

Citation: §63-3025B —corporate income tax; §63-3622o —sales tax.

Publications: *Nonprofit Groups and Churches, An Educational Guide to Sales Tax in the State of Idaho; Retailers & Wholesalers: Making Exempt Sales* are available from the contact office.

Requirements: 501(c)(3)s, fraternal benefit societies, and certain agricultural organizations are exempt from income taxes other than unrelated business income taxes; sales tax exemptions on sales to, or purchases by, non-profit hospitals, educational institutions, the Idaho Food Bank Warehouse, and certain other health-related entities are specifically exempt

by law. However, sales to most religious, charitable and nonprofit organizations are taxable. Sales by nonprofit, charitable, and religious organizations are usually taxable but some incidental sales by religious organizations are exempt by law.

Application Procedure: If exempt, provide the vendor with a completed ST-101 form.

CHARITABLE SOLICITATION

Contact:

> Office of the Attorney General
> Consumer Protection Unit
> 700 W. State Street
> PO Box 83720
> Boise, ID 83720-0010
> (800) 432-3545 (in Idaho)
> (208) 334-2424

Citation: *Idaho Charitable Solicitation Act,* Chapter 12, 48-1201 et seq.

Publications: A copy of the statute is provided by the contact office.

Initial Registration: None.

Annual Reports: None.

Organization Solicitation Disclosure Requirements: It is unlawful to utilize unfair, false, deceptive, misleading, or unconscionable acts or practices.

Paid Solicitor Requirements: None.

Fundraising Counsel Requirements: None.

Illinois

Central Switchboard: (217) 782-2000
State Web Home Page: http://www100.state.il.us/

INCORPORATION

Contact:

> Secretary of State
> Business Services Department
> Corporation Division
> 501 S. Second Street, Room 328
> Springfield, IL 62756
> (217) 782-6961

Citation: *Illinois General Not-For-Profit Corporation Act of 1986 (Public Act 88-691).*

General Requirements: Articles of Incorporation must set forth corporate name; purposes; address; name and address of each incorporator; and the names and addresses of first board of directors (must have at least three members).

Corporate Name: Must be distinguishable from existing Illinois corporations; may not imply that it is organized for a purpose other than what is set forth in its Articles of Incorporation; must not contain a name of an established political party without permission of that party; and must be written in English letters with Arabic or Roman numerals.

Name Check/Name Reservation: Verify that a name is available by telephoning (217) 782-9520. Names may be reserved for a $25 fee for a period of 90 days by written request or by filing a form NP-104.10. Can be checked online at: *http://www.cyberdriveillinois.com*

How to File: Deliver two copies of the Articles of Incorporation (using form NP-102.10), one of which must be the original copy, with a $50 certified check, money order, law firm check, or cashiers check to the Secretary of State. Articles of Incorporation and certificate from the Secretary of State must be filed with the county Recorder of Deeds in the home county of the organization within 15 days after receiving them.

Other Filings/Reports: An annual report must be filed with the Secretary of State before the first day of the corporation's anniversary month on forms provided by the Secretary of State 60 days before the due date. The report discloses general information, including information about officers and directors, and a brief description of the affairs that the corporation is conducting in the state. The fee is $10.

LOBBYING

Contact:

> Secretary of State
> Department of Index
> Lobbyist Division
> 111 East Monroe Street
> Springfield, IL 62756
> (217) 782-7017

Citation: *The Lobbyist Registration Act, 25 ILCS § 170/1 et seq.*

Registration Required: All lobbyists who for compensation or otherwise undertake to influence executive, legislative, or administrative action, and those who employ such persons, must register on or before January 31 and July 31 every year or before lobbying activity occurs, but in any event no more than two business days after being employed or retained. Registrations expire on December 31 each year. There is a $350 annual fee for each lobbyist and/or each employer employing a lobbyist. The fee is reduced to $150 for organizations and their lobbyists with 501(c)(3) tax-exempt status.

Forms to Use: Registration is performed electronically at: *http://www.cyberdriveillinois.com*. All registration fees must be submitted electronically.

Reporting Requirements: Registered entities must file First Half Year Expenditure Reports and Second Half Year Expenditure Reports of expenses. These reports include schedules for reporting Non-itemized, Itemized, Large Gatherings, Giveaways, and Grass Roots Lobbying expenditures.

TAX EXEMPTIONS

Contact:

Local Government Services Bureau-MC3-520
Illinois Department of Revenue
101 W. Jefferson Street
Springfield, Il 62702
(800) 732-8866
(217) 782-8881

Citation: 35 ILCS 5/ §205(a)— corporate income tax; 86 Ill. Admin. Code Section 130.2007(b)— Illinois Retailers' Occupation Tax.

Requirements: Organizations exempt from federal income tax are exempt from state corporate income tax, other than unrelated business income tax. The Retailers' Occupation Tax exemption extends to tangible personal property sold to a "governmental body, to a corporation, society, association, foundation, or institution organized and operated exclusively for charitable, religious, or educational purposes, or to a not-for-profit corporation, society, association, foundation, institution, or organization that has no compensated officers or employees and that is organized and operated primarily for the recreation of persons 55 years of age or older." Exemption also exists for various other entities, including property sold to a "not-for-profit music or dramatic arts organization that establishes, by proof required by the Department by rule, that it has received an exemption under Section 501(c)(3) of the Internal Revenue Code and that it is organized and operated for the presentation of live public performances of musical or theatrical works on a regular basis." More details about exemptions can be found in publications at: *http:// www.revenue.state.il.us/publications/pubs/ pio37.htm*

Application: No special petition is required for exemption from the state income tax. For exemption from the Illinois Retailers' Occupation Tax, submit request by letter to the Illinois Department of Revenue; include copy of Articles of Incorporation, constitution, and bylaws; a narrative explaining purposes, functions, and activities; the IRS determination letter, if available; most recent financial statement (other than for religious organizations); brochures; and other relevant information.

CHARITABLE SOLICITATION

Contact:

Office of the Illinois Attorney General
Charitable Trusts Bureau

100 W. Randolph Street
3rd Floor
Chicago, IL 60601
(312) 814-2595

Citation: *The Illinois Charitable Trust Act* (760 ILCS 55/1) and the *Solicitation for Charity Act* (225 ILCS 460/1) as amended (August 1999).

Initial Registration: Organizations that solicit, or intend to solicit, must file a registration statement (Form CO-1) with the Attorney General. The fee is $15. The late registration fee is $200. If the organization has been in operation for less than one year, it must also file a financial information form (CO-2). Organizations must also provide governing documents such as Articles of Incorporation, annual financial reports for the previous three years, IRS determination letter or copy of exemption application, copies of contracts with fundraisers, and bylaws.

Annual Reports: Organizations that receive more than $150,000 in contributions in a calendar or fiscal year, or that receive more than $25,000 from paid professional fundraisers, must file audited financial statements in addition to Form AG 990-IL and federal tax returns. There is a $15 fee. The AG 990-IL discloses how the organization spent donations, how much went to professional fundraisers, the amount it paid to the three highest paid persons, and the value of end-of-year assets and liabilities.

Solicitation Disclosure Requirements: The public member shall be promptly informed by statement in verbal communications and by clear and unambiguous disclosure in written materials that the solicitation is being made by a paid professional fundraiser. The fundraiser, solicitor, and materials used shall also provide the professional fundraiser's name and a statement that contracts and reports regarding the charity are on file with the Illinois Attorney General and additionally, in verbal communications, the solicitor's true name must be provided.

Paid Solicitor requirements: Must register annually and file financial reports. A $10,000 bond is required if the fundraiser takes control or possession of charitable funds.

Fundraising Counsel requirements: Must register every two years.

Indiana

Central Switchboard: (317) 232-3140
State Web Home Page: http://www.in.gov

INCORPORATION

Contact:

Secretary of State
Business Services Division
302 W. Washington Street
Room E018
Indianapolis, IN 46204
(317) 232-6576

Citation: *Indiana Nonprofit Corporation Act of 1991,* IC 23-17-1.

Publications Available: Forms and *Indiana Entrepreneur's Guide* are available from the contact office or Web site at: *http://www.sos.in.gov*

General Requirements: Articles of Incorporation must set forth the corporate name; that the corporation is either a public benefit corporation, mutual benefit corporation, or a religious corporation; the street address of the corporation's initial registered office and the name of the initial registered agent at that office (must be either a person who resides in Indiana or a corporation with an office in the state); the registered office address (may not be a post office box); the name, address, and original signature of each incorporator; whether the corporation will have members; provisions relating to distribution of assets upon dissolution; and optional information, which may include purposes, names and addresses of the initial board of directors, and internal regulating provisions.

Corporate Name: Must include the word "corporation," "incorporated," "company," or "limited," or the abbreviation "corp.," "inc.," "co.," or ltd." Must be distinguishable from any other domestic corporation or have written consent from the other corporation.

Name Check/Name Reservation: Call (317) 232-6576 or search at Web site to check corporate name availability; may be reserved for a 120-day period for a fee of $20.

How to File: File Articles of Incorporation along with a filing fee of $30. Online filing is $25.

Other Filings/Reports: An annual report must be submitted to the Secretary of State each year that provides contact information. The due date is the last day of the month in which the corporation was originally incorporated. The filing fee is $10 ($5 if filed online).

LOBBYING

Contact:

Indiana Lobby Registration Commission
10 W. Market Street
Suite 1760
Indianapolis IN 46204-1927
(317) 232-9860

Citation: IC-2-7; Acts 1981, PL 9 as amended.

Publications: *Indiana Lobbyist Handbook* is available online at: *http://www.in.gov/ilrc*

Registration Required: Lobbyists who receive or spend at least $500 in any registration year must register with the Commission. Separate registrations are required for employer lobbyists (those that compensate others to lobby on their behalf) and compensated lobbyists. Registration statements must be filed within 15 days of becoming a lobbyist or no later than January 15, whichever is later. Registrations terminate on December 31. There is a fee of $100 for each lobbyist registration statement; $50 for 501(c)(3) or (c)(4)s, or an employee who performs lobbying services for the employer as part of the employee's salaried responsibilities.

Forms to Use: Employer Lobbyists file the *Employer Lobbyist Registration Statement;* others file *Compensated Lobbyist Registration Statement; Report on Employer Lobbyist Activities; Report on Compensated Lobbyist Activities.*

Reporting Requirements: Employer lobbyists and compensated lobbyists file semi-annual reports on or before May 31 and on or before

November 30 for activities for the six-month periods of November 1-April 30 and May 1-October 31. The January 31 report includes totals for the full year. Expenses are itemized by compensation to others (employer lobbyists only), reimbursement to others (employer lobbyists only), receptions, entertainment, lobby registration and penalty fees, and other expenses. Gifts and the subject of lobbying activity must also be reported. A lobbyist must file a written report with both the Commission and with the relevant member of the General Assembly within 30 days of gifts worth in excess of $100 or more (or aggregating more than $250) and certain purchases valued at more than $100 from a member of the General Assembly, or more than $1,000 from a partner of a General Assembly member.

TAX EXEMPTIONS

Contact:

Indiana Department of Revenue
Not-for-Profit Section
IN Government Center North-Room N203
100 North Senate Avenue
Indianapolis, IN 46204-2253
(317) 233-2188 (sales tax)

Citation: Indiana Code 6-2.1-3.

Publications: *Nonprofit Organization Unrelated Business Income Tax Booklet, Sales Tax Information Booklet, Application of Sales Tax* (NP-20A) are available from the contact office or at: *http:// www.in.gov/dor/business*

Requirements: Income received by institutions, trusts, groups, and bodies organized and operated exclusively for religious, charitable, scientific, fraternal, education, social, and/or civic purposes and not for private benefit are exempt from the Gross Income Tax. Generally, 501(c)(3)-type organizations, business leagues, cemetery associations, churches, labor unions, hospitals, and most schools are exempt from paying sales tax. Organizations that conduct selling activities or fundraising events during more than 30 days in a calendar year may be required to register as a retail merchant for the collection and remittance of sales tax to the Department.

Application Procedure: File form NP-20A with a copy of Articles of Incorporation and bylaws, and a copy of the IRS determination letter. If not incorporated, include a copy of the Constitution and/or bylaws, Articles of Association, Declaration of Trust, and copies of amendments.

CHARITABLE SOLICITATION

Contact:

Office of the Attorney General
Consumer Protection Division
Indiana Government Center South, Fifth Fl.
302 West Washington Street
Indianapolis, IN 46204-2770
(317) 232-6330

Citation: Indiana Code 23-7-8-1 et seq.

Publications: A copy of the statute and forms are available from the contact office and by visiting the Web site at: *http://www.in.gov/ attorneygeneral*

Initial Registration: None.

Annual Reports: None.

Paid Solicitor Requirements: Must register with the Division and pay an initial $1,000 registration fee. Renewals are annual (before July 2) and have a fee of $50. Must have a contract filed with the Division that specifies the gross contributions to be received by the charity; must file a solicitation notice with the Division specifying the projected dates of the campaign, the location and telephone number where solicitation will be conducted, the names and address of each person responsible for supervising the campaign, and a certification from the charity that the information is correct to the best of its knowledge. At time of solicitation, professional solicitors must disclose before the donor agrees to making a contribution the name of the charity, and if requested, the charity's address; the fact that the solicitor is being compensated; the name of the solicitor and a number to call for the donor to confirm information; the charitable purpose for which the funds are being raised; the name of the professional solicitation company; the name of the solicitor; the phone number and address of the location from which the call is being made; and the percentage of charitable contribution that will be expended for charitable purposes after administrative costs and the costs of the solicitation. Other requirements apply.

Fundraising Counsel Requirements: Must register ($1,000 initial fee and $50 renewal) and comply with most provisions that apply to professional solicitors.

Iowa

Central Switchboard: (515) 281-5011
State Web Home Page: http://www.state.ia.us/

INCORPORATION

Contact:

> Secretary of State
> Business Services
> Lucas Building, 1st Fl.
> 321 E. 12th Street
> Des Moines, IA 50319
> (515) 281-5204

Citation: *Revised Nonprofit Corporation Act,* 504.

Publications Available: *Iowa Principles and Practices for Charitable Nonprofit Excellence* and nonprofit forms are available online at: *http://www.sos.state.ia.us*

General Requirements: Articles of Incorporation must set forth the name of the corporation; the address of its initial registered office and the name of the registered agent at that office; the name and address of each incorporator; whether the corporation will have members; provisions not inconsistent with law regarding the distribution of assets upon dissolution; and the signature of at least one incorporator.

Corporate Name: May not contain any language stating or implying that it is organized for a purpose other than that permitted by 504.301 and its articles of incorporation; must not be identical to another corporation.

Name Reservation: May be reserved for a non-renewable 120-day period by filing an application with the contact office along with a $10 fee.

How to File: File the original of the Articles of Incorporation with the Secretary of State with a $20 filing fee.

Other Filings/Reports: A biennial report must be filed with the Secretary of State each odd-numbered year, due between January 1 and April 1. The report discloses general information. Notices are mailed to the registered agent in early January. Corporations may file electronically using the notice or request a paper report. There is no fee.

LOBBYING

Contact:

> Chief Clerk of the House
> Statehouse
> Des Moines, IA 50319
> (515) 281-5381
> (515) 281-5403 (Secretary of the Senate)

For lobbying the executive branch:

> Iowa Ethics and Campaign Disclosure Board
> 510 E. 12th Street, Suite 1A
> Des Moines, IA 50319
> (515) 281-4028

Citation: Iowa Code section 68B.2, subsection 13, paragraphs a and b (definitions); section 68B.36 (registration procedures).

Publications: *General Information for Persons Lobbying Before the Iowa General Assembly; Overview of Lobbying the Legislature; House Rules Governing Lobbyists;* and *Senate Rules Governing Lobbyists* are available from the contact office.

Registration Required: Lobbyists must file at the beginning of each calendar year. House and Senate rules require each registered lobbyist to file a statement with the chief clerk on the general subjects of legislation of interest, the file number of the bills that will be the target of lobbying, whether the lobbyist intends to lobby for or against the bills, and on whose behalf the lobbyist is lobbying. There is no fee.

Forms to Use: *Iowa General Assembly Lobbyist Registration Statement; Iowa General Assembly Lobbyist Report; Iowa General Assembly Lobbyist Client Report; House and Senate Lobbying Declarations.*

Reporting Requirements: Reports are due not later than 25 days following any month the General Assembly is in session and on or before July 31, October 31, and January 31 for months when not in session. Reports must contain a list of the lobbyist's clients, information on campaign contributions made by the lobbyist, and expenditures. Lobbyists' clients are required to file semi-annual reports on salaries, fees, and retainers paid to lobbyists for lobbying purposes.

Lobbyist clients must file no later than July 31 each year and disclose all salaries, fees and retainers paid by the lobbyist's client to the lobbyist during the preceding 12 calendar months. The July 31 report provides a cumulative total for the preceding fiscal year.

TAX EXEMPTIONS

Contact:

> Taxpayer Services
> Iowa Department of Revenue
> PO Box 10457
> Des Moines, IA 50306-0457
> (515) 281-3114
> 1-800-367-3388 (in Iowa only)

Citation: § 422.34 —corporate income tax exemption; § 422.45 —sales tax exemption.

Publications: *Iowa Tax Guide for Non-Profit Entities* is available from the contact office.

Requirements: Organizations with federal tax-exempt status are automatically exempt from Iowa corporation tax other than unrelated business income; they must file form IA 1120 to report unrelated business income; they may be subject to the alternative minimum tax (requires filing of form IA 4626). Charities are treated the same as other businesses when purchasing goods and taxable services at retail—they pay sales taxes on goods and taxable services, except when the goods or services are for resale. Only organizations explicitly named in Iowa law are exempt from sales tax. These include the following: American Red Cross; Navy Relief Society; USO; governmental units; federal corporations created by the federal government that are exempt under federal law; private nonprofit educational institutions located in Iowa; community health centers; migrant health centers; certain residential care, ICF, and group homes for the mentally retarded and mentally ill; foster care residential facilities; rehabilitation facilities for the disabled; adult day care facilities; community mental health centers; nonprofit legal aid organizations; nonprofit private museums; nonprofit organizations that lend property to the general public for nonprofit purposes (such as libraries); statewide nonprofit organ procurement organizations; and sales of tangible personal property and services made to nonprofit hospitals.

Application Procedure: Organizations qualify for income tax exemption automatically upon receiving their IRS determination letters certifying federal exemption.

CHARITABLE SOLICITATION

Contact:

> Iowa Attorney General
> Consumer Protection Division
> 1305 E. Walnut Street
> Des Moines, IA 50319
> (515) 281-5164

Citation: Iowa Code, Chapter 13C

Publications: A copy of the solicitation law and the application for registration permit are available from the contact office and Web site.

Initial Registration: Registration applies only to professional commercial fundraisers. There is a $10 registration fee. Charitable organizations are not required to register.

Annual Reports: None.

Organization Solicitation Disclosure Requirements: Must disclose upon request, and without cost, financial disclosure information concerning contributions received and disbursements for the organization's last complete fiscal year, or for the current year if the organization has not completed an entire fiscal year. This information must be provided within five days of the request. Charitable organizations may not solicit contributions by claiming that all or a portion of the proceeds will be given to another charity in Iowa without permission from that other charity.

Paid Solicitor Requirements: Must register annually with the Attorney General and pay a $10 registration fee.

Kansas

Central Switchboard: (785) 296-0111
State Web Home Page: http://www.kansas.gov

INCORPORATION

Contact:

Secretary of State
Memorial Hall, 1st Floor
120 SW 10th Avenue
Topeka, KS 66612-1594
(785) 296-4564

Citation: Kansas General Corporation Code, K.S.A. 17 §6001 et seq.

Publications Available: *Filing Suggestions for Not-for-Profit Corporations* is available from the contact office.

General Requirements: Articles of Incorporation must set forth the corporate name; name and address of registered office and agent at that address; the purpose(s); whether the corporation is authorized to issue capital stock; if there are members and the conditions for membership; the names and addresses of incorporators (only 1 required); the names and addresses of directors if the powers of incorporators end upon filing; the term of existence of the corporation; and other lawful provisions. Setting a duration for the corporation is optional.

Corporate Name: Must include one of the words of incorporation such as "association," "company," "church," "corporation," "club," "foundation," "fund," "incorporated," "institute," "society," "union," "syndicate," or "limited," or one of the abbreviations "co.," "corp.," "inc.," "ltd.," or words or abbreviations of like import in other languages. Must be distinguishable from other names without written consent.

Name Check/name reservation: May be reserved for a period of 120 days for a $35 fee ($27 if filed online).

How to File: File an original of the Articles of Incorporation with a $20 filing fee. A certified original is returned.

Other Filings/reports: An annual report must be filed with the Secretary of State with an $80 privilege fee. The first report is not required until the corporation is six months old; blank annual reports are provided by the contact office and on the Web site. The report is due on the 15th day of the 6th month following the close of the taxable year.

LOBBYING

Contact:

Kansas Governmental Ethics Commission
109 SW Ninth—Suite 504
Topeka, KS 66612-1287
(785) 296-4219

Citation: K.S.A. 46-215 et seq. and administrative regulations K.A.R. 19-60-1 through 19-63-6.

Publications: *Handbook for Legislative Lobbyists* is available from the contact office.

Registration Required: Lobbyists must register with the Secretary of State prior to engaging in lobbying activity. Registration expires annually on December 31. Registration for succeeding calendar years may begin on or after October 1. There is a $35 registration fee if spending $1,000 or less in the registration year; $300 if spending more than $1,000; $360 fee if an employee of a lobbying group or firm and not an owner or partner.

Forms to Use: *Lobbyist Registration Statement.*

Reporting requirements: Expenditure reports must be filed on the 10th of the month following each of the six reporting periods (January, February, March, April, May-August; September-December). The report includes lobbying expenditures itemized for food and beverages; entertainment, gifts, or payments; mass media communications; recreation; communications; and other. No itemization is required if expenditures did not exceed $100.

TAX EXEMPTIONS

Contact:

> Kansas Dept. of Revenue
> Docking State Office Building
> Room 150
> 915 SW Harrison Street
> Topeka, KS 66625
> (785) 368-8222

Citation: § 79-32, 113.

Requirements: Organizations exempt from federal income taxes are exempt from Kansas corporate income taxes. Some organizations are explicitly exempt under Kansas law from the sales and compensating use tax including YMCAs; YWCAs; the Salvation Army; church entities; nonprofit educational institutions; nonprofit hospitals; nonprofit blood tissue and organ banks; nonprofit historical societies and museums that are 501(c)(3)s; and non-commercial, educational TV and radio stations. Other organizations should write to the Department (2nd Floor, Docking State Office Building, Topeka, KS 66625) and request a private letter ruling. Applicants may call the Taxpayer Assistance Center (785-291-3614) in advance of the written request to informally explore whether their activities qualify the organization for exempt status. Each type of organization has a specific exemption certificate. The Department will assign a Tax Exemption Entity Identification Number to each exempt organization and issue a Tax Exempt Entity Exemption Certificate (Form PR-78), which is furnished by the organization to the retailer. For details, visit: http://www.ksrevenue.org/pdf/forms/pub1510.pdf

CHARITABLE SOLICITATION

Contact:

> Secretary of State
> 1st Floor, Memorial Hall
> 120 SW 10th Avenue
> Topeka, KS 66612
> (785) 296-4564 or
> (785) 296-4565

Citation: Charitable Organizations and Solicitations Act, K. S. A. 17-1760 et seq.

Publications: Forms and a copy of the statute are available from the contact office.

Initial Registration: Charitable organizations that raise more than $10,000 or have paid fundraisers must file a Form SC registration statement with a $35 registration fee, or may instead file a Uniform Registration Statement (URS). Some organizations are exempt from registering under Section 17-1762. The form discloses general information, purpose of the organization, IRS tax exemption status, purpose for contributions, names of professional fundraisers, fundraising costs, costs of fundraising as a percentage of contributions, and previous year financial statements. Must include Articles of Incorporation, Form 990, and IRS determination letter.

Annual Reports: Registrations expire on the last day of the sixth month following the month in which the fiscal year of the charitable organization ends, and must be renewed each year. A financial statement must be enclosed with each registration (IRS annual returns are acceptable for this purpose). If the organization received contributions exceeding $500,000, it must also file an audited financial statement. The registration statement, in addition to general information, requires a calculation of total costs as a percentage of contributions received.

Organization Solicitation Disclosure Requirements: See below.

Paid Solicitor Requirements: Must register annually. Registrations expire on June 30. All solicitations by professional solicitors must disclose the name, address and telephone number of the charity; the registration number for the charity; the solicitor's registration number; and that an annual financial report for the preceding fiscal year is on file with the Secretary of State. The fee is $25.

Fundraising Counsel Requirements: If counsel meets the definition of a professional fundraiser, then he/she must register as one. The fee is $25.

Kentucky

Central Switchboard: (502) 564-3130
State Web Home Page: http://www.kentucky.gov

INCORPORATION

Contact:

> Office of the Secretary of State Business
>   Filings
> State Capitol Building—Room 154
> 700 Capital Avenue
> PO Box 718
> Frankfort, KY 40602
> (502) 564-2848

Citation: KRS Chapter 273.

Publications Available: Kentucky Business Organizations Law and Rules (2002-2003 edition) is provided for a fee by calling 1-800-562-1197.

General Requirements: Articles of Incorporation must set forth the corporate name, purposes, street address, name of the initial registered agent, mailing address, number of directors constituting the initial board of directors and their names and addresses, and the name and address of each incorporator. At least three directors are required.

Corporate Name: Shall include the word "corporation" or "incorporated" or the abbreviation "Inc.," or the word "company" or the abbreviation "Co." If the word "company" or the abbreviation "Co." is used, it may not be immediately preceded by the word "and" or the abbreviation "&." This does not apply to corporations existing on June 13, 1968. Must be distinguishable upon the records from other business names in Kentucky. Shall not imply that the corporation is organized for purposes not permitted by law. May not have appositives or acronym/full name combinations.

Name Reservation: May be reserved for a nonrenewable period of 120 days for a $15 fee.

How to File: File one original and two copies of the Articles of Incorporation with the Secretary of State with an $8 fee. Two copies are returned; one copy must be filed with the county clerk of the county in which the registered office is located.

Other Filings/Reports: An annual report must be filed with the Secretary of State with general information, including the names and business addresses of the directors and principal officers. The first report is due between January 1 and June 30 after the year following the calendar year of incorporation. Subsequent reports are due between January 1 and June 30. There is a $4 filing fee, which can be paid online when filing electronically.

LOBBYING

Contact:

> Kentucky Legislative Ethics Commission
> 22 Mill Creek Park
> Frankfort, KY 40601
> (502) 573-2863

Citation: KRS 6.807.

Publications: Kentucky Legislative Ethics Code, statutes, relevant forms, and legal opinions are provided by the contact office.

Registration required: All lobbyists must register with the Commission. There is a two-year registration period, expiring on December 31 of each odd-numbered year. A $250 fee is required to be paid by the employer and covers one or more lobbyists. Registration requires the name of the lobbyist, employer, and a description of the bill or legislative action that is to be the target of the lobbying activity.

Expense Reporting: Required to be filed on the 15th day of January, February, March, April, May, and September. Expenditures reported include food, beverages, lodging, transportation, entertainment, and other expenses.

TAX EXEMPTIONS

Contact:

> *Office of Sales and Excise Taxes*
> *Division of Sales and Use Tax*
> *200 Fair Oaks Lane*
> *PO Box 181, Station 53*
> *Frankfort, KY 40620*
> *(502) 564-5170 (sales and use tax)*

Citation: §136.010—income tax exemption; § 139.010 et seq. —sales and use tax exemption.

Publications: Forms and instructions for applying for sales and use tax exemption are provided by the contact office and are available on the Web site.

Requirements: Organizations with federal 501(c) tax exemptions such as religious, educational, charitable, cemeteries that are exempt from property taxes, historical sites (must include a validation letter from the Kentucky Historical Commission) or like corporations not organized or conducted for pecuniary profit are exempt from income tax. All 501(c)(3)s are exempt from paying tax on the sales of tangible personal property or services to them, provided the property or services are used solely for the educational, charitable, or religious function. Most sales by such organizations are taxable. All nonprofits not engaged in the business of selling are exempt on the first $1,000 of sales made in any calendar year.

Application Procedure: Submit a 51A125 *Application for Purchase Exemption, Sales and Use Tax* (downloadable at: *http://www.revenue.ky.gov/forms/cursalefrm.htm)* to the contact office along with Articles of Incorporation, a detailed schedule of receipts and disbursements, and the IRS determination letter.

CHARITABLE SOLICITATION

Contact:

> *Consumer Protection Division*
> *Office of the Attorney General*
> *The Capitol, Suite 118*
> *700 Capitol Avenue*
> *Frankfort, KY 40601*
> *(502) 696-5389*

Citation: *Kentucky Charitable Solicitations Act,* KRS 367.650, et seq.; *Telephone Solicitations Act,* KRS 367.46951.

Publications: Both statutes and relevant forms are provided by the contact office.

Registration Requirements: All charitable organizations that are required to file a federal 990 with the Internal Revenue Service are required to register.

Initial Registration: Prior to solicitation, the organization must file its latest federal form 990 or, if newly formed, a notice of intent to solicit on a *Uniform Registration Statement* (see Chapter 15).

Annual Reports: Charitable organizations must file a copy of their federal 990s each year.

Organization Solicitation Disclosure Requirements: If solicitation is by telephone, the organization must disclose immediately the name of the solicitor, name of the charity, telephone number or address where the charity is located, and the town where the solicitor is physically located. The solicitor must immediately discontinue the solicitation "if the consumer responds in the negative."

Paid Solicitor Requirements: There is a $300 annual registration fee and $25,000 bonding requirement ($50,000 bonding for telephone solicitors); must undergo a background check by the Attorney General's Office paid for by the solicitor ($5 fee for "Request for Conviction Record").

Fundraising Consultant Requirements: Must pay a $50 annual fee plus the costs of a background check.

Louisiana

Central Switchboard: (225) 342-6600
State Web Home Page: http://www.state.la.us/

INCORPORATION

Contact:

Secretary of State
Corporations Section
PO Box 94125
Baton Rouge, LA 70804
(225) 925-4704

Citation: *Nonprofit Corporation Law*, R.S. 12 § 201 et seq.

General Requirements: One or more natural or artificial persons capable of contracting may form a nonprofit corporation. Articles must be notarized and must set forth corporate name; purpose(s), in general terms; duration if other than perpetual; that it is a nonprofit corporation; location and street address of the registered office and name and address of each registered agent; name, address, and signature of each incorporator; names, addresses, and terms of office of each initial director; whether it is organized on a stock basis, nonstock basis, or both, and information about shares if it is organized, in whole or in part, on a stock basis; qualifications of members if it has members; its tax ID number (optional); and optional provisions relating to the rights of shareholders and members. Filing must include a notarized affidavit of any registered agent accepting his or her appointment.

Corporate Name: Must be expressed in English letters or characters; shall not imply that it is an administrative agency of any parish, the state, or the U.S.; shall not contain the words "bank," "banking," "savings," "trust," "deposit," "insurance," "mutual," "assurance," "indemnity," "casualty," "fiduciary," "homestead," "building and loan," "surety," "security," "guarantee," "cooperative," "state," "parish," "redevelopment corporation," "electric cooperative," or "credit union." Shall be distinguishable from others without written consent.

Name Reservation: May be reserved for a 60-day period for a fee of $25. May be renewed for two 30-day periods.

How to File: File Articles of Incorporation with the Secretary of State with a $60 filing fee. A certified copy is returned along with a certificate of incorporation. File the certified copy and a copy of the certificate with the Office of the Recorder of Mortgages of the parish in which the registered office is located, within 30 days of filing with the Secretary of State.

Other Filings/Reports: An annual report must be filed with the Secretary of State on or before the anniversary date of incorporation each year disclosing general information and tax I.D. number. There is a $5 filing fee (which does not apply to churches).

LOBBYING

Contact:

Louisiana Board of Ethics
2415 Quail Drive, 3rd Fl.
Baton Rouge, LA 70808
(225) 763-8777 or (800) 842-8780

Citation: *Lobbyist Disclosure Act*, R.S. 24:50 et seq.; R.S. 49:71 et seq.

Publications: *Summary of Lobbyist Disclosure Act* is available from the contact office or by visiting the Web site at: *http://www.ethics.state.la.us*

Registration Required: Persons employed to lobby state legislators or executive branch officials or who receive compensation of any kind to lobby such persons and who make expenditures of $500 or more in a calendar year for lobbying purposes must register with the Board. Registration must occur within five days of employment as a lobbyist or within five days after the first activity requiring registration as a lobbyist. The registration form includes general information, the name of the employer, names of clients, a 2-inch by 2-inch photograph, and a $110 registration fee. Registrations expire on December 31 of each year.

Forms to Use: For Legislative Lobbying: *Lobbying Registration Form, Supplemental Lobbying Form, Lobbying Expenditure Report.* For Executive Branch Lobbying: *Executive Lobbying Registration Form, Executive Lobbying Supplemental Lobbying Form, Executive Lobbying Expenditure Reporting Designation, Executive Lobbying Expenditure Report, Executive Lobbying Expenditure Report Attachment, Executive Lobbying Principal/Employer's Expenditure Report, Executive Lobbying Principal/Employer's Expenditure Report Attachment.*

Reporting requirements: Legislative lobbying and executive lobbying require separate reporting. An aggregate total of all lobbying expenditures for a reporting period and an aggregate total of all lobbying expenditures for a calendar year must be included in every report. Expenditures on a legislator or executive branch official exceeding $50 on any one occasion or totaling an aggregate of more than $250 in a six-month reporting period require listing the legislator's or executive branch official's name and the total expenditures made on that person. Legislative lobbyists must also disclose expenditures for receptions or social gatherings to which the entire legislature or committees or delegations thereof are invited, and executive branch lobbyists must disclose expenditures for receptions and social gatherings to which more than 25 executive branch officials are invited. Reports must be filed semi-annually. Reports are due by August 15 for the period January 1-June 30 and by February 15 for the period July 1-December 31.

TAX EXEMPTIONS

Contact:

> Department of Revenue
> Taxpayer Services Division
> PO Box 201
> Baton Rouge, LA 70821
> (225) 219-7356 (sales tax)
> (225) 219-0067 (corporate income & franchise)

Citation: R.S. 47 §287.501; R.S. 47:301(8)(d);(10)(q).

Requirements: Most organizations exempt from federal income taxes are exempt from state income taxes. Purchases of songbooks, bibles, and literature for classroom instruction by nonprofit religious organizations are statutorily exempt from sales/use tax, although a court ruling, on appeal, requires this tax to be collected. Approved nonprofit private and parochial schools that have been certified by the Department of Education as having complied with the Dodd-Brumfield decision may purchase books, workbooks, computers, computer software, films, videos, and audiotapes for classroom instruction exempt from the sales/use tax, provided Department approval of the exemption is obtained prior to its being claimed. See *http://www.rev.state.la.us/ forms/publications/1002(6_03).pdf* for details about current exemptions.

CHARITABLE SOLICITATION

Contact:

> Department of Justice
> Consumer Protection Section
> PO Box 94005
> Baton Rouge, LA 70804-9005
> (225) 326-6465

Citation: Act 1053, 1995 Regular Session, R.S. 51:§1901 et seq.

Initial Registration: At least 10 days prior to soliciting for contributions, charities utilizing professional solicitors must file a *Charitable Solicitations Questionnaire* with the Consumer Protection Section. The questionnaire includes general information; whether the organization is federally tax-exempt (a copy of the IRS determination letter must be attached, if so); how funds will be raised; information about professional solicitors used; and financial information (must attach a copy of a certified financial statement or current budget or annual report).

Charities that utilize a professional solicitor must register. There is a $25 filing fee. They must include a copy of their Articles of Incorporation and bylaws, IRS determination letters, copies of current financial statements and/or annual reports, copies of all contracts with professional solicitors, and lists of other states in which the organizations are registered.

Annual Reports: Registration must be renewed annually.

Organization Solicitation Disclosure Requirements: Any charitable organization solicitor, upon request to a donor, must provide information substantiating the claims of the charity that it is a bona-fide charity or that the organization delivers certain goods or services; its disclosure statement; the names and residential addresses of incorporators, shareholders, directors, officers, sales persons, and employees; and any information or documentation required under the *Louisiana Unfair Trade Practices and Consumer Protection Law.*

Paid Solicitor Requirements: Not less than 10 days prior to doing business in the state, professional solicitors must register with the Department by filing an application, application fee, and bond. The fee is $150; the bond is $25,000. Registration is valid for one year. Professional solicitors must, prior to an oral solicitation or at the same time a written solicitation is made, disclose a clear and conspicuous statement that the solicitation is being performed by a for-profit fundraising firm; the identity of that firm; and the specific charitable purpose for which the solicitation is being conducted. Upon request, they must state the percentage of funds that go to the charity, the percentage of funds that go to the for-profit fundraising firm, and the percentage of funds to the charitable organization that is used for a charitable purpose.

Fundraising Counsel Requirements: None.

Maine

Central Switchboard: (207) 624-9494
State Web Home Page: http://www.maine.gov

INCORPORATION

Contact:

Secretary of State
Bureau of Corporations, Elections and
    Commissions
101 State House Station
Augusta, ME 04333-0101
(207) 624-7752

Citation: *Maine Law on Nonprofit Corporations,* Title 13-B, §401 et seq.

Publications Available: *Maine Law on Nonprofit Corporations* is available at: *http://ww.maine.gov/portal/government/law.htm/#laws*

General Requirements: Articles of Incorporation must set forth the corporate name; whether the organization is a public benefit or mutual benefit corporation, purpose(s); name of registered agent (must be a Maine resident or another corporation other than your own) and address of the registered office; number of directors (must be at least 3); minimum and maximum number of directors; whether the corporation will have members; whether no substantial part of the activities of the corporation shall be the carrying on of propaganda, or otherwise attempting to influence legislation and whether the corporation will be prohibited from intervening in any political campaign on behalf of any candidate for public office, consistent with 501(c)(3) status; provisions relating to corporate dissolution and private inurement; other provisions relating to regulation of the internal affairs; the names, addresses, and signatures of each incorporator (only one required); and the signature of the registered agent.

Corporate Name: Shall not contain language stating or implying that the corporation is organized for a purpose other than that permitted by Section 201 and the corporation's articles of incorporation; must be distinguishable from others.

Name Reservation: May be reserved for 120 days for a $5 fee.

How to File: File Articles of Incorporation using form MNPCA-6 with a $40 filing fee.

Other Filings/Reports: An annual report must be filed with the Secretary of State disclosing general information, including the names and addresses of the president, treasurer, registered agent, secretary or clerk, and directors. Reports are due no later than June 1 of the following year for each corporation on file as of December 31 in any year. The filing fee is $35.

LOBBYING

Contact:

Commission on Governmental Ethics &
    Election Practices
#135 State House Station
Augusta, ME 04333
(207) 287-4179

Citation: 3 M.R.S.A. §§311 et seq.

Publications: *Lobbyist Disclosure Procedures* is available from the contact office or at: *http://www.maine.gov/ethics*

Registration Required: Lobbyists who lobby at least eight hours in any calendar month must register with the Commission. The fee is $200 for each lobbyist and $100 for each "lobbyist associate" (partners, associates, or employees of lobbyists who lobby on behalf of the employer named on the lobbyist registration and lobby more than eight hours in any calendar month).

Forms to Use: *Lobbyist/Employer Joint Registration* form. Must be filed no later than 15 business days after a lobbyist is required to register.

Reporting Requirements: Monthly reports are required to be filed, due by 5 p.m. on the 15th day following the month that is the subject of the report, or the next business day when the 15th day is on a weekend or holiday. The report specifies the dollar amount of compensation received for lobbying, preparation of documents, and research; the dollar amount of lobbying expenditures; and the legislative action taken by bill number or topic. Each registered lobbyist and employer must file an annual disclosure report by 5 p.m. on December 30 following the year that is the subject of the report. Itemization includes expenses made on behalf of any official in the legislative branch or a member of that person's immediate family totaling $25 or more in any calendar month.

TAX EXEMPTIONS

Contact:

> Maine Revenue Services
> PO Box 1065
> Augusta, ME 04332-1065
> (207) 624-9693

Citation: 36 M.R.S.A., Section 1760; Rule No. 302 (08-125 CMR 302).

Requirements: Must be eligible for exemption under Section 1760 of the Sales and Use Tax Law. That section lists the types of organizations eligible for exemption, which include hospitals, schools, libraries, community action agencies, and more than three dozen other types of organizations. Organizations exempt from federal income taxes are exempt from state income tax.

Application Procedure: Apply for an exemption certificate from the Maine Revenue Services; include a copy of the IRS determination letter. Call (207) 624-9742 for an exemption application. Each type of organization has a different application form.

CHARITABLE SOLICITATION

Contact:

> Department of Professional and Financial
>   Regulation
> Office of Licensing and Registration
> 35 State House Station
> Augusta, ME 04333-0035
> (207) 624-8624

Citation: Title 9, Chapter 385 §5001 et seq.

Publications Available: Forms and a copy of the statute are available from the contact office or *http://www.state.me.us/pfr/olr/categories/cat10.htm*

General Requirements: Charitable organizations that intend to solicit contributions in the State of Maine or to have contributions solicited on their behalf are required to register with the Department. Registrations expire on November 30. Initial and renewal charitable organization registration fees are $100 annually. Initial applicants must submit a $100 application fee along with a photocopy of the charity's IRS determination letter. If upon renewal a charitable organization's contributions in the previous fiscal year exceed $30,000, a $100 filing fee must be submitted. IRS Form 990s must be submitted with renewal applications. Organizations exempt from registration requirements include those that solicit primarily within their membership and solicitation is conducted by members; those soliciting contributions for the relief of any individual specified by name at the time of solicitation when all of the contributions collected are turned over to the named beneficiary for that person's use; and charities that do not intend to solicit and receive, and do not solicit and receive, contributions in excess of $10,000 during the calendar year or do not receive contributions from more than ten persons during a calendar year if fundraising is carried out by volunteers and none of the income inures to the benefit of any officer or member. Bona fide religious organizations are also exempt. Exempt organizations must annually submit a $10 fee to the Department; a notarized affidavit; the most recent financial form submitted to the IRS; and, unless already provided, a copy of its IRS determination letter. Renewals are $25.

Annual Reports: See above. Charities must file a report by September 30 of each year covering the previous calendar year's activities.

Organization Solicitation Disclosure Requirements: See below.

Paid Solicitor Requirements: Must pay a $200 registration fee, post a $25,000 bond, and pay a $50 application fee. Solicitors must disclose prior to a request for contributions the name and address of the charitable organization. Professional solicitors, fundraising counsel, or commercial coventurers must fully disclose prior to the request for contributions their name and address, and the following statement: "(Insert name of professional fundraising counsel, professional solicitor or commercial coventurer) is a professional charitable fundraiser." A fundraising activity report is due by September 20 of each year covering the previous calendar year's activities.

Fundraising Counsel Requirements: Must pay a $200 registration fee, post a $25,000 bond, pay a $50 application fee, and file a report by September 30 each year covering the previous calendar year's activities. See *Paid Solicitor Requirements* above.

Maryland

Governor's Office: (410) 974-3901
State Web Home Page: http://www.maryland.gov

INCORPORATION

Contact:

> State Department of Assessments and
>   Taxation
> Corporate Charter Division
> Room 801
> 301 West Preston Street
> Baltimore, MD 21201
> (888) 246-5941 (in Maryland)
> (410) 767-1340

Citation: Annotated Code of Maryland, Section 2-101 et seq.

Publications Available: *Guide to Legal Aspects of Doing Business in Maryland* is available at: *http://www.oag.state.md.us/legalaspects.doc*

General Requirements: Articles must set forth the names and addresses of incorporators (minimum of one; must be at least 18); corporate name; address of the principal place of business (cannot be a PO Box); name and address of registered agent (must be in Maryland and cannot be a PO Box); that the corporation has no authority to issue capital stock; the number and names of initial directors; and provisions that are optional, such as IRS-required language for tax-exempt status.

Corporate Name: Must contain the word "company," (if it is not preceded by the word "and" or a symbol for "and"), "Corporation," "Incorporated," "Limited," "Inc.," "Corp.," or "Ltd." Cannot be misleadingly similar to a name already on record in Maryland. May not contain any word or phrase that indicates or implies that it is organized for any purpose not contained in its charter.

Name Check/Name Reservation: May be reserved for a period of 30 days for a fee of $25.

How to File: File Articles of Incorporation using sample form found at: *http://www.dat.state.md.us/sdatweb/nonstock.pdf* of the organization plus a $120 filing fee.

Other Filings/Reports: Every corporation is required to file an annual report each calendar year following the year in which it was incorporated. These forms are provided automatically by the Department and are due by April 15. There is no fee for nonprofit corporations.

LOBBYING

Contact:

> State Ethics Commission
> 45 Calvert Street, 3rd Fl.
> Suite 200
> Annapolis, MD 21401
> (410) 260-7746
> (877) 669-6085

Citation: *Maryland Public Ethics Law*; Md. Code Ann.; Title 15, Subtitle 7.

Publications: *Maryland Public Ethics Law— Lobbying Law Requirements* is available online and from the contact office.

Registration Required: Lobbyists who incur more than $500 in lobbying-related expenses during a reporting period or receive $2,500 or more as compensation for lobbying must register. Similar expense-related registration requirements apply to those who lobby the executive branch. There is a $50 registration fee. Those who expend $2,000 or more for grass-roots lobbying in a reporting period must also register. The registration form consists of general information disclosure, the matters that will be subject of lobbying, and employer identification. Registration expires each October 31.

Forms to Use: Ethics Commission Form No. 3.

Reporting Requirements: Lobbyists must file a *General Lobbying Activity Report* (Form No. 4) by May 31 for activities during the period November 1- April 30; and by November 30 for activities May 1- October 31. These reports cover itemized expenses of compensation, meals, special events, meetings, gifts, office expenses, professional and technical research, publications, witness fees, and other expenses. Gifts of more than $75 must be disclosed on a separate reporting schedule; gifts of tickets, meals, and beverages to a legislator or member of a legislator's immediate family worth more than $20 must be reported on a separate form.

TAX EXEMPTIONS

Contact:

> Comptroller of Maryland
> Revenue Administration Division
> 301 W. Preston Street, Room 408
> Annapolis, MD 21411
> (410) 260-7980
> 1-800-MD Taxes (corporation taxes)
> 1-800-492-1751 (sales taxes)

Citation: §10-104—income tax exemption; §11-204— sales and use tax exemption.

Requirements: 501(c)(3) organizations are exempt from the corporate income tax other than on unrelated business taxable income. Sales and Use Tax exemptions are codified in Section 11-204 of the Tax General Article. Consult the statute or the contact office for more details.

Application Procedure: For income tax exemption, file IRS determination letter with a cover letter requesting that the Comptroller recognize the federal exemption. For sales and use tax exemption, file a combined Registration Application with the Comptroller (obtained by requesting document #2001 when calling 410-767-1300 or 800-492-1751) and include a copy of the IRS determination letter and Articles of Incorporation.

CHARITABLE SOLICITATION

Contact:

> Office of the Secretary of State
> Charitable Organizations Division
> State House
> Annapolis, MD 21401
> (410) 974-5534

Citation: Maryland Solicitations Act, Business Regulation Article §6-101 et seq.

Publications: Giving Wisely, a copy of the statute and forms, and a Registration Instructions and Check List sheet are available from the contact office.

Initial Registration: Every charitable organization must submit a registration statement to the Secretary of State and receive a letter of approval before contributions are solicited if it collects $25,000 or more in a year or uses a professional solicitor. Organizations receiving less than $25,000 in contributions are required to submit a one-page annual "Exempt Organization Fund-Raising Notice." The registration fees vary with contributions collected ($0 if less than $25,000, $50 for $25,000-$50,000; $75 for $50,001-$75,000, $100 if $75,001-$100,000, and $200 for at least $100,001). An annual fee of $50 is required for charitable organizations that collect less than $25,000 but that use the services of a professional solicitor. In addition to general information, the registration requires a copy of the IRS determination letter and Articles of Incorporation; a copy of the federal 990 or financial information in a form required by the Secretary; an audit of gross contributions if they are at least $200,000, or a review if gross income from contributions is between $100,000 and $200,000; and a copy of any contracts with fundraising counsel or professional solicitors.

Annual Reports: Charitable organizations must submit annual reports within 6 months after the end of each fiscal year containing financial information and supporting audit/review and any changes to the previous annual report or registration statement.

Organization Solicitation Disclosure Requirements: Written solicitations must provide a disclosure statement that information filed can be obtained from the Secretary of State.

Paid Solicitor Requirements: Must register by filing an SS-PS-0001 form, pay a $300 fee, and post a $25,000 bond or irrevocable letter of credit. Written agreements are required with the charity. Copies of these agreements must be provided to the Secretary of State.

Fundraising Counsel Requirements: Must register and pay a $200 registration fee. Written agreements are required with the charity. Copies of these agreements must be provided to the Secretary of State.

Massachusetts

Central Switchboard: (866) 888-2808 (toll-free)
State Web Home Page: http://www.mass.gov/

INCORPORATION

Contact:

> Corporations Division
> Secretary of the Commonwealth
> One Ashburton Place; Room 1717
> Boston, MA 02108
> (617) 727-9640

Citation: General Laws, Chapter 180.

Publications Available: Sample Articles of Organization and all other forms are available from the contact office and the Web site at: *http://www.state.ma.us/sec/cor*

General Requirements: Articles must set forth the corporate name; purpose; information about its members if it chooses to have members (or may be included in the bylaws); provisions relating to conduct and regulation of the business, voluntary dissolution, and limiting or defining powers of the corporation, its members or directors; that the bylaws have been duly adopted by the board and its officers and initial directors have been duly elected; the effective date of the incorporation; the street address of the principal office (not a PO Box); the name, residential address, and post office address of each director and officer; the fiscal year of the corporation; the name and business address of the resident agent; and signatures of incorporators (may be another corporation represented with the signature of someone with authority). It must include one of the following words: Limited (Ltd.), Incorporated (Inc.), or Corporation (Corp.), unless it is a religious organization. The name must not be the same as, or similar to, another entity operating or having recently operated in the Commonwealth.

Name Check/Name Reservation: May be reserved for 60 days for a $30 fee, and renewable once for an additional 60 days, in writing, for an additional $30 fee. A preliminary name check is available by calling (617) 727-9640 or by checking the name reservation section and corporate database on the Web site.

How to File: All forms are available at the Web site at the "download corporate forms" link. The Articles may be filed with a $35 fee either online, by fax filing, or mailed to the Division's office. Copies are not mailed back unless specifically requested, the photocopy enclosed with the filing, and accompanied by a postage-paid return envelope. All filings can be viewed as images in the corporate database.

Other Filings/Reports: An annual report must be filed online, by fax, or by mail with the Secretary of the Commonwealth's Corporations Division. This report is due November 1. The fee is $15.

LOBBYING

Contact:

> Secretary of the Commonwealth
> Public Records Division
> Lobbyist Section
> One Ashburton Place
> Room 1719
> Boston, MA 02108-1512
> (617) 727-2832

Citation: M6L Chapter 3, Sec. 39-50.

Publications: *Lobbying In Massachusetts* is available from the contact office.

Registration Required: All lobbyists and employers of lobbyists must register annually by December 15, using Form 1 *(Notice of Employment Agreement)*, 2 *(Executive or Legislative Agent Registration)*, or 3 *(Authorization of Executive or Legislative Agent)*, and provide three passport size photographs (or have them taken at the registration office). The registration fee of $1000 for lobbying entities and $100 for each lobbyist is waived for nonprofit organizations upon written request. Registration and photos expire at the end of each legislative session for that year. Registration is permitted by mail for lobbyists located outside the 508 or 617 area codes, but they must provide three passport-size photographs.

Reporting Requirements: Financial disclosure reports *(Form 43-Executive and Legislative*

Reporting Statement) must be filed semi-annually covering the periods of January 1- June 30 (due July 15) and July 1-December 31 (due January 15). The reports must include the total amount of lobbying expenses, and must be itemized when the amount during a single day is $35 or more. Itemization categories include information about the amount, date, to whom the expenditure was paid, purpose, bill number, and campaign contributions (to be reported on Form 43C). If the expenditure was made for meals, entertainment, or transportation, all persons participating must be listed.

TAX EXEMPTIONS

Contact:

> Department of Revenue
> Customer Service Bureau
> PO Box 7010
> Boston, MA 02204
> (617) 887-MDOR
> (800) 392-6089 (in Massachusetts)

Citation: AP 301.2 —corporate excise—G.L. c. 63, § 30, 1 and 2; AP 101—sales and use tax.

Publications: A Guide to Sales and Use Tax booklet and Massachusetts Trustee Tax Form TA-1, Application for Registration and Instructions are available from the contact office.

Requirements: Generally, 501(c)(3) organizations are exempt from paying sales/use tax and all 501(c) organizations are exempt from paying corporate excise tax, other than unrelated business income tax.

Application Procedure: All businesses file TA-1 forms. There are lines on the form that indicate application for tax-exempt status that require an attached copy of the IRS determination letter. An organization that has a 501(c)(3) determination by the IRS pending may apply for a temporary certificate of exemption from sales by submitting IRS Form 1023, a copy of its Articles of Incorporation, and bylaws. If issued, the certificate is effective for two years or until 30 days after a determination by the IRS is provided. To obtain exemption, exempt purchaser must submit a Sales Tax Exemption Certificate (Form ST-5C) and a copy of the Certificate of Exemption issued to the organization by the Department (Form ST-2).

CHARITABLE SOLICITATION

Contact:

> Division of Public Charities
> Office of the Attorney General
> One Ashburton Place (for mailing)
> 100 Cambridge Street (for visits)
> Boston, MA 02108-1698
> (617) 727-2200 x1701

Citation: G.L. c. 68, §§ 18-35 and G.L. c. 12 §§ 8 et seq.

Initial Registration: The initial registration fee is $50. Must register annually and pay a $35-$250 license fee unless the organization raises less than $5,000 in the calendar year or does not receive contributions from more than ten persons. Registration information includes copy of charter, Articles of Incorporation, statement of purpose, and bylaws. Organizations must have a valid Certificate of Solicitation prior to soliciting for contributions. See additional requirements and exemptions at: http://www.mass.gov/ago

Annual Reports: Financial statements (Form PC) must be filed within 4½ months of the end of the fiscal year; audited financial statements must be included if the organization receives $500,000 or more. A reviewed financial statement is required if gross support and revenue is between $100,000 and $500,000.

Organization Solicitation Disclosure Requirements: See below. Information may not be deceptive. Disclosure required only if using a paid fundraiser.

Paid Solicitor Requirements: Must register, post $10,000 bond, and pay a $300 fee; must file Form 11-A solicitation campaign reports by February 28 of the year after a campaign takes place; must file Form 10-A and a copy of the contract with the charity for each solicitation campaign; professional solicitors must state that they are paid fundraisers; the potential donor must be given the name, address, and telephone number of the charitable organization; when selling advertising space for a publication, the solicitor must tell the potential donor how many copies will be published and where the copies will be distributed; they may not solicit for organizations that are not themselves registered and in compliance; if asked, they must tell a potential donor how much is going to the charity.

Fundraising Counsel Requirements: Must pay a $200 fee. Commercial coventurers must post a $10,000 bond and pay a $50 registration fee. Commercial coventurers must register and file like solicitors, but pay a $50 registration fee.

Michigan

Central Switchboard: (517) 373-1837
State Web Home Page: http://www.michigan.gov

INCORPORATION

Contact:

*Michigan Department of Labor and
    Economic Growth
Bureau of Commercial Services
Corporation Division
PO Box 30054
Lansing, MI 48909-7554
(517) 241-6470*

Citation: M.S.A. 21.101 et seq.

Publications Available: Forms and publications are available at the Web site: *http://www.michigan.gov/corporations*

General Requirements: Articles of Incorporation must set forth the corporate name; purposes (it is not sufficient to state that the corporation may engage in any activity within the purposes for which corporations may be organized under the Act); whether organized on a stock or non-stock basis; description of real property assets; address of the registered office; name of the resident agent at that office; name, address, and signature of each incorporator; and additional provisions that are optional.

Corporate Name: May not contain a word or phrase implying a purpose different than permitted by the Articles; shall not be the same as, or confusingly similar to, another entity of the state; shall not contain a word or phrase or abbreviation or derivative thereof that is prohibited or restricted by any other statute unless that restriction has been complied with.

Name Reservation: May be reserved for four calendar months following the calendar month that contains the date the reservation was made for a fee of $10; up to two extensions of two months may be granted.

How to File: File one legible original form C&S 502 Articles of Incorporation with $20 Filing fee. The document must be signed in ink by each incorporator, but incorporators may, by resolution, designate one incorporator to sign on their behalf, provided a copy of that resolution is attached.

Other Filings/Reports: An annual Corporate Information Update is required to be filed with the administrator on or before October 1 each year after the year of formation containing general information about the corporation, the nature and kind of business that the corporation has engaged in during the year covered by the report, and the names of officers and directors. The fee is $20. Domestic nonprofit corporations can file online.

LOBBYING

Contact:

*Michigan Department of State
Bureau of Elections
PO Box 20126
Lansing, MI 48901-0726
(517) 373-2540*

Citation: *The Michigan Lobby Registration Act,* Public Act 472 of 1978, MCL 4.411 et seq.

Publications: A copy and summary of the statute and forms are available from the contact office.

Registration Required: Lobbyists who make expenditures of more than $2,125 to lobby a number of public officials, or spend at least $550 to lobby a single public official, in any 12-month period, must register within 15 calendar days after exceeding these thresholds. Lobbyist agents (those who receive compensation or reimbursement of more than $550 for lobbying on behalf of employers or clients during any 12-month period) must register within three calendar days of exceeding the threshold. These thresholds are adjusted annually based on the Detroit Consumer Price Index (the amounts quoted are for 2007).

Forms to Use: LR-1E, *Registration.*

Reporting Requirements: Lobbyists and lobbyist agents must submit a financial report on August 31 (covering the period January 1-July 31) and January 31 (covering the period August 1-December 31) each year detailing activities and expenditures. They must submit a list of persons compensated or reimbursed in excess of $21 for lobbying on their behalf. Expenditures are categorized by food and beverage for public officials, mass mailings and advertising, and all other lobbying expenses.

TAX EXEMPTIONS

Contact:

Michigan Department of Treasury
Richard H. Austin Building
430 West Allegan St.
Lansing, MI 48922
(517) 636-4730 (Customer Contact Div.)
800-827-4000 (income tax information)

Citation: MCL 205.54a—sales tax; MCL 205.94—use tax

Publications: *Revenue Administrative Bulletin 1995-3, Sales and Use Tax— Nonprofit Entities* is available from the contact office or at: *http://www.michigan.gov/treasury*

Requirements: Organizations exempt from federal income taxes are exempt from state income tax, other than unrelated business income tax; most 501(c)(3) and 501(c)(4) organizations, nonprofit schools, nonprofit hospitals, and churches are statutorily exempt from Michigan sales and use taxes. Some sales by such organizations are exempt if less than $5,000 for the calendar year.

Application Procedure: A 1994 law eliminated the application process for sales and use tax exemptions. For exemption, the vendor should be presented with a copy of the IRS determination letter and a Form 3372, *Michigan Sales and Use Tax Certificate of Exemption* form, which is available from the contact office or at: *http://www.michigan.gov/treasury*

CHARITABLE SOLICITATION

Contact:

Department of Attorney General
Charitable Trust Division
Williams Building

525 W. Ottawa St.--6th Fl.
Lansing, MI 48933-1067
(517) 373-1152

Citation: *Charitable Organizations and Solicitations Act,* 1975 PA 169, as amended, MCLA 400.271, et seq.

Publications: A copy of the statute is available from the contact office and Web site.

Initial Registration: All those who request or receive charitable contributions in excess of $8,000, or intend to receive more than $8,000 annually or who pay or compensate persons for fundraising services, with some statutory exemptions, must obtain a license prior to solicitation, and file financial statements with the Attorney General before solicitations. The license application must include general and detailed financial information about the charitable organization, all methods by which solicitations will be made, and copies of contracts between the organization and professional fundraisers. Copies of solicitation materials must be supplied upon request of the Attorney General. The license expires six or seven months after the close of each fiscal year. There is no registration fee.

Annual Reports: Renewal applications should be submitted 30 days before the expiration date of registration.

Organization Solicitation Disclosure Requirements: None.

Paid Solicitor Requirements: Must post $10,000 bond and be licensed annually (using form DAG 009-007). The application form must include the surety bond, Articles of Incorporation (if incorporated), copies of all contracts with organizations that solicit contributions, the *Registration of Professional Solicitor* form for individual solicitors hired by the professional fundraiser, and campaign financial statements for certain campaigns and special events. Licenses expire each year on June 30th.

Fundraising Counsel Requirements: Same requirements as paid solicitors.

Minnesota

Central Switchboard: (651) 296-2803
State Web Home Page: http://www.state.mn.us/

INCORPORATION

Contact:

Secretary of State
Business Services
60 Empire Drive
Suite 100
Saint Paul, MN 55103
(877) 551-6767

Citation: *Minnesota Nonprofit Corporation Act,* Minnesota Statute Chapter §317A.001 et seq.

Publications Available: A blank form is provided by the contact office, and all forms are available at: *http://www.sos.state.mn.us*

General Requirements: One or more adult natural persons may act as incorporators. Articles of Incorporation must include corporate name; street address for the registered office (PO Box not acceptable); number of shares that the corporation is authorized to issue (nonprofit corporations may issue shares); name, address, and signature of each incorporator (only one required); and a contact name and telephone number.

Corporate Name: A corporate designation is not required; must be in the English language or expressed in English letters or characters; shall not contain a word or phrase that shows or implies that it may not be incorporated under Minnesota law; must be distinguishable from others or, if not distinguishable, must obtain written permission to use the name.

Name Reservation: May be reserved for 12-month periods for a fee of $35, Renewals of name reservations are permitted.

How to File: File form *State of Minnesota Secretary of State Articles of Incorporation, Business and Nonprofit Corporations* along with a $70 filing fee. Incorporators may file their own form of Articles if the standard form does not meet their needs and requirements.

Other Filings/Reports: An annual registration is required on forms provided by the Secretary of State. The report is due on or before December 31. There is no fee for annual registration, unless the corporation is not in good standing.

LOBBYING

Contact:

Campaign Finance and Public Disclosure
Board
1st Floor South, Centennial Building
658 Cedar Street
St. Paul, MN 55155-1603
(651) 296-5148

Citation: Minn. Stat. § 10A. and Minn. Rules 4501, 4511 and 4525.

Publications: *Lobbyist and Lobbyist Principals Handbook* is available from the contact office.

Registration Required: All lobbyists must register within five days of meeting the criteria for registration. Lobbyists file a *Lobbyist Registration Form* with the Board. The registration threshold is being paid more than $3,000 in a year or, if not paid, spending more than $250 in a calendar year for lobbying, including grassroots lobbying. Registration is permanent until a termination report is filed.

Reporting Requirements: Lobbyists must provide reports due June 15 (for January 1-May 31 reporting period); and January 15 (for June 1-December 31 reporting period). Reports must be filed even if there are no reportable receipts or disbursements. Reports of those who employ lobbyists are due March 15 for the previous calendar year reporting period.

TAX EXEMPTIONS

Contact:

Minnesota Department of Revenue
Sales and Use Tax Division
Mail Station 6330

St. Paul, MN 55146-6330
(651) 297-5199 (corporate franchise tax)
(651) 296-6181 (sales tax)
(800) 657-3777 (toll free)

Citation: M.S. §290.05— corporate income taxes; M.S. §297A.70— sales tax.

Requirements: Organizations that are exempt from federal income tax are exempt from the corporate income tax, but must pay taxes on unrelated business income, using Form M4NP. The statute provides limited exemptions from the sales tax for certain nonprofits, including 501(c)(3)-type organizations, senior citizens groups, and youth groups.

Application Procedure: File form ST-16 for sales tax exemption. For exemption, organizations present Form ST-3 to vendor.

CHARITABLE SOLICITATION

Contact:

Office of the Attorney General
Charities Division
Suite 1200, Bremer Tower
445 Minnesota Street
St. Paul, MN 55101-2130
(651) 296-6172

Citation: The *Social and Charitable Organizations Act,* Minnesota Statutes §§ 309.50 et. seq.

Publications: *Fiduciary Duties of Directors of Charitable Organizations* booklet; *A Guide to Minnesota's Charities Laws* booklet; and a copy of the registration forms are available from the contact office.

Initial Registration: Organizations must register with the Attorney General's Office before they solicit contributions, unless they do not have paid staff or professional fundraisers and receive or plan to receive less than $25,000 in total contributions during an accounting year. The registration statement must include a financial statement using a form provided by the Attorney General, IRS 990, or an audited financial statement. There is a $25 registration fee. The Articles of Incorporation and IRS determination letter should also be attached.

Annual Reports: Charities must file an annual report no later than the fifteenth day of the seventh month after the close of the organization's fiscal year. The report must include a balance sheet, a statement of income and expense, and a statement of functional expenses; a list of its five highest paid directors, officers, and employees that receive total compensation of more than $50,000 together with total compensation paid to each; and a list of the five highest paid directors, officers, and employees of any related organization if that organization receives funds from the charity. Registered charities with total revenue in excess of $350,000 must provide an audited financial statement. There is a $25 fee to file the annual report.

Organization Solicitation Disclosure Requirements: Along with a written request or prior to an oral request for contributions, organizations and professional fundraisers must disclose the name and location of the charity by city and state; the tax deductibility of the contribution; a description of the program for which the solicitation is being carried out and, if different, a description of the programs and activities of the organization generally.

Paid Solicitor Requirements: Must register annually, pay a $200 fee, and post a $20,000 bond if the fundraiser will have custody or access to the contributions at any time; must provide a copy of the contract between themselves and the charity that, among other things, discloses the percentage or reasonable estimate of the amount raised that will go to the charity; must provide a completed "solicitation notice" providing information about the fundraising campaign, and a post-solicitation campaign financial report within 90 days after a campaign. Professional fundraisers must disclose their names during solicitations and that the solicitation is being conducted by a "professional fundraiser."

Fundraising Counsel Requirements: Must register and pay a $200 fee.

Note: The contact office specifically requested a statement that those interested in these requirements refer to the statute for specific definitions and requirements.

Mississippi

Central Switchboard: (601) 359-1000
State Web Home Page: http://www.ms.gov

INCORPORATION

Contact:

Office of the Mississippi Secretary of State
PO Box 136
Jackson, MS 39205-0136
(601) 359-1633
1-800-256-3494

Citation: *Mississippi Nonprofit Corporation Act,*
Section 79-11-101 et seq. of the Mississippi Code
of 1972.

Publications Available: All forms are available at
the Web site: *http://www.sos.state.ms.us*

General Requirements: Articles of Incorporation
must set forth whether the corporation is for-profit
or nonprofit; the corporate name; the future
effective date (if applicable); the period of duration;
the name and street address of the registered
agent and registered office; the name, address, and
signature of each incorporator; and other optional
provisions.

Corporate Name: Nonprofit organizations are not
required to provide a corporate name ending. No
language shall be included that implies a purpose
other than permitted by law or its Articles; must be
distinguishable from others on the record.

Name reservation: May be reserved for a 180-day
period for a non-refundable fee of $25.

How to File: File Articles on bar-coded form F0001
along with a $50 filing fee; forms must be com-
pleted suitable for scanning by a computer.

Other Filings/Reports: Any amendment, agent
changes, mergers, or corrections can be filed upon
the completion of the proper bar-coded application
and submission of the appropriate filing fees. At
the preference of the Secretary of State, a status
report shall be filed by each nonprofit corporation
every five years.

LOBBYING

Contact:

Mississippi Secretary of State
Lobbyist Registration and Reporting
401 Mississippi Street
PO Box 136
Jackson, MS 39205-0136
(601) 359-6353

Citation: *Lobbying Law Reform Act of 1994,* Miss.
Code Ann. §5-8.

Publications: *Lobbying in Mississippi Handbook,*
forms, and a copy of the statute are provided by
the contact office and at the Web site.

Registration Required: Lobbyists must register by
January 1 or within five days of becoming employed as a lobbyist. The lobbying cycle extends
from January 1 through December 31, and registration is required on a calendar year basis. The
registration form discloses general information
about the lobbyist and the lobbyist's client and the
specific issues to be lobbied. The fee is $25 annu-
ally per registration. Clients may employ more
than one lobbyist, and lobbyists may represent
more than one client. A numbered certificate is
issued for each registration.

Forms to Use: *Lobbyist's Registration Form* (Form
R); *Lobbyist's Legislative Expenditure Report* (Form E);
Lobbyist's Annual Report (Form A); *Lobbyist's Client
Annual Report* (Form C).

Reporting Requirements: Lobbyists are required
to file two legislative expenditure reports (Form E)
and an annual report (Form A) for each registration.
Additionally, the lobbyist's client is required to file
one annual report (Form C). The first legislative
report period is from the legislative convening date
through February 25. The report is due February 25.
The second legislative report covers February 26
through *sine die* adjournment, and is due 10 days
after *sine die*. The form requires itemized disclosure of each reportable expenditure made or
promised to a public official or employee. The report
also discloses the provider's name, the value of the
payment, the object that was given or promised,
the date, and the place given or promised. Lobbyists must file a separate annual report for each

registration. A notarized original and two copies must be filed by January 30 of the year following registration. The lobbyist's annual report (Form A) is used to disclose all lobbying expenses and receipts during the calendar year. Lobbyist's clients must also file an annual report (Form C) disclosing all lobbying expenses during the calendar year. A notarized original and two copies must be filed by January 30 of the year following registration. Clients file a single annual report for all registrations.

TAX EXEMPTIONS

Contact:

> Mississippi State Tax Commission
> PO Box 1033
> Jackson, MS 39215-3338
> (601) 923-7015 (sales tax)
> (601) 923-7099 (corporate income tax)

Citation: §27-7-29 —corporate income tax; §27-13-63 —corporate franchise tax; §27-65-111 —sales tax exemption.

Requirements: Most corporations exempt from the federal income tax are also exempt from the state corporation income tax and corporation franchise tax. Limited exemptions are provided from the sales tax for certain named organizations, including nonprofit schools. Churches must pay sales tax. Consult the contact office or the statute for more information.

Application Procedure: Write a letter to the Department requesting the exemption; the Department will respond with an exemption determination letter. While none is required, most vendors request to see the determination letter from the Department certifying that the exemption is legitimate.

CHARITABLE SOLICITATION

Contact:

> Secretary of State
> Business Regulation and Enforcement
> PO Box 136
> Jackson, MS 39205
> (601) 359-1350
> 1-888-236-6167

Citation: Miss. Code Ann. §§79-11-501 et seq. (Supp. 1992).

Publications: A copy of the statute is available from the contact office.

Initial Registration: Prior to solicitation, charitable organizations must register with the Secretary of State, unless they have contributions less than $4,000 and have unpaid solicitors. Organizations with contributions of less than $4,000 must still file a Notice of Exemption in order to be exempt from registration requirements. There is a $50 nonrefundable annual registration fee. Registration is accomplished by using the Unified Registration Statement (URS), along with the Mississippi Supplement to the URS. The form discloses general information about the organization, its officials, and professional fundraisers, if any. Copies of any and all IRS forms must be filed. An audited financial statement for the most recently completed fiscal year must be filed if contributions are over $100,000 and/or a professional fundraiser is used. If a professional fundraiser is used, copies of contracts between the organization and the fundraiser must be filed. With the initial registration only, the organization must file a copy of its Articles of Incorporation, bylaws, and IRS determination letter. Registration remains in effect for one year.

Annual Reports: Registration must be renewed annually before the expiration date of the current registration using the Unified Registration Statement, Mississippi Supplement to this statement, and the Annual Financial Report Form (Form FS).

Organization Solicitation Disclosure requirements: All solicitations must be compliant with §79-11-523. The charity may not use registration to imply endorsement by the state.

Paid Solicitor Requirements: Must register annually, pay a $250 registration fee, and post a $10,000 bond. A Solicitation Campaign Notice must be filed prior to beginning a campaign, and a Campaign Finance Report must be filed at the end of a campaign. Prior to orally requesting a contribution or contemporaneously with written requests for a contribution, the solicitor/fundraiser must disclose the name of the fundraiser on file with the Secretary of State, that the solicitation is being conducted by a professional fundraiser, the name of the charity on file, and a description of how the contribution will be used for charitable purposes. Each written solicitation or confirmation must state: "The official registration and financial information of (insert charity's legal registered name) may be obtained from the Mississippi Secretary of State's office by calling 1-888-236-6167. Registration does not imply endorsement by the Secretary of State."

Fundraising Counsel Requirements: Must register, pay a $250 nonrefundable registration fee, and file copies of contracts. Registration expires on June 30 of each year.

Missouri

Central Switchboard: (573) 751-2000
State Web Home Page: http://www.mo.gov

INCORPORATION

Contact:

Secretary of State
Corporation Division
Kirkpatrick Information Center
PO Box 778
Jefferson City, MO 65102
(573) 751-4153

Citation: Chapter 355 RSMo.

Publications Available: *Corporation Laws Handbook* and a sample form are provided by the contact office.

General Requirements: Each corporation must have at least a president and/or chairman, secretary, and treasurer. The same person may hold more than one office simultaneously. At least three directors are required. Articles of Incorporation must set forth the corporate name; whether the corporation is a public or mutual benefit corporation; the period of duration; the name and street address of the registered agent and registered office; the name, address, and signature of each incorporator; whether the corporation has members; provisions relating to the distribution of assets on dissolution; the corporate purposes; and the effective date of the document if other than when filed.

Corporate Name: May not contain language stating or implying that it is organized for a purpose other than permitted by law and its articles of incorporation; must be distinguishable from other domestic or foreign corporations or limited partnerships authorized to transact business in the state.

Name Check/Name Reservation: May be reserved for a period of 60 days for a $25 fee; name check may be made by telephone, but this does not guarantee availability of the name.

How to File: File Corp. #52 *Articles of Incorporation of a Nonprofit Corporation* form in duplicate with original signatures and a $25 filing fee.

Other Filings/Reports: An annual report must be filed each year with the Secretary of State listing officers and directors. The fee is $45 if filed in hard copy or $20 if filed electronically. This report is due August 31 for other than new corporations. It may be filed online at: *http://www.sos.mo.gov/BusinessEntity/annualreport/reportstart.asp*

LOBBYING

Contact:

Missouri Ethics Commission
PO Box 1370
3411A Knipp Drive
Jefferson City, MO 65109
(573) 751-2020
1-800-392-8660

Citation: Section 105.470-482 RSMo.

Publications: See the office's Web site at: *http://www.mec.mo.gov* for current information and publications.

Registration Required: There are four types of lobbyists under the act—executive lobbyist, legislative lobbyist, judicial lobbyist, and elected government official lobbyist. Lobbyists must register annually with the Commission if they are engaging in lobbying activities. Registration must occur within five days of beginning lobbying activity. The names and addresses of persons employed by the lobbyist for lobbying purposes and the names and addresses of the clients of the lobbyist or his/her employer must also be disclosed. There is a $10 fee for registration, as well as a $10 annual renewal fee.

Forms to Use: *Lobbyist Registration Statement* is used for initial registration and renewal; all other reports are filed online.

Reporting Requirements: Lobbyists must file monthly expenditure reports electronically with the Commission, due on the tenth day of the following month. The report discloses the total expenditures the lobbyist or his or her lobbying principals made on behalf of public officials, their staff and employees, and spouses and dependent children, itemized by printing and publication; media and other advertising; travel; entertainment; honoraria; meals, food, and beverages; and gifts. The report also discloses group expenditures and other ethics-related lobbying disclosures.

TAX EXEMPTIONS

Contact:

> Department of Revenue
> Customer Services Division
> 301 West High Street, Room 330
> Jefferson City, MO 65101
> (573) 751-4541 (corporate income tax)
> (573) 751-2836 (sales tax)

Citation: §143.441 —corporate income tax; §144.030(19) and (20) —sales tax.

Requirements: Nonprofit organizations that file federal 990s are not required to file a Missouri corporation income tax return unless the organization files a 990T (unrelated business income) or 990(C) and at least $100 of gross income is from Missouri sources. Nonprofits are exempt from the Missouri franchise tax. Sales made to religious and charitable organizations and institutions in their religious, charitable or educational functions and activities; not-for-profit civic, social service, or fraternal organizations; not-for-profit public and private institutions of higher education; eleemosynary and penal institutions; benevolent, scientific, and educational associations formed to foster, encourage, and promote the progress and improvement in the science of agriculture and in the raising and breeding of animals; and nonprofit summer theatres are eligible for exemption from the sales and use tax. Certain sales made by certain organizations are also eligible for exemption. Consult the contact office or Regulation 12 CSR 10-110.950 for details.

Application Procedure: Use Form DOR-1746 and the *Missouri Sales/Use Tax Exemption Application.* Include a copy of the Articles of Incorporation, bylaws, a copy of the IRS determination letter, and financial statements for the previous three years indicating sources of revenue and a breakdown of disbursements, or, if just beginning the organization, an estimated budget for one year.

CHARITABLE SOLICITATION

Contact:

> Attorney General's Office
> Consumer Protection Division
> 207 W. High Street
> PO Box 899
> Jefferson City, MO 65102-0899
> (573) 751-3321

Citation: *Charitable Organizations and Solicitations Law,* § 407.450, Missouri Revised Statutes.

Initial Registration: All charities must register before soliciting in the state. The registration fee is $15.

Annual Reports: Must file an annual report within 75 days after the end of the fiscal year. There is a $15 filing fee.

Organization Solicitation Disclosure requirements: If a professional fundraising organization is used, a charity, upon request, must disclose the percentage of funds spent on the costs of fundraising in the last 12-month period for which an annual report was filed; fundraising literature must state that a portion of funds contributed pay marketing expenses, if this is the case.

Paid Solicitor Requirements: All solicitors for a professional fundraising organization must register at the time they are initially employed. There is no fee for solicitor registration. A solicitor must disclose the fact that he/she is a paid solicitor for a professional fundraising organization.

Fundraising Counsel Requirements: Fundraising counsels are exempt from registration, but must contact the Attorney General's Office in writing with exemption information.

Montana

Central Switchboard: (406) 444-2511
State Web Home Page: http://www.mt.gov

INCORPORATION

Contact:

> Secretary of State
> Business Services Bureau
> PO Box 202801
> Helena, MT 59620-2801
> (406) 444-3665

Citation: Montana Code Annotated, Title 35, Chapter 2.

Publications Available: A sample Articles of Incorporation form is available from the contact office.

General Requirements: Articles of Incorporation must set forth the corporate name; a statement that it is a public benefit, mutual benefit, or religious corporation; the street address of the initial registered office, and, if different, the mailing address; the name of the initial registered agent at that address; the name, address, and signature of each incorporator; whether the corporation will have members; and provisions consistent with law regarding the distribution of assets upon dissolution.

Corporate Name: Must consist of English letters or Arabic or Roman numerals; may not contain language stating or implying that it is organized for a purpose other than permitted by its Articles; must be distinguishable from other corporate names in the state unless it has consent; may not be the same as, or identical to, another.

Name Reservation: May be reserved for a non-renewable, 120-day period.

How to File: File an original Articles of Incorporation form and a $20 filing fee with the Secretary of State. The Articles of Incorporation form may be used but is not required.

Other Filings/Reports: Each corporation must file an annual report with the Secretary of State providing the name of the corporation, address of its registered office and registered agent at that address, address of its principal office, the names and business or residence addresses of its directors and principal officers, a brief description of the nature of its activities, and whether or not it has members. The first annual report is due between January 1 and April 15 of the year following the calendar year of incorporation; subsequent annual reports are due between January 1 and April 15. The fee is $15 if filed by April 15 and $30 if filed after that date.

LOBBYING

Contact:

> Commissioner of Political Practices
> 1205 Eighth Avenue
> PO Box 202401
> Helena, MT 59620-2401
> (406) 444-2942

Citation: §5-7-101 et seq.

Publications: *Lobbying* booklet of forms and the statute are available from the contact office and at: *http://politicalpractices.mt.gov*

Registration Required: Lobbyists who receive at least $2,300 for lobbying must register with the Commissioner. Licenses expire on December 31 of each even-numbered year. There is a $150 license fee. Disclosure consists of general information and the name, address, and telephone number of each principal and specific subjects of legislation for each principal. Principals must disclose the subjects on which they authorize the lobbyist to represent them, the date the individual was employed to lobby, and provide an authorization statement authorizing their lobbyist.

Forms to Use: Lobbyists register by filing Form L-1; principals file Form L-2. Both filings are required along with the $150 license fee for the lobbyist to receive a license; L-5 (see below).

Reporting Requirements: Principals who make payments exceeding $2,300 in a calendar year for lobbying must file L-5 reports listing each lobbyist to whom they have made payments of more than $25 to the benefit of any public official; payments of more than $100 to the benefit of more than one public official; contributions or membership fees of $250 or more paid to the client for lobbying expense; the issue, if any, for which the payment was earmarked; and an itemized list of lobbying expenses categorized by printing, advertising, postage, travel expenses, salaries and fees, entertainment, communication, and other office expenses.

TAX EXEMPTIONS

Contact:

Department of Revenue
Customer Service
PO Box 5805
Helena, MT 59604
(406) 444-6900

Citation: Montana Code Annotated §15-31-102(1).

Publications: A copy of the exemption statute is provided by the contact office.

Requirements: Nonprofit corporations may be exempt from the Montana Corporation License Tax. There is no sales and use tax in Montana. Once an organization has qualified for tax-exempt status from the Department, it is not required, in most cases, to file a return other than when it has unrelated business income tax liability exceeding $100. Those that do have this liability must file a copy of their federal 990T with the Department.

Application Procedure: Provide an affidavit showing the character of the organization, the purpose for which it was organized, its actual activities, the sources and disposition of its income, and whether or not any of its income may inure to the benefit of any private shareholder or individual. Attach a copy of the Articles of Incorporation; a copy of the bylaws; copies of the latest financial statements showing the assets, liabilities, receipts, and disbursements; and, if applicable, a certified copy of the IRS tax exemption determination letter.

CHARITABLE SOLICITATION

There is no statute governing charitable solicitation activities by Montana nonprofit organizations.

Nebraska

Central Switchboard: (402) 471-2311
State Web Home Page: http://www.nebraska.gov

INCORPORATION

Contact:

*Secretary of State
Corporations Division
Suite 1301
PO Box 94608
Lincoln, NE 68509-4608
(402) 471-4079*

Citation: § 21-1901 et seq., revised Statutes of Nebraska.

Publications Available: None provided.

General Requirements: Articles of Incorporation must set forth corporate name; period of duration (optional); purposes (optional); provisions relating to the internal management and regulation of the organization (optional); street address of the initial registered office; name of the initial registered agent at that office; the number of directors constituting the initial board of directors (optional); the names, addresses, and signatures of each incorporator; if the corporation is a public benefit, mutual benefit, or religious corporation; if the corporation will or will not have members; and provisions not inconsistent with the law regarding the distribution of assets upon dissolution.

Corporate Name: Shall not contain any word or phrase that indicates or implies that it is organized for any purpose other than the one or more purposes contained in its Articles of Incorporation; shall not be the same as, or deceptively similar to, another; shall be transliterated into letters of the English alphabet if it is not in English.

Name Reservation: May be reserved for a non-renewable, 120-day period for a fee of $30.

How to File: File an original and a copy of the Articles with the Secretary of State. The fee is $10 plus $5 per page.

Other Filings/Reports: A biennial report must be filed with general information on forms provided by the Secretary of State. The reports are due on or before April 1 every odd-numbered year. The first report is due April 1 of the odd numbered year next succeeding the year of incorporation. There is a $20 filing fee.

LOBBYING

Contact:

*Nebraska Accountability and Disclosure
Commission
11th Floor, State Capitol Building
PO Box 95086
Lincoln, NE 68509
(402) 471-2522*

Citation: *The Nebraska Political Accountability and Disclosure Act*, 49-1401 et seq.

Registration Required: All lobbyists, whether compensated or not, must file an *Application for Registration* with the Clerk of the Legislature prior to lobbying. The registration is valid through the end of the calendar year. The registration fee is $200 for lobbyists who receive compensation for lobbying and $15 for those who do not. Employees who lobby are considered lobbyists for compensation.

Forms to Use: NADC Form A, *Application for Registration as a Lobbyist*; NADC Form B, *Nebraska Registered Lobbyist Quarterly Report*; NADC Form C, *Nebraska Principal Quarterly Report*; NADC Form D, *Nebraska Lobbyist Statement of Activity*. Call (402) 471-2608 to have the current forms mailed to you.

Reporting Requirements: Each lobbyist and client must file quarterly reports disclosing itemized expenditures categorized by miscellaneous, entertainment, lodging, travel, lobbyist fees, and receipts. Special monthly reports are required for expenditures of more than $5,000 for lobbying purposes during any calendar month in which the Legislature is in session, due 30 days after the end of that month (does not apply to fees for lobbying services previously disclosed on the registration statement). There are gift limitations and gift-reporting provisions, as well. The registration form includes general information, compensation given or planned to be given to the lobbyist, and identification of matters on which the client or lobbyist expects to lobby.

TAX EXEMPTIONS

Contact:

> Department of Revenue
> 301 Centennial Mall South
> PO Box 94818
> Lincoln, NE 68509-4818
> (402) 471-5729

Citation: §77-2704.12—sales and use tax; §77-2714 —income tax.

Requirements: Sales and use taxes are not imposed on the gross receipts from the sale, lease, or rental of, and the storage, use, or other consumption of, purchases by the following: any organization created exclusively for religious purposes; any nonprofit organization providing services exclusively to the blind; any private educational institution established under certain specified statutes; any private college or university established under certain specified statutes; any hospital; any health clinic when two or more hospitals or the parent corporations of the hospitals own or control the health clinic for the purpose of reducing the cost of health services or when the health clinic receives funds under certain federal programs; skilled nursing facilities, intermediate care facilities, or nursing facilities licensed under certain statutes and organized not for profit; certain facilities that serve the mentally retarded, provide home health, hospice, or respite care; organizations that provide community-based services for persons with developmental disabilities; any licensed child-caring agency; and any licensed child placement agency. To qualify, organizations must be nonprofits. Organizations that are exempt from federal income tax are generally exempt from the corporate income tax, but this does not include those required to file federal 990T unrelated business income tax returns.

Application Procedure: File Form 4, *Nebraska Exemption Application,* with the Department. The statute and regulation provides enumerated exemptions by type of organization purchasing and type of organization selling. Form 4 discloses general information; requires disclosure of the Social Security numbers, names, and addresses of corporate officers; and the basis for exemption. A copy of the organization's bylaws, Articles of Incorporation, or current license may be required to be provided.

CHARITABLE SOLICITATION

Contact:

> Secretary of State
> Suite 2300 Capitol Building
> Lincoln, NE 68509-4608
> (402) 471-2554

Citation: As of March 1, 1996, the Nebraska Charitable Solicitor registration laws have been repealed as a result of a ruling by the Nebraska Supreme Court.

Nevada

Central Switchboard: (775) 687-5000
State Web Home Page: http://www.nv.gov

INCORPORATION

Contact:

> *Secretary of State*
> *New Filings Division*
> *206 N. Carson Street*
> *Carson City, NV 89701-4299*
> *(775) 684-5708*

Citation: NRS Chapter 82, §82.006-82.541; Nonprofit Corporations.

Publications Available: A compilation of applicable law and forms is available from the contact office. Forms are available at: *http://secretaryofstate.biz*

General Requirements: Articles of Incorporation must set forth the corporate name; name and address of the resident agent; that the corporation is a nonprofit corporation; the nature of the business or objects, or purposes; names and addresses of the board of directors/ trustees; the organization purposes; the names and addresses of incorporators (at least one required); and optional provisions relating to dissolution, voting, and internal management.

Corporate Name: Must be distinguishable from the names of all other artificial persons formed, organized, or registered under Title 7 of NRS and on file in the office of the Secretary of State, unless accompanied by written consent from the holder of the name. May not be a name appearing to be that of a natural person and containing a given name or initials except with an additional word or words such as "Incorporated," "Inc.," "Limited," "Ltd.," "Company," "Co.," "Corporation," "Corp.," or other word that identifies it as not being a natural person. It must not be the same as another corporation, or deceptively similar, without permission of the other corporation, partnership, or limited liability company. May not contain the words "bank," "trust," engineer," "engineered," "engineering," "professional

engineer," "licensed engineer," "mortgage," or "insurance."

Name Reservation: May be reserved for a renewable period of 90 days for a fee of $25.

How to File: File original Articles of Incorporation with the Secretary of State with a $50 filing fee plus $30 for each certified copy requested.

Other Filings/Reports: An annual list of officers/directors and resident agent must be filed on or before the last day of the first month after the filing of articles and annually thereafter. The fee is $25. Filings may be done online.

LOBBYING

Contact:

> *Legislative Counsel Bureau*
> *Lobbyist Registration Office*
> *Room 1199*
> *401 S. Carson Street*
> *Carson City, NV 89701-4747*
> *(775) 687-6800*

Citation: *Nevada Lobbying Disclosure Act,* NRS §218.900 et seq.

Registration Required: Every lobbyist, within two days after lobbying activity begins, must file a registration statement with the director of the Legislative Counsel Bureau. The form discloses general information, a list of lobbyist clients, a list of direct business associations and partnerships with any member of the Legislature, a description of the principal areas of interest, and a statement that compensation is not contingent upon the production of any legislative action. Fees for nonprofit organizations and their paid lobbyists are $15 for unpaid lobbyists, and $95 plus $1 for each additional client for paid lobbyists.

Forms to Use: *Lobbyist Registration; Lobbyist's Expenditure Report.*

Reporting Requirements: Each lobbyist must file an itemized final expense report within 30 days after the close of each legislative session, and interim reports within 10 days following the close of each month during sessions. Expenses are itemized by entertainment, parties, gifts and loans, and other. Lobbyists must wear identification badges when lobbying.

TAX EXEMPTIONS

Contact:

Nevada Department of Taxation
1550 E. College Parkway STE 115
Carson City, NV 89706-7921
(775) 684-2000

Citation: Nevada Revised Statutes, Chapter 372, Sales and Use Taxes, §372.326, §372.348, and §372.3261.

Requirements: There is no corporate income tax. Qualifying organizations created for religious, charitable, or educational purposes may be exempt from sales tax on sales of tangible personal property to and/or by the organization upon application review and approval.

Application Procedure: File a *Sales and Use Tax Exemption for Religious, Charitable and Educational Organizations* form (APP-02.01, available at: *http://www.state.nv.us/taxation/eforms)* with the Department, and attach by-laws, Articles of Incorporation, IRS determination letter, list of volunteer activities, and financial statements. Include other relevant information, such as pamphlets, brochures and fact sheets. If the application is for a charitable organization, an outline of charitable activities, fundraisers, goals, and a copy of the business plan must be attached. If the application is approved, the organization is issued a sales tax exemption letter. Exemption letters must be renewed by reapplication every five years. Copies of the letter are given to vendors in order to not be charged sales tax.

CHARITABLE SOLICITATION

There is no Nevada law regulating charitable solicitation.

New Hampshire

Central Switchboard: (603) 271-1110
State Web Home Page: http://www.nh.gov

INCORPORATION

Contact:

*Secretary of State
Corporation Division
107 N. Main Street
Concord, NH 03301-4989
(603) 271-3246*

Citation: RSA Chapter 292, 292:1 et seq.

Publications Available: *New Hampshire Non-profit Corporations* booklet is available from the contact office.

General Requirements: At least five or more individuals of lawful age are required to form a nonprofit corporation. Articles of Agreement must set forth the corporate name; object for which the corporation is established; provisions for establishing membership and participation in the corporation; provisions relating to distribution of assets upon dissolution; address where business will be carried on; amount of capital stock, if any; provisions limiting liability of directors and/or officers (optional); and the signature and post office address of each of the persons forming the corporation.

Corporate Name: Must be distinguishable upon the record but not similar to any other reserved or registered business name.

Name Reservation: Nonprofit corporation names may not be reserved.

How to File: Articles of Agreement must first be filed with the Department of State's Corporation Division and then with the clerk of the city or town in which the business of the corporation will be carried out. The fee for filing locally is $5; the fee for filing with the state is $25. File form NP 1, *Articles of Agreement of a New Hampshire Nonprofit Corporation.*

Other Filings/Reports: Corporations must file a "return" during the calendar year 2005 and every five years thereafter. The return fee is $25. The forms for returns are provided by the Department. The return includes the corporation's principal address and the names and addresses of all of the officers and directors.

LOBBYING

Contact:

*Department of State
State House
Room 204
Concord, NH 03301
(603) 271-3242*

Citation: RSA 15 15:1 et seq.

Publications: A copy of the statute is available from the contact office.

Registration Required: All registrations expire each year on December 31; the fee is $50 for each lobbyist and $50 for each client. Lobbyists must wear a clearly visible name tag when lobbying in the state house or the legislative office building. The badge must have white lettering on a hunter orange background and be at least 2.5 inches high and 2.5 inches long with their first and last names and the word "lobbyist" at least .25 inches high.

Reporting Requirements: Lobbyists must file itemized statements on April 15, August 15, and December 15 covering the periods of registration March 31, April 1-July 31, and August 1-December 1, respectively. The form requires disclosure of lobbyist fees and other compensation; expenditures made directly by the lobbyist; and lobbyist expenditures charged by the lobbyist to the client. All disclosures are itemized by date received, who paid, and the amount of expenditure.

TAX EXEMPTIONS

Contact:

> Department of Revenue Administrator
> 45 Chenell Drive
> PO Box 457
> Concord, NH 03302-0457
> (603) 271-2191

Citation: 77-A:1—Business Profits Tax.

Requirements: Corporations exempt from the federal income tax are exempt from the state business profits tax. There is no corporate sales tax. Nonprofit corporations other than 501(c)(3)s are subject to the Business Enterprise Tax.

CHARITABLE SOLICITATION

Contact:

> Department of Justice
> Office of the Attorney General
> Charitable Trusts Unit
> 33 Capitol Street
> Concord, NH 03301-6397
> (603) 271-3591

Citation: RSA 7:28 et seq.

Publications: *Guidebook for Charities* is available from the contact office and from the web site:
http://www.doj.nh.gov/publications/pdf/ New_Charitable_Guidebook_2005.pdf

Initial Registration: Charitable organizations must register with the Register of Charitable Trusts one time only using Form NHCT-1. There is a fee of $25. Registration discloses general information about the charity. Charitable corporations must attach Articles of Incorporation and bylaws; other types of organizations must attach a copy of Articles of Agreement or other governing document; names, home addresses, telephone numbers, and titles of at least five trustees/directors and officers; a copy of the most recent balance sheet or financial information (copy of checkbook register and/or savings passbook account if newly formed and without a balance sheet); a copy of the organization's conflict of interest policy; whether the organization has applied to the IRS for a tax exemption and a copy of the IRS determination letter, if applicable. Must disclose the month the fiscal year ends. Every charitable organization must adopt a conflict-of-interest policy, pursuant to RSA 7:19 II.

Annual Reports: Must file financial reports (or federal 990 form) within 4 months and 15 days after the end of each fiscal year along with a $75 filing fee.

Organization Solicitation Disclosure Requirements: see below.

Paid Solicitor Requirements: Must register, pay a $500 filing fee and post a $20,000 bond. Contracts with charities must be in writing. Paid solicitors must clearly and conspicuously disclose prior to orally requesting a contribution, or contemporaneously with a written request, the name of the paid solicitor, that the solicitation is being conducted by a paid fundraiser, and that the charity shall receive a fixed percentage of the gross revenue, or the reasonable estimate, which is included in the contract between the solicitor and the charity. There are restrictions on solicitations involving tickets to events. Prior to soliciting, must file a Solicitation Notice with the Attorney General disclosing the contract with the charity, a description of the campaign, general information, and a $200 fee.

Fundraising Counsel Requirements: Must register, pay a $150 fee and post a $10,000 bond. Within 90 days after a solicitation campaign, and on the anniversary of a campaign lasting more than one year, a fundraising counsel shall account to the charitable trust for all contributions collected and expenses paid, in writing. Each contribution collected shall, within five days of receipt, be deposited at a bank or other federally insured financial institution in the name of the charity. The charity shall have sole authority to make withdrawals.

New Jersey

Central Switchboard: (609) 292-2121
State Web Home Page: http://www.state.nj.us/

INCORPORATION

Contact:

New Jersey Division of Revenue
Corporate Filing Unit
225 West State Street
PO Box 308
Trenton, NJ 08625-0308
(609) 292-9292

Citation: *New Jersey Nonprofit Corporation Act;*
N.J.S.A. 15A:1-1 et seq.

Publications Available: "Starting a Nonprofit Organization in New Jersey" is available at: http://www.state.nj.us/treasury/taxation/pdf/pubs/exemptfaq.pdf. Forms and instructions are available from the contact office and Web site.

General Requirements: One or more individuals at least 18 years of age or corporations may act as incorporators (10 or more persons are required to serve as incorporators of volunteer fire companies). Filing must include name, type of entity, purpose, duration, contact information, names and addresses of initial trustees (may not be less than three), address and signature of each incorporator (at least one), whether there will be members and their classes, how trustees will be elected, and how assets will be distributed.

Corporate Name: Shall contain one of the following: "a New Jersey nonprofit corporation," "incorporated," "corporation," "inc." or "corp;" shall not contain any word or phrase, or abbreviation or derivation thereof, which indicates or implies that it is organized for any purpose other than permitted by its Certificate of Incorporation; shall not be the same as, or confusingly similar to, another without written permission; shall not contain any word or phrase, abbreviation, or derivation thereof, the use of which is prohibited by any other statute.

Name Check/Name Reservation: Call (609) 292-9292 for name search. There is a charge for expedited telephone name search (credit cards accepted). The name may be reserved for 120 days for a $50 fee. A name availability lookup service is offered for $15.

How to File: File Form NJ-REG, which includes 23 questions that apply to all new business organizations plus additional questions for new nonprofit corporations. The filing fee is $75. Expedited service is available by fax for an additional fee of $10 plus $1/page. Same day service is available for an additional $50 charge plus $1/page. If you desire exemption from state sales and use taxes, file NJ-REG-1E instead of NJ-REG.

Other Filings/Reports: An annual report must be filed along with a $25 filing fee. The report discloses general information, including the names and addresses of trustees and officers, on forms provided by the contact office. The contact office notifies each corporation within 60 days prior to the due date, and the report must be filed during the anniversary month of the organization's initial incorporation. Businesses that fail to file an annual report in two consecutive years will be revoked.

LOBBYING

Contact:

Election Law Enforcement Commission
PO Box 185
Trenton, NJ 08625-0185
(609) 292-8700

Citation: 52:13C-18 et seq.

Registration Required: Lobbyists must register with the Commission before lobbying, or within 30 days of being hired as a lobbyist. The registration form discloses general information, information about clients, a description of lobbying interest, whether the lobbyist is a paid lobbyist, and the legislation or regulation of interest. The fee is $425 and lobbyists must provide two 2" x 2" color photos.

Reporting Requirements: Quarterly reports on lobbying activity must be filed describing the target of lobbying activity that was actively promoted or opposed. These reports are due between the first and tenth days of each calendar quarter covering activity during the preceding calendar quarter. If receipts or expenditures exceed $2,500 in any calendar year, an annual report of financial activity is required to be filed.

TAX EXEMPTIONS

Contact:

Department of Treasury
Division of Taxation—Regulatory Services
  Branch
50 Barrack Street
PO Box 269
Trenton, NJ 08695-0269
(609) 292-5994

Citation: 54 §10A-3, Exempt Corporations—corporate income taxes; 54 § 32B-9—sales and use taxes.

Publications: *Starting a Nonprofit Organization in New Jersey* booklet is available at: *http://www.state.nj.us/treasury/taxation/pdf/pubs/exemptfaq.pdf*

Requirements: Nonprofit corporations are exempt from the Corporation Business Tax Act. Certain nonprofit organizations, churches, scientific, charitable organizations with 501(c)(3) status, and veterans' organizations may apply for sales tax exemption status.

Application Procedure: All 501(c)(3) organizations are exempt upon application. Complete and file an REG-1E Form *(Application for Exempt Organization Certificate)* with the Regulatory Services Branch of the Division of Taxation, and include your organization's bylaws, Articles of Incorporation, and IRS determination letter. Once approved by the Branch, submit an ST-5 *(Exempt Organization Certificate)* to vendors.

CHARITABLE SOLICITATION

Contact:

NJ Division of Consumer Affairs
Charities Registration Section
124 Halsey Street
PO Box 45021
Newark, NJ 07101
(973) 504-6215 (Charities Hotline)

Citation: *Charitable Registration and Investigation Act,* New Jersey Statutes Annotated Title 45, Subtitle 2, Chapter 17A 45:17A-18 et seq.

Publications: *Charitable Registration and Investigation* booklet, forms, general information, and copy of the law are available from the contact office. Call, telephone, or visit the Web site.

Initial Registration: Annual registration is accomplished by using the long form (CRI-150I) or short form (CRI-200, for organizations that did not receive more than $10,000 in gross contributions during the preceding year and whose fundraising was conducted entirely by volunteers). Most religious organizations, schools, and libraries are exempt. Fees range from $60 to $250 depending upon contributions raised (minimum $60 fee for organizations filing the long form). Generally, organizations must submit audited financial reports and IRS 990s, IRS determination letters, information about paid fundraisers and solicitors, and information about organizational misconduct. If a charity's total gross revenue exceeds $100,000, a certified audit is required. The URS form is accepted as long as all New Jersey requirements are included.

Annual reports: Charities must file *Renewal Registrations* each year. Renewals are due within six months of the end of the charity's fiscal year along with an annual fee ranging from $60 to $250 based on amount raised. The statement provides for itemized receipt and expenditure disclosures, conflict of interest disclosures, information about how contributions were used, information about paid fundraisers, and financial information. The IRS 990 and certified audit are due when applicable.

Organization Solicitation Disclosure requirements: Solicitation materials must contain a disclaimer "Information filed with the attorney general concerning this charitable solicitation may be obtained from the attorney general of the state of New Jersey by calling (973) 504-6215. Registration with the attorney general does not imply endorsement." Upon request of the donor, written confirmation, receipts, or written reminders must be sent. The charity must honor requests from the public for written literature on the organization.

Paid Solicitor Requirements: Must register annually and pay a $250 fee and post a $20,000 bond. There is also a $15 fee for persons working with a paid solicitor. Renewal of registration for solicitors is $15. At least 10 days prior to initiating a solicitation campaign, the solicitor must send the contract with a $30 fee to the Attorney General describing the nature, purpose, and the proposed dates and location of the solicitations. Charities must establish and exercise control over fundraiser activity. Charities must review and approve of all telephone scripts, printed solicitations/pledge documents, and contribution collection processes.

Fundraising Counsel Requirements: Must register; pay a $250 fee and, if applicable, post a $20,000 bond if they have access to the charity's funds at any time. Contracts with a charity must be in writing and must be filed along with a form CRI-500 to assure that the contract meets the requirements of the law.

New Mexico

Central Switchboard: (800) 825-6639
State Web Home Page: http://www.newmexico.gov

INCORPORATION

Contact:

> Public Regulation Commission
> Corporations Bureau
> PO Box 1269
> Santa Fe, NM 87504-1269
> (505) 827-4502
> (800) 947-4722 (N.M. residents only)

Citation: *New Mexico Nonprofit Corporation Act,* NMSA 53-8-1 et seq.

Publications Available: *Requirements for Incorporating a New Mexico Corporation for Nonprofit* and forms and instructions are available from the contact office.

General Requirements: One or more persons may serve as incorporators. The Articles of Incorporation must set forth the corporate name; period of duration; purpose(s); provisions relating to the distribution of assets upon dissolution; provisions relating to internal regulation; the address of the initial registered office and the name of the registered agent at that address; the number of directors constituting the initial board of directors (must be at least three), their names, and addresses; and the name and address of each incorporator.

Corporate Name: Shall not contain any word or phrase that indicates or implies that it is organized for any purpose other than contained in its Articles of Incorporation; shall not be the same as, or confusingly similar to, another.

Name Reservation: May be reserved for 120 days for a $10 fee.

How to File: File duplicate originals of the Articles of Incorporation with the contact office along with a $25 filing fee. There is an additional fee of $10 if a certified copy is requested plus a copying fee of $1/page, minimum $5, if provided by the Commission. The initial registered agent must submit an affidavit accepting appointment as that agent.

Other Filings/Reports: An annual report is required to be filed disclosing general information, including the names and addresses of its directors and officers, and a brief statement of the character of the affairs the corporation is actually conducting in the state. Forms for the report are sent out at least 30 days before the due date by the contact office. There is a $10 fee to file this report, which is due on the 15th day of the fifth month following the end of the organization's tax year.

LOBBYING

Contact:

> Office of the Secretary of State
> Ethics Administration
> 325 Don Gaspar—Suite 300
> Santa Fe, NM 87503
> (505) 827-3600

Citation: *Lobbyist Regulation Act,* Chapter 2, Article 11 2-11-1 et. seq. NMSA 1978.

Publications: *Am I a Lobbyist?,* the occasional newsletter *Lobbyist Letter, Highlights of the Lobbyist Regulation Act,* and a copy of the statute are available on the web site: *http://www.sos.state.nm.us/*

Registration Required: Lobbyists must register with the Secretary of State. Lobbyists must also pay a $25 fee for each employer for which compensation is received. If no compensation is provided, then no fee is required. Each lobbyist must also file a lobbyist authorization form for each client/employer.

Forms to Use: LOB-REG-*Lobbyist Registration Form; Lobbyist Authorization Form; Lobbyist Report of Expenditures and Contributions.*

Reporting Requirements: Reports of expenditures and contributions are due by January 15 for all expenditures and political contributions made/incurred during the preceding year and not previously reported; within 48 hours, expenditures of $500 or more must be reported;

reports are due May 1 for all previously unreported expenditures and political contributions made or incurred since the January filing. The reports are divided as follows: *Lobbyist Reporting Form A* is a general overview of the entire report; *Lobbyist Reporting Form B* itemizes expenditures; *Lobbyist Reporting Form C* provides for disclosure concerning special events; *Lobbyist Reporting Form D* discloses information about political contributions; and *Lobbyist Reporting Form E* discloses information about bundling of political contributions. Itemized expenditures are categorized by meal and beverage, entertainment, gift, other, special events, and political contributions.

TAX EXEMPTIONS

Contact:

Taxation and Revenue Department
Tax Information/Policy Office
1100 S. St. Francis Drive
PO Box 630
Santa Fe, NM 87504-0630
(505) 827-0700

Citation: §7-2-4.

Publications: *FYI-103, Information for Non-Profit Organizations* booklet and *Nonprofit Groups & New Mexico's Gross Receipts Tax* are available from the contact office or online.

Requirements: Organizations granted 501(c)(3) status by the IRS are exempt from gross receipts taxes on income related to their mission statement. Unrelated income is fully taxable under both the gross receipts and compensating tax and income tax. For purposes of the gross receipts tax, there is a difference between what a 501(c)(3) organization sells and what it buys. It may buy only tangible personal property "tax free" upon delivery of the appropriate New Mexico non-taxable transaction certificate (NTTC). It may not purchase services nor may it lease property free of the gross receipts tax.

Application Procedure: Complete and mail form ACD 31015, *Application for Business Tax Identification Number* and a copy of the organization's IRS determination letter.

CHARITABLE SOLICITATION

Contact:

Attorney General
Charitable Organization Registry
111 Lomas Blvd. Suite 300
Albuquerque, NM 87102
(505) 222-9046

Citation: *Charitable Organizations and Solicitations Act,* Section 57-22-1, et seq., NMSA 1978.

Publications: A copy of the statute and *Registration and Annual Reporting Requirements* leaflet are available from the contact office.

Initial Registration: All 501(c)(3) charities or those that have applied for such status or hold themselves out as having a charitable purpose must register with the Registrar of Charitable Organizations within 30 days of operations. Charities must submit a copy of the Articles of Incorporation and Certificate of Incorporation, bylaws, a copy of their IRS tax exemption determination letter; a copy of the completed *Request for Exemption* (federal Form 1023 or 2024); a copy of the most recent IRS Form 990 or, if not required to file it, a completed *Charitable Organization Registration Form* provided by the Attorney General's office. There is no fee. Religious and educational organizations are generally exempt.

Annual Reports: A charity must file its federal 990 with the contact office each year, due within six months after the close of the charity's fiscal year. Organizations that do not file a 990 may file Form CCO-2 *(Charitable Organization Annual Report Form)* that provides contact information, names and addresses of all trustees, total revenues, expenses, and assets.

Organization Solicitation Disclosure requirements: Upon request, all charities must disclose the percentage of funds solicited that are spent on the costs of fundraising.

Paid Solicitor Requirements: Paid solicitors must complete a registration form provided by the Attorney General's office accompanied by a $25,000 bond. Each campaign must be registered to include all solicitation materials and contacts.

Fundraising Counsel Requirements: None.

New York

Central Switchboard: (518) 474-2121
State Web Home Page: http://www.ny.gov

INCORPORATION

Contact:

> Department of State
> Division of Corporations
> 41 State Street
> Albany, NY 12231-0001
> (518) 473-2492

Citation: *Not-for-Profit Corporation Law,* Articles 1-15, Sec. 101 et seq.

General Requirements: Certificate of Incorporation must set forth the name, address, and signature of each incorporator; corporate name; purpose(s); the county where the corporation will be located; the names and addresses of initial directors (Type A, B & C only—see below); the duration; a statement designating the Secretary of State as its agent for service of process; and provisions that will facilitate approval by the IRS of federal tax-exempt status.

Type A: corporations formed for any lawful non-business purpose or purposes, including, but not limited to, any one or more of the following non-pecuniary purposes: civic; patriotic; political; social; fraternal; athletic; agricultural; horticultural; animal husbandry; and for a professional, commercial, industrial, trade or service association.

Type B: corporations formed for any one or more of the following non-business purposes: charitable, educational, religious, scientific, literary, cultural, or for the prevention of cruelty to children or animals.

Type C: corporations formed for any lawful business purpose to achieve a lawful public or quasi-public objective.

Type D: corporations formed when such formation is authorized by any other corporate law of NY for any business or non-business, or pecuniary or non-pecuniary, purpose or purposes specified by such other law, whether such purpose or purposes are also within types A, B, C above or otherwise. If a corporation is formed for purposes that are both type A and B, it is type B. If a corporation has among its purposes any purpose that is within type C, it is type C.

Corporate Name: Shall contain the word "corporation," "incorporated," or "limited," or an abbreviation, unless it is formed for charitable or religious purposes; shall be distinguishable from others; may not include words or phrases restricted by other statutes unless the nonprofit has complied with that restriction; may require the approval of another agency before filing if the organization is engaging in certain activities, such as day care centers, hospitals, or substance abuse programs. Review Section 404 of the Nonprofit Corporation Law for information related to consents and approvals.

Name Check/Name Reservation: May be done in writing; telephone inquiries are not accepted; the fee for the name search is $5 for each name. To reserve a name, file DOS-635 form *Application for Reservation of Name.* The fee is $10; the name will be reserved for 60 days with two extensions permitted for additional $10 fees.

How to File: Forms for filing Certificate of Incorporation are available from the contact office or the Web site at: *http://www.dos.state.ny.us*
The filing fee is $75. File DOS-1511 if seeking tax-exempt status from the IRS. All documents must be on white paper, single-sided, using black ink on 8 1/2" x 11" paper.

Other Filings/Reports: None.

LOBBYING

Contact:

> New York State Temporary Commission on
>   Lobbying
> Two Empire State Plaza
> 18th Floor
> Albany, NY 12223-1254
> (518) 474-7126

Citation: *Lobbying Act,* (L. 1999, Chapter 2, as amended by Chapter 17, Laws of 2001).

Publications: A copy of the statute and *Guidelines* are available from the contact office or through its web site *(http://www.nylobby.state.ny.us).*

Registration Required: Lobbyists and public corporations must register and report annually if they expend or receive more than $2,000 of combined reportable compensation and expenses for lobbying activities. Registration discloses general information about the lobbyist and client. Written lobbying contracts must be attached or a summary of any oral agreement. The dollar amount of compensation must be included. The general subject of lobbying must be disclosed as well as the nature of the client's business. Clients of lobbyists must report semi-annually, although they are not required to register. The registration fee is $100 if compensation and expenses from a client exceeds $5,000.

Forms to Use: Lobbyists use *New York State Lobbyist Statement of Registration;* public corporations use *New York State Public Corporation Statement of Registration.*

Reporting Requirements: Six itemized spending reports are required disclosing compensation and expenditures for the periods ending February 28 (due March 15), April 30 (due May 15), June 30 (due July 15), August 31 (due September 15), October 31 (due November 15), and December 31 (due January 15). Any lobbying expense in excess of $75 must be fully identified. Clients must file semi-annual reports for January-June (due July 15) and July-December (due January 15).

TAX EXEMPTIONS

Contact:
> NY State Department of Taxation and Finance
> Taxpayer Assistance Bureau
> WA Harriman Campus
> Albany, NY 12227
> 1-800-698-2909 (sales tax)
> 1-800-698-2908 (corporation tax)

Citation: §§209.9-Article 9A—Business Corporations —corporation tax; §1116 —sales and use tax.

Requirements: Organizations exempt from federal income tax are exempt from state corporation income taxes, other than unrelated business income tax. Generally, 501(c)(3) organizations are exempt from sales and use tax.

Application Procedure: To apply for exempt organization status, complete and submit Form ST-119.2, *Application for an Exempt Organization Certificate.* Upon approval, an organization can issue Form ST-119.1. *Exempt Organization Certificate,* to make purchases for the organization exempt from tax. However, if an organization makes sales through a shop, store, restaurant, tavern, or similar establishment, it must register as a vendor and collect and pay sales tax.

CHARITABLE SOLICITATION

Contact:
> New York State Attorney General's Office
> Charities Bureau
> 120 Broadway
> New York, NY 10271
> (212) 416-8401

Citation: Article 7-A of the Executive Law.

Initial Registration: Charitable organizations must register with the Attorney General prior to soliciting contributions. Exemptions can be found at: *http://www.oag.state.ny.us/charities/forms/char401i.pdf.* Charities register by filing a Form CHAR 410 *Charities Registration Statement* or the Unified Registration Statement (URS) and paying a one-time $25 fee. The registration form includes general information; a list of professional fundraisers and fundraising counsel; the purposes of the organization; the purposes for which contributions are solicited; the names, addresses, titles and terms of directors, trustees and officers; other entities that share in the revenues raised; names of banks, addresses, and account numbers; and information about previous organizational misconduct. Charities must enclose their Certificate of Incorporation, IRS tax exemption determination letter, and previous year's financial report.

Annual Reports: Charities must file CHAR 497, *Annual Financial Report,* and IRS 990 if they have one. The CHAR 497 provides a financial summary of support, revenue, and expenses; a balance sheet; itemizations of public support and government grants; descriptions of campaigns; and information about professional fundraisers, fundraising counsel and commercial coventurers. An accountant's review is required of organizations with income between $100,000 and $250,000 and an audit is required of organizations with income over $250,000. The organization's 990 must be attached. The report is due within 4½ months following the close of the fiscal year.

Organization Solicitation Disclosure Requirements: Must include the statement: "A copy of the latest annual report may be obtained from the organization or from the Attorney General's Charities Bureau, Attn: FOIL Officer, 120 Broadway, NY, NY 10271."

Professional Fundraiser Requirements: Registration is required, along with payment of an annual fee of $800 and the posting of a $10,000 bond. There is an $80 registration fee for individuals employed by a professional fundraiser.

Fundraising Counsel Requirements: Annual registration is required along with an $800 fee.

North Carolina

Central Switchboard: (919) 733-1110
State Web Home Page: http://www.ncgov.com

INCORPORATION

Contact:

> Corporations Division
> Department of Secretary of State
> PO Box 29622
> Raleigh, NC 27626-0622
> (919) 807-2225

Citation: *North Carolina Nonprofit Corporation Act,* N.C. Gen. Stat. §55A.

Publications Available: *North Carolina Nonprofit Corporation Guidelines* is available online at: *http://www.sosne.com* and link to the corporations divisions page.

General Requirements: Must have at least one director. Articles of Incorporation must set forth the corporate name, designation as a charitable or religious corporation if applicable; the name and address of its registered agent who must be a resident of the state; the address of a registered office and the county where it is located; the name and address of at least one incorporator; a statement that the corporation has or does not have members; provision for the distribution of assets upon dissolution and termination; and the address of its principal office. The Articles may also, but are not required to, contain a statement of the corporation's purposes; the names and addresses of the initial directors; provisions relating to the corporation's management and regulation; provisions defining, limiting, or regulating the powers of the corporation, its members, or directors; provisions relating to the qualifications, rights, and responsibilities of members; and provisions relating to personal liability of directors.

Corporate Name: May not imply a purpose other than a purpose that is lawful and permitted by its Articles of Incorporation; must be distinguishable from names of other corporations authorized to transact business in North Carolina.

Name Check/Name Reservation: May check with the Office of the Secretary of State to see whether a proposed name is available; may be reserved for a 120-day period for a $30 fee, but is not renewable.

How to File: One original copy of the Articles of Incorporation must be submitted to the Office of the Secretary of State by mail or in person with a $60 filing fee.

Other Filings/Reports: Update contact information when applicable.

LOBBYING

Contact:

> Lobbyist Registration
> Department of the Secretary of State
> PO Box 29622
> Raleigh, NC 27626-0622
> (919) 807-2170

Citation: Article 9A, Chapter 120, General Statutes of North Carolina.

Publications: A copy of the statute and *Lobbying Guidelines—General Information* sheet (Form LR-GI) and relevant forms are available from the contact office.

Registration Required: Lobbyists must register with the Department of Secretary of State before lobbying; registration is effective from date of filing to January 1 of the following odd-numbered year; filing fee is $200 for each lobbyist's client/employer (the entity on whose behalf the lobbying is performed); a written authorization must be filed by each lobbyist client/employer within 10 days of registration that the lobbyist is authorized to lobby for the client.

Forms to Use: LR-1 for Lobbyist Registration; LR-2 for Authorization statements; LR-3 for Lobbyist Expense Reports; LR-4 for Principal Expense Reports.

Reporting Requirements: Expense reports are filed with respect to each client/employer within 60 days after the last day of the regular legislative session. These reports are divided into the following categories: transportation, lodging, entertainment, food items with a cash equivalent of greater than $25, and contributions. Supplemental reports must be filed for the period after the legislative session ends but by February 28th of the following year.

TAX EXEMPTIONS

Contact:

> North Carolina Department of Revenue
> PO Box 25000
> Raleigh, NC 27640-0640
> (919) 733-4668
> (877) 252-3052

Citation: G.S. Subchapter 5b —Franchise Tax; 5c— Corporate Income Tax; 105-125, 105-130.11, 105-130.12.

Publications: *State Taxation and Nonprofit Organizations* is available from the contact office and at: *http://www/dor.state.nc.us/publications/ nonprofit2002.pdf*

Requirements: Upon incorporation, the Department of State sends a notice to the Department of Revenue. The Department of Revenue sends a letter of notification to the corporation with a six-part questionnaire (CD-345) that is used to determine tax-exempt status. Generally, nonprofit organizations pay sales taxes on their purchases, but they may be eligible for semi-annual refunds of sales taxes they pay.

Application Procedure: The corporation should submit the questionnaire along with its Articles of Incorporation, bylaws and, if applicable, any tax-exempt organization provisions. The Department notifies the corporation by mail as to whether it is exempt from franchise and income taxes.

CHARITABLE SOLICITATION

Contact:

> Department of the Secretary of State
> Charitable Solicitation Licensing Section
> PO Box 29622
> Raleigh, NC 27626-0622
> (919) 807-2214
> (888) 830-4989 (NC residents only)

Citation: Charitable Solicitations Act; N.C. Gen. Stat. (PP)131F-1-131F-33.

Publications: A copy of the statute, regulations, and forms are available from the contact office and at the Web site at: *http://www.sosnc.com*

Initial & Renewal Registrations: Applies to organizations that receive more than $25,000 in contributions in any calendar year and/or provide compensation to any officer, trustee, organizer, incorporator, fundraiser, or solicitor. Many types of organizations, such as hospitals, volunteer fire and rescue squads, educational institutions, non-commercial radio and TV stations, and YMCA/ YWCAs are exempt. Registration must disclose general information; the purpose for which the contributions will be used; the organization's fiscal year end date; a list or description of major program activities; the names of individuals in charge of solicitation activities; a financial report that includes a balance sheet, a statement of support, revenue and expenses and any changes in the fund balance; a statement of program, management and general, and fundraising expenses (or a copy of its federal 990 with schedule A); a budget for the current year if it is newly formed and does not have a financial history; a statement including whether it is authorized by any other state to solicit contributions; whether any of its officers, directors, trustees, or paid staff have engaged in unlawful practices relating to solicitation or otherwise have been implicated in unlawful solicitation practices; the names, addresses, telephone numbers, and compensation/terms of reimbursement for expenses of any solicitor, fundraising consultant, or coventurer; and (for initial registration only) when and where the organization was established; the tax-exempt status of the organization; and a copy of any IRS tax determination letter. Fees for registration are $0 for contributions received during the previous fiscal year if under $5,000, $50 for $5,000-$99,999, $100 if $100,000-$199,999, and $200 if $200,000 or more in contributions.

Annual Reports: see above. Reports are due within 4 1/2 months after the end of the fiscal year.

Organization Solicitation Disclosure Requirements: Must display in at least 9-point type a statement that *"Financial information about this organization and a copy of its license are available from the State Solicitation Licensing Division at 1-888-830-4989. The license is not an endorsement by the State."* The statement must be made conspicuous by either underlining, a border, or bold type.

Paid Solicitor Requirements: A $200 registration fee is required for both initial and renewal licenses; license expires on March 31 of each year. A bond of $20,000 is required if contributions received for the last fiscal year were less than $100,000; $30,000 if at least $100,000 and less than $200,000; and $50,000 if at least $200,000.

Fundraising Counsel Requirements: Same as above, except that no bond is required.

North Dakota

Central Switchboard: (701) 328-2000
State Web Home Page: http://www.nd.gov

INCORPORATION

Contact:
> *Secretary of State*
> *Business Division*
> *Department 108*
> *600 East Boulevard Avenue*
> *Bismarck, ND 58505-0500*
> *(701) 328-4284*

Citation: *ND Nonprofit Corporation Act,* North Dakota Century Code, Chapter 10-33.

Publications Available: A copy of the *ND Nonprofit Corporation Act* is available from the contact office.

General Requirements: Articles of Incorporation must set forth the corporate name; that it is organized under Chapter 10-33 of the North Dakota Century Code; the address of the registered office; the name of the initial registered agent at that office; the effective date of the corporation; and the names, addresses, and signatures of the incorporators (at least one required).

Corporate Name: May not contain any word or phrase that indicates or implies that it is organized for any purpose other than a legal purpose for which a nonprofit corporation may be organized; may not be the same as, or deceptively similar to, another without written consent; must be transliterated into letters of the English language if it is not in English.

Name Reservation: May be reserved for a renewable period of one year for a $10 fee.

How to File: Submit to the Secretary of State an original of the Articles of Incorporation, a signed consent of the registered agent form, a filing fee of $30 for the Articles of Incorporation, and $10 for the consent form.

Other Filings/Reports: An annual report must be filed disclosing general information, a brief statement describing the purpose that is actually pursued in the state, the names and addresses of officers and directors, and federal tax exemption information. The report, submitted on forms provided by the Secretary of State, is due on or before February 1 each year; the first report is due February 1 of the year following the year of incorporation. There is a $10 filing fee.

LOBBYING

Contact:
> *Secretary of State*
> *Licensing Division*
> *600 East Boulevard Avenue*
> *Department 108*
> *Bismarck, ND 58505-0500*
> *(701) 328-3665*

Citation: North Dakota Century Code, Chapter 54-05.1- 01 et seq.

Publications: A copy of the statute is available from the contact office or the Web site at: *http://www.state.nd.us/sec*

Registration Required: All lobbyists must register with the Secretary before engaging in lobbying. Registration includes general information, the code of primary activities of the entity, and a letter of authorization from each entity represented. The fee is $20 for the first entity represented and $5 for each additional one.

Forms to Use: SFN 11106 *Lobbyist Registration;* NDCC 54-05.1 *Authorization Letter for Lobbyist.*

Reporting Requirements: A detailed report is required to be submitted on or before August 1 each year of expenditures of $50 or more during the legislative session for lobbying.

TAX EXEMPTIONS

Contact:

North Dakota Office of State Tax Commissioner
600 E. Boulevard Avenue, Dept. 127
Bismarck, ND 58505-0599
income tax: (701) 328-2046
sales tax: (701) 328-3470

Citation: §57-38-09 —state income tax; §57-39.2-04 —sales tax.

Requirements: Organizations exempt from paying federal income tax are exempt from the state income tax. There are limited exemptions provided under the sales tax law. Consult the statute or the contact office.

CHARITABLE SOLICITATION

Contact:

Secretary of State
Department 108
600 East Boulevard Avenue
Bismarck, ND 58505-3665
(701) 328-3665
(800) 352-0867 ext. 8-3665

Citation: North Dakota Century Code, Section 50-22-01 et seq.

Publications: A copy of the statute is available from the contact office or at the Web site: http://www.nd.gov/sos

Initial Registration: All charitable organizations must register with the Secretary of State. The registration form discloses contact information, the form of the organization, date and place of organization, name and address of the person with custody over books and records, total compensation paid to employees and its affiliated organization, tax-exempt status, fiscal year, purposes, how charitable contributions will be used, methods by which solicitation will be made, names of those with authority to distribute and use the contributions, and amount of total contributions received during the previous fiscal year. The registration fee is $25, and must also include a financial statement of the organization's operations for its most recent 12-month period.

Annual Reports: Must file an annual report to the Secretary of State before September 1, with a $10 fee. The report includes a 12-month financial statement, including total receipts, total income, cost of management and general, program services, cost of fundraising, cost of public education, funds or properties transferred out of state, total net amount disbursed within the state, names of professional fundraisers, and total compensation paid to employees. Charities must include copies of tax and information returns.

Paid Solicitor Requirements: Must register apply for a license and pay a $100 annual fee. Registration expires every September 1. Registration discloses contact information, type of fundraising conducted, name of person who maintains the fundraiser's records, a list of those who work under the registrant's direction, and a list of all licensed charities which the registrant contracts with in the state. Registrants must post a $20,000 bond.

Fundraising Counsel Requirements: Must apply for a license and pay a $100 annual fee.

Ohio

Central Switchboard: (614) 466-2000
State Web Home Page: http://ohio.gov

INCORPORATION

Contact:

> Secretary of State
> Business Services
> 180 East Broad Street
> 16th Floor
> Columbus, OH 43215
> (614) 466-3623
> (877) 767-3453

Citation: *Nonprofit Corporation Law, §1702.01 et seq.*

Publications Available: *Legal Guide for Nonprofit Organizations* is being updated and is available soon from the contact office or online at: *http://www.state.oh.us/pubAffairs/businessPubs.aspx?Section=102*

General Requirements: Any person, without regard to residence, may act as an incorporator. Articles of Incorporation must set forth purposes (must not be too general), the names and street addresses of at least three natural persons who will serve as initial trustees, and the corporate name and location of the principal office. The articles must be signed by the incorporators.

Corporate Name: Is not required to end in "Incorporated" or "Inc."; must be distinguishable from others without written permission.

Name Reservation: May be reserved for 60 days for a fee of $50.

How to File: File Articles of Incorporation with the Secretary of State using Form 532. The filing fee is $125.

Other Filings/Reports: A statement of continued existence must be filed within five years from the date of incorporation or previous corporate filing. The Secretary of State provides the form and notice. The fee is $25.

LOBBYING

Contact:

> Office of the Legislative Inspector General
> Joint Legislative Ethics Committee
> 50 W. Broad Street—Suite 1308
> Columbus, OH 43215-3365
> (614) 728-5100

Citation: Section 101.70 et seq., Ohio Revised Code; Section 121.60 et seq., Ohio Revised Code. Section 101.90 et seq., Ohio Revised Code.

Publications: *Ohio Lobbying Handbook; Scenarios and Reporting Requirements for Legislative Agents and Employers,* and a copy of the statute and rules are provided by the contact office.

Registration Required: Every lobbyist and employer, within 10 days after hiring a lobbyist, must file an initial registration statement with the Committee disclosing general information, a brief description of the type of legislation being lobbied, and the category of the principal business or activity of the employer. There is a $25 filing fee, which is waived for state employees. Lobbyists and employers of lobbyists must file an updated registration statement by the last day of January, May, and September, covering four-month periods ending in the month prior to the month in which the report is filed. There is no fee for that filing. The updated registration reports provide for itemized expenditure reporting. For-profit business arrangements between lobbyists or their employers (including immediate family) and members of the general assembly and certain other public officials, including staff, also require disclosure.

Forms to Use: *Legislative Agent/Employer Initial Registration Statement; Legislative Agent Updated Registration Statement; Employer of Legislative Agent Updated Registration Statement*

Reporting requirements: See above.

TAX EXEMPTIONS

Contact:

> *Ohio Department of Taxation*
> *Business Tax Division*
> *PO Box 2476*
> *Columbus, OH 43216-0232*
> *(614) 387-0232*
> *(614) 466-4810 (sales and use tax)*

Citation: ORC §5733.01 and 5339.02

Publications: *Ohio Business Tax Guide* from the web site at *http://tax.ohio.gov/* (Choose "research" and then "publications."

Requirements: Nonprofit corporations organized under ORC Chapter 1702 are exempt from the corporate franchise tax. Churches, nonprofit and charitable organizations, and 501(c)(3) tax-exempt organizations are exempt from paying Ohio sales or use tax on their purchases. Sales by these same organizations require the collection of sales or use tax if the number of days of the sales exceeds six in any calendar year. Nonprofit organizations are not required to register for or to file returns or make payments for the commercial activity tax. For purposes of the commercial activity tax only, the term "nonprofit organization" is narrowly defined as an entity that (1) is organized other than for pecuniary gain or profit; (2) does not distribute its net earnings to the entity's members, directors, officers, or other private persons, unless otherwise permitted by law; and (3) operates consistent with its mission.

Application Procedure: There is no application process for sales tax exemption. Exempt organizations present vendors with a certificate of exemption that is available on the Web site at: *http://tax.ohio.gov.* There is no application or filing process for commercial activity tax exemption.

CHARITABLE SOLICITATION

Contact:

> *Attorney General—Charitable Law Section*
> *150 E. Gay Street, 23rd Floor*
> *Columbus, OH 43215-5148*
> *(614) 466-3180*

Citation: Chapter 1716, Section 1716.01 et seq.

Initial Registration: Most charitable organizations that compensate those primarily to solicit contributions or that raise more than $25,000 during their most recent fiscal year must register with the Attorney General. Initial registration must include a copy of the Articles of Incorporation or other organizational charter, bylaws, a copy of the IRS determination letter, and general information. The filing fee ranges from $0 (less than $5,000 in contributions) to $200 (more than $50,000 in contributions) for the last calendar or fiscal year, received from persons within Ohio. Renewals also include general financial and contact information; information about organizational misconduct; names and addresses of all officers, directors, trustees, and executive personnel; and specific financial arrangements with outside fundraisers.

Annual Reports: Registration statements must be refiled on or before the 15th day of the fifth calendar month after the close of each fiscal year. The fees apply to renewal registrations as well. Charities that are required to register must file annual financial reports that include a balance sheet; a statement of support, revenue, expenses, and changes in the fund balance; the names and addresses of fundraising counsel, professional solicitors, and commercial coventurers used and the amounts received from each; a statement of functional expenses itemized by categories of program, management/general and fundraising; and a financial statement, report, or IRS 990 tax return.

Organization Solicitation Disclosure Requirements: Whether or not required to register by the law, every charitable organization must make disclosures at the point of solicitation of the name of the charity and the city of the principal place of business of the charity. The particular charitable purpose to be advanced with the funds raised if no 501(c)(3) determination letter has been received and is currently in effect must also be disclosed.

Paid Solicitor Requirements: Must register, pay a $200 fee and post bond in the amount of $25,000. Prior to the beginning of a solicitation campaign, professional solicitors must file a *Solicitation Notice* with the Attorney General. The Notice includes a copy of the contract with the charity, a certification statement by the charity, and general information about the campaign. Not later than 90 days after the campaign has been completed or on the first anniversary of the campaign, the solicitor must file a financial report.

Fundraising Counsel Requirements: Those with custody of contributions at any time must register, post a $25,000 bond, and pay a $200 fee.

Oklahoma

Central Switchboard: (405) 521-2011
State Web Home Page: http://www.state.ok.us/

INCORPORATION

Contact:
> Secretary of State
> 101 State Capitol
> 2300 N. Lincoln Boulevard
> Oklahoma City, OK 73105-4897
> (405) 521-3912

Citation: Title 18, *Oklahoma General Corporation Act, 18 § 1001 et seq.*

Publications Available: *Title 18-Oklahoma General Corporation Act* is available from the contact office; forms and *Procedures for Organizing an Oklahoma Business Corporation* are available from the contact office.

General Requirements: Three or more incorporators are required. Any person (without regard to residence), partnership, or corporation may act as an incorporator; must set forth the name; address of registered office; the name of the registered agent at that office; the nature of the business or purposes; the name, addresses, and signatures of each incorporator; that the corporation does not afford pecuniary gain, incidentally or otherwise, to its members; the name and mailing address of each trustee or director and the number to be elected at the first meeting; optional provisions relating to the internal regulation and management; and the duration, unless it is perpetual. Must indicate that the organization does not have authority to issue capital stock.

Corporate Name: Must contain one of the following words: association, company, corporation, club, foundation, fund, incorporated, institute, society, union, syndicate, or limited, or one of the abbreviations "co.," "corp.," "inc.," "ltd.," or words or abbreviations of like import in other languages provided that such abbreviations are written in Roman characters or letters. The name must be distinguishable from other corporations, limited partnerships, or limited liability companies or reserved names,

including those that existed at any time during the preceding three years.

Name Check/Name Reservation: May be reserved for 60 days for a $10 fee by filing a name reservation application; may be checked by telephone or in person by calling (405) 521-3912.

How to File: File Certificate of Incorporation with the Secretary of State with a $25 fee.

Other Filings/reports: None.

LOBBYING

Contact:
> Ethics Commission
> B-5 State Capitol
> Oklahoma City, OK 73105
> (405) 521-3451

Citation: 74 § 4249 et seq; 74 CH 62 App., §257:23-1-1 et seq.; § 257:1-1-2.

Publications: *Constitutional and Statutory Provisions and Constitutional Ethics Rules governing the Ethical Conduct of State Officers and Employers and Campaigns for State Office or State Issues* and *1999-2000 Lobbyist Registration and Regulation* are available from the contact office.

Registration Required: Lobbyists who are employed or retained by another for compensation to perform services that include lobbying must register with the Commission. Registration must occur within five days after engaging in lobbying for a new client, or during the month of January of each odd-numbered year. The form requires general information and the names and addresses of the lobbyist's clients.

Forms to Use: L-1, *Lobbyist Registration;* L-2 *Lobbyist or Other Person Gift Report.*

Reporting Requirements: All lobbyists and those who give things to state officers or state employees with a value of more than $50 in the aggregate during any six-month period (January 1-June 30 and July 1-December 31) must submit an L-2 report.

TAX EXEMPTIONS

Contact:

> Oklahoma Tax Commission
> Taxpayer Assistance Division (sales tax)
> PO Box 26850
> Oklahoma City, OK 73126-0920
> (405) 521-3160

Citation: 68 § 2359— income tax; 68 § 1356— sales tax.

Requirements: Organizations that are exempt from paying federal income tax are exempt from paying state income taxes other than on unrelated business income. There are limited exemptions provided to charities and educational institutions provided in the statute, such as churches, council organizations of the Boy Scouts and Girl Scouts, accredited museums, meals on wheels programs, PTAs, certain Older Americans Act-funded programs, nonprofit private schools, youth camps, nonprofit community blood banks, federally qualified health care facilities, and the Camp Fire Girls. Consult the contact office or the statute for more information.

Application Procedure: File Form 13-16-A with the Commission. The form includes information about paying taxes on unrelated business income. Attach a copy of the federal 990 annual tax return.

CHARITABLE SOLICITATION

Contact:

> Oklahoma Secretary of State
> 2300 N. Lincoln Boulevard
> Room 101
> Oklahoma City, OK 73105-4897
> (405) 521-3911

Citation: *Oklahoma Solicitation of Charitable Contributions Act*, 18 §552.1 et seq.

Initial Registration: All charitable organizations must register with the Secretary of State using the *Uniform Registration Statement— Charitable Organization* form or the form provided by that office. The Unified Registration form requires more information than is required by Oklahoma. The statement discloses general information; information about organizational misconduct; information about use of outside professional fundraisers, solicitors, counsel and coventurers and amounts paid to them during the previous year; total contributions in the previous year; total fundraising costs in the previous year; and information about methods of solicitation. There is a $15 fee for new registrations and renewal registrations each year.

Annual Reports: Financial reports are required to be filed along with registration statements and renewals.

Organization Solicitation Disclosure requirements: None.

Paid Solicitor Requirements: Must register, pay a $10 fee.

Fundraising Counsel Requirements: Must register, pay a $50 fee and post a $2,500 bond.

Oregon

Central Switchboard: (503) 378-6500
State Web Home Page: http://www.oregon.gov

INCORPORATION

Contact:

Secretary of State
Corporation Division
255 Capitol St. NE; Suite 151
Salem, OR 97310-1327
(503) 986-2200

Citation: Chapter 65 ORS65.001 et seq.

Publications Available: A copy of Chapter 65, Nonprofit Corporations law, is available from the Legislative Counsel (503-986-1243). The Business Information Center (503-986-2200) provides online information that includes Articles of Incorporation forms and the *Oregon Business Guide* at: *http://www.filinginoregon.com*

General Requirements: Articles of Incorporation must set forth corporate name; a statement that the corporation is a public benefit corporation, a mutual benefit corporation, or a religious corporation; the address of the corporation's initial registered office and the name of its initial registered agent at that location; the name and address of each incorporator; an alternative corporate mailing address until the principal office has been designated in the annual report; whether the corporation will have members; provisions regarding distribution of assets upon dissolution; and optional provisions.

Corporate Name: May not contain language stating or implying that it is organized for a purpose other than permitted by law or its articles; shall not contain the word "cooperative" or the phrase "limited partnership." Shall be written in the alphabet used for the English language, but may include Arabic and Roman numerals and incidental punctuation; and shall be distinguishable from others.

Name Reservation: May be reserved for a renewable 120-day period for a processing fee of $50.

How to File: File one original with the Secretary of State with a $50 filing fee. Documents can be faxed in with a Visa or MasterCard number. The fax number is on the form; faxed documents will be filed within 72 hours.

Other Filings/Reports: An annual report with a $50 processing fee must be filed with the Secretary of State on the first anniversary of the corporation. The report includes general information, a brief description of the nature of the activities, and the names and addresses of the president and secretary. Forms are mailed by the Secretary of State in advance of the due date, but failure to receive the form does not relieve the corporation of its duty to file it. After the first year, corporations are renewed with a coupon and $50 filing fee. Any updates to officers and addresses can be made by completing Form 139 (Amendment to Annual Report). There is no processing fee. This form is available at the Web site.

LOBBYING

Contact:

Oregon Government Ethics Commission
3218 Pringle Road, SE
Suite 220
Salem, OR 97302-1544
(503) 378-5105

Citation: ORS 171.725 et seq.

Publications: *Guide to Lobbying in Oregon* is available from the contact office and the Web site: *http://www.gspc.state.or.us*

Registration Required: All lobbyists who spend more than 24 hours lobbying in any calendar quarter, or spend more than $100 for lobbying in a calendar quarter must register, within three working days of achieving these thresholds. There is no registration fee. Registrations expire on December 31 of each odd-numbered year.

Forms to Use: *Lobbying Registration Statement; Lobbyist Expenditure Report; Entity Expenditure Report; Lobbyist Termination Form.*

Reporting Requirements: All registered lobbyists and entities employing them must submit quarterly itemized expenditure reports. Lobbyist and entity reports are due 15 days following the end of each quarter. Expenditure categories include food, refreshment, and entertainment; expenditures reimbursed by the client or organization employing the lobbyist; and itemized expenditures made on behalf of a legislator or executive branch official of over $50 on any single occasion. Note: Regulations implementing a revised state lobbying law that took effect on January 1, 2008, had not been developed before this publication went to press.

TAX EXEMPTIONS

Contact:

> *Oregon Department of Revenue*
> *955 Center Street, NE*
> *Salem, OR 97301-2555*
> *(503) 378-4988*
> *1-800-356-4222 (toll free within Oregon)*

Citation: Chapter 317.080, Oregon Revised Statutes —corporate excise/income tax.

Requirements: Organizations with federal tax-exempt status are automatically exempt from state corporate excise taxes/income taxes other than unrelated business taxable income. If organizations have unrelated business taxable income, they need to file a Form 20 (Oregon Corporate Excise Tax Return) and attach a copy of their federal tax return.

Application Procedure: Organizations qualify for exemption automatically upon receiving their IRS determination letters certifying federal exemption.

CHARITABLE SOLICITATION

Contact:

> *Department of Justice*
> *Charitable Activities Section*
> *1515 SW 5th Avenue, Suite 410*
> *Portland, OR 97201*
> *(971) 673-1880*

Citation: *Charitable Trust and Corporation Act,* ORS 128.610 et seq.; Oregon Administrative Rules, Chapter 137, Section 10-005 et seq.

Publications: Forms and a copy of the statute are available from the contact office and the Web site: *http://www.doj.state.or.us*

Initial Registration: Charitable corporations and trusts must register with the Department of Justice. Corporations must include Articles of Incorporation; bylaws; IRS determination letter; printed brochures, reports, and newsletters; and a list of directors. Charitable trusts must include a trust agreement or will, the IRS determination letter (if applicable), and a list of trust officers. The registration form discloses general information and a brief description of the mission and activities of the organization. Organizational publications may substitute for a specific narrative statement. There is no fee for the initial registration, which is accomplished by filing the *Registration of Charitable Corporation or Charitable Trust* form.

Annual Reports: An annual financial report must be submitted on either a calendar year or fiscal year basis, and is due four months and 15 days after the close of the accounting year. Forms are mailed at the end of each accounting year. A filing fee ranges from $10 (for less than $25,000 in income and receipts) to $200 (for more than $1 million in income and receipts), plus an additional fee of .18% of the fund balance up to $10 million. No fee based on fund balance is required if the fund balance is less than $50,000.

Organization Solicitation Disclosure Requirements: None.

Paid Solicitor Requirements: Must register and pay an annual registration fee of $250; must file a fundraising notice with the Attorney General and a written financial plan with the charity. Solicitors must disclose that the solicitor is operating under the direction and control of a named professional fundraising firm. Must submit a financial report to the Attorney General within 90 days after a solicitation campaign is completed.

Fundraising Counsel Requirements: Must register and pay a $250 fee if they have access to contributions.

Pennsylvania

Central Switchboard: (717) 787-2121
State Web Home Page: http://www.state.pa.us/PaPower

INCORPORATION

Contact:

Department of State
Corporation Bureau
206 North Office Building
Harrisburg, PA 17120
(717) 787-1057

Citation: Title 15, 5101 et seq.

General Requirements: One or more natural persons of full age are required to incorporate. Articles of Incorporation must set forth the corporate name; address of the initial registered office (PO Box is not allowed); name of its commercial registered office provider; purpose(s); that the corporation does not contemplate pecuniary gain or profit, incidental or otherwise; that it is organized on a nonstock basis; whether the corporation will have members; whether the incorporators constitute a majority of the members of the committee authorized to incorporate; the name, address, and signatures of each incorporator; the effective date; and additional optional provisions.

Corporate Name: Corporate designation is not required. May not contain the word "cooperative" or its abbreviation. Must be in the English language or letters; may not contain a blasphemy; may not contain language that the corporation is organized for a purpose other than those stated in the Articles, or that it is a government agency of Pennsylvania or the U.S., a bank or savings institution, a trust company, insurance company, or a public utility. May not be the same or similar to another corporation or any other reserved or registered name.

Name Check/Name Reservation: Telephone (717) 787-1057 for a name search at no charge; name check will be provided in writing for a $15 fee. Names may be reserved for a renewable 120-day period for a fee of $70.

How to File: Provide the $125 filing fee, one original of the Articles of Incorporation (Form DSCB:15-5306) and a copy of docketing statement form DSCB:15-134A. The docketing statement asks 16 questions, including whether the association solicited or intends to solicit contributions in Pennsylvania. Incorporators must advertise their intention to file or the corporation shall advertise the filing of the Articles. The advertisement must appear in both a general circulation newspaper in the home county of the corporation and a legal journal.

Other Filings/Reports: Most nonprofit corporations must annually notify the Corporation Bureau of any changes in officers, using the DSCB:15-5110 form. There is no fee for this report.

LOBBYING

Contact:

Pennsylvania Department of State
210 North Office Building
Harrisburg, PA 17120
(717) 787-5280

Citation: *Lobbying Disclosure Law, Act 134 of 2006*

Publications: Required forms are available from the contact office and on the Web site (see below).

Registration Required: All lobbyists, lobbying forms, and principals must register unless otherwise excluded by the act. There is a biennial fee of $100.

Forms to Use: Form DSBE-1305-A is used for principals, lobbyists, and lobbying firms. The forms are available at: *http://www.dos.state.pa.us*

Reporting Requirements: Registered principals must file quarterly expense reports no later than 30 days after the last day of the quarter. Each expense report includes the total costs of all lobbying during the period. It includes office expenses, personnel expenses, expenditures related to gifts, hospitality, transportation, and lodging to state officials, employees, or their immediate family members and any other lobbying costs; and the costs of direct and indirect communication. The law requires a lobbying firm or a lobbyist not associated with such a firm to sign the reports submitted by each principal to attest to its validity and accuracy. A lobbying firm or lobbyist may attach a statement to the report of a principal describing the limits of the knowledge of that lobbying firm or lobbyist concerning the information in the expense report.

TAX EXEMPTIONS

Contact:

Department of Revenue
Bureau of Collections & Taxpayer Services
Strawberry Square—10th Fl.
Harrisburg, PA 17128-1041
(717) 787-1064

Citation: 72 P.S. §7204(1)—corporate income tax 61 Pa. Code §§32.1 and 32.21—sales and use tax.

Requirements: All nonstock, nonprofit corporations are exempt from the corporate income tax. For sales and use tax exemption, organizations must demonstrate that they meet a five-part test (advance a charitable purpose; donate or render gratuitously a substantial portion of its services; relieve government of some of its burden; serve a substantial, indefinite class of persons who are legitimate subjects of charity; and operate entirely free from private profit motive) emanating from a 1985 Pennsylvania Supreme Court decision.

Application Procedure: Submit PA-100 combined form along with REV-72 form.

CHARITABLE SOLICITATION

Contact:

Department of State
Bureau of Charitable Organizations
207 North Office Building
Harrisburg, PA 17120
(717) 783-1720
1-800-732-0999

Citation: Act 90-202, Solicitation of Funds for Charitable Purposes Act, 10 P.S. § 162.1 et seq.

Publications: A copy of the statute and required forms are available from the contact office or the Web site at: http://www.dos.state.pa.us/charities

Initial Registration: Every charitable organization that raises $25,000 or more must register with the Bureau within 30 days after contributions in excess of $25,000 are received. A charitable organization that uses paid solicitors must register with the Bureau prior to such persons conducting solicitations. Registration fees range from $15 (organizations filing a short form, or those with $25,000 or less in gross contributions annually) to $250 (for organizations with more than $500,000 in gross contributions). The form to use is BCO-10, and may be filed electronically.

Annual Reports: Renewal registrations using Form BCO-10 are due within 135 days after the close of the organization's fiscal year. Reports vary with amount of gross contributions: No financial statement is required to be filed for charities eligible to file a short form registration. They may file their IRS 990 tax return and schedule A, and Form BCO-23. $0-<$50,000 in gross contributions require internally prepared, compiled, reviewed, or audited financial statements, Form BCO-23; and federal 990 (for those required to file it with the IRS) along with Schedule A. $50,000 to less than $100,000 in gross contributions: require a compiled, reviewed, or audited financial statements; Form BCO-23; federal 990 (for those required to file it with the IRS) with Schedule A. $100,000 to <$300,000 in gross contributions require a reviewed or audited financial statement; with Form BCO-23; and federal 990 with Schedule A. >$300,000 in gross contributions require an audited financial statement, Form BCO-23; federal 990, with Schedule A. The BCO-23, Pennsylvania Public Disclosure Form, discloses information about contributions; receipts; contributions received from federated fundraising organizations; gross contributions; program service revenues; government grants and contracts; administrative expense; membership dues receipts; fundraising expenses; fund balances; and other fiscal information. Most organizations may file their 990 Annual tax return rather than the BCO-23.

Organization Written Solicitation Disclosure Requirements: Every written confirmation, receipt or reminder of a contribution shall conspicuously state:

The official registration and financial information of (insert legal name of the charity registered with the Department) may be obtained from the Pennsylvania Department of State by calling toll free, within Pennsylvania, 1 (800) 732-0999. Registration does not imply endorsement.

Paid Solicitor Requirements: Must register, pay a $250 annual fee, and post a $25,000 bond; must file a copy of the contract with the charity with a solicitation notice, which has a $25 fee.

Fundraising Counsel Requirements: Must register and pay a $250 annual fee.

Rhode Island

Central Switchboard: (401) 222-2000
State Web Home Page: http://www.state.ri.us/

INCORPORATION

Contact:

> Secretary of State
> Corporations
> 148 W. River Street
> Providence, RI 02904-2615
> (401) 222-2185

Citation: *Rhode Island Nonprofit Corporation Act,* Chapter 7-6-1 et seq. of the General Laws of Rhode Island.

Publications Available: The blank forms are provided by the contact office or online at: *http://www.state.ri.us*

General Requirements: Articles of Incorporation must set forth the corporate name; period of duration; purpose(s) (must be specific); provisions, if any, not inconsistent with the law, which the incorporators elect to set forth in the Articles for the regulation of the internal affairs of the corporation; address of the initial registered office and the name of the initial registered agent at that address; the number of directors constituting the initial board of directors; their names and addresses; the name, address, and signature of each incorporator; and the date when the corporate existence is to begin. This date cannot be more than 30 days after the Articles are filed.

Corporate Name: Must be distinguishable from others. Shall not contain any word or phrase that indicates or implies that it is organized for any purpose other than one or more purposes contained in its Articles of Incorporation; shall not be the same as, or deceptively similar to, the name of another; shall be transliterated into letters of the English alphabet if it is not in English.

Name Check: Name may be reserved for 120 days for $20. May be checked by telephoning the contact office or online at: *http://www.state.ri.us*

How to File: File original Articles of Incorporation using Form 200 with a $35 filing fee.

Other Filings/Reports: Annual reports must be filed in June; annual reports are mailed by the contact office prior to the due date. There is a $20 filing fee. Forms may also be obtained online at: *http://www.state.ri.us*

LOBBYING

Contact:

> Department of State
> Lobbyist Registrar
> 82 Smith Street
> Providence, RI 02903
> (401) 222-2357

Citation: 22 §10-1 et seq., General Laws of Rhode Island.

Publications: *Guide to Rhode Island Lobbying Laws* is provided by the contact office and online at: *http://www.sec.state.ri.gov/pubinfo/ lobbying/lobby_guide.html*

Registration Required: Lobbyists must register with the Department of State within seven days of employment as a lobbyist; disclosure includes general information and the legislation by bill number or subject matter that is the target of lobbying. Those who hire a lobbyist must have the name of their lobbyist entered into the lobbyist register of the Secretary of State. Lobbyists must wear identification badges. The registration fee is $5.

Reporting Requirements: Lobbyists and those who hire lobbyists must file updated expense reports on the 15th of each month starting in March until final adjournment of the General Assembly, and a final report is due no later than 30 days after adjournment. The reports disclose compensation paid to the lobbyist, itemizations of expenditures, and gifts and honoraria in excess of $25, and which bills they promote and/or oppose. Bills are listed by bill number or subject matter.

TAX EXEMPTIONS

Contact:

Department of Administration
Division of Taxation
One Capitol Hill
Providence, RI 02908-5800
(401) 222-1120 (corporate taxes)
(401) 222-2950 (sales and excise taxes)

Citation: §44-18-30.1 —sales and use tax; §44-11-1(iv) —business corporation tax.

Requirements: Organizations with federal tax exemption status are not required to file corporate or franchise tax returns unless they have a filing requirement with the IRS (such as unrelated business income taxes). Organizations exempt from RI Sales and Use tax are: nonprofit hospitals, educational institutions, churches, orphanages, institutions operated exclusively for religious or charitable purposes, nonprofit interest-free loan associations, nonprofit youth sporting leagues and bands for youth under 19, PTAs, state chapters of certain vocational student organizations, and certain senior citizens organizations.

Application Procedure: File an *Application for Certification of Exemption for an Exempt Organization From the Rhode Island Sales and Use Tax*, and include a $25 application fee.

CHARITABLE SOLICITATION

Contact:

Department of Business Regulation
Division of Securities Regulation
Charitable Organizations Section
233 Richmond Street
Providence, RI 02903-4232
(401) 222-2246

Citation: §5-53-1 et seq. Note: An amended Charitable Solicitation Law was enacted in 1999.

Initial Registration: Charities that do not intend to receive or do not receive more than $25,000 in contributions during a calendar year are exempt, as well as 14 other categories of organizations. File *Application for Registration as a Charitable Organization in Rhode Island*. The filing fee is $75 for annual registration and $75 for annual renewals. The form discloses general information; EIN number; IRS status; the percentage of contributions received that is spent on fundraising and administration; information about officers, directors, trustees and CEO; a description of solicitation methods; purposes of contributions; and the percentage of contributions spent on fundraising and administration. Submit an audited financial report if annual gross income is more than $500,000; include the organization's latest federal form 990 annual tax return. Other disclosure is required. Renewal forms are sent automatically each year by the Department.

Annual Reports: Same as registration (see above).

Organization Solicitation Disclosure Requirements: None.

Paid Solicitor Requirements: Must pay a $200 registration fee and post a $10,000 bond.

Fundraising Counsel Requirements: Must pay a $200 annual registration fee.

South Carolina

Central Switchboard: (803) 896-0000
State Web Home Page: http://www.sc.gov

INCORPORATION

Contact:

Secretary of State
1205 Pendleton Street
PO Box 11350
Columbia, SC 29211
(803) 734-2158

Citation: *South Carolina Nonprofit Corporation Act, §33-31-101 et seq.*

Publications Available: A sample Articles of Incorporation form is provided by the contact office.

General Requirements: Articles must set forth corporate name; that it is either a public benefit, mutual benefit, or religious corporation; the address of the initial registered office; the name of the initial registered agent at that office; the name, address, and signature of each incorporator; whether it will have members; provisions relating to the distribution of assets upon dissolution; the address of the principal office; and optional provisions relating to the internal regulation and management, directors, and rights of members.

Corporate Name: Must contain the word "corporation," "incorporated," "company," or "limited," the abbreviation "corp.," "inc.," "co.," or "ltd.," or words or abbreviations of like import in another language. May not contain language stating or implying that it is organized for a purpose other than that permitted by law or its Articles of Incorporation. Must be distinguishable from others without written permission.

Name Reservation: Names may be reserved for a non-renewable 120-day period for a $10 fee.

How to File: File two copies of the Articles of Incorporation (the original and either a duplicate original or a conformed copy) and a $25 filing fee with the Secretary of State.

Other Filings/Reports: An annual report may be required to be filed with the South Carolina Department of Revenue.

LOBBYING

Contact:

State Ethics Commission
5000 Thurmond Mall
Suite 250
Columbia, SC 29201
(803) 253-4192

Citation: *Lobbyists Registration Act, §2-17-10, Code of Laws of South Carolina.*

Registration Required: Lobbyists must register with the Commission and pay a $100 fee. The form discloses general information about the lobbyist and client(s) and the legislative, agency, or gubernatorial action to which the lobbying relates. Clients must also register with the Commission and pay a $100 fee. Registration is on an annual basis and must be done prior to January 5 of each year, or within 15 days of being retained.

Forms to use: SEC—L1A.2 *Lobbyist Registration* (green form); SEC—L4A *Lobbyist Disclosure Statement*; SEC—L2A.2 *Lobbyist's Principal Registration;* and SEC—L5A.2 *Lobbyist's Principal Disclosure Statement.*

Reporting Requirements: Lobbyists and their clients/employers must file itemized income and expenditure reports prior to June 30 and January 31. The report discloses all income and expenses related to lobbying, categorized by supplies, rent, utilities, compensation of support personnel, and other expenditures.

TAX EXEMPTIONS

Contact:

> Department of Revenue
> 301 Gervais Street
> PO Box 125
> Columbia, SC 29214
> (803) 898-5000

Citation: Code Section 12-36-2120(41)—sales tax; §12-6-540 and §12-20-110—income tax.

Requirements: Corporations exempt from federal income tax pursuant to IRC Section 501 are exempt from the state license on capital (franchise tax) and income tax. Sales tax exemption covers only items bought and sold by certain exempt charitable organizations, if used for exempt purposes with no inurement to any individual and the organization purchases the items for resale.

Application Procedure: File form ST-387, *Application for Sales Tax Exemption Under Code Section 12-36-2120(41), "Exempt Organizations."* Include charter and bylaws; most recent income statement and balance sheet; IRS determination letter; and disclose general information, including the purpose of the organization, the items the organization purchases or will purchase, how proceeds from the sales will be used, and what other retail sales are made by the organization. Mail to: SC Department of Revenue, License and Registration, Columbia, SC 29214-0140.

CHARITABLE SOLICITATION

Contact:

> Secretary of State
> Division of Public Charities
> PO Box 11350
> Columbia, SC 29211
> (803) 734-1790

Citation: *South Carolina Solicitation of Charitable Funds Act of 1994,* Title 33, 33-56-10 et seq.

Publications: A copy of the statute and forms are available from the contact office.

Initial Registration: Charities raising at least $5,000 in a calendar year must register with the Division annually. The filing fee is $50. The uniform registration statement discloses general information, outside professionals used for fundraising, the amount paid to them in the previous year, total contributions during the previous year, and total fundraising costs during the previous year. Charities renew registrations 4½ months after the end of the organization's fiscal year.

Annual Reports: Each charity must submit an annual financial report no later than 4½ months after the end of its fiscal year, but may submit its federal 990 or 990-EZ in lieu of the form provided by the Secretary of State's Office. Attached schedules itemize contributions, and disclose information about contracts with professional fundraising solicitors, fundraising counsels, and commercial coventurers.

Organization Solicitation Disclosure Requirements: See below.

Paid Solicitor Requirements: Must register annually, pay a $50 filing fee, and post a $15,000 bond. They must deliver information about the charity, purpose of contributions, and financial statements upon request of a solicited party; must disclose his/her status as a professional solicitor, the name of the fundraising organization, and the charity represented at the initial time of solicitation. Joint financial reports are due 90 days after the end of each campaign when they last less than one year, and on the anniversary date of the campaign when they last a year or more.

Fundraising Counsel Requirements: Must register and pay a $50 annual filing fee.

South Dakota

Central Switchboard: (605) 773-3011
State Web Home Page: http://www.sd.gov

INCORPORATION

Contact:

Secretary of State
State Capitol
500 E. Capitol
Pierre, SD 57501-5077
(605) 773-4845

Citation: *South Dakota Nonprofit Corporation Act,* SDCL 47-22.

Publications Available: Sample incorporation forms are available from the contact office.

General Requirements: Three or more natural persons of legal age are required to act as incorporators. Articles must set forth the corporate name; period of existence; purposes; whether the corporation will have members and provisions relating to members; how directors will be elected or appointed if not elected or appointed by members; provisions relating to internal affairs and provision for the distribution of assets upon dissolution; street address of the initial registered office (or a statement that there is no street address); the name of the initial registered agent at that address; the number of directors and their names and addresses; and the name, address, and signature of each incorporator. A consent of appointment must also be provided by the registered agent.

Corporate Name: Shall not contain a word or phrase that indicates or implies that it is organized for a purpose other than permitted in the Articles; may not be the same as or must be distinguishable upon the records of the Secretary of State from the name of any other corporation; shall be transliterated into letters of the English alphabet if not in English.

Name reservation: May be reserved for a non-renewable period of 120 days for a $20 fee.

How to File: Send an original and one exact or conformed copy of the Articles with a $25 filing fee.

Other Filings/Reports: Domestic nonprofit corporations must file a corporate report annually. The form is mailed by the Secretary of State's Office as a reminder to the registered agent listed with the office. The report is due the anniversary month of the original filing of the incorporation. The fee is $10. An additional penalty fee is assessed if the report is not filed by the last day of the month following the anniversary month.

LOBBYING

Contact:

Secretary of State
State Capitol, Suite 204
500 East Capitol Avenue
Pierre, SD 57501-5070
(605) 773-3537

Citation: Chapter 2-12, 2-12-1 et seq.

Publications: A copy of the statute and forms are available from the contact office.

Registration Required: Lobbyists must register with the Secretary of State and pay a $35 fee. The registration form discloses general contact information, employer, and subject of interest. All lobbyists must file the lobbyist employer's written authorization with the Secretary of State within 10 days after registration.

Forms to Use: SOS form *Lobbyist Registration; Lobbyist Expense Report Form; Lobbyist Employer Expense Report form.* There is also a form to authorize lobbying on behalf of a client/employer. Lobbyists and their employers, on separate forms, must report the date, amount, and purpose of each lobbying expense; lobbyists must wear lobbyist badges within the Capitol complex.

Reporting Requirements: Expense reports must be filed by lobbyists and their employers on or before July 1 each year. The compensation to the lobbyist is not required to be reported.

TAX EXEMPTIONS

Contact:

> Department of Revenue
> 445 East Capitol Avenue
> Pierre, SD 57501-3100
> (605) 773-3311

Citation: §10-45-13; 10-45-14.

Requirements: Charities must submit an application form to the Department for exempt status. For exemption from sales tax, the organization must be organized and conducted solely for the benefit of the general public and for the relief of public burden, may not turn away someone in need of the agency's service if not able to pay for it, may not provide for gain or profit for any private member of the agency, and must be recognized as a 501(c)(3) by the Internal Revenue Service.

There is no corporate income tax or personal income tax in the state.

Application Procedure: Submit ST-130 form with bylaws, Articles of Incorporation, constitution, and IRS determination letter. Exemption must be renewed every five years.

CHARITABLE SOLICITATION

Contact:

> Office of the Attorney General
> Division of Consumer Protection
> 1302 E. Highway 14
> Suite 3
> Pierre, SD 57501-8503
> (605) 773-4400

Citation: Chapter 37-30, 37-30-1 et seq. (for paid solicitors).

Publications: A copy of the telephone solicitation statute is available from the contact office and on the Web site at: http://www.state.sd.us/atg

Initial Registration: None.

Annual reports: None.

Organization Solicitation Disclosure Requirements: None.

Paid Solicitor Requirements: Paid solicitors must register no less than 30 days before conducting any solicitation. Registration is annual. A bond of $10,000 is required if the applicant solicits contributions but does not have physical access to contributions, and a $20,000 bond is required if physical access is available. Must file solicitation notices with the Department; contracts between solicitor and charity must be in writing and shall state the minimum amount the charity will receive as a percentage of gross revenue and may not include expenses of the solicitor paid by the charity. Financial reports must be filed by the solicitor within 90 days after a solicitation campaign has been completed or on the anniversary of the commencement of a campaign that lasts more than one year.

Fundraising Counsel Requirements: None.

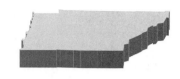

Tennessee

Central Switchboard: (615) 741-3011
State Web Home Page: http://www.tennessee.gov

INCORPORATION

Contact:

> Department of State
> Division of Business Services
> 312 Eighth Avenue North
> 6th Fl.; William R. Snodgrass Tower
> Nashville, TN 37243
> (615) 741-2286

Citation: *Tennessee Nonprofit Corporation Act,* Tennessee Code Annotated Section 48-51-101 et seq.

Publications Available: A *Non-Profit Filing Guide* and all forms are available from the contact office, and can be accessed at: *http://www.state.tn.us/sos*

General Requirements: Charter must set forth the corporate name; whether it is a public benefit, mutual benefit, or religious corporation; the address of the initial registered office and the name of the initial registered agent at that office; the name, address, and signature of each incorporator; the address of the principal office; that the corporation is a nonprofit corporation; the effective date of charter; provisions regarding the distribution of assets upon dissolution; and optional provisions.

Corporate Name: May not contain language stating or implying that it is organized for a purpose other than permitted by law or its charter; or organized as, or affiliated with, or sponsored by, any fraternal, veterans', religious, charitable, or professional organization unless it is certified by those organizations in writing; must be distinguishable from others without written permission; must not state or imply that it is or is affiliated with an agency or instrumentality of a government agency unless if such is true and is certified in writing.

Name Reservation: May be reserved for a renewable four-month period upon payment of a $20 fee.

How to File: File the original with the Secretary of State with a $100 filing fee.

Other Filings/Reports: An annual report is required to be filed disclosing general information. The report is due the first day of the fourth month following the close of the corporation's fiscal year. The fee is $20, plus an additional $20 if there are changes to the registered agent or registered office.

LOBBYING

Contact:

> The Tennessee Ethics Commission
> 201 4th Avenue. North
> Suite 1820
> Nashville, TN 37248
> (615) 741-7959

Citation: *Tennessee Lobbyist Registration and Disclosure Act of 1975,* 3-6-101 et seq.

Publications: *Campaign Financial Disclosure Guidelines* (includes lobbying information) is available from the contact office.

Registration Required: All lobbyists must register with the Registry of Election Finance within 5 days after becoming lobbyists. There is a $100 registration fee. Registration is annual and expires on December 31. Disclosure includes general information and a listing of general subject matter that is the target of lobbying activity. Paid lobbyists are subject to an annual $400 occupational privilege tax.

Reporting Requirements: Reports are required to be filed no later than 30 days after the end of the annual General Assembly session or July 30, whichever is later, and December 31. The reports disclose information on business arrangements with public officials or candidates and an itemized list of political contributions in excess of $100.

TAX EXEMPTIONS

Contact:

Department of Revenue
Taxpayer Services Division
500 Deaderick Street
Nashville, TN 37242
(615) 253-0752 (sales tax)

Citation: T.C.A. Section 67-6-322 —sales tax; §67-2-104 —income tax on stocks and bonds.

Requirements: Exemptions from sales and use tax are provided by statute to churches, temples, synagogues, and mosques; colleges and universities; schools; orphanages; institutions for homeless and foster children; homes for the aged; hospitals; girls' and boys' clubs; community health councils; volunteer fire departments; organ banks; organizations such as the USO; property owned by the state and operated by the historical commission; nonprofit community blood banks; senior citizen centers; nonprofit beauty contest organizations; and 501(c)(3)s, (c)(5)s and (c)(19)s. Exempt organizations are exempt on items they buy, not items they sell. Organizations exempt from federal income taxes are generally exempt from the corporate franchise and excise tax.

Application Procedure: Submit an RV-0462 form to the Department.

CHARITABLE SOLICITATION

Contact:

Department of State
Charitable Solicitations and Gaming
312 Eighth Avenue, North
William A. Snodgrass Tower—8th Floor
Nashville, TN 37243
(615) 741-2555

Citation: *Tennessee Charitable Solicitations Act,* Tennessee Code Annotated 48-101-501 et seq.

Publications: A copy of the statute and forms are available from the contact office or from the Web site at: *http://www.tennessee.gov/sos*

Initial Registration: Charitable organizations that raise or intend to raise more than $30,000 annually must register annually with the Division. There is a $50 filing fee for initial registrations. Registrants must disclose the birthdate and 10-year employment history of the charity's key employees; information about the charity's most recent fiscal year; information about officers, managers, and misconduct; methods of how solicitations will be made; and purposes for which contributions will be used. Must provide audited financial reports if they received more than $300,000 in gross revenue. All registering organizations must submit their federal 990s. New organizations must submit their corporate charters and bylaws, and copies of their IRS determination letter. Contracts with professional fundraisers must be provided. Religious, educational, volunteer fire, rescue, and local civil defense, and hospitals are generally exempt from registration requirements.

Annual Reports: Registration renewal statements must be accompanied by a renewal fee ranging from $100 for organizations that have gross revenues of less than $49,000 annually to $300 for those with gross revenues of more than $500,000. All registrations expire on the anniversary date of the organization (the last day of the sixth month following the month in which the fiscal year of the organization ends). During the first year of operation, charities must submit quarterly financial reports due within 30 days of the end of each quarter, disclosing gross amounts of contributions; amount of contributions disbursed; aggregate amounts paid to any professional solicitor or fundraising counsel; and the amounts spent for overhead, expenses, commissions, and similar purposes. For subsequent years, reports must be filed annually, within six months after the close of the fiscal year.

Organization Solicitation Disclosure Requirements: Every solicitor, paid or otherwise, must furnish identification indicating that the solicitor is authorized by the organization to solicit.

Paid Solicitor Requirements: Must register annually, pay an $800 fee, and post a $25,000 bond. Registrations expire December 31. Prior to an oral solicitation and at the same time as a written one, professional solicitors must disclose their names, the names of their employers, and that they are professional solicitors who will receive as costs, expenses, and fees a portion of the solicited funds. For written solicitations, the disclosure must be in at least 12-point type.

Fundraising Counsel Requirements: Must register annually, pay a $250 fee, and post a $25,000 bond.

Texas

Central Switchboard: (512) 463-4630
State Web Home Page: http://www.texasonline.com

INCORPORATION

Contact:

Secretary of State
Business and Public Filings Division,
Corporations Section
PO Box 13697
Austin, TX 78711-3697
(512) 463-5555

Citation: *Texas Business Organizations Code.*

General Requirements: Must set forth corporate name; a statement that it is nonprofit; purpose(s); a statement that it will have no members, if such is the case; optional provisions relating to internal regulation and management; the street address of its initial registered office; the name of the initial registered agent at that office; the number of directors or trustees of the initial board and their names and addresses; and the name, address, and signature of each organizer.

Corporate Name: Shall not contain any word or phrase that indicates that it is organized for any purpose other than authorized by its Certificate of Formation; shall not be similar to another without written consent; may not contain the word "lottery."

Name Reservation: May be reserved for a period of 120 days for a fee of $40.

How to File: File an original and a copy of the Certificate of Formation with the Secretary of State along with a $25 fee.

Other Filings/Reports: A report is required to be filed not more often than once every four years when requested by the Secretary of State disclosing general information, including the names and addresses of directors and officers. The report is due within 30 days of receiving a notice from the Secretary of State that the report needs to be filed.

LOBBYING

Contact:

Texas Ethics Commission
PO Box 12070
Austin, TX 78711-2070
(512) 463-5800

Citation: § 305.001 et seq.

Publications: *Guide to Lobbying In Texas* available at:
http://www.ethics.state.tx.us/guides/lobby.htm

Registration Required: All lobbyists who spend $500 or more in a calendar quarter on lobbying or who receive at least $1,000 per quarter in compensation for lobbying must register with the Commission. The fee is $500. The fee is reduced to $300 for lobbyists employed by 501(c)(3) and 501(c)(4) organizations. Registration discloses general information, names of clients, subject matter/docket number, and amount of compensation.

Reporting Requirements: Itemized expenditure reports are required to be filed with the Commission. Itemized spending categories include transportation and lodging, food and beverages, entertainment, gifts, awards and mementoes, expenditures made to attend fundraisers and charity events, and certain mass media expenditures. Reports are due between the first and tenth days of each month.

TAX EXEMPTIONS

Contact:

Comptroller of Public Accounts
Exempt Organizations Section
PO Box 13528
Austin, TX 78711-3528
1-800-252-5555 (exempt organizations)

Citation: V.T.C.A. §151.309-151.310 —sales, excise and use taxes; §171.051-171.087— franchise tax.

Publications: *Exempt Organizations—Sales and Purchases (Pub. 96-122), Guidelines to Texas Tax Exemptions (Pub. 96-1045)* and *Exemption Organizations and Taxpayer Identification Numbers (Pub. 98-103)* are available from the contact office.

Requirements: While the general details are in the statutes and rules (see Rule 3.322, accessible at the FAQ at: *http://www.window.state. tx.us/taxinfo/sales*), religious, charitable, educational and organizations granted a federal exemption under 501(c)(3), (4), (8), (10), and (19) are some of the organizations that qualify for sales tax exemptions. The exemption is on purchases made by the organization for its own use, provided the item is not used for the personal benefit of a private stockholder or individual. Religious, charitable, educational, and organizations granted a federal exemption under certain sections of the Internal Revenue Code are among the corporations that qualify for exemption from the franchise tax. There is no corporate income tax.

Application Procedure: Charitable organizations must file Form AP-205 for exemption from the sales, franchise, and hotel occupancy taxes. The request must include a detailed description of the activities conducted; Articles of Incorporation if a corporation; bylaws, constitution, or articles of association if the organization is not a corporation; services performed by the organization; an actual or proposed two-year budget; brochures; Web site address; and IRS determination letter. More details can be found in Publication 96-1045.

CHARITABLE SOLICITATION

Contacts:

> *Office of the Attorney General*
> *Charitable Trusts Section*
> *PO Box 12548*
> *Austin, TX 78711-2548*
> *(512) 463-2185 (for LETSA)*
> *(800) 621-0508*

Citation: T Tex. Rev.Civ. Stat. Ann. art. 9023e for telephone solicitation; Tex. Occ. Code Chapter 1803 for public safety organizations and 1804 for veterans' organizations

Publications: Copies of the statutes are available from the contact office.

Initial Registration: Veterans' organizations and public safety organizations must register with the Secretary of State before beginning solicitations. They have separate statutes governing their solicitation requirements and for their professional solicitors. Each statute requires a registration fee, bond for professional solicitors, and the filing of annual reports and disclosures. Bond is also required for veterans' organizations and public safety entities. Telephone solicitations by charitable organizations raising funds for law-enforcement-related charities are regulated by the *Law Enforcement Telephone Solicitations Act (*LETSA). These organizations must register annually with the Attorney General's office and pay a registration fee.

Annual Reports: Each type of organization has separate requirements for annual reports. Details are provided by the contact office.

Organization Solicitation Disclosure Requirements: Disclosure requirements are extensive for organizations raising funds for veterans' and public safety organizations, and for telephone solicitation on behalf of law enforcement organizations. For requirements, contact the Charitable Trusts Section staff at: (512) 463-2185.

Paid Solicitor Requirements: Bonding requirements and fees vary depending on whether fundraising is for a law enforcement, public safety, or veterans' organization. There are extensive registration and disclosure requirements. For details, contact the Charitable Trusts Section staff at: (512) 463-2185.

Fundraising Counsel Requirements: None.

Utah

Central Switchboard: (801) 538-3000
State Web Home Page: http://www.utah.gov

INCORPORATION

Contact:

> Department of Commerce
> Div. of Corporations and Commercial Code
> Heber M. Wells Building
> 160 East 300 South
> PO Box 146705
> Salt Lake City, UT 84145-6705
> (801) 530-4849
> (877) 526-3994 (Utah residents only)

Citation: *Utah Revised Nonprofit Corporation Act;* Chapter 6A; 16-6a-101 et seq.

Publications Available: *Revised Nonprofit Corporation Act; Business Licensing Guide; Why Register Your Business?* are available from the contact office (a fee is charged for some of these publications, but they are free if accessed at the Web site: *http://www.corporations.utah.gov).*

General Requirements: Articles of Incorporation must be filed in duplicate, and set forth the business purpose(s); corporate name; the Utah street address of the registered office; the name and signature of the registered agent at that address; the name, addresses, and signatures of each incorporator (at least one required); a statement of whether the corporation will have voting members; the number of shares the corporation is authorized to issue; names and addresses of directors; and whether the organization intends to apply for 501(c)(3) status.

Corporate Name: Must contain the word "corporation," "incorporated," or "company," or the abbreviation "corp.," "inc.," or "co." or words or abbreviations of like import in another language; may not contain language stating or implying that the corporation is organized for a purpose other than permitted by law or its Articles of Incorporation; may not, without the written consent of the US Olympic Committee, contain the word "Olympic," "Olympiad," or "Citius Altius Fortius." Must be distinguishable

from other corporations unless it has consent from the other corporation.

Name Reservation: May be reserved for 120 days for a fee of $20; the reservation may be renewed for an additional 120 days.

How to File: No form is required; send Articles of Incorporation (a sample can be found at: *http://www.corporations.utah.gov/pdf/ incnonprofit.pdf)* with original signatures on one copy with the $22 filing fee. Forms may be faxed (801-530-6438) if valid Visa/MasterCard information is provided.

Other Filings/Reports: Each corporation must file an annual report on an approved form that includes the corporate name; state or country under which it is incorporated; street address of its registered office; name of its registered agent at that office; street address of its principal office; name and addresses of its directors and principal officers; and a brief description of the nature of its business.

LOBBYING

Contact:

> Lt. Governor's Office
> Elections Division
> Utah State Capitol Complex
> East Office Building, Suite E325
> Salt Lake City, UT 84114
> (801) 538-1041

Citation: *Lobbyist Disclosure and Regulation Act,* Utah Code 36-11-101-106.

Publications: *Utah Election Laws* and *Information Pamphlet for Lobbyists* are available from the contact office and on the Web site at: *http://www.elections.utah.gov*

Registration Required: Lobbyists must register with the Lt. Governor's Office prior to lobbying. There is a $25 fee for a lobbyist license. The license expires on December 31 of even-numbered years.

Forms to Use: *Lobbyist Registration* form; *Lobbyist Disclosure Report* with attached schedules. Registration is available online.

Reporting Requirements: Any lobbyist, client, or government officer who makes expenditures to benefit public officials or members of their immediate families in any calendar quarter of the calendar year must file a financial disclosure report. Lobbyists who have spent $50 or more during a reporting period or any calendar quarter must file an interim report. All lobbyists, principals, and government officers must file a year-end report even if expenditures were zero.

TAX EXEMPTIONS

Contact:

> Utah State Tax Commission
> Religious and Charitable Section
> 210 North 1950 West
> Salt Lake City, UT 84134
> (801) 297-2200

Citation: Utah Code Ann. Section 59-7-102; 59-12-104.1.

Requirements: Corporations that have federal exempt status under Section 501(c) are exempt from the Utah corporation franchise tax.

Sales and Use tax: Exemption is limited to those with 501(c)(3) tax-exempt status; sales tax must be collected on any sales income arising from unrelated trades or businesses unless the sales are otherwise exempt by law.

Application Procedure: For exemption from the corporate franchise tax, send a letter to the contact office requesting exemption, along with a copy of the federal IRS determination letter and Articles of Incorporation. For sales and use tax exemption, apply using Form TC-160.

CHARITABLE SOLICITATION

Contact:

> Department of Commerce
> Division of Consumer Protection
> 160 East 300 South
> Box 146704
> Salt Lake City, UT 84114
> (801) 530-6601
> (800) 721-7233 (Utah residents only)

Citation: *Charitable Solicitations Act*, UCA §13-22-1—13-22-21.

Publications: The text of the statute and forms are provided by the contact office.

Initial Registration: Must include a $100 application fee; bylaws; Articles of Incorporation; IRS tax exemption determination letter; most recent federal 990 or financial audit; telephone scripts (if applicable); copy of contractual agreement with parent foundation (if applicable); copy of contracts with professional fundraisers, counsel, or consultants; and an acknowledgment that fundraising in Utah will not begin until the organization, its parents, professional fundraiser, counsel, or consultant are registered and in compliance with the law. The permit card must have a disclaimer statement:

"THE STATE OF UTAH DOES NOT WARRANT THAT THE INFORMATION CONTAINED ON THIS CARD IS TRUE."

Annual Reports: Must report annually; newly registered organizations must file quarterly financial reports during their first year, due within 30 days after the end of each quarter. Each report must disclose the gross amount of contributions; amount of contributions disbursed; aggregate amounts paid to any professional fundraiser, amount spent on overhead, expenses, commissions, and similar purposes; and the name and address of any paid solicitors.

Organization Solicitation Disclosure Requirements: See below.

Paid Solicitor Requirements: Must include a $250 application fee; provide a copy of the contractual agreement with each charitable organization; provide a copy of the telephone script (if applicable); and an acknowledgment that fundraising in Utah will not begin until the professional fundraiser or professional fundraising counsel, or consultant, and the charity, its parent foundation (if any) are registered and in compliance with the law. The permit card must have a disclaimer statement: "THE STATE OF UTAH DOES NOT WARRANT THAT THE INFORMATION CONTAINED ON THIS CARD IS TRUE."

Fundraising Counsel Requirements: Same requirements as paid solicitors.

Vermont

Central Switchboard: (802) 828-1110
State Web Home Page: http://vermont.gov

INCORPORATION

Contact:

Secretary of State
Division of Corporations
81 River Street, Drawer 09
Heritage Building
Montpelier, VT 05609-1104
(802) 828-2386

Citation: Title 11B, Vermont Statutes Annotated.

General Requirements: Nonprofit organizations file Articles of Incorporation that require one or more persons who are at least 18. Articles must set forth the corporate name; duration; purpose; whether public or mutual benefit; provisions relating to internal regulation (optional); the address of the registered office; name and address of its registered agent; names and addresses of initial board of directors (must be at least three); the name and address of each incorporator; and optional provisions relating to 501(c)(3) status.

Corporate Name: May not be the same as, or deceptively similar to, another registered or reserved name; may not contain any word or phrase that implies a purpose other than contained in the Articles; must be transliterated into the English alphabet if it is not in English. Must include an ending word denoting the corporate status (e.g., "corporation" or "Inc.")

Name Reservation: May be reserved for a 120-day period for a fee of $20; may be renewed up to two additional times.

How to File: Mail Articles of Incorporation form in duplicate to the contact office. The fee is $75.

Other Filings/Reports: A report is due between January 1 and April 1 every two years. Forms are mailed by the contact office. The filing fee is $15.

LOBBYING

Contact:

Secretary of State
Attention: Elections Division
26 Terrace St.
Montpelier, VT 05609
(802) 828-0771
(800) 439-8683

Citation: Title 2, § 261 et seq., Vermont Statutes Annotated.

Registration Required: Lobbyists who are paid more than $500 annually to lobby or who expend more than $500 in any calendar year on lobbying activities must register with the Secretary of State within 48 hours after commencing lobbying activity. Registration discloses general information, a description of the matters for which lobbying has been engaged, and a signed registration form from the client/employer authorizing the lobbying. Registration is valid for two years and expires on December 31 of every even-numbered year. Every employer and every lobbyist must pay an initial registration fee of $25. An employer pays a fee of $5 for each lobbyist engaged. A lobbyist pays a $5 fee for each employer represented.

Reporting Requirements: Every lobbyist and employer of a lobbyist must file expense reports. The reports are due April 25 covering January-March; July 25 covering April-June; and January 25 covering July-December. Employers must disclose the total of all lobbying expenditures to the nearest $200, the amount of compensation paid to lobbyists to the nearest $200, and provide an itemized list of every gift valued at more than $5. Lobbyists must disclose the total of all lobbying expenditures to the nearest $200, and provide an itemized list of every gift valued at more than $5.

TAX EXEMPTIONS

Contact:

> Department of Taxes
> 133 State Street
> Montpelier, VT 05633-1401
> (802) 828-2551 (sales and use tax)
> (802) 828-5723 (corporate income tax)

Citation: 32 § 9743 —sales taxes; § 5811 — income taxes.

Requirements: Corporations organized for religious, charitable, scientific, or educational purposes are exempt from Vermont income taxes provided no part of net earnings inure to the benefit of any private stockholder or individual member. 501(c)(3)s are exempt from sales and use taxes, provided they have obtained a Vermont exemption certificate and their prior year sales did not exceed $20,000. Special rules apply to amusement charges, certain flower sales, and agricultural organizations qualified for exempt status under 501(c)(5).

Application Procedure: For exemption from sales and use taxes, corporations must obtain an exemption by calling (802) 828-2551 and requesting Form S-3 *(Resale and Exempt Organization Registration).*

CHARITABLE SOLICITATION

Contact:

> Office of the Attorney General
> 109 State Street
> Montpelier, VT 05609-1001
> (802) 828-3171

Citation: T.9, Chapter 63, Subchapter 2, § 2471 et seq.

Publications: A copy of the statute is available from the contact office and accessed at the web site: *http://www.state.vt.us/atg/ consumerprotectionstatutes.htm*

Initial Registration: None.

Annual Reports: See below.

Organization Solicitation Disclosure Requirements: None.

Paid Solicitor Requirements: All paid fundraisers must file a *Notice of Charitable Solicitation* at least 10 days prior to the start of a fundraising campaign; must post a $20,000 bond; must file a financial report no later than 90 days after the campaign has been completed or no more than 90 days after the anniversary of a campaign that lasts more than one year.

Fundraising Counsel Requirements: None.

Virginia

Central Switchboard: (804) 786-0000
State Web Home Page: http://www.virginia.gov

INCORPORATION

Contact:

> Clerk's Information Office
> State Corporation Commission
> Tyler Building
> 1300 East Main Street
> PO Box 1197
> Richmond, VA 23218-1197
> (804) 371-9767
> (866) 722-2551 (Virginia residents only)

Citation: Chapter 10 of Title 13.1 of the Code of Virginia.

Publications Available: *Business Registration Guide* is available at the Web site. It includes the Articles of Incorporation form for nonstock corporations.

General Requirements: Articles of Incorporation must set forth the corporate name; whether the corporation will have members and provisions relating to members; how directors will be elected or appointed; the address of the initial registered office; the name of the initial registered agent and whether that agent is either an initial director, a member of the Virginia State Bar, or a professional corporation or professional limited liability company of attorneys; optional provisions; the names and addresses of initial directors; and the signature of each incorporator.

Corporate Name: Shall not contain any word or phrase that indicates or implies that it is organized for a purpose other than for what it is authorized to conduct; must be distinguishable from other corporations without written permission.

Name Reservation: May be reserved for up to 120 days and may be renewed for successive 120-day periods for a fee of $10.

How to File: File the original Articles of Incorporation along with a filing fee of $75 with the Clerk of the State Corporation Commission at the contact office.

Other Filings/reports: An annual report must be filed with the Commission disclosing general information including the names and addresses of the corporation's directors and principal officers on forms provided by the Commission. There is an annual registration fee of $25. The report and fee are due by the last day of the seventh month of incorporation date.

LOBBYING

Contact:

> Secretary of the Commonwealth
> Lobbyist Specialist
> Post Office Box 2454
> Richmond, VA 23218-2454
> (804) 786-2441

Citation: Chapter 49, § 2.2-418 et seq.

Publications: A copy of the statute is available from the contact office.

Registration Required: All lobbyists who receive more than $500 for compensation and reimbursements in a calendar year or who spend more than $500 in a calendar year for lobbying must register with the Department prior to engaging in lobbying. There is a $50 registration fee per principal. Disclosure includes general information, an identification of the subject matter, and information about the client.

Forms to Use: *Lobbyist's Registration* form.

Reporting Requirements: Annual expenditure reports are due July 1 covering the preceding 12 months ending May 1. The report includes a list of executive and legislative actions lobbied for and a description of the activities conducted; expenses itemized by entertainment, gifts, office expenses, communications, personal living and travel expenses, compensation of lobbyists, honoraria, registration costs, and other; and the dollar amount of the lobbyist's compensation.

TAX EXEMPTIONS

Contact:

Department of Taxation
Office of Customer Services
PO Box 1115
Richmond, VA 23218-1115
(804) 367-8037

Citation: § 58.1-401 —corporate income tax; § 58.1-608 —retail sales and use tax.

Publications: *Business Registration Guide.*

Requirements: Nonprofit corporations with federal income tax exemptions are exempt from the state corporation income tax, other than unrelated business income tax; certain 501(c)(3) organizations are statutorily exempt; consult the statute or the contact office. Limited exemptions are available from Retail Sales and Use taxes (use Form NP-Nonprofit Application).

Application Procedure: All companies doing business in Virginia must register with the Department of Taxation by completing and filing a Form R-1, *Combined Registration Application Form.* Request a *Tax Exempt Questionnaire Form* from the contact office, which will be used by the Department to determine eligibility for tax-exempt status. Charities must show they are registered with the Dept. of Agriculture (see below).

CHARITABLE SOLICITATION

Contact:

Department of Agriculture
Division of Consumer Protection
Office of Consumer Affairs
PO Box 1163
Richmond, VA 23218-0526
(804) 786-1343

Citation: *Virginia Solicitation of Contributions Law,* §§ 57-48 et seq. of the Code of Virginia, as amended.

Publications: A copy of the statute and rule are available from the contact office.

Initial Registration: Every charitable organization must register annually with the contact office and file an initial registration statement, using Form 102. The initial statement must include an IRS 990 or balance sheet and income and expense statement with the opinion of an independent public accountant, complete information on fundraising activities and expenses (organizations with gross revenue of less than $25,000 may submit a balance sheet and income and expense statement verified under oath or affirmation by the Treasurer), the general purpose(s) for which funds will be used, the names of those who will have final responsibility for the custody of the funds and how they will be distributed, information about previous misconduct, and a copy of governing documents. Annual fee ranges from $30 (for not more than $25,000 in contributions during the preceding year) to $325 (for contributions in excess of $1 million annually). The initial registration fee is $100 plus the registration fee above. Less stringent notification requirements apply to organizations that raise (or intend to raise) less than $5,000 annually, and 11 classes of organizations that may request exemption from registration.

Annual Reports: Annual registration renewals on Form 102 are due on the 15th day of the fifth month following the end of the fiscal year. The renewal must include a copy of the federal 990 or a certified annual audit (or a certified treasurer's report, if annual income is under $25,000), updates to information provided in the initial registration, and much of the information required by the registration.

Organization Solicitation Disclosure requirements: Registered organizations must disclose that a copy of their financial statements are available from the contact office.

Paid Solicitor Requirements: Must register annually using Form 104; pay a $500 fee annually and post a $20,000 bond; and must file a copy of an authorization, *Consent to Solicit* form, from two officers of the charity. In the course of each solicitation, they must identify themselves by disclosing their own real first name and surname, disclose that they are paid solicitors, disclose the primary name under which they are registered, identify their employing charitable or civic organization, and file an accounting report not later than 90 days following a fundraising campaign or 90 days after the anniversary of the beginning of a campaign. A *Notice of Solicitation* form must be filed with each contract. There is a late registration fee of $250 for paid solicitors who begin fundraising before registering. There is a late final accounting report filing fee for each 30 days or any portion thereof. Companies may request a 90-day extension to file the final accounting report.

Fundraising Counsel Requirements: Must register and pay a $100 fee, and provide a copy of all contracts.

Washington

Central Switchboard: (360) 753-5000
State Web Home Page: http://access.wa.gov

INCORPORATION

Contact:

*Office of the Secretary of State
Corporations Division
PO Box 40234
Olympia, WA 98504-0234
(360) 753-7115*

Citation: *Washington Nonprofit Corporation Act,* RCW 24.03 et seq.

Publications Available: A form for filing Articles of Incorporation is available from the contact office or on the web site: *http://www.secstate.wa.gov/corps*

General Requirements: Shall set forth corporate name; period of duration; purpose(s); provisions relating to the distribution of assets upon dissolution; the name and address of the initial registered agent and registered office; the names and addresses of each initial board director and incorporator, and signature of each incorporator.

Corporate Name: Cannot include or end with "Incorporated," "Company," "Ltd.," "Corporation," "Partnership," "Limited Partnership," "limited liability company," "Ltd," or an abbreviation thereof, but may use "club," "league," "association," "services," "committee," "fund," "society," "foundation," or "..., a nonprofit corporation." Shall not contain any word or phrase that indicates or implies that it is organized for any purpose other than contained in its Articles of Incorporation; shall not be the same as, or deceptively similar to, another; shall be transliterated into letters of the English alphabet if it is not in English; may not include the term "public benefit" unless designated as such by the Secretary.

Name Reservation: May be reserved for a non-renewable period of 180 days for a fee of $20.

How to File: File an original of the Articles with the Secretary of State along with a $30 filing

fee. To receive expedited service (processing within 24 hours of receipt), enclose $20 per entity in addition to the filing fee and write "EXPEDITE" on the outside envelope. Online filing is available at: *http://www.secstate.wa.gov/corps/eforms_notice.aspx*

Other Filings/Reports: An annual report is required to be filed before the last day of the corporation's annual renewal month of incorporation along with a $10 filing fee. The report discloses general information including the names and addresses of directors and officers, a brief statement of the character of the affairs that the corporation is actually conducting, and registered agent/office.

LOBBYING

Contact:

*Public Disclosure Commission
711 Capitol Way
Room 206
PO Box 40908
Olympia, WA 98504-0908
(360) 753-1111*

Citation: Chapter 42.17 RCW, *The Public Disclosure Law.*

Publications: *Employers of Lobbyists*; and *Lobbyist Reporting* booklets and forms are available at the Web site: *http://www.pdc.wa.gov*

Registration Required: All lobbyists must register within 30 days of being employed as a lobbyist or before doing any lobbying, whichever comes first. Registrations are valid until the second Monday of each odd-numbered year. Anyone who attempts to influence legislation or the rulemaking action of state agencies is a lobbyist. Persons who receive some form of compensation to lobby must register and file monthly expenditure reports.

Forms to Use: PDC Form L-1. Lobbyists must provide a brief biographical sketch and a 2" x 2" glossy photo taken within the last 12 months.

Reporting Requirements: Lobbyists must submit PDC Form L-2 *Monthly Expense* reports. These reports are due the 15th of each month and cover activity of the previous calendar month. "Zero" reports may be filed even if there is no reportable lobbying activity. The reports itemize compensation; some personal expenses; entertainment, gifts, and travel; contributions to elected officials; advertising, printing, and informational literature; and other lobbying expenses. The report must describe the subject matter lobbied for each client. Employers of lobbyists must file PDC Form L-3 annual comprehensive expense reports that are due by the last day of February covering the previous year's compensation and expenditures for lobbying during the previous year.

TAX EXEMPTIONS

Contact:

Department of Revenue
PO Box 47478
Olympia, WA 98504-7478
1-(800) 647-7706 (Telephone Information Center)

Citation: Chapter 82.04 RCW —Business and Occupation Tax; Chapter 82.08 RCW —Retail Sales Tax; Washington Administrative Code 458-20-169

Requirements: There is no corporate income or franchise tax, but there is a Business and Occupation Tax (B&O). Nonprofit corporations are generally liable for the same B&O and retail sales taxes as their for-profit counterparts. There are some limited exemptions for qualifying nonprofit organizations relating to fundraising activities, childcare resource and referral activities, and emergency lodging.

CHARITABLE SOLICITATION

Contact:

Secretary of State
Charities Program
PO Box 40234
Olympia, WA 98504-0234
(360) 753-0863
(800) 332-4483 (toll free, WA only)

Citation: Chapter 19.09 RCW, *Washington State Charitable Solicitations Act; Charitable Trust Act, 11.110 RCW*

Initial Registration: All charities that raise at least $25,000 in an accounting year, have paid employees, or which use paid fundraisers, must register annually unless otherwise exempted. The fee for new registrations is $20; fee for renewals is $10. Renewals are due no later than the 15th day of the fifth month after the end of the fiscal year.

Annual Reports: See above. Financial reporting includes total revenue, total expenses, expenses applied to charitable purpose, information about paid fundraisers, types of solicitations and how conducted, names of the three highest employees or officers, and the names and addresses of officers.

Organization Solicitation Disclosure Requirements: Must disclose the name of the person making the solicitation, the identity of the charity, the city of the principal place of business, and the published number of the secretary for the donor to obtain financial disclosure information filed with the Secretary. Some types of solicitation require the published number of the Secretary (1-800-332-4483) to be included in the solicitation materials.

Paid Solicitor Requirements: Commercial fundraisers must register, pay an initial filing fee of $250 ($175 for renewals), and post a $15,000 bond. They must disclose at the point of solicitation the name of the person making the solicitation, employer (paid fundraiser), the name and city of the charitable organization, and the published number of the Secretary (see above). Mass media advertising or mass distribution solicitation must disclose that the solicitation is being conducted by a paid fundraiser if it is; that the notice of solicitation is on file with the Secretary, and that financial disclosure information may be obtained at the published number of the Secretary. Those who contract for fundraising services must submit a *Fundraising Service Contract* with a copy of the contract and a $10 fee prior to the start of any fundraising campaign.

Fundraising Counsel Requirements: None.

West Virginia

Central Switchboard: (304) 558-3456
State Web Home Page: http://www.wv.gov

INCORPORATION

Contact:

> Secretary of State
> Corporations Division
> Building 1, Suite 157-K
> 1900 Kanawha Blvd. East
> Charleston, WV 25305-0770
> (304) 558-8000

Citation: *West Virginia Corporation Act*, W. Va. Code 31-1-136 et seq.

Publications Available: A copy of the form is available from the contact office.

General Requirements: Notarized Articles of Incorporation must set forth the corporate name; principal office (may be in another state); the address of the principal place of business in the state; the name of the "agent of process" (registered agent); that the corporation is organized as a nonprofit; the purposes (may not be general); whether or not the corporation will have members; whether the provisions regulating the internal affairs of the corporation are set forth in the bylaws or in the Articles (and attached if the latter); the names and addresses of incorporators; and information relating to the corporation's land ownership or land that it expects to own. Note: A fee of five cents/acre in excess of 10,000 acres is charged.

Corporate Name: Must include the term "corporation," "company," "incorporated," "limited," or an abbreviation of one of those terms; may not contain any word or phrase that implies that it is organized for a purpose other than contained in the Articles; may not be the same as, or deceptively similar to, another corporation; if not in English, shall be transliterated into letters of the English alphabet.

Name Check/Name Reservation: May be reserved for a period of 120 days for a $15 fee; may be checked by telephone (304-558-8000), but this is not a guarantee that the name is available.

How to File: Incorporators must sign an original using Form CD-1NP *West Virginia Articles of Incorporation.* The filing fee is $25 plus the "Attorney-In-Fact Fee." That fee is required if the principal place of business is outside the state, and ranges from $10 to $30 depending on the month of the filing. Include an additional copy if you want a filed copy returned to you. See: *http://www.wvsos.com/forms/business/2004/cd-1np.pdf*

Other Filings/Reports: An annual report is required of corporations formed before May 1 preceding the report filing, due July 1. This report discloses general information, including the names and addresses of directors and officers, and a brief statement of the character of affairs conducted. The fee is $25.

LOBBYING

Contact:

> West Virginia Ethics Commission
> 210 Brooks Street, Suite 300
> Charleston, WV 25301
> (304) 558-0664
> (866) 558-0664 (toll free)

Citation: West Virginia Code Sections 6B; WV Ethics Commission Legislative Rules: Series 12 Lobbying, 158-12-1.

Registration Required: Persons who lobby the legislature or state regulatory agencies must register if they receive compensation for lobbying, or if they spend money on a public servant in furtherance of their lobbying activities. Lobbyists must register with the Commission before engaging in lobbying. Volunteer lobbyists or those whose total lobbying expenditures do not exceed $150 during any calendar year are exempt. The application requires a *Lobbyist Registration Statement,* a recent 2" by 2" passport style photo, a *Lobbyist Employer Authorization* for each employer, and a $100 registration fee. Registration expires at the end of each even-numbered year and must be renewed before engaging in lobbying in the new year. Registration forms are available online.

TAX EXEMPTIONS

Contact:

Department of Tax and Revenue
Taxpayer Services Division
PO Box 3784
Charleston, WV 25337-3784
1-800-982-8297 (in W.Va)
(304) 558-3333

Citation: Taxation, § 11-24-5(a)—Corporate Net Income Tax; §11-15-9—Consumers Sales Tax.

Publications: A copy of the statute and *Special Sales and Use Tax Rules for Nonprofit Organizations* flyer are available from the contact office.

Requirements: Corporations exempt from federal income tax are generally exempt from corporate income tax, but this does not apply to unrelated business income. Many 501(c)(3)s and (c)(4)s are exempt from the consumers sales tax or use tax, if four conditions are met. Consult the contact office for details.

Application Procedure: File the *Business Registration Certificate* application (WV/BUS-APP) with the Department, and include a copy of the IRS determination letter.

CHARITABLE SOLICITATION

Contact:

Office of the Secretary of State
Charitable Organization Registration Division
Building 1. Suite 157K
1900 Kanawha Boulevard, East
Charleston, WV 25305-0770
(304) 558-6000

Citation: Chapter 29, Article 19 of the West Virginia Code, *Solicitation of Charitable Funds Act.*

Initial Registration: All charities except those exempt under §29-19-6 (accredited educational institutions, individual relief funds, nonprofit hospitals and nursing homes, membership organizations that solicit only their members, churches and synagogues, and charities that do not employ a professional fundraiser and do not intend to solicit or receive contributions greater than $25,000 in a calendar year) must register annually with the Secretary of State. The registration fee is $15 for organizations collecting less than $1 million, and $50 for those collecting more. The registration form must include a copy of a balance sheet and a report of income and expenses for the preceding year. If more than $100,000 is solicited, an audit by an independent CPA is required showing the kind and amount of funds raised, costs and expenses, and where and for what purposes the funds were disbursed. Registrants must include their IRS 990 and a copy of their IRS determination letter. If they are not required to file a federal 990, they need to complete the *Computation of Fund-raising Percentage* form.

Annual Reports: Annual renewal of registration requires disclosure of general information, purposes of the contributions, tax-exempt status, information about professional solicitors and fundraising counsel, copies of contracts with them, information about organization misconduct, information about funds raised and disbursed, and a detailed itemized report of income and expenses.

Organization Solicitation Disclosure Requirements: Must disclose in writing the name of a representative of the charity to whom inquiries can be made; the charity's name; the purpose of the solicitation; upon request of the person solicited, the estimated percentage of the money collected that will be applied to the cost of solicitation and administration and how much will be applied directly to the charitable purpose; and the number of any raffle, bingo, or other state permit used for fundraising. Every printed solicitation must include the following statement:

> West Virginia residents may obtain a summary of the registration and financial documents from the Secretary of State, State Capitol, Charleston, West Virginia 25305. Registration does not imply endorsement.

The disclosure statement must be conspicuously displayed on any written or printed solicitation. When the solicitation consists of more than one piece, it must be displayed on a prominent part of the materials.

Paid Solicitor Requirements: Must register annually, pay a $100 registration fee, and post a $10,000 bond.

Fundraising Counsel Requirements: Must register, pay a $100 fee, and post a $10,000 bond.

Wisconsin

Central Switchboard: (608) 266-2211
State Web Home Page: http://www.wisconsin.gov

INCORPORATION

Contact:

Department of Financial Institutions
Division of Corporate & Consumer Services
Corporate Section
PO Box 7846
Madison, WI 53707-7846
(608) 261-7577

Citation: *Nonstock Corporations*, Chapter 181, Wisconsin Statutes.

Publications Available: *Articles of Incorporation* (Form 102) is available from the contact office; all forms are available at the web site: *http://www.wdfi.org*

General Requirements: Articles of Incorporation must set forth a statement that the corporation is incorporated under Ch. 181; the corporate name; mailing address of the initial principal office; street address of the initial registered office and the name and address of the registered agent at that address; the name and address of each incorporator; and whether the corporation shall have members or no members.

Corporate Name: Corporate name must contain the word "corporation," "incorporated," "company" or "limited" or the abbreviation of one of those words.

Name Reservation: May reserve a corporate name for 120 days. The fee for a written request is $10.

How to File: Submit Articles of Incorporation in duplicate, at least one with an original signature of an incorporator. The filing fee is $35, payable by check to *Department of Financial Institutions.*

Other Filings/Reports: Corporations are required to continuously maintain a registered agent resident in Wisconsin and to file an annual report. The report must be made on the form provided by the Department. Forms are distributed to each corporation's registered agent in Wisconsin during the calendar quarter in which they are due for filing. Failure to file the report may establish grounds for administrative dissolution of the corporation. There is a $10 fee.

LOBBYING

Contact:

Wisconsin Ethics Board
44 E. Mifflin Street
Suite 601
Madison, WI 53703
(601) 266-8123

Citation: Wisconsin Statutes, Subchapter III, Chapter 13; §§ 13.61-13.75.

Publications: Several publications on lobbying rules, a copy of the statute, and relevant forms are available from the contact office.

Registration Required: Lobbyists are required to register before the fifth day on which the first lobbying communication occurs. The license expires December 31 every even-numbered year. Lobbyists are required to have only one license regardless of the number of clients they represent; organizations authorizing lobbyists must file registration/authorization forms no later than before the fifth day on which a lobbyist communicates on the organization's behalf. The license fees are $250 to lobby on behalf of one employer and $400 to lobby for multiple employers. The registration fee is $375 for the organization and $125 for each authorization of a licensed lobbyist. Organizations that have lobbying expenditures not exceeding $500 annually pay a fee of $20 for a two-year period.

Forms to Use: *Registration of Organization Employing a Lobbyist and Authorization of Lobbyists* (Eth-805); *Application for Lobby License* (Eth-807); and *Principal's Statement of Lobbying Activities and Expenditures (Eth 810).*

Reporting Requirements: Each lobbying organization must report to the Ethics Board each bill, budget bill subject, proposed rule number, or topic on which the organization makes a lobbying communication, within 15 days of the first lobbying communication. In January and July, each lobbying organization must file a *Statement of Lobbying Activities and Expenditures* for the preceding six-month reporting period.

TAX EXEMPTIONS

Contact:

> Department of Revenue
> Customer Service and Education Bureau
> PO Box 8949
> Madison, WI 53708
> (608) 266-1143 (corporation franchise & income)
> (608) 261-6261 (sales and use)

Citation: §77.54, Wisconsin Statutes Annotated— sales and use tax; §71.22 —corporate income tax.

Requirements: Occasional sales of tangible personal property or services by nonprofit organizations may qualify for exemption. Consult the statute or the contact office for more information. Organizations exempt from federal income taxes are exempt from the state corporate income tax, other than on unrelated business income.

Application Procedure: File an S-103 form, *Application for Wisconsin Sales and Use Tax Certificate of Exempt Status,* with the Department and include Articles of Incorporation and bylaws, a statement of expenditures and receipts, and a copy of the IRS determination letter if there is one.

CHARITABLE SOLICITATION

Contact:

> Department of Regulation and Licensing
> Division of Professional Credential Processing
> Charitable Organizations
> PO Box 8935
> Madison, WI 53708-8935
> (608) 266-2112

Citation: Chapter 440, Subchapter III, Stats; Chapter RL 5, Wis. Admin. Code.

Publications: A copy of the statute and forms are available from the contact office.

Initial Registration: Organizations that solicit contributions for a charitable purpose must file a notarized Form 296, *Information Regarding Charitable Organization Registration Statement,* along with a $15 filing fee. Each organization must include a copy of its certificate of incorporation, charter, Articles of Incorporation and bylaws; a statement explaining how the contributions will be used; a copy of the organization's IRS determination letter if it has one or a copy of its application for exemption if a determination is pending; its federal 990 annual return with Form #1952 or a Form #308 *(Charitable Organization Annual Financial Report)* for those with more than $5,000 in contributions during the most recently completed fiscal year (or a Form #1943 for those with $5,000 or less in contributions); the name and address of any professional fundraiser or fundraising counsel used by the organization; a list of government agencies that have formally authorized the organization to engage in charitable solicitation; and information about organizational misconduct concerning solicitations.

Annual Reports: Organizations that raise more than $5,000 must submit, within six months after the end of each fiscal year, a financial report that includes a balance sheet; a statement of support, revenue, expenses, and changes in the fund balance; and a statement of functional expenses divided into, at least at a minimum, categories of management and general, program services, and fundraising. Organizations that raise more than $100,000 during the fiscal year must submit an audited financial statement within six months after the end of that fiscal year, consistent with generally accepted accounting principles. Financial reports must be made on approved forms and are provided automatically by the Department within two weeks of the close of the organization's fiscal year. Organizations that raise less than $5,000 must file Form 1943, *Affidavit In Lieu of Annual Financial Report.* Renewal registration is $15 annually, and is due by July 31.

Organization Solicitation Disclosure Requirements: Those required to register must, at the time of the solicitation, disclose the name and location of the charitable organization; that a financial statement disclosing assets, liabilities, fund balances, revenue and expenses of the preceding fiscal year will be provided upon request; and a clear description of the primary charitable purpose for which the solicitation is made. This does not apply to those organizations that solicit less than $50,000 in their fiscal year and limit solicitation to the county where they are headquartered.

Paid Solicitor Requirements: Must register by paying a $53 fee (renewal fee is $93) and posting at least a $20,000 bond ($5,000 bond if they do not have custody of funds), must have a written contract with the charitable organization, and must file a solicitation notice with the Department disclosing information about the terms of the solicitation.

Fundraising Counsel Requirements: May not have custody of contributions unless they are registered, must pay a $53 registration fee and have a bond of at least $20,000 if they intend to earn more than $1,000/year, and must have a written contract with the charitable organization.

Wyoming

Central Switchboard: (307) 777-7011
State Web Home Page: http://wyoming.gov

INCORPORATION

Contact:

*Secretary of State
Business Division
State Capitol, Room 110
200 W. 24th Street
Cheyenne, WY 82002-0020
(307) 777-7311*

Citation: *Wyoming Nonprofit Corporation Act,* Wyoming Statutes 17-19-101 et seq.

Publications Available: Forms are available from the contact office and the web site: *http://www.soswy.state.wy.us/*

General Requirements: Articles of Incorporation must set forth the corporate name; whether it is a religious, mutual benefit or public benefit corporation; the street address of the initial registered office and the name of the initial registered agent at that office; the name and address of the incorporator; whether it will have members; provisions regarding the distribution of assets upon dissolution; and, for name availability purposes, the type of business the corporation will be conducting. Articles must be accompanied by a written consent to appointment executed by the registered agent (this form is available at the Web site).

Corporate Name: May not contain language stating or implying that it is organized for a purpose other than permitted by law or its Articles of Incorporation; shall not be the same as, or deceptively similar to, the name of any trademark or service mark registered, and shall be distinguishable upon the records from other registered business names.

Name Reservation: May be reserved for a non-renewable, 120-day period for a fee of $10.

How to File: File Articles of Incorporation with one conformed copy and a *Consent to Appointment by Registered Agent* form with a $25 filing fee.

Other Filings/Reports: An annual report must be filed disclosing general information, and any profit or pecuniary advantage paid directly or indirectly to any officer or director. The report is due on the first day of the month of corporate registration of every year. There is a $25 license fee for filing.

LOBBYING

Contact:

*Secretary of State
Elections Administration
State of Wyoming
State Capitol—Room B-17
200 W. 24th Street
Cheyenne, WY 82002
(307) 777-7186*

Citation: W.S. 28-7-101 et seq.

Publications: Forms may be accessed at the web site: *http://soswy.state.wy.us/election/forms.htm* or obtained from the contact office.

Registration Required: Lobbyists must register with the Office within 48 hours of commencing lobbying activity. The registration fee is $25, but a $5 fee applies if reimbursement or compensation is expected to be less than $500 or if the lobbyist receives only travel and per diem expenses. Registrations expire in April.

Reporting Requirements: Lobbyist activity reports are due by June 30 for activities during the preceding May 1-April 30. Activity reports include the date of expenditure, the lobbyist's source of funding, the item or activity, the name of the recipient, and the amount of the expense.

TAX EXEMPTIONS

Contact:

Department of Revenue
Herschler Building
2nd Floor West
122 W. 25th Street
Cheyenne, WY 82002-0110
(307) 777-2459

Citation: §39-15-105 (a)(iv)(B,C)

Requirements: Religious and charitable organizations, and nonprofits providing meals or services to senior citizens, are exempt from sales/use tax on their purchases. There is an exemption from the sales tax for occasional sales made by religious and charitable organizations for fundraising purposes.

Application Procedure: Organizations seeking tax-exempt status must apply for exemption approval and registration in writing and include Articles of Incorporation; charter; mission statement; budget; income and expense statements. Submit a copy of the IRS determination letter or advise the Department that no determination has been issued, if that is the case. Organizations that are recognized by the IRS as a 501(c)(3) tax-exempt organization will be issued an exemption approval letter based on documentation verifying such status. Any nonprofit organization that does not have 501(c)(3) tax-exempt status must be a religious or charitable organization that has expended at least 65% of its annual net income during the previous three years on programs and activities related to its charitable purpose, or a nonprofit organization that provides meals or services to senior citizens. New organizations can expect one-year exemptions until they have a history of meeting the 65% threshold and/or obtain their 501(c)(3) status. Exempt purchasers present to the vendor an exemption certificate *(Streamlined Sales/Use Tax Agreement Certificate of Exemption)*. For more information, see: *http://revenue.wyoming.gov/ PortalVBVS/uploads/Exemption%20Matrix6 (revised)8-10-06.pdf*. Occasional sales of tangible personal property or services by religious or charitable organizations for fundraising purposes for the conduct of their regular religious or charitable functions and activities are exempt from sales taxes. *Occasional* is defined as an event occurring four or fewer times over a calendar year. There is no corporate income or franchise tax for in-state corporations.

CHARITABLE SOLICITATION

Note: There is no registration/reporting law.

State Government Web Sites of Interest to Nonprofit Organizations

Alabama

Incorporation: http://www.sos.alabama.gov
Lobbying: http://www.ethics.alalinc.net/
Tax Exemptions: http://www.ador.state.al.us/
Charitable Solicitation:http://www.ago.state.al.us/consumer_charities.cfm

Alaska

Incorporation: http://www.commerce.state.ak.us/occ/home.htm
Lobbying: http: //www.state.ak.us/apoc/lobcov.htm
Tax Exemptions: http://www.tax.state.ak.us/
Charitable Solicitation: http://www.law.state.ak.us/department/civil/consumer/cpindex.html

Arizona

Incorporation: http://azoc.gov/divisions/corporations
Lobbying: http://www.azsos.gov/election/lobbyist/
Tax Exemptions: http://www.revenue.state.az.us/
Charitable Solicitation: http://www.azsos.gov/business_services/Charities/default.htm

Arkansas

Incorporation: https://www.ark.org/sos/ofs/docs/index.php
Lobbying: http://www.arkansasethics.com/
Tax Exemptions: http://www.arkansas.gov/dfa
Charitable Solicitation: http://www.ag.state.ar.us/

California

Incorporation: http://www.sos.ca.gov/business/business.htm
Lobbying: http://www.soc.ca.gov/prd/prd.htm
Tax Exemptions: http://www.ftb.ca.gov/
Charitable Solicitation: http://caag.state.ca.us/charities/forms.htm

Colorado

Incorporation: http://www.sos.state.co.us/pubs/business/main.htm
Lobbying: http://www.elections.colorado.gov/DDefault.aspx?/lobbyist.htm
Tax Exemptions: http://www.revenue.state.co.us/main/home.asp
Charitable Solicitation: http://www.sos.state.co.us/pubs/bingo_raffles/main.htm

Connecticut

Incorporation: http://www.sots.ct.gov/
Lobbying: http://www.ct.gov/ethics/site/default.asp
Tax Exemptions: http://www.ct.gov/drs/site/default.asp
Charitable Solicitation: http://www.dcp.state.ct.us/licensing/all.htm#charity

Delaware

Incorporation: http://www.corp.delaware.gov/
Lobbying: http://depic.delaware.gov/
Tax Exemptions: http://www.state.de.us/revenue/default.shtml
Charitable Solicitation: (none)

District of Columbia

Incorporation: http://dcra.dc.gov/dcra/site/default.asp
Lobbying: http://www.ocf.dc.gov
Tax Exemptions: http://cfo.dc.gov/
Charitable Solicitation: http://brc.dc.gov/nonprofit/nonprofit.asp

Florida

Incorporation: http://ccfcorp.dos.state.fl.us/index.html
Lobbying: http://www.leg.state.fl.us/Lobbyist/index.cfm?Tab=lobbyist&submenu=1
Tax Exemptions: http://myflorida.com/dor
Charitable Solicitation: http://www.800helpfla.com/~cs/registration.html

Georgia

Incorporation: http://www.sos.state.ga.us/corporations/
Lobbying: http://ethics.georgia.gov/EthicsWeb/lobbyists/lobbyist.aspx
Tax Exemptions: http://www.etax.dor.ga.gov/
Charitable Solicitation: http://ethics.georgia.gov/00/channel_title/0,2094,26886019_27327507,00.html

Hawaii

Incorporation: http://www.hawaii.gov/dcca/areas/breg
Lobbying: http://www.state.hi.us/ethics/
Tax Exemptions: http://www.state.hi.us/tax/tax.html
Charitable Solicitation: http://www.hawaii.gov/ag/charities

Idaho

Incorporation: http://www.idsos.state.id.us/corp/corindex.htm
Lobbying: http://www.idsos.state.id.us/elect/lobbyist/lobinfo.htm
Tax Exemptions: http://tax.idaho.gov/index.html
Charitable Solicitation: (none)

Illinois

Incorporation: http://www.cyberdriveillinois.com/departments/business_services/home.html
Lobbying: http://www.cyberdriveillinois.com/departments/index/lobbyist/home.html
Tax Exemptions: http://www.revenue.state.il.us/
Charitable Solicitation: http://www.illinoisattorneygeneral.gov/charities/index.html

Indiana

Incorporation: http://www.in.gov/sos/business/corporations.html
Lobbying: http://www.in.gov/ilrc/
Tax Exemptions: http://www.in.gov/dor/
Charitable Solicitation: http://www.in.gov/attorneygeneral/

Iowa

Incorporation: http://www.sos.state.ia.us/business/nonprofits/index.html
Lobbying: http://www.state.ia.us/ethics/
Tax Exemptions: http://www.state.ia.us/tax/index.html
Charitable Solicitation: http://www.state.ia.us/government/ag/consumer/index.html

Kansas

Incorporation: http://www.kssos.org/business/business.html
Lobbying: http://www.accesskansas.org/ethics/
Tax Exemptions: http://www.ksrevenue.org/
Charitable Solicitation: http://www.kssos.org/business/business_charitable.html

Kentucky

Incorporation: http://sos.ky.gov/business/filings
Lobbying: http://klec.ky.gov
Tax Exemptions: http://revenue.ky.gov
Charitable Solicitation: http://ag.ky.gov/consumer/charity/regs.htm

Louisiana

Incorporation: http://www.sos.louisiana.gov/comm/corp/corp-index.htm
Lobbying: http://www.ethics.state.la.us/lobby.htm
Tax Exemptions: http://www.rev.state.la.us/
Charitable Solicitation: http://www.ag.state.la.us/

Maine

Incorporation: http://www.maine.gov/sos/cec/corp
Lobbying: http://www.maine.gov/ethics/lobbyists/index.htm
Tax Exemptions: http://www.maine.gov/revenue
Charitable Solicitation: http://www.maine.gov/pfr/professionallicensing/index.shtml

Maryland

Incorporation: http://www.dat.state.md.us/sdatweb/corp_forms.html
Lobbying: http://ethics.gov.state.md.us/
Tax Exemptions: http://www.comp.state.md.us/
Charitable Solicitation: http://www.sos.state.md.us/charity/charityhome.htm

Massachusetts

Incorporation: http://www.sec.state.ma.us/cor/coridx.htm
Lobbying: http://www.sec.state.ma.us/pre/prelob/lobfaq.htm
Tax Exemptions: http://www.massdor.com/#
Charitable Solicitation: http://www.ago.state.ma.us/sp.cfm?pageid=972

Michigan

Incorporation: http://www.michigan.gov/cis/0,1607,7-154-35299---,00.html
Lobbying: http://www.michigan.gov/sos/0,1607,7-127-1633_11945-30292--,00.html
Tax Exemptions: http://www.michigan.gov/treasury
Charitable Solicitation: http://www.michigan.gov/ag/0,1607,7-164-17334_18095---,00.html

Minnesota

Incorporation: http://www.sos.state.mn.us/business/index.html
Lobbying: http://www.cfboard.state.mn.us/lob_overview.htm
Tax Exemptions: http://www.taxes.state.mn.us/
Charitable Solicitation: http://www.ag.state.mn.us/charities

Mississippi

Incorporation: http://www.ms.gov/frameset.jsp?URL=http%3A%2F%2Fwww.sos.state.ms.us%2F
Lobbying: http://www.sos.state.ms.us/elections/Lobbying/
Tax Exemptions: http://www.mstc.state.ms.us/
Charitable Solicitation: http://www.ms.gov/frameset.jsp?URL=http%3A%2F%2Fwww.sos.state.ms.us%2F

Missouri

Incorporation: http://www.sos.mo.gov/business/corporations
Lobbying: http://www.moethics.mo.gov/Ethics/Lobbying/Lobbying.aspx
Tax Exemptions: http://dor.mo.gov/tax/business
Charitable Solicitation: http://ago.mo.gov/checkacharity/charityregistration.htm

Montana

Incorporation: http://sos.mt.gov/BSB/index.asp
Lobbying: http://politicalpractices.mt.gov/
Tax Exemptions: http://mt.gov/revenue/default.asp
Charitable Solicitation: http://www.doj.mt.gov/

Nebraska

Incorporation: http://www.sos.state.ne.us/business/corp_serv/
Lobbying: http://nadc.nol.org/
Tax Exemptions: http://www.revenue.state.ne.us/
Charitable Solicitation: (none)

Nevada

Incorporation: http://sos.state.nv.us/business/forms/corporations.asp
Lobbying: http://www.leg.state.nv.us/lcb/admin/lobbyist/index.cfm
Tax Exemptions: http://tax.state.nv.us/
Charitable Solicitation: (none)

New Hampshire

Incorporation: http://www.sos.nh.gov/
Lobbying: http://www.sos.nh.gov/
Tax Exemptions: http://www.nh.gov/revenue/
Charitable Solicitation: http://doj.nh.gov/charitable/charitable.html

New Jersey

Incorporation: http://www.state.nj.us/njbgs
Lobbying: http://www.elec.state.nj.us
Tax Exemptions: http://www.state.nj.us/treasury/taxation/
Charitable Solicitation: http://www.state.nj.us/lps/ca/charhlp.htm

New Mexico

Incorporation: http://www.nmprc.state.nm.us/cb.htm
Lobbying: http://www.sos.state.nm.us/displayContent.asp?id=110
Tax Exemptions: http://www.tax.state.nm.us/
Charitable Solicitation: http://www.nmag.gov/office/Divisions/Civ/charity/faq.aspx

New York

Incorporation: http://www.dos.state.ny.us/corp/crpfaq.html
Lobbying: http://www.nyintegrity.org/forms/lobbying.html
Tax Exemptions: http://www.tax.state.ny.us/
Charitable Solicitation: http://www.oag.state.ny.us/charities/charities.html

North Carolina

Incorporation: http://www.secretary.state.nc.us/corporations/the page.aspx
Lobbying: http://www.secretary.state.nc.us/lobbyists/default.asp
Tax Exemptions: http://www.dor.state.nc.us/
Charitable Solicitation: http://www.secretary.state.nc.us/csl/

North Dakota

Incorporation: http://www.nd.gov/sos/businessserv/
Lobbying: http://www.nd.gov/sos/lobbylegislate/
Tax Exemptions: http://www.nd.gov/tax
Charitable Solicitation: http://www.nd.gov/sos/nonprofit/charitableorg/index.htm

Ohio

Incorporation: http://www.sos.state.oh.us/sos/businessservices/corp.aspx
Lobbying: http://www.jlec-olig.state.oh.us/
Tax Exemptions: http://tax.ohio.gov/
Charitable Solicitation: http://www.ag.state.oh.us/business/char_organizations.asp

Oklahoma

Incorporation: http://www.sos.state.ok.us/business/business_filing.htm
Lobbying: http://www.ethics.state.ok.us/
Tax Exemptions: http://www.oktax.state.ok.us/oktax/
Charitable Solicitation: http://www.sos.state.ok.us/forms/FORMS.HTM#Charity

Oregon

Incorporation: http://bluebook.state.or.us/state/executive/Corporations/corporations_home.htm
Lobbying: http://www.oregon.gov/OGEC/index.shtml
Tax Exemptions: http://www.or.gov/DOR/index.shtml
Charitable Solicitation: http://www.doj.state.or.us/charigroup/howtobe.shtml

Pennsylvania

Incorporation: http://www.dos.state.pa.us/corps/site/default.asp
Lobbying: http://www.ethics.state.pa.us/ethics
Tax Exemptions: http://www.revenue.state.pa.us/
Charitable Solicitation: http://www.dos.state.pa.us/char/site/default.asp

Rhode Island

Incorporation: http://www.sec.state.ri.us/corps
Lobbying: http://www.sec.state.ri.us/resources_for/lobbyist.html
Tax Exemptions: http://www.tax.state.ri.us/
Charitable Solicitation: http://www.dbr.state.ri.us/divisions/banking_securities/charitable.php

South Carolina

Incorporation: http://www.scsos.com/corporations.htm
Lobbying: http://ethics.sc.gov
Tax Exemptions: http://www.sctax.org/
Charitable Solicitation: http://www.scsos.com/charities.htm

South Dakota

Incorporation: http://www.sdsos.gov/busineservices/corporations.shtm
Lobbying: http://www.sdsos.gov/adminservices/lobbyistreg.shtm
Tax Exemptions: http://www.state.sd.us/drr2/revenue.html
Charitable Solicitation: http://www.state.sd.us/attorney/office/divisions/consumer/default.asp

Tennessee

Incorporation: http://www.state.tn.us/sos/bus_svc/index.htm
Lobbying: http://www.state.tn.us/tref/lobbyists/lobbyists.htm
Tax Exemptions: http://www.state.tn.us/revenue/
Charitable Solicitation: http://www.state.tn.us/sos/charity.htm

Texas

Incorporation: http://www.sos.state.tx.us/corp/index.shtml
Lobbying: http://www.ethics.state.tx.us/
Tax Exemptions: http://www.window.state.tx.us/
Charitable Solicitation: http://www.oag.state.tx.us/

Utah

Incorporation: http://www.corporations.utah.gov
Lobbying: http://www.elections.utah.gov/lobbyists.html
Tax Exemptions: http://tax.utah.gov/
Charitable Solicitation: http://consumerprotection.utah.gov/registration/charitableorganization.html

Vermont

Incorporation: http://www.sec.state.vt.us/corps/corpindex.htm
Lobbying: http://vermont-elections.org/elections1/lobbyist.html
Tax Exemptions: http://www.state.vt.us/tax/
Charitable Solicitation: http://www.atg.state.vt.us/display.php?smod=10

Virginia

Incorporation: http://www.scc.virginia.gov/division/clk/index.htm
Lobbying: http://www.commonwealth.virginia.gov/index.cfm
Tax Exemptions: http://www.tax.virginia.gov/index.cfm
Charitable Solicitation: http://www.vdacs.virginia.gov/consumers/oca-regulatory.shtml

Washington

Incorporation: http://www.secstate.wa.gov/corps/
Lobbying: http://www.pdc.wa.gov
Tax Exemptions: http://dor.wa.gov/
Charitable Solicitation: http://www.secstate.wa.gov/charities/

West Virginia

Incorporation: http://www.wvsos.com/common/startbusiness.htm
Lobbying: http://www.wvethicscommission.org/lobby.htm
Tax Exemptions: http://www.state.wv.us/taxdiv/
Charitable Solicitation: http://www.wvsos.com/charity/formsfees.htm

Wisconsin

Incorporation: http://www.wdfi.org/corporations/
Lobbying: http://ethics.state.wi.us/LobbyingRegistrationReports/LobbyingOverview.htm
Tax Exemptions: http://www.dor.state.wi.us/
Charitable Solicitation: http://drl.wi.gov/boards/rco/index.htm

Wyoming

Incorporation: http://soswy.state.wy.us/corporat/corporat.htm
Lobbying: http://soswy.state.wy.us/election/lobby.htm
Tax Exemptions: http://revenue.state.wy.us/
Charitable Solicitation: (none)

Appendix A

SAMPLE BYLAWS (BASED ON THE BYLAWS OF THE PENNSYLVANIA JEWISH COALITION)

BYLAWS
OF
(INSERT)

ARTICLE I- CORPORATE NAME

1. The name of the corporation shall be (insert).

ARTICLE II - PURPOSE

1. The corporation shall have unlimited powers to engage in and do any lawful act concerning any and all lawful activity for which non-profit corporations may be incorporated under the Act of November 15, 1972 P.L. 1063, as amended, under the provisions of which the corporation is incorporated.

2. The corporation shall undertake such acts as it deems necessary to (insert purpose of the corporation).

ARTICLE III - OFFICES

1. The principal office of the corporation shall be located in (insert), Pennsylvania.

2. The corporation may also have offices at such other places as the Board of Directors may from time to time appoint or the activities of the corporation may require.

ARTICLE IV - SEALS

1. The corporate seal shall have inscribed thereon the name of the corporation, the year of its organization and the words "Corporate Seal, Pennsylvania."

ARTICLE V - MEMBERS

1. The corporation shall have no members. All powers, obligations and rights of members provided by law shall reside in the Board of Directors.

ARTICLE VI - DIRECTORS

1. The business and affairs of this corporation shall be managed by its Board of Directors. The number of directors shall not exceed (insert number). The minimum qualifications of members of the Board of Directors shall be (insert).

2. In addition to the powers and authorities by these Bylaws expressly conferred upon them, the Board of Directors shall have the maximum power and authority now or hereafter provided or permitted under the laws of the Commonwealth of Pennsylvania to Directors of Pennsylvania non-profit corporations acting as a Board.

3. The Annual Meeting of the Board of Directors shall be held annually during the calendar year at such time and place as the Board of Directors shall designate in the notice of the meeting.

4. Regular meetings of the Board of Directors shall occur at least (insert) at such times and places as it shall designate from time to time.

5. Special meetings of the Board of Directors may be called by the Chairperson at such times as the Chairperson shall deem necessary.

6. Written or personal notice of every meeting of the Board of Directors shall be given to each Director at least five (5) days prior to the day named for the meeting.

7. A quorum for the transaction of business shall consist of (insert). The acts of a majority of directors present and eligible to vote at a Board meeting shall be the acts of the Board of Directors. Any action that may be taken at a meeting of the Directors may be taken without a meeting, if the consent or consents in writing setting forth the action so taken shall be signed by at least a majority of all directors in office, and shall be filed with the Secretary of the corporation.

8. Except where inconsistent with law or these bylaws, corporate proceedings shall be governed by the latest edition of Robert's Rules of Order.

9. The Board of Directors may, by resolution adopted by a majority of the Directors in office, establish one or more committees to consist of one or more Directors of the corporation to report back to the Board on the matter(s) within the committee's jurisdiction. A quorum for the purpose of holding and acting at any meeting of a committee shall be a simple majority of the members thereof.

10. All Board members shall be nominated and elected to serve on the Board. The Board may designate one or more directors as alternate members of any committee, who may replace any absent or disqualified member at any meeting of the committee. In the absence or disqualification of a member of a committee, the member or members thereof present at any meeting and not disqualified from voting, whether or not he, she or they constitute a quorum, may unanimously appoint another director to act at the meeting in the place of any such absent or disqualified member. Each committee of the Board shall serve at the pleasure of the Board.

11. The Board of Directors may, by resolution adopted by a majority of the Directors in office, establish an Advisory Committee to advise and assist the Board of Directors in carrying out its responsibilities. The Advisory committee shall consist of (insert).

12. One or more persons may participate in a meeting of the Board or a committee of the Board by means of the conference telephone or similar communications equipment by means of which all persons participating in the meeting can hear each other. Participation in a meeting pursuant to this section shall constitute presence in person at such meeting.

13. The Board of Directors may declare vacant the office of a director if he or she is declared of unsound mind by the order of court or is convicted of felony, or if within sixty (60) days after notice of his or her selection, he or she does not accept such office either in writing or by attending a meeting of the Board of Directors, and fulfill each other requirements of a qualification as the Bylaws may specify.

14. Any Director or Officer of the corporation is authorized to receive reasonable compensation from the corporation for services rendered and for actual expenses incurred when authorized by the Board of Directors or its designee. No director of the corporation shall receive compensation merely for acting as a director.

ARTICLE VII - OFFICERS

1. The executive officers of the corporations shall be natural persons of full age, shall be chosen by the Board, and shall be a Chairperson, Vice Chairperson, Secretary, Treasurer and such other officers and assistant officers as the needs of the corporation may require. They shall hold their offices for a term of (insert) and shall have such authority and shall perform such duties as are provided by the Bylaws and as shall from time to time be prescribed by the Board. The Board of Directors may secure the fidelity of any or all such officers by bond or otherwise. There shall be no limit on the number or terms an officer can serve.

2. Any officer or agent may be removed by the Board of Directors whenever in its judgment the best interests of the corporation will be served thereby but such removal shall be without prejudice to the contract rights of any person removed.

3. The Chairperson shall be the chief executive officer of the corporation; he or she shall preside at all meetings of the Directors; he or she shall have general and active management of the affairs of the corporation; shall see that all orders and resolutions of the Board are carried into effect, subject, however, to the right of the Directors to delegate any specific powers, except as may be by statute exclusively conferred on the Chairperson to any other officer or officers of the corporation. He or she shall execute all documents requiring a seal, under the seal of the corporation. He or she shall be EX-OFFICIO a member of all committees and shall have the general powers and duties of supervision and management usually vested in the office of Chairperson.

4. The Vice Chairperson shall act in all cases for and as the Chairperson in the latter's absence or incapacity, and shall perform such other duties as he or she may be required to do from time to time.

5. The Secretary shall attend all sessions of the Board and act as clerk thereof, and record all the votes of the corporation and the minutes of all its transactions in a book to be kept for that purpose; and shall perform like duties for all committees of the Board of Directors when required. He or she shall give, or cause to be given, notice of all meetings of the Board of Directors, and shall perform such other duties as may be prescribed by the Board of Directors or Chairperson, under whose supervision he or she shall be. He or she shall keep in safe custody, the corporate seal of the corporation, and when authorized by the Board, affix the same to any instrument requiring it.

6. The Treasurer shall have custody of the corporate funds and securities and shall keep full and accurate accounts or receipts and disbursements in books belonging to the corporation, and shall keep the moneys of the corporation in a separate account to the credit of the corporation. He or she shall disburse the funds of the corporation as may be ordered by the Board, taking proper vouchers for such disbursements, and shall render to the Chairperson and Directors, at the regular meeting of the Board, or whenever they may require it, an account of all his or her transactions as Treasurer and of the financial condition of the corporation.

7. Elections of officers shall be held every (insert) at the Annual Meeting of the Board of Directors.

ARTICLE VIII - VACANCIES

1. If the office of any officer or agent, one or more, becomes vacant for any reason, the Board of Directors may choose a successor or successors, who shall hold office for the unexpired term in respect of which such vacancy occurred.

2. Vacancies in the Board of Directors shall be filled in the same manner as provided for the designation of Directors in Article VI - Directors.

ARTICLE IX - BOOKS AND RECORDS

1. The corporation shall keep an original or duplicate record of the proceeding of the Directors, the original or a copy of its Bylaws, including all amendments thereto to date, certified by the Secretary of the corporation, and an original or a duplicate Board register, giving the names of the Directors, and showing their respective addresses. The corporation shall also keep appropriate, complete and accurate books or records of account that shall be reviewed on an annual basis. The records provided for herein shall be kept at either the registered office of the corporation in this Commonwealth, or at its principal place of business wherever situated.

ARTICLE X - FISCAL YEAR AND ANNUAL REPORT

1. The fiscal year of the corporation shall commence on (insert) and end on the following (insert).

2. The Board of Directors shall cause a report of the activities of the corporation to be prepared annually and sent to such persons as the Board of Directors shall determine.

ARTICLE XI - AMENDMENTS

1. The Board of Directors may alter, amend, suspend or repeal these Bylaws at any regular or special meeting called for that purpose, except as restricted by the Pennsylvania Non-Profit Corporation Law of 1972, as amended.

ARTICLE XII - LIMITED LIABILITY OF DIRECTORS

1. A director shall not be personally liable for monetary damages as such for any action taken, or any failure to take any action, unless the director has breached or failed to perform the duties of his or her office under section 8363 of the Directors' Liability Act (relating to standard of care and justifiable reliance); and the breach or failure to perform constitutes self-dealing, willful misconduct or recklessness. The provision of this section shall not apply to the responsibility or liability of a director pursuant to any criminal statute; or the liability of a director for the payment of taxes pursuant to local, State or Federal Law.

Appendix B

New Year's Resolutions for Nonprofit Executives

by Gary M. Grobman
(reprinted with permission from Pennsylvania Nonprofit Report)

It's December, and another year has slipped by. Replacing calendars on the wall is often an excuse for introspection. I've made some New Year's resolutions of my own, and it's not too late for you to do so if you haven't. Let me make a few suggestions.

1. Become an exemplary, ethical individual, every minute, every day. Don't use organizational resources for personal use and don't tolerate others in your organization who do. Consider whether you are creating conflicts of interest with your decisions. Don't cheat on your expense account. Register your organization with the state agency that regulates charitable organizations if you are required to do so. Consider registering with that agency and disclosing information even if you are not required to do so because your fundraising is under the threshold requirements. Be honest with your board and staff (most boards are much more tolerant of mistakes made than they are of lying about it, anyway!). Your standard of ethics reflects not only upon you and your organization, but also upon our sector as a whole. The shock waves surrounding the New Era debacle and the United Way fiasco in the 1990s are still being felt. The public is becoming more cynical about how charities operate. Don't be someone who adds to this sense of cynicism. It's also easier to sleep at night when you know you didn't do something dishonest or questionable during the day.

2. Make sure you have a healthy, vibrant personal life. It is so easy running an organization to become consumed by the pressures, challenges, and demands that accompany leadership and neglect your health, family, hobbies, and vacation needs. If you are one of those who find it impossible to leave the office to take vacation, remember that even the President plays golf and takes vacations, and he's a really busy executive! If your organization is such that it can't survive with you away for a few days, then that is a sign that something is unhealthy with either you or the organization. Fix it. And then go take a hike (on the Appalachian Trail). If you are getting too many evening calls from your board chair or (God forbid!) unnecessary calls in the middle of the night, politely inform him or her that you are no longer willing to take these calls, and that there are 900 numbers available for late night companionship needs.

3. If your organization can afford it, consider making a voluntary contribution to a local government or a foundation established to support local governments. There is some legitimacy to the view of local governments that charities use their services and do not pay for it, and this places a strain on their ability to function. There is also legitimacy to our sector's view that as charities, we should be exempt from taxes or involuntary monetary payments. Yet many in our sector recognize that we have a partnership with local governments to make society better. One way to do so is to help our local governments, on a voluntary basis, when we can do so. If your organization cannot or will not provide money, then offer services.

4. Be sensitive to the legitimate concerns of small business. Small business people are not the enemies of charities. They serve on our boards. They provide us with valuable products and services. They purchase our products and services. How would you feel if you invested not only your entire life savings but your entire emotional capital in a business, and a local charity used its profits as venture capital to establish a commercial business (i.e. designed not to serve any charitable mission but to generate net revenue) to compete head-to-head with yours, and had the advantage of not paying taxes, paying cheaper postage rates, had volunteers, access to capital, and the public relations value that comes from being a "charity"? There is clearly a role for charities to generate revenue to fund services for the community. But there is a right way and a wrong way of doing this. The Jewish Community Center or YMCA that places advertisements in general circulation newspapers seeking corporate memberships touting that its fees are slightly lower than the private health club a mile away is probably not violating any laws. But they are violating the spirit of why the JCC health club and YMCA are eligible for tax-exempt status. The hospital that markets its laundry service to the general public may be paying unrelated business income taxes on its revenue, but this style of marketing creates tensions within the small business community, and for good reason. Should my public library be offering best-sellers and videos for fees that undercut existing small businesses? A gray area, and we could argue that one for a long time. But my point stands: Before establishing or expanding a commercial business under the aegis of charitable tax-exempt status, even if it is not violative of any unfair business competition provisions of your state law, think twice. There are ways to generate income by providing services and products that don't step on toes.

5. Join and support a state advocacy association. The non-profit charitable community faces problems and challenges that are too big for any individual to face alone. There are associations based in most state capitals and Washington whose job is to identify these problems and challenges, devise a strategy to meet them head on, and coordinate advocacy. Many of these organizations are starved for membership and resources because it is easy for a charity to avoid its responsibilities and let the burden fall on the "other guy." There is strength in numbers, and if you run an agency that thinks it can save a few dollars by not making an investment in its future, you're being short-sighted. And while you are at it, join a professional organization, as well.

6. Get some continuing education to improve your ability to manage your organization. Whether it is in the grants writing, computer, management, strategic planning, time management, or board/staff relations areas, virtually every nonprofit organization manager can benefit by some outside training. Taking a course also offers a break from the office routine and brings you in contact with peers from other disciplines. It's good for networking, good socially, good for your brain, and, best of all, many organizations will pay all of the costs!

7. Take advantage of the Internet, and set up a Web page that hawks your products and services. The communications revolution shouldn't leave you and your organization behind. Each day, thousands of "newbies" access the Web, which has become the access point of choice for information about volunteering, charitable giving, news and views, demographic data, and contacts within your field. A modest home page, blog, and online store can be established and maintained for surprisingly low cost and effort. And, believe it or not, it's lots of fun.

8. Invite your local legislators to visit your agency and/or meet with your board. Whether at the City Council/County Commissioner, state legislature, or Congressional level, the decisions made by our elected officials affect our organizations, our clients, our volunteers, our board members, and us. There are many benefits in establishing a relationship with these officials *before* you need something from them. This is especially important if your agency is the recipient of government funding, or hopes to be in the future.

Appendix C: Sample Financial Reports: Association for Research on Nonprofit Organizations and Voluntary Action (ARNOVA)

FINANCIAL SUMMARY

Statement of Activities
Year Ended December 31, 2003
(With Comparative Total for the Year Ended December 31, 2002)

	2003 Unrestricted	2003 Temporarily Restricted	2003 Total	2002 Total
2003 Support and Revenue				
Grants	$ -0-	$92,500	$92,500	$729,905
Membership dues	103,831	-0-	103,831	98,445
Conference revenue and sponsorships	120,060	40,753	160,813	156,394
Contributions	9,922	19,585	29,507	18,001
Interest income on cash and cash equivalents	1,154	49	1,203	2,950
Other	19,810	-0-	19,810	15,040
Net assets released from restrictions	395,467	(395,467)	-0-	-0-
Total support and revenue	650,244	(242,580)	407,664	1,020,735
Expenses				
Program:				
Conference	165,649	-0-	165,649	139,815
Publications	109,184	-0-	109,184	142,108
Membership services	91,628	-0-	91,628	91,402
Scholarships and awards	22,480	-0-	22,480	28,553
Other	34,136	-0-	34,136	41,489
	423,077	-0-	423,077	443,367
Management and general:				
Office	162,324	-0-	162,324	155,242
Marketing publication portfolio study	-0-	-0-	-0-	21,521
Collaboration	9,505	-0-	9,505	10,181
Board development	24,772	-0-	24,772	21,988
	196,601	-0-	196,601	208,932
Fundraising *	25,164	-0-	25,164	23,499
Total expenses	644,842	-0-	644,842	675,798
Increase (decrease) in net assets from operations	5,402	(242,580)	(237,178)	344,937
Other Income (Expense)				
Investment return, net	18,402	-0-	18,402	31,693
Change in net assets	23,804	(242,580)	(218,776)	376,630
Net Assets, Beginning of Year	451,647	693,622	1,145,269	768,639
Net Assets, End of Year	$475,451	$451,042	$926,493	$1,145,269

* Includes staff time for grant proposal writing

Note: Financial statements are prepared using Generally Accepted Accounting Principles (GAAP). Therefore, grants and contributions are recognized as revenues in the year the monies are received or promises made (although they may be designated for several years). The net assets released from restriction shows restricted grant money released for use in a given year. ·

Financial Information Excerpted From the Audited Financial Statements Provided by Blue & Co., LLC

Statements of Financial Position
December 31, 2003 and 2002

Assets

	2003	2002
Cash and cash equivalents	$294,642	262,950
Cash held by others	99,640	63,620
Investments	618,582	795,155
Grants receivable	11,152	50,000
Other receivables	10,263	23,935
Prepaid expenses	7,144	3,426
Property and equipment, net	41,482	48,086
	$1,082,905	$1,247,172

Liabilities and Net Assets

	2003	2002
Liabilities:		
Accounts payable	$86,824	$23,288
Accrued payroll and benefits	25,393	27,140
Deferred member dues	44,195	51,475
Total liabilities	156,412	101,903
Net Assets:		
Unrestricted:		
Undesignated	402,107	381,152
Board designated	73,344	70,495
Temporarily restricted	451,042	693,622
Total net assets	926,493	1,145,269
	$1,082,905	$1,247,172

Appendix D
About the Author...

Gary M. Grobman (B.S. Drexel University, M.P.A. Harvard University, Kennedy School of Government, Ph.D., Penn State University) is special projects director for White Hat Communications, a Harrisburg-based publishing and nonprofit consulting organization formed in 1993. The title of Dr. Grobman's doctoral dissertation is *An Analysis of Codes of Ethics of Nonprofit, Tax-Exempt Membership Associations: Does Principal Constituency Make a Difference?* He is an adjunct faculty member of Indiana University of Pennsylvania, Marylhurst University, and Gratz College. He is an officer of the teaching section of the Association for Research on Nonprofit Organizations and Voluntary Action (ARNOVA)

He served as the executive director of the Pennsylvania Jewish Coalition from 1983-1996. Prior to that, he was a senior legislative assistant in Washington for two members of Congress, a news reporter, and a political humor columnist for *Roll Call.* He also served as a lobbyist for public transit agencies. In 1987, he founded the Non-Profit Advocacy Network (NPAN), which consists of more than 50 statewide associations that represent Pennsylvania charities. He currently is the Harrisburg Contributing Editor for *Pennsylvania Nonprofit Report.*

He serves on the board of directors as Vice President of the Greater Harrisburg Concert Band. He also served on the board of directors of the Citizen Service Project, and was the Treasurer of that statewide 501(c)(3), which was established to promote citizen service in Pennsylvania. He is the author of *The Holocaust—A Guide for Pennsylvania Teachers, The Nonprofit Handbook, Fundraising Online: Using the Internet to Raise Serious Money for Your Nonprofit Organization* (co-authored with Gary Grant), *Improving Quality and Performance in Your Non-Profit Organization, The Nonprofit Organization's Guide to E-Commerce,* and other books published by White Hat Communications and Wilder Publications (now Fieldstone).

Appendix E

Nonprofit Handbook—Fifth Edition
Reader Survey/Order Form

Return Survey To:
White Hat Communications
PO Box 5390
Harrisburg, PA 17110-0390

My name and address (please print legibly):

1. I would like to suggest the following corrections:

2. I would like to suggest the following topics for inclusion in a future edition:

3. I have the following comments, suggestions, or criticisms:

4. I would like to order _____ additional copies @$29.95 each plus $8 shipping and handling first book, $1 each additional book. Pennsylvania purchasers please add 6% sales tax or include a copy of exemption certificate from the Pennsylvania Department of Revenue. Note: Quantity discounts are available.

Bibliography

Note: References to Chapters 32, 33, 34, and 35 may be found at the end of each of those chapters.

General

Conners, Tracy D. *The Nonprofit Handbook: Management. New York: Wiley & Sons.* (1997).

Hopkins, Bruce R. *Starting and Managing a Nonprofit Organization: A Legal Guide.* New York: Wiley & Sons. (2000).

Mancuso, Anthony. *How to Form a Nonprofit Organization* (National Edition). Berkeley, CA: Nolo Press.

Ott, J. Steven and Shafitz, Jay M. *The Facts on File Dictionary of Nonprofit Organization Management.* New York, NY: Facts on File Publications, 1986.

Chapter 1/Chapter 2/Chapter 3

Debnam, Robert J. *Handbook of Legal Liabilities for Nonprofit Executives.* Washington, DC: Rural America.

Hopkins, Bruce R. *Starting and Managing a Nonprofit Organization: A Legal Guide.* New York, NY: Wiley & Sons, 1989.

Kirschten, Barbara L. *Nonprofit Corporate Forms Handbook.* New York, NY: Clark Boardman Co., 1990.

Lane, Marc J. *Legal Handbook for Nonprofit Organizations.* New York, NY: Amacon, 1980.

Mandel Center for Nonprofit Organizations. *Legal Issues in Nonprofit Organizations.* Mandel Center for Nonprofit Organizations Discussion Paper Series. Cleveland, OH: Case Western Reserve University, 1988.

Majmudes, Carol S. and Weiss, Ellen. (eds.). *Tax-Exempt Organizations* (2 vol.). Englewood Cliffs, NJ: Prentice-Hall, 1988.

Philadelphia Volunteer Lawyers for the Arts. *Guide to Forming a Non-Profit, Tax-Exempt Organization.* Philadelphia, PA: Philadelphia Volunteer Lawyers for the Arts, 1980.

Treusch, Paul E. and Sugarman, Norman A. *Tax-Exempt Organizations.* Philadelphia, PA: American Law Institute, 1983.

Whitaker, Fred A. *How to Form Your Own Non-Profit Corporation in One Day.* Oakland, CA: Minority Management Institute, 1979.

Chapter 4

Andringa, Robert C. and Egstrom, Ted W. *Nonprofit Board Answer Book.* Washington, DC: Board Source. (2002).

Anthes, Earl, et. al. (ed.). *The Nonprofit Board Book.* Independent Community Consultants, West Memphis, Ark., Independent Community Consultants, 1985.

Bates, Don. *How to Be a Better Board Member: Guidelines for Trustees.* Voluntary Action Leadership (Winter 1983).

Black, Ralph. *What Do You Do With a Do-Nothing Board Member?* American Symphony Orchestra League (1987).

Brooklyn In-Touch Information Center. *Building a Board of Directors*. Brooklyn, NY: Brooklyn In-Touch Information Center, 1984.

———*How To Conduct a Meeting*. 1988.

———*How To Develop a Board of Directors*. 1988.

Conrad, William R. Jr. and Glenn, William E. *The Effective Voluntary Board of Directors: What is it and How it Works*. Chicago, IL: Swallow Press, 1983.

Donovan, James A. *50 Ways to Motivate Your Board*.Lake Monroe, FL: Donovan Management, 1997.

Duca, Diane J. *Nonprofit Boards: A Practical Guide to Roles, Responsibilities and Performance*. Phoenix, AZ: Oryx Press, 1986.

Independent Community Consultants. *The Nonprofit Board Book: Strategies for Organizational Success*. West Memphis, Ark: Independent Community Consultants, 1983.

Kirk, W. Astor. *Nonprofit Organization Governance: A Challenge in Turbulent Times*. New York, NY: Carlton Press, 1986.

Kile, Robert W. and Loscavio, J. Michael. *Fredrick, Strategic Board Recruitment, The Not-for-Profit Model*. New York: Aspen Publishers, 1996.

Klein, Kim & Roth, Stephanie. *The Board of Directors* (Revised Edition). Oakland, CA: Grassroots Fundraising Journal, 2000.

O'Connell, Brian. *The Role of the Board and Board Members*. Nonprofit Management Series (#1). Washington, DC: Independent Sector, 1988.

——— *Finding, Developing and Rewarding Good Board Members*. Nonprofit Management Series (#2). Washington, DC: Independent Sector, 1988.

——— *The Board Member's Book: Making a Difference in Voluntary Organizations*. New York, NY: The Foundation Center, 1985.

Widmer, Candace and Houchin, Susan. *The Art of Trusteeship: The Nonprofit Board Member's Guide to Effective Governance*. San Francisco, CA: Jossey-Bass. 2000.

Chapter 5

About.com. (2003). *How to draft a mission statement*. Retrieved June 9, 2003, from http://management.about.com/library/howto/ht_stmt.htm

Deal, J. (1997). *How to create and use a mission statement*. Retrieved June 9, 2003, from http://www.dealconsulting.com/strategy/mission.html

Grobman, G. (2001). Mission/vision statements remain key to successful npo governance. *Pennsylvania Nonprofit Report*. Retrieved June 9, 2003, from http://www.panonprofitreport.com/reports/vision.html

Morrisey, George. *A Guide to Strategic Thinking: Building Your Planning Foundation*. San Francisco:Jossey-Bass,1996.

Chapter 6

Albert, K. J, editor. *The Strategic Management Handbook*. New York: McGraw-Hill, 1983.

Barry, Bryan W. *Strategic Planning Workbook for Nonprofit Organizations*. St. Paul, Minnesota: Amherst H. Wilder Foundation, 1997.

Department of Hospital Planning and Society for Hospital Planning. *Compendium of Resources for Strategic Planning in Hospitals*. Chicago, IL: American Hospital Association, 1981.

Armstrong, J. S. *The Value of Formal Planning for Strategic Decisions: Review of Empirical Research*. Strategic Management Journal (Ill, 1982:197-211).

Barry, Bryan. *Strategic Planning Workbook for Nonprofit Organizations*. St. Paul, MN: Amherst H. Wilder Foundation, 1997.

Burkhardt, Patrick J. & Reuss, Suzanne. *Successful Strategic Planning: A Guide for Nonprofit Agencies and Organizations*. Newbury Park CA: Sage Publications, 1993.

Bryson, John M. & Alston, Farnum K. *Creating and Implementing Your Strategic Plan: A Workbook for Public and Nonprofit Organizations* (Second Edition). San Francisco: Jossey-Bass, 1995.

Mintzburg, Henry. *The Rise and Fall of Strategic Planning*. NY, NY: MacMillan, 1994.

Newman, W. H., Summer, C. E. and Warren, E. K. *The Process of Management*. Englewood Cliffs, NJ: Prentice Hall, 1982.

Pennings, J. M. *Organizational Strategy and Change*. San Francisco, CA: Jossey-Bass, 1985.

Peters, J. P. *A Guide to Strategic Planning for Hospitals*. Chicago, IL: American Hospital Association, 1979.

Rhenmann, E. *Organizational Theory for Long-Range Planning*. NY, NY: Wiley & Sons, 1973.

Steiner, G. A. *Strategic Planning: What Every Manager Must Know*. NY, NY: Free Press, 1979.

Chapter 7

Carver, John. *Boards That Make a Difference: A New Design for Leadership in Nonprofit and Public Organizations* (Second Edition). San Francisco: Jossey-Bass, 1997.

Chapter 8

Anderson, Albert. *Ethics for Fundraisers*. Bloomington, IN: Indiana University Press, 1996.

Harmon, Curran, Spielberg & Eisenberg, LLP. *The "Intermediate Sanctions" Law Means for Nonprofit Organizations*. Washington, DC: Alliance for Justice, 1996.

Independent Sector. *Ethics and the Nation's Voluntary and Philanthropic Community*. Washington, DC.

Josephson Institute of Ethics. *Making Ethical Decisions*. Marina del Rey, CA.

Chapter 9

Blazek, Jody. *Tax Planning and Compliance for Tax-Exempt Organizations: Forms, Checklists, Procedures* (Third Edition). New York: John Wiley & Sons, 1999.

Godfrey, Howard. *Handbook on Tax-Exempt Organizations.* Englewood Cliffs, NJ: Prentice-Hall, 1983.

Hansmann, Henry. *The Rationale for Exempting Nonprofit Organizations From Corporate Income Taxation.* New Haven, CT: Institute for Social Policy Studies, 1981.

Harmon, Gail and Ferster, Andrea. *"Dealing With the IRS."* Nonprofit Times (May 1988).

Hopkins, Bruce R. *The Law of Nonprofit Organizations* (6th Edition). New York: John Wiley & Sons. (1992).

Hopkins, Bruce R. *The Second Legal Answer Book for Nonprofit Organizations.* New York: John Wiley & Sons, 1998.

Kirschten, Barbara L. *Nonprofit Corporate Forms Handbook.* New York: Clark Boardman Co., 1990.

Lang, Andrew and Sorrells, Michael. *Completing Your IRS Form 990: A Guide for Tax-Exempt Organizations.* Washington, DC: American Society of Association Executives, 1999.

Larson, Martin A., and Lowell, C. Stanley. *Praise the Lord for Tax Exemption.* Washington, DC: Robert B. Luce, 1969.

Mancuso, Anthony. *How To Form Your Own Nonprofit Corporation.* Berkeley, CA: Nolo Press, 1990.

Skousen, Mark. *Tax-Free.* Merrifield, VA: Mark Skousen, 1982.

Stralton, Debra J. *"A Guide for Dealing With the IRS."* Association Management (August 1979).

Sughrue, Robert N. and Kopnski, Michele. *Qualifying as a Nonprofit Tax-Exempt Organization.* New York: Quorum Books (1991).

Trompeter, Jean E. *"Formation and Qualification of a Charitable Organization."* Milwaukee Lawyer (Fall 1983).

Chapter 10

Brooklyn In-Touch Information Center. *How to Assess Board Liability. Fact Sheet for Nonprofit Managers* (#6). Brooklyn, NY: Brooklyn In-Touch Information Center, 1988.

Chapman, Terry S.; Lai, Mary L; and Steinbock, Elmer L. *Am I Covered For? A Guide to Insurance for Nonprofit Organizations.* San Jose, CA: Consortium for Human Resources, 1984.

Council on Foundations. *Directors and Officers Liability Insurance.* Washington, DC: Council on Foundations, 1983.

Davis, Pamela. *Nonprofit Organizations and Liability Insurance: Problems, Options and Prospects.* Los Angeles, CA: California Community Foundation, 1987.

Drucker, Peter F. *Managing the Nonprofit Organization.* New York, NY: Harper Collins, 1990.

Johnson, R. Bradley. *Risk Management Guide for Nonprofits.* Alexandria, VA: United Way of America, 1987.

Minnesota Office of Citizenship and Volunteer Services. *Planning It Safe: How to Control Liability & Risk in Volunteer Programs.* Minneapolis, MN: Author. 1998

Peat, Marwick, Mitchell and Co. *Directors' and Officers' Liability: A Crisis in the Making.* New York, NY: Peat, Marwick, Mitchell and Co., 1987.

Chapter 11

American Institute of Certified Public Accountants. *Audits of Certain Nonprofit Organizations.* New York, NY: American Institute of Certified Public Accountants, 1981.

Brooklyn In-Touch Information Center. *How To Prepare a Budget.* New York, NY: Brooklyn In-Touch Information Center, 1988.

Conners, Tracy D. (ed.). *The Nonprofit Organization Handbook.* New York, NY: McGraw-Hill Book Co., 1980.

Dropkin, Murray and La Touche, Bill. *The Budget-Building Book for Nonprofits: A Step-by-Step Guide for Managers and Boards.* San Francisco: Jossey-Bass, 1998.

Drucker, Peter F. *Managing the Nonprofit Organization.* New York, NY: Harper Collins, 1990.

Foster, Mary, Becker, Howard; & Terrano, Richard. *Miller Not-for-Profit Reporting.* New York: Aspen Publishing, 2001.

Gross, Jr., Malvern J. and Warshauer, William. *Financial and Accounting Guide for Nonprofit Organizations.* New York, NY: John Wiley, 1983.

Matthews, Lawrence M. *Practical Operating Budgeting.* New York: McGraw-Hill, 1977.

Olenick, Arnold J. and Olenick, Philip R. *Making the Non-Profit Organization Work: A Financial, Legal and Tax Guide for Administrators.* Englewood Cliffs, NJ: Institute for Business Planning, 1983.

Public Management Institute. *Bookkeeping for Nonprofits.* San Francisco, CA: Institute for Business Planning, 1983.

————- *Budgeting for Nonprofits.* San Francisco, CA: Institute for Business Planning, 1980.

Quint, Barbara Gilder. *Clear and Simple Guide to Bookkeeping.* New York: Monarch Press, 1981.

Ragan, Robert C. *Step-By-Step Bookkeeping.* New York, NY: Sterling Publications, 1987.
Jae K. Shim, Joel G. Siegel, and Abraham J. Simon. *Handbook of Budgeting for Nonprofit Organizations.* Old Tappen, NJ: Prentice Hall 1996.

Sladek, Frea E. and Stein, Eugene L. *Grant Budgeting and Finance.* New York, NY: Plenum Press, 1981.

Smith, G. Stephenson. *Accounting for Libraries and Other Not-for-Profit Organizations* (Second Edition). Chigaco, IL: American Library Association, 1999.
Stevens, Susan Kenny and Anderson, Lisa. *All the Way to the Bank: Smart Money Management for Tomorrow's Nonprofit.* St. Paul, Minnesota: The Stevens Group, 1997.

Vinter, Robert D. and Kikish, Rhea K. *Budgeting for Not-for-Profit Organizations.* New York, NY: Free Press, 1984.

Wacht, Richard F. *Financial Management in Nonprofit Organizations.* Atlanta, GA: Georgia State University, 1984.

Waldo, Charles N. *A Working Guide for Directors of Not-for-Profit Organizations.* Westport, CT: Greenwood Press, 1986.

Chapter 12

Albert, Sheila. *Hiring the Chief Executive: A Practical Guide to the Search and Selection Process.* Washington, DC: National Center for Nonprofit Boards, 2000.

Anthes, Earl W. and Cronin, Jerry (eds.). *Personnel Matters in the Nonprofit Organization.* West Memphis, AR: Independent Community Consultants, 1987.

Anthony, Robert N. and Herzlinger, Regina E. *Management Control in Nonprofit Organizations.* Chicago, IL: Richard D. Irwin, 1975.

Becker, Sarah and Glenn, Donna. *Off Your Duffs and Up the Assets: Common Sense for Non-Profit Managers.* Rockville, NY: Farnsworth Publishing Co., 1988.

Bernstein, Leyna. *Creating Your Employee Handbook: A Do-It-Yourself Kit for Nonprofits.* San Francisco: Jossey-Bass Publishers, 1999.

Borst, Diane and Montana, Patrick J. (eds.). *Managing Nonprofit Organizations.* New York, NY: Amacon, 1977.

Broadwell, Martin M. *Supervisory Handbook: A Management Guide to Principles and Applications.* New York, NY: Wiley, Inc., 1985.

Brown, James Douglas. *The Human Nature of Organizations.* New York, NY: Amacon, 1973.

Chruden, Herbert J. *Personnel Management.* Cincinnati, OH: South-Western Publications, 1976.

DeLuca, Matthew. *Nonprofit Personnel Forms & Guidelines.* New York: Aspen, 1994.

Drucker, Peter F. *Managing the Nonprofit Organization.* New York, NY: Harper Collins, 1990.

Gillis, John (Ed.). *Nonprofit Personnel Policies.* New York: Aspen. 1997.

Goldberg/Rosenthal, Montgomery, Mc Cracken, Walker & Rhoads, and Paychex, Inc. *Accounting, Legal and Payroll Tax Guide for Nonprofit Organizations.* Philadelphia: Community Accountants, 1991.

Hauge, Jennifer C. & Herman, Melanie. *Taking the High Road: A Guide to Effective and Legal Employment Practices for Nonprofits.* Washington, DC: Nonprofit Risk Management Center, 1999.

Pynes, Joan E. *Human Resources Management for Public and Nonprofit Organizations.* San Francisco: Jossey Bass, 1997.

Chapter 13

Bagley, Esq., Bruce. *Necessary v. Nosey—Guidelines and Strategies for Hiring.* PA Society of Association Executives' *Society News.* April 1996. pp. 20.

Gelatt, James P. *Managing Nonprofit Organizations in the 21st Century.* Phoenix, AZ: The Oryx Press, 1992.

Half, Robert. *On Hiring.* New York, NY: Crown Publishers, 1985.

Pennsylvania Human Relations Commission. *Pre-Employment Inquiries: What May I Ask? What Must I Answer?* Harrisburg, PA.

Rogers, Henry C. *The One Hat Solution—Rogers' Strategy for Creative Middle Management*. New York, NY: St. Martin's Press, 1986.

Thompson, Brad. *The New Manager's Handbook*. Burr Ridge, IL: Irwin Professional Publishing, 1995.

Chapter 14

Adams, Katherine. *"Investing in Volunteers: A Guide to Effective Volunteer Management."* Conserve Neighborhoods (1985).

Brown, Kathleen M. *Keys to Making a Volunteer Program Work*. Richmond, CA: Arden Publications, 1982.

Conners, Tracy D. (ed.). *The Nonprofit Organization Handbook*. New York, NY: McGraw-Hill Book Co., 1980.

de Harven, Gerry Ann. *"Fostering the Voluntary Spirit: Motivating People to Serve."* Fund Raising Management (March 1984).

Ellis, Susan J. *From the Top Down: The Executive Role in Volunteer Program Success*. Philadelphia, PA: Energize, 1996.

Fisher, James C. and Cole, Kathleen M. *Leadership and Management of Volunteer Programs: A Guide for Volunteer Administrators*. San Francisco: Jossey-Bass, 1993.

Flanagan, Joan. *The Successful Volunteer Organization: Getting Started and Getting Results in Nonprofit, Charitable, Grassroots and Community Groups*. Chicago, IL: Contemporary Books, 1984.

Fletcher, Kathleen Brown. *The 9 Keys To Successful Volunteer Programs*. Taft Group: Rockville, MD., 1987.

Graff, Linda. Beyond Police Checks: *The Definitive Volunteer & Employee Screening Guidebook*. Dundass, Ontario: Graff and Associates, 1999

Independent Sector. *Americans Volunteer, 1981*. Washington, DC: Independent Sector, 1982.

Lauffer, Armand and Gorodezky, Sarah. *Volunteers*. Beverly Hills, CA: Sage Publications, 1977.

London, Mark. *"Effective Use of Volunteers: Who, Why, When and How."* Fund Raising Management (August 1985).

McCurley, Stephen H. *"Protecting Volunteers From Suit: A Look At State Legislation."* Voluntary Action Leadership (Spring-Summer 1987).

O'Connell, Brian. *America's Voluntary Spirit*. New York, NY: The Foundation Center, 1983.

Rauner, Judy. *Helping People Volunteer*. San Diego, CA: Marlborough Publications, 1980.

Stafford, J. et. al. *Fundamentals of Association Management: The Volunteer*. Washington, DC: American Society of Association Executives, 1982.

Taylor, Shirley H. and Wild, Peggy. *"How to Match Volunteer Motivation With Job Demands."* Voluntary Action Leadership (Summer 1984).

Van Til, Jon. *Mapping the Third Sector: Volunteerism in a Changing Social Economy*. New York, NY: The Foundation Center, 1988.

Vineyard, Sue and McCurley, Steve. 101 More Ideas for Volunteer Programs. Downers Grove, IL: Heritage Arts Publishing 1995.

Volunteer—The National Center. *New Challenges for Employee Volunteering.* Arlington, VA: Volunteer—The National Center, 1982.

Chapter 15

Kramer, Donald. *"Pa. Passes Solicitation Act With New Rules, Penalties."* Nonprofit Issues (December 1990).

Morgan, Lewis & Bockius. *"The Solicitation of Funds for Charitable Purposes Act."* Philadelphia: Morgan, Lewis & Bockius, May 1991.

Wickham, Kenneth. *Testimony Presented to House Finance Committee Regarding HB 2046 and HB 2047: November 1, 1989.* Harrisburg, PA: United Way of Pennsylvania, 1989.

Chapter 16

Dannelley, Paul. Fundraising and Public Relations. Norman, OK: Univ. of Oklahoma Press, 1986.

Des Marais, Philip. *How To Get Government Grants.* New York, NY: Public Service Materials Center, 1975.

Dove, Ken. *Conducting a Successful Fundraising Program: A Comprehensive Guide and Resource.* San Francisco: Jossey-Bass, 2001.

Kelly, Kathleen. *Effective Fund-Raising Management.* Mahwah, NJ: Lawrence Erlbaum Associates, 1997

Kletzien, S. Damon, ed. *Directory of Pennsylvania Foundations.* Springfield, PA: Triadvocates Press, 1990.

Margolin, Judith B. (ed.). *The Foundation Center's User Friendly Guide—Grant Seeker's Guide to Resources.* New York, NY: The Foundation Center, 1990.

Mussoline, Mary Louise (Ed.). *Small Nonprofits: Strategies for Fundraising Success.* San Francisco: Jossey-Bass, Inc., Publishers, 1998.

Nelson, Paula. *Where to Get Money for Everything.* New York, NY: William Morris & Co., 1982.

Raybin, Arthur D. *How to Hire the Right Fundraising Consultant.* Washington, DC: Taft Group, 1985.

Seltzer, Michael. *Securing Your Organization's Future: A Complete Guide to Fundraising Strategies.* New York, NY: The Foundation Center, 1987.

White, Virginia (ed.). *Grant Proposals That Succeeded.* New York, NY: Plenum Press, 1983.

Chapter 17

Blum, Laurie. *The Complete Guide to Getting a Grant.* New York, NY: Poseidon Press, 1993.

Chelekis, George C. *The Action Guide to Government Grants, Loans and Giveaways.* New York, NY: Perigee Books, 1993.

Collins, Sarah & Dion, Charlotte. *The Foundation Center's User-Friendly Guide: A Grantseeker's Guide to Resources* (Fourth Edition). New York: The Foundation Center, 1996.

Dermer, Joseph. *How to Write Successful Foundation Presentations.* New York, NY: Public Service Materials Center, 1984.

Dumouchel, J. Robert. *Government Assistance Almanac.* Washington, DC: Foggy Bottom Publications, 1985.

Educational Funding Research Council. *Funding Database Handbook.* Arlington, VA: Funding Research Institute, 1992.

Geever, Jane C. *The Foundation Center's Guide to Proposal Writing.* New York, NY: The Foundation Center, 1993.

Hillman, Howard and Chamberlain, Majorie. *The Art of Winning Corporate Grants.* New York, NY: Vanguard Press, 1980.

Margolis, Judith. *Foundation Fundamentals: A Guide for Grantseekers.* New York: Foundation Center, 1991.

_____ *The Foundation Center's User Friendly Guide: Grantseeker's Guide to Resources.* New York: The Foundation Center, 1992.

Quick, James M. & New, Cheryl C. *Grant Seeker's Budget Toolkit.* New York: Wiley and Sons, 2001.

Sanlon, Eugene. *Corporate and Foundation Fund Raising: A Complete Guide from the Inside.* Sudbury, MA: Jones & Bartlett Publishers, 1997.

Smith, Craig W. and Skjei, Eric W. *Getting Grants.* New York: Harper and Row, 1979.

Chapter 18

Avner, Marcia. *The Lobbying and Advocacy Handbook for Nonprofit Organizations.* St. Paul, MN: Wilder Foundation, 2002.

Brandt, Sanford F. *Tax-Exempt Organizations' Lobbying and Political Activities Accountability Act of 1987: A Guide for Volunteers and Staff of Nonprofit Organizations.* Washington, DC: Independent Sector, 1988.

Caplan, Marc and Nader, Ralph. *Ralph Nader Presents a Citizen's Guide to Lobbying.* New York, NY: Dembner Books, 1983.

Gaby, Patricia V. and Gaby, Daniel M. *Nonprofit Organization Handbook: A Guide to Fundraising, Grants, Lobbying, Membership Building, Publicity and Public Relations.* Englewood Cliffs, NJ: Prentice-Hall, 1979.

Independent Sector. *Advocacy Is Sometimes an Agency's Best Service: Opportunities and Limits Within Federal Law.* Washington, DC: Independent Sector, 1984.

Mental Health Association. *A Layman's Guide to Lobbying Without Losing Your Tax Exempt Status.* Roslyn, VA: Mental Health Association. 1976.

Migdail, Rhonda G. *"Lobbying and Political Activities: What Every Nonprofit Should Know."* Nonprofit World Report 3 (May-June 1983).

Richan, Willard. *Lobbying for Social Change* (Second Edition). Binghamton, NY: Haworth Press, 1996.

Smucker, Bob. *Nonprofit Lobbying Guide* (Second Edition). Washington, DC: Independent Sector. 1999.

Speeter, Greg. *Playing Their Game Our Way. Using the Political Process to Meet Community Needs.* Amherst, MA: University of Massachusetts, 1978.

Suhrke, Henry C. *" 'Political' Advocacy by Non-Profits."* Philanthropy Monthly (Feb 1983).

United States House of Representatives, Ways and Means Committee, Subcommittee on Oversight. *Tax Administration: Information on Lobbying and Political Activities of Tax-Exempt Organizations.* Gaithersburg, MD: U.S. General Accounting Office, 1987.

Webster, George D. and Krebs, Frederick. *Associations and Lobbying: A Guide for Non-Profit Organizations.* Washington, DC: Chamber of Commerce of the United States, 1979.

Chapter 19

Gates, Lowell, J.D. (Killian and Gephart). *Political, Lobbying and Grassroots Activities of 501(c)(3) Organizations.* LTC Legal Briefs; July 28, 1988.

Harvard Law Review. *Political Activities of Non-Profit Corporations;* May 1992.

Independent Sector. *Update on Permissible Activities of 501(c)(3) Organizations During a Political Campaign.* July 29, 1988.

Montgomery, Richard C. *Charitable Organizations and Prohibited Political Activities.* Pennsylvania Bar Association Quarterly; April 1992.

Wharton, Linda. *Guidelines for 501(c)(3) and 501(c)(4) Organizations Regarding Electoral Activities Under the Federal Tax Laws.* Memorandum of March 1, 1990.

Chapter 20

Booth and Associates. *Promoting Issues and Ideas: A Guide to Public Relations for Nonprofit Organizations* (Second Edition). Washington, DC: The Foundation Center, 1987.

Committee to Defend Reproductive Rights of the Coalition for the Medical Rights of Women. *The Media Book: Making the Media Work for Your Grassroots Group.* San Francisco, CA: Committee to Defend Reproductive Rights, 1981.

Council on Foundations. *Communications and Public Affairs Guide.* Washington, DC: Council on Foundations, 1984.

Dannelley, Paul. *Fundraising and Public Relations.* Norman, OK: Univ. of Oklahoma Press, 1986.

Drucker, Peter F. *Managing the Nonprofit Organization.* New York, NY: Harper Collins: 1990.

Foundation for American Communication. *Media Resource Guide.* Los Angeles, CA: Foundation for American Communications, 1981.

Gaby, Patricia V. and Gaby, Daniel M. *Nonprofit Organization Handbook: A Guide to Fundraising, Grants, Lobbying, Membership Building, Publicity and Public Relations.* Englewood Cliffs, NJ: Prentice-Hall, 1979.

Green, Alan. *Communicating in the '80s: New Options for the Nonprofit Community.* Washington, DC: Benton Foundation, 1983.

Gross, Sallie and Viet, Carol H. *For Immediate Release: A Public Relations Manual.* Philadelphia, PA: Greater Philadelphia Cultural Alliance, 1982.

Kinzey, Ruth Ellen. *Using Public Relations Strategies to Promote Your Nonprofit Organization.* Binghamton, NY: Haworth Press, 2000.

Chapter 21

Gerwig, Kate. *Putting Your Mark on the Web.* NetGuide Vol. 3 No. 2 (February 1996) pp. 87.

Gibbs, Mark and Smith. Richard. *Navigating the Internet.* Carmel, Indiana: Sams Publishing 1993.

Gilster, Paul. *The New Internet Navigator.* NY, NY: Wiley & Sons, 1995.

LaQuey, Tracy and Ryer, Jeanne. *The Internet Companion Plus.* Reading, MA: Addison-Wesley Publishing Co. 1993.

Johnston, Michael. *The Nonprofit Guide to the Internet: How to Survive and Thrive* (Second Edition). New York: Wiley & Sons, 1999.

Manger, Jason J. *The Essential Internet Information Guide.* Berkshire, England: McGraw-Hill, 1995.

Chapter 22

Grobman, Gary and Grant, Gary. *Fundraising Online.* Harrisburg, PA: White Hat Communications

Tureen, Edward. *The Nonprofit Internet Companion,* Second Edition. Washington, DC: SEK Publications, 2000.

Warwick, Mal; Hart, Ted; & Allen, Nicj (Eds). *Fundraising on the Internet: The ePhilanthropyFoundation.org's Guide to Success Online* (2nd Edition). San Francisco: Jossey-Bass, 2001.

Chapter 23

Grobman, Gary. *The Nonprofit Organization's Guide to E-Commerce.* Harrisburg, PA: White Hat Communications, 2001.

Holden, Greg. *Starting an Online Business for Dummies* (Second Edition). Foster City, CA: IDG Books Worldwide.

Rich, Jason. *The Unofficial Guide to Starting an Online Business.* Foster City, CA: IDG Books Worldwide.

Sanders, Michael. *Joint Ventures Involving Tax-Exempt Organizations* (Second Edition). New York: Wiley and Sons, 2002.

Chapter 24

Brown, Cherie R. *The Art of Coalition Building— A Guide for Community Leaders.* New York: American Jewish Committee, 1984.

Clifton, Robert L. & Dahms, Alan. *Grassroots Organizations: A Resource Book for Directors, Staff, and Volunteers of Small, Community-Based, Nonprofit Agencies* (Second Edition). Long Grove, IL: Waveland Press, 1993.

Kahn, Si. *Organizing: A Guide for Grassroots Leaders.* Washington, DC: NASW Press, 1991 (Revised Edition)

MacEchern, Diane. *No Coalition, No Returns.* Washington, DC: Environmental Action.

Tydeman, Ann. *A Guide to Coalition Building.* Washington, DC: National Citizen's Coalition for Nursing Home Reform, 1979.

Chapter 25

Dabel, Gregory J. *Saving Money in Nonprofit Organizations: More Than 100 Money-Saving Ideas, Tips, and Strategies for Reducing Expenses Without Cutting Your Budget.* San Francisco: Jossey-Bass, 1998.

Kirschten, Barbara L. *Nonprofit Corporate Forms Handbook.* New York, NY: Clark Boardman Co., 1990.

Mancuso, Anthony. *How To Form Your Own Nonprofit Corporation.* Berkeley, CA: Nolo Press, 1990.

Norsworthy, Alex (ed.). *The Nonprofit Computer Sourcebook.* Rockville, MD: The Taft Group, 1990.

Chapter 26

Deja, Sandy. *"Nonprofit Organizations, Business Ventures, and the IRS: Your Guide to the Unrelated Business Income Tax Law."* Whole Nonprofit Catalog 6 (Spring 1988).

Dewan, Bradford N. *"Operation of a Business by Non-Profit Tax-Exempt Organizations."* Economic Development and Law Center (March-April 1986).

Gallaway, Joseph M. *The Unrelated Business Income Tax.* New York, NY: John Wiley, 1982.

Grobman, Gary. *"The Issue of Competition Between Non-Profit and For-Profit Corporations"* Harrisburg, PA: Pennsylvania Jewish Coalition, 1994.

Hopkins, Bruce. *"Hearings on Nonprofit 'Competition' ".* Nonprofit World 5 (Sept-Oct. 1987).

Kotler, Philip and Andreasen, Alan R. *Strategic Marketing for Nonprofit Organizations.* Englewood Cliffs, NJ: Prentiss-Hall, Inc., 1987.

Lehrfeld, William J. *"More Unrelated Business Tax Issues.* Philanthropy Monthly (October 1984).

Skloot, Edward (ed.). *The Nonprofit Entrepreneur.* New York, NY: The Foundation Center: 1988.

United States Congress, Joint Committee on Taxation. *Tax Policy: Competition Between Taxable Businesses and Tax-Exempt Organizations.* Gaithersburg, MD: U.S. General Accounting Office. 1987.

Wellford, Harrison and Gallagher, Janne. *The Myth of Unfair Competition by Nonprofit Organizations.* New York, NY: Family Service Association of America, 1985.

Chapter 27

Grobman, Gary. *"The Issue of Tax-Exempt Status for Pennsylvania Non-Profit Charities."* Harrisburg, PA: Pennsylvania Jewish Coalition, 1994.

National Council of Nonprofit Associations. *State Tax Trends.* Volume 2, No. 4; Summer 1994.

Wellford, Harrison and Gallagher, Janne. *The Myth of Unfair Competition by Nonprofit Organizations.* New York, NY: Family Service Association of America, 1985.

Chapter 28

Bookman, Mark. *Protecting Your Organization's Tax-Exempt Status.* San Francisco: Jossey Bass, 1992.

Gillespie, Catherine H. *Court Denies Tax Exemption for Nonprofit Nursing Home.* Nonprofit Issues, Philadelphia, PA: Montgomery, McCracken, Walker and Rhoads, March 1992.

Hopkins, Bruce. *The Law and Tax-Exempt Organizations, 6th edition.* New York: John Wiley and Sons. 1992.

Stepneski, Rob. *Rising Tax Pressure Hits Nonprofits.* NonProfit Times: April 1993.

Van Til, Jon. *Tax Exemptions Reconsidered.* NonProfit Times: June 1993.

Chapter 29

Cavadel, Joel. Nonprofit Mergers. Unpublished report on legal consideration relating to nonprofit mergers in Pennsylvania, 1996.

La Pinana, David. *Nonprofit Mergers: The Board's Responsibility to Consider the Unthinkable.* Washington, DC: Center for Nonprofit Boards, 1994.

La Piana, David. *Nonprofit Mergers Workbook: The Leader's Guide to Considering, Negotiating, and Executing a Merger.* St. Paul,, MN: Amherst H. Wilder Foundation, 2000.

McCormick, Dan H. *Nonprofit Mergers: The Power of Successful Partnerships.* New York: Aspen Publishers, 2000.

McLaughlin, Thomas A. *Nonprofit Mergers and Alliances: A Strategic Planning Guide.* New York: Wiley and Sons, 1996.

Morgan, William, Mattaini, Paul and Doliner, Ann. *Is a Merger in Your Future?* Presentation to the Pennsylvania Association of Nonprofit Organizations (PANO), 1996.

Chapter 30

Crosby, Philip B. *Quality is Free*. New York: McGraw Hill, 1979.

Garvin, David A. *Management Quality: The Strategic and Competitive Edge*. New York: Free Press, 1988.

Grobman, Gary. *Improving Quality and Performance in Your Non-Profit Organization*. Harrisburg, PA: White Hat Communications, 1999.

Martin, Lawrence. *TQM in Human Service Organizations*. San Francisco: Jossey-Bass, 1993.

Pappas, Alceste T. *Reengineering Your Nonprofit Organization: A Guide to Strategic Transformation*. New York: John Wiley & Sons, 1995.

Chapter 31

Bunker, Barbara Benedict and Alban, Billie T. *Large Group Interventions: Engaging the Whole System for Rapid Change*. San Francisco: Jossey-Bass, 1997.

Bunker, Barbara Benedict and Alban, Billie T. *What Makes Large Group Interventions Effective?* Journal of Applied Behavioral Science 28(4), 1992.

Carter, Reginald. *The Accountable Agency*. Thousand Oaks, CA: Sage Publications, 1983.

Creech, Bill. *The Five Pillars of TQM: How to Make Total Quality Management Work for You*. New York: Penguin Books, 1994.

Crosby, Philip B. *Quality is Free*. New York: McGraw Hill, 1979.

Deming, W. Edward. *On Some Statistical Aids Toward Economic Production. Interfaces,* v5, n4. Aug. 1975. The Operations Research Society of America and the Institute of Management Sciences, 1975.

Friedman, Mark. *A Guide to Developing and Using Performance Measures in Results-Based Budgeting*. Washington, DC: The Finance Project, 1997.

Greenway, Martha Taylor. *The Status of Research and Indicators On Nonprofit Performance In Human Services*. Alexandria, VA: United Way of America, 1996.

Hammer, Michael. *Reengineering Work: Don't Automate: Obliterate. Harvard Business Review,* July-Aug. 1990, pp. 104-112, 1990.

Hammer, Michael. and Champy, James. *Reengineering the Corporation: A Manifesto for Business*. New York: HarperBusiness, 1993.

Hammer, Michael and Stanton, Steven A. *The Reengineering Revolution: A Handbook*. New York: HarperBusiness, 1994.

Peters, Thomas J. and Waterman, Jr., Robert H. *In Search of Excellence: Lessons from America's Best-Run Companies*. New York: Harper and Row, 1982.

Richmond, Frederick and Hunnemann, Eleanor. *What Every Board Member Needs to Know About Outcomes.* Management and Technical Assistance Publication Series n2, Harrisburg, PA: Positive Outcomes, 1996.

Rouda, R. & Kusy, M., Jr. *Organization Development—The Management of Change. Tappi Journal* 78(8): 253 ,1995.

Steckel, Richard and Lehman, Jennifer. *In Search of America's Best Non-Profits.* San Francisco: Jossey-Bass, 1997.

Watson, Gregory H. *The Benchmarking Workbook: Adapting Best Practices for Performance Improvement.* Portland, OR: Productivity Press, 1992.

Chapter 32

Festen, Marcia & Philbin, Marianne (2006). *Level Best: How Small and Grassroots Nonprofits Can Tackle Evaluation and Talk Results.* San Francisco, CA: Jossey Bass.

Wholey, Joseph S., Hatry, Harry P., & Newcomer, Kathryn E. (2004). *Handbook of Practical Program Evaluation.* San Francisco, CA: Jossey-Bass.

Gray, Sandra T. (1997). *Evaluation with Power: A New Approach to Organizational Effectiveness, Empowerment, and Excellence.* San Francisco, CA: Jossey-Bass.

KEY WORD INDEX

A

abuse, 67, 94, 97, 100, 102, 215, 229, 250, 252, 278, 300, 365
accountability, 26, 27, 29, 55, 71, 72, 75, 78, 80, 84, 97, 98, 100, 101, 105, 118, 147, 174, 177, 205, 275, 278, 300, 301, 306, 311, 316, 326, 332, 345, 356, 360, 364, 366
accounting, 23, 26, 29, 60, 63, 98, 100, 103, 108, 113, 124, 214, 242, 298, 326
accrual basis of accounting, 103, 106, 113
advertisement, legal, 23
advertising, 61, 94, 126, 150, 151, 174, 182, 184, 187, 189, 193, 194, 197, 198, 200, 205, 211, 212, 238, 240, 248, 249, 267, 273, 274, 283, 355, 357
affiliate marketing, 248, 249
AIDS, 15, 200, 278, 359, 365
Amazon.com, 245, 248, 249
American Cancer Society, 15, 232
American Society of Association Executives, 78, 81, 374
Americans With Disabilities Act, 92, 118
AmeriCorps, 135, 136, 338
annual meeting, 37, 128, 314
annual report, 17, 28, 183, 191, 195, 262
application service provider (ASP), 51, 78, 153, 196, 198, 199, 210, 211, 215, 219, 221, 231, 232, 234, 235, 239, 244, 342, 355, 368
applications, 32, 43, 44, 47, 85, 87, 125, 126, 153, 154, 157, 159, 163, 188, 203, 207, 235, 253, 264, 323, 334, 335, 340
   for EIN, 23, 45, 120
   for 501(c)(3) status, 24, 32, 33, 34, 83-87, 145
   for funding and grants, 47, 55, 148, 153, 154, 157, 158, 159, 162, 163, 203, 207, 309
   for domain name (see *domain names*)
ARNOVA, 20, 102, 337
articles of incorporation, 26, 28, 31, 35, 43, 83, 85, 86, 145, 262, 267, 316
auctions, charity (see *charity auctions*)
audit, 28, 43, 65, 68, 77, 97, 101, 106, 107, 108, 153, 162, 206, 289, 356, 358
authentication, 252
awards, 72, 92, 126, 138, 140, 153, 154, 158, 166, 168, 173, 176, 177, 181, 206, 248, 340

B

balance sheet, 100, 102, 103
bank accounts, 18, 23, 28, 32, 256, 317
benchmarking, 295, 299, 303
blogs, 180, 185, 187, 188, 194, 196, 199, 202, 212, 366
board development, 42, 44
board minutes, 27, 28, 38, 42, 43, 45, 46, 56, 64, 67, 96, 107, 262, 267
board of directors, 16, 23, 25, 27, 31, 33, 34, 37, 39, 41, 46, 49, 94, 106, 117, 129, 274, 292, 300, 315

bookkeeping, 23, 28, 105, 106, 109, 261, 262, 264
budget, 16, 25, 27, 28, 43, 44, 54, 56, 62, 65, 67, 73, 76, 78, 86, 97, 99, 100, 104, 109, 110, 111, 112, 129, 132, 135, 136, 145, 146, 151, 154, 162, 194, 204, 238, 247, 248, 256, 257, 261, 262, 264, 277, 278, 289, 297, 301, 340, 358, 359, 364, 365, 367
budget deficits
   federal, 326, 330, 358, 359, 370
   organization, 60, 83, 111
bulk mail, 213, 230, 265, 269
Bush, George W., 136, 165, 339, 342, 359, 365
business process reengineering (BPR), 295, 297, 298, 300, 302
bylaws, 18, 23, 26, 27, 31, 34, 37, 39, 46, 86, 130, 262, 275, 289

C

campaigns, 34, 72, 73, 143, 145, 155, 167, 170, 171, 173, 175, 200, 201, 209, 211, 215, 219, 221, 223, 227, 229, 231, 246, 247, 250, 334, 357, 358
   fundraising, 72, 73, 143, 145, 155, 209, 215, 219, 227, 231, 233, 234
   political, 34, 167, 173, 174, 175, 211, 221, 223, 227, 250, 357, 358, 366
capital campaigns, 200, 201, 215, 228, 229
cash, 99, 100, 102, 106, 113, 146, 209, 237, 241, 244, 288, 317, 323, 335
cash basis of accounting, 103, 106, 113
cash-flow, 60, 104, 105, 157
cause-related marketing, 232, 233, 362, 366, 367
Census Bureau, 323, 353, 354, 359, 369
chairperson (of the Board), 27, 38, 39, 41, 43, 45, 46, 47, 56, 57, 61, 76, 111, 117, 129, 130, 135, 168
change management, 20, 295, 297, 299, 301, 303
charity auctions, 231, 237, 243, 245, 355
child labor law, 119
Chronicle of Philanthropy, 126, 138, 153, 154, 204, 209, 211, 246, 329, 342, 355, 361, 365, 370, 374
churches and synagogues, 15, 88, 135, 199, 216, 223, 228, 323, 332, 333, 334, 337, 341, 357, 365
civil liability, 92
Clinton, Bill 76, 93, 338, 339, 347
coalitions, 49, 180, 185, 205, 255, 258, 259, 338, 366, 371
code of ethics, 77, 80, 107, 363, 364, 366
colleges and universities, 15, 16, 17, 20, 26, 33, 51, 77, 88, 97, 112, 114, 131, 135, 139, 147, 150, 190, 196, 199, 207, 218, 219, 223, 225, 226, 228, 229, 234, 261, 263, 272, 273, 292, 298, 305, 307, 322, 328, 330, 333, 334, 336, 337, 340, 342, 350, 354, 355, 362, 363, 366, 370, 372, 374
commercial nonprofits, 272, 347
commercial property insurance, 94
Commission on Private Philanthropy, 336
committees, 27, 38, 39, 42, 44, 46, 64, 68, 77, 125, 167, 168, 173, 174, 177, 183, 259, 320, 363
   advisory, 146, 149, 179

NOTES

NOTES

NOTES

NOTES

Are you a staff or board member of a nonprofit organization?
Do you want your organization to be excellent?
Are you a busy person?

If you answered **YES** to all three questions, *How to Manage an Effective Nonprofit Organization*, with more than a thousand practical tips, is the one book you need.

- Board members will learn how to run effective meetings and get and keep the best people on their teams.
- Busy staff members will learn how to raise substantial funds for their agency in the least amount of time.
- Grant writers will learn how to prepare better proposals and manage funds once they get them.
- Agencies will learn how to establish an outstanding volunteer program and form community coalitions that work.
- Everyone will learn effective strategies to help improve their supervisory, personnel, and general management skills.

Agency professionals at every level will find themselves referring to *How to Manage an Effective Nonprofit Organization* when they have a problem and need helpful, practical, and to-the-point advice from an acknowledged leader in the field.

About the Author: *Michael A. Sand heads Sand Associates, a management consulting firm based in Harrisburg, PA. For more than 25 years, he has led practical workshops for representatives of nonprofit groups. He also provides assistance in board development, strategic planning, grant writing, and fundraising. In addition, he has formed a Grant Writing and Grant Management Group to assist nonprofits in researching, writing, and managing grant funds.*

ORDER FORM—WHITE HAT COMMUNICATIONS

Name_____Organization_____

Address_____City_____State___Zip_____

Telephone_____ E-mail_____

# of Nonprofit Handbooks Ordered ____@$29.95 each $_____

# of Fundraising Online ordered ____@$29.95 each $_____

# of How to Manage an Effective NP Organization ordered ____@14.95 each $_____

Shipping and Handling ($8.00 first book, $1 ea. add'l book) $_____

6% PA sales tax (PA residents only) $_____

Please charge: ☐Mastercard ☐Visa ☐AmEx ☐Discover   TOTAL ENCLOSED $_____

Expiration Date_____

Card Number _____

3-4 digit CVV Number _____ (back of card for VISA/MC/DISC; front of card for AMEX)

Cardholder's Name (Print)_____

Cardholder's Signature_____

Billing Address (if different)_____

For information about rush orders or quantity discounts, call (717) 238-3787.
Make check or money order payable to: White Hat Communications. Pennsylvania orders: Please add 6% sales tax or enclose copy of PA Department of Revenue exemption certificate. Pre-payment must accompany all orders. Please allow two weeks for delivery. Call for rush delivery.

Mail to: **White Hat Communications, PO Box 5390, Harrisburg, PA 17110-0390**
telephone: 717-238-3787   fax: 717-238-2090
Visit Our Website at: http://www.whitehatcommunications.com   3e108

Fundraising Online: Using the Internet to Raise Serious Money for Your Nonprofit Organization

by Gary Grobman and Gary Grant

Fundraising Online helps nonprofit organizations get the most out of the Internet for fundraising and selling goods and services. This 189-page book will help fundraisers learn how to—

- Find grants from foundations, corporations, and government agencies
- Put together an online fundraising strategic plan
- Engage in effective search engine marketing
- Set up an online store to sell and market products and services, handle Internet payments, fulfill orders, provide customer service, and protect sensitive customer data
- Partner with commercial providers to bring in valuable revenue
- Set up an online charity auction
- Develop blogs, podcasts, and online communities to enhance their fundraising efforts
- Assess the value of working with application service providers (ASPs)
- Respond to questions donors ask about third-party charity evaluation sites

This book also includes—
- Practical advice about what works and what doesn't to generate donations and grants
- Capsule site reviews of more than 100 Web sites where readers can download free online store software and tools for their Web pages, find information about affiliate programs, and partner with online retailers
- Information about regulation of online fundraising

This is a valuable resource for executive, development, marketing, planning, major gifts, grant development, prospect research staff, and board members of nonprofit organizations, as well as Webmasters, leadership of organizations that fund nonprofit organizations, and fundraising consultants who advise them.

Published September 2006 ISBN: 1-929109-18-0 189 pages $29.95

The Nonprofit Handbook, 5th Edition

by Gary M. Grobman

The Nonprofit Handbook, Fifth Edition is the most up-to-date and useful publication for those starting a nonprofit or for those already operating one. This 518-page, 36-chapter *Handbook* is based on *The Pennsylvania Nonprofit Handbook,* a book originally published in 1992 with the help of more than two-dozen nonprofit executives and attorneys and now in its 7th edition. Each easy-to-read chapter includes a synopsis, useful tips, and resources to obtain more information. This essential reference tool includes:

- Information about current laws, court decisions, and regulations that apply to nonprofits—two full pages devoted to each state and the District of Columbia
- Practical advice on running a nonprofit, including chapters on grant-writing, communications, fundraising, quality management, insurance, lobbying, personnel, fiscal management, nonprofit ethics, and 27 other chapters
- Information on applying for federal and state tax-exempt status
- How to write effective grant applications
- How to hire and fire
- Internet resources for nonprofits
- How to develop a strategic plan
- How to plan for a program evaluation
- A guide for students that includes information about the scope, history, theory, and future of the nonprofit sector

We know you will find *The Nonprofit Handbook* to be an essential resource for every library's reference collection.

ISBN13: 9781929109203
8½" x 11" softcover
518 pages including index
$29.95 U.S. $30.95 Canada

Table of Contents

From the very first edition, Grobman's handbook has been a treasure. I have passed along copies to those with no knowledge of non-profit organizations as well as those with lots of hands-on experience. Its usefulness lies in its practicality and accessibility... a great resource to have on your bookshelf!

Pam Leland, Ph.D.
Center for Community Development and Family Policy, University of Delaware

The Nonprofit Handbook is must reading. While it will have value as a reference tool to be consulted when needed, I highly recommend that you read the book cover-to-cover to familiarize yourself with the panoply of issues that face the modern nonprofit in the United States.

Joe Geiger, Executive Director
Pennsylvania Association of Nonprofit Organizations

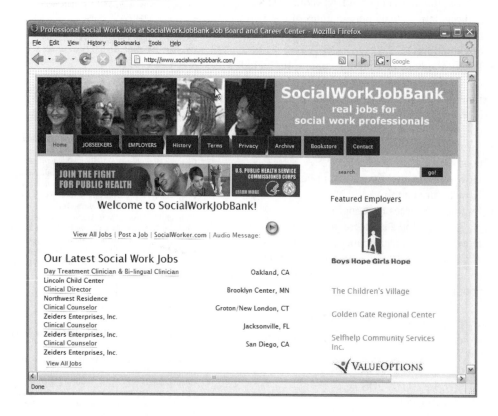

Related Titles Published by White Hat Communications

Introduction to the Nonprofit Sector, 2nd Ed. (2007)

Days in the Lives of Gerontological Social Workers (2007)

Fundraising Online (2006)

More Days in the Lives of Social Workers (2005)

The Social Work Graduate School Applicant's Handbook, 2nd Edition (2005)

The Pennsylvania Nonprofit Handbook, 7th Edition (2005)

Days in the Lives of Social Workers, 3rd Edition (2005)

The Field Placement Survival Guide (2002)

The Nonprofit Organization's Guide to E-Commerce (2001)

Improving Quality and Performance in Your Non-Profit Organization (1999)

PLEASE SHIP MY ORDER TO:

NAME _____

ADDRESS _____

ADDRESS _____

CITY/STATE/ZIP _____

TELEPHONE NUMBER _____

❑   Enclosed is a check for $_____ made payable to "White Hat Communications."

❑   Please charge my credit card (VISA, MasterCard, AmEX, or Discover)

Card #_____

Expiration Date _____

3- or 4-digit Security Code (found on back of card) _____

Name as it appears on card _____

Signature _____

Billing address for credit card (if different from above) _____

Billing City/State/Zip _____

Please send the following publications:

QUANTITY	TITLE		AMOUNT
_____	THE PENNSYLVANIA NONPROFIT HANDBOOK, 7TH EDITION		$29.95 _____
_____	FUNDRAISING ONLINE		$29.95 _____
_____	THE NONPROFIT HANDBOOK, 5th EDITION		$29.95 _____
_____	OTHER_____ (Visit Our Web Site for available titles and pricing)		$_____

Shipping charges: $8.00 first book/
$1.00 each additional book in U.S.
*Please contact us for rates on rush orders,
other methods of shipping, or shipping
outside the U.S.*

SHIPPING $ _____
SUBTOTAL $ _____
PA SALES TAX (6%) $ _____

TOTAL DUE $ _____

(3e)

Federal EIN: 25-1719745